FRANCE REBORN

ROBERT ARON

FRANCE REBORN

Translated by HUMPHREY HARE

THE HISTORY OF THE LIBERATION

JUNE 1944 – MAY 1945

CHARLES SCRIBNER'S SONS, New York

Picture Acknowledgments

THE AMERICAN-SWEDISH NEWS EXCHANGE (*Copyright A. B. Text and Bilder*): 15

JEAN COLLAS: 26

DOCUMENTATION FRANÇAISE: 2, 7, 10

FRENCH EMBASSY PRESS AND INFORMATION DIVISION: 1, 3, 4, 5, 6, 9, 11, 12, 14, 16, 17, 18, 20, 25

PICTORIAL PARADE (*From A.F.P.*): 13

UNITED PRESS INTERNATIONAL PHOTOS: 19, 22, 24

WIDE WORLD PHOTOS: 8, 21, 23

FOREWORD

THE history of the Liberation is the history of 36,000 communes and ninety departments. There is no town, no locality, in France that did not participate in this tremendous event.

To reduce the inevitable lacunae to the minimum, it has been necessary to make a prolonged investigation over a period of more than three years, and has involved gathering information on the spot in nearly every region in France. Many paths have led to dead ends and the evidence gathered has sometimes proved contradictory. In the endeavour to unravel the tangled skein, we have acquired information from more than four hundred people, belonging to every political camp, Resistance and Vichy supporters, Frenchmen and foreigners, most of whom sincerely desired to arrive at the truth. Some of these have permitted their names to figure among the sources for this book. We also owe a great debt of gratitude to our assistant, Y. Garnier-Rizet, whose intelligence, intuition, and sense of method have enormously reduced the problems and difficulties of writing it.

It may well be that, a few decades hence, the opening of the official archives, which in France occurs after a delay of fifty years, will allow of certain statements in this story to be amplified or corrected. But one may doubt whether the historian of the future, poring over documents in libraries, will know the joys the author of this book has been afforded by the excitement of discovery and of contact with living witnesses.

The history of the Liberation could not have been written earlier because of the passions that were still alive; while, conversely, to have waited too long would have meant losing eye-witness accounts from many principal actors, some of whom are already dead.

This is a first attempt to record objectively one of the most complex and dramatic periods France has ever known.

CONTENTS

Part One

THE BAYEUX BRIDGEHEAD

Chapter I

D-DAY

ON D-DAY, 6 June 1944, perhaps the most gigantic plan in the whole of military history was put into operation. It was called *Overlord*, and the British and American staffs looked on it as the decisive campaign of World War II. The operation had first been suggested in 1940, decided on in principle in April 1942, and finally confirmed in January 1943, when Churchill and Roosevelt met at Casablanca. An Anglo-American Combined Chiefs of Staff had been set up. In May 1943, the assault on "Fortress Europe" was being planned for the following spring. In August 1943, at the Quebec Conference, in spite of Churchill's reservations, the plan was approved: the Combined Chiefs were ordered to study the operation in the minutest possible detail, even though its commander had not yet been appointed. Eisenhower was nominated at the end of 1943, after the Cairo and Teheran Conferences.

Under his supreme command, the three commanders of the operation were British officers: Admiral Sir Bertram Ramsay, Air Chief Marshal Sir Trafford Leigh-Mallory, and Field-Marshal Lord Montgomery of Alamein, who was "responsible to the Supreme Commander for the planning and execution of the military side of the landings, as well as for the eventual conquest of the zone of consolidation."

Eisenhower, the Supreme Commander, "a military statesman rather than a true generalissimo," "imprisoned behind the bars of that brilliant hive of top brass known to the world as the Supreme Headquarters of the Allied Expeditionary Forces," was himself indeed something of an Overlord for, being in a position to take a bird's-eye view of events, his decisions were on the general plane rather than concerned with detail.

This led, on occasion, to certain conflicts, with Montgomery among others, but the senior commanders were nevertheless at one in their confidence in the crusade they were conducting, which was after all for civilization itself.

"The Lord mighty in battle," declared Montgomery in his personal

message to the troops on their departure for France, "will go forth with
our armies and his special providence will assist our battle."

Such convictions appear to have been generally held throughout the
military hierarchy. During the Battle of the Bulge, in December 1944,
an American army commander, Patton, when delayed by bad weather,
summoned his chaplain and told him to pray for Heavenly intervention. When the chaplain demurred, Patton said: "Who the hell are
you working for? Are you an officer of the Third Army, yes or no?" A
suitable prayer was composed and distributed throughout the army,
upon which the sun immediately reappeared and the air force was able
to go into action.

We do not know whether, at four o'clock on 5 June, when present
at the final conference, Patton had recourse to similar invocations to
confirm the experts' opinions. But the huge armada, whose setting out
for France was then decided on, had two sound reasons to expect victory: belief in a Divine mission, and immensely detailed military and
technical preparations. It was a prefabricated crusade.

Eisenhower's decision set the wheels of the immense machine in
motion. At H-hour the following day 5,000 ships, 2,000 aircraft and
23,000 parachutists would set out for the French coast. Commandos
and assault troops were to follow, amounting in all to a total of 176,000
men and 20,000 vehicles during the first two days. The operation was
to be in two phases: between midnight and three o'clock in the morning, three complete divisions were to land from the air: one British
division to the east of Caen at the eastern end of the invasion front;
and two American divisions at its western end in the Cotentin. At dawn
five hours later, at 06.30, five seaborne divisions were to begin landing
under the covering fire of a terrific bombardment from the sea and the
air: these consisted of three British and Canadian divisions on the
beaches north of Caen, and two American, one on the beach of Saint-
Laurent, code-named "Omaha," and the other in the Cotentin, south
of Saint-Vaast.

Millions of men were living in the shadow of secrecy; and it was only
gradually, and with the greatest precautions, that the units which were
to take part in the battle began to see their horizons clear as H-hour
approached. It was essential that on landing the terrain they were
individually to capture should be familiar to them in every detail. Yet
it was imperative that the actual landing-places should not be known
till the last moment. Successive series of maps were issued, first without place-names, then with borrowed Polish or Russian names, and
finally only during the very last hours with the actual names of the

French villages. In barracks and billets, in improvised lecture halls, officers delivered increasingly informative briefings during the last days before the landings, and enlarged photographs were shown the troops of the roads and streets down which they would march, of the spinneys and thickets in which they would take cover, of the buildings they were to capture or by-pass. "At the western entrance to the village," a soldier recorded of one of these photographs, "after a fork, the road ran straight on towards a minor crossroads. Continuing east, another road running north and south cut it. At this crossroads there was a big square shaded by trees. Close to it, one could clearly make out a truck parked on the right and men loading it with large boxes and petrol tins. There were two other trucks, also on the right but nearer the square, and we could see that there were vehicles parked under the trees. There were many pedestrians at the crossroads and in the main street." By means of photographs the village was already theirs.

For the warships detailed for supporting fire, which required the greatest precision, there were models in relief made of foam rubber; and those taking part were enabled, as it were, to handle their targets.

At last the night came which was to end for most of them beyond the Channel. Unit commanders assembled their officers and men for a last word of advice and to wish them good luck. Near Southampton, Lord Lovat, commanding the 1st Special Service Brigade, a mixed commando brigade of 800 British and 180 French, explained that the success of the operation depended on the establishment of bridgeheads, on the successful completion of the tasks assigned to such units as theirs, which was set out in a few minutes' time for the casino at Ouistreham. Then, turning to the French, he added in their own language with a smile: "*Demain matin, les Boches, on les aura.*" At last they knew their landing-place for certain.

The airmen of the Lorraine group, who were to set off among the first to lay a smoke-screen along the French coast and mask the landing, also spent a night of waiting. There were indications that the moment was at hand: all personnel was confined to the airfield; the telephone was cut off; painters were busy putting three white bands on the fuselages of the aircraft; and then, finally, the order of battle was posted in the mess.

Briefing took place at two o'clock in the morning and the last orders were given. Breakfast in the mess. "Well, gentlemen, this is the day. . . ." The aircraft set off.

On board the warships the captains and senior officers read the plans given them under seal a few days before and put the last-minute corrections into effect. They now knew the precise targets to neutralize. They knew the beaches on which they must give the infantry supporting fire. The immense armada had assembled during the night south of Portsmouth in the concentration zone known as Piccadilly Circus, so crowded was it. "It was from there," wrote Admiral Lemonier, describing these ultimate moments, "that 5,000 ships set a course for the coasts of France."

While every participant in Overlord, down to the private soldier, now knew that D-day was fixed for the morrow and had been told the precise area in which he was to go into action, the German leaders, on the other hand, did not believe the real landings were to take place in Normandy. At 02.40 on 6 June, nearly two hours after the first landings, the Chief of Staff to Rommel, commanding Army Group B, which controlled the Channel and North Sea coasts from Finistère to the Zuider Zee, was still telephoning: "We do not think this is going to be an important operation." At 04.00, Hitler telephoned in person to forbid von Rundstedt to use his reserve divisions: "You should await daylight to get a clear view of the situation." In fact, the O.K.W. waited until 16.55 the following evening before ordering an energetic counter-attack. It was already eighteen hours since four detachments of parachutists had landed in France, eighteen hours since regular units of the French Army had begun to fight once more on the soil of their country. This is a little-known episode and some account must be given of it.

The first detachments preceding the actual Allied landings, indeed the first to fight in France and shed their blood there, were French. They belonged to the 2nd Chasseurs Parachute Regiment, which was entirely composed of Frenchmen who had succeeded in joining, by many devious and adventurous paths, the Free French Forces either in England or Algiers.

During the period of training this regiment underwent in English and Scottish camps, it had beaten several records, including the marksmanship record over the battle course.

Fit and tough, wearing the red beret and the badge of the Cross of Lorraine, which distinguished its members from those of the other units of the British Brigade of the Special Air Service, to which the regiment was attached, it was finally concentrated in the secret camp at Fairford while awaiting Overlord in which it was to play the initial role.

After a seven-day leave period, during which the men were able to appreciate the prestige their uniform conferred on them in the eyes of the British public, they began to receive huge cases of weapons and equipment, of which the contents, when D-day came, would be divided up and carried in their packs. The scale, however, was so generous and the weight proved so excessive that they were obliged to discard much of their equipment during their approach marches. Every possible contingency had been foreseen by the British authorities, and each man was expected to carry: "Compass, field-glasses, watch, felt-soled boots, American dagger, rucksack, sleeping bag, camouflaged overalls, parachute overalls, life jacket, explosives, ammunition, and as many grenades as required." Their equipment also included phials of morphia in case of wounds, and a pullover which when unravelled would make thirty feet of rope strong enough to bear the weight of a man and assist him to escape in case of capture. There were also "a chemical to confuse police dogs, a little metal saw, which could be slipped into a shoulder-strap or the sole of a boot, a battledress button that would pivot on another button to make a compass, a map of France on a silk handkerchief, and two banknotes for a thousand francs each which could be rolled up thin and slipped into a lapel." Also "a little flat box, called 'a commando pack,' which contained sufficient food for three days, a few tablets of chewing-gum, a few cubes of solidified concentrated milk, cubes of vitamins, a tablet of chocolate (which tasted rather nasty), four pieces of sugar, a miniature razor with a blade and a minute piece of soap, a fishing line and two hooks, a needle and thread, a file for escaping, and three sheets of toilet paper," corresponding to the three days on which it was expected the parachutists would have to be self-supporting.

According to Lieutenant Henry Corta, who recorded these details, the care devoted to these preparations greatly encouraged the French paratroops, as did the precise tactical instructions given them on D-minus-1. Every officer in command of a stick, which varied from three to ten men, received a secret file of detailed orders: beneath its orange cover, it contained all the relevant information concerning the principal mission and the secondary missions assigned to each patrol; also two air photographs of the principal objective, one taken from 300 feet, giving a detailed view of the objective to be sabotaged, the other from 1,500 feet, showing the neighbourhood. Two further photographs, taken from the same altitudes, showed the landing zones. When these photographs were placed side by side, the approach route from the landing zone to the objective could be studied in its entirety. The route laid down could, however, be altered. Every commander, having studied the photographs, was at liberty to refuse his landing zone and demand an alternative. He might well suspect a field, which at first sight appeared safe enough, to contain tree stumps or camouflaged traps of one sort or another after stereoscopic study. An aircraft would be sent out at once to reconnoitre his alternative selection, after which a decision could be arrived at.

The file also contained two maps of 1 : 50,000 which together formed a rectangle of 32 × 42 kilometres, and three maps of 1 : 250,000 covering the whole of Brittany.

Splendidly equipped and trained, the 2nd R.C.P. was to be dropped in Brittany, half in the north, in the Côtes du Nord, half in the south, in the Morbihan. In a first phase, on 5 June, during the night preceding the landings, two groups, each consisting of an officer and seven men, were to be parachuted into each sector. Their job was to set up bases called, respectively, Agamemnon and Beatrice in the north, Charlotte and Dudule in the south, and to establish contact with the local Resistance, which throughout Brittany was known to be both numerous and aggressive. Two days later, on the 7th, eighteen sabotage missions, divided between the two departments, were to join the first sticks. Finally, in a third phase, the rest of the regiment would land in groups of ten from D-plus-2 to D-plus-10.

Thus the first operation in the Liberation of France was confided to a French parachute regiment. It was known as Operation Stanwest, and began on the night of 5 June, at 23.00, two hours before all else. Why was Brittany selected? Why did the landings in Normandy open with the parachuting of four French detachments into the adjacent province?

In the first place, Brittany was one of the most densely occupied parts of France. Enemy troops stationed there were estimated at 150,000. Secondly, the German formations in Brittany were well placed to attack the Allied bridgehead in Normandy from the rear. These were the decisive reasons for the 2nd R.C.P.'s mission. By sabotaging railways and roads it was hoped to render the enemy's movement difficult, and by organizing and encouraging the Maquis to take the offensive it might be possible to inflict casualties and hold him up.

In the Morbihan, in particular, German armoured divisions were in the region of Ploërmel-Guer and formed a considerable threat to the bridgehead. A whole series of demolitions was planned to isolate them and prevent their using the railways. The Ploërmel-la-Gousnière, the Ploërmel-Guer, the Ploërmel-Malestroit, the Messac-Guer, the Messac-Rennes, the Messac-Redon, and the Messac-Châteaubriant lines were the parachutists' objectives, while the two preliminary detachments under Lieutenants Marienne and Deplante were to reconnoitre the terrain and make preparations for the operations.

The men of these two sticks, heavily laden and their faces blackened with burnt cork, were escorted to the boundary of Fairford Camp by the whole regiment. Two hours later, they were over France. Red lights came on in the fuselages—warning signals. The green lights followed— and they jumped.

Lieutenant Deplante's detachment was dropped some ten kilometres from its objective. Lieutenant Marienne's had better fortune. An hour later, after they had regrouped, they heard voices talking a foreign language in the night. Were they Germans? A soldier from Lorraine, who knew German, said: "No." Were they natives talking Breton? A Breton in the detachment, Corporal Bouétard, did not recognize it as such.

Whoever they were, they opened fire. The detachment replied and then dispersed to meet again at the assembly point. Having reached it, they realized one of their number was missing. They were not unduly anxious, thinking he must have got lost. In fact, Corporal Bouétard had been killed in the skirmish, though the incident remained a mystery. Bouétard was a sailor from the Côtes du Nord, who had joined the Free French Forces. He was the first man to die on the battlefield of the Liberation and also the first Frenchman to be killed in reconquering his native land.

Hardly had Lieutenant Marienne and his men landed on the Breton heaths, near the Plemelec windmill, which was a German anti-parachutist observation post, than delegates from the Resistance came to see them. "You ought to see the farmers who leave their fields, herds, wives and children. They're on the move in big groups by 'byways,' as they say, to join the headquarters of the Saint-Marcel Maquis. They set off by twos and arrive by fifties. They come from all parts, from Redon, Vannes, Josselin, Ploërmel, Pontivy and Lorient, a few individuals even come from the neighbourhood of Rennes. Some, having heard tell of the parachutists, are longing to fight, and come from villages in Finistère, arriving exhausted after the long march. You can see their feet swollen and bleeding through their worn shoes. But they don't care: all they want is arms so that they can make their contribution to victory."

Surprised and delighted by this splendid influx of volunteers, Lieutenant Marienne set up his portable radio and sent the following message to his colonel. It was the first news of the landing to be received in London: "Pierre I—Call Sign 101—Confirm message from Commandant F.F.I.—Confirm 10 Companies out of 25 poorly armed—Send urgently all available officers, troops and weapons, in particular Bren guns—Your presence here indispensable—Urgent—Delighted with organization and its immense possibilities—Resistance Headquarters confirms aid to Stanwest from here—Charlotte and Dudule heard—Will be strongly established and defended—Inform all missions that assembly areas O.K. . . .   Signed: Pierre I Marienne."

This signal was followed by another: "Pierre I—Call Sign 101—Confirm signal sent last night to Commandant Bourgoin—Situation splendidly re-established in spite of bad landings—Have found Pierre II and Fernand—Have made contact with Resistance—Am at Headquarters—Great Success—3,500 men in organized formations await you—Your presence here indispensable—Hope to give you details during course of the day—Confirm DZ will be guarded by 500 men night of your arrival —Confirm—Urgent—Weapons and men."

These signals summed up the F.F.I. situation in the Morbihan on the arrival of the first parachutist elements. They confirmed that from the very start of the operations, both by the blood of the first man killed in the campaign and by the surprising influx of reinforcements, France made her presence felt, despite the fact that the preparations for them had been made entirely without her knowledge.

During the morning of 6 June, Pierre Laroque, secretary-general to the French administrative services in London, directed an indoor tactical exercise for the administrative liaison officers; it was these officers who, when the day came, were to accompany the Allied divisions to France and establish relations with the local population. The basis selected for the exercise that morning was: "A landing between Cotentin and the Seine, followed by an advance on Caen." While the students were considering the details of the operation and the part they would have to play in it, the announcement was made that landings were actually taking place in the precise districts envisaged in the exercise. It was a dramatic moment; and the students were persuaded that their instructor had been in the secret.

In fact, it was pure coincidence, the result merely of common-sense reasoning. Pierre Laroque, impressed by the fact that the Allied equipment was suitable for landings on beaches, had drawn the logical conclusion that he must set exercises for the districts between the Cotentin and Le Havre, and in the region of Paris-Plage. There may also have been among the French in London a few officers who remembered that in September 1937 the army staff, with considerable foresight, had organized large-scale manœuvres in Basse-Normandie, the plan being based on an invasion from the sea to the west of the mouth of the Orne, and the occupation, at the earliest possible moment, of a bridgehead running from Bayeux to Cabourg and including Caen.

That very morning, in London, Colonel Rémy, of the French Intelligence Service, received a telephone call on arriving at his office. It was from a woman who had been worrying him for weeks to send her on a secret mission to France.

"Really, *madame*, I have already asked you to wait till the landings are an accomplished fact before asking me for an interview."

"But, *monsieur*, that's why I'm telephoning you."

"What do you mean?"

"Really, *monsieur*, haven't you heard? It's happened; they landed last night."

These two anecdotes show how little the French knew about the landings. Everyone was aware that an operation was about to take place; but no one, from the humblest to the highest, whether soldier or civilian, whether in France or in exile, knew either the date or the locality.

The officials of the Vichy government kept in touch with the authorities of the occupying power in the hope of gaining information; but the Germans knew no more than they did and contradicted each other.

The sub-prefect of Bayeux, P. Rochat, who was to have a ringside seat when the time came, got no information from the Germans. He was merely aware that the famous Atlantic Wall in his district did not appear to be particularly well maintained. When, on 1 June, five days before the landings, Marshal Rommel arrived on a tour of inspection in the neighbourhood of Bayeux, the German authorities, to the amusement of the local population, asked the farmers to remove their cattle from the pastures on which they had encroached for several months past so that the marshal might be led to believe they were minefields. Notices announced: "*Mined area. Lebensgefahr*"; but when Rommel had gone, the cattle returned to graze peacefully till D-day.

Nor was the local Resistance any better informed.

Triboulet, who was to become the first Gaullist sub-prefect of the liberated territories, was taken completely by surprise by the landings. For the previous two months he had frequently been out of radio contact with London and had received no information. During the night of the 5th, he was awakened by the noise of the German troops evacuating a neighbouring château and by the sound of the bombardment twelve kilometres away. The explosions drew nearer and increased in intensity; the horses were restless in the stables. Everyone took refuge in the cellars, where he spent the whole day of the 6th. On the 7th, when the Germans had finished moving out, Triboulet went off on a bicycle to find out what was happening.

Louis André, President of the Bayeux Liberation Committee, unexpectedly found himself in the front line of the battle. His whole area was subjected to a deafening, terrifying uproar. His staff had taken refuge in a farm, where he joined them. He suddenly realized with astonishment that the farmer, having milked his cows, was harnessing his float to go to sell the milk in Bayeux. "I shouldn't, if I were you," André said. "Why not? Today's Tuesday, isn't it?" D-day was market day in Bayeux.

Not a single Frenchman, whether in the area of the beaches, the battlefield, or the bombed towns knew of the landings. Were there any in London or Algiers who, being nearer the headquarters, were better informed?

Maurice Schumann was spokesman for France Combattante on the B.B.C. To his millions of listeners he seemed particularly well-informed, as well as being a man whose opinions mattered and whose heartening eloquence produced a profound effect. On the evening of 30 May, when he reached the studio, he was informed that Colonel Drexel-Biddle wished to see him at once. As soon as he had finished his broadcast, Maurice Schumann went to see him. "It is essential," the colonel said without explanation, "that you should leave tomorrow morning without a word to anyone." Schumann pointed out that, if his daily broadcast were not heard on the Continent, it would seem odd and might give the alarm. It was decided that Schumann should spend the night at the B.B.C. recording talks to be broadcast on the following days. The next morning, he embarked with a British commando in a flotilla of landing-craft, without any idea of his destination. At sea, on 4 June, the colonel assembled his officers and opened a sealed envelope from which he took a map of the Cotentin.

"We have no harbour in our landing zone," he said, "but Churchill has had the brilliant idea of building artificial harbours. We should be able to land three divisions during the course of the first eight days. If Rommel has reserve divisions he can concentrate against the danger points, we risk being thrown back into the sea. But we have two trump cards: superiority in the air, and the French Resistance."

It was thus, far removed from all chance of being indiscreet, that the French B.B.C. spokesman first heard the secret. It was also the first time he had heard a senior British officer recognize the value of the Resistance.

In Algiers, there were certain people who were traditionally well-informed: the Inspectors of Finance. However, one of them, Didier Gregh, when he heard of the landings, cried: "This is a disaster! The exchange rates have not been fixed." Could there be better proof that the French knew nothing of them?

Let us turn to the senior soldiers: General Koenig, the hero of Bir-Hakeim, exercised from London command not only of the French troops stationed in England, who were to take part in the landings, but also of the F.F.I. in France. A double claim to be put in the picture, one might have thought. In fact, not only was he not invited to the final high-level meeting held on 15 May, which was attended by King George VI, a great number of Allied generals, and the principal members of the British General Staff and the War Cabinet, including Churchill and Field-Marshal Smuts, but it was not until 4 June that two Allied officers came to see him and told him that the messages to alert the French Resistance would be sent out that night by the B.B.C.[1]

General de Gaulle was in the same case. He no doubt knew, of course, that when, on 2 June 1944, Winston Churchill invited him to come urgently to London and placed his private aircraft at his disposal, it was to take part in the landings. The President of the Provisional Government of the French Republic was accompanied by a military and civilian staff—Generals Béthouart and Billotte, Palewski, Geoffroy de Courcel, Teyssot—which was reinforced in London. But, officially at least, no information had been vouchsafed him about the impending operation. Both General Eisenhower and the Prime Minister have made no attempt to conceal the fact that they waited till the very last moment before informing their unmanageable ally. On 4 June, Churchill wrote to Roosevelt in somewhat flippant terms to inform him of the General's coming. "De Gaulle's Committee by a large majority decided that he should accept my invitation to come here. He hemmed and hawed, but Massigli and several others threatened to resign if he did not do so. We expect him on D-minus-1. If he arrives Eisenhower will see him for half an hour and explain to him the position exclusively in its military aspect. I shall return to London during the night of D-day. I do not expect that very much can be done with de Gaulle."

Eisenhower confirms the impression given by this letter in a single phrase of his *Crusade in Europe*: "One of our last visitors was de Gaulle." And Churchill describes General de Gaulle's visit in terms which leave no doubt about the reserve observed towards him: "Presently Mr. Eden arrived with General de Gaulle, who had just flown in from Algiers. I told de Gaulle that I had asked him to come because of the forthcoming operation. I could not do this by telegraph and I felt that the history of our two countries required that the liberation of France must not be undertaken by the British and Americans without the French being

[1] Cf., page 90.

informed. I had intended to invite him a little before D-day, but the weather had forced us to postpone the assault for twenty-four hours, and it might even be later. . . . The General was bristling."

And, indeed, every Frenchman would have felt the same. D-day, which had been so long awaited by France, looked propitious for her neither in its military nor in its political aspects.

Militarily speaking, the French forces engaged in the battle of Normandy played only a marginal role. The great formations that had been built up—the 2nd Armoured Division under Leclerc, and the First French Army under General de Lattre de Tassigny—set foot on the soil of their country only two months later, in August.

The French land forces engaged in Normandy on the first day with the eight British, American and Canadian divisions, amounted to no more than one company of some 180 men, under the command of Captain Kieffer. It was attached to a British unit, 4 Commando, which comprised 800 British. Small though the French contingent was, it distinguished itself. It was the first unit to land in Normandy, at Ouistreham, to seize the fortified villas transformed into blockhouses, and also the first to come under enemy fire on the beach. "Already," related one of the survivors, "the most extraordinary rumours were flying about. So-and-so had been wounded, so-and-so killed, his head blown off, his legs shot away. . . . One of the French platoons had terrible casualties. A mortar-bomb landed among them as they were emerging from the sea. The officers were all casualties. A non-commissioned officer took over and commanded it throughout the operation." They were also the first to meet the French who had stayed in France. It was a moving experience. "Suddenly, on the right of the road, we saw a head appear out of a shelter. A number of civilians emerged, both men and women. 'Here you are at last! We've been waiting for four years for you.' They were wild with excitement and weeping for joy. So it was really true, after all. Here we were in France and these people were waiting for us. We were in a field of fire, but no one gave it a thought. We gathered round them and stared at them, almost incapable of speech. These were the first French we met."

Then a veteran of the 1914 war joined the little group. "Give me a rifle. I'm no raw recruit. I went through the whole of the other war. To hell with these damned Boches!" On the strength of his service record, he wanted to take command of the platoon. It was explained to him with some difficulty that Overlord was not Verdun.

These moments were all too short. The Commando had to move on.

It was continuously in the line for ninety days. "But at the cost of considerable losses: of the 180 men who landed on 6 June, there remained sixty-five at the end of the campaign, all the rest having been killed or wounded."

Heroic enough, but they were only an infinitesimal part of the troops engaged in the landing.

As for the navy, the French flag was somewhat better represented, though even here the Gaullist ships had only an accessory role.

The warships engaged in Overlord numbered in all 467: two battleships, three battle cruisers, fifteen cruisers, 107 destroyers, 48 corvettes, 64 armed trawlers, 228 light coastal craft, without counting the 5,000 landing-craft. The French contribution to the fleet was two 7,000-ton cruisers, the *Georges Leygues* and the *Montcalm*, which were in support of the offensive headed for Bayeux, and the 10,000-ton cruiser, the *Duquesne*, which was used as a supply ship. Near Ouistreham was the destroyer *Combattante*, in which de Gaulle crossed the Channel on 14 June for his first visit to France. Eight months later this ship was blown up by a German mine.

Only three ships, therefore, two cruisers and a destroyer, took part in the actual landings. Besides these, four frigates, new, fast and well-found ships, mounted guard over the convoys heading for the French coast: *Aventure*, *Découverte*, *Surprise* and *Escarmouche*. The corvettes *Estienne d'Ovres*, *Aconit*, *Renoncule* and *Moselys* were submarine-chasing. There were also other smaller ships on escort duty. Besides these, there was an old battleship, the *Courbet*, a veteran of the First World War, which had been the first ship to fly the flag of the Free French Naval Forces, and which had bombarded the German tanks in the Cotentin in June 1940; a passenger ship, the *Fortin*, which at the time of the Armistice had brought a Czech regiment to England; and two old cargo boats, the *Formigny* and the S.N.A. 8, which were deliberately sunk on the coast of France to create the artificial harbours.

These ships were under Allied command. The supreme authority was the Allied Naval Commander-in-Chief, and they were split up, according to the different zones, between the Commander-in-Chief Portsmouth, the Vice-Admiral Dover and the officer commanding the British assault. A French admiral, Rear-Admiral Jaujard, who was in command of the two cruisers, was the only French flag officer with a command on D-day.

But here again it was only a token force: compared to what the French fleet had been before the tragedies of Mers-el-Kebir and Toulon, compared even to the ships still available in Algiers, Alexandria and Martinique, French participation, though distinguished, was infinitesimal.

As for aircraft, France was represented by approximately 100 machines out of the 9,000 engaged in the operation: there were seven groups of which three were fighter groups (*Ile-de-France, Alsace, Cigognes*), two medium bomber groups (*Lorraine* and *Berry*), and two heavy bomber groups (*Tunisie* and *Guyenne*).

On 6 June, the *Lorraine* group was the first to set off to spread a huge smoke screen in front of the ships and the British landing craft which, at approximately 07.00, were making for the beaches of Courseulles and Langrune. "To maintain the smokescreen, it was necessary to go continuously to and fro so close to the ground that one of our aircraft broke off the two smoke pipes under the fuselage against a chimney."

The bombers of the Guyenne and *Tunisie* groups set off two hours later to bomb the German elements trying to re-form. Meanwhile, to maintain mastery in the air, the fighters were making constant sorties: one squadron alone made four during the day, from 09.00 to 11.10, from 14.40 to 16.05, from 17.25 to 19.30, and from 20.00 to 22.15, of which the last sortie was to escort gliders.

On the beach at Ouistreham a monument commemorates the first disembarkation of Allied troops on French soil; it bears the following inscription: "On this beach, at dawn on 6 June 1944, the troops of Field Marshal Montgomery and the French Commando of Captain Kieffer were the first to set foot on the soil of France." The inscription is significant. A field-marshal for the British and a captain for the French. There could be no clearer proof than this of the small part, militarily speaking, played by the French.

From the political point of view, France appeared to be in no better situation. On 14 March 1944, in a speech to the Assemblée Consultative d'Alger, de Gaulle had deplored "the relative absence of France from the great political and strategic problems."

Indeed, in the spring of 1944, General de Gaulle and his government were still a long way from having succeeded in their prolonged efforts to get what was in fact the only French government outside France recognized by the Allies. It was an effort that had run into many difficulties since June 1940.

These efforts were based on Churchill's letter to de Gaulle of 20 June 1940: "It is no longer possible to consider the government of Bordeaux as the government of an independent country. . . . His Majesty's government declares that it will recognize the French National Provisional

Committee and will treat with it on all questions that concern the prosecution of the war, for as long as the Committee continues to represent all those French elements which are determined to fight the common enemy."

On 23 September 1941, de Gaulle announced the creation of the French National Committee in London, which was no longer to be merely provisional, and he defined its aims:

"It is not only essential that France should fight, with every means in her power, beside the Allies and in particular beside the British Empire to defeat Hitler by force of arms, but the Committee must be organized in such a way as to be able to express the will of France, serve her interests, assemble all the French forces of resistance both within and without the country, and prepare itself for those duties which will be incumbent upon it both in France itself and in the Empire as the liberation proceeds." For the first time, the functions of the French National Committee, which had originally been limited to purely military matters, were defined as extending to the administration of the country after it was liberated.

Twenty-one Allied governments, including the U.S.S.R. and those in exile in London, successively recognized the French National Committee. On 13 January 1942, de Gaulle attended the Inter-Allied Conference in London, which was a first definite token of recognition. As for the U.S.A., in a memorandum dated 9 July 1942, it went so far as to allow the Gaullist Committee a symbolic value; it "recognized the contribution of General de Gaulle and the efforts of the French National Committee in keeping alive the traditional spirit of France, and considered that the common objectives would be more easily attained by giving all possible military assistance and support to the French National Committee as a symbol of general French Resistance against the Axis powers. The government is prepared to treat with the functionaries of the Free French, wherever they exercise effective authority."

In November 1942, the satisfaction felt by the Gaullists in London at the liberation of North Africa was considerably mitigated by disappointment that another government organization should be set up there, soon to come under the leadership of Giraud. It was in vain that de Gaulle proposed to Giraud that the French National Committee should move to Algiers and be enlarged by representatives from the newly liberated territories. It required six months of negotiation before the French Committee of National Liberation, as distinct from the French National Committee, was set up in Algiers on 3 June 1943, under the authority of the two leaders. Nor was it till 26 August 1943, that the U.S.A.,

Great Britain and the U.S.S.R. established official relations with the C.F.L.N., and then the formulas employed were somewhat grudging and reserved. The U.S.A. and Great Britain recognized the C.F.L.N. "as the administrator of French territories overseas which are under its authority." The U.S.S.R. recognized the C.F.L.N. "as representing the interests of all French patriots fighting against the Hitlerian tyranny and has decided to proceed to an exchange of plenipotentiaries."

On the eve of the landings, the French Committee for National Liberation, with the approval of the Assemblée Consultative, decided, in May 1944, to assume the title of Provisional Government of the French Republic. But neither the British, nor the Americans, ratified this unilateral act. As far as they were concerned France had no official government on D-day.

What was the reason for this reticent attitude? As far as the Americans were concerned, it was due above all to lack of information.

The American Army had been improvised: in peace-time it consisted of 200,000 men, but by June 1944, it numbered 7,800,000. This resulted inevitably in inexperienced staffs and, on various occasions at the beginning of the campaign, they had recourse to British or French officers to organize their battles. In Tunisia, where American divisions met the Germans for the first time, the Americans asked French officers, in November 1942, to draw up orders for an attack. Though their fighting units soon acquired experience of battle, and their supply organization brought off prodigies unequalled by other armies, there were nevertheless certain departments that never acquired a competence comparable to those of countries with longer traditions: in particular, American Intelligence and counter-espionage always felt inferior to their British equivalents. The American Army was a huge wave of tough, ardent, eager and idealistic young men breaking over the old world. Red-faced, often truculent generals, not unlike those of the French Revolution or the War of Secession, frequently flouted the conventions customary at more traditional headquarters.

American policy was no better prepared than the American Army for intervention in Europe. Well-intentioned but ingenuous, it had, in France, consistently backed the wrong horse ever since the Armistice. "I learned," wrote an American diplomatist, recording his European experiences, "this difficult lesson for Americans, that neither nations nor individuals are entirely black or white." Faced with the complications of the French political situation between 1940 and 1944, American policy was one of hoping for the best, defensible *a priori*, but bearing little relation to the facts. It sought a *modus vivendi* with the Vichy government: "We wish to show our friendship for *all* the French, whether they have been able or not to escape the Occupation and whatever their political opinions may be. We have never approved the policy of Vichy, we have openly criticized it, but we have never condemned a Frenchman for sincerely believing that this policy was the best solution for France." Looking upon every Frenchman as "a potential ally," they sought among French soldiers and politicians for a statesman in whom loyalty to Pétain and hostility to the Germans were combined; and their selections were not always happy. They first supported General Fornel de la Laurencie, who in 1941 had sought to become head of the internal Resistance and who believed he was displaying remarkable political acumen by replying to the question: "What will you do with de Gaulle?" with the memorable phrase: "We shall give de Gaulle an amnesty." They then turned to Weygand, who refused their advances, declaring that he was too old to become a rebel. Then, finally, they took up Giraud who, since he was as deficient in political experience as they were themselves, was an ideal partner.

The one man whom they refused to accept was de Gaulle, who seemed to them at once intolerable and incomprehensible.

Intolerable, because of his haughtily expressed cult of the greatness of France, which conflicted with the contempt in which many of the American leaders held France at that time.

In a letter, of 10 February 1943, to a personal friend, Zabrouski, Roosevelt envisaged the creation of a new international organization in which he attributed to France the secretaryship of the "universal tetrarchy" with the United States, U.S.S.R. and Great Britain, but with advisory but not deliberative powers, as being at once a recompense for her resistance and a punishment for her previous fall. France was, moreover, to remain within the British orbit, though with a broad autonomy. This, of course, would have amounted to dominion status, to which de Gaulle would certainly not have submitted. Furthermore, the General's very personality was incomprehensible to Americans. Eisenhower, whose political sense was far above the average, expressed the following opinion with, moreover, considerable tact: "I personally liked General de Gaulle, as I recognized in him many fine qualities. We felt, however, that these qualities were marred by hypersensitiveness and an extraordinary stubbornness in matters which appeared inconsequential to us."

De Gaulle was certainly not the man to smooth over the incidents that were bound to occur between America and France, allies of such unequal power and standing at that time. His innate sense of his own superiority, combined with the collective inferiority complex from which the French were then suffering because of their defeat—and from which he was not exempt—drove him to adopt modes of speech and action which tended to upset and bewilder American statesmen. The sudden attack on Saint-Pierre and Miquelon by the Free French Forces in December 1941, in spite of American opposition, the anti-American broadcasts from Brazzaville, the lack of co-operation with the United States in New Caledonia and in the Pacific, and the mistakes made by certain Gaullist representatives in the United States, in particular by Adrien Tixier, all made de Gaulle unacceptable to the American leaders.

Also to his disadvantage were the accounts given of the leader of the Free French by certain Frenchmen themselves. The little clans of exiles in New York and London were, indeed, far from unanimous in their recognition of his merits.

In London, there was left-wing opposition to him in the journal *France*. Comert, Louis Lévy and Gombault were not of much importance in French circles, but they nevertheless succeeded in disquieting Allied opinion about the General. Similarly, André Labarthe, the editor of *France Libre*, who left London for Algiers in 1943, retailed detrimental gossip about de Gaulle and his ministers.

In New York, Camille Chautemps, making use of his prestige as an ex-Prime Minister, who had been democratically elected, persuaded the White House that he was a better representative of France than the man of 18 June, who owed his leadership entirely to a B.B.C. microphone.

In these circumstances, it only required some of his more zealous and faithful supporters to commit an indiscretion or two in manifesting their cult of loyalty to the General for the rumour to become widespread that de Gaulle was no democrat. It seemed that he and his entourage were intending to establish a military dictatorship, that he was a *coup d'état* general, who was fighting Vichy and the Nazis merely to perpetuate their authoritarian practices.

The British knew de Gaulle better and perfectly understood the situation in France. One of the least tendentious accounts written during the war on the real state of France is to be found in the *French Basic Handbook*, a publication issued in June 1944, to British officers serving in France. As one may imagine, it is far from pro-Vichy, yet it gives an impartial account of the efforts Vichy had made to resist the Germans, and of what it had done to ameliorate the sufferings of the French. From 13 December 1940, till Pierre Laval's return to power in April 1942, the Marshal's government had done all it could to counter the demands of the Germans. Under Darlan's premiership, a large majority of the population, particularly among the *bourgeoisie* and the peasants, had supported the government. The *French Basic Handbook* recognized that there had been profoundly anti-German, even though reactionary, elements at Vichy—Gillouin and Fernet, for example. Nor, therefore, was the Marshal accused of being a traitor.

On the other hand, the *French Basic Handbook* did not accuse de Gaulle of being a factionist. It recognized how popular the Resistance had been in the country since 1943, and the extent of de Gaulle's following.

Were the British then going to give de Gaulle their wholehearted support? First and foremost, they remained British, searching empirically for the solution which would be of the greatest immediate advantage to their country. The difference between the British and the Americans was that the British were more realistic and had, moreover, for four years past, been in direct contact with the extraordinary man who was trying to regenerate France; they were aware of his greatness, and they knew his faults; they were capable of apprehending the pressures behind de Gaulle's arbitrary actions for the very good reason that they would themselves, in similar circumstances, have done the same or more.

The British, therefore, understood both France and de Gaulle: but they behaved towards them as they would have done towards any other country. De Gaulle's masterly description of their craftiness coincides precisely with that of the American Ingersoll: evasiveness that wears down their allies, overt courtesy concealing a secret contempt, tenacity that surely but imperceptibly gains the day for British policies and interests, and a mixture of candour and hypocrisy, of egoism and disinterestedness. Certainly, the British Army was not an army of boy-scouts, but an army led by astute professionals who, far from believing that the accumulation of goodwill was necessarily an essential to success, were well aware that to gain one's political ends it was sometimes necessary to put sentiment aside. Churchill, who took every opportunity of proclaiming his sincere love for France, received de Gaulle on D-day in the company of Field-Marshal Smuts, who made no attempt to conceal his hostility. It was a piece of good fortune for France that the Janus of hatred was in this instance subordinated to that of friendship.

To everyone, both Americans and British, de Gaulle seemed politically intolerable owing to his touchy and exigent patriotism. But the British esteemed and admired him, even when they were trying to do him down; in his presence, they fell victims to what one might call the Hudson Lowe complex about the prisoner of St. Helena, or perhaps that of

Bedford about the martyr of Rouen. As Churchill humorously remarked of de Gaulle: "We nickname him Joan of Arc and are looking for bishops to burn him."

And, indeed, the General's and his Committee's position, both with regard to the British and the Americans, seemed far from established on the eve of D-day. France, it seemed, could not be assured of a government recognized by the Allies proceeding to her liberation. AMGOT weighed, an extra menace, over the French coasts vowed to devastation and over the cities threatened with destruction. The prize to be won in the battle that was to begin during the night of 5–6 June was, therefore, not precisely the same for liberators and liberated. And this dissimilarity must be clearly understood if the real problems that had to be faced on D-day in the Bayeux bridgehead are to be comprehended.

For England and America, the order of priorities was first to liberate Europe, and then to restore their independence to the various conquered countries, among which France would have to take her turn with the rest.

That the landings took place on the coast of France and that France was the first country to be liberated had nothing whatever to do with political or sentimental considerations; the reasons were purely practical. Originally, C.O.S.S.A.C. had had a choice of six landing zones, not all of which were situated in France. It had studied them, and progressively eliminated those that seemed inconvenient. Bayeux had been selected because of the tides and the supposed state of the coastal defences.

For the French themselves, whatever party they belonged to, this battle ran in double-harness with another in which the prize was political. France must recover her rank as a great power as soon as possible; she must have a free government, devoid of all foreign interference, and whose sovereignty was recognized without restriction. To de Gaulle, the problem presented itself in an even more precise form: it was his own government whose recognition must be obtained.

This was the profound, if human, misunderstanding that existed between the British and the Americans on the one hand and the French on the other. A little while before the landings, Montgomery, in the presence of the King, Eisenhower and Churchill, delivered a lecture on the operations to the commanders of the sea, land and air forces. A relief map of Normandy, wide as a street, lay on the floor of a hall in St. Paul's School. With rare ability, Montgomery explained the tactical plans of 21 Army Group, moving about the map like a giant amid a crowd of Lilliputians. But this France, which had been reduced to so unreal a size for the benefit of the Anglo-Saxon generals, was no Lilliput to the French, but a man-sized country with which their destinies were involved. "Here," wrote Pierre Bourdan, recording his return to France, "the very land takes you in its arms, surrounds you, seizes you by its robust and moving scents. . . \ There is a special odour common to all the land of France. It is an odour you can breathe nowhere else. It is a mixture of man, beast, and work; it consists of the breath of animals, smoke, ploughed earth, dried herbs; it is a unique combination of the land and hard work. And it was this odour that we found and recognized, with such incredulity, as our own, in the Cotentin during that night. . . ."

This was the contrast between the two attitudes towards the land of France. A contrast between the concrete fatherland to be liberated and the strategic and political abstractions necessary to its liberation. A contrast which became evident at Bayeux during those first days in the differences that arose between the French and their Anglo-Saxon allies.

Chapter II

BAYEUX THE CAPITAL

(6 TO 14 JUNE 1944)

NOTHING, apart from their tide-table and the shape of their beaches, had preordained the Bessin and its sub-prefecture Bayeux for the part they were to play in a world cataclysm.

Taken by and large, the population of the area had been less affected by the Occupation than that of most districts in France. On good terms with the local Vichy administration, which toned down German demands and dealt with day-to-day problems without over-much reference to the central government, it was well fed, and supplied the rest of the nation, as well, of course, as the Wehrmacht, with butter, cheese, eggs and meat; indeed, it suffered only from the less vital shortages: coffee, wine and, to some extent, bread. It knew nothing of the physical sufferings that incite to rebellion. After the landings, its main danger lay in the over-production of foodstuffs. On 6 June, the people of Bayeux had to eat the supplies destined for Paris themselves, or risk their total loss. Montgomery was shocked to find them so healthy-looking: the *Daily Mirror* correspondent in the bridgehead wrote on 14 June for his English readers: "If you're short of anything, ask the French people, there's a good chance they've got it"; and a hasty decree of the Gaullist authorities led to the inopportune stockpiling of 40,000 camemberts.

The inhabitants of Bayeux, a sub-prefecture of 7,000 souls, famous for its relics of the Middle Ages (Queen Matilda's tapestry and the eleventh-century cathedral), were no fanatics and had, indeed, a profound sense of civic decorum. In that country of meadows and sunken lanes that slope gently down towards the sea, the Resistance had not shown that intransigence which elsewhere had so violently opposed Frenchmen to other Frenchmen. When Maurice Schumann, the first Gaullist envoy, arrived on 8 June and paid a visit to the mayor of Ver-sur-Mer, whom he had been told in London was a sympathizer, he saw a portrait of Marshal

1. The return of General de Gaulle to Metropolitan France: Bayeux, 14 June 1944.

2. *François Coulet, the first Commissaire de la République to be appointed on Metropolitan soil.*

3. *Some publications of the underground press.*

Pétain hanging above his desk. "In this part of the country," the mayor explained with a certain irony, "if you don't display it, you're looked on as a collaborator."

This, presumably, is what is known as having a sense of realities. Pierre de Chevigné, military delegate for the G.P.R.F. for the northern zone, made his first contact with the local inhabitants on arriving from London on 15 June. He was surprised and disappointed by the anxieties they voiced. "You won't," they said, "requisition our butter, or mobilize us, will you?" Admiral Jaujard and Captain Laurin received a visit on board the cruiser *Georges Leygues* from the mayor of a coastal district, wearing his sash, and accompanied by his deputy, the postmistress, a young woman carrying a bunch of roses, and a delegation. The cruiser's guns had been bombarding the neighbourhood during the preceding days.

"You must have had a number of casualties," the sailors said to these first fellow-countrymen they had met, "you have been continually in our thoughts these last days."

The party looked very depressed.

"How many casualties have you had?"

"Alas, a great many."

"Do you know how many?"

"At least sixty."

The sailors were greatly shocked. Then the mayor added: "And who's going to pay, I should like to know?" [1]

They were relieved to discover that the mayor was referring to head of cattle.

But when things changed, and shells and bombs, instead of falling on fields and barns, destroyed their houses, these same Normans, who displayed so much concern for their interests and comforts, were to set an outstanding example of steadfastness and courage.

During the crossing, Maurice Schumann had made for broadcasting a romantic paraphrase of the *"Debout les Morts"* of Verdun about the peoples awaiting them on the other side.

"The living, in their deep sleep, did not yet know that we were coming. But the dead knew it. They had been awakened from their frail rest."

Three days later, on 11 June, at Trévières, the devastated chief town of a canton, he found himself in the presence of the dead in all their appalling reality. Trévières was the first little town to be liberated by the American troops, but only after a three-day bombardment. During those three days, the inhabitants, led by the priest and a retired captain,

[1] Admiral Lemonnier: *Paisible Normandie*, page 147.

had brought in the wounded and dead under fire. On the 11th, in the roofless church among the shattered houses, a funeral service was held for the twenty-two dead. Maurice Schumann attended in uniform. In spite of their tears, the survivors embraced him, for his was the first French uniform to be associated with their mourning. At the cemetery, Schumann made a speech that was moving because it was heartfelt.

In the liberated arrondissement there were no more than about twenty collaborators, and they had not been particularly virulent. The Resistance during the Occupation had numbered about a hundred, and were all the more deserving for that fact. There, as elsewhere, they increased considerably after the Germans had left.

The Resistance did not form a very cohesive organization either in Bayeux or in its neighbourhood. Some were preparing acts of sabotage for D-day, though events forestalled them, and others were doing intelligence work.

Jean Sainteny, who, in September 1940, had created a local organization, which later became part of the "Alliance" network, at first recruited its members among his childhood friends, peasants, sailors from Port-en-Bessin, Norman country gentlemen, workmen, plumbers and electricians. There were no class distinctions; they were all imbued with the same spirit and worked in the closest accord. Most of them, some fifteen, were arrested and imprisoned in Caen in April 1944 and executed on 7 June.

Among them was Dounin, the art master of the Caen Lycée, whose clandestine duty was to keep the headquarters' map of the district up-to-date. He made bicycle rides along the coast, took notes of the German defences and reported them to Sainteny, who sent them on. One day the latter received an enormous map, some fifty feet long, of the zone between the mouth of the Dives and the Cotentin.

There was not a hedge, or barbed-wire fence, or fisherman's hut or concrete blockhouse missing. It was sent to S.H.A.E.F., in London, and put to good use in preparing the plans for D-day.

It occurred to Thomine, a fisherman, that there was information at his disposal that might be of value to the Allies. Whenever the Germans installed a new coastal defence battery, they made a practice shoot out to sea and a notice was posted in the mairie showing the area closed to shipping. Thomine filched the notices and handed them in to the right quarters. From these the Allies gained information about the fields of fire they were likely to encounter during the landings.[1]

It was due to such humble assistants as these that the Allies were able

[1] Thomine and Dounin were among those executed in Caen on 7 June.

to complement the information available from air-photography by intelligence derived from the very land itself.

The great danger at this moment was that there would be a hiatus in the administration of the liberated territories—a danger of which both Algiers and Vichy were equally conscious. And, indeed, it was a major danger for any lapse of administrative authority might well be taken advantage of either by the Communist Party, or by the Allies, to endanger French independence.

The Communist Party was practically non-existent in the Bayeux region. The sole danger was, therefore, American or British interference in French affairs. And this danger, in the atmosphere ruling at the time, appeared far from negligible, and seemed to be confirmed by a number of indications preceding and accompanying the landings.

In the first place, in the April and May before D-day, there had been disagreements in London between General Koenig and his staff and General Lee, the head of British Civil Affairs, whose job it was to establish liaison with the liberated population of France. These quarrels were concerned in particular with the instructions given the Allied liaison officers.[1]

There was also, on D-day itself, Eisenhower's proclamation to the people of western Europe, of which one passage particularly concerned France. In the view of de Gaulle and his government, it was an infringement of French independence.[2]

From 6 June, these indications and many others appeared to be receiving confirmation. The Allied armies were abundantly supplied with French money "made in U.S.A."—vulgarly designed notes resembling dollars—and the French had not been consulted about its issue. "Your forged notes," de Gaulle called them. Notices, which were rather too reminiscent of those posted by the Germans, were posted on the walls of the liberated towns. They conferred on the Allied authorities police powers normally exercised by the French themselves. They concerned, in particular, the black-out, the possession of arms, and the use of field-glasses and cameras. In Cherbourg, a notice of the sort, posted on 29 June, made the American notes legal tender, and even bore the signature of the mayor, who had clearly allowed himself to be influenced. Was this a new form of "collaboration?" There were also, at the beginning, misunderstandings about requisitioning.

Laval in Vichy and de Gaulle in Algiers had equally foreseen the danger from their own standpoints and had both tried to parry it. As

[1] Cf., page 41.
[2] Cf., page 41.

early as April, the Vichy government had sent out instructions to prefects and sub-prefects to take all necessary measures to assure the safety
and feeding of the inhabitants should they find themselves isolated from
the central authority. Credits had been agreed for the treasuries of the
threatened departments to finance essential public services. Moreover,
directives had been issued concerning the attitude—one of "correct"
neutrality—to be adopted towards the German and, eventually, towards
the Allied military authorities.

The Algiers government from its side had organized, as we shall see,
a whole new administrative establishment, which was to replace that
of Vichy on the arrival of the Allies and thus assure the immediate continuity of authority.[1]

In fact, this organization only began to take over, and on a much
reduced scale, nine days after the landings, from 15 June onwards. Nine
days during which the Vichy instructions prevailed over those of the
G.P.R.F.

These nine days are therefore of considerable interest, for they constituted not only the sole period in which the Vichy administration
functioned in the presence of the Allies, but they also contributed to
the maintenance of national independence.

What would have happened if, on landing, the Allies had found the
administration abandoned and the civil power abdicated in the first
arrondissement they liberated? It would undoubtedly have been a temptation to increased interference and possibly to the installation of
AMGOT.

These days began tragically with a hail of bombs on the Norman
towns, which in some cases continued until they were completely destroyed.

In April 1944, there had been a conference of British and American
leaders at which the question of the bombing of French towns had
been discussed.

It was a dramatic conference not only because of what was at stake,
but also because of the open clash of two different conceptions of war,
two human attitudes towards the exigencies of battle. The purely military considerations were obvious and General Eisenhower did not lack
arguments justifying the destruction of strategic bridges, marshalling
yards and main railway lines. His adversaries estimated that the bombing
would cost some 80,000 civilian casualties. "Such a catastrophe would
certainly be of a nature to fill the French nation with bitterness."
Churchill opposed it with all his authority, saying in particular: "Post-

[1] Cf., Part II, Chapter 1.

war France must be our friend. It is not alone a question of humanitarianism. It is also a question of high state policy." But, between strategic necessities and political and human considerations, the former won the day. "Finally," Eisenhower says, "the Prime Minister and his government and General Pierre Joseph Koenig, the commander of the French Forces of the Interior, all agreed that the attacks had to be executed as laid down, with the hope that the measures we adopted for warning the population would be effective in minimizing casualties."

The first bombing of Caen took place in the afternoon of the 6th with heavy bombs and a few phosphorus. Interrupted at 20.00, it began again more heavily during the night, destroying dwelling-houses and public buildings, making the streets impassable and causing a large number of casualties, particularly in the Saint-Jean district. During the night of 8 June, there was a naval bombardment. During that of 12 June, there was bombing with incendiaries, followed later by high explosive. The town was three-quarters destroyed.

At Saint-Lô, the bombing began on 5 June at 17.00. It began again at 20.00 and lasted throughout the night. The population fled into the countryside or took refuge in a cave behind the hospital. The town was completely destroyed; and a thousand dead were found among the ruins.

Vire was almost entirely destroyed by high explosives and incendiaries during 6 and 7 June.

Coutances suffered two bombing attacks on 6 June. The inhabitants immediately took to the countryside. And they were right for, on 7 June, a third raid completed the destruction of the town, sparing merely a few public buildings. Of these, the cathedral, the mairie and the hospital were finished off by incendiaries on the night of the 13th.

Lisieux was largely destroyed by bombs on 6 and 7 June. The cathedral and the law courts were still standing, but with all their windows broken. But the prison was in ruins—and what was to be done with the convicts?

On 6, 7, 10 and 12 June a great part of Falaise was destroyed and looting began.

Avranches was spared on 6 June; but during the next three days practically the whole of the business centre was reduced to rubble.

At Pont-L'Évêque there were both destruction and casualties.

Argentan and Domfront both suffered severe bombing. So did Alençon, during the nights of 9 and 24 June. Nevertheless, the courts were still functioning and the magistrates at their posts on the bench. The prisoners, however, took advantage of the bombing to escape. Misfortune to some meant liberty to others.

Throughout the whole of this widespread operation, Bayeux was the one town spared. It had been planned that the army would advance beyond it on the second day and, owing to the fact that it was an important road junction, it would be useful to the liberators as a military and administrative centre. It had, therefore, to be left intact.

On 6 June, at five o'clock in the morning, the inhabitants were brought from their beds by gunfire and began queuing at the bakers' shops. During the morning, German posters appeared on the walls, framed in red, proclaiming an intensified state of siege. Civilians were to remain in their houses, close their windows and leave their doors on the latch. The sale of alcohol was forbidden, as also was riding bicycles. The troops had orders to fire on anyone disobeying these orders. "Anyone giving information to the enemy will be considered as committing espionage . . ." as also for lending "assistance to the enemy. . . ." It was from these notices that it was learned that the "enemy" was in the neighbourhood and that the landings had taken place.

Though they brandished these last thunderbolts, the Germans were beginning to move out. The employees of the civil administration and the administrative services of the Todt organization left the Place du Château. Then the archives were evacuated in the care of the interpreter. By the evening of 6 June, there were no Nazis left, except for eight telephone-operators in the basement of the Post Office and three German policemen, who continued to control the traffic even after the arrival of the first Allied troops.

The next day, 7 June, at eight o'clock in the morning, the British reached Bayeux, preceded by a crowd of small boys bearing cigarettes heralding the event. The first arrivals, a corporal and two privates of the Essex Regiment, took a good look at the roofs, while fifty or sixty civilians cheered them. While the suspicious conquerors were taking up firing positions in the prone position in the Place, a *Feldgrau* stood beside them directing such little German traffic as still passed.

The advancing and retreating armies ignored each other till the single skirmish that marked the capture of Bayeux took place at the Post Office. It was watched by a crowd completely heedless of its danger. A woman in smart summer clothes was busy taking holiday snaps. A few British soldiers, more prudently, climbed along the walls and fired through the shutters of the *Feldpost*. Two French policemen tried to move the spectators back. A Bayeux citizen advised the British to take the Post Office from the rear through the marie garden. Seven Germans came out, their hands above their heads. A shot rang out: their chief had committed suicide. Bayeux was liberated; a French town had been freed from the Occupation. A few Sherman tanks arrived—"huge, dusty, belted with gigantic floats." They were cheered. In an instant, the whole street was full of flags. "It was like Corpus Christi Day," said an old woman.

On 8 June, Bayeux began to function as a capital. At nine o'clock in the morning, Maurice Schumann arrived in his steel helmet dating from the "phoney war." The resistant school-mistresses, Mlles. Limeuil and Picot, sent their pupils to the mairie for tricolour streamers to decorate his car. At 14.00, there was a meeting at Mercader's, where Schumann was introduced to the principal resistants. From there, in his beribboned car, in which he was accompanied by a South African major, an American captain, and an English private soldier, he drove to the Place du Château, and stopped in front of the sub-prefecture. At 15.00, he made a speech to the crowd, largely passive till now, and succeeded in raising it to a high pitch of enthusiasm.

Behind the iron gates of the sub-prefecture there was another interview taking place. At 17.00, the Vichy sub-prefect, Rochat, who had taken no part in Schumann's welcome, received two visitors, the British Major Goodings, the Allied town-major designate, and a Field Security lieutenant. In the presence of two British officers, it might be supposed this Pétain official would carry no weight and perhaps suffer from a guilty conscience.

He was a Protestant, thirty-one years of age, and had occupied this, his first post as sub-prefect, for two years. Before the war he had been a junior official in the Ministry of Public Works, but he was one of those servants of the State who are prepared to do their jobs under any government whatever. It so happened that in 1941, when Pierre Pucheu was Secretary of State for Industrial Production, one of his senior civil servants had recommended Rochat for his personal Secretariat in this technical ministry. Pierre Pucheu changed his department and was appointed to the more formidable post of Minister of the Interior. Rochat went with him and, ill-advisedly, remained loyal to him, even when his chief was no longer in power, indeed even after he was shot. He was also, equally inadvisedly, the son-in-law of Bruneton, a high Vichy official at the time of the landings. Hardly circumstances conducive to being the right man to receive two British officers.

Nevertheless, Rochat impressed them and, once the ice was broken, the British gave him the significant and friendly nickname of "King of the Liberated Territories." This "king," so quickly anointed, stood up to them and proved by his example how permanent the French administration was. To begin with, Gooding's attitude was that of a paternalistic conqueror who presumed he was in a starving and disorganized country. Furnished with cigarettes and military francs, with food rations for the nourishing of the poor fellows whose healthy appearance he had as yet had no time to gauge, he proposed to take over the police, the administration and perhaps even to set up some tentative form of AMGOT.

The presence of the two British officers in that sub-prefecture's very ordinary room, which had a portrait of Pétain that was to become, as we shall see, notorious, no doubt marked an important hour for France. Rochat received them politely, but with the dignity of a man who was sure of his position and of his capacity to organize the public administration. He refused to have anything to do with their American francs: they were an assault on the autonomy of the French finances which even the Germans had never attempted. He gave his visitors the figures of the holdings in the arrondissement: in all 5,635,000 francs, of which 560,000 were at the Recette des Finances, 460,000 at the P.T.T., 2,000,000 in the Crédit Lyonnais, 700,000 in the Société Générale, 450,000 in the B.N.C.I., 1,500,000 in the Crédit Industriel, and 15,000 at the Caisse d'Épargne. This was sufficient to deal with all immediate necessities.

As for the food they offered, it was, on the other hand, the sub-prefect who was able to assure the Allies that he could supply them with fresh vegetables, butter, eggs and, of course, cheese. Police powers? Apart from the particular requirements of the armies on active operations, he proposed to control them himself.

Most of the regulations in force before the landings were accepted by the Allies: the French police and gendarmerie continued to keep order, together with the Allied military police. The cafés remained open for the same hours, except those that might become centres of espionage— though how these were to be recognized was not stated. The brothel, which remained closed, was nevertheless inspected by the new town-major. As for the loot left behind by the Germans, it was mostly used for the benefit of the inhabitants: the Wehrmacht's gasoline ensured the civilian ration; the stakes defending the fields were used as fuel by the Bayeux bakery; and the wagons and German horses were divided up among the farmers.

Everything was arranged in detail, except the fate of eighteen piglings found at the *Soldatenheim*. This was one of the uncertainties of war. Were they French or English? Who was to eat them? In short, the administration carried on under the new régime as it had under the old; and, by the evening of D-plus-2, the sub-prefect of Bayeux had permitted nothing to be done that could in any way compromise French sovereignty.

On 9 June, as a matter of urgency, he addressed a Circular No. I to the mayors of the devastated towns laying down the steps to be taken for lodging the bombed-out, for food supply, for the prevention of looting, and for the burial of the dead. For lack of coffins, the dead were temporarily to be put straight into the earth. On this day, too, Rochat received the first French liaison officers, under the command of Colonel Chandon, from London.[1] It was a cordial meeting. The newcomers had little to do in Bayeux in any case, where liaison had already been established by the sub-prefect of Vichy.

On the 10th, the administrative machine was working at full blast. Rochat wrote to the bishop informing him that he had obtained an assurance from Goodings that no observation post would be set up in the cathedral towers. He sent out circulars to the mayors about the fate of the German horses and the organization of milk collection; it ended in the style of the Grande Armée: "I know I can count on you." He sent out a circular to employers about unemployment; it began with a remarkable euphemism: "There has been a certain disturbance of the economic life of the district during the past week . . ."

To be the "king of the liberated territories" was clearly no sinecure. Let us look a little further into the minor events of his "reign."

The 11th was a Sunday, and there was a luncheon for the members of the Resistance presided over by Maurice Schumann. Owing to the secrecy in which they had worked, these men had not known each other, and were now surprised to discover that their ranks included Catholics and atheists, freemasons and priests, and members of both the right and left. At the *hors d'œuvre*, the loyal unity of the Resistance still existed. But, by the dessert, the old disagreements had broken out again, and everyone was passionately arguing the question of the Catholic schools.

On the 12th, the sub-prefect was busy with civil affairs; his post consisted of three or four letters and circulars.

On the morning of 13 June, his duties extended into the military sphere. The Allied armies required supplementary hospitals. They approached the sub-prefect through Colonel Chandon, and during the next twenty-four hours hospitalization was organized for some 900 wounded. Rochat put some into the Hôtel du Luxembourg, the ex-*Soldatenheim*, some into the schools and the college, and some into the asylum. He

[1] Cf., page 42.

succeeded in finding bedding and set up an operating theatre. He recruited doctors and nurses. The town-crier went round the streets to ask the civilian population to supply such minor articles as were still lacking. The whole was ready to function the following day. The British General Lewis came to thank this new ally officially on behalf of the British Army.

On Wednesday, 14 June, the sub-prefect's secretary was overwhelmed with memoranda, circulars and letters: it was the culminating point of the "reign." The bombed-out were to be given urgent financial assistance. Five managers were appointed for the supplementary hospitals. A list of the medical supplies required for the liberated region was drawn up. Eggs and butter were collected, cigarettes and tobacco allowed to be sold freely, and a bilingual notice issued to be placed in bars. Life was becoming normal again.

The Vichy adminstration had imposed itself on the Allies thanks to its efficiency. But it was a Capitol that did not yet suspect how close was the Tarpeian Rock.

But this busy 14 June has its place in history for more important reasons than these. Bayeux, Isigny and other places in the neighbourhood received a visit from General de Gaulle.

This was the most moving day of all; the man who, during four long years, had been the incarnation of the refusal to accept defeat, was making contact once again with the soil of metropolitan France and with its population. It was a decisive day in the history of the Liberation and in that of France's independence.

But for sub-prefect Rochat it was the beginning of the end.

Chapter III

BAYEUX THE CAPITAL

(14 TO 24 JUNE 1944)

ON 14 June, the conflict between General de Gaulle and the Allies, which had been latent ever since 21 April, came to a head. On that day, a measure taken by the British in preparation for the landings had forbidden the transmission of ciphered signals between the government in Algiers and its representatives in London, that is to say Viénot, the ambassador, and Koenig, the military delegate. This measure, of which the object was to preserve the secret of the forthcoming landings and which, from that point of view, was justified, seemed to the General a personal affront or rather an affront to the France he represented. He retorted from Algiers by forbidding Viénot and Koenig to "negotiate anything at all so long as the Allies insist on knowing the orders we give and the reports that are sent us."

There was also another question, which had been dragging on for a long time, to aggravate the discord: the Allies' failure to recognize the Algiers Committee as the government of France.

The struggle between de Gaulle and the Allies came to a head in London over the newly created corps of French administrative liaison officers. It consisted of two sections, one male numbering approximately 160 officers, and one female numbering about fifty. This organization, under the command of Lieutenant-Colonel Hettier de Boislambert, with Captain de Rothschild in charge of the female contingent, had been set up in August 1943 by Pierre Laroque, secretary-general of the French Services in London, together with Boislambert himself, under the name of M.M.L.A. (Military Mission for Administrative Liaison).

The liaison officers had been recruited either in Algiers or in London, not for their military abilities but because of their administrative experience in civilian life. Whether they had ever worn uniform before or not, they were put into khaki and given white badges of rank. They were sent on a course to Camberley designed to fit them, after the landings, to be attached to the Allied staffs and to ensure liaison with the French civilian authorities and population.

The course was designed to cover both practice and policy.

After the Camberley course, most of the administrative liaison officers attended courses at the training school for their British equivalents, the officers of Civil Affairs, and this made useful personal contacts possible: on the other hand, the American officers of Civil Affairs, trained in schools on the other side of the Atlantic, had no contact with the French liaison officers and from this many misunderstandings were to arise.

On 25 April 1944, official negotiations to define the respective functions of M.M.L.A. and Civil Affairs in liberated territory began. In particular, who was to appoint officials to replace those with Vichy affiliations? In this French sovereignty was involved.

The first meeting took place under the auspices of Lieutenant-General Grasett, of S.H.A.E.F., and General Koenig.

The atmosphere was friendly; both sides expressed their point of view in general terms and these appeared to be reconcilable: "The policy put forward by the Allies showed no profound incompatibility with that which the French officers had been ordered to support."

There was no question of AMGOT, nor of contesting French sovereignty on any point. It merely seemed to the French that their opposite numbers were ill-informed about the situation in France, and above all about the preparations the C.F.L.N. had made to ensure the administration of the liberated territories.

Two days later, the practical work between the authorities of Civil Affairs and M.M.L.A. began.

On 3 May 1944, General Koenig gave a talk on the role the liaison officers were to play.

But on 4 May, these preliminaries ceased on an order from Algiers. General de Gaulle forbade all official relations between the French in London and the Allies.

On 7 May, in a speech to the Assemblée Consultative in Algiers, de Gaulle said: "So long as communications are not restored between Algiers and London, it is impossible to allow General Koenig to negotiate on his own."

On 15 May, the Committee of Algiers transformed itself of its own volition into the Provisional Government of the French Republic. At the same time, de Gaulle denounced the Clark-Darlan agreement, which had been concluded by the Americans on the morrow of the Allied landings in North Africa. And then, agreeable to these prestige measures,

Koenig, on 17 May, gave orders to his subordinates in London that all contact with the Allies, even unofficial, be broken off. As a French liaison officer wrote in his private diary: "We mustn't even know each other any more."

The rupture was complete, though the British did their best to improve the situation. On 18 May, the King received General Koenig and personally authorized him to send a signal to General de Gaulle in Algiers.

On 21 May, the British Sunday Press recognized the difficult position in which the cessation of communications had placed the Gaullist authorities and showed understanding of French reactions.

On 24 May, Churchill made a speech in the House of Commons, which was calculated to ease the situation. He enumerated the reasons which had prevented him *till now* from recognizing the C.F.L.N. as the government of France. He had invited de Gaulle to come to London, and the General had accepted. And, finally, he recognized France as "the fourth great power." He made no precise promises, but his speech was courteous and friendly.

On 25 May, Eden also made a speech in the House which cleared the atmosphere. The House in general showed itself to be favourably disposed towards the provisional government of the French Republic.

On 1 and 2 June, the British Press made it clear that it did not agree with the "negative position of the U.S.A." It discussed the monetary and sovereignty questions over which the Americans were being intransigent.

On 3 June, the bombardment of the coast of the Pas de Calais could be heard in the suburbs of London. Was this the beginning of the great event?

On 4 June, in the morning, General de Gaulle arrived in London.

He had made the journey in Churchill's personal York, which had been politely placed at his disposal, and there was a second British plane for his staff, which consisted of two civilians, his *chef de cabinet*, Palewski, and a diplomat, Geoffroy de Courcel, and three soldiers, Generals Béthouart and Billotte, and Lieutenant Teyssot. There was no minister with the head of the provisional government; and this was deliberate, since the General refused to permit any political negotiations so long as he had not obtained satisfaction on the two controversial points.

On his arrival in London at the Connaught Hotel, where he had lived before leaving for Algiers, de Gaulle received a friendly letter from Churchill.

In the train, 4 June 1944.

My dear General de Gaulle,

Welcome to these shores! Great military events are about to take place. I would be happy if you would come to see me here, in my train, which is very close to General Eisenhower's headquarters, and that you should bring one or two members of your staff with you. General Eisenhower is hoping for a visit from you and will explain the military situation which is extremely important and imminent. If you could be here by 1.30 I would be happy to give you luncheon; we will then go to General Eisenhower's headquarters. Send me a telephone message early so that I may know whether this suits you or not.

Sincerely yours.

De Gaulle accepted the invitation to luncheon and was accompanied by General Béthouart, Ambassador Viénot, the diplomatic representative of the G.P.R.F. in London, and the military representative, General Koenig. Eden picked them up at their hotel and drove them down to the Prime Minister's train, which was near Portsmouth. Churchill's British guests were Eden, Bevin, General Ismay, and Field-Marshal Smuts.

There was a certain lack of harmony about the meal. Could it be otherwise, given the situation of the guests and their hosts? For de Gaulle and the French this was an essential meeting. The independence of France was at stake, as were the recognition of their government and the success of their whole policy during the last four years. For de Gaulle, this was the greatest struggle of his life.

For the British, on the other hand, this was merely an episode which, though it had a certain importance no doubt, was in no sense decisive. Churchill had thought it proper that the French be informed of the forthcoming liberation of their country. The Allies needed them for certain matters of detail; indeed, Eisenhower, recognizing the possible military importance of the Resistance, preferred to have an understanding with de Gaulle, without whom he might find it difficult to gain the support of the F.F.I. Similarly, it was hoped that the presence of French liaison officers would facilitate relations with the population during the forthcoming operations. But these considerations, whether military or merely sentimental, were of very minor importance among the problems that the huge operation necessarily posed. What weight could these Frenchmen, so stiff in their pride and so intransigent in their demands, carry in the face of the huge masses of men to be launched on the morrow, or of the great empires on whose fate the future of the world depended? One has the impression that this entertaining of the French to luncheon was for Churchill merely a two-hour break amid more pressing cares: his correspondence with the King, who had just dissuaded him from embarking in a warship to watch the landings; his relations with Stalin, whom he was keeping minutely informed of the progress of the war; his permanent and intimate contacts with Roosevelt; and, for that matter, his deliberations with Eisenhower and Montgomery, who were at this moment in conclave about the landings.

This 4 June, on which the not very amicable luncheon took place, was indeed the day on which the decision was made as to whether Overlord should go forward or be postponed. The meteorologists' reports were clearly of far greater importance to Churchill than the opinions of these Frenchmen, these outsiders, about the conduct of the war. And his somewhat curt and abrupt treatment of them was no doubt due to these facts. De Gaulle was "bristling," but Churchill immediately got down to detail. He told him of the imminence of the landings. He recapitulated the efforts the Allies had made, and particularly those made by Great Britain. He explained the military reasons for which, to his great regret, it had been necessary to bomb French towns. He described the broad outlines of Overlord with sincerity and brilliance. "At that moment in history," de Gaulle writes in his *Mémoires*, "a similar emotion of respect and friendship affected both the French and British present."

More simply, General Béthouart, who was present at the luncheon, remembered having heard de Gaulle say a laconic "thank you" when the Prime Minister had finished speaking.

Churchill then turned to the more thorny political problems. He could make no decision about the future government of France without consulting the Americans. De Gaulle should accept Roosevelt's invitation to go to America to discuss the matter with him. The General curtly refused. His government existed—why should he negotiate its recognition?

The British reacted violently. Bevin intervened to say that if General de Gaulle refused to negotiate, the Labour Party would consider his attitude as offensive to Great Britain.

This did not frighten de Gaulle: if they wanted him to talk, he would do so. He spoke of the infringements of French sovereignty intended by the Allies; he demanded once again the right to communicate in cipher between Algiers and London; and he criticized the false money that had been printed for France without the consent of the French. In these circumstances, what guarantee had he that the Americans would not take over the government of France as soon as they landed? "How can you expect us," said de Gaulle, "to negotiate on bases such as these?" To treat with allies who were holding a knife to his throat?

There was mounting exasperation on both sides. Churchill's reply had a bluntness that can be explained only by the urgencies and anxieties of the day.

If he had to decide between the United States and France, the Prime Minister's decision was already made: "If there was a split between the committee of national liberation and the United States we should almost certainly side with the Americans. About the administration of liberated French soil, if General de Gaulle wanted us to ask the President to give him the title deeds of France the answer was 'no'." De Gaulle replied that he quite understood that if the U.S.A. and France disagreed Britain would side with the U.S.A. On that, the interview ended.

Churchill then took de Gaulle to headquarters, where Eisenhower gave greater evidence of diplomacy than the statesman. De Gaulle was received "most ceremoniously." "Ike and Bedell Smith vied with one another in their courtesy," Churchill writes. "Ike took him to their map tent, and for twenty minutes imparted to him the whole story of what was about to happen."

The Commander-in-Chief was even more amiable, or perhaps cleverer, than Churchill records. He not only gave de Gaulle all the details of the landings, but asked his advice on the essential decision that had to be made during the next twenty-four hours: was Overlord to be posponed or not? "What do you think?" he asked his visitor, who clearly could not have as much information on which to base a decision as himself. But it was a mark of deference to which, in the circumstances, de Gaulle could not but be sensible. He replied, as a head of state who wished to leave freedom of action to the military authority, that it was a decision which could only be Eisenhower's and that he approved in advance whatever he decided. "I will only say this," he added, "that in your place I would make no postponement. The risk from the weather seems to me less than the dangers of several weeks' delay which is bound to exacerbate the moral tension of the troops taking part and to compromise the secret."

This was the only bright spot in the relations between France and the Allies that day. And it was very transient. Before de Gaulle left, Eisenhower, looking somewhat embarrassed the French thought, handed him the proclamation he was proposing to make on D-day to the people of western Europe.

This proclamation did not contest France's right to administer herself, but on the other hand it did not exclude the possibility of being "otherwise instructed" by the Allied military authorities; it included no formula either recognizing or disowning de Gaulle's government, but it was clear that at best it could be considered only a temporary organization covering the interregnum before complete liberation had been achieved. From Eisenhower's point of view this was a compromise between Roosevelt's instructions and his desire not to offend the General's susceptibilities. The Commander-in-Chief's position was a far from easy one: on the one hand, from the military point of view, he needed the General: "We were depending," he wrote in *Crusade in Europe*, "on a considerable assistance from the insurrectionists in France. They were known to be particularly numerous in the Brittany area and in the hills and mountains of south-east France." Moreover, he "particularly desired de Gaulle to participate with me in broadcasting on D-day to the French people so that the population, avoiding uprisings and useless sacrifices at non-critical points, would still be instantly ready to help us where help was needed." A statement which, as we shall see, is somewhat disingenuous.

On the other hand, Eisenhower knew that President Roosevelt viewed with disfavour de Gaulle's desire to be recognized as the only head of the government. In Roosevelt's view, no single person should be singled out, but there should be co-operation with all the French groups fighting the Germans; above all, the future must not be prejudiced. The people would choose a government after the Liberation. The most he would allow Eisenhower was to recognize General Koenig as commander of the French Forces of the Interior, attached to the Allied organization.

The proclamation as drafted did not satisfy de Gaulle. The next day, 5 June, he sent an alternative proclamation to Eisenhower's headquarters; but he was told that it was now too late.

De Gaulle's interview with Eisenhower ended in no more friendly an atmosphere than his luncheon with Churchill. "I had expected," writes Churchill, "that de Gaulle would dine with us [in the train] and come back to London by this, the swiftest and most convenient route, but he drew himself up and stated that he preferred to motor with his French officers separately."

On 5 June two further conflicts arose between de Gaulle and the Allies. The French had been informed that the landings would take place during the following night. Charles Peake, whom the Foreign Office had appointed as British representative with the leader of Free France, made two requests of de Gaulle. The first was that he should talk on the radio in a chain of broadcasts to the peoples of Occupied Europe. The order of these broadcasts was to be as follows: first, the heads of states of western Europe: the King of Norway, the Queen of Holland, the Grand Duchess of Luxembourg; then the Prime Minister of Belgium; then Eisenhower, who would make his proclamation; and, finally, de Gaulle would speak to France.

Secondly, he was asked to place at the disposal of the Allied forces, who were on the point of landing, the French liaison officers who had been recruited and trained for this purpose over many months.

De Gaulle refused both requests. He refused to grant anything whatever till the two points of disagreement between himself and the Allies had been resolved: free communications between London and Algiers and the recognition of his government. Otherwise, he would seem to be underwriting the Allied declarations.

Churchill learnt of de Gaulle's intransigence during the night of the landings, when a prey to far greater anxieties. He sent for Ambassador Viénot and asked him to intervene with de Gaulle. At two o'clock in the morning, when the first Allied and French commandos were already in France, Viénot transmitted Churchill's message to de Gaulle. It was an interview which he later summed up in these terms: "Never have I received such a rocket in my life."

De Gaulle absolutely refused to take part in the chain of broadcasts planned for that morning. Nor would he allow the 170 liaison officers, who were champing at the bit now that the moment had come at last, to sail.

The most he would concede, and the Allies had to be content with it, was that a first contingent of twenty liaison officers, under the command of Colonel Chandon, should sail on 8 June; and even then he laid it down that they were to have no liaison duties with regard to the civil authorities, which would imply, in de Gaulle's view, approval of the British and American policy towards France; they would not be called liaison officers for civil administration, but "general liaison officers and observers."

With regard to the broadcast, de Gaulle refused to take part in the morning programme so as to avoid the question of precedence which was clearly unfavourable to him, but spoke alone in the evening. He spoke to France at 18.00, but his speech made no reference whatever to Eisenhower's demands.

"The supreme battle has begun. . . . It is, of course, not only the battle of France, but France's battle! . . . For the sons of France, wherever they may be, whatever they may be, their simple and sacred duty is to fight the enemy by every means at their disposal. . . . The orders given by the French government and by the French leaders it has appointed must be implicitly obeyed. . . . From behind the dark cloud of our blood and tears, the sun of our grandeur is appearing once more!"

It was no doubt a splendid message, but in it de Gaulle, who had no direct military responsibilities, entirely ignored the points made by the responsible Commander-in-Chief.

If the circumstances had not been so grave, and the personalities involved so eminent, one might well say that the differences between de Gaulle and the Allies were a case of the deaf listening to the deaf. De Gaulle refused to listen to anything that failed to correspond to his own conception of the grandeur of France and of his personal mission. He mistook his apprehensions for realities; and as a result his telegram of 9 June to the ministers who had remained in Algiers, Henri Queuille and Massigli, asserted that Eisenhower's proclamation to the French people introduced "in principle AMGOT into France," which would seem exaggerated. Or again, on the eve of the landings, he could refer to the "honour" he had done Eisenhower by placing "under his command a great part of the French Army." When one knows how many men were involved, the remark appears a trifle excessive.

But at this moment de Gaulle was playing for the highest stakes, and as he did so presented a human problem that was to condition both his own future and that of France. As the day approached on which he was to regain the contact he had been denied for four years with the soil of his native land, his personality achieved fulfilment, and his destiny its apogee in history as he conceived it.

On his first coming into power as head of a prentice state, there was certainly less spontaneity in de Gaulle's attitude to history than to France herself. His country was not only a physical reality, but also a sort of sublime allegory against which he was projected. To him, history was no merely temporal thing for, even as he lived it, it assumed the stylization of the past. For de Gaulle, history was transmuted into heroic legend even as it was being made. The memoirs in which he records it are a *Chanson de Roland* written by Roland himself, with all the compulsive distortions and simplifications that must imply. As a man who felt himself to be a part of all the centuries—though he was really of none—a man for whom *Grandeur, Gloire* and *Patrie* were always, inevitably written with initial capitals, he was inclined to conjure with the names of Clemenceau, Napoleon and Joan of Arc. And, indeed, in the perspective in which he viewed them, were they not his equals, almost his contemporaries? Contemporary in legend, in eternity and in the history of France, in which only heroes counted. For de Gaulle himself was, after all, tradition made man; and this was sometimes a disservice to him when it was merely a matter of making contact with the contiguous and ephemeral lives of those who have simply to suffer history and have no pretensions to making it. Fated to have to take extraordinary decisions, he was, during this period of his career in which he achieved supreme power for the first time, as ineffectual when the tension was relaxed as he was brilliantly lucid at moments of extreme crisis. Like Baudelaire's albatross, it occasionally happened that "his giant wings prevented his walking."

And this was the extraordinary man who, his greatness wrapped about him like a cloak, was making preparations, on 6 June, for his rendezvous with history on the liberated soil of France.

As the decisive moment approached, his figure seemed to acquire a greater stature, an increasing grandeur—as it were, a bronze cast for all eternity, majestic, powerful, but in search of its plinth. And the truest and finest of plinths, at this crucial moment, was his native land—that earth in which, four years before, his mother had been buried, and who had said of him, on 16 July 1940, before dying: "Charles has always succeeded in everything he has undertaken. I know he is doing the right thing."

The fourteenth of June was the day on which his destiny was put to the test. When, four days earlier, on 10 June, Winston Churchill, accompanied by Field-Marshal Smuts and the three American Chiefs of Staff, had landed in his Norman apanage, Field-Marshal Montgomery was awaiting him on the shore. But, for General de Gaulle, on 14 June, the welcome was less elaborate. There was a guard of honour of the Scots Guards, commanded by a captain, and a few officers of the Royal Navy to welcome him. This was the usual proportion, which indeed corresponded to the proportions of the forces involved: a captain for the French, a field-marshal for the Allies.[1]

The week between the 6th and the 14th had been one of continuous crisis growing more acute each day. On 8 June, Eden had dined with de Gaulle: he had insisted that the French government agree to negotiate and send Massigli to London. The sole result was that next day de Gaulle sent a telegram to Queuille, Vice-President of the Council, who was acting for him in Algiers, and to Henri Massigli, saying: "I consider it essential that my journey should strictly adhere to the character origi-

[1] Cf., page 16.

nally intended for it and that no other member of the government come to negotiate here."

Finally, on 14 June, Churchill was questioned in the Commons about his policy towards France. He made an evasive reply. That same day, on French soil, de Gaulle was organizing his counter-attack. Together with the Service chiefs and civilians who had accompanied him to Bayeux, General Koenig, General Béthouart, Admiral Thierry d'Argenlieu, Ambassador Viénot, Gaston Palewski and Commandant de Boislambert, he sailed that evening for London. François Coulet, Commandant de Chevigné and Pierre Laroque remained in France. Their job was to play the part of the Trojan horse among the Allied administrative personnel.

De Gaulle's first day in France was a mixture of grandeur and stratagem. But, above all, like a mystic in search of God as the crown of his aspirations, de Gaulle was expecting France to justify his vocation.

He left London at five o'clock in the morning, on the 14th, with his staff. The day before, he had summoned François Coulet, who had been for three months the first secretary-general of the prefecture in Corsica after the departure of the Germans and Italians, and had therefore some experience of the problems of liberated territories. De Gaulle told him in detail of his difficulties with Churchill and concluded: "I am leaving tomorrow for the bridgehead. I shall take you with me and leave you there as Commissaire Régional of the Republic."

From this, François Coulet gathered that his appointment had been made without the knowledge of the Allies, and probably contrary to their intentions. With Colonel de Chevigné, who was to be the military delegate appointed to reorganize the liberated sub-divisions, and Commandant Laroque, who was to be his legal assistant, he spent the night of the 13th making preparations for his departure to take up his duties in France.

They embarked at Portsmouth at ten o'clock, on board *La Combattante*, which hoisted a tricolour flag bearing the General's initials. "It is not altogether in accordance with regulations," a chief petty officer admitted. "We improvised it the first time the General came to visit us in England."

During the crossing, de Gaulle and his staff remained on deck. The General, wearing a leather tunic and a *képi* with the single oak leaf corresponding to his temporary rank, was silent, gazing at the coastline appearing on the horizon through his field-glasses. Everyone shared his unexpressed emotion. But silence weighed on them as the moment, for which they had risked everything, approached. As they spoke in low tones about their silent leader, their voices seemed to be carried away by the winds of sea and history. Ambassador Viénot heard one of his companions remark that this crossing was the anniversary of the saddest date of all: that of the entry of the Germans into Paris. Taking the opportunity to break the spell in which the General seemed to be enveloped, he went to him and mentioned this dramatic fact. Without taking his eyes from the horizon, de Gaulle remarked curtly: "Well, they were wrong. It was an error. . . ." And they all fell silent again.

At 14.00, *La Combattante* dropped anchor a few hundred yards from the shore. There was a certain amount of sea running and they had to wait for a D.U.K.W. to come off to the destroyer and take them ashore, which it did in two trips. There were two villages on the low coast, Courseulles and Graye-sur-Mer, both of which were later to claim the honour of having been first to receive the General. The roofs of their houses were shattered and their churches partly ruined. The beach was covered with tents, bivouacs and packing-cases. The sky was alive with anti-aircraft balloons. How would their native land respond to their own emotion?

The D.U.K.W. landed the headquarters of Free France near the Courseulles' calvary. Amid the uniforms, François Coulet, in plain clothes, sat on a trunk brought from London containing 25,000,000 francs in French banknotes for the immediate requirements of the Gaullist administration and so that they should not have to have recourse to the American "false money."

Two Allied officers introduced themselves to the General. They each had a jeep to transport the party. One was a Canadian major, wearing a tartan-trimmed beret with a pom-pon on top; the other was one of the most popular officers in the British Navy, the bearded Commander Colin Maud, wearing shorts and carrying his legendary blackthorn.

The General and his suite split up into three parties. The Canadian major's jeep took de Gaulle, General Béthouart and Ambassador Viénot to Montgomery's headquarters. Montgomery had asked de Gaulle to luncheon. "We have not come to France," replied de Gaulle, "to have luncheon with Montgomery."

A mere visit would be enough.

Commander Colin Maud's jeep took Admiral Thierry d'Argenlieu, General Koenig, Gaston Palewski, and Colonel de Boislambert straight to Bayeux. They were to make preparations for de Gaulle's entrance into the liberated sub-prefecture.

Finally, the rearguard, comprising François Coulet, Colonel de Chevigné, Commandant Laroque and Commandant de Courcel, remained for some time on the beach till invited by a British liaison officer to join the General at the Bayeux sub-prefecture. Commandant Laroque inaugurated his functions as secretary-general of police by guarding the treasure: he sat on the 25,000,000 francs.

De Gaulle reached Montgomery's headquarters at about 14.30. Montgomery was in all his glory as a victorious general. From the extra thick soles he wore on his shoes, to make him look taller, to his famous black beret which, so it was said, he had one day lost and gone to look for under heavy fire, this little man, with his nasal voice and corduroy trousers, had created for himself a personality that was in keeping with his public acclaim. Even his pet bitch seemed conscious of his fame. He had also adopted a way of living that will go down to history. He received de Gaulle in his trailer. On the walls were two photographs: one, signed, of Eisenhower; the other, unsigned for obvious reasons, of Rommel. But he remarked in his most martial manner of the latter: "I missed him in Africa, but I hope to get him this time." Montgomery explained the battle he was in process of winning. Then he asked de Gaulle to say a few words to his staff. De Gaulle was delighted to do so. But these formalities, more or less necessitated by etiquette, were for him of minor importance. The one important matter was a sentence he had let drop during the conversation, and to which Montgomery paid no particular attention: "I have brought with me Commandant Coulet, who will be concerned with the administration at Bayeux." And so, when de Gaulle left Montgomery's headquarters to attend to "his business" in Bayeux, he had placed his Trojan horse in position, more or less unbeknown to the British commander.

Meanwhile, the French advance party had reached Bayeux. Maurice Schumann, wearing a beret, had come to meet it. At about 14.30, Admiral d'Argenlieu, General Koenig, Gaston Palewski, and Boislambert, went to Mercader's shop. Together with Colonel Chandon, they arranged General de Gaulle's reception.

From there, the party went on foot to the sub-prefecture in the Place du Château. Koenig led the way, clutching a bunch of peonies, followed by Admiral d'Argenlieu, Palewski, Boislambert and a war-correspondent called Jeannerat. On the way, they gathered an escort of a few resistants and women and children: the first triumphal progress. When they arrived at the Place du Château, they formed a circle in front of the fountain, while two mobile loudspeakers, organized by the local electricians, drove round Bayeux announcing: "General de Gaulle will speak at four o'clock on the Place du Château. . . ." Meanwhile, Commander Colin Maud's jeep was driving through the streets with one of the leaders of the Resistance, Desprairies, the future regional public relations officer, who was inaugurating his functions by shouting the same announcement at the top of his voice.

Another team of resistants was busy erecting a little platform and draping it with the Tricolour. The gathering would be concealed from the air by the closely growing trees—the enemy was only some six miles away.

In Bayeux excitement was mounting. The man who was to bring it to a climax had, in the meantime, left Montgomery's headquarters and was on his way to the town, wondering what sort of reception was in store for him.

On the way, he met two policemen bicycling towards Courseulles. De Gaulle stopped the jeep and called them over.

"The policemen got off their bicycles, came across and smartly saluted the unknown officer in the long coat buttoned up to the neck. . . . They clearly had no idea to whom they were talking. The officer introduced himself: 'I am General de Gaulle. . . .'

"The policemen at once dropped their bicycles," recorded Colonel Rémy.

" 'My friends,' said the General, 'I'm going to ask you to do me a service. I'm on my way to Bayeux; would you be kind enough to go back there and tell them I'm coming, so that I take no one unawares? We shall not move from here for a quarter of an hour.' " [1]

Half an hour later, at 15.30, de Gaulle reached Bayeux. At the entrance to the town, where the road he had followed from the coast met the first houses, the General encountered a civilian, called Banse, who indicated the way. Then the captain of the gendarmerie and the commissaire of police met him and guided him in. Finally, there was Maurice Schumann.

The streets were more or less empty; the whole population, warned by the loudspeakers, had gathered in the Place du Château round the platform. The General, his face drawn with fatigue and emotion, reached the sub-prefecture without having made any significant contact with the population.

In front of the sub-prefecture, his suite grouped themselves round him: not only the advance party, consisting of General Koenig, Thierry d'Argenlieu and Boislambert, but also the rearguard who, with happy timing, arrived at this moment: Commandant de Chevigné, Laroque, Commandant de Courcel and François Coulet in plain clothes.

When, therefore, Rochat, the sub-prefect, came out to the gates of

[1] Rémy: *Les Mains Jointes*, page 147.

the sub-prefecture, he was able to welcome the whole Gaullist headquarters. De Gaulle shook him by the hand. The new arrivals crossed the courtyard, climbed the horseshoe steps, and crossed the hall and the big reception-room. Hardly had Rochat heard them refuse a *champagne d'honneur*, for which it hardly seemed an appropriate moment, when he found himself closeted in the little adjacent room with General de Gaulle, General Koenig and Coulet. The conversation lasted a quarter of an hour, and was merely interrupted for a moment by the doorkeeper, who was Gaullist, bringing the General a glass of lemonade with a trembling hand. This conversation marked the first taking over of a liberated territory by the G.P.R.F.

De Gaulle, with somewhat distant courtesy, questioned the sub-prefect about bombings, the damage and the morale of the Norman population. Then Koenig and Coulet, who were even stiffer, asked him for information about supplies, stocks of food and reserves of currency: "How much money have you got? How much flour?" Rochat, who felt as if he were appearing before a particularly harsh board of examiners, came very well out of the interview. His behaviour and attitude towards the Allies aroused no criticism.

But, alas, as he came out of the room everything suddenly went wrong. One of the new arrivals, Boislambert, who was standing in the big reception-room, had seen a portrait of Marshal Pétain on the wall. He indicated it to Rochat with an imperious gesture of the chin. The latter, fearing an incident, summoned the doorkeeper and had the photograph removed.

For several interminable seconds there was a meaningful silence; the photograph resisted all the doorkeeper's efforts to remove it. At last, Rochat climbed on to a chair and together they succeeded in taking it down.

This *coup d'état* accomplished, the General was introduced to the notables of the town: Monseigneur Picaud, who had been hastily summoned from the bishop's palace; Dedoman, the mayor; and the president of the court.

De Gaulle and his staff then returned to the square, where the crowd gave him an enthusiastic welcome, throwing flowers and trying to touch him. Mothers held out their children to him. It was an apotheosis consecrating de Gaulle head of the French government. It was the long-awaited moment which legitimized all his actions. He was so moved that, as he shook hundreds of hands, he could find nothing to say but: "How are you?" Maurice Schumann presented the local resistants.

"Then, General de Gaulle went up on to the platform and put his *képi* down; the background consisted of a Tricolour, waist high, with an American flag on the right and a British flag on the left; above, at head height, there was a long red, white and blue streamer, fixed to the lime trees, marking the apex of the triangle into which the crowd pressed forward. Higher still, hanging from the branches above, was a big flag with the Cross of Lorraine." [1]

Then followed the first speech General de Gaulle delivered on French soil:

We are all moved to find ourselves together again in one of the first Metropolitan French towns to be liberated; but it is no moment to talk of emotion. What the country expects of you, here behind the front, is to continue the fight today as you have never ceased from fighting since the beginning of the war and since June 1940. Our cry now, as always, is a war-cry, because the path of war is also the road to liberty and to honour. This is the voice of the Mother Country. . . . I promise you that we shall continue to fight till sovereignty is re-established over every inch of our soil. No one shall prevent our doing that.

We shall fight beside the Allies, with the Allies, as an ally. And the victory we shall win will be the victory of liberty and the victory of France.

I am going to ask you to sing with me our national anthem, the *Marseillaise.*

To assert that this peaceable population—despite the Occupation, it had been far from discontented with its lot—had not ceased fighting since June 1940 would in other circumstances have made these good Normans smile. But hearing the *Marseillaise* once more temporarily overcame all their mental reservations. For the time being, de Gaulle succeeded in raising his captivated audience to his own plane.

The crowd showed great enthusiasm. When the *Marseillaise* was over, the General went towards the jeeps which were waiting in front of the École de la Poterie, next door to the sub-prefecture. The crowd pressed in on him. It was only with great difficulty that de Gaulle and his escort succeeded in making their way through it. The jeeps tried to start moving, but they were surrounded, taken by assault. They had to stop; and the General stood up in the leading jeep and said a few more words to the crowd. At last, the police and the military police succeeded in opening a way for the vehicles.

The three jeeps set off towards Isigny.

Unlike Bayeux, Isigny was in a part of Normandy that had suffered considerable damage.

[1] Raymond Triboulet: *Arrivée de de Gaulle en France.*

They drove to the bridge where the ruins began. The inhabitants, be- coming aware of the excitement, though most of them were ignorant of its cause, began to emerge from the cellars. Some of the women, their nerves tense, became hysterical as they heard the cheering from amid the ruins of their houses. "The Germans have come back," they cried. "Listen to the hand-to-hand fighting." But a passer-by shouted: "It's de Gaulle!" They quickly donned such respectable clothes as still remained to them—one a tweed jacket, another a fur coat—and hurried out to the General's jeep.

A crowd had gathered at what had been the crossroads of the Grand- Rue and the Rue de la Mairie. For three hundred yards in every direc- tion there was nothing to be seen but broken walls and still-smoking rubble, yet from amid the devastation tricolour flags began to appear. Guns and half-tracks were passing through the town; there was shelling not far away; the Germans were still within two and a half miles.

The General stood on the base of a fallen lamp-post and made a speech precisely attuned to the sufferings his audience had undergone:

"I am so glad to see assembled here the beloved, suffering population of our beloved and suffering town of Isigny. I know the sufferings Isigny has undergone. These are the sufferings every part of France will have to undergo before attaining liberation. But I know, as you do, that this ordeal will not be useless. It is through ordeals such as this that we shall achieve the unity and grandeur of France. I want you to have, as I have, hope in your hearts and, out of that hope, to sing the *Marseillaise*."

Before the General had even had a chance to lead them, they burst out into the national anthem. And here, even more than at Bayeux, it was France's response to the man who had never despaired, a consecra- tion of the past four years of effort. The inhabitants came forward and introduced themselves, proud of the part they had played in the clan- destine struggle, accepting the price they had had to pay for victory. "My daughter was killed in the air-raids," a woman said; "but I am happy now."

From Isigny the General went to Grandcamp, the last halt before re- embarking.

Grandcamp, a fishing village, had also been warned by Maurice Schu- mann of the General's coming, but he had been unable to give them a precise time. The mayor, called Gouye, an old salt with a tanned face, grew tired of waiting and was leaving the Place de la Mairie with his staff at about 17.30, when the jeeps arrived.

"The Mairie was hurriedly reopened. The General and his suite went up to the first floor and talked to the staff, while the news was quickly spreading and fishermen in caps and jerseys gathered on the Place. . . . The General went back to his jeep, stood up in it, made his third speech, and once again led the *Marseillaise,* which the fishermen sang heartily."

At Courseulles, during the half-hour he was waiting for a D.U.K.W., the General talked with a number of resistants, who showed him a secret radio set. He gave last instructions to those he was leaving behind. "You're staying," he said to Coulet; "don't act on a political basis, the population doesn't want it."

According to the official statistics of the Gaullist headquarters in London, the General had shaken 3,000 hands in four hours. The success of his journey was celebrated by the crew of *La Combattante* with a party as they sailed back to England.

On the morning of the 15th, sub-prefect Rochat went on with his job as if nothing had happened. He appointed Camille Brée, of Bayeux, to organize beds and bedding for the supplementary hospitals. He appointed Dalmier to look into the question of tires and batteries so as to get motor transport back on to the road. And, finally, he appointed a butcher to supply Port-en-Bessin with meat.

These were the last official acts of his "reign." Normal and serene as they may appear, in fact the atmosphere in the sub-prefecture had changed profoundly since the day before. In the morning, the visitors of the previous day, who had not left with the General—François Coulet, Pierre Laroque and the Commandant de Chevigné—accompanied by members of their immediate staffs, came to see him. Most of them showed no open hostility; though one among them, aware that Rochat had served under Pucheu, boasted of having had a hand in that minister's execution. Coulet and Laroque took over offices in the sub-prefecture. Clearly, the two administrations could not co-exist. In the afternoon, the new régime began. Coulet had a poster distributed informing the population of his accession to office. It was the first Gaullist notice posted on metropolitan French soil. It had a government tone.

To the Liberated Population.

The Provisional Government of the French Republic has placed upon me the duty of representing it and exercising the rights of French sovereignty in the liberated territories of the Rouen region.

I thank, on behalf of the Nation, all those who, during the last four years, under the menace of the enemy and his accomplices, have carried on the struggle for the liberation of their country.

I extend, on behalf of the government, solicitude and sympathy to every-one who has suffered, or is still suffering, the daily hardships of war.

The war continues. The battle of France is being fought among us. Be-hind the lines, the combatants of the interior are harassing the enemy with-out cease and with an ardour and courage that are the admiration of the world. They must be our inspiration and our example. The French, who have already been liberated by the stupendous efforts of the Allied armies, have themselves a duty to give all their strength to the service of the struggle for the liberation and grandeur of France. To our British and American friends, you owe every assistance you can render, fraternally united, as we are, in the same battle and for the same ideals.

All this General de Gaulle told you yesterday as he passed through our liberated towns and villages. As one man, we shall go forward along the path he has traced for us.

Bayeux, 15 June 1944.
FRANÇOIS COULET, Commissaire Régional de la République.

While drawing up this proclamation, François Coulet received cer-tain members of the local Resistance; among them, a young landowner, Raymond Triboulet. During his clandestine activities, he had been in contact with Bourdeau de Fontenay, the future Commissaire de la République at Rouen, and with Daure, the future prefect of Caen. He gave François Coulet an account of the situation in the Bessin.

He went back to his estate of Saint-Croix-Grande-Tonne, between Bayeux and Caen, only to see a car drive up during the course of the afternoon: it was Coulet sending to fetch him. "You belong to the dis-trict," said the Commissaire de la République, in substance, "I need a sub-prefect to replace the Vichy one. You are the only man who can do the job. . . . You are appointed sub-prefect." Then he gave him his instructions: "Establish French sovereignty at once; show the Allies that we can administer ourselves competently; and give such an example in the first liberated town that the whole of France will soon be responsible for her own destinies."

Triboulet bore little relation to the usual idea of a sub-prefect. He was more like a character out of Colette, for he was nonchalant, wore a small moustache and had charm. As soon as he had begun to get used to his job, he was to be seen with his hat on one side of his head and a camera slung over his shoulder, tripping about the centres of government and the seats of conferences like a nonchalant tourist wandering through the gaieties and tragedies of his time. There was nothing formal or preten-tious about him. His appointment to an administrative job, of which he knew absolutely nothing, amused him as a challenge presented by unwitting fate, but also of course as an opportunity to serve his country.

It was, in a sense, "a dare," and he went straight to Rochat's office, and in the most courteous way in the world introduced himself as his successor. Handing over took place at once. Triboulet knew very well that Rochat had nothing to reproach himself with, and saw to it that he was not persecuted. Rochat went off with his family to live in a neighbouring village, quietly to await his official dismissal. He continued temporarily to draw his salary as a sub-prefect though without the expenses for which there were no longer any justification. Before moving out, however, he stayed on in the sub-prefecture of Bayeux for a few days longer, though there was nothing for him to do. One day, as he was walking down a passage, he heard through the wall Maurice Schumann recording a broadcast for the B.B.C.: "We have sacked the Vichy administration and restored Republican legality." The ex-sub-prefect could not help smiling: so the Republic had been restored, had it!

Triboulet went to his office and at once entered upon this new game. In the ante-room were a crowd of callers, both French and British, waiting to see the Vichy sub-prefect. Triboulet stayed there till half past eight that night and interviewed them all.

On what was Coulet's and Triboulet's hastily assumed power based? Apparently on nothing more than a kind of *coup d'état*.

In fact, when Coulet took over the offices of the sub-prefecture, issued a proclamation, sacked a sub-prefect and appointed another, he had no official power to do so at all. His appointment as Commissaire de la République for the liberated district needed to be confirmed by a decree of the Algiers government, which was only dated 17 June, forty-eight hours after he had taken over. Moreover, the decree took several days to reach London and then Bayeux. And, furthermore, it had been made by a government which had merely proclaimed itself to be such and which the Allies, who had actually liberated Bayeux, had not recognized.

François Coulet's position was also somewhat irregular with regard to the internal Resistance. As we shall see, the Resistance in the months preceding the Liberation had, in liaison with Algiers, nominated Commissaires de la République and prefects from their own ranks to replace the Vichy officials on the departure of the Germans. On this list, Bourdeau de Fontenay was to be the Commissaire Régional for Normandy, with his headquarters at Rouen. When he learned, on 6 June, that another Commissaire de la République had been installed in the part of his province which had been liberated, his first reaction was to treat him as a "usurper." However, when he realized the circumstances which had led de Gaulle to appoint a provisional colleague, he awaited the liberation of Rouen to take up the post that was his right.

François Coulet had therefore no regularized powers. If a local policeman or a British military policeman had asked him for his papers on the day he took over the sub-prefecture, he might well have found himself in difficulties. His appointment depended on a purposely vague sentence dropped by General de Gaulle during his interview with Montgomery. It was also the result of a private conversation, none of which has been recorded, with General de Gaulle, during which the General gave him verbal orders.

There was therefore no legal authority for his sudden seizure of power. Yet there was no effective opposition from the French. On the Allied side, all resistance soon yielded to the determination of the Gaullists.

During the four years they had lived far removed from the metropolitan population, the Gaullists had gradually created a revolutionary image of the nation corresponding to their own outlook. When they received reports that were at variance with their preconceived ideas, they put them aside as suspect. They were indeed prepared to paraphrase the famous words of Saint-Just at the trial of Louis XVI: "If Louis is innocent, the Revolution is guilty." And, since they were the incarnation of the Resistance, Vichy had similarly to be guilty and disowned by the country.

It was therefore of vital importance to them that the population should coincide with their own aspirations. It was necessary that Bayeux, that peaceful sub-prefecture, should become an important centre of the Resistance, as if proved by Schumann's report: "I am writing to you in the shadow of Bayeux Cathedral, in the back shop from which for the last four years the leader of the local Resistance has directed his sector of the French front." It was necessary that the placid Normans should be athirst for reprisals and be demanding a purge; at least, this was what Pierre Viénot asserted in his speech of 18 June: "The population is demanding the departure of the Vichy supporters; the sub-prefect is a collaborator. Is he to keep his job?"

The new sub-prefect, who had been a member of the Resistance himself, did his best to make the French from London understand the real state of public opinion. Triboulet told them that "non-resistant" was not synonymous with "collaborator."

In some cases, however, their harsh and intransigent attitude was due to the fact that they had originally been excommunicated by the Vichy government. They were pariahs, persecuted men, who were recovering their human dignity.

Nor was the take-over in Normandy their first experience of invincibility. François Coulet had been appointed secretary-general of the prefecture in Corsica, in 1943, after the liberation of the island. He had
remained there three months, and his experiences had been calculated
to make him all the more intransigent thereafter.

He had seen the complete collapse of the whole administration of the
French state. Commandant Vittini, head of the Légion des Combattants
at Bastia, wrote on 12 September 1943 to Raymond Lachal, the director-
general at Vichy, giving him an account of the events in Corsica after
the Italian surrender, as follows:

"The prefect of Corsica and the sub-prefect of Bastia, both of whom
only recently arrived in Corsica, have gone over to the dissident party
immediately on the surrender of Italy, at the first demand from the
Front National."

Similarly, in Normandy, he met with no resistance from the authorities of the French state, to whom indeed Vichy had given instructions
to avoid all conflict. His objects were to restore to France her standing
as a great power, to shake this first liberated region out of its indifference
and to prevent an attempt to seize power by the Communists, if not in
Bayeux itself, possibly in Cherbourg, which was liberated on 24 June.

He was the new "king of the liberated territories," and was in a better
position to justify the title than his predecessor. He did more than administer. By virtue of an ordinance issued in Algiers on 30 December
1943, approving the appointment of Commissaires Régionaux de la
République Française, he had all necessary powers to govern in case of
a break with the central power. And Coulet, on the morrow of his assuming his functions, began to legislate.

On 16 June, he issued a decree blocking all bank accounts, as had been
done in Corsica.

On 17 June, another decree sequestered all newspapers appearing in
the liberated territories: this was the beginning of a policy which was
later to have unexpected developments.

On 18 June, François Coulet organized the first public ceremony held
in the liberated arrondissement; it was to commemorate the appeal made
by General de Gaulle on 18 June 1940 on the B.B.C. Nothing, one might
have thought, could be more obvious. In fact, Coulet quickly realized
that his fellow-countrymen where far from ready for a commemoration
of the kind.

However anti-German the leading citizens of Bayeux might be, it
became evident that they had certain reservations. The bishop, Monseigneur Picaud, was a good patriot, but no Gaullist. François Coulet

4. The devastation at Saint-Lô.

5. *This thirteen-year-old boy, an F.F.I. mascot, was responsible for killing thirteen Germans during the battle of Carpentras in the Rhône Valley.*

6. *One of the groups of the Brittany F.F.I.*

had to plead with him for an hour and a half to persuade him to hold a *Te Deum*. Louis André, president of the C.D.L., kept a photograph of Pétain in his office out of personal conviction. When Coulet talked to him about the 18th of June, he showed considerable astonishment. The date meant nothing to him. He had never heard of de Gaulle's first broadcast.

And it was at this time that a clash took place between the British officers of Civil Affairs and the new incumbent of the Bayeux sub-prefecture. The British had no idea either how he had got there or what he was doing there.

When General Lewis heard that sub-prefect Rochat, whose general attitude he approved, had been replaced without reference to him by unknown men of whom he knew nothing, he expected the newcomers to make themselves known to him.

Since nothing happened, he sent Colonel Chandon to tell Coulet that he and certain officers from Montgomery's headquarters would call upon him. The Commissaire de la République, together with Pierre Laroque and Geoffroy de Courcel, received them in his office.

This visit took place only a fortnight after Major Goodings had made contact with Rochat. General Lewis and his officers passed through the same ante-room and entered the same office, where only the incumbent had changed. At both these interviews, the French object was precisely similar: to maintain French independence against all Allied interference. The tone of the interview was, however, very different. Coulet displayed a forcefulness which was in contrast with Rochat's moderation.

The British marched into his office as if they were proposing to bring him to judgement, and made no overture to shake hands. General Lewis got down to business at once and spoke in a tone suited to an ultimatum. "These," he said, "are our plans, and the methods we propose to adopt in the districts we have liberated. We do not intend to have to deal with French administration and we expect order to be maintained. As for you," he said, looking Coulet straight in the eye, "we know you're here without the agreement of our government but we're prepared to accept your presence and that of your colleagues, though only on a provisional basis."

François Coulet replied calmly and in English. He first thanked them for liberating Normandy. He then spoke of the war aims common both to the French and Allies. "This war is ours too; our friends are the same; our methods are very similar." In Coulet's view, the maintaining of order by the imposition of his authority was rendering a service to the Allies. He then changed his tone. Banging the desk with his fist, he said: "As for my presence here, it has nothing to do with you. I have received the order to be here from General de Gaulle's government and I shall leave only on his orders." Upon which François Coulet got to his feet and made it clear that the interview was at an end.

His outburst confirmed François Coulet in his job. And now he began to take in hand the differences existing between the Allies and the Gaullists. In spite of all the difficulties and recriminations, he succeeded gradually in restoring French sovereignty in its integrity, as well as the authority of the G.P.R.F.

Among his first "most secret" communications to Koenig in London, he asked urgently for rubber stamps to surcharge the postage stamps bearing the effigy of the Marshal. And this was a matter of considerable importance. The Allies were hostile to any tampering of the sort. The British opposed it on the grounds that the surcharged stamps would become the object of speculation by philatelists. The Americans took a more moral stand: the effigy of that noble old man should be respected. In the end, Coulet won the day.

Having gained his point, he was, however, faced with a number of far greater problems.

In the first place, of course, the problem of the "false money," which had curious consequences. In spite of Gaullist opposition, these francs, "made in U.S.A.," were widely accepted by the Bayeux shopkeepers and were in general circulation among the population. The Normans manifested their practical good sense: since they had no confidence in this imported money, they showed great zeal in paying their taxes in advance with it. There were queues at the tax-collector's office. The tax-gatherers protested. At their request, Coulet summoned the officers of Civil Affairs and the French financial agents on 25 June. The meeting was far from harmonious and resulted in a compromise: Coulet authorized the tax-collector's office to receive "the false money" in payment, but the Allies guaranteed to exchange it for real French francs of which they had a reserve. It was another victory for Coulet.

Little by little Coulet and his staff wore down the resistance and prejudice of the Allies. On 24 June, Cherbourg was taken. Coulet went there at once.

At first sight, the population seemed to him more Gaullist than that of Bayeux. He recorded that there was "a considerable difference from what we have seen in the agricultural regions of Calvados, in Bayeux in particular, where the innate conservatism of the population seems

From the Normandy Beaches to Paris

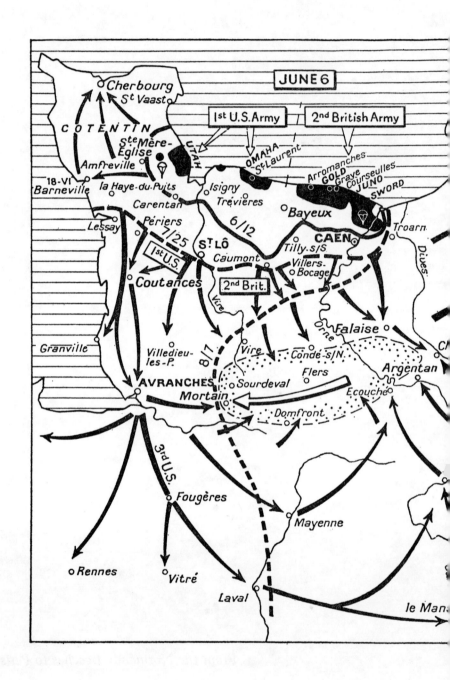

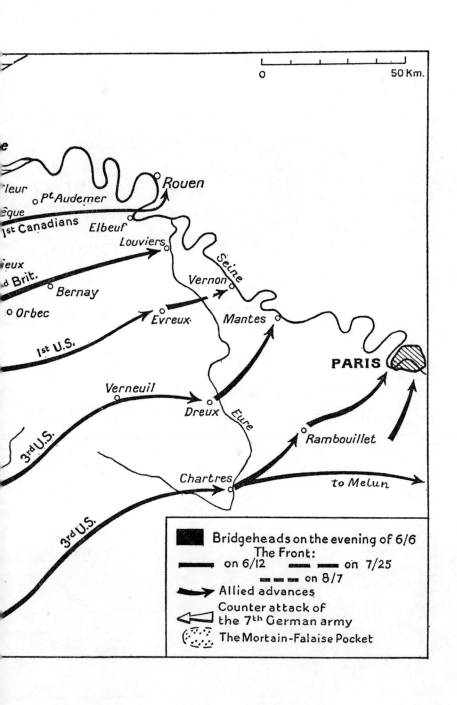

0   50 Km.

'leur
ò Pt Audemer
ìque
1st Canadians   Elbeuf
Rouen
Louviers
Seine
'eux
d Brit.   Bernay
Vernon
ò Orbec
Evreux
Mantes
1st U.S.
PARIS
Verneuil
Dreux   Eure
Rambouillet
3rd U.S.
Chartres   to Melun
3rd U.S.

Bridgeheads on the evening of 6/6
The Front:
on 6/12   on 7/25
on 8/7
Allied advances
Counter attack of
the 7th German army
The Mortain-Falaise Pocket

able to survive any revolution." There were more acclamations than there had been in Bayeux of "Vive de Gaulle! Vive la République!" as Coulet made his official entry into the town.

In a week great progress had been made towards the recognition of French sovereignty and the provisional government of the French Republic. Coulet and his staff appeared to be nearing their goal, and Cherbourg seemed to promise a solution to the problems he had had to face in Bayeux.

From now on the French administration was to function without anyone contesting its right to do so. Making use of the almost unlimited powers conferred on him by the decree of 30 December 1943, Coulet could act as a sovereign. He dissolved the municipal councils appointed by the Vichy government. He reserved his right to endorse or reject the appointments of mayors made by the Allied armies. He sacked and replaced certain of the Préfecture Maritime's officers as well as certain magistrates, who had shown a lack of courage during the hostilities. He appointed temporary managers to private companies which had been deprived of their directors. He proceeded to make arrests and place people under house-arrest. And, finally, making the utmost use of the exceptional powers conferred on him, he promulgated an order suspending the application of the principal laws of the Vichy government, among others "the constitutional law of 10 July 1940, and all other constitutional acts and decrees showing discrimination against Jews, all decrees relating to secret societies, and all laws giving jurisdiction to exceptional courts. . . ."

Barely a fortnight after he had taken over, Coulet had won the day. The Allies recognized him. His power, exercised as a delegate of the G.P.R.F., was absolute. In the person of the first Commissaire de la République to be appointed on metropolitan soil, de Gaulle was recognized *de facto* as head of the government from which all civil and military authority proceeded.

This was the considerable event that took place in Bayeux. The Vichy sub-prefect had laid the foundations for it. The super-prefect from Algiers reaped the harvest.

One day, sub-prefect Rochat, living in retirement in his village, was handed a note by a dispatch-rider summoning him to the Bayeux sub-prefecture. What could they want with him?

His successor received him with the greatest possible politeness.

"My dear sir, you can do me a service."

And as Rochat looked at him in some astonishment, Triboulet went on: "The fact is, I have no sub-prefect's uniform. We're about the same size. Would you mind giving me yours?"

"Of course," said Rochat, enjoying the irony of the situation; "but don't forget to change the buttons, mine bear the axe."

Apart from this detail, the transference of Rochat's uniform to Triboulet was symbolical of the continuity of the French civil administration.

Part Two

THE FIRST LIBERATIONS

Chapter I

THE POLITICAL SITUATION IN FRANCE
ON THE EVE OF THE LIBERATION

"You are not a Gaullist, but all France is," said General de Gaulle in London in 1944 to a Frenchman of whose reservations he was aware.

In fact, at the time of the landings, France was not wholly Gaullist. The political picture resembled a triptych, of which one panel was still Pétainist, another Communist and a third Gaullist. But these panels varied greatly in importance and consisted, on D-day, of very unequal forces both as to numbers and effectiveness.

As for the Marshal's partisans, a document published in June 1944 by the French Special Services in London (D.G.S.S.) gives certain indications. It consisted of the report of a foreign observer in France, dated 31 May, that is to say, D-minus-6:

According to our informer, ten per cent of the French are fairly satisfied with the situation in France. . . . Of the ninety per cent who are anti-German, he considers fifty per cent to be Pétainist, notably in Paris. These consider that Pétain had the great merit of saving numerous lives during the exodus along the roads, and that the Marshal does what he can to make the German yoke less heavy.

The other forty per cent are frankly against Pétain and overtly anti-German.

This analysis appears to be at once exact and insufficient. It is clear that the real partisans of the Germans were only a very small fraction by May 1944: even ten per cent is probably an exaggeration. It is nevertheless true that among the vast anti-German majority there were many for whom Pétain, if not his government, still represented resistance to Hitler. The enthusiastic welcome given the Marshal during his last visits to French towns, particularly in Paris on 26 April 1944 and Saint-Étienne on 6 June 1944, on the very day of the landings, is clear evidence that his personal prestige had survived the failure of his policy.

But the high percentage of the Marshal's supporters no longer amounted to a political force by 1944.

As a government, Vichy no longer had much hold on public opinion or over the life of the nation. It was a sort of legal abstraction dissociated from the real life of the country. Its main institutions, such as the Conseil National and the Légion des Combattants, had long ceased to function. Of the latter, only the most extreme elements, the militiamen, still existed, and were detested by almost everyone. Their excesses had rung the knell of the "Révolution Nationale" in whose name, in spite of the Marshal, they still continued to act.

All that still remained of Vichy was, on the one hand, the corrupt chivalry that constituted the Militia and, on the other, the administrative organization which continued to function more or less until it was relieved, sometimes politely and sometimes not, by the Gaullist administration.

Originally, the Militia had pretensions to being a sort of "chivalry," the active élite of the great and rather amorphous mass of the Légion des Combattants. Darnand, its chief, had played an heroic part in both wars; he was a leader of coups de main and corps-francs who, though fundamentally anti-German, ended up in the uniform of the Wehrmacht.

In July 1918, in Champagne, on the eve of the last German offensive, he had led a decisive attack which had paved the way for victory,[1] and Pétain had decorated him with the Medaille Militaire in the presence of the troops. This scene, which profoundly affected Joseph Darnand, had considerable bearing on his future actions. Twenty-two years later, obedient to the great leader in the rays of whose fame he had basked in his youth, he engaged with the same enthusiastic and ingenuous heroism upon the path of collaboration. He believed Pétain had preceded him along it, but he was unaware that for the Marshal this apparent attitude was merely part of a subtle game, which the circumstances made it impossible to reveal. And how could the "poor bloody infantryman" of 1918, which was what Darnand had essentially remained, grasp the complexities of the double game the Marshal was playing? He engaged in it, and lost his way in it. It was his undoing. In the end, Pétain disowned him.

To start with, he gathered about him comrades from the Légion who were as courageous as he was, but equally devoid of subtlety and politi-

[1] This attack had brought him a letter from the President of the Republic, Raymond Poincaré, congratulating him on being "one of the principal artisans of victory."

cal awareness. Brave and naïve, they lacked a sense of realities. In the first instance it was from lack of common sense, rather than from defects of heart or character that most of them became traitors. The first cadres of the Militia included some of the great names of France, Vaugelas, Bernonville, Bourmont, whose ancestors had fought for France and her Christian civilization. By fighting for Hitler, their descendants believed they were following their example. In the same way, many highly respectable people joined the Militia from blind anti-Communism. Recruiting varied from department to department, sometimes attracting old members of the Ligues, and sometimes young men disgusted by the defeat.

But they were soon joined by gangsters, toughs and recidivists, to whom the Militia afforded an opportunity to gratify their sadism. But since their crimes were disguised as idealism, the original militiamen were never quite able either to condemn or disown them, particularly since these gangsters often displayed a courage under fire that was worthy of a better cause.

The Militia claimed to be a great movement of national regeneration; it consisted of some 15,000 men; and it set up a training school for its cadres at Uriage, where the future masters of the country were to be educated to think and act on its behalf. They were adjured to be honest. "Power," wrote Darnand, "affords many temptations. Should our cause lose the day, I hope no one will be able to accuse us of having embezzled a centime." This did not, however, prevent some members looting and raping, crimes which Darnand punished severely.

They were trained to a condition of aggressive and chauvinistic absurdity; and most of them retained it to the very end, even when wearing German uniform or in the ranks of the Wehrmacht. Could anything be more fantastic than their self-congratulation, when retreating with the German Army through Alsace, whose population regarded them with the utmost hatred, on being the first to hoist the French flag on the soil of that annexed province? Or again, when they had crossed the Rhine and were at Neu Ulm, with what derision one contemplates their marching past with the French flag at their head, proud that the Germans should salute their glorious standard, and their deliberately selecting for manœuvres the hill of Michelsberg, so evocative of memories of Napoleon and French uniforms of other days!

How was it that these Darnands, Vaugelas and Bernonvilles failed to realize that they were leading nothing more than a pitiful caricature of a French Army under a degraded flag? How were they able to continue the pretence that they were "saving French military honour" from the injury done it by the disaster of June 1940? Unconscious of their folly, they yet tried to justify themselves by saying that they had never fought against French regular forces; that maquisards were outlaws and bandits; or, on occasion, they would make an arbitrary distinction between the combatants of the Maquis: the secret army, consisting of ex-soldiers, might pass, but the F.T.P., those Communist terrorists, were to be utterly condemned. They denounced them to the Germans and, when they took them prisoner, shot them out of hand.

To justify these punitive expeditions, Darnand would plead the seventy-five militiamen assassinated, apart from the women scalped, the children killed and the old men whose throats had been cut. He replied to these atrocities with others equally abominable. As a result, "the glorious deeds of the Militia" were apt to degenerate into the foulest crimes. In January 1944, there was a first expedition against the Savoy Maquis. On 7 April 1944, a witness, who was at Vichy station when the Militia returned from fighting the F.F.I. in the Vercors, reported much shouting, singing, drinking, tales of derring-do and showing of trophies in the pure, ageless tradition of military victors. But these had fought against their brothers and set fire to French villages. These Frenchmen, who pretended to be saving France from the danger of Communism and protecting Europe from atheistical materialism, were in fact the supporters of a pagan totalitarianism, which was an even greater menace to their country at that time.

It is difficult to determine precisely how many senior Vichy officials were transferred, retired or dismissed on German insistence. It is known, however, that, on 24 January 1944, twelve prefects were removed at one stroke at the demand either of the occupying power or the Militia. In one German concentration camp there were interned the prefects Didkowski, Cousin, Chaigneau, Hontebeyrie, Benedetti de Vileneuve and Faugère, while their colleagues Théry, Duprech, Bonnefoy, Jacques Bussière and others died in captivity. A list of the Vichy prefects and sub-prefects who fell foul of the Germans has been drawn up by Georges Hilaire, who was secretary-general for administration to the Ministry of the Interior. It contains six who either died in captivity or were shot, twenty deported, seven arrested who remained in France, and fifteen dismissed or compelled to resign. Of those who stayed at their posts till the arrival of the Allies, the majority showed a courage which was often equal to that of the resistants themselves.

At Caen, that martyred town, which was for over a month in the front line of the battle (6 June to 10 July 1944), the Vichy prefect, Cacaud, stayed among his people not only to ensure supplies, but to protect them from the Gestapo and the Militia. To prevent intervention by the Militia, he organized a local security police, which moreover became a refuge for most of the resistants. He freed many French whom the Germans had arrested. He and his wife showed great heroism in bringing assistance to the inhabitants during the bombardments, and this the leaders of the Resistance acknowledged in writing. Nevertheless, on 10 July, when the siege was over, Daure, the prefect nominated by de Gaulle, entered the town with the President of the Departmental Committee of the Liberation, Léonard Gille, and his brother-in-law, Coulet, Commissaire de la République.

This family party went to the prefecture and entered the prefect's private drawing-room. He received them in uniform. Draped over the piano was the prefecture's flag which Cacaud had carried in his brief-case since the beginning of the battle. The day before, as the first Allied troops entered the town, he had hoisted it over the prefecture. But the Resistance had insisted he take it down, for they desired the Tricolour with the Cross of Lorraine to be the only flag to fly officially over the town. Coulet told the prefect that, though he was the representative of a hated government, he had nothing against him personally. He shook him by the hand. After which, he led Cacaud into the office where the ceremony of handing over took place in the usual way. Cacaud was thus turned out, though his behaviour had been irreproachable.

Similar ceremonies, though with local variations, took place in most of the liberated prefectures in the northern zone.

There are two things that should be said about this: in the first place, the Vichy administration carried on nearly everywhere to the end; and, in the second, its departure aroused neither protest nor resistance. "The Vichy administration," records Chevigné, who was present on many of these occasions, "made no resistance to the arrival of the government from London. . . ."

It can therefore be asserted that the Vichy administration carried on till the end without indulging in politics.

Let us now turn to the extreme opposite camp: the Communists, who formed the second panel of the French political triptych. Between 1939 and 1945, the French Communist Party alternated between repressing and inciting its members' patriotism, though, for the most part, they were eager enough to show their devotion to France. Why did the Party's policy so often constrain them to disguise or repress their feelings? Individually, the Communists in the Resistance showed themselves to be among the most courageous. To many of them, clandestine action against the Nazis was the climax of their militancy, for their revolutionary ardour could at last be placed at the service of their country. Marrane, a militant Communist and leader of the National Front in the southern zone, tells with emotion of his innumerable bicycle rides through southern France, of bearding the Germans and risking his life. Often sleeping in fields, he fought the occupying power for many months.

Colonel Eon, who was far from being a Marxist, and whom General Koenig appointed to the command of the F.F.I. in Brittany, has this to say of his Communist personnel:

"Most of the F.T.P. volunteers were determined militants, apostles devoted body and soul from the beginning to a cause for which they were prepared to make every sacrifice. . . . I always found the F.T.P. volunteers ready to fight and imbued with a far greater hatred of the Germans than was the case in units formed from other groups."

But, before they reached this fulfilment, from what tergiversations and crises of conscience they suffered!

In the first instance, immediately upon the signing of the German-Soviet pact in August 1939, the Party directed its activities against the French war effort. Florimond Bonte and Ramette, in a letter to the President of the Chamber, demanded the cessation of hostilities. Both *L'Humanité* and *L'Humanité du Soldat*, which were appearing secretly, as well as numbers of tracts and pamphlets, were constantly encouraging the sabotage of factories producing materials of war. In June 1940, at the time of the Armistice, two of the Party's militants made contact with the German authorities in Paris and asked permission to publish *L'Humanité* openly. In August of the same year, there was an appeal to the French people signed by Maurice Thorez and Jacques Duclos in the still secretly published *L'Humanité*. There was no mention made of the occupying power. It was concerned with replacing the Vichy government by a government "of manual workers and intellectuals" who would sign "a real peace by concluding a pact of friendship between France and Russia." This was still far from the spirit of the Resistance.

If, as a whole, the Party repressed its patriotism in these early days, there were nevertheless many individual members who openly avowed their feelings—a proof of independence which, in the long or short run, generally led to their expulsion as undesirables. At the time of the signing of the German-Soviet pact, five members of Parliament, Gustave Saussot and Paul Loubardou, for the Dordogne, Jules Fourrier and Marcel Brout, for Paris, and Gilbert Declercq, for the Nord, resigned. "We condemn the German-Soviet pact which has made the Nazi aggression against Poland possible. . . . We condemn those who, disregarding

French interests, have been either unwilling or unable to dissociate themselves from the new orientation of Stalin's policy."

It was also at this time that certain Communists, without resigning from the Party, began individually to become militants in the Resistance. The Party, though it was glad to make use of them later, when the wind had changed, never quite forgave them their indiscipline. Among these early volunteers were Pierre Hervé and Auguste Lecœur.

An army within the army of the Resistance, as well as a state within the State, the Communist organizations had, from their point of view, good reason to behave as they did.

In the first place, they felt, and not without some justification, that their comrades in arms were not always very open with them.

It was certainly the case that some local distributors of supplies treated the Communists unfairly from political prejudice. A leader of the Secret Army in the Grésivaudan informed us that when parachuted arms were delivered to the A.S., the F.T.P. were, in principle, excluded. But it is also true that in some districts, the Gard for instance, the precise opposite occurred, and it was the F.T.P. who received the arms deliveries.

But there were other, and more profound, reasons why the Communists so often failed to co-operate.

Here is part of a very significant, and hitherto unpublished, document:

Plan D.
Military Headquarters of Greater Paris.
Memorandum concerning measures to be taken at the opening of a second front for the liberation of the country.

All leaders at every level must bear clearly in mind that, in case of an Allied landing on French soil, certain measures must be taken to ensure the liberation of the country. There are, in particular, two general measures of capital importance:
A general strike;
National insurrection . . .
. . . H-hour, on D-day, will be the hour for a general rising. . . .

This document, signed by the national military commissaire of the F.T.P., is clear evidence that for the Communists insurrection was the essential means to Liberation. But it was also the object: Order of the Day No. 2 from the High Command of the F.T.P.F. (southern zone), after the landings, is a call to arms in the tradition of revolutionary Paris or the peasant Jacqueries:

Arm the railwaymen, the miners, the metal workers and the builders, and through them make yourselves masters of the important industrial centres

of the country. . . . In the countryside, arm all the peasants, recover the
guns deposited at the mairies. . . . Let the tocsin ring out from village to
village calling everyone to arms. . . .

Such documents as these are clear evidence of the F.T.P.'s isolation
at the time of the Liberation. Theirs was the political objective of
achieving power in a sufficient number of localities to bring about a
general action and thereby eventually set up a revolutionary government.

This was apparent not only in the way they participated in the fighting
but also in their political activities. In the latter, they set out to infiltrate
into all the organizations which, however remotely, controlled the Resistance. In the first instance, they sought to gain control by creating
new organizations specifically for the purpose: the Front National and
the Milices Patriotiques. They formed groups into which they welcomed adherents from all sections of opinion, but of which they themselves firmly retained all the key posts. The Front National was a
political grouping which recruited its members from every movement of
the French Resistance and tried to federate them under the Communist
yoke, while concealing its ends by appointing priests and members of
the extreme Right to its organizing committee. The Milices Patriotiques
was a para-military organization similarly recruited from the Resistance
movements.

Apart from their strictly military activities, their role included others
which were essential to the Communists: purging; police; control of
movement, telephones and post; and national insurrection in co-operation with the tactical units of the F.F.I.

In an appeal to the people of Paris, broadcast on D-plus-1, the Paris
Committee of Liberation, on which the Communists held three seats out
of six, declared: "Not a block of houses, not a quarter, not a district,
not a factory should be without its patriotic militia. Form yourselves
into groups of eight or ten, appoint a group leader, the best, the most
capable and the bravest. And let the group leaders appoint their detachment leaders."

The Milices Patriotiques, at once supplementary police and a para-
military force, formed a basic element in the Communist tactical plan
for insurrection and the seizing of power.

This process of achieving power through specially created crypto-
Communist organizations ran parallel to the similar proceedings of the
provisional government itself. In the spring of 1944, Closon, whom the
government of Algiers entrusted with the organization of the future
Committees of Liberation (C.D.L.), described Communist infiltration in

these terms: "Considered for some months past as non-existent, the F.N. is now reappearing in most departments, though it is impossible to discover whether it really has troops and, if so, whether they are organized. Apart from the big towns, where its existence was known before the war, the situation with regard to the C.P. is similar. It asserts it is present everywhere and takes credit for the exploits of the F.T.P." The two Communist organizations endeavoured to acquire a majority in the C.D.L. and demanded that the three non-Communist Resistance movements, Combat, Liberation-Sud and Franc-Tireur, which were grouped in the federation of the M.U.R. (Mouvements Unis de Résistance), should exercise only one vote instead of three. At the same time they claimed that such crypto-Communist organizations as the Front Uni de la Jeunesse Patriotique and the Union des Femmes Françaises had a right to be represented, which would increase the number of Communist or fellow-travelling delegates. Moreover, some Communists infiltrated into the C.D.L., as representatives of the C.G.T., of the F.T.P., as peasants or even as "Catholics." There were, therefore, a certain number of C.D.L.s in which the Communists succeeded in obtaining a majority, as for instance in the Isère, where the addition of the "Jeunes" and the "Femmes" gave them a preponderance. But Communist infiltration was even more concentrated on the central organizations than it was on the local committees. And by its ability and tenacity the C.P. achieved formidable and lasting results.

One of the prime causes of this situation was that extremely important episode in the history of the Resistance, the arrest, on 21 June 1943, of Jean Moulin at Caluire, near Lyons. At that time, Jean Moulin was the only delegate of the government of Algiers in Metropolitan France. He held two posts, which were later to be dissociated, those of president of the Délégation Générale, which represented the government of Algiers in the occupied territories, and president of the Comité National de la Résistance (C.N.R.), which co-ordinated the actions of the various Resistance movements in France. After his arrest, there was a period of confusion during which communications with Algiers and de Gaulle became difficult and consequently the taking of essential decisions impossible. The Communists took advantage of the situation to consolidate their influence in the C.N.R. In the provisional directorate of the organization, which consisted of six members, their influence was preponderant.

Though Villon was the only member who was overtly Communist, Saillant, the delegate of the C.G.T., was a "crypto"; as was Pascal Copeau, the representative of the M.U.R.

There were two definitely non-Communist members: Blocq-Mascart, who represented the three non-political movements of the northern zone, Ceux de la Libération (C.D.L.L.), Ceux de la Résistance (C.D.L.R.) and the Organization Civil et Militaire (O.C.M.); and Laniel, of the Alliance Démocratique, who was not, however, very assiduous about it. Everything depended on the sixth member, Georges Bidault, concerning whom there were curiously diverse opinions among his colleagues in the Resistance. Debu-Bridel thought his appointment as president of the C.N.R. "disastrous"; Parodi, Daniel Mayer, Blocq-Mascart and Laniel thought him first-class. By background and political conviction, this university educated Christian-Democrat journalist, who, before the war, had been on the staff of *L'Aube,* had presumably nothing whatever in common with the Communists. And yet, at a secret session of their Central Committee, they decided, all unknown to him, to vote for him.

The fact was that Bidault, as writes René Hostache, "was at once a member of a party (and therefore the symbol of the resurrection and restoration of the political parties) and of a Resistance movement; a man of the internal Resistance as well as the head of a branch of the Delegation (the Service d'Information et de Presses)"; and therefore in a position to create an opposition to de Gaulle's power in France while endued with the prestige of being its representative.

Bidault, indeed, had peculiar qualifications and equally peculiar qualities. He would appear to have been precisely the man required to keep the rivalries in the internal Resistance alive by the double process of, on the one hand, preventing an open row and, on the other, ensuring that the rivalries were never resolved. His singular qualities enabled him to play the delicate part of an umpire who never made a decision; while even his faults contributed to his being tolerated by both sides at once.

The fact was that Bidault, a writer, an intellectual, an orator, a party leader and an honest man, could never wittingly play the Communist game; he was too loyal and sincere for that. And, indeed, he frequently opposed it. Nevertheless, he was subject to the sudden intoxication of some plan, some bright idea, which blinded him to the precise significance of impending events and to the real characters of the men who embodied them. He combined in his nature the attributes of both the glow-worm and the moth. He glowed and was dazzled by his own light; his thought buzzed and fluttered about itself till he was unable to see the issues. Here clearly was the man the C.P. required to turn the majority of the committee if not red, at least pink. German repressive measures made it impossible, or at least dangerous, to hold meetings of the C.N.R. and the committee. Two secretaries, Meunier and Chambeyron, both Communist fellow-travellers, made up for this by making personal contacts with the members. And it was therefore, after a series of conversations held between no more than two or three people at a time, followed by a postal vote organized by the two liaison agents, that Georges Bidault was elected by twelve votes to one, with three abstentions. In fact, if there was a ballot at all, it was so secret that no one except the scrutineers knew precisely what procedure had been adopted. With Bidault's election to the presidency of the C.N.R., the organization, without being actually under Communist control, nevertheless seemed no longer able to oppose the C.P. openly.

To counter this obvious danger, General de Gaulle decided, in March 1944, to reorganize the Délégation Générale, which was thereafter composed as follows: Parodi, delegate-general, and in order of succession in case of arrest by the Germans, Serreulles, Bingen, Émile Laffon, J. Maillet and Closon. Shortly before the liberation of Paris, on 31 July 1944, General de Gaulle sent instructions to the delegate-general which, despite the bouquet he handed out to the Resistance, made it clear that the role of the delegation was predominant and that of the C.N.R. merely advisory:

"You are the representative of the government. That is to say that your orders must in the last analysis be obeyed. We naturally attach the greatest importance to the advisory role and the inspiring activities of the Council of the Resistance and the local Committees of Liberation. . . . I recommend you always to speak precisely and authoritatively in the name of the State. The multiple organizations and activities of our admirable internal Resistance are the means by which the nation is fighting for its salvation. But the State stands above all these organizations and activities."

This is a first example of the tactics employed by General de Gaulle to set limits to Communist infiltration. When the C.P. threatened to dominate some directing organization, the General used all his authority to substitute some complementary organization, either by giving new life to one that already existed or by creating a new one.

Much the same thing took place with the C.O.M.A.C. (Comité d'action Militaire) as it had with the civilian organization of the C.N.R.

Thus the principal military posts of the internal Resistance were as much in the hands of Communists as were the principal civilian posts. In view of this danger, General de Gaulle once again created an organization of his own, which was to rank higher than the Resistance command. In April 1944, in London, he appointed General Koenig Commander-in-Chief of the F.F.I., and henceforth the C.O.M.A.C. and the national headquarters came under his orders. Hence the conflicts, sometimes concealed, sometimes open, between Villon, Joinville, Kriegel-Valrimont on the one hand, and Koenig, assisted by the whole of his D.N.R. network in France, on the other.

The Communists had mounted a huge conspiracy in the very heart of the Resistance and General de Gaulle had to thwart it. The best that can be said for the members of the C.P., whether they were really patriotic, as most of them were, or inclined to treason, as were a few, can be summed up in the words of a delegate of the F.T.P. when, in 1945, he was demanding decorations for his men: "They have served France as well as the Party."

But was there not an even greater majority of resistants in France who served her for herself and independently of any party?

We must now turn to the third panel of the French political triptych at the time of the Liberation: the non-Communist Resistance. If it was not always Gaullist, it at least rallied to General de Gaulle's government.

By June 1944, Gaullism was at once a climax and a point of departure. It was the more or less direct result of a whole series of spontaneous rebellions against the occupying power; and these rebellions had been going on in France ever since the capitulation. In the free zone, a first movement had been organized in Marseilles, in July 1940, under the leadership of Henri Frenay, then a Regular officer. Most of its recruits came from the Army of the Armistice. In the occupied zone, in the same month of the same year, another movement came to birth in the Musée de l'Homme in Paris, founded by the ethnologist Boris Vilde.

His organization was destroyed in February 1941 and his leaders shot at Mont-Valérien. From these beginnings, many further movements came into being during the next four years; and, broadly speaking, three main sources of recruitment can be distinguished during the Occupation: from the spontaneous resistants who, as we have seen, did not wait upon events and often paid for their patriotism with their lives; from the defaulters from the S.T.O. who, from 1942 onwards, chose the Maquis rather than go to work in Germany; and from the Regular officers and other ranks serving in June 1940, who, after the dissolution of the Army of the Armistice in November 1942, found in the Maquis another way of serving.

Until 1943, this branch of the Resistance had no political affiliations and, in particular, none that bore any relation to the Third Republic and its parties. Till 1942, it was not, properly speaking, even Gaullist. Indeed, many of its leaders still viewed the activities in London with suspicion; and the unification of the internal Resistance, under the aegis of the General, was the work of Jean Moulin, parachuted into France on the night of 1 January 1942, and arrested by the Germans on 21 June 1943, who, during the course of the year 1942, co-ordinated the great Resistance movements in the southern zone (Libération, Francs-Tireur, Combat) and set up the first secret organizations of the Resistance, the Bureau d'Information et de Presse (B.I.P.) in April 1942, and the Comité Général d'Études (C.G.E.) in June 1942.

To begin with, de Gaulle was as hostile as most of the resistants to a return to party politics, or to any form of policy likely to revive or prolong the Third Republic. He was, however, prevented from maintaining this attitude to the end, was constrained in 1943 to act in contradiction to his most profound aspirations, and was in 1945 the victim of a dilemma from which he could escape only by renouncing his task, owing to the fact that history from June 1940 onwards had placed him in a tragically paradoxical position. De Gaulle was the man who should have brought about a National Revolution in France. There was everything to incite him to do so: family tradition, youthful friends, a temperament hostile, as he was to say later, to *"democrasouillerie,"* his conception of the State, his religious background, and his inflexible patriotism.

The tragedy was that he was ground politically between the millstones of Pétain, whom he knew well, whose background was in many respects similar to his own, and into enmity with whom he had been forced by the events of 1940, on the one hand, and, on the other, of the Communists, with whom he had nothing whatever in common, but whom he was forced, from June 1941 onwards, to treat with a certain diplomacy, were it merely to curb their increasing power. Between an enemy who, in the last analysis, was of his own circle, and allies who were members of a party that had always been opposed to his own, he was often compelled to adopt a policy and a mode of action that were not necessarily in keeping with his convictions and had, indeed, often to manœuvre and compromise—activities that were then profoundly alien to his conception of authority, and in which he was not invariably successful. When he spoke of "national insurrection," it was because he could not safely utter the words "National Revolution."

His was an uncomfortable situation, consisting as it did of combating all he had once admired, and compromising with everything he had always disliked. Nor was it a situation whose discomfort could be concealed for long. It came into the open in the spring of 1943, when the Resistance, which till then had been in favour of its directing organizations consisting only of representatives of the various movements, as advocated by Brossolette, began to tolerate the reappearance on them of representatives of the old political parties. De Gaulle had to make a decision. Was he to reintroduce the pre-June 1940 political parties, which would be playing the game of the politicians and the Communists, or was he to insist on creating a new instrument of power from the new men who had emerged from the Resistance? At the beginning of April 1943, he received, through Georges Buisson, a letter from Léon Blum, who was then a prisoner: "I realize," wrote Léon Blum, "that you adhere unreservedly to the democratic principle and I take it to be a constant that a democratic state—whatever its constitution, whatever role is left to parliamentary representation—cannot exist and cannot even be rationally conceived without the existence of political parties.

"The Resistance organizations which have emerged on French soil in response to your call cannot in any degree be a substitute for these parties. . . . Nevertheless, the men who compose this *élite* will, in the new France, of necessity be distributed among the various parties, which they will also refresh and rejuvenate, and continue to impregnate their diversity with a fundamental solidarity, a true spirit of French unity." We must not anticipate the form this "rejuvenation" of the parties was to take, but we may record here Léon Blum's impression of French political life when he returned from captivity in May 1945:

"Since . . . I have returned once more to French soil—I admit that I am much disappointed—I have not found what I expected—I expected to find something that was at once purged and tempered and, in many respects, I have the impression of being in a country which is—how shall I put it?—corrupted. I do not feel that any of the vital functions of the country has as yet recovered its normal form. I have the feeling that there is a sort of weary, casual, slothful convalescence, which is a condition liable to every sort of infection."

Blum's letter of April 1943 was one of the determining factors that led de Gaulle to agree that the Conseil National de la Résistance (C.N.R.) should consist of representatives from the political parties as well as from the Resistance movements. He was thus caught in the trap he had wished to avoid—the trap set by the veterans of the Third Republic.

This political influence of the Resistance on the directing bodies was not always popular with the Maquis and the other organizations.

In general, the Resistance had as its first objective to rid France of the enemy, and as its second to construct, after the Liberation, a France which would be democratic certainly, but rejuvenated, and free from the influence of the old political groupings which had led it to disaster. This was made abundantly clear by the reactions of its leaders when, after July 1943, they went on missions to Algiers; they were sickened by the place-hunting they found going on in the Assemblée Consultative and in the Lycée Fromentin, where the government offices were. And the fighting F.F.I. in France felt the same.

When the Liberation took place, therefore, Gaullism was the outcome of a spontaneous movement of resistance to the enemy, which had originally been free of all politics and had indeed remained so in so far as the actual combatants were concerned, but had nevertheless degenerated among many of the leaders at the top into a return to the habits of thought existing before the defeat.

But, above all, it was an effort towards a reconstruction that would enable the nation, once it had been liberated, to escape revolution and assert its independence. This was not, however, properly understood at the time by the Allies, who believed they would find on landing a country in a state of anarchy, a sort of administrative "no man's land," from which nothing could immediately emerge except vestiges of the Vichy régime; and they were much surprised to discover how precisely the new wheels of the French administrative machine began to turn as the Nazis retreated. And this, perhaps almost the greatest achievement of the Gaullist government, is still largely unrecognized by the French themselves.

As is no doubt natural in a Cartesian land, the administrative restoration was heralded by a flood of instructions. With the assent of the Assemblée Consultative, innumerable decrees and ordinances were promulgated in Algiers by the appropriate departments, representing ministries, which were in contact with the internal Resistance organizations, and in particular with C.G.E. (Comité Général d'Études).

From the red tape angle, when Commandant de Lignières landed in France as the first administrative officer with the duty of reorganizing the regional districts and recruiting for the army, he took with him the following printed documents: a notice to be posted at his office door concerning the enlistment of foreigners in the metropolitan army; another concerning their enlistment in the colonial army; an appeal conceived in the usual attractive terms of this particular kind of literature encouraging the liberated French to join up; another dealing with re-enlistment; an enormous quantity of notices dealing with the maintenance of a state of siege, arbitrary search and arrest, the carrying of arms and, of course, looting; further notices dealing with a census of officers and non-commissioned officers, and for all Frenchmen between the ages of eighteen to forty-eight; an establishment for subdivisional staff; establishments for units to be formed; instructions to the police about enlistment and re-enlistment; instructions about registration and identity cards for officers and men; registration cards and log-books for motor vehicles; and, finally, since every eventuality—even the end of the war—must be anticipated, leave passes and discharge certificates.

There were trunks and trunks of papers, as if every French quill-driver had been feverishly and secretly at work furbishing new weapons ever since the Armistice of 26 June 1940.

From the personnel angle, of course, there were evident a remarkable sureness, precision and breadth of view about the training, both in Algiers and London, of the men who were to ensure the continuity of the State in France. In a B.B.C. broadcast on 3 June 1944 at 21.30, "a high French official," Pierre Laroque, Conseiller d'État, spoke of the conditions in which these improvised civil servants would have to work:

"When the liberation of French territory takes place, the administration will find itself faced with heavy responsibilities. Amid the chaos caused by military operations, all the civilian services will have to be taken in hand with energy and authority. Men who have the confidence of the population, as well as the necessary qualities of character and competence, will have to take over the whole public administration at once. . . ."

Each service and ministry, whether in Algiers or London, was busily recruiting competent men.

The Défense Nationale appointed to each Resistance region in France a military delegate, who was to co-ordinate the Resistance's activities before the Liberation and, after it, supervise the transition from the army of maquisards to the Regular Army, which was to be reconstituted. Of these, Rondenay, Fassin, Benier, Abeille and Kammerer were shot by the Germans.

The Ministry of Justice organized three delegations for the three possible theatres of operations.

The first delegation landed in Normandy in June 1944, and then moved into Brittany behind the Allied lines. It re-established courts in Rouen and Caen. The second landed in August on the coast of Provence and followed up General Patch's army group and the First French Army, re-establishing courts in Aix, Grenoble, Chambéry, Nîmes, Montpellier, Toulouse, Lyons and Dijon. In January 1945, it undertook a similar task in liberated Alsace-Lorraine.

The third never landed in France and was dissolved in Algiers.

The Admiralty, determined to assert its authority at the earliest possible moment over the harbours liberated by the Allies, had detachments in readiness; and these, from Cherbourg on 24 June 1944 to Toulon on 28 August 1944, hoisted the French flag beside those of the Allies on arsenals and bases, thereby staking their claim to them as "the property of the French government."

There were also, as we have seen, the liaison officers of the Mission Militaire de Liaison Administrative (M.M.L.A.), who had instructions to play the part of administrative jacks-of-all-trades at the Liberation. They were expected to deal with everything from protecting ancient monuments to coping with the evacuated population and sick children, from repairing broadcasting stations and cinemas to exercising control over the first newspapers issued by the Resistance, and from burying the victims of bombardment to maintaining coal mines, power stations and gas and water supplies.

They were assisted by women members of the M.M.L.A., who worked among the population—a purely civilian activity which did not, however, prevent one of them, who had strayed into the German lines, from returning in triumph with two prisoners.

There was above all the improvised corps of Commissaires de la République and the prefects of the Liberation, whom we have already seen in action in the bridgehead, playing a decisive part in the re-establishment of order in France. The appointing of these high functionaries, their "prefabrication" in secret, and the dramatic circumstances in which they took office in the liberated French towns, constitute one of the most dramatic and astonishing episodes of this extraordinary period.

It had all begun in July and August 1943 in Paris, in the grill room of the Medicis, a Latin Quarter restaurant. "In a corner two lovers—the classic spectacle at this season in this type of establishment. By the door a waiter was complaining of the heat. The commission entered."

The "commission," as he signed himself on reports to London and Algiers, was Michel Debré, *maitre des requêtes* to the Conseil d'État, alias Michel, alias Turquan, alias Jacquier, alias Fontevrault. With all these aliases, which he abandoned successively for security reasons, he was indeed almost a "commission" in himself, and he hoped to impress his correspondents beyond the Channel by signing himself as such. Sitting at a café table, the "commission" was soon joined by two assistants. The first was Bouchinet-Serreulles, alias Pellerin, smartly dressed in an English suit and shirt, and wearing English spectacles and a very English moustache. Indeed, the very sight of him could not but raise suspicions that he had contacts in London.

The other was Pierre-Henri Teitgen, alias Tristan, who was invariably late. Ill-dressed and ill-shaven, it was certainly not anxiety over his personal appearance that made him unpunctual; and he would always have some story as an excuse—wildly improbable, but true. He seemed to move in a fantastic world; indeed, he had something fey about him—which was perhaps not without its advantages in secret work.

The agenda at this first meeting consisted of the nominations of the prefects and Commissaires de la République who were to be appointed at the Liberation. The three conspirators drew up a preliminary list. During the twelve or thirteen months which were to elapse before the new authorities took post, the "commission" moved from place to place, sometimes alone, sometimes accompanied by his secret collaborators. He held sessions in unusual places from which no prefect had ever been appointed within living memory.

Michel Debré first lived in a comfortable flat, which had two exits—a very necessary precaution—one on to the Boulevard Saint-Germain, the other on to the Rue de l'Université, while dealing with the possible candidates for the North (Libé-Nord). For the West, Central and South (O.C.M.) he went openly to the parliamentary office of the Chamber, where he was escorted and announced by a German *Feldgrau*. There, he had an interview with a devoted official, M. Jeanjean, who in the very shadow of the Wehrmacht took him to his office and produced files containing the names of ninety prefects who were nominated to administer France after the Germans' departure. He acquired the Ceux de la Résistance list in a little top-floor flat near the Lamarck-Caulaincourt underground station; and the Ceux de la Libération list in the Café Scossa on the Place Victor-Hugo. Coquoin, alias Lenormand, who was shot a few weeks later, brought him this short list. The Front National, which was Communist, furnished no list of names.

He took tea, an extraordinary luxury at that time, with Villey, a former prefect of the Seine dismissed by Vichy, and with Verlomme, a former prefect of the Nord and once secretary-general to the Ministry of the Interior, who was now reduced by the difficulties of the times and the mistrust of Pucheu to being manager of a lunatic asylum. These two high officials had very precise ideas about the appointments that should be made to the liberated prefectures: they must be prefects and, more particularly, men whom Vichy had sacked. "You're in the trade, M. Verlomme. . . ."

On other occasions, Michel Debré met colleagues at the secret headquarters of the C.G.E. (Comité Générale d'Études), the "brains trust" of the Resistance. These meetings often took place on Sundays and were held in the shadow of Saint-Sulpice, in a room lent by the elderly M. Francisque Gay in the Rue Garancière. On the wall were large-scale maps on which the progress of the war was marked up in accordance with the communiqués from the B.B.C. There were also shelves containing hundreds of dusty books in which Bib (Bidault) and many others concealed their secret papers. And it was in this room that lawyers met to discuss the new institutions; and here too that the title "Commissaire de la République" was first uttered.

There was a grey, intellectual dust in Francisque Gay's study which was in contrast to the black, administrative dust of another room in which, so it was said, the Régent had once met his mistress. And it was here, in the Conseil d'État, in Michel Debré's official office, that he hid the prefectorial, or rather pre-prefectorial, documents in the nineteenth-century files. Another batch was concealed in a drawer that had obviously never been opened, if not within living memory, at least for a great number of years, for Michel Debré found in it a document thick with dust that had been "written and signed by a very old councillor when he was a quite junior civil servant," which was reassuring as to the secrecy of the drawer as a hiding-place.

Further meetings, as the work developed and the establishment of regular contact allowed of discussion of the Paris proposals with Algiers, took place in the Rue Séguier, in the Juris Classeur building, to which a professor of law, René Courtin, managed to give them the entry. Others again took place in the cafés round the Trocadero; and it was there that Avinin, alias Talbert, alias Ansot, the delegate of the Mouvements Unis de Résistance, who constituted in his own person the "commission" for the southern zone, met Debré, at first on one Wednesday in each month, then on two Wednesdays, and later each week. As their work advanced they were able to watch progress of another order taking place at a nearby table; a gentleman, clearly of standing and sporting a decoration in his buttonhole, held frequent assignations with an elegant, charming young woman. As spring began to turn to summer, it became clear that the two couples, Avinin and Debré, the gentleman and the young woman, had simultaneously attained their so different ends. They bowed to each other ceremoniously—and never saw each other again.

Another unexpected scene took place one day at the Juris Classeur where the "commission" was meeting in a small, dark, cold kitchen. "The sight," wrote Michel Debré, "had a certain quality of fantasy. The host (whose real name was Jacques Charpentier), President of the Paris Bar, was sitting on the stove, and Tristan (Pierre-Henri Teitgen), a future Minister of Justice, on the sink. Primis (Bastid), a former minister, had to be content with the dignity of a deal chair. . . ."

These meetings, held under the constant menace of death, led to three highly dramatic incidents.

The first, which might easily have been fatal, took place in the métro. Marguerite, the secretary of the C.G.E., lost his brief-case containing a large sum of money and part of the archives. As may well be imagined, this aroused considerable concern. The next day, on inquiring at the terminus, it was learned that the brief-case had been found by a passenger who had left his name and address. Greatly anxious, Marguerite went to see him, wondering whether he was a member of the Militia or the Gestapo. As it turned out, he was fortunately a good Frenchman who had quickly realized the nature of the documents he had found. All he asked as reward was that he should be given a job as a civil servant when the Liberation took place. This was later done by Tristan, when he became Minister of Justice.

The second was the occasion of the arrival in Paris of a messenger from London. This was Laffon, alias Lachaud, alias Martet, who had adopted the second pseudonym that very day. He was wearing next to his skin a little bag filled with tightly folded papers. These were the decrees naming the future prefects, the future Commissaires de la République and appointing a commission of three members to continue investigations till the Liberation took place.

The third was tragic. It occurred over the transmission to the southern zone of the final list of prefectorial appointments drawn up in the capital. This list was to be transmitted by word of mouth so as to avoid the danger of the written word. Michel Debré strolled up and down the Rue Daru with Jacques Bingen, who was to leave the next day, repeating to him the names of the prefects department by department. When he was word-perfect, Jacques Bingen went off. Next day he left for the southern zone, but was arrested at Clermont-Ferrand station. He committed suicide for fear of revealing the names under torture.

And thus, after a year of secret work, of danger and of emotions that varied between laughter and horror, the most important reorganization of the prefectorial system in French history, since it covered nearly every prefecture,[1] was ready on D-day for the landings. Of the eighty prefects nominated, in fact only forty-five took up their jobs. Between 6 June and 30 August, ten designated prefects had been arrested by the Germans. Five or six did not receive notice of their appointment in time. While, after the liberation of Paris, certain changes were made with regard to the departments that had not yet been liberated. In some ten departments only did incidents arise out of the change in the prefectorial administration.

In a very high proportion of cases the "prefabricated" reorganization succeeded in attaining its ends.

Of the new prefects, rather less than a third were professionals. A

[1] There were eight prefectures, corresponding more or less to the eastern departments, which had not been dealt with.

similar proportion came from outside the civil service, both from the liberal professions and from workers. The greater number were drawn from officials who did not belong to the prefectorial service (ministers, senior civil servants, technicians, university professors).

Of the Commissaires de la République, all had been appointed by the Liberation, except five, who were nominated in the following weeks on the suggestion of Lachaud (E. Laffon). Three did not take up their duties: Fourcade, who was denounced by the Militia and shot by the Germans; and Cassou and de Bouhey who were both seriously wounded on reaching their posts. On the other hand, two Commissaires de la République, who had not been on the original list, took over the job in the first territories liberated by the two landings: Coulet at Bayeux in the northern zone,[1] and Aubrac at Marseilles in the southern zone.[2]

The commissaires and prefects took up their posts amid the enthusiasm engendered by the Liberation, with the desire to efface the shame that had fallen upon their country, and with expectations, that were sometimes perhaps a little exaggerated, for the achievement of their great task. As one of them, Yves Farge, Commissaire de la République at Lyons, wrote: "Everything needs to be built anew, morality in the first place."

The political situation in France on D-day was such as to justify the worst prognostications. The government in power had completely collapsed; there was an almost hysterical hatred between the more excitable elements of the two parties; and there had been constant undermining by the Communists. France might easily have awakened to find herself subject to AMGOT, civil war, or Communism.

That she did not have to suffer these extremes was due to de Gaulle and his adherents. The course of French political life after the Liberation has certainly achieved no ideal tomorrows. But that is another story and belongs to the aftermath of the Liberation. But, on D-day, due to de Gaulle, every preparation had been made to ensure that the Liberation would take on the appearance of a successful revenge by France not only on the occupying power but also on her own past.

[1] For the circumstances of Coulet's appointment, cf., page 45.
[2] The complete list of Commissaires de la République who actually exercised their functions is as follows: Rouen: Bordeau de Fontenay; Rennes: Le Gorgeu; Angers: Debré; Orléans: Mars; Poitiers: Schueller; Limoges: Boursicot; Bordeaux: Cusin; Toulouse: Bertaux; Montpellier: Bounin; Marseilles: Aubrac; Clermont-Ferrand: Ingrand; Lyons: Farge; Dijon: Mairey; Lille: Closon; Saint-Quentin: Penne; Châlons-sur-Marne: Grégoire; Nancy: Chailley-Bert; Strasbourg: Blondel, then Boellaert.

Chapter II

THE "PERSONAL MESSAGES"
FROM LONDON

WE may now continue the narrative.

In the spring of 1944, Lucien Rachet, called Socrates, a member of the internal Resistance, spent a short time in London and then returned to France on an important mission assigned him by General de Gaulle. He was to make contact with the Resistance leaders, Colonel Ely, alias Algebra, Chaban-Delmas, alias Arc, the national military delegate, and Parodi alias Quartus, the delegate-general of the Comité Français de la Libération Nationale (C.F.L.N.) in France, to give them instructions from London for Resistance action on D-day. He explained to them that it would be folly to mount a general action. The liberation of territory by the Allies, even on the most favourable supposition, could only be progressive. The Resistance operations in France must therefore be launched in succession, district by district, and on orders from London. In no circumstances were they to assume the nature of a general insurrection, but to be limited to local sabotage operations and such guerrilla warfare as the Allied authorities might require. A memorandum signed by Algebra, Arc, Quartus and Socrates embodied these decisions.

During the night of 4–5 June 1944, a French officer in London, Captain Mamy, of the Premier Bureau of the F.F.I. headquarters, was duty officer in the Intelligence department. He made a tour of the offices to make sure that there were no documents lying about, and that the filing cabinets, drawers and safes were properly closed. At 11.30, when he had done his rounds, he turned on the wireless to listen to the "Personal Messages" which the B.B.C. broadcast twice a day to France. For the French in London, the B.B.C. consisted of two floors in the building between Aldwych and the Strand: the fourth floor and the second basement floor. The offices where the programmes were prepared were upstairs. And it was here that the men principally responsible for the broadcasts which had sustained French morale for four years and which directed underground action in France met. There were basically three types of broadcast. Firstly, the "Personal Messages" which emanated directly from the higher command, that is to say, from Eisenhower's headquarters, or from the headquarters of Koenig, who was in command of the F.F.I. These were strictly controlled, since they dealt with military activities, sabotage or local actions in France, in accordance with the Allied plans, and might well result in casualties. The announcers were merely agents of the Intelligence and Operations departments and were subject to military authority. Secondly, there were broadcasts of a political tendency: the half-hour of the "French speaking to the French," directed by Jacques Duchêne, whose real name was Michel Saint-Denis, with a team consisting of Pierre Bourdan, Jean Oberlé, Jean Marin, Maurice van Moppés and others, gave commentaries on the news and other programmes, among which was the famous "The Three Friends" which was very popular in France. Jacques Duchêne, who was a temporary employee of the B.B.C., and therefore under British control, managed to preserve his freedom of speech in face both of British directives and a good deal of outrageous talking and thinking among certain French circles in London. Thirdly, a series of broadcasts, the "Five Minutes," were the daily preserve of Free France, and emanated directly from the Gaullist government. These were directed by Maurice Schumann. It was in this series that André Gillois spoke at the time of the landings; while French ministers and other important persons frequently used the programme to address their fellow-countrymen in France. General de Gaulle himself, white-gloved and smoking a cigarette, spoke during the daily "Five Minutes" on several occasions. In general these broadcasts were more polemical in tone than the "French speaking to the French," and tended to be more condemnatory of the followers of Pétain and Giraud and indeed of all Frenchmen who were not Gaullists.

The French broadcasts from the B.B.C. showed therefore considerable disparity; they reflected the diversities of French dissident thought, the disagreements among themselves, the conflicts with their allies, and the quarrels with their fellow-countrymen who had difficult political affiliations. They were all, however, subject to a dual control which in general functioned amicably enough. In the first place, there was a commission of "orientation" on which Gillie, the British director of French broadcasts, and Michel Saint-Denis, responsible for the "French speaking to the French," represented the B.B.C., while officers or officials from the Free French and from British ministries represented their respective governments. They kept the editors informed on the military and political situation and agreed with them the general line to be pursued during the week's broadcasts.

Secondly, from the spring of 1944, a smaller committee met every day at noon consisting generally of Georges Boris, delegate of the French government, André Gillois, responsible for the "Five Minutes" of the Free French, Michel Saint-Denis, responsible for the "French speaking to the French," and Gillie. They, too, discussed the line the broadcasts were to take. But they also had power to censor the scripts. Indeed, every script for the evening broadcasts was first typed with a number of carbons and submitted before five o'clock to the British Minister of Information, Gillie and Jacques Duchêne. Even General de Gaulle's talks were subject to this censorship.

The broadcasting studio was on the second floor of the basement, safe from the bombing.

Between the two floors there was a lift, which on occasion reflected the accelerated rhythm of history. On 18 June 1942, both the British and the French in London were waiting anxiously for news of the fate of Koenig's troops who, surrounded at Bir-Hakeim, had been ordered on 10 June, after a fortnight of desperate fighting, to cut their way out and make contact with the Eighth Army. For two days nothing had been heard of this handful of heroes who, at that moment, were the incarnation of the renaissance of French power. Towards evening, at the very hour General de Gaulle was broadcasting, the British duty officer on the fourth floor received a cable announcing that the junction had been made. He hurried to the lift and rang four times, which was the recognized signal to the liftman for urgent priority. The lift appeared at once and the Englishman, his eyes glued to the signal, hurried into the lift, treading heavily on the toe of a passenger who had been unexpectedly hoisted to the fourth floor. He looked up. De Gaulle, wearing white gloves, had finished his broadcast and had been on his way out of the building. "General, here's a signal saying Koenig had made contact." De Gaulle, pale with emotion, seized the Englishman's hand and said: "Thank you, thank you"—doubtless the only time the General ever thanked anyone for treading on his toe.

At 11.30 on 4 June, Captain Mamy had no reason to expect messages of exceptional importance. There had, of course, been certain warning messages broadcast to France during the four previous days, but they might well have been intended to deceive the Germans. This had occurred before; for instance, in October 1943, the B.B.C. had transmitted certain warning orders which had never been followed up.

On this evening of 4 June, therefore, Captain Mamy expected nothing special. Nevertheless, as soon as the "Personal Messages" began coming over, he realized there was something unusual afoot.

In normal circumstances, the time given to messages to France was strictly limited. Since April 1944 the British Ministry of Information had reduced it to sixteen minutes in the twenty-four hours: four minutes at 14.30, six minutes at 19.30, and again at 21.30. This was sufficient for the transmission of between thirty-five to sixty-five messages a day, according to the length of the message.

Moreover, the messages were, in general, phrased in such a way that they could be understood only by the local Resistance whose particular operational concern they were. They dealt with the parachuting of arms; particular circumstances of sabotage or guerrilla action; transmitted news and warnings; or gave some individual Maquis information by which a parachuted agent might be identified. "The messages were couched in individual codes which," writes Galimand in an unpublished report, "only the recipients, the authors of the message, and the intelligence departments were in a position to interpret correctly." Each message consisted of two parts: the "reference phrase," equivalent to a postal address, which indicated originator and recipient, and the message itself, containing military instructions in words that to the uninitiated appeared not only ludicrous but often utterly senseless.

Indeed, unless he held the clue, who could possibly suppose that "the centipede is a mammal" had anything to do with parachuting arms, or that the "crocodile is thirsty" and the "ostrich pecks its stomach" were preludes to sabotage? Who could imagine that "the doctor buries all his patients" announced the secret sailing of a motor-boat for Finistère, that "Flora has a red neck" and "Kiou is nice" indicated secret landing-grounds for aircraft from London, or that "from Baba to Coco" was a message to a Resistance leader with the pseudonym of Bacot? Had the B.B.C. gone crazy? Or simply turned libertine, to judge from certain messages that seemed to contain the most intimate avowals? "I hope to see you again, darling, twice," meant that two aircraft were to drop weapons.

Nevertheless, amid these apparent incoherencies, an attentive listener could sometimes discern a singular continuity. He would be told one day that "Melpomene uses heliotrope scent," which was not, however, particularly surprising, considering the fantastic mythology to which the B.B.C. apparently subscribed. But a few days later the Muse of Tragedy would be scenting herself with iris, then with jasmine, then with carnation, and finally with violet. These messages were to give a certain Maquis the date for a particular Operation: operation Melpomene. The scent indicated the selected date: heliotrope, since it began with the eighth letter of the alphabet, meant that the operation would start eight days after a previously arranged date. Then there was a counter-order: the operation was to be postponed for twenty-four hours: iris replaced heliotrope. After which, there were further delays: and scent succeeded to scent. Finally, in the last message, which fixed the action for the twenty-fourth day, the unfortunate Melpomene, unable to find a scent beginning with the letter X that pleased her, was reduced to informing her anxious correspondent that she bought her perfume at Xenophon's.

As he listened-in that evening, Captain Mamy was merely expecting broadcasts of this kind destined for recipients in the various Maquis throughout France, all isolated from each other, and as yet in no position to carry out joint operations. Yet the broadcast was to surprise him on two counts.

In the first place, it was longer than usual: there were some seventy code messages. Secondly, instead of being directed to a series of dispersed and isolated listeners, Captain Mamy soon realized that the whole broadcast seemed to be unusually integrated and consistent. Indeed, he began to recognize the messages, for he had written them himself. They concerned sabotage and guerrilla operations. But what surprised him was that this series applied to the whole of France, to every military district of the Resistance.

Captain Mamy had reached London in June 1942, from France, where he had been employed in the intelligence service of the Army of the Armistice, which worked in liaison with both Vichy and the British. He had been posted to the operations staff of the B.C.R.A.

His first job, in July 1942, under Commandant Saint-Jacques, had been to allot code words to the various plans the Resistance were to put into operation on D-day. He had named "Plan Vert," dealing with sabotage of the railways, "Plan Tortue," dealing with the roads, which was to develop later into "Plan Bibendum," and "Plan Bleu," dealing with electric power, to which was later added "Plan Violet," which dealt with the sabotage of the Post Office underground cables.

At the beginning of 1944, a new organization was set up, known as "Bloc Planning," concerned with preparing "organized intervention by the Resistance to assist the Allies" on D-day. Its directors, Colonel Gombaud and Captain Michke, an officer of the Czechoslovak Army, who had been through the French École de Guerre, reported that the Resistance might with advantage replace the bombing activities of the

Allies, which often caused casualties among French civilians, by sabotage.

In collaboration with its British opposite number, S.O.E., "Bloc Planning" submitted three reports. The first, dated 20 January 1944, was entitled "The Military Conditions for a Landing in France." It was a study of possible Resistance action in support of the various probable landing zones. The British staffs were interested and asked for further information.

A second report, "Military Action by the French Resistance," maintained that the Resistance's activities should be limited mainly to the enemy's rear areas. It would, however, amount to no less than an army and must act in close contact with the Allied High Command. In the mountainous district (Massif Central, Alps, Pyrenees, Vosges, Dura, and Morvan) the Resistance must create redoubts and mobilization centres from which the personnel could be reinforced when the moment came. The report also suggested the formation of the "Jedburgh" teams, consisting of a French officer and two Allied officers, one British, the other American, who could be parachuted into the Maquis to co-ordinate their activities with London's.

S.O.E. asked that the conclusions reached by "Bloc Planning" be distributed immediately to the military leaders in all districts. A third report, dated 31 March 1944, "Instructions for Military Action by the French Resistance," was sent to the various D.M.P.s in France. In some districts, it was sent to the Maquis commanders in the form of sealed orders, which were not to be opened before the "Personal Messages" from London announced D-day. Anyone disobeying this order would be shot out of hand.

These orders were mostly for sabotage operations—of which the "Plan Vert" against the railways was the most vital—and also, in some districts, for guerrilla action. They were never intended to be put automatically into effect in every district on the same day, for in localities far removed from the main Allied battle the only results could be to subject the civilian population to unnecessary risks and German reprisals, and involve the ill-equipped Maquis forces themselves in hopeless battles against the Wehrmacht and the Militia.

Mamy knew these messages well. For those which concerned the "Plan Vert," he had thought out a number of rural phrases evoking the colour green: "I'm looking for four-leaved clovers," "reeds must grow, leaves rustle." The "Plan Violet" was referred to in such phrases as: "The tomatoes must be picked."

When Mamy, sitting alone in his office, heard these phrases over the air, he knew that D-day was at hand. But what most surprised him was that he heard the whole range of code phrases, those ordering both sabotage and guerrilla activities, and not only in the northern zone but in the southern zone as well.

Captain Mamy's excitement at the fact that operations in France were imminent was mingled with considerable anxiety. He was excited at the thought that the whole secret machine of renascent France, which he and his fellow-countrymen, whether resistant or dissident, had watched being assembled piece by careful piece, was now at last to be set in motion. These messages would alert a whole new army and administration, a whole new political organization, both in France and beyond her borders. But he was profoundly anxious because he had reason to believe that no French military leader would have given the B.B.C. instructions to read the whole of the personal messages at the same time.

He imagined, therefore, that the Allies had taken it upon themselves to do so.

Could it be that Allied headquarters had decided on simultaneous landings in the north and south and were therefore calling for hostilities over the whole country? But even in that case the Allied advance would take time and Mamy, from the viewpoint of a junior officer, wondered anxiously what could have gone wrong.

He feared what would happen if the listeners in France obeyed the summons to a general and simultaneous rising.

It has taken many years for the questions Captain Mamy asked himself that night to find an answer.

General de Gaulle does not mention this incident in his *Mémoires*. And Jacques Soustelle, in his, merely says: "This was one of the most tragic incidents of the period and I can give no satisfactory explanation of it." Various tendentious explanations have been given both by the Communists and the Americans, but these appear to be vitiated by political considerations.

Nevertheless, a certain amount of light can now be brought to the elucidation of this mysterious occurrence.

We have gone very carefully into the circumstances and have had the advantage of General Koenig's help. There is no doubt that the decision for general action was taken by Allied headquarters and communicated *in extremis* to the French. On 4 June 1944, the day before the messages were broadcast, two Allied officers, the British General Gubbins and the American Colonel David Bruce, called on General Koenig—Colonel

Passy being present—and inquired whether the French had any objections to messages for a general rising being passed over the air. In fact, this was no more than a polite gesture, for the decision had already been taken and the orders issued.

Faced with the accomplished fact, the French do not seem to have reacted. General Koenig, who represented the military authority, made no objection. General de Gaulle, who incarnated the civil power, was immediately informed and appears not to have protested against these orders being given directly to French combatants by the Allied authorities. His broadcast on 6 June, after his row with Eisenhower,[1] contained no reservations concerning the Allied decision.

. . . For the sons of France, wherever they may be, whatever they may be, their simple and sacred duty is to fight with every means at their disposal. The enemy must be destroyed, the enemy who is crushing and polluting the fatherland, the hated enemy, the dishonourable enemy.

. . . France will fight this battle with fury. She will conduct it with precision. . . .

For a nation, fighting with her feet and hands tied against an oppressor armed to the teeth, to fight a battle with precision necessitates a number of conditions.

The first is that the orders given by the French government and by the French leaders who have been called on to issue them, whether on a national or a local level, must be implicitly obeyed.

The second is that the action we take in the enemy's rear should be as closely integrated as possible with the offensive conducted from the front by the Allied and French armies. . . .

There was certainly no criticism of the Allied decision here; nor indeed anything to suggest that it was not in accord with the intentions of the French government.

Is there matter for astonishment in the fact that neither Koenig nor de Gaulle protested against the orders of the Allied High Command unleashing a rising of the French Resistance? Though they were not directly responsible for the broadcast of the messages, are they to be considered indirectly responsible for not having opposed it? These were the views put forward later by the Communists and others, who blamed General Koenig for the premature insurrection.

Evidence from French officers who were in responsible positions in London at the time,[2] including General Koenig, makes it perfectly clear

[1] Cf., page 42.
[2] Among others, Colonel Zigler and Colonel Passy.

that the French did not protest because they could not. Nor should they have protested.

They could not, for the simple reason that they were, in the military hierarchy, subordinate to Allied headquarters; General Koenig was under the command of General Eisenhower. It was S.H.A.E.F. and Eisenhower who were responsible for Overlord; and they alone, being in possession of all the facts, were in a position to decide on the appropriate use of the French Resistance on D-day. If Allied headquarters, at the risk of having certain units of the Maquis prematurely decimated, ordered sabotage and guerrilla warfare throughout France, it was clearly from no casual decision but for overriding strategical reasons. Had S.H.A.E.F., in order to economize the Resistance forces, broadcast messages applicable only to the regions in which military operations were to take place, it would have meant informing the Germans of the precise localities of the landings and of the areas in which to concentrate their available forces. But Allied tactics were concerned with leaving the Wehrmacht not only uncertain as to where the invasion forces were to land, but also in ignorance of the invasion's true nature. Was it the main operation, or merely a diversion planned to attract the German reserves away from the real battlefield? We have seen [1] how successful the cover plan was. Indeed, it was one of the main reasons for the success of the landings.

Furthermore, the broadcasting of all the messages at once was based on two other considerations: "To hinder to the maximum extent, and at one blow, the whole of the enemy's strategic and tactical transport system; and to demoralize the enemy to the extent that he could no longer feel secure anywhere in French territory." [2]

The orders given the French Resistance to go into action everywhere at once were therefore necessary to the operation that was to liberate France. De Gaulle, Koenig and all the French in responsible positions might well deplore that their fellow-countrymen should be exposed to premature dangers in secondary operations. They were later able to do a good deal to minimize them, but they could not oppose the order at the time.

The drama was not, therefore, being played out in London but in France. The resistants, as they listened-in to the B.B.C., had every reason to interpret the personal messages in the widest and most dangerous sense. In the first place, most of them were not in circumstances favourable

[1] Cf., page 6.
[2] Unpublished letter from General Koenig, dated 21 November 1957.

to a clear and balanced analysis of what they heard. Jamming from German and French stations controlled by the Nazis often caused considerable interference. Moreover, these personal messages, so carefully weighed and phrased by the Allied Command, were on occasion accompanied during the Free French programme by eloquent appeals from militarily irresponsible speakers. They sometimes got carried away and went further than was prudent. For instance, on 6 June, the B.B.C. broadcast certain sentences that, if heard out of their context and taken in isolation, could easily lead to misunderstandings: "Let everyone respond to the appeal of the nation, in whose service today every Frenchman and Frenchwoman is mobilized." Or again: "You are all mobilized. Obey the orders of your government." This was enough to persuade the Maquis that the hour for a general insurrection had struck. The F.F.I., whether Gaullist or Communist, all felt by D-day a psychological tension from having waited so long, and were inclined, therefore, to interpret the London broadcasts in terms of their own enthusiasm and impatience.

The almost general rising of the Maquis over the whole country on D-day was therefore the result, on the one hand, of the simultaneous broadcasting of all the personal messages concerning sabotage and guerrilla warfare and, on the other, of unofficial talks that seemed to sanction general mobilization and insurrection. In fact, the order for general insurrection was never given to the Maquis either by the French command of the F.F.I. or by the Supreme Allied Command, whatever the opponents of Gaullism may have declared. But it may well be that the simultaneous broadcasting of messages for sabotage and guerrilla action for the whole of France, combined with imprudent speeches from the B.B.C., and aggravated by the psychological condition of the French, led to their recipients believing that an appeal for a general rising had been made. As a result, there were many tragedies, of which the following is a poignant example.

In the Vosges mountains on the evening of 5 June, the thirty-four Corcieux maquisards received the messages they had been long awaiting: "Reeds must grow, leaves rustle"; and: "I will bring the eglantine." They interpreted them as an order for general insurrection.

On 6 June, at four o'clock in the morning, this handful of F.F.I. went off to attack the German garrison at Taintrux, which consisted of some hundreds of men. Captain Vichard divided his men into three sections. The first was to attack the mairie, where most of the enemy was billeted; the second to assault the Café Girard, where the non-commissioned officers lived; while the third was to capture the remaining Germans billeted in the school.

At 04.45, the first section was seen by the enemy and a shot gave the alarm. The ten men entered the mairie, but had to retreat. There were fortunately no casualties, and the withdrawal was made in good order.

The third section took the enemy by surprise and captured forty-eight prisoners, of whom some were wounded.

But the second section, having entered the café and taken fourteen non-commissioned officers prisoner, was surrounded. Four maquisards were killed. Their comrades continued the fight. The five survivors were captured only when they had fired their last round. The Germans stripped them and beat them. After many hours of torture, they were executed by machine-gun fire on the morning of 7 June.

Ten thousand Germans descended on the village and created a reign of terror. Some of the leading inhabitants were shot.

Owing to their having been sent prematurely into action, these brave men never saw the final victory.

By inciting the local resistants, the broadcasts from London caused similar tragedies throughout the country, in the Ain, the Drôme, the Ardèche, the Aveyron, the Dordogne, the Isère, the Haustes-Alpes, the Basses-Alpes, the Vaucluse, the Haute-Loire, the Lozère, the Cantal, the Creuse, the Haute-Vienne, the Lot, the Hautes-Pyrénées, the Haute-Garonne, the Vosges, the Vercors, Vienne, Haute-Provence, Franche-Comté, Dauphiné and Savoy. This list is in accordance with de Gaulle's speech of 25 July 1944.

The Gaullist authorities, who were not responsible for broadcasting the messages, did their best to limit the consequences as soon as they became aware of the tragedies that were resulting. On 10 June, General Koenig sent something in the nature of a counter-order, correcting the erroneous impression certain Gaullist and Communist Maquis had derived from the B.B.C. messages. It was, he said, a matter merely of limited operations, not of a general insurrection.

On 12 June, in the middle of a battle, the Vercors Maquis received orders to limit their operations and to send men, who had been prematurely mobilized, back to their homes.

On their own level, the military delegates, in closer contact with the combatants, were in a better position to assess the dangers that premature operations were bound to entail, not only for the Maquis but also for the civilian population. The national military delegate (D.M.N.), Chaban-Delmas, declared on 21 June at a meeting of the Comité d'Action Militaire (C.O.M.A.C.): "The D.M.N. . . . considers that the national insurrection should not take place till the disorganization of the enemy army has reached a pitch sufficient to prevent its having the means at its disposal to effect the reprisals it is capable of carrying out today and for which he does not think the Resistance should render itself responsible." Similarly, Gilbert Grandval, D.M.R. of the Nancy (Vosges and Lorraine) region, in orders distributed to his organizations, wrote significantly on 16 June: "Immediately on the first landings, those formations which already had arms went into action, others occupied the parachuting zones, expecting arrivals which did not in fact take place. These partial actions, though they were undertaken with a spirit worthy of all praise, have nonetheless resulted in the enemy's increased alertness, which complicates the situation."

It was the conflict, or lack of synchronization, inevitable in any war, between the decisions made by headquarters, whether military or political, and the interests of the combatants.

There was nothing scandalous or disgraceful about all this; but one fact emerges and bears repetition: in France's situation in 1944, it was sometimes inevitable that Frenchmen should be sacrificed to effect her liberation.

Chapter III

THE LIBERATION OF NORMANDY

THE form the Liberation took varied from province to province. Accompanied in some places by tragedy, in others it was heroic-comedy; immediate in certain localities, elsewhere it was long delayed, while the defenceless inhabitants, sometimes liberated by the Maquis, sometimes by the Allied regular forces, were here subjected to a bloody battle and there scarcely heard a shot fired. France had become the unhappy battlefield of huge opposing forces.

From D-day onwards there was a continuous flow of reinforcements to both sides in the theatre of operations.

The Allied Intelligence services, working either in Germany or in occupied territory, reported an increase in military traffic at the railway junctions: in Strasbourg, between 10 and 13 June 1944, eighteen trains of troops or munitions passed through from Germany towards Nancy. Six troop trains and 150 tanks went to Belfort. One hundred troop-carriers took the road to Nancy.

At Singen, between 8 and 10 June 1944, twenty trains carrying fresh divisions passed through each day as well as fifteen trains of munitions moving from Bavaria to France.

A few days later, there was another wave or reinforcements: between 14 and 20 June, five trains carrying infantry and artillery were moving from Germany towards the Strasbourg and Nancy region every twenty-four hours. At the same time, two thousand trucks coming from Baden passed through Cologne on the way to France by road.

These troop movements increased the German order of battle in the army in the west, but no divisions were brought across from the Russian front. The Wehrmacht had now to deal with war on two fronts. At the end of April, a month before the landings, there were fifty-two divisions in France, six in Holland, six in Belgium and twenty-four in Italy, compared to 202 in Russia. There was a general reserve, mostly stationed in the region of Wesel-Aix-la-Chapelle-Wiesbaden, consisting of twenty divisions. On 1 July, a month after the landings, the number of divisions in Russia had scarcely diminished, there were 200 as against 202. In Holland and Belgium the number had remained almost constant (six and five). In Italy, it had risen to twenty-six. In France, however, there was a considerable increase, the number rising from fifty-two to sixty. And, finally, there were varying reports of the strategic reserve stationed on the banks of the Rhine having risen to thirty-two or, as some said, fifty divisions.

Moreover, in France itself, units from the south and south-west were sent north; and it will be seen that the Resistance did not facilitate their movement.

The Allies, meanwhile, were quickly and methodically reinforcing the landings, and pumping supplies into the expanding bridgehead. According to the official Canadian Army documents, by 15 June half a million men and 77,000 vehicles had been landed in France and two artificial harbours were working to capacity. A month after D-day there were a million Allied soldiers deployed in Normandy; and Pluto had come into service to supply their vehicles with gasoline. In this instance, Pluto was not the god of fable, but a submarine pipe-line which derived its name from its initials (Pipe-Line-Under-The-Ocean). It ran from the Isle of Wight to Cherbourg. Similar pipe-lines were quickly set up in the liberated territory. Only four days after 6 June there was a pipe-line already in service. It was extended progressively as the Allies advanced. By the end of the war, it consisted of 2,400 kilometres of pipe of 150 m. diameter. Four more were begun in June 1944. At the same time, American engineers in great numbers, together with the French railway workers who had stayed at their jobs, opened up the railways. On 11 July, the first regular train was running between Cherbourg and Carentan, on a line roughly parallel to the front.

Road transport was also quickly organized. A fast road, called the Red Ball Express, began to function on 15 August to connect Normandy with the Paris region. Saint-Lô was its point of departure and Chartres the first terminus in the east. It was gradually extended to Soissons, and then to Château-Thierry. Five thousand trucks were allotted to it.

Such was the great controlled flood that was spreading across the soil of France. It was directed by the Allied staffs in London and by the campaigning generals, who decided their objectives in their caravan headquarters.

Some districts were liberated by the Allies. And in these it was the regular military forces who took over, while the Maquis played only a secondary part and the Liberation, with but few exceptions, presented no urgent political problems and provoked but few acts of revenge. On the other hand, there were districts which liberated themselves, were in fact liberated by their own local Maquis and F.F.I., without direct support from the Allied armies. In these cases, it was not always easy to keep order; political difficulties came to the fore, there was sometimes a tendency towards civil war and mob rule, while the rancours that had accumulated during four years found release in spontaneous and un-controlled reprisals. In general it can be said that the Liberation north of the Loire and east of the Rhône, which was effected by British, Ameri-can or French regular units, aroused no, or few, political difficulties. On the other hand, in the centre of France and in the south-west, where the F.F.I. and the F.T.P. were generally operating on their own, events took a very different course.

The first advance of the Allied armies after the landings spread over two provinces north of the Loire, Normandy and Brittany. Though both these provinces were liberated by regular armies, and suffered no revolu-tionary incidents of any significance, there was nevertheless a profound difference in the course of events according to whether the areas lay east or west of the Cotentin. In the east, in the Normandy plains, it took six weeks, from 6 June to 20 July, for the northern half of the depart-ment of the Manche and a coastal region of some thirty kilometres in depth between the Vire and the Dives to be liberated. It was a period of heavy bombardments by both sides, reminiscent of the war of posi-tion in Champagne or at Verdun, during which whole towns and vil-lages were destroyed by artillery fire or bombing from the air.

For five days, from 22 to 27 June, Cherbourg was the centre of a des-perate battle, which ended with street-fighting and a final assault against the arsenal. Caen, which had been in the front line since the landings, was not liberated till 9 July, after a battle lasting twenty-four hours and a final bombing by 460 aircraft, each of which, during the forty minutes it lasted, dropped five tons of bombs.

From 20 July to 18 August, the Allies in France and Normandy ad-vanced somewhat more rapidly. Two departments were completely liberated, the Calvados and the Manche, as well as half the Orne. The territory conquered by the Allies had almost tripled, but progress was still comparatively slow, and varied in different areas, entailing great hardships for the civilian population. In front of Caen, the Second British Army, which was trying to break out to the east, was temporarily contained and had to mark time. On the other hand, the First Ameri-can Army succeeded in breaking through the German lines towards the south on 25 July. A war of movement began again with the celerity of a *blitzkreig*. Coutances was taken on 28 July; Granville and Avranches fell to the tanks on 30 and 31 July. A breach was opened, through which Eisenhower could unleash a double prong towards both the west and the east.

In the west, Patton's Third American Army, which had been held in reserve, advanced on 2 August to conquer Brittany. This manœuvre was completed within a week, except for enemy pockets on the coast to which 75,000 Germans retreated to make a stand in the principal ports, Saint-Malo, Brest, Lorient and Saint-Nazaire. Brest, the most important, held out till 18 September. The Americans took Rennes on 5 August; the next day they reached the outskirts of Brest, 200 kilometres away. On the 10th, they were in Nantes. This rapid advance, carried out in liaison with the F.F.I., saved most of the Breton population from the bombardments suffered by the Normans. In general, only the ports were subjected to the destruction entailed by a war of position.

In the east, before overrunning unravaged districts and debouching towards Paris, the Allied advance was involved in some very dramatic episodes indeed during the Normandy battle. There was a German counter-attack on Mortain and Avranches, followed by the encirclement of the German Fifth and Seventh Armies in a pocket, some seventy by twenty-five kilometres, stretching approximately from Argentan in the east to Mortain in the west.

Within these two hundred square kilometres the fate of the campaign was decided. "It is impossible to tell," declares a witness, "how many German dead there are or how many prisoners have been taken, but the trucks, wagons, troop-carriers, guns and burnt-out tanks run into thousands; and hundreds of horses have been killed. . . . Some 1,500 or 2,000 horses, many of them wounded, stampeded in the plain and the devastated fields, and peasants from the whole department soon turned out to make a selection among them. In this cemetery of vehicles and tanks, among the corpses which were to infect the air for many months, it became clear how wide and general had been the Seventh German Army's systematic pillaging of the districts it had crossed; food, merchandise of every kind, furniture, plate, clothes, linen, even account books, visiting cards, and headed writing paper. All these were strewn about the progress of this army which had now been crushed at last."

Then the advance to the Seine began. There was no question of the Germans putting up any resistance; their problem was to evacuate the districts they had occupied for the last four years as quickly as they could. Harassed by the F.F.I., demoralized by civilians who kept advising the *Feldgrau* to surrender, and here and there indulging in final atrocities, the German Army began to learn what the natural obstacle of a river could mean to routed troops.

Four Allied armies took part in the pursuit.

The First Canadian Army, moving along the Channel coast, crossed the Seine near Elbeuf and advanced on Rouen which it reached on 27 August and liberated on the 30th. Farther south, the Second British Army took the offensive on 16 August, crossed the Dives, and successively liberated Lisieux, Pont-L'Évêque and Louviers; after which it also reached the Seine south of Rouen. The Third American Army advanced on Paris. Starting from Alençon and Le Mans, its corps reached Verneuil, Dreux and Mantes in the north, and Chartres and Rambouillet, its ultimate objectives, in the south. Meanwhile, the First American Army advanced towards the Basse-Seine, downstream from Paris, by Évreux and Vernon. After the taking of Paris and the crossing of the Seine the campaign completely altered its nature. There were few battles and the armoured advance continued to the northern frontier.

The battle of Normandy, said Churchill in the House of Commons, on 28 September 1944, had been "the greatest and most decisive single battle of the entire war. Never has the exploitation of victory been carried to a higher perfection." More precisely, General Eisenhower recorded the enemy losses in the Normandy operations as follows: "The enemy had lost 400,000, killed, wounded or captured. Half the total were prisoners of war, and 135,000 of these had been taken in the month subsequent to 25 July. German material losses included 1,300 tanks, 20,000 other vehicles, 500 assault guns, and 1,500 pieces of artillery.

What part did the French, and the F.F.I. in particular, play in this cataclysm?

In the Bayeux region, as we have seen, the Maquis consisted of 200 adherents. In the Orne, there were 1,800 F.F.I. of which one-third was armed. In the Eure, there were 5,000, of which 1,000 were in the Évreux region. They were not all properly equipped, nor could they all devote their whole time to Resistance activities; but the Resistance was nevertheless an heroic aspiration. Among the hundreds of thousands of superbly equipped troops who had come to grips in Normandy, this handful of men without uniforms could have no real effect upon the battle's issue.

But they could have some influence on its minor episodes; and it was thanks to them that France was represented at the liberation of this first province. And it was due to them, too, that some tragedies were averted.

In Caen, on 5 June, the theatre was presenting *Véronique*. Hardly had the swing ceased from swinging when the bombing began. A former prefect of the Corrèze, Lecornu, who had been sacked by Vichy and had joined the Resistance, made contact with the Intelligence services and informed the Vichy prefect of the areas of the towns in which it would be safe for the population to take refuge. At the same time, on the orders of Léonard Gilles, a midwife, Madame Himbert, wearing a Red Cross brassard, set off on a bicycle to cross the lines on a similar mission. The Germans let her go through. She found herself alone in no-man's-land, which was littered with corpses and broken weapons. She reached a village occupied by the Canadians, who took her for a spy. She spent two hours in prison, and several more being interrogated. Then she was taken to Captain Fitzgerald, of the Intelligence. He promised that the Saint-Étienne quarter would be spared and that the civilian population could take shelter there.

This was the sort of thing the Resistance could do. Many other towns owed to its intervention the fact that they were not destroyed during the last battles.

On 22 August, the Americans got within range of Évreux, and were preparing to bombard it. Before doing so, however, they wished to make sure the Germans were still in the town. Two young resistants, Pierre Miguet, a medical student, and Jean-Michel Heyraud immediately set out from Dreux to Évreux with a verbal message for the F.F.I. commander. Their bodies were found at the entrance to the village of Couture-Boussey, bearing traces not only of bullet-wounds, but of kicks and blows from rifle butts. In the meantime, however, another messenger had brought Thierry, the mayor, a "letter from the American Divisional Commander." It told the Resistance "to see that the town of Évreux was completely evacuated by enemy troops before dawn on 23 August 1944. . . .

"We must remind you, Monsieur le Maire, that this evacuation is the only thing that can save your town from destruction.

"We feel sure that the inhabitants and authorities of the town of Évreux will do the necessary."

It was an ultimatum and, however well-intentioned, carried grave menace. Thierry, the Vichy mayor, told his principal secretary to take the message to Commandant Stouls, the leader of the local Resistance, and to Georges Bernard, the Gaullist mayor designate.

On the morning of the 23rd, at 5.30, only a short while before the American general's ultimatum was due to expire, nine people set off to see him in the prefecture open Renault, among whom were Commandant Stouls and Bernard. The car blew up on a mine. There were two dead, six wounded, and only one unhurt. The accident might well have entailed appalling consequences for the town. Stouls and Bernard, though both wounded, continued on foot and reached the American lines. They were immediately taken to Hobbs's headquarters. Dawn was breaking and they were only just in time.

On 26 August, the American troops entered Évreux without encountering resistance, and the American general wrote to the mayor: "It gives me great pleasure to inform you that thanks to the splendid and devoted efforts of the F.F.I., who have been of the greatest assistance to us in our common cause, we have been enabled to enter your important town without having to use the offensive power of our troops."

Other towns were saved by the Resistance in similar circumstances. In the Orne, there were Laigle, Bellême and Mortagne where the F.F.I. took a thousand Germans prisoner. In the Seine-Maritime, Dieppe owed to them its liberation without a battle. In the Eure-et-Loir at Nogent-le-Rotrou, and in the Eure, at Vernon, they provided the British troops with guides for the crossing of the Seine. At Elbeuf, on 24 August, an F.F.I. commandant, aged twenty-three, gave the order to attack and liberated the town before the arrival of the Americans, killing forty Germans and taking 200 prisoner.

"At Elbeuf, from 21 August onwards," records a witness, "the German retreat began to look extraordinarily like a rout. The troops looked as if they had had enough. They went into the houses to ask for food and somewhere to sleep. Their tanks tore up the pavement and chipped bits off the buildings. Their vehicles were driving two or three abreast. There was a traffic block at every crossroads. Here was a pathetic recapitulation of the 'retreat of the Ten Thousand' but their cries were not hailing the sea but the Seine. The whole mass of men, horses, wagons, trucks, tanks, guns and bicycles were pressing on towards the river.

"But the Seine could no longer be crossed! The ferry by the suspension bridge had had a 'misfortune' and so had the one by the fairground; as for the big ferry at Écluses, with its decked-over twin barges, which normally carried seventy tons of cargo every half-hour, it had a remarkable fate. A patriot from Saint-Aubin, the heroic Arsène Guerbette, joined the crew, and sabotaged and sank it under the very noses of the Germans. . . . He was arrested and mercilessly shot in the Plaine de Cléon." (Charles Brisson.)

These were typical Resistance actions; but they were performed against a background of civilian casualties and ruined towns. The dramatic and heroic episodes emerged from widespread scenes of horror.

At the bombed and burning village of Roque-Dugnard, near Pont-l'Évêque, English soldiers calmly warmed their billycans on a still burning wall. Or again, at Carentan, near Mortain, which was in flames, the inhabitants fought the fire by pouring barrels of cider on it. These were the disasters of war and also its unexpected, if sombre, absurdities.

On the other hand, peacetime protocol often subsisted amid the ruins. In the middle of July, Caen was still cut in two by the battle. The prefecture had been liberated, but the front was only some thousand yards away. Bombs and shells were still scouring its walls every day, but the offices were functioning. A French liaison officer, Colonel Lion, conducted two British brigadiers to it through considerable mortar fire, moving from cover to cover on the way. In the hall, they were met by a *huissier* wearing a chain, who gave them forms to fill in: "Object of visit. . . . Surname and Christian names. . . ." Having complied with the formality and while waiting for the *huissier* to submit the precious document to the newly installed prefect, one of the brigadiers remarked: "You really are a great people." The British officers were introduced into the prefect's office, and Daure apologized for the fact that a shell-burst had made the chairs rather dusty.

But none of these lighter facets could alter the terrible reality of the tragedy. They could not relieve the sufferings of the civilian population. And this was the reality of the life of the French during the battle of Normandy.

From the military point of view, the civilians did not, could not, count in the plans of the military commanders.

On 20 July, General Bradley, on the eve of an offensive, gave a press conference to explain the plan of attack: "At the close of the briefing, one of the newsmen asked if we would forewarn the French living within the bounds of the carpet. I shook my head, as if to escape the necessity of saying no. . . . The success of Cobra hung upon surprise; it was essential to have surprise even if it meant the slaughter of innocents as well."

The "innocents" in question, therefore, suffered the consequences of a plan of which they had no knowledge.

"For two hours on end," wrote an inhabitant of a village in the front line, "the coming and going of bombers took place amid a roar of engines, a thunder of exploding bombs of all sizes, and a quivering of the air. When coming out of a shelter, it was better not to close one's mouth if one wished to avoid fracturing one's tympanum; smoke from one's cigarette rose in the air in an extraordinary, jerky way. The birds were panic-stricken and flew to more clement districts." And this particular "innocent" concluded: "To suffer war in one's own territory is an appalling experience."

The cities were harder hit even than the countryside. When Caen was eventually liberated, after a month's fighting in the town, the population had declined from thirty-two thousand to twelve thousand. Avranches, which underwent an even worse ordeal, had no more than thirty-five left out of six thousand. Saint-Lô, which the Americans called the "capital of ruins," sheltered, if one can call it that, no more than ten inhabitants. Both there and elsewhere whole families were buried under the rubble.

Le Havre, the last Normandy town to be liberated, was among those to suffer most severely. From the city centre, the sea was now visible in every direction. Nothing had survived but the plinth of a statue. And yet, amid the appalling destruction, there were still inhabitants clinging to the pulverized earth.

On 5 September, an Allied emissary made contact with the German commander. But in vain. The *Petit Havre* announced: "The commander of the Fortress has declared to an officer of the opposing forces, who came to see him as an emissary, that the fortified camp of Le Havre would be defended to the last." And, on the other side, the Canadian general let it be known that it was impossible to suspend hostilities for the evacuation of civilians. Once again, the French population was caught in the giant vice of war. It was not always aware of the ordeal it was to undergo.

At six o'clock in the evening, when everyone in Le Havre was expecting a land battle and street fighting, a Pathfinder aircraft "roared funereally across Le Havre, dropping four flares enclosing an area of a third of the town. The noise in the streets, which was still considerable at that hour, prevented most of the inhabitants being warned. For two appalling hours, this demarcated area, which was also the finest part of the town, was bombed mercilessly with high explosives and incendiaries, street by street, house by house, according to a prearranged plan: "There was an indescribable chaos of crashing buildings; huge flames roared from the ruins and were spread ever farther by the strong west wind which seemed to be the breath of Satan himself. And within the brazier was caught a whole population that had been overconfidently going about its business. Thousands were killed in this inferno, burned alive whole families at a time. Fifteen hundred tons of high explosives were dropped according to the wireless. But how many incendiaries?

"In that week of 5 to 12 September [the day the town was liberated], the population suffered between 2,000 and 3,000 dead while 35,000 were completely bombed out of 10,500 houses. The flags that had been prepared to welcome the liberators were burned with the rest. The Allied troops, who entered the town on 12 September, were at first surprised by the reserve with which they were received. But when they had advanced farther into the ruins, the soldiers saw and understood. How could these people, mourning their many thousand dead, most of them burnt alive as a result of useless bombing, welcome their liberators? . . . British soldiers were seen in tears by the graves in the Place Gambetta, for they too could not accept this devastation for which there was no military necessity whatever." (Julien Guillemord.)

In the Saint-Lô district improvised shelters were turned into operating theatres. Doctors performed a Caesarean on a kitchen table. Elsewhere, two young people, a boy and a girl, who had been wounded in the same bombardment, were placed side by side in the same bed; but the girl was already dead when the doctor amputated the boy's leg by the light of a candle.

At Brest, which owing to the fact that it was in a "pocket" suffered destruction comparable to the Norman towns, one of the principal shelters was the Sadi-Carnot, which could hold about a thousand refugees. To start with they were all French; but when the bombing got worse, the Germans turned 600 French civilians out to make room for soldiers.

On Saturday, 9 September, at two o'clock in the morning, the German soldier responsible for running the motor for the shelter's lighting tripped as he was pouring gasoline into the tank. There was a burst of flames. "*Achtung, Achtung, munitions kaput,*" cried the Germans, making a dash for the exit. But the fire was too quick for them and too quick also for the French, most of whom were asleep.

"There was a deep, terrifying roar that shook the roof. . . . A wave of burning smoke drove those who had passed the gate into the open air as if they were brands of straw. Bruised and black from head to foot, there were some fifty of them, shattered and horrified. Behind them, a great cloud of smoke poured out of the gaping tunnel of the shelter. . . . A great draught fanned through it as if it were a long chimney. All the ammunition stored in it exploded, immediately turning the long tunnel into a gigantic cannon. Apart from the fifty who escaped, ejected up the steps like the wad of a blank cartridge, all the occupants of the shelter, of which 393 were French, became cinders on the instant." (Albert Vulliez.)

At Caen, during the siege, hundreds of the bombed-out camped in the nave of Saint-Étienne cathedral. From the washing-lines between the columns not over-clean linen hung to dry. A sour smell of dirty, crowded humanity replaced the odour of incense. Shells were falling all around, and the cathedral roof afforded no more than precarious shelter. Nevertheless, official pressure to get these unfortunate people to move out was met only by inertia or flat refusal. The cathedral had become a sanctuary again as it had been in the Middle Ages.

A lay building, the Lycée Malherbe, was also full of refugees. Between them, the saint and the poet sheltered some eight thousand people. It so happened, however, that two or three shells fell on the school whereas the cathedral was spared. This made the refugees in the latter refuse even more stubbornly to leave it.

Lisieux, in these desperate times, turned to prayer. Rarely, during the course of a battle, have such religious ardours alternated with the brutalities of war.

The bombing began on 6 June with bombs on the station. On the night of the 6th to 7th, at about half past one in the morning, flares lit up the sky and a rain of fire and steel fell on the Saint-Désir quarter, where the religious communities were grouped, the Benedictines of the Abbey, the Little Sisters of the Poor, the Providence with its hospital, and the Refuge. When day came, it was at last possible to gauge the extent of the destruction. The Abbey of the Benedictines had been destroyed; and with it disappeared all the memorials of the First Communion of Saint Theresa of the Infant Jesus. Twenty nuns had been burnt to death; sixteen nuns in the Providence killed; and eleven young girls in the Foyer. In the town it was reported that there were altogether over a thousand dead. Msgr. Germain, Father Augros, the priests of the Mission de France, the parochial clergy, and the youth groups set about searching for them among the delayed-action bombs which claimed further victims during the next few days. At the hospital, continuous operations were being performed in extremely difficult circumstances. Over a hundred were performed that night under the direction of Dr. Marie.

There were other religious buildings destroyed: Saint-Jacques, a fifteenth-century church with wonderful glass, was no more than a skeleton; the church of Saint-Désir was a ruin. The ancient cathedral of Saint-Pierre and the new basilica of Saint Theresa then became the centres for prayers of intercession.

"On 11 July, the bombed-out who had taken refuge in the crypt celebrated with great emotion the unforgettable date of 11 July 1937, when the new basilica had been consecrated by the Legate of Pius XI, the future Pius XII." And next day there began a fervent novena before the exposed Holy Sacrament.

When the novena was over, on 20 July, in the presence of a great congregation drawn from all the surrounding districts, the three vicars of the town, of whom two had lost their churches by bombing, made a vow to Saint Theresa of the Infant Jesus, binding themselves most solemnly to celebrate her feast-day on 30 September each year. They invited all their parishioners to take part in a procession of her relics from the cathedral of Saint-Pierre to the basilica.

A little later, as if in answer to the vow, the radio announced that the Pope had made representations to the belligerents to respect the religious buildings still existing in Lisieux, in particular the Carmel and the basilica. As a result, on 16 August, the German headquarters asked the sub-prefecture for detailed information about the two buildings. This was readily furnished and emphasis laid on the international character of the cult of Saint Theresa. But since the Kommandantur had to retreat precipitately, no further information as to the effect of this plea is available.

On 19 August the liberation battle began. A shell pierced the cloister wall of the Carmel. The gap had to be filled in quickly to prevent looting.

During the night of the 21st to 22nd, the population of the crypt, which was already overcrowded by refugees from the countryside, received the unwelcome addition of two hundred German soldiers. There was some fear that their having forced their way into the basilica would be signalled by Intelligence agents to the Allies and result in a bombardment of the sanctuaries.

On Tuesday the 22nd, at the hour of Vespers, the first British tanks arrived. There was a skirmish with the German rearguard. Shells whistled over the cathedral and one fell in the courtyard leading to the crypt of the basilica, throwing huge blocks of granite about. "It was as if," wrote one of the faithful, "the basilica was collapsing on top of us."

Nevertheless, the basilica was saved.

"Our Saint," continued the narrator, turning hagiographer, "was watching over her church and we had tangible proof of it on the morrow of the battle, when a British officer, told that the Holy Father's request did not appear to have been taken into consideration, replied: 'The church was scheduled to be destroyed. We received an order to destroy it, because we were informed it was sheltering German troops. The shoot had been actually laid on when someone told us there were no soldiers in it. Naturally, we didn't want to destroy an important building like that without good cause. We sent several scouts to find out whether there were troops really hidden in it or not. Eventually, the shoot was countermanded, but you escaped by the skin of your teeth.'

"On 27 August, after a solemn service, the Carmelites returned to their monastery in procession, bearing on their shoulders the shrine of their beloved saint, and escorted by a large and sympathetic crowd, telling their beads." Canon G. A. Simon, who described the ceremony, compared it to the recovery of the holy relics after the great barbarian invasions of the Middle Ages.

The Wehrmacht was in confusion. The civilian population took note of its marching and counter-marching. At first, units in good order, followed by supply columns, advanced hastily towards the front. Soon, however, the retreat began and the traffic changed direction. Sad columns of exhausted, harassed troops returned down the roads they had once known in all the splendour of their pristine equipment. Later, it became a general rout, during which the mocking French peasants gathered many stories that were long to be retailed at the fireside. For those living on the banks of the Seine, there was indeed an abundant harvest. It was said in Rouen that, between 25 and 27 August, Field-Marshal von Klug had shot one of his subordinates with a revolver, because the unfortunate officer had omitted to inform him that the crossing of the Seine was impracticable. "My armoured divisions have nothing left to do but die," von Klug was supposed to have said as he pressed the trigger. Unfortunately, this story bears little relation to historical fact, since von Klug had committed suicide on 18 August, a week earlier and 500 kilometres away, between Metz and Verdun. It is a grave loss to Norman folklore.

On the heels of the Wehrmacht, the Allied army was enthusiastically welcomed, but the Normans felt a certain disappointment that it had no need of their aid.

This "machine which had been so patiently organized over four years of preparation," a witness remarked, "brought so much with it that one might have thought it was going to fight in the desert and not in a friendly country, where there were still houses, beds, barns, tables, chairs and even butter."

In battle, they noted, the invading armies were careless of what they crushed beneath the tracks of their tanks or the wheels of their guns. The Allies did not go round obstacles, but straight through them. To get from one place to another they made tracks across the countryside, metalled them, and drove their way through the ruins impeding their advance with bulldozers. To cross the Orne, they built half a dozen bridges, of which one or two were bound to remain intact. Every advance over doubtful terrain was supported by hundreds of aircraft.

Four days after the landings, when the first monuments had already been shattered into ruins by the Allied air forces, the American Professor Dinsmore, a member of the "Inter-Allied Commission for the Safeguard of Historic Monuments" and of a similar American commission, promised the M.M.L.A. to protest energetically to one of the chiefs of the Allied air forces. But it was of no use. Destruction was added to destruction.

Much was due to the Allied bombardments preceding the operations, and to the action of high explosive bombs was added that of the incendiaries. On the coast, the navy ranged on the churches: the steeple of Saint-Pierre at Caen was destroyed by naval guns. But some was also due to demolitions carried out in cold blood by engineer officers of the British and American Armies after the battle was over. The British Royal Engineers and the American Corps of Engineers finished off the work of the guns to facilitate the advance. The church at Valogne was blown up with dynamite by the American Corps of Engineers; while the Royal Engineers actually prepared charges to blow up a gem of medieval architecture, the church at Norroy, which had been damaged but not destroyed. It was only the arrival of Captain Lafarge, an American monuments officer, and of Leroy, the French architect for historic monuments, which saved it at the last moment. Elsewhere, the liaison officer Albert Gilou prevented a bulldozer destroying the remains of the Hôtel d'Escoville in Caen.

Further damage was due to looting and vandalism. At Caen, the Musée des Antiquaires was sacked by British troops.

The best one can say of the initial behaviour of the Allies in the liberated territories is that it lacked any sense of friendliness. They were advancing through a conquered country, or rather through a country that had been dehumanized by war, and every standing stone was no more than an obstacle to their progress.

All armies when campaigning commit similar abuses. The only conclusion one can draw is that for all that Normandy was friendly territory, the British and Americans treated it as if it were not. In spite of the exploits of the F.F.I., Normandy played only a marginal part in the campaign which liberated it. And the Normans suffered the proof of it in the treatment they received.

In Brittany, the second province to be liberated, things were very different.

Chapter IV

THE LIBERATION OF BRITTANY

As a province, Brittany was an exceptional case in the Liberation of France. The Resistance was associated with the Allies not only in minor skirmishes but in high level military operations. It was not confined merely to sabotage and guerrilla action, but fought pitched battles and conducted siege operations, for which it sometimes took the complete responsibility, requiring no help from the Allied forces.

For France, at this particular moment in her history, this was of capital importance. As a result, Koenig, who was in command of the F.F.I., and his headquarters in London were able to play a part, together with the British, Canadian and American staffs, in the direction of the battle.

The Resistance in Brittany was a national army, and its remarkable discipline and admirable courage could not be disregarded by the authorities responsible for running the war. There were other regions in which, though it was exceptional to join the F.F.I. before D-day, the organization was more or less approved by most of the population; but in Brittany, from the very start, the whole countryside was practically at one in its rebelliousness. For the first time in France, total war was launched. In June 1940, General de Gaulle inspected one of the first units of the Free French Forces in England and questioned the soldiers about their homes. When he discovered how many of them came from the Ile de Sein off Finistère, he remarked: "Sein must be a quarter of France." In peacetime Sein had 1,144 inhabitants.

At Christmas 1941, de Gaulle wrote to the Bretons of the Free French Forces and extended his admiration for the islanders to the whole of Brittany: "Among the good and loyal French sailors, soldiers and airmen, who are still fighting for France, one out of three is Breton."

The inhabitants of the northern and western coasts of the peninsula were engaged in a constant traffic across the Channel. In Finistère, five coastal mayors were shot by the Germans; one of them, Pierre Guéguin, mayor of Concarneau, was executed on 22 October 1941, at Châteaubriant, the others, Louis Mehu, mayor of Polmeur, Alain Budes de Guébriant, mayor of Saint-Pol-de-Léon, François Le Dilasser, mayor of Heulgoat, and Louis Krebs, mayor of Lanriec, during the Liberation, in June and August 1944.

In the schools, conspiracies among the under-twenties became an established part of the syllabus, indeed almost figured in the timetables. Though two-thirds of the Tour d'Auvergne Lycée at Quimper were occupied by the German Army, it was at the same time one of the centres of the Resistance.

All the sector commanders, under the leadership of Colonel Berthaud, departmental head of the F.F.I., met two or three times a week in the science laboratories. Vice-Principal Bellan's private flat and the physics and chemistry laboratory were the meeting-places of the Resistance leaders of the whole arrondissement.

The cyclo-style was used for secret publications. One day the Gestapo made a search and there was only just time to mingle the sheets carrying orders and information for the Maquis with others for the use of the pupils. Fortunately, the chemistry assistant, Alain le Guillou, was a member of the Resistance. Out of school hours he manufactured explosives for the F.F.I. In March and April 1944, his somewhat irregular proceedings were still further extended. Mademoiselle Micheline, a young second-lieutenant, was parachuted in from London and, under the auspices of the physics master, Barbe, gave courses in explosives and the approved methods of sabotaging railways, bridges and so on. A decidedly "optional" subject, which did not yet figure in examination syllabuses.

This secret war, admits Abel Villard, president of the Lycée Old Boys Association, was not always "fun and games." Pupils were arrested by the Gestapo, one in the Lycée itself, in spite of the protests of the headmaster, and five others at home. Three succeeded in escaping while being transferred to Germany; the others were never heard of again.

Extraordinary incidents took place all over Brittany. On the moors, a prehistoric menhir was destroyed by the Germans, perhaps because it was nicknamed "la Républicaine." On the coasts, most of the lighthouses were extinguished or demolished. In Finistère only nine out of eighty-nine still functioned. The others had their domes blown up, their lenses smashed with sledgehammers, and the mercury from the rotating mechanism removed to Germany. Meanwhile, the churches echoed with the sermon preached in the cathedral by the Bishop of Quimper, Monseigneur Duparc. He appealed for a crusade against the spirit of violence and injustice. Six priests of his diocese, who responded to his appeal, were executed between June and August 1944, while seven others were deported, of whom six never returned.

"The Breton," acknowledged a report drawn up by the B.C.R.A. in London, "together with the inhabitants of certain provinces in eastern France, had the reputation of being the best type of resistant. It was therefore reasonable to expect that the armed Resistance in Brittany would have considerable importance."

The Maquis' fighting personnel increased as the time for military operations approached.

In June 1944, when the landings took place, their numbers in the five departments were estimated to be as follows:

Morbihan: 7,000 men, mostly armed.

Finistère: 1,000 men, of whom 100 were armed.

Côtes-du-Nord: 2,500 men, of whom 900 were armed.

Ille-et-Vilaine: 2,500 men, unarmed.

Loire-Inférieure: 6,500 men, not yet mobilized.

Total: 19,500 men, of whom no more than half at the most were in a position to fight.

By the end of July 1944, when the real campaign in Brittany was about to begin, the situation was as follows:

Morbihan: 9,000 men, of whom 7,000 were armed.

Finistère: 10,000 men, of whom 3,500 were armed.

Côtes-du-Nord: 3,500 men, of whom 2,000 were armed.

Ille-et-Vilaine: 2,500 men, of whom 1,000 were armed.

Loire-Inférieure: 6,500 men, of whom 250 were armed.

Total: 31,500 men, of whom 13,750 were armed.

When operations began against the enemy pockets, the number of effective combatants had risen to 20,000 men.

On 1 November 1944, after the liberation of their province, the F.F.I. joining the Regular Army amounted to the greater part of the personnel of two newly formed divisions, the 19th Infantry Division, and the 25th Airborne Division.[1]

There was another characteristic peculiar to Brittany: the F.T.P. acted jointly with the F.F.I. in a spirit of almost complete loyalty and discipline.

From the human point of view, it is interesting to compare the F.F.I. with the F.T.P. during this first campaign in which they were associated. They were both recruited largely from the lower classes, mainly from the Breton peasants, who had been infantrymen in every war in history.

[1] Each division consisted at that time of about 14,000 men.

It was merely that in the F.T.P., there was a greater admixture of workers from the towns. And, due above all to their environment and the way they were officered, the spirit in the two types of unit was very different.

The F.F.I., drawn from the A.S. (Armée Secrète), the O.R.A. (Organisation de Résistance de l'Armée), Libération, O.C.M. (Organisation Civile et Militaire), belonged to a political tradition that was still a living thing in the western departments, the tradition of the Chouans who had once fought for their God and their King. Now, no doubt, with the Nazis as enemies and the Communists as allies, the problem wore a somewhat different complexion: God might perhaps be endangered, but the King clearly had no part. It may well be that the Chouans would be Republicans today. In any case, their descendants of the F.F.I. were above all patriots who, recruited by the leading men of the province and by officers of the Regular Army, whether on the active list or the reserve, wanted both to drive out the Germans and maintain order. The F.T.P., on the other hand, were inspired by the example of the Spanish Left. Their fighting technique had been taught them by an ex-officer of the Republican Air Force, who had taken refuge in France after General Franco's victory. They also included certain units of ardent "guerrilleros," who were determined to take their revenge against Fascism.

Even today, when meeting ex-leaders of the F.F.I. and F.T.P., one is struck by the fact that they are a different type of man. One is reminded of certain portraits by French painters contemporary with the Revolution and the Empire, for instance Baron Gros and David. In these family portraits of two successive generations, the father, an aristocrat, having passed nearly all his life in a society that was apparently stable and, in any case, careless of the menace under which it lay, preserves from his youth and middle age the calm and dignified expression of an aristocrat, whose future is assured, and whose position and influence are uncontested. Even the flesh of his face, so regularly and delicately nurtured with unguents, perfumes and powder, has acquired a certain heavy, soft placidity. No mystery lies behind his eyes, which seem concentrated entirely on external things—his estates, his château—and they contain no expression of disquiet, no latent anxiety of the soul, no distress for the times. But the expression in the eyes of his children nearby is very different. Having grown up in the maelstrom of the Revolution, when their world was reeling and their whole future collapsing about them, their eyes are both watchful and anxious. The flesh of their faces seems firmer, healthier, tanned by the brisk airs of great events, the suns of revolutionary days, and formed and moulded by danger. One feels that, between the two generations, so close in time and by blood, a great chasm has opened. The Revolution has swept away a society tranquilly assured of its hierarchies and castes.

Though no doubt less acute, there was a similar difference between the leaders of the F.F.I. and the leaders of the F.T.P. In the first place, a difference in age: in the Morbihan, the senior officers of the Francs-Tireurs et Partisans were still boys—battalion commanders of twenty-one and twenty-two, under a regimental commander of barely twenty-five.

The leaders of the F.F.I. were on the average ten to fifteen years older. Moreover, they were not inexperienced: the soldiers had held commands in the army, and the civilians known responsibility in civil life. Professional officers in the navy or army, lawyers and businessmen, who had served as officers on the Reserve, they brought to the Resistance the techniques of command and organization they had learned in the Services. The mobilization of the F.F.I. took place in two stages. As in 1914 and 1939, there was an active nucleus round which the influx of Reservists was grouped on D-day.[1] Its officers were in contact by radio or messenger with the professionals in London—the B.C.R.A., Koenig's headquarters, and the Allied staffs. Within their districts, they applied the knowledge acquired during their service: security, defence, operational centres in farms and woods—classical tactics applied to secret warfare.

The tactics of the F.T.P., on the other hand, were those of guerrillas. They were not so much concerned with organizing trained units as with dispersal to avoid being caught. Farms and woods were too easily searched and surrounded. The F.T.P. spread out over the countryside, and took refuge among the hills and moors. No comfort or organization was possible in the conditions in which they lived, but they were at once invisible and ubiquitous, part of the landscape into which they merged. And even when they had to have recourse to the F.F.I. for arms or for the purposes of some action, they criticized their plans, and disliked their discipline. There was no nonsense about practicing arms drill, marching in step or moving in formation about the F.T.P. There was frequently, too, a certain lack of deference in their attitude towards the leaders of the F.F.I. They were apt to call them "mothballs," and to sing irreverent songs about them:

> *Ça sent la naphthaline*
> *Oui, ça sent le renfermé*

[1] Cf., the Saint-Marcel Maquis, page 120.

Ça sent la naphthaline
Quand passent ces beaux messieurs!

Nor had they any greater respect for the Americans, whom they called "Ricains." They claimed to be superior in military tactics and would quote Lorient as a case in point. The Americans, they said, had allowed the Germans to form the pocket because they refused to follow the advice of Le Yarric, the F.T.P. commander, and, instead of making a detour by side roads as he advised, had advanced straight down the main road with their columns of tanks, only to fall into an ambush and be compelled to retire. As a result, the Germans, who had been preparing to evacuate the town, took heart, and Lorient was liberated only after a siege lasting several months.

Another example concerned the F.F.I. This was over the camp of Saint-Marcel, where on 18 June 1944 the first pitched battle between the F.F.I. and the Germans took place. According to the F.T.P., the camp was a strategic mistake due to a too classical conception of war. Instead of concentrating all their forces at one point, said Le Yarric, they ought to have dispersed them over the countryside.

The Allies were rather suspicious of these undisciplined bands. How could they include them in their plan of campaign? How could they insert them into the precise machinery of their elaborately detailed planning? They naturally preferred the officers of the F.F.I. They talked the same language and had the same war aims: to liberate the country without revolution and to drive out the Germans without opening the way to Communism.

During the fighting in Brittany, however, these two very different organizations were nevertheless blended into the single army of the Resistance. The F.T.P. even agreed to serve under leaders other than their own. Two battalions, renowned for their offensive spirit, both of which were to play an important part in the battles for the pockets—the "Stalingrad" battalion, and the "Normandie" battalion, named thus in honour of the French squadron fighting on the Russian front—were commanded by Lieutenants "Équivalence" and Bernard, who were sent out from London. The Commissaire of the F.T.P., Maurice Devillers, alias Michel, became head of the Troisième Bureau on the departmental staff of the F.F.I.; and Commandant Le Yarric accepted a post on the staff of Colonel Morice.

Both the F.F.I. and the F.T.P. contributed to the victory in Brittany. The F.T.P. on their own, because of their lack of staff organization and discipline, could have played no significant part in the battle conducted by the Allies. Yet, without them, the F.F.I. would have proved less effective in demoralizing the enemy and embarrassing his troop movements towards the Normandy front.

It has often been said that in Brittany the F.F.I. were the infantry of the American divisions. If this is correct, the F.T.P. acted as irregular guerrillas to the infantry of the F.F.I. Their dispersed but effective bands contributed not a little to showing the Americans how valuable the maquisards were.

The campaign can be divided into five periods.

The first was previous to 6 June, a preparatory period in which the F.F.I. and F.T.P. suffered the terrible losses inevitable to clandestine activities.

The second period, from 6 to 18 June, included the mobilization of the Breton Maquis, sabotage and guerrilla activities, and the first pitched battle, fought at the camp of Saint-Marcel, in the Morbihan, between the Breton Resistance and the Wehrmacht. This battle showed the maquisards that they could not take on the German Army in regular operations alone and without the support of the Allies. They therefore dispersed.

The third period was from 18 June to 2 August, that is to say from Saint-Marcel to the opening of the Allied offensive in the peninsula, during which the Resistance re-formed in view of the approaching operations. Liaison was re-established between the Resistance and London; the F.F.I. Command was reorganized; and arms were parachuted.

The fourth period, from 2 August, D-day for Brittany, to 20 August, was that of the successful operations and the Allied advance. During these two weeks, Brittany was liberated with remarkable speed by the combined actions of the Third American Army and the F.F.I., whose importance was becoming increasingly recognized.

Finally, during a fifth period, from 21 August to 10 September, the German centres of resistance in the interior of the peninsula were mopped up. The American Army, putting their trust in their French allies of the Maquis, left the mopping-up process largely to them, and were thus able to send the greater part of their troops to the east to take part in the battles that were to lead them to the Rhine.

By 10 September, the whole of Brittany had been cleared except for the coastal pockets. Thanks to the F.F.I., the liberated province was held by French troops and its administration, both civil and military, was in French hands.

The first and clandestine period was exceptionally murderous, particularly during its last months.

The F.F.I. Command in London had organized the Resistance into regions, and Brittany, together with Normandy, the Vendée, the Mayenne and the Sarthe, formed region "M." Four of its departments, Morbihan, Finistère, Côtes-du-Nord and Ille-et-Vilaine were grouped in subdivision "M3": the fifth department, the Loire-Inférieure, was technically attached to the subdivision "M2" with the Vendée and the Maine-et-Loire. In fact, during the actual fighting, it frequently came under "M3."

"M3" had the advantage of a very select cadre, largely recruited from Regular officers; General Audibert, head of the A.S. in Brittany, had been instructed to organize it as early as 1942. He was a distinguished officer who had been on Foch's staff in September 1914. After the Armistice in 1918, on being appointed to the General Staff, he had drawn up plans for demobilization and for the reorganization of the army, based on the hypothesis that Germany, though temporarily crushed, would be prepared for war once again between 1935 and 1940. When this, in fact, happened, he was commanding the Nantes reserve division, which was on the Meuse in June 1940. He joined the clandestine forces immediately after the Armistice, founding a Resistance centre in Alix Eraud's house, in the Chaussée de la Madeleine, in the centre of Nantes. Then he became head of the Secret Army in Brittany and soon had under his command all the F.F.I. forces, parachutists and maquisards. Everyone recognized his authority. He had only one defect, about which there was nothing he could do: he was sixty-eight and no longer young. Though he shared all the risks of the Maquis in an extreme degree, he could not always lead the life they did.

Under his command, in Loire-Inférieure, was Commandant Yaco, who had been evacuated sick from Dieppe in 1940 to Nantes, where he refused to surrender to the Germans. He had been a member of the Resistance since October. Not only had he organized false papers, work certificates, and sure hiding-places for fugitives, but had led the attacks on the Petit-Port vehicle park and the Soldatenheim (the German soldiers' club) in Nantes. Appointed on 16 October 1943 as head of the departmental Maquis of Loire-Inférieure by the regional Maquis of Brittany (Henri Bourret, known as Jean-François), he received instructions for D-day from Colonel Alma, chief of the A.S. in Paris, under whom General Audibert became commander of the western district.

Among these Regular officers there was also, from 1941 onwards, the commander of the Morbihan gendarmerie, whose name was Guillaudot, alias Yodi. Most of his companies co-operated with him in his under-cover activities. It was these servants of the law who from 1943 onwards arranged the parachuting of arms with London, concealed Allied air-men and, in August 1943, trained the Maquis volunteers in the use of the weapons received. Arrested on 10 December, Guillaudot was re-placed at the head of the Action organization in the Morbihan by Chenailler, a retired naval officer, known as Colonel Morice. He, assisted by his second-in-command, Commandant le Menach, a Regular artillery officer, and Colonel Muller, was in command of all the F.F.I. in the Morbihan.

And so, by New Year's Day, 1944, which was to be the year of Libera-tion, Brittany was organized. Alas, after several of the departmental leaders of the F.F.I. had already been arrested, there was a real catas-trophe in February. Audren, the head of Audibert's Deuxième Bureau, was arrested and talked under torture. General Audibert was arrested as well as the woman liaison agent of the departmental command, Agnès de Nanteuil. Morice, warned in time, had taken to the Maquis. The head of his Premier Bureau, Berrigant, also went into hiding. His Chief of Staff, Lieutenant of Gendarmerie Guillot, who had succeeded in es-caping, was arrested on 31 March.

The situation had therefore become critical at the very moment the decisive operations were being prepared. The danger was that the Re-sistance would be disorganized and incapable of playing its part. Within three months, however, by devoted work in increasingly dangerous con-ditions, the Maquis was reorganized and liaison renewed with the secret headquarters in Paris and with London. Broch Florette, the departmental head of Finistère, made a dangerous journey to Paris to see the regional military delegate, Fantassin, who was in direct contact with London. He had to stay in Paris eighteen days before he could contact Fantassin —and then the interview lasted only seventeen minutes in perilous cir-cumstances. But they sufficed. Contact had been re-established.

On the very day of his return to Brest, Broch Florette was arrested by the Gestapo. He protested that his journey to Paris had been in con-nection with supplies for the Wehrmacht. His cover story was accepted. After a night in the Hôtel du Commerce at Morlaix, he was set free.

He went to pay his bill. "No, please," an S.S. officer said politely, "we shall settle it for you. We Germans always like to show our gratitude to those who serve us."

For Finistère, therefore, essential liaison was restored just in time for the landings. In the Morbihan, the highly complex work of reorganization had been completed a few weeks earlier, which gave the Resistance an opportunity to hold a sort of general rehearsal for D-day.

This episode is little known but it was important.

During April, an officer called Barrat, alias Hauteur, was parachuted in from London, made contact with Colonel Morice, and one night inspected the companies of the F.F.I. assembled on the moors. He was satisfied with their soldierly bearing and reported favourably to London.

This report may well have had an influence on what followed.

On 5 May, the Comité d'Action Immédiate in Paris, which was one of the centres for communications between the F.F.I. and London, sent an officer named Rivière to the Morbihan with orders for general sabotage of the railways. What did this mean? Were the landings about to take place? In fact, what had happened was that the Morbihan had been selected to give proof of the Resistance's ability to hold up the movement of the German divisions on D-day, to make sure that "Bloc Planning" was effective. If this rehearsal were successful, the High Command could safely leave the job of destroying railways and roads to the F.F.I.; and concentrate the air forces on other objectives. Apart from the tactical advantages to the Allies, the rehearsal was clearly of vital importance to the civilian population, who would be spared many casualties if it were successful.

During the night of 6 to 7 May, exactly a month before the landings, the Resistance went into action. The F.T.P. groups commanded by Le Yarric, de Larmort, d'Auray, le Frapper, de Vannes and de Landevant were particularly active. At midnight every railway was blown up: the Paris-Quimper line was cut in three places; the Ploërmel-Cuer line was cut three kilometres from the Coëtquidan Camp; and the Augan line was destroyed for 150 yards, as were the points at Augan and Loyal stations.

The Locminé group was sent to Dol to blow 100 yards of line.

But mere sabotage was not enough. The problem was to maintain the demolitions. London insisted that the lines should remain cut for eight days.

The second part of the experiment proved much more difficult and costly than the first. Yet it succeeded. The railways remained cut for the eight days, but only at the cost of some hard-fought skirmishes during which the Germans had some thirty men killed and the Resistance twenty-two. But the Resistance had given proof that it could play the part for which London wished to cast it. When H-hour struck a month later, sabotage of the railways preventing the movement of German divisions to the landing zones was confided entirely to the Brittany Resistance, which thus deserved well not only of the Allies but of the civilian population.

On 4 June, Brittany, like the other provinces, received the "Personal Messages" from London. Two of them applied to the whole of France: "The dice are thrown," and "It is hot in Suez." A third was specifically directed to the Breton Resistance: "The arrow will not pierce." As soon as they heard these messages, the Breton F.F.I., as indeed did the F.F.I. all over France, put their prepared plans into effect. In Brittany there were two:

(1) The Green Plan: Sabotage of railway lines. All trains ceased running, except on the Brest-Rennes line, where a few managed to get through in spite of numerous cuts: one took eighteen days to get from Brest to Redon, where an Allied air attack blew it up together with the shells and torpedoes it was carrying.

(2) The Violet Plan: Guerrilla operations. Telephone lines both above and below ground were systematically cut. German convoys had to move on bicycles, in wagons, and sometimes on foot and were harassed continuously. One unit had to march 150 miles to reinforce the Normandy front.

At the same time Colonel Morice issued orders for general mobilization.

The mobilization centre was at Saint-Marcel, or more precisely, in a farm called La Nouet near the village of that name. It was isolated amid some 150 acres of fields and woods. Three huts had been erected in the woods the previous month: one for radio equipment, another for staff offices, and a third for personnel. Close to the camp, a landing-ground had been organized for the parachuting of arms. Inconspicuous though these arrangements were, in the end they proved to be too vulnerable in guerrilla warfare.

The mobilization of the Maquis took place at this improvised camp in two stages: the first consisted of an influx of some 8,000 Reservists, who were enrolled and distributed among the twelve battalions of the Morbihan F.F.I. Then the battalions came in turn to Saint-Marcel to be issued with the parachuted arms stocked there.

These operations were, however, detected by the Germans and, on 18 June, led to an attack on the camp and the dispersion of the troops there.

The battle of Saint-Marcel is still matter for contention. To the majority of the F.F.I. who took part in it, it remains a great feat of arms, a sort of Dunkirk of the Resistance, in which the battalion, having fought most valiantly, succeeded in breaking off the engagement in peculiarly difficult circumstances. For many of the civilian members of the Resistance, such as the Committees of Liberation in the towns, Saint-Marcel was a sort of gratuitous act; they took the view that the stake was not worth the price paid in human lives. While for the F.T.P. this first battle fought by the Breton Resistance stank not of blood only but of mothballs. In their view, the Regular officers in command were perpetuating the errors of the phoney war by engaging in a pitched battle which was entirely unjustifiable and, moreover, was lost even before it began.

In fact, the Saint-Marcel action, which appeared to be no more than rashly heroic, was an operation important to the success of the Allied landings; and it must be considered from the viewpoint of the general strategic plan.

The course events took at the camp was as follows. As soon as the "Personal Messages" had been received during the night of 4–5 June, the departmental commander, Colonel Morice, together with his staff, immediately went to his secret command post, from which he issued orders for mobilization. Of the four battalions in the west of the department, one was to move immediately to Saint-Marcel to be its permanent garrison; the other three were to stay where they were and await further instructions.

The other eight F.F.I. battalions in the department were to remain in their concentration areas in a state of readiness, except for one company from each battalion which was to go into the Maquis with the battalion commander to execute the various planned actions.

The department of the Morbihan and the neighbourhood of Saint-Marcel in particular afforded an extraordinary spectacle in those days. Recruits in clogs and overalls were coming from all directions to join up, as if reporting to barracks in the regular way. You could stop in any little café and, before you could even ask the way, they would say: "Oh, so you're going to Saint-Marcel! . . ."

There was something heroic but also rather artificial in setting up in secret a military organization that conformed so closely to the Regular Army pattern. At the time, the population, after four years of repression, welcomed the reappearance of units that were almost like those of the Regular Army.

Besides the five hundred men guarding the command post and the terrain under Colonel Morice's command, the camp also became the concentration point for four hundred officers, non-commissioned officers and men of the 4th Parachute Regiment of Chasseurs, who had been parachuted from London and made their way to the camp when they had completed their mission. Among them was Lieutenant Marienne's detachment which had had the first fatal casualty of the campaign.[1]

During the night 10 June, Colonel Bourgoin, commanding the 4th Regiment, was parachuted in. Since he had only one arm, the Germans soon had his description and placed a price of a million francs on his head. The Gestapo set about arresting all the one-armed men in the department, including an old man of seventy-five. But their efforts were of no avail.

His arrival gave new impetus to the mobilization.

At his request, Colonel Morice ordered the various battalions to come in turn to the camp to get their arms. Some came by small detachments, others as complete units.

It was at this time that the Pontivy-Ouest battalion, commanded by Le Coutaller, crossed the whole department despite the Germans with four trucks full of arms and ammunition. Escorted by eighty cyclists armed with sub-machine-guns, the convoy reached its destination. But there was a skirmish on the way, and a van was sent out next morning to bring in the dead. All these comings and goings, including the flying over of some 150 Allied planes within three kilometres of a German observation post, could hardly fail to attract the enemy's attention. From 15 June, enemy searchlights on a neighbouring airfield had been lighting up the Allied aircraft as they dropped their containers. Moreover, several pilots, deceived by enemy signals, had dropped their containers of arms and ammunition on the Germans. The troops at Saint-Marcel were therefore prepared for an attack at any moment.

It came on 18 June. Two F.F.I. battalions were guarding the camp together with the S.A.S. troops. These were the 8th Morbihan F.F.I. Battalion under the command of Commandant Caro, and the 12th F.F.I. Battalion under the command of General de la Morlaix, who had resumed the badges of rank of a commandant for the honour of leading his maquisards in battle. Another battalion, the 2nd, under the command of Lieutenant-Colonel Le Carrec, had just reached the camp to be equipped, after a number of skirmishes with the enemy on the way. It was issued with arms during the night of the 17th and was to use them next day.

On the German side, the battle was fought by deploying troops in an almost geometrical progression: first a patrol, then a battalion, then a brigade, and finally a division. At dawn on the 18th, precisely at 04.30,

[1] Cf., page 9.

the sound of rifle and machine-gun fire gave the alarm. It was a reconnaissance patrol of the Feldgendarmerie, come from the west in two
vehicles. Of the eight men, seven were killed or taken prisoner. The
F.F.I. had one casualty, Sergeant-Major Le Canut, and two wounded.
On the report of the one German who escaped, a battalion arrived at
06.30. Two hundred Germans attacked the French positions on the east,
near the Château de Les Hardys. They succeeded in infiltrating. A gallant counter-attack by a detachment under the command of Lieutenant
Marienne almost entirely annihilated the attacking troops with fire from
automatic weapons. At 09.00, a brigade of German troops arrived and
debussed on Route Nationale No. 774, a few kilometres from the camp.
They tried to break through the French positions and seize the château;
but, in spite of continually renewed attacks, they failed to reach their
objective. Meanwhile, however, the Intelligence staff in the camp, who
were kept well informed by the neighbouring villagers, heard that numerous convoys of troops were on their way towards Saint-Marcel. These
reinforcements, which amounted to a division, included Georgian units,
anti-parachute troops, and artillery. There was also information of
armoured cars coming from Coëtquidan and La Baule. Colonel Bourgoin
immediately asked by radio for British air support. At 16.00, the R.A.F.
appeared and harassed the enemy. But it was unable to prevent the
enemy's concentration. The French Command decided that the camp
must be evacuated at 22.30 and that, after breaking off the engagement,
the men should disperse throughout the Morbihan and the neighbouring
departments. This decision was confirmed by signals from London,
which also carried the information that a plan for a landing in southern
Brittany, at Suscinio near Quiberon, had been abandoned; and this, it
may be noted, was the first indication of the real reason for the concentration of troops at Saint-Marcel.

But it was impossible to break off the engagement before nightfall.
From 18.00 onwards, the Germans, continually reinforced, intensified
their attacks. Fresh units were arriving all the time by the main road
and being sent straight into the battle. At 19.00 the battle was still
raging. The Germans set fire to the woods behind the French lines with
incendiary bullets, and this made contact between the forward troops
and headquarters almost impossible.

Meanwhile the F.F.I. units were containing the enemy at all points.
"With their machine-gun fire, the outposts literally scythed the enemy
down as they advanced through the cornfields." (Lieutenant-Colonel
Le Garrec.) Sections armed with sub-machine-guns succeeding in dis-

engaging units in danger of being surrounded. It was now 19.30. There were still another three hours during which they must hold out. The Germans, however, seemed to be taking a breather.

But then another attack came in at the farther end of the French position. It made progress, and Lieutenant Rio's unit was in danger. Brilliantly led, his men drove the enemy back with grenades. But, climbing on to the parapet by his machine-gunner to look at the situation, he was killed by an enemy burst of fire.

At 20.00, the French mounted a counter-attack to reduce enemy pressure. The enemy was driven back in disorder with heavy losses. But, a quarter of an hour later, further reinforcements enabled the Wehrmacht to recapture the ground gained. For two hours, till contact was broken off, the two lines were face to face and continuously engaged. Between 22.00 and 22.30, the withdrawal was carried out. One platoon per company stayed in their positions to cover the withdrawal of the rest.

Some companies were able to keep to the timetable, others, more closely engaged, were unable to begin withdrawing before 23.00.

At 23.30 there was an explosion behind what remained of the French positions—the ammunition had been blown up. The Wehrmacht had taken no prisoners and were being denied booty as well.

During the course of the day, the Germans had 560 men killed. The French had fifty paratroops and 200 maquisards killed or missing—losses which do not include non-combatant casualties. Notices were posted to the effect that any civilian who had given assistance in any circumstances to paratroops or maquisards would be shot without trial. Daily perquisitions terrorized the neighbouring villages. All movement either by car or bicycle was forbidden. The civilian population was subjected to the most appalling reprisals

The price was a heavy one; and the prestige both the Maquis and France earned by this battle would appear, at first sight, too hardly gained. But, both from information available at the time and from the more recent study by Colonel Le Menach, based on both French and Allied documents, it would seem that the battle fought at Saint-Marcel cannot be judged purely on its immediate results.

Though the establishing of the camp at Saint-Marcel was convenient for mobilizing and arming some ten thousand Breton maquisards recruited from the Morbihan, and also as a concentration point for the paratroops from London, its main importance for Allied headquarters was undoubtedly that it formed part of a cover plan which came into operation on D-day. Its object was to persuade the German High Command that the landings in Normandy were not the principal operation.

It was hoped that the setting up of a camp at Saint-Marcel and the concentrating of troops there, under conditions which made German ignorance of these activities impossible, would persuade the enemy that another bridgehead was planned at Suscinio in the Quiberon area. It was, indeed, the second stage of the Overlord cover plan, the first being directed at misleading the Germans into believing that the landings would take place in the Pas-de-Calais and the Nord.

This then was the fate of the maquisards of Morbihan. They had to fight a battle that was lost in advance, unaware of its importance or of what was at stake, or even that it was in support of an offensive which it was never intended should take place. But it is to their undying glory that they were thought worthy to play so perilous a part in the concert of operations which was destined to liberate France.

After Saint-Marcel the third period began. The scene shifts between Brittany, where the dispersed but undefeated Maquis continued hostilities in ever more difficult circumstances, and London, where the Allied military authorities were doing their best to support, arm and organize it.

In Brittany, the Resistance forces were scattered. Lieutenant Marienne remained in the Morbihan to reorganize the Maquis, but was taken prisoner and executed by, it appears, the Militia. Colonel Bourgoin withdrew to Finistère. Two other F.F.I. leaders, "Hauteur" and "Fonction," joined the Saffré Maquis in the Loire-Inférieure, near which a parachute dropping zone had been organized as at Saint-Marcel. At Saffré, the Saint-Marcel drama began all over again. Mobilization took place on 15 June, and a camp was set up under the command of Commandant Yaco. The battle also began in much the same way. On the morning of 28 June there was an attack by 1,500 S.S. and 500 to 600 Militia. As at Saint-Marcel, the Maquis had to break off contact. The Germans took thirty-five prisoners, mostly very young men between eighteen and twenty. They were tried by drumhead court martial in the Château de la Bouvardière; but the verdicts and sentences were a foregone conclusion: twenty-seven were "condemned to death, the sentence to be carried out immediately, together with confiscation of property to the Reich." A German chaplain gave them collective absolution in the room in which the court sat, and they were shot within the hour. Introducing himself, the chaplain said: "I am a Catholic priest. I cannot confess you individually, but I will give you general absolution." Three were "condemned to death subject to the assent of the French minister in Paris," which meant de Brinon. Two of them were executed fifteen days later and were buried as "unknown Germans," a phrase in the German Army code applied to deserters. One was reprieved. The cases of the remaining five were adjourned for "further evidence."

This episode is revelatory of the appallingly dangerous conditions in which the Maquis fought from the middle of June till the end of July. Exasperated by their activities, the Germans looked on them as terrorists against whom all measures were permissible. If captured, they were shot, with or without the simulacrum of a trial. On 9 August, the Commissaire de la République, Le Gorgeu, reviewed some paratroops in liberated Vannes and asked their commander what proportion they had had of killed to wounded. The latter replied: "We have had only dead." And, indeed, those who were shot on the spot were relatively lucky. Others were handed over to the Militia and tortured on behalf of the Nazis before being executed. At Bourbriac, the prisoners were put in a cellar. Two armed militiamen stood by the door. "A wounded prisoner, whose arm was swelling badly, asked them to loosen his handcuffs. One of the jailers, pretending to accede to his request, took a key from his pocket, and instead of loosening the handcuffs tightened them, saying: 'I'll make you comfortable, you bastard!'"

Between 10 July and 4 August, in the department of the Côtes-du-Nord alone, the following results were obtained:

2,500 Germans put out of action.

300 telephone lines and high tension cables cut.

200 acts of sabotage to the railways.

40 derailments.

50 convoys ambushed and 200 vehicles captured.

10,000 gallons of German gasoline destroyed at Saint-Brieuc.

30 attacks on German observation posts.

Capture of the prison of Saint-Brieuc on 3 August and the liberation of thirty-two French condemned to death by the Gestapo.

While these guerrilla activities were continually being intensified, the staffs in London were perfecting their liaison with the 30,000 F.F.I. in the peninsula and organizing their integration with the Allied forces who were to liberate Brittany.

Liaison was operated by a whole series of organizations that were parachuted in for the purpose: the S.A.S. (Special Air Service), the Jedburghs, the O.G. (Operational Groups) and the Aloès mission. These organizations varied in composition and tactical purpose. The S.A.S., whom we have already met at the landing at Bayeux,[1] were a British formation of airborne troops under the command of Brigadier Macleod. Apart from their British personnel, they included a Belgian company

[1] Cf., page 6.

and the 3rd and 4th French battalions. It was they who on D-day had carried out the sabotage operations preliminary to Overlord and who, having accomplished their mission, regrouped at the Saint-Marcel camp. They were then used in conjunction with the F.F.I., being placed at the disposal of Colonel Eon, appointed by London as commander of the Brittany F.F.I.

The Jedburghs were inter-allied teams of parachutists specially trained in a school in England, and consisted of three members, a French officer, an Allied officer (either American or British) and a radio-operator, generally a non-commissioned officer, who might be of any Allied nationality.

These teams, of whom there were about ninety, were specially trained to be parachuted into France; they were to assure liaison with the F.F.I., assist in the organization and training of Resistance groups, and carry out such guerrilla activities as might be ordered by London.

They played a great part during the Brittany campaign; and their prestige with the Maquis was immense because:

"(1) The team being parachuted in struck the imagination of the young men and aroused their admiration.

"(2) The F.F.I. felt that the teams had the confidence of General Headquarters and that they could ask for parachute drops, air support, and so on.

"(3) The feeling the leaders had that the 'Jed' was their only means of obtaining the arms they had so long desired."

The O.G. (Operational Groups) were airborne commandos of thirty-two men, who could be split up into two or four independent groups. They were trained for special missions, the destruction, or indeed the protection, of some precise objective and came directly under headquarters in London. Once their particular mission had been carried out, the O.G. had orders to join the nearest F.F.I. and assist them in their ordinary activities.

The Aloès Mission was a very different type of organization. It had wider responsibilities and was to take part in operations only when the Allied offensive in Brittany began. It was neither more nor less than a complete headquarters with four sections. Organized in detail in London, it was to be parachuted into France at the beginning of the battle.

Its duties and organization were determined during long and detailed discussions between Supreme Headquarters and Koenig's staff.

During 8 to 10 July, Eon visited the various Jedburgh teams ready to leave for Brittany, and briefed them on the following points:

The general character of guerrilla warfare in Brittany.

The precise objects of this warfare.

The process by which the B.B.C. code words were to be given effect.

The organization of guerrilla units—fluidity, mobility, ability to live off the country and operate in teams of five to ten men.

On 21 July, Colonel Eon accompanied General Koenig to Twenty-first Army Group Headquarters, where General de Guingand, Montgomery's Chief of Staff, gave them luncheon and an outline of the forthcoming operations in Brittany.

About the same date, General Patton, commanding the Third American Army, which was to liberate Brittany, sent two of his officers to Colonel Zigler, of Koenig's staff, to discuss the support he required from the F.F.I.

Patton had already planned the surprise manœuvre he was to put into effect on 3 August, which consisted of using two of his three armoured corps in a left hook towards Laval and Angers.

Originally, the whole of his army was to be engaged in Brittany, but the support of the F.F.I. contributed to his being able to engage only Middleton's Eighth Corps in the peninsula, while his Twentieth Corps was deployed towards Angers and his Fifteenth Corps towards Laval.

During 2 and 3 August, the F.F.I. Operations Room in London was always full. Reports were constantly coming in of the rapid advance of the Third American Army towards Rennes and Dinan.

On 3 August, at 18.00, the B.B.C. broadcast the code phrase for general guerrilla action in the five Brittany departments.

On 4 August, at midday, General Koenig asked Colonel Eon whether he could arrange to be dropped that very evening with all his staff, whether trained parachutists or not, into the central region of Brittany.

Eon was himself not "parachutable," for he had never had any training in jumping from an aircraft. Nevertheless, he agreed without hesitation.

The whole headquarters was dropped on the "Bonaparte" zone near Kerien, fifteen kilometres south of Guincamp, during the night of 4–5 August.

After crushing the 70th German Division and breaking through at Avranches, Patton's army deployed through the breach towards Brittany. Rennes, on 3 August, was the first city to be liberated. It served, in Colonel Morice's words, as a turntable for the great American formations in their triumphant exploitation of the break-through. One prong was directed towards the east, by Vitré, Laval and Le Mans, to take the German troops in Normandy in the rear. Another was directed south, with Nantes as its objective, to isolate the Armorican peninsula. In the interior of the peninsula, the American advance had three axes: Rennes-Brest, by Saint-Brieuc, Guingamp and Morlaix; Rennes-Lorient, by Ploërmel, Josselin and Locminé; and Rennes-Saint-Nazaire by Redon.

Pontivy, Josselin, Ploërmel and Locminé were all liberated on 4 August. Vannes was liberated on 5 August by the F.F.I. On the same day, the armoured elements advancing to the west reached a point some eighty kilometres from Brest, while in the Côtes-du-Nord the F.F.I. liberated Saint-Brieuc. To the west of the town, they forced what remained of the 260th German Infantry Division, which was trying to make its way to Normandy, to withdraw towards Brest. On 6 August, the whole of Ille-et-Vilaine was overrun with the exception of Saint-Malo, where the German garrison, under the command of Colonel von Aulock, held out till the 17th. There were heavy losses on both sides and the old town was destroyed by bombing and artillery fire—as if Adolf Hitler cared! When asked to declare Saint-Malo an open town, he replied: "No historical town matters. You will fight to the last man and the last stone."

On 6 August, the Germans tried to recapture Vannes from the F.F.I. They failed. The next day, the Americans entered the town. Also, on that day, an American column reached the Loire to the west of Angers. Brittany was cut in half, from the Vilaine to the sea.

The American VIIIth Corps continued its advance, liberating Morlaix and Châteaubriant on the 8th, and Quimper on the 9th.

On 11 August, Nantes and Angers were taken by the Americans.

On the 13th, it was the turn of Châteaulin and Quimperlé.

In nine days, between 4 and 13 August, four German divisions stationed in Brittany and two divisions come from Normandy were either destroyed or surrounded. An American corps, supported by 30,000 maquisards, took 60,000 prisoners.

The Germans abandoned the whole interior of the peninsula and concentrated their forces on the ports of Brest, Saint-Nazaire and Lorient.

During this lightning campaign, the F.F.I. were in continuous support of the American VIIIth Corps. They were constantly in action in the gaps the Germans still occupied between the axes of the American advance.

In a Finistère Maquis, near Rosporden, on the evening of 3 August, Lieutenant Mercier heard on the radio the order for the launching of hostilities. The Americans had only reached Pontorson, 260 kilometres away. But the officer decided not to wait for them. Mercier, a Regular officer of the Army of the Alps, had already fought in the Vercors and been in the Resistance in Paris. "His subordinates were all good men: Pierrot le Naour, a Regular sergeant-major, who had gone into the scent business on being demobilized, was to die heroically on 5 August leading his company; Le Coz, a schoolmaster, was an ensign on the reserve of the artillery; René Gall, a restaurant proprietor, was the supply officer, and organized rations in difficult circumstances for two hundred men— one day, he calmly threw back a grenade that had fallen among a group of men; Corporal Ricco, who maintained liaison with the departmental commander at Quimper; and Aubert (or Albert) who was a brilliant company commander and became mayor of Rosporden." [1]

As soon as he heard the message, Mercier assembled his men in a farmyard. He said merely a few words to them: "I have only one thing to say to you: they're the rabbits now, and we're going to hunt them down. . . ."

The next morning the Rosporden Maquis attacked the German garrison of the town at 05.00.

There were similar incidents throughout Brittany. From fields and villages, from farms and woodlands, these soldiers without uniforms emerged and gradually the Americans learned how to use them. The F.F.I. in Brittany played many parts, of which one was the gathering of information. On 3 August, the F.F.I. received urgent instructions from London to send volunteers through the enemy lines to make contact with American units and inform them of fortified localities, troop concentrations, and tank harbours. The information, which they transmitted at the peril of their lives, proved to be of the highest importance. On 9 September the Intelligence officer of the American Ninth Army, after spending two days at the F.F.I. headquarters, stated that the F.F.I. Intelligence work represented ninety per cent of all the useful military information he had received.

Later on, they played the part of flank guards. So rapid was the American advance that the army had no time to consider its flanks, and entrusted the following duties to the maquisards:

(1) Protection of the Brest railway line running along the north coast of the Brittany peninsula;

(2) Occupation of the heights north of Vannes;

(3) Provision of guides both to advanced elements of the American Army and to the main body;

(4) Protection of all lines of communication in Brittany;

[1] From an unpublished report sent to the B.C.R.A.

(5) Prevention of the movement of German reinforcements from south of the Loire.

(6) Assistance in mopping up the area.

The maquisards did not fail in the execution of these orders.

On 4 August, 6,000 of them occupied the high ground north of Vannes and contained the German attack till the Americans arrived to relieve them.

On 5 August, in conjunction with 150 S.A.S., who had been parachuted in, 2,000 F.F.I. protected the viaducts of Morlaix and Plougastel.

On 7 August, the American 83rd Infantry Division informed the F.F.I. that it urgently required their help. They wanted detachments to occupy the regions between Cancale and Saint-Malo. When they had completed this operation, the F.F.I. received orders to occupy the right bank of the Rance, to establish advance-posts, organize patrols and prevent the Germans crossing the river while the 83rd Division attacked Dinard from the south.

During these operations, the F.F.I. of Ille-et-Vilaine took 1,400 prisoners and destroyed 100 vehicles. Here is a list of the towns they liberated in the Côtes-du-Nord:

    3 August: Callac, Bourriac, Loudéac, Corlay;
    5 August: Saint-Brieuc, Port-du-Lègre;
    8 August: Guincamp, Portrieux, Plouac;
    10 August: Lannion, Perros-Guirec;
    11 August: Pleuvenant, Saint-Quay-Portrieux;
    13 August: Tréguier (recaptured by the Germans during the night);
    14 August: Tréguier (retaken by the F.F.I.);
    15 August: Lezardrieux;
    16 August: Paimpol;
    17 August: Ploung, Pointe-du-Guilhen, L'Ile-à-Bois, Bréhat Island.

On 13 August, at Vannes, General Wood, commanding the American 4th Armoured Division, decorated Colonel Morice, leader of the Morbihan, F.F.I., with the first Bronze Star given to a maquisard.

This, for the Brittany F.F.I., brought the liberation of the province to an end. There remained only the pockets, in which the enemy was solidly entrenched and where, for the moment, he was able to defy all the F.F.I.'s assaults. At Brest, there were two, one on the north and the other on the south of the entrance to the harbour. On the north the pocket consisted of the Capes of Corsen and Conquet, which dominated Brest; and, on the south, of the Crozon peninsula.

The battle for the northern pocket came to an end on 9 September on the Conquet Cape. In the final phase of the attack, which progressed from fortification to fortification and from trench to trench, two companies of F.F.I., in support of the Americans, were the first to enter the German battery at Lochrist, which commanded the position. At midday, the garrison surrendered, and its commander conducted the American Colonel Rudder, Commandant Foucher of the F.F.I. and an officer of a Jedburgh team, Major Sommers, to the command post of the commander of the Conquet defences. At 13.00, he agreed to surrender. There were 1,435 prisoners taken. The act of surrender was signed jointly by an American officer and an F.F.I. officer. It was a recognition of the part the maquisards had played in this siege operation in conjunction with the Rangers and the armour.

The battle for the southern pocket on the Crozon peninsula was commanded by Colonel Eon. Between 17 August and 4 September, with units of the F.F.I. supported by American armour, he took the Menez-Hom massif, whose summits, ranging from 1,000 to 1,200 feet, dominated the battlefield and provided a base for the reduction of the pocket. For seven days, the maquisards advanced stubbornly along the flanks of Hill 299 and Hill 330. By 26 August, before the arrival of American support, the F.F.I. had achieved considerable progress on their own. On the 27th, with the support of one American tank, elements of the F.T.P. "Normandy" Battalion reached the foot of their objective of Sainte-Marie du Menez-Hom, which they took the following day, in spite of minefields and concentrated mortar fire.

To the north of Menez-Hom, other elements were advancing to the north-west. On the 29th, under cover of fog, an attack was launched on Menez-Hom itself. But the F.F.I. ran into heavy German machine-gun fire while the American and French artillery was bombing Hill 330. The decisive attack on the summit was launched on 1 September at 10.00, by the "Normandy" Battalion. After fighting for three-quarters of an hour, they took the position. Two 77 guns, three Hotchkiss machine-guns, three 20 guns and five light machine-guns were captured.

During the afternoon, the F.F.I. and the Americans took possession of all the heights and began to debouch into the plain. Thanks to the fall of Menez-Hom, the American armour was able to advance more than ten kilometres.

On 2 September, three battalions of F.F.I. and American reinforcements cut through the peninsula from the Poulmic inlet to Hill 133. The Germans withdrew to the west round Crozon.

This victory in a war of position for which the F.F.I. were entirely untrained, reached its culmination in the Crozon peninsula. On 4 September, Colonel Eon suggested to General Earnest, the commander of the Task Force, that the F.F.I. should cease to be engaged in siege operations, where the superiority of American weapons was bound to carry the day. He withdrew to Châteaulin, from where, on 10 September, he was summoned to Paris by General de Gaulle.

The German positions on Crozon were taken between 15 and 19 September by American troops, who completed the victory the F.F.I. had begun.

It was thus that the maquisards became total allies.

Nevertheless, as in all recent and unequal associations, there was a certain residual lack of sympathy that was never entirely dissolved. This was sometimes apparent in a sort of competitive heroism due to the maquisards' sense of inferiority, and sometimes in inevitable incidents between the Americans, those lords of war, with their jeeps and tanks, and the heroic, ragged foot-soldiers, who were so insufficiently armed, in spite of parachute drops, that they had sometimes to fight the enemy merely with their clogs.

It was partly to overcome this complex that the Brittany F.F.I. performed such great deeds. They wanted to rehabilitate the French Army, held in contempt since June 1940, in the eyes of the Americans. For instance, when an F.F.I. detachment was advancing between Brest and Le Conquet with an American company, the American officer asked the F.F.I. commander whether he wished to go ahead or follow behind the Americans. "Ahead, it's our duty," he replied.

Though they were associated with American tactical plans, and won victories at their side, the F.F.I. never felt that the American Command considered them to be equals or an integral part of the victorious army.

In the result, they became touchy and bitter whenever they felt they were being underestimated by their allies.

On the morning of 6 August, Colonel Morice asked the Americans, who had reached Vannes, to continue their advance on Lorient at once. He knew, through agents, of the confusion existing among the German troops under Colonel Rumann, who was in command of the approaches, and of the discouragement of Vice-Admiral Matthie, the naval commander. He assured them the town could be taken without striking a blow.

But the American commander insisted on keeping to his timetable. His troops required rest, and his vehicles maintenance. The attack took place as planned twenty-four hours later, during the morning of the 7th. During the 6th, however, the Germans had taken advantage of the unexpected respite to mine roads and bridges, and organize the defence. When the American tanks began their advance again on the 7th, with a company of the 1st F.F.I. Battalion in the lead, they could not get through Hennebont, where the bridges had been blown and the centre of the town destroyed by a tremendous artillery concentration. During the next three days, every attack failed. On 11 August, the Allied commander came to the conclusion that tank attacks could not succeed; and General Wood, commanding the American 4th Armoured Division, asked Colonel Morice to be responsible for containing the town.

On 3 September a much graver incident took place between the French and the Americans. Owing to faulty liaison, which the F.F.I. interpreted as complete disregard for their lives, two successive waves of American aircraft bombed the village of Telgruc, which was occupied by the F.F.I. The place was reduced to rubble and 108 F.F.I. and civilians were killed. Colonel Eon protested angrily to General Middleton:

"My conclusions as to the results to be expected from these methods of attack are as follows:

(a) Terrifyingly effective on units without proper cover and even more so on dwelling-houses and the civilian population. . . .

(b) Not in the least effective against any form of defence, even if it is only just below ground. . . .

(c) Complete absence of tactical intelligence by the American formations in question."

Hearing that there was some question of the Americans renewing the attack, Eon pleaded vehemently for his soldiers:

"If these civilians have no uniforms, they are . . . nonetheless your soldiers and have a right to expect some other reward from you than to be massacred as they were at Telgruc on 3 September, which appears to have been an unpleasant foretaste of what is to come.

"The German troops comfortably sheltered from your bombing in the fortifications of which my Deuxième Bureau have given you details, will be delighted to witness the massacre of patriots who have been till now their most redoubtable enemies in Brittany."

This bitterness was due not only to the grave mistake the Americans had made, but it reflected also the F.F.I.'s sense of inferiority towards them.

Here is another example of their extreme sensitivity:

"Certain American units have behaved in a way which is profoundly demoralizing so far as we are concerned; we have seen them systematically destroy guns captured from the enemy, and prevent our men, who are very short of footwear, from acquiring boots from prisoners; while the Americans cram German prisoners with food and give them new boots, our own units die of hunger and march barefoot through the gorse."

Brittany was the first example of a liberation during which the French from London and the French who had remained at home met in the heat of battle. And here, too, we can discern for the first time that atmosphere of dramatic, if sometimes rather confused, exaltation which swept across the country on the departure of the Germans.

On 8 August, four days after the liberation of Vannes, the American head of Civil Affairs met the local authorities and principal officials in a room in the prefecture.[1] Onfroy, the new prefect, had just replaced Constant, the Vichy prefect, who was regretted even by some of the Resistance. Onfroy, who did not belong to the district, was finding difficulty in coping with the situation. On taking up his post, he found that there were two committees of liberation in the department, one of which had been formed as recently as June or July and was Communist in allegiance. It was headed by Lucie Aubrac, and included the curé of Pontivy among its eighteen members to give it an air of respectability. It was ready to assume power in the department. Unfortunately for this committee, another C.D.L. had existed in secret ever since the beginning of 1943. At its head was a barrister, Maître Camenen, and on the committee was another lawyer, Maître Perrot, president of the Chamber of Notaries.

"Ladies and gentlemen," said the barrister when the two committees met, "I am delighted to meet you. But where the devil have you sprung from? We don't seem ever to have seen you before. . . . You're Communists? Splendid. We have reserved four places for you on our C.D.L., which has functioned till now with a reduced membership: one for the Party, one for the United Youth Front, one for the National Front, and one for your women's organization. You are now members. Please take your seats!"

The four elected members obeyed, and the other fourteen disappeared. Much to the surprise of Maître Camenen and Maître Perrot, Onfroy awarded the four new members Resistance medals. However, this first incident had been smoothed over. Alas, there were to be others and, at the meeting on 9 August, Onfroy gave an account of them. He painted a sombre picture of the situation: the population was in a state of excitement and one of the Resistance leaders was demanding his prefecture and threatening to take it by assault; no one would obey orders; and there

[1] Cf., Branges de Civriac: *La Libération dans le Morbihan*, page 30.

were many arbitrary acts of revenge. Indeed, some German prisoners had been executed without trial in front of the prison gate, which had infuriated the Americans. The Civil Affairs officer was so angry that his immediate reaction was towards some form of the now outmoded AMGOT: "There's such chaos in the department that I'm seriously considering removing jurisdiction from the French authorities and exercising it myself." What had occurred in Vannes to produce this sudden atmosphere of civil disorder?

The liberation in Brittany, as later elsewhere, may be compared to the eagre which occurs in estuaries with the changing tide. The tide falls quietly, but the flow hurls itself against the current and the result is turbulence.

The F.F.I., the flowing tide of French patriotism after four years of occupation, was hardly likely to remain quiescent in these days of revenge; and, in particular, the F.T.P., whom the Militia and the Germans had hunted down with peculiar virulence, was apt to take speedy and violent reprisals.

The maquisards had undergone many ordeals of which the soldiers in uniform of the Regular armies knew nothing. They had suffered the tortures of the Gestapo and the Militia. They had been denounced by traitors who had infiltrated into their ranks.

There were French secret political organizations in the service of the occupying power, such as the Revolutionary Anti-Communist Committee, which sent warnings to people suspected of Gaullism or Marxism. Here is an example:

This letter is to warn you that from now on we shall hold you responsible for your words and actions, and for those of your friends.

We are prepared to make this warning public, if necessary, and at whatever cost to you.

We are also prepared to make you expiate, when the time comes, the crimes you are so ready to encourage.

There were also Breton autonomists. Though their numbers, even according to the Germans, were very small, from their ranks were drawn some hundreds of armed militiamen, on the pattern of Darnand's, though their uniform was different and they were formed into independent units. While the ordinary Militia had its headquarters in Rennes, these had theirs at Saint-Brieuc, at 39, Rue Renan, where they kept the flag of the Autonomist Party. They had a newspaper, L'Heure Bretonne, which was read less and less as the years of occupation drew on. Their leader was Jean de Suelen, a notorious collaborator. The

Resistance called them "Perrot's" Militia, from the name of the curé of Finistère, the Abbé Perrot, of whom they had made, so to speak, their martyr and patron saint. An ingenuous and misguided political idealist, this unfortunate man, who even the Resistance admitted had never denounced or tortured anyone, allowed himself to be seduced by the Germans and paid with his life for his mistake. On information broadcast from London, some maquisards killed him in December 1943. And then there were, of course, the Gestapo and the S.S. who, with the support of the French members of the two brands of Militia, as well as informers, indulged in every form of sadistic cruelty in an attempt to frighten their opponents.

At Kerhouden, a Morbihan village, a group of F.T.P. was denounced to the Germans. They all succeeded in escaping except one. The Germans "employed as an instrument of torture a little bevelled anvil on which the peasants sharpened their scythes. They hammered their victim till his flesh was in bloody rags." [1] The village was considered to be solid for the Maquis. The men were arrested and assembled under guard. There were no executions, but the farms were sacked and burnt.

"Under the horrified eyes of the unfortunate peasants, the officer . . . set fire to the centre of the village, having first lighted a cigarette with the torch. . . . A poor old woman came running from her flaming cottage, carrying her little hoard of savings with her, doing her best to hide it in the folds of her apron; but a soldier saw it, seized it and made off with it. The peasants had to watch their homes and outbuildings, their clothes and furniture, their tools and their reserves of fodder, even their livestock in the barns, consumed."

At Vannes, Georgians wearing the Wehrmacht uniform castrated the patriots they arrested.

This atmosphere of horror spread and grew ever darker during the last battles. When retreating German troops passed through a village which had been evacuated by its original garrison, they made it pay dearly for the joy it had shown. This was particularly the case in Finistère, where German units were retreating from every direction into the fortified camp of Brest. At Lesneven, the Germans shot everyone they saw; and slaughtered the wounded. They fired their guns point-blank at the houses and set them on fire. At Saint-Pol-de-Léon, on 4 August, there were twenty-five killed.

On the other hand, the Germans were often shot at by local snipers and provoked into taking reprisals that might well have been avoided. At Cleder, on 8 August, as a German column was passing the Lamen-

[1] Louis de Brazidec: *Saint Yves la Vérité, Village Breton,* page 175.

nais school, a sergeant was shot dead. In reprisal, the Germans executed five hostages they had with them, though they had no connection whatever with the village.

These incidents were typical of the Liberation in the towns and villages of Brittany. The dead lay everywhere and the first hours of their reconquered liberty had to be spent by the population in burying them. In their treks across country, the F.F.I. often found heaps of anonymous corpses.

In a wood near Uzel, in the Côtes-du-Nord, they found three ditches containing the bodies of sixty patriots, who had been tortured and mutilated. Similar discoveries were made at Plesnay, Malaunoy, in the forest of Loudéac and near Saint-Brieuc. The resistants exhumed in the forest of Lorges were unrecognizable. They were identified only by scraps of clothing, or because they bore a number traceable in the list of names the Gestapo had omitted to take away with them.

Is it astonishing that the Breton maquisards, who had suffered such tortures and disasters, should react to reprisals such as these by taking their revenge?

It was a vicious circle of violence; and though vengeance often fell on those who had inaugurated it, the innocent did not always escape. With so much horror to avenge, the primitive law of blood for blood temporarily overwhelmed the detachment essential to justice. On the whole, however, it would appear unlikely that the victims of revenge equalled those subjected to the atrocities of the Germans and the Militia; the F.F.I., in Brittany, committed fewer cruelties than those they had had to endure.

At the Liberation, the civil authorities who had maintained some semblance of ordinary life in the province all disappeared at once.

Apart from the regional prefect of Nantes, who received the liberators "sitting behind his desk, dressed in an immaculate gold-braided uniform" [1] and reproached them for having kept everyone waiting so long, the leading Vichy officials, prefects, sub-prefects, and mayors, felt their power tottering the moment the Allies arrived; it was clearly no use counting on them to prevent reprisals. On the other hand, as soon as a department, or even a zone of action, was liberated, the F.F.I. and the maquisards found that their whole official organization, their whole operational cadre, lapsed. The Jedburgh teams either returned to England or left for new fields of action. The American liaison units disappeared. The French regional authorities took some days to get organized.

[1] Rémy: *Les Mains jointes*, page 267.

And during this period of transition there was a military and adminis-trative void.

It was during this interregnum that the excesses took place. It was no use the Americans reproaching the F.F.I. with having "a somewhat dif-ferent conception of the laws of war and the Geneva Convention from those of regular troops," for indeed it made no more sense than the reproaches levelled by virtuous and well-fed foreigners against the starv-ing French for having recourse to the black market. At Rennes, during the night before the Liberation, "elements of the Resistance arrested fifty militiamen," who in that town had subjected the population to "the harshest treatment and the most atrocious cruelty." While, accord-ing to an M.M.L.A. report, "detachments of the F.T.P., acting inde-pendently of the Resistance, have made a number of arrests and, in cer-tain cases, appear to have committed outrages."

At Vannes, in the discreet phrase of a new Gaullist civil servant, "joy at the Liberation resulted in certain extravagances." German soldiers who had fired on the population were executed by the cemetery. Georgians, who had been taken prisoner, were shot against the prison wall in re-prisal for the cruelties they had inflicted when they were jailers them-selves. At Locminé, five Germans were executed without trial for having kicked in the face of an F.F.I. liaison agent who refused to talk. A few French collaborators, or reputed collaborators, were killed. Even before the Liberation, irresponsible elements of the Resistance, without the prior knowledge of the Committee of Liberation, had killed three un-fortunate suspects: one, called Rivière, was killed in the prefecture itself, because he had belonged to a para-military organization. Bonnamy, the Marshal's "propaganda delegate," was assassinated in his own house. And a woman was killed for similar activities. In the Baud district, where the Communists were particularly numerous, they set about eliminating all the local notables, and the Gaullist authorities were forced to im-prison these unfortunate people to save their lives. In the same district, the curé of Bieuzy was killed.

These summary executions, on the evidence even of those who re-ported them, were exceptional. More often, the German supporters arrested at the Liberation were eventually brought to trial. Such was the fate of a group of traitors, near the Saffré Maquis, who had helped the Germans to organize their perquisitions. Their leader, a ruined country gentleman, who had drawn 2,000 francs a month from the Gestapo, was condemned to death by the Nantes court and shot. The others were sentenced to varying terms of hard labour.

Moreover, every act of revenge in this period of turmoil, whether it consisted of execution without trial or merely arrest as a preliminary to trial, nourished a curious tendency to exaggeration. Rumour flew from village to village. "If one believed all one heard," said an F.F.I. official, "we should have to arrest the whole of the Morbihan." He might have added that, conversely, rumour also had it that the whole of the Morbihan, or nearly, had already suffered either arrest or execution.

By the end of August, order had been more or less restored in the liberated province. The new authorities were beginning to take the measure of their jobs; and the F.F.I. had sown their wild oats and now marched past in disciplined ranks like seasoned troops. In some towns, they even lived in barracks and held inspections like those of peacetime.

The public authorities, prefects and mayors, made great use of the F.F.I. Deuxième Bureau, which had given proof of its capacity during operations and was now, from the very nature of its duties, in a position to assist in restoring order. It arrested and held imprisoned many people who had committed only very minor crimes because their release would have endangered them. It secured the documents the enemy had left behind, and these provided the necessary evidence in the more serious cases. It kept track of enemy agents. Indeed, it facilitated the transition between the critical period and the progressive restoration of order.

And this transition was all the easier in Brittany because, unlike some other districts, there was no real attempt to seize power by revolutionaries. The presence of Allied troops and the competent organization of the F.F.I. enabled the province gradually to recover its customs and traditions.

Part Three

THE NATIONAL INSURRECTION

Chapter I

SABOTAGE

THE Normandy and Brittany F.F.I. and F.T.P. were certainly insurgents. But their insurrection formed part of a definite plan of campaign carried through by the Allied armies.

In the rest of France, where between June and August there was no Allied advance, the maquisards were masters of their terrain and national insurrection burst out unalloyed. The Resistance deployed its own forces and its activities assumed the forms peculiar to it. These were essentially sabotage, guerrilla tactics and the anticipatory liberation of various fragments of territory.

At 15.30 on 6 June 1944, General Revers, head of the O.R.A. (Organization de Résistance de l'Armée) took the train from Paris to Toulouse. He had just heard at the Cour des Comptes that the landings had taken place. He wanted to make sure on the spot that the Green Plan for the sabotage of the railways was being properly executed. The train took three days to reach its destination, and this in itself augured well.

For three days, the train was held up by sabotage activities and was obliged to zigzag on by secondary routes. General Revers was delighted by each delay, but his travelling companions became increasingly exasperated. Finally, an indignant lady said: "One might almost think you're pleased that the whole line's blown up!" After that, the General was more careful to conceal his feelings.

The Green Plan covered the whole railway network, but more particularly the localities where intervention by the Allied air forces was difficult or impracticable.

In the northern zone, in the region of Chartres, sabotage was less necessary than elsewhere, since the destruction of the Loire bridges and the bombing of the Trappes marshalling yards had brought all railway traffic to a standstill. This was also true of the Orléanais, the neighbourhood of Tours and the district north of Poitiers.

In the Bordelais an invisible and subtle form of sabotage was practiced; it proved just as effective as the destruction of material; and we shall have occasion to record examples of it. The Toulouse district was an apanage of the Maquis, and there the cutting of railway lines alternated with the sabotage of locomotives.

In the Aveyron and the Hérault, where the railway network was far less dense, and every line therefore of great importance to the Germans, derailments were generally effected in tunnels which complicated clearing the line. But the Maquis' masterpiece of sabotage was undoubtedly in Burgundy, in the region between Lons-de-Saunier, Chalon, Dijon and Besançon. From 7 June onwards, not a single train was able to cross this quadrilateral through which ran all the main and secondary lines joining the valley of the Rhône to Alsace and the Palatinate. In the Dijon district alone, thirty-seven lines were cut on 7 June.

In the south-east, on the old P.L.M. network, approximately a thousand trains were held up by the F.F.I. for a fortnight.

These acts of sabotage by the French railwaymen are recorded in an Intelligence Bulletin produced by the British Air Ministry immediately after the landings. It was, however, only a first report and far from complete. They were the climax to a long-term period of sabotage activities which, first undertaken spontaneously by railway personnel, had later been organized and co-ordinated by the B.C.R.A. in London.

From the beginning of the Occupation, the railways had been of particular concern to the German authorities.

According to the terms of Article 13 of the Armistice Convention, the railways in the occupied zone were to be placed "at the full and complete disposition of the chief of German transportation." A complete administrative hierarchy of Germans moved in on every level.

In July 1940, Colonel Goeritz, Director-General of Transportation in Paris, informed representatives of the S.N.C.F. that, in accordance with Article 155 of the German Military Code of Justice, they were subject to the laws of war: "The German laws of war are extremely severe, they provide in almost every case for the death penalty, life sentences or hard labour. . . . Everyone should remember that the German military courts are harsh and pay no attention to circumstances." The price paid by the S.N.C.F. for refusing to obey Goeritz's instruction was 300 shot and more than 3,000 deported.

The railwaymen's behaviour was due not only to their patriotism, but also to professional pride. They strongly objected to the interference of German railway officials.

In 1944, fearing a rising in mass, the occupation authorities "found it necessary to bring in urgently some 25,000 German railway technicians to keep the main lines running, if the French railwaymen failed them. Some of these men still wore on their arms Kief or Kharkov badges as souvenirs of their victories."

Meanwhile, on 28 January, the Vichy Minister for Communications associated himself with the Nazi threats: "The occupation authorities have . . . informed me in unequivocal terms that, if there is no improvement in the situation within the next few days, they will impose sanctions on all those responsible."

But the railwaymen had more than one string to their bow. For four years, they had been competing with each other in guile and cunning. And, indeed, for the whole of that period German military transportation had been dependent on the services of the enormous army of spies and rebels which constituted the personnel of the S.N.C.F. The signalman in his box, the labourer on the permanent way, and the stationmaster on his platform had unrivalled opportunities for taking note of the movements of the Wehrmacht. Indeed, they often had previous knowledge of them. Approximately sixty trains were required to move a German division. And for these operations the Germans, in their poetic way, favoured the names of flowers or birds. And London would be informed through the French station that "T.C.O." Edelweiss, consisting of twelve trains every twenty-four hours, would be routed in such and such a way on such and such dates. In the result, the bird was often plucked of its feathers or the flower of its petals.

To prevent these "constant leakages" the Germans soon began delaying as long as possible before communicating their programmes to the French railways. They often altered the routing at the very last moment and changed the convoys' code names two or three times during the course of the journey. But in spite of all these precautions, and till the very last day of the German Occupation, Eisenhower was kept informed by French railwaymen—even when the Normandy battle was raging—of the German reinforcements moving up from Germany, Belgium or the south. But reporting troop movements was not enough. They had also to be prevented. Drivers, firemen and engineers were as zealous in suspending or slowing down the traffic as they had been in normal times in running it to schedule.

In May 1944, on the eve of the landings, a goods train arrived in a station some eighty kilometres south-east of Paris, where a German troop train had broken down. The driver of the goods train was ordered to couple his engine to the troop train and drive off at once. Night was falling. He had no light on his engine. Could he borrow one from the

German train, or from the station stores? There was much delay and the troop train left only at nine o'clock. It got no farther than the next station. "The coal, replenished the night before, nevertheless appeared to give out extraordinarily quickly, except that one knows that for every shovelful that went into the furnace at least two were tipped on to the permanent way." The engine had run out of fuel. It was sent to coal. Meanwhile, the driver and the fireman disappeared. By the time the locomotive was ready, there was no one to drive it. Another driver had to be found. In the event, the train was thirty hours late.

The station of Bordeaux-Saint-Jean specialized in working so scrupulously to rule that it amounted to sabotage.

On 8 June, it happened that a German train was derailed (by accident) between Bordeaux and Saintes. There was a failure to inform officially the assistant stationmaster responsible for traffic on that particular line. He therefore continued imperturbably to direct more German trains to the site of the accident. Indeed, for once, he made a point of sending them off on time, or even before time. The result was chaos. First, a south-bound goods train ran full speed into the wreck to increase the scope of the accident. Then eleven north-bound German trains carrying tanks were quickly piled up behind it. Eventually, they had to be backed out, and sent on a very complicated itinerary, during which one of them was derailed by the Maquis. In the end, the trains reached the Loire nine days late.

The railwaymen did not limit their activities to the sabotage of the railways. They could put them to good use for the benefit of British and American airmen, who had been shot down over France. Dressed in caps bearing the letters S.N.C.F. and the red and green railwayman's brassard, they were dispatched to the Spanish frontier. The Americans, however, were not always easy to disguise owing to their patently transatlantic appearance.

A group of fugitives would be collected at a station, with a French guide to lead them. They moved at intervals, pretending not to know the man ahead. Compartments were avoided because of the danger of having to enter into conversation. They generally stood in the corridors, gluing their faces to the windows for hours at a time, or pretending to sleep with their heads on the brass bar. On one occasion, a ticket-collector, who was not in the secret, spoke to an American, who was quite incapable of replying. Exasperated, the ticket-collector threatened to turn him off the train at the next station. The French leader of the group intervened. Pretending to be merely an obliging traveller, he endeavoured to smooth things over. But things had gone too far; he had to burn his boats. He whispered to the ticket-collector: "Shut up, he's an American." "Why the hell didn't you tell me that before?" replied the ticket-collector and went on his way down the train.

But the best *coup* the railwaymen brought off was making use of Laval's special train to pass couriers across the demarcation line on their way to London. The railway Resistance soon realized that this train afforded the maximum of security. Who could possibly suspect it? Even the Germans would hardly dare to search it. For greater security, Colonel Goeritz's staff insisted that the same locomotive always be used with the same driver. The driver accepted the risk, as did his fireman. Certain alterations were made to the tender. A false floor was installed half-way up the water tank, above the coal bunker. The secret passengers could lie concealed in it but not without some danger of being drowned, if an accident took place, or if some too zealous German railwayman opened the cocks on the side of the tender. However, under the involuntary auspices of the Vichy Prime Minister, the Resistance's courier passed through the station at Moulins with full honours from a detachment of the Gestapo. A number of well-known members of the Resistance, Médéric in particular, were privileged in this way.

Resistance Fer, with its ingenious and courageous personnel, became organized into a secret army which also took part in the insurrection.

Early in 1943 a young railway engineer, René Hardy, alias Didot, met Henri Frenay, head of the Combat movement. Condemned to death in 1940, when he was working at the Gare Montparnasse, he had had the singular good fortune to be set free after fifteen months' imprisonment. Having convinced Frenay and the leaders of the M.U.R. (Mouvements Unis de Résistance), Didot organized the "Bloc Fer" which was soon attached to the N.A.P. (Noyautage des Administrations Publiques).

It was a real G.H.Q. that was organized in the underground. It thought out sure and economical methods of paralyzing whole regions. Making spectacular raids and destroying material that would be invaluable to France after the Liberation seemed unnecessary. It would be just as effective to destroy one particular part in every locomotive throughout the region. In the southwest, it was the water-injector. In agreement with the B.C.R.A., which had modelled its "Bloc Planning" organization on that of the Resistance, and had its teams of inspectors to verify the results obtained, the "Bloc Fer" prepared the five hundred line-cuttings under the Green Plan and exchanged essential information with London by secret radio or microphotographs. Didot was arrested in June 1943. Jean-Guy Bernard, alias Thalès-Navarre, replaced him. He undertook to put the second part of the Green Plan into operation, and made contact with the high officials of the S.N.C.F., of which many were already affiliated to Intelligence networks, or in direct liaison with London. Arrested early in 1944, he never returned from being deported. But his work and that of the teams he organized bore fruit on D-day.

This systematic action had important military results. At Mailly-le-Camp, motorized S.S. entrained for Avranches. The lines leading from Troyes to Chalons-sur-Marne, and from Vitry-le-François to Sézanne and Épernay were cut one after the other, so that for several days the trains went round in circles unable to get through. They reached Normandy a fortnight late, after Rommel's counter-attack had failed. It may well be that the absence of such fanatical troops as the S.S. from Mailly-le-Camp contributed to his failure. Continually blocked and scattered by the joint action of the Resistance and the Allied air forces, the German troops became frustrated and demoralized.

"One important convoy," relates a French document, written immediately after the Liberation, "was coming from Belgium in a compact mass of forty or fifty trains; by the time it reached the Somme, this railway armada amounted to only a third or a quarter of its original size. Trains had been blocked, deviated and delayed. The troops were exhausted by their seemingly endless journey and demoralized by the constant accidents. One should also be able to relate incident by incident the odyssey of another convoy from the Bordeaux region which became stuck in the sands of the Loire. The troops had to abandon it in indescribable disorder four hundred kilometres from their base." But the most famous example of all concerned the crack Das Reich Armoured Division. It was moving up to the Normandy front and was signalled as being near Souillac on 7 June. It at once became the target for the whole Resistance of the district. The Maquis harassed it and tried to block its progress. At Souillac itself, at Cressensac and, on 9 June, at the Bretenaux Bridge over the Dordogne F.F.I. patrols sacrificed their lives to delay it. It took the Germans four hours to cross the river. Das Reich brought its heavy machine-guns and mortars into action and was held up from 6.30 till 10.30 in the morning by twenty-eight F.F.I., of whom fifteen were killed and two wounded.

During the forty-eight hours the division was delayed, other secret organizations came into action against it. They were invisible but nonetheless effective for that. These were the Maquis Intelligence services who located the convoys and signalled the information to London in the hope, which was soon realized, that they would be attacked by the R.A.F. One of these groups was commanded by André Malraux, alias

Colonel Berger. As one might expect, with such a leader the use made of the information was not lacking in ingenuity. André Malraux's role was a triple one. He had first to gather information about Das Reich's order of march and the direction of its movement. He learned that the division had split up at Brive: the light elements going to Limoges, by way of Tulle and Oradour, while the heavy elements were directed towards Périgueux, where they were to entrain for Normandy.

Secondly, in liaison with the Dordogne Maquis, he had not only to impede the movement of the heavy elements, but above all, by concentrated sabotage, compel them to take the single line railway to Angoulême and Poitiers. Once they were engaged on this line from which there was no possible deviation or return, Malraux, who was in contact by radio with London, had, thirdly, to inform the R.A.F. that Das Reich was running into a "bottleneck." Hour by hour, London was kept informed first of the progress of entraining and then of the train movements. Eventually, the R.A.F. had merely to spend twenty-five minutes bombing the target that had been so carefully prepared for it.

Here is an account of what happened:

The railway was blown up and the roads cut; rocks were blown down to block them. . . . The trains were derailed in the cuttings. . . . In short, the main body of the Panzer division was delayed and lost another six days at Périgueux while their tank patrols circled round trying to break the vice which the Dordogne F.F.I., under the command of Martial, was tightening every day.

However, they eventually managed to get away, due (1) to the complete exhaustion of the Maquis' stocks of explosives, and (2) to the support of the armoured trains they had organized. They entrained at Périgueux and Libourne a fatal fifteen days late, for London, which had been warned, had the trains of tanks bombed at Libourne, Angoulême and Poitiers. Only a few tanks reached Normandy, and then so late that they could have little effect on the situation. . . .

The other Panzer divisions (Gross-Deutschland and Goering) made a detour round the Dordogne. This delayed them and they also arrived too late.

French estimates place the number of enemy divisions which the Resistance prevented either from moving to the north or escaping to the east at ten to fifteen.

As well as the Green Plan for sabotaging the railways, there was the Tortoise Plan for sabotaging the roads. On 18 July 1944, the pro-Nazi leader Doriot wrote an indignant letter to Ambassador Otto Abetz: "It is no longer possible today for private persons or for Wehrmacht vehicles to travel along the roads of France. It is impossible to go freely from Paris to Lyons, from Lyons to Bordeaux, from Paris to Châteauroux, from Châteauroux to Angoulême, from Angoulême to Toulouse, from Poitiers to Bordeaux or to Clermont-Ferrand. The roads of Brittany are impracticable. Behind the Normandy front, the Chief of Staff of the Army, whose headquarters are at Le Mans, has told me that German convoys are far from safe owing to particularly active maquisards. The roads from Paris to Nancy and Verdun, and from Paris to Mézières, have been cut by the Maquis, that is to say that within a short distance from the German frontier the men of the Maquis attack officers of the Wehrmacht. . . .The Maquis forces are so numerous that one is forced to the conclusion that, since the month of May, a veritable mobilization has taken place in the towns and villages of central France, as well as in the south and south-east."

The strategic consequences of the Tortoise Plan were important, but its psychological effects were no less so. During this period of the Liberation, German post-bags often fell into the hands of the Maquis. Many letters gave evidence of the Wehrmacht's and, even more, of the Gestapo's obsessive feeling that they were besieged. Here is a letter from a Gestapo officer to his wife: "Once again, it looks as if I have a chance of writing to you. The last days and weeks have been tragic, but they are nothing to the fate that is in store for us. We are completely surrounded by the Americans, on the north, the south and the south-west. And to them must be added bands of thousands of armed men, terrorists who practise lynch law. . . . Believe me, my angel, I am no coward, and you have no need to be ashamed of me, but, you know, to be completely surrounded like the unfortunate chaps at Stalingrad and to have no hope . . ."

Besieged by the Green Plan on the railways, and by the Tortoise Plan on the roads, the German Army was also deprived of its normal communications by a third form of sabotage operated by the P.T.T.

The Violet Plan, unlike the Green and Tortoise Plans, was not controlled by the regional military delegates, the representatives in France of Supreme Headquarters in London. The P.T.T. administration itself was made entirely responsible for its execution. "You will receive by next courier plan of action against telecommunications called Violet Plan which will come into action on the following phrase: 'I can no longer hear your voice.' Teams will go into action on same warning phrase as for other plans. Violet Plan sent you for information and co-ordination. Central P.T.T. administration responsible for executive action." On 1 June, this message was sent by the B.C.R.A. in London to every D.M.R. It is evidence of the efficiency of the Resistance organizations of the P.T.T. The Post Office employees, like the railwaymen, and for similar reasons, had been among the first resistants.

From the moment the demarcation line cut France in two and interrupted the normal postal traffic between the two zones, there was a natural temptation to use post wagons for dispatching secret communications, escaped prisoners and fugitives from the Gestapo.

As a result, a whole network of secret post and telephone communications, as well as a plan for the sabotage of long-distance lines, the Violet Plan, was organized in the Ministry of the P.T.T. in the Rue de Grenelle. It also had subsidiary organizations, some to make sure the plan worked, others to repair the sabotage immediately after the Liberation.

The first essential was to destroy the telephone cables used by the enemy, as well as to transmit with the utmost speed information about German forces to the Allies.[1]

This subversive activity had various branches. There was, of course, an Intelligence service. Post Office and Radio employees were well placed to communicate with London by secret radio. The secret radios constantly changed location to avoid detection. Nevertheless, there was always the danger of being detected by the Feldgendarmerie on the roads when moving from one place to another.

A more satisfactory method was adopted later on. It consisted in using several transmitters simultaneously on the same wave length. . . . One transmitter would send the beginning of a message for one minute, then a second transmitter would take it up for another minute, followed by a third and so on. The enemy was faced with a very difficult problem of detection.

Another unofficial activity of the P.T.T. consisted in sending correspondence to the Allied Intelligence services. A secret network of postmen and sorters was organized with the same efficiency as the official departments.

During the first months of 1943, a member of the Resistance accompanied every Post Office railway van. "At every important station, a member of the organization took delivery and in exchange handed over the mail he had collected. He delivered the mail received in person. . . . This took place daily between Paris and Arras, Amiens, Lille, Nancy, Nîmes, Montpellier, Toulouse, Bordeaux, Limoges, Nantes, Quimper,

[1] For information about the P.T.T. Resistance and, in particular, Radio Liaison, we are indebted to E. Debaumarche and J. Laversanne: *La France et son Empire dans la Guerre*, Vol. II (Littéraires Françaises, Paris, 1947).

Saint-Brieuc, Rennes, Le Mans, Cherbourg, Caen, Rouen, Le Havre and Dieppe." (E. Debaumarche.)

The post for England, the most important of all, which often consisted of several mailbags, was directed to Concarneau, in Brittany, embarked on a trawler and transhipped at sea to a British ship, in spite of German naval patrols. At the beginning of 1944, the secret postal services were so regular and sure that the Secret Army confided the whole of its official correspondence to it: orders, reports and plans, as well as the transference of funds. In the same way, the liaison between the various Maquis also required a sure and secret postal service.

But, apart from all this, the resistant Post Office employees also carried out technical sabotage.

The network of cables used in France by the Wehrmacht had a two-fold origin: on the one hand there were the special circuits installed by German engineers. These did not survive the Liberation, for there was no point in keeping them and they could be totally destroyed. On the other, was the network of French underground cables the Nazis reserved entirely for their own use; these reverted to the use of the State after the Liberation. For these latter, sabotage had to assume a form which would make repairs possible as France was progressively evacuated by the Germans.

But, in both cases, the cuts must be difficult to repair at once and the method of sabotage simple enough to be effected by nonspecialist members of the P.T.T. or even by the F.F.I.

This was the main outline of the sabotage organized by the central P.T.T. administration. But it was in the local post offices that extraordinary courage and cunning were manifested daily.

Every official telegram, both on sending and reception, whether from Vichy, the Reich, the Italian or the German embassy, was copied and sent to the proper—or perhaps improper—quarters.

Letters were also sorted, and interesting information copied, before they were sent on their way. The Post Office employees were thus often able to warn the Resistance or fugitives in danger of arrest.

Information of a more general nature culled from this unofficial censorship was sent to the headquarters of the P.T.T. every two days and sometimes every day.

Some of it was of the highest importance: for instance, within a two-month period, the location of forty V.1 positions; the discovery of underground reserves of extremely powerful liquid explosive (for the V.2s situated at Chartres); and the solving in five days and nights of Joseph Darnand's code.

Moreover, the post offices were specially organized to supply refugees with identity cards, either for Paris or the provinces, P.T.T. identity cards, paybooks of the Production Industrielle, labour certificates and mobilization documents, official copies of birth certificates, blank sickness warrants already stamped by hospitals, and ration cards. Even German discharge certificates were forged to enable prisoners and workers escaped from Germany to draw their ration cards.

When awarding their flag the medal of the Resistance and the Croix de Guerre, General de Gaulle published the following citation in Army Orders:

P.T.T. Resistance:
A magnificent movement which numbered over 10,000 members of the corps of administrators and employees of the Post, Telegraph and Telephone services.

From 1940 it took part in the underground movement, helping to convey documents and relay orders, particularly by radio posts.

Later on, it worked in liaison with the intelligence services, fighting against the pro-German movements and contributing to keep communications open throughout the country.

From the first moment of the Liberation, it played a major part in destroying the enemy's means of communication, while successfully protecting installations necessary to the Allied forces.

It paid heavily in the struggle against the invader with nearly 500 dead and 1,500 deported.

Chapter II

THE CADRES OF THE NATIONAL INSURRECTION

THE National Insurrection was mainly directed from London and Algiers by three men, none of whom, in May 1940, could have expected to play so important a part. Their careers, in this revolutionary period of the Resistance and the Liberation, were somewhat similar to those of the generals and ministers of the Revolution and the Empire, who due to some gallant charge on a victorious field of battle or during some night of riot were suddenly promoted to the summits of power. But now the night lasted for the four years of the Occupation and the charges were motorized.

At their head was General Koenig, commanding the Free French Forces in Great Britain and the French Forces of the Interior, and he was therefore in charge of organizing the National Insurrection.

Koenig's *curriculum vitae*, as he drew it up himself for the archives of the National Assembly when he first entered Parliament, is rather similar to a radio broadcast suffering from "fading."

His promotion was curiously lacking in a regular rhythm: commissioned second lieutenant on 3 September 1918, at the end of the First World War, Koenig mentioned no other rank before that of lieutenant-colonel, in November 1940. It was with the three gold and two silver stripes that he was appointed by General de Gaulle as military commander in the Cameroons, which had joined the Free French Forces.

When was he promoted lieutenant? No doubt after the two normal years as second-lieutenant, on 3 September 1920. And captain? He must have served a long time in this rank, for at the Armistice in 1940 he had still risen no higher. His promotion between the two wars had been extremely slow as was generally the case for officers who had risen from the ranks and whose services, however distinguished, did not compensate for their lack of training in a military school. Commandant? In fact, if not officially, he attained to this rank on the fishing-boat which, in June 1940, was taking him with six companions from Brittany to Jersey, from where he made his way to London.

From London, he went to the Cameroons; and from the Cameroons to the Sudan, Palestine, Syria, Libya and Tunisia. From lieutenant-colonel he became colonel, then brigadier-general, which he remained till the moment came, which we shall deal with later, when he was appointed to commands of the highest importance and became a legend in the process.

Koenig's scholastic career, his intellectual *cursus honorum*, has also a good deal of "fading" about it. From his own autobiographical note, it would appear that he never got further than his *baccalauréat*: "He was educated at the Sainte-Marie College," he wrote of himself, "and, after taking the first part of the *baccalauréat*, completed his studies at the Lycée Malherbe" at Caen.

During the next thirty-five years he seems to have achieved no further scholastic distinction. Then, suddenly, on 5 March 1951, the "fading" stops on Koenig's election to the Academy of Moral and Political Sciences. He must have been the only member of the Institute who had never got further than his *baccalauréat*. How did this singular event come about?

Koenig owed all his promotion, both civil and military, to the gallant defence of Bir-Hakeim, of which he was the hero. The members of the Institute, in their green uniforms, were still deeply excited by this epic of the sands; and for once *cedant armis togae*.

At Bir-Hakeim, in May 1942, Brigadier-General Koenig defended a desert strong point which consisted of a quadrilateral four kilometres square, surrounded by mines and barbed wire. The garrison was made up of two battalions of the Foreign Legion, the Pacific Battalion formed from volunteers from Tahiti and New Caledonia, a motorized battalion from Equatorial Africa, a regiment of artillery armed with 75's, anti-tank gun batteries armed with 75's and 47's, a battalion of marines armed with anti-aircraft guns, engineer and signal units, and a medical unit—some 10,000 men in all. But this handful of soldiers represented at that moment the only hope of the renaissance of French arms. It was the first time since the Armistice that French troops in regular formation had confronted the Axis.

The "box" was a threat to the Afrika Korps. "Bir-Hakeim," wrote Lutz Koch, the German war correspondent with Rommel's army, "is like a stake driven deep into the flesh of the German front. It must be destroyed at all costs."

On the morning of 26 May, the Italian Ariete Armoured Division opened the attack which was to continue till 11 June. Six tanks penetrated into the box. The Foreign Legion took them by assault, climbing on to their armour plating, harassing them with grenades and firing through the slits in their turrets. The Italians withdrew.

Further attacks were mounted on the 28th, 29th and 30th. Forty-four tanks out of sixty, eight armoured cars, numerous trucks and 180 prisoners, remained in French hands.

On 31 May, the Italians and Germans withdrew temporarily; but on 1 June, bombing by Stukas began. On 2 June, Rommel, returning to the attack with over 1,000 vehicles, issued an ultimatum:

All further resistance can lead only to useless bloodshed. Your fate will be similar to that of the two British brigades which were annihilated the day before yesterday at Goat-Ualeb. We will break off the battle as soon as you hoist the white flag and come forward without arms.

ROMMEL
General Oberst.

Koenig's reply was to issue orders to fire on every vehicle that came within range. He made the following proclamation to his men:

We must expect a heavy attack with every possible combination of arms. . . . It will be a powerful one.

I renew my orders with the certainty that every man will do his duty without weakening, and will hold his ground whether cut off from his comrades or not. . . . Good luck to you all!

KOENIG.

For five days, from the 6th to the 10th, the battle raged continuously. The 90th German Infantry Division of the Afrika Korps attacked with the Italian Trieste Division.

It was two divisions against little more than a brigade, which was running very short of both food and water. The French fighting day and night in great heat had no more than a litre of water a day, and soon not even that. They were also running out of ammunition. They were unremittingly bombed by sixty Junkers. On the 9th, they drove off another general assault.

On the 10th, they received orders from the British Command to evacuate Bir-Hakeim. The brigade fought its way out during the night of the 10th. It had exactly twenty-two shells left.

It was a great feat of arms, whose significance went much further than its strategic importance, though this was real enough. France was recognized once more as a belligerent power. The traditions of its army had been renewed. From then on Koenig became a symbol of victory and triumphant Gaullism. He had earned his position by a fortnight of fighting that was to become almost legendary.

He was and remained an ardent and patriotic Gaullist, but he retained his prejudices, his ambition and a certain harshness. When he received Pétain on the Marshal's return to France after the collapse of Germany, both in speech and action he conformed with the utmost rigour to the then official view of the victor of Verdun, and refused to shake hands with him.

However, when exercising command of the F.F.I. from London, and during the leading part he played at the Liberation, he showed great aptitude for attention to detail, diplomacy and clear thinking, while always concerned to spare the lives of his soldiers out of uniform.

He was both a great soldier and a great servant of his country, and these surely constituted a greater claim to a seat under the dome of the Institute than many weighty volumes.

Together with Koenig, the two other directors of the National Insurrection were Colonel Passy, whose real name was Dewavrin, the head of the B.C.R.A. in London, and Jacques Soustelle, who was at one time his assistant in London and later his chief in Algiers, where he was head of the Special Services (D.G.S.S.).

There seemed to be no particular reason why Dewavrin, a captain of Engineers, should have been destined to play so important a part—or why, for that matter, he should have selected a métro station for pseudonym. He was a mathematician, and had entered the Engineers from the École Polytechnique.

In June 1940, immediately on the organizing of the Free French Forces in London, General de Gaulle had appointed him to be head of the Deuxième Bureau, the Intelligence section of his staff. This was his road to Damascus. He was embarked on a career to which he was perfectly suited, that "most passionately exciting of all trades, though in it one receives more kicks than halfpence, that trade which brings you into contact with the best and the worst of the human species, but rarely with mediocrities who are afraid of risk and adventure."

He was an inspired amateur, who to start with upset the professionals of espionage. French officers, grown grey in the service of the Deuxième Bureau, as it was run on conventional pre-war lines, and British Intelligence officers, who had been trained in a famous tradition and thought they had nothing to learn, were completely nonplussed by this novice and his innovations, by his determination to adapt well-tried methods to the peculiar conditions then existing in his country.

It seemed almost scandalous that he should wish to reduce secret agents to the minimum; and undoubtedly the most shocking revolution that had ever taken place in the sacrosanct corps of the S.R. was the recognition that "there existed throughout the occupied territory an infinite number of eager and willing assistants." He placed his faith in patriotic amateurs rather than in professionals. "If," wrote Passy, "I agreed in urgent cases to send an occasional special mission to some precise and vital point, I believed it essential to make the utmost use of the goodwill manifest throughout the country. . . . Who could give us more accurate information about troop movements than a senior official of the S.N.C.F.? Who could tell us what was going on at Brest, Lorient, Le Havre or Bordeaux so well as a ship's officer or a pilot from one of those ports?" The only limit Passy set to membership of his particular service was the whole population of France. It was a far from traditional approach. When Passy first explained his policy to de Gaulle, the General "seemed not much impressed" and suggested "that he strictly limit himself to gathering military intelligence."

But Passy was obstinate. No orders, risks or disappointments could stop him. From the S.R. to the B.C.R.A.M. (the first name of the B.C.R.A.), from the B.C.R.A.M. to the B.C.R.A., from the house in Carlton Gardens, where he was limited to the third floor, to the commercial offices at 10 Duke Street where, from March 1942, he occupied twenty-seven rooms, Passy reigned over a numerous staff of officers, neophytes as zealous as himself, and organized an elaborate filing-system which grew month by month.

His officers, "unaware of the sacrosanct custom of the Secret Service by which one must retain the same initials," adopted the names of the Paris métro as pseudonyms: Lagier became Bienvenue, Duclos Saint-Jacques, Fourcaud Barbès, Lecot Drouot, and Dewavrin Passy. It was nostalgia for France and the occupied capital.

From the first the B.C.R.A. was determined to acquire clear and precise Intelligence and accept the risk entailed. The work of the office was based on three sets of files. The first, the Holy of Holies of this "strange organization born of a no less strange a situation" was devoted to the "agents." Every new arrival in London was interrogated by Passy's officers and asked for the names of people he thought capable of undertaking secret missions, with particular reference to the districts they knew and the contacts they had. "One officer, Lieutenant Bienvenue, was made responsible for filing these names. . . . They were classified by departments. The cards bore no names, merely numbers, and the relationship of name to number was known only to one other officer, Lieutenant Drouot, and to Passy himself."

This most secret of files, which comprised originally only some hundreds of names, was soon paralleled by another, which ran to no less than 100,000. It consisted of a list of all Frenchmen who had remained in France and of whose political views there was some sort of information available. Were they active Gaullists? Sympathizers? Indifferent? Pétainists or collaborators? "Of course," concedes Passy, "the information, since it was not the result of detailed enquiries about the people concerned, but derived merely from appreciations, more or less informed, more or less limited, from sources whose value and objectivity could not always be checked, had only . . . the value of indications" on which final judgement had necessarily to be reserved.

Indeed, these were presumptions not certainties and they were sometimes errors due to personal animosities and irresponsibility; but the card-index nevertheless proved its usefulness, not least as a means of verifying the stories of new arrivals in London, among whom enemy agents were always a possibility.

To these two filing-systems, one devoted to agents of the B.C.R.A., of whom many came to London, and the other to Frenchmen who had remained in occupied France, was soon added a third in which the secret landing and parachuting grounds in France were listed. A file was opened for each ground, containing a description of its physical characteristics and correspondence concerning it with the B.C.R.A. agent responsible and with the British.

These files and card-indexes represented the bureaucratic aspect of Passy's activities. But he was also concerned with the more purely military. In August 1944, together with Colonel Eon, he was to fight in Brittany on a terrain he had organized from London.

Whether he was in London or in France, Passy was one of the invisible but powerful leaders directing and controlling the Resistance effort. At the time of the landings, he was still in London where he came under the command of his former assistant, Jacques Soustelle, who was head of the D.G.S.S., which co-ordinated all the secret organizations, in Algiers.

There was nothing in Jacques Soustelle's background either to qualify him for such a post. He had been to the university, but had made his own way entirely. His whole career, whether as schoolboy, student or graduate, had taught him to work hard and take risks. His father was a mechanic and his mother worked in an office at Villeurbanne, near

Lyons. His ancestors had been Protestants who had suffered for their faith, and he had perhaps inherited from them a disinclination for the easy life.

At seventeen, he had passed first into the École Normale Supérieure. At twenty he had taken a degree in philosophy. At twenty-five, he had taken his doctor's degree and was assistant director of the Musée de l'Homme. His career had been both brilliant and remarkably rapid. Hardly had he taken his degree, when he set off for Mexico to write a thesis on the Otomis, an Indian tribe living on the high Mexican plateau, and on the Lacondons, a branch of the Maya people in danger of extinction, who lived on the borders of Mexico and Guatemala. On 7 November 1932, he landed at Vera Cruz, went to Ixtlahuoca, which lies some 8,000 feet above sea-level, and then travelled some 300 kilometres through an almost uninhabited district to attend an Otomi festival.

From having studied these more intuitive and less rational civilizations, so different from our own, he derived a rule of life. The Aztecs believed in a particular "luck" in every human being's destiny. If it slept, that man was subject to every kind of misfortune. Jacques Soustelle was the type of man who never allowed his luck to slumber. He knew the Aztec legends which exalt courage, particularly the one about the creation of the sun and the moon: "The gods saw with terror that the two heavenly bodies did not move. They remained immobile above the horizon, burning the world with their fires. They were dead and required blood to bring them back to life. So the gods decided to sacrifice themselves. 'Let us all die,' they said, 'so that the sun may be revived by our death.'" One of them, Eecatl, the god of the winds, took it upon himself to kill the rest . . . "Upon which, below the sacrificed gods, drawing life from their death, the sun and the moon began their courses across the sky."

The history and legend with which Soustelle became imbued had no relevance to the shabby, peacetime, political scene. His friends the Mayas had been a flourishing, civilized, prosperous people till the day the Spaniards landed in the New World and caused their rapid disappearance.

What Soustelle, both as a resistant and, later, as a statesman who had emerged from the Resistance, seemed to have retained from his Mexican period was the belief that a national catastrophe was always possible, but that it depended on the will of man, made manifest in desperate and tragic effort, whether the nation succumbed to it or surmounted it. "There are," he wrote, "moments in the life of a nation when its destiny seems to be hesitating: rare moments when the beam of the balance seems to oscillate between grandeur and disaster. Load the will on to one of the scales, and the balance will incline, however imperceptibly, towards life or towards death. . . ."

Such moments were not peculiar to the Mayas. In our own day, and in particular between 1940 and 1944, the fate of France seemed to be hesitating. Thus it was that Soustelle rallied at once to the cause of Free France in June 1940, and gave his unstinted support to de Gaulle in London and Algiers, and rather less frequently after his return to Paris. While others wavered in their loyalty according to their estimate of the General's political ability and his chances of success, Soustelle remained loyal to him, or rather to the grandeur he felt he embodied: "The provisional immortality accorded by the memory of a nation to particular names is never relative to their usefulness but to their grandeur: in the list of great men, Napoleon always comes before Parmentier. One may deplore it, but so it is. Perhaps it is due to the fact that our species is bored and instinctively recognizes those rare deeds which give to its dull life a lustre of free will."

It was also from this attitude that, conversely, his contempt for politicians was derived. To use a simile, most politicians are like weathercocks: they orient themselves to the direction of the wind. Soustelle, on the other hand, was more like a seismograph responding to earthquakes. Sensitive to the deep and sudden quakings of history, conscious of all the possible catastrophes that could be the ruin of our whole civilization, there was an apocalyptic quality about his approach to politics.

Soustelle was typical of a whole generation of young men who rallied to Gaullism. Nevertheless, the seismograph is not an entirely useful instrument for the conduct of one's life from day to day. Whatever its precision in an earthquake, it lacks exactitude as a guide to more stable terrains. And so Soustelle, like many others, found it difficult to adapt himself to the situation in France after the cataclysm was over. A man of strong conviction but uncertain opinion, for they do not necessarily inhabit the same plane, he symbolized both the outstanding rectitude of the men who rallied to de Gaulle while France was still occupied, and their singular fluctuations of opinion after the Liberation. He seemed at times to be oscillating in the most singular way between exaggerated authoritarianism and a sort of nostalgia for liberalism.

Koenig, Passy and Soustelle were the external organizers of the insurrection in France and were typical of the three types of Frenchmen who became the earliest Gaullists. The first, already middle-aged, with an inconspicuous career behind him, was given his great chance. The second was a young adventurer, in the best sense of that word, to whom the four years of the war brought much opportunity and also many dangers, which he would never otherwise have encountered, and of which when peace returned he might well feel the lack. The third discovered in London and Algiers a vocation for politics, of which he might never have become aware in normal times.

They were three companions through epic days, three neophytes to power, three spiritual descendants of the Jacobins and of Napoleon's veterans. Murat at one moment, Fouché at another, they manipulated the strings of one of the most astonishing political and military revivals France had ever known. On the farther side of the Channel or the Mediterranean, in the interior of France, a whole nation of resistants was in close liaison with them and fought under their orders.

The F.F.I. headquarters were opened in London in the spring of 1944 under Koenig.

On 17 June, there was a conference at S.H.A.E.F. and an important agreement was drawn up concerning the F.F.I. command and its relationship to Allied headquarters:

General Koenig will command all the French Forces of the Interior under the supreme command of General Eisenhower and his position will be that of all Allied commanders serving directly under the orders of S.H.A.E.F.

It is agreed that it is General Koenig's duty to advise the Supreme Commander if the orders he receives are in conflict with the directives from the French Committee of National Liberation, as all superior British and American commanders have a duty to do in case of a serious conflict between the orders they receive and the policies of their respective governments.

This document implicitly recognized the C.F.L.N. as a French government equivalent to the other Allied governments.

Parallel to the F.F.I. headquarters proper, the D.G.S.S. (Direction Générale des Services Spéciaux) under Soustelle was very active during the period of the landings. It had two bases, one in Algiers under Pélabon, the other, previously the B.C.R.A., in London under Manuel. Each of these bases had three functions, counter-espionage, intelligence and action.

At the time of the landings, the London base, which remained the principal one, was receiving as many as 6,000 reports a day from occupied France. A special department had to be created to deal with them. Under the command of Colonel Rémy, it sorted out the information from France, had forty-five copies of it duplicated, and reproduced maps and plans with special machines.

The quantity of this information became so great that the Allies had to set up a special Operations staff of French-speaking officers so that the information might be used directly since there was far too much of it to translate. And from this was derived a new plan, known as Plan Sussex, which paid great dividends when the Allied advance began.

This last-born of the great plans hatched in London envisaged parachuting teams consisting of a French Intelligence officer, an Allied officer and a radio-operator behind the retreating enemy lines. The teams were to retreat with the enemy, and transmit information to London about the organization of the rear areas. Some went all the way from Normandy to Holland. With the help of the civilian population, they created Intelligence cells in the various sectors and played an important part in counter-espionage and radio-detection. Moreover, as the Wehrmacht retreated, the Germans left many radio posts behind them. The Plan Sussex teams made contact with the operators, many of whom had been recruited from the population of the occupied countries, and were authorized to promise them their lives if they continued to send signals in accordance with information passed to them from London or Algiers.

The D.G.S.S. was thereby able to use the German agents for what the Deuxième Bureau called "intoxication." A "Deuxième Bureau Bis" was set up whose job it was to pass false information to the Germans. Operational cover plans were split up and fragments signalled by means of these double agents. By the time the Wehrmacht staffs had sorted all the information they were in possession of a "notional" plan covering the real intentions of the Allies.

Among other successes, four German armoured divisions were held for four months between Hamburg and Basle in the expectation of an offensive of which German Intelligence mistakenly believed it had pieced together the secret plan of operations.

In France itself, a double hierarchy was set up for the F.F.I.; the first, which was internal, corresponded to the various formations of the armed Resistance, whose unification was attempted and partly realized by the C.N.R. in February 1944: the Armée Secrète (A.S.), which had grouped the para-military elements of the various Resistance movements of the southern zone, merged under the title M.U.R. (Mouvements Unis de Résistance), the F.T.P.F. (Francs Tireurs et Partisans

Français), the para-military organization of the Front National, which was of Communist obedience, and the Organization de Résistance de l'Armée (O.R.A.) which, after the dissolution of the Army of the Armistice in November 1942, was recruited from among the demobilized officers and men. After February 1944, these three organizations, fused in principle, created their own hierarchy. In each department there was a military leader, generally chosen from the civilian Resistance movements, that is to say the A.S. or the F.T.P., and a Chief of Staff who was more often than not a professional soldier from the O.R.A. This first hierarchy was linked to the C.N.R., and more precisely to its Committee for Military Action, the C.O.M.A.C. In the months preceding D-day, and particularly from April to June 1944, a whole series of tragic happenings reinforced the Communist influence. In April 1944, the arrest of Claude Bourdet, the head of the Combat movement since Frenay had joined the government in Algiers, destroyed one of the barriers to infiltration by the extreme Left. At that time, Bourdet exercised great influence within the Resistance. He was a political theorist with an impressive and persuasive, though sometimes misleading, gift of speech, and had shown exceptional qualities of efficiency in underground organization. His arrest opened a period of argument and intrigue as to who was to succeed him at the head of Combat. After a while, Dormoy replaced him as the political head and Rebattet, called Cheval, the only non-Communist, as military leader. The post on the C.O.M.A.C., made vacant by Dormoy's appointment to another command, was given to the crypto-Communist Kriegel-Valrimont who, as we have seen, brought the military direction of the internal Resistance under the influence of Moscow.

As well as Bourdet's arrest, there were others which disorganized the non-Communist cadres of the internal Resistance. In the spring of 1944, the arrest of Pontcarrel de Jussieu, chief of the national staff of the F.F.I., left the way open to the Communist Villon, who then became the head of this central organization, while the arrest of Lefaucheux, military chief of the Paris region, permitted the appointment of the Communist Rol-Tanguy to this vacant post. It looked very much as if everything, during this period immediately preceding the landings, was playing into the hands of the Communists.

Faced with this hierarchy which, though born spontaneously from the internal Resistance, had been infiltrated at the top by the Communists, the Gaullist authorities superimposed another. It consisted of the D.M.N. (National Military Delegates), D.M.Z. (Zonal Military Delegates) and D.M.R. (Regional Military Delegates).

The object of these appointments was twofold: the political need to preserve the loyalty to de Gaulle of the Resistance organizations which were in danger of being subjected to Communist influence; and the purely military necessities of organizing supplies to the Resistance and achieving proper co-ordination between the various regions and the F.F.I. headquarters in London.

At the time of the National Insurrection, the two hierarchies, one internal and the other imposed by London, though never actually fused, were nevertheless sufficiently co-ordinated, and they constituted for the F.F.I. in general an organization that was indeed sometimes complex, but which worked and was clear in its main outline.

At the top was the D.M.N. appointed by London, who was given the rank of general. Bourgès-Maunoury, a great-nephew of General Maunoury, one of the victors of the Marne, had been a pupil at the Polytechnique. He was twenty-one when parachuted into France as D.M.R. for the Lyons region. In June 1944, he became D.M.Z. for the whole of the southern zone. He was very nearly appointed D.M.N. for the whole country. But the British opposed it on the grounds that he was much too young. Bourgès-Maunoury then put forward the name of Chaban-Delmas for the appointment. Chaban-Delmas was a junior Treasury official with great charm, vitality and courage but scarcely older than Bourgès-Maunoury. By the time the British realized the fact, it was too late.

Chaban-Delmas became a general, while Bourgès-Maunoury, to whom he owed his appointment, remained merely a colonel as delegate to the southern zone. Jarry-Rondenay, delegate to the northern zone, also held the rank of colonel. He was later arrested and deported to Germany, where he died.

The National Military Delegate was an important personage, whose "standing and standard of living" differed considerably from those of his subordinates, the D.M.R., and even more from those of the leaders of the F.F.I. who did the actual fighting.

He was well dressed, frequently lunched in the best restaurants, enjoyed a certain social life even, and his car was driven by pretty young ladies. None of this, however, altered the fact that he was running fearful risks.

The D.M.R.s, on their regional level, were also important people, but nearer to the troops, closer to the life of the Maquis, and enjoyed merely such advantages as high rank has always conferred in every period and under all régimes. The fact that they were in direct contact with London through the B.B.C. gave them facilities for communication that were obviously lacking to subordinate officers. In the great majority of cases, they used them exclusively for the benefit of the service and military operations. On occasion, however, "Personal Messages," which were indeed such, were sent over the secret radios. A.D.M.R. might inform his family in London as to the state of his health or, alternatively, ask for news of them.

The effectiveness of the D.M.R. varied greatly according to the region he controlled and his own personality. Recruited more often than not from the bourgeoisie, senior civil servants, industrialists, or sometimes members of the liberal professions, they tended to establish satisfactory relations with the professional officers of the O.R.A., particularly with the departmental Chiefs of Staff, but were not always so successful with the leaders of the F.F.I., who were often less disciplined.

On looking through the list of D.M.R.s in office at the time of the National Insurrection, those who played a really important part can be determined at once. There was, for instance, Hirsch-Ollendorff, alias Grandval, a splendid organizer and true war leader, in Region C (Châlons). Or again, in Region M (Le Mans), Abeille, D.M.R. from September 1943 to January 1944, when he was shot, held a much more important position than any of those who succeeded him.

In certain districts, the relationship between the military delegates and the F.F.I. leaders was one of great difficulty. On the other hand, many of the F.F.I. were enthusiastically loyal to the hierarchy in London and its representatives in France, such as General Lajouanie, at Amiens, and Colonel Allard, at Le Mans, who were accepted even by the most independent of maquisards; or Colonel de Chezelles, who was sent to the P2 (Paris-Sud) region by General Revins, head of the O.R.A., and did magnificent work in reorganizing the district in very difficult circumstances following on a wave of arrests; or again, Commandant Descours, a regular cavalry officer, who at Larnes succeeded in gaining everyone's confidence and integrating the various elements of the armed Resistance as early as 1943.

On the other hand, in the adjacent regions R3, R4, and R5, Montpellier, Toulouse and Limoges, the Communist and crypto-Communist F.F.I leaders behaved as if they had been appointed to bring about the Liberation solely for the benefit of the Party. These three regions were liberated by the Maquis without the help of Regular armed forces, whether French or Allied. In consequence the Liberation had more of the nature of an insurrection than elsewhere and Communist domination appeared to be a graver menace.

In these three regions, as in Paris, the Communists made great efforts to staff the Resistance with officers on whom the C.P. could count. It looked very much as if this area of the south-east, together with the capital, had been selected by Communist headquarters as a trial of strength, if not as a base for seizing power.

This organization for the Maquis set the frame within which the extraordinary adventure of the National Insurrection was played out during the first nine months of 1944. The realities of the situation are evident in a series of secret signals exchanged between April 1944 and September 1944 (the liberation of Nancy), between the headquarters in London and Region C. (Ardennes, Bas-Rhin, Haut-Rhin, Marne, Meuse, Meurthe-et-Moselle, Moselle, Vosges) of which the D.M.R. was Grandval.

On 4 April 1944, the following was sent by General Koenig on assuming command:

Appointed by the French Committee of National Liberation to the command of the north-west theatre of operations of the French Forces both in the Interior and the Exterior under the supreme command of General Eisenhower, I shall henceforth send you your orders. You should accept no orders other than those signed by me for anything directly concerning the plans for the employment of the French Forces of the Interior—both measures for their execution and orders for attack.

This does not in any way change the orders and plans already transmitted for D-day. These are still to be put into execution on phrases from the B.B.C. for alert and action as already agreed.

On 6 June, a signal announced the start of the operations:

P. 61—6 June: Order of the Day by General Koenig: (1) The battle for the liberation is begun. I ask the representatives of the F.T.P. and O.R.A. movements to realize the necessity for total integration so as to drive the enemy from France.

P. 62—6 June: (2) All the military leaders of the Army of the Interior must be asked in my name to take their proper places in the hierarchy of command in this army.

(2) The following local ranks are conferred on those who do not at present hold a rank of at least equivalent grade: as Military Head of a Region you are appointed to the rank of lieutenant-colonel; the departmental leaders will be commandants; the leaders of groups of thirty, aspirants or second lieutenants.

P. 63—6 June: Continuation of appointments to local rank: leaders of 100 men, lieutenant; leaders of 300 men, captain; of 1,000 men, commandant; of 2,000 men and above, lieutenant-colonel. Holders of these ranks are authorized to wear the corresponding badges and will be recognized as such by French and Allied troops. The fact of holding title and wearing badges of rank is equivalent to accepting military law and discipline.

The General was setting up two hierarchies of rank within the F.F.I., one corresponding to the area and the other to the number of men under command.

On 10 June, P. 68 contained an order of great military importance since it concerned the over-hasty and too general launching of the National Insurrection:

London—P. 68—10 June: Order from General Koenig: Restrict guerrilla activities to the minimum. Impossible supply you at the moment with sufficient arms and munitions. Break off contact wherever possible to permit phase of reorganization. Avoid large concentrations, organize small isolated groups.

This order was confirmed by three succeeding signals, P. 75 to 77, dispatched on 16 June and bearing the title of General Operational Order No. 1:

The mission of the whole Army of the Interior is to fight. Nearly the whole of the air force at the disposal of the Commander-in-Chief is being used for immediate support of the bridgehead. The arming and equipping of the F.F.I. can be affected only progressively. In consequence we are limited to equipping units in an order of priority corresponding to the zones involved in the development of the battle for the liberation of France. Until the plan for arming and equipping can be realized you will avoid concentrating unarmed elements in the neighbourhood of forces already equipped. . . .

After this date, there were no further secret signals directly from Koenig. On the other hand, the D.M.R. sent him increasingly numerous appeals:

P. 210 to 215—12 July: Personal to General Koenig. I am completely destitute of money. The situation of the clandestine troops is critical. In order to live, they will soon be compelled to take action which will give the F.F.I. a bad name and upset the population. . . .

Another request from Grandval: the Germans had refused to allow the F.F.I. the status of combatants, and the D.M.R. asked London to obtain that his men be recognized as soldiers:

P. 115—12 June: May I hope that the wearers of brassards and forage caps will shortly be considered as regular members of the French Army and not as Francs-Tireurs.

The B.C.R.A. sent the F.F.I. all the information they thought might be useful to them, particularly about German espionage:

P. 83—19 June: Germans are dumping carrier pigeons in wicker baskets with English cigarettes. Carrier pigeons from England may be identified by English newspaper always placed in containers. Never give names or addresses. Merely send pigeon back.

London also organized secret rendezvous for the D.M.R. with parachuted couriers bringing him information. On 3 July, Grandval signalled:

P. 170—3 July: Your 95 of 29 June. Where will Maximum arrive? Inform you of great difficulties of movement. No trains. No cars. Some forbidden cars and bicycles in certain departments. Important I should meet Maximum to inform him political aspect of F.F.I. Alsace. Suggest Nancy on date you must inform me noon in front of cathedral. Maximum will have *Signal* in left hand. I shall have *Actu* in right hand. Shall accost Maximum and ask him way to Place d'Alliance. He will reply comes from Verdun.

London replied four days later:

P. 102—7 July: Maximum left night 6–7 via Ain department. Place and time of rendezvous agreed also recognition and passwords. Maximum will be at rendezvous every Friday and Saturday from Friday, 14 July. Description of Maximum: forty-five years of age, looks sixty, very tall, bald and with very blue eyes, heavy in body, charcoal suit, possibly blue-grey overcoat, smokes pipe.

On 14 September, the Germans began evacuating the town. They were a routed army. Grandval, who had vainly tried to hasten the American advance, decided to intervene. He signalled his intention in P. 370, whose telegraphic style failed to conceal his emotion. It was marked doubly urgent:

P. 370—14 September—D.D.—D.D.: F.F.I. launch tonight action for liberation Nancy. Considering small reserves of arms and above all munitions ask you insist Third American Army hasten entrance into the town or at least send us some tanks. *Vive de Gaulle. Vive la Lorraine. Vive la France.*

By the early hours of 15 September, all the public services were in the hands of the F.F.I. The Germans were still holding only a few positions on the outskirts of Nancy. The town had been liberated. The flags that had been made in secret were being flown. Colonel Grandval and his staff, who only yesterday had been soldiers without uniforms, were now properly dressed to receive the Allied troops.

A last message to General Koenig closed this secret exchange of signals which had been going on for so many months:

P. 376—15 September—D.D.: Personal to General Koenig: *Mon Général*, I have the honour and joy of informing you of the liberation of the capital of Lorraine. The people of Nancy are awaiting with calm and order the arrival of the Allied armies. In this splendid hour, their thoughts are turned towards the man who, during these last four years, has shown them the road to honour and liberty. *Vive de Gaulle! Vive la France éternelle!*

Colonel Grandval—Planète.

Chapter III

THE MAQUIS

1. MONT–MOUCHET

The development of the Maquis, like that of Gaullism, also took place in three phases.

Its first embryonic stages dated from the beginning of the Occupation. These consisted of simple Resistance cells inspired by men who refused to resign themselves to defeat, such as Lecompte-Boinet, Commandant Guérou, Léon des Landes and Colonel Heurtault. Most of their early members were either deported or shot.

After June 1941, the Maquis entered a second phase which was that of political recruitment. On Germany going to war against Russia, the militant socialists, trade unionists and, of course, the Communists were hunted down by the Gestapo and the Vichy police. They went into hiding outside the towns and formed cells which became the bases for the armed movements of the Resistance. Still weak in numbers, scattered and ill-armed, the Maquis was already assuming "that double character, patriotic and revolutionary, which it was to preserve until the common victory."

In 1942, there was a third phase during which the Maquis increased the number of its members by the arrival of deserters from the S.T.O. and men who had been demobilized from the Army of the Armistice. Soon they were organized by "tens" and "thirties" in a rudimentary military organization.

After the Wehrmacht marched into the free zone, the Maquis took on its final form: it became a real army, capable not only of fighting a guerrilla war, but of manœuvring and taking part in regular operations. The camp commander became a company commander and dealt with all matters of discipline, training, supply, arms and security.

In each sector a "sedentary" Maquis leader exercised control over the administrative organization. It was he who paid the men, at the rate of ten francs a day, and organized supplies; the total budget of the Maquis amounted to approximately 300 francs per day per man, covering his food, clothes and arms, as well as the "creation of six training schools, academies of guerrilla warfare, which functioned a few kilometres from the enemy garrisons, the covering of all France with a network of liaison agents, the provision of trucks for transporting arms and touring instructors, who carried sub-machine-guns in their suitcases." (Lieutenant-Colonel Michel Brault-Jérôme.)

The timetable in many Maquis was organized like that of a training camp. "After reveille and cleaning up," wrote a leader of the F.F.I., "the flag was hoisted. Then swabbing and general fatigues. After that, the time was divided into weapon training, general military instruction and games. . . . Some Maquis had sports grounds as well equipped and organized as so-called official ones. In one camp there was even a model swimming-pool. However, none of this was much use in bad weather when we had to stay indoors. . . . Some Maquis were particularly well off. One of them had tapped a power cable at a pylon on the road. They could dance in their well-lit dugouts to radio music from London." (Commandant Pierre-Paul Bernard.)

The Maquis' greatest excitement was the parachute drops by night. "Long before the time announced, the men set out the guiding lights on the terrain. When they heard the sound of engines in the distance, they lit the lights and waited impatiently for the aircraft to turn into the wind and drop its cargo, which it did from 6,000 feet. They searched for the containers in the brushwood and brambles and transported them to a previously selected hiding-place. On their return to camp, the young men made hammocks and scarves from the parachutes and used the cords for pistol lanyards."

Then the arms were issued and instructors arrived to teach the young maquisards how to use them.

All the Maquis went into action at the outset of the National Insurrection. They existed all over the country, but in certain regions, in agreement with the B.C.R.A. in London, or the D.G.S.S. in Algiers, they had created positive reduits, with mobilization centres for the incorporation of reservists on D-day with the active core. The northern zone of France, with its dense industrial population, its lack of moutains, and its great network of roads and railways, was not very favourable to the Maquis. It was only in Brittany and in the east, in that mountainous triangle dominated by the Morvan, the Jura and the Vosges, that they were at all thick on the ground.

The southern zone, on the other hand, presented great possibilities

owing to its mountainous terrain, its comparatively sparse rural population, and the fact that it had been occupied two years later than the
northern zone. From April 1943 onwards, the B.C.R.A. made great
efforts to organize and arm it. Indeed, in the southern zone, there were
great reduits which covered several departments. The Maquis did not,
of course, occupy the whole of the terrain but, organized into veritable
fortresses, it could fall on the enemy at will, keep him in a state of
permanent insecurity, harass him, inhibit his movement, and cause
him casualties.

One of these reduits was the Massif Central. A region of Maquis
mobilization centres and fortified strongpoints, it faced the Loire on the
north, the Canal du Midi and the valley of the Garonne on the south,
and the valley of the Rhône on the east. Beyond the Rhône began the
Alpine reduit. On the south, it ran down almost to the Mediterranean
coast; on the north it joined the Swiss frontier; and on the east it backed
on to the Italian frontier. But it was mostly in the west, towards the
Rhône valley, essential to the Wehrmacht's communications, that it
did most of its fighting.

A third reduit was that of the Pyrenees, which started at the Atlantic
and ceased a few miles short of the Mediterranean. It controlled the
Spanish frontier to the south, and operated towards the Garonne and
the Canal du Midi on the north.

Within these immense fortresses, there were certain points where the
fighting rose to a pitch of particular intensity. Such were, among others,
the neighbourhood of Mont-Mouchet, near Clermont-Ferrand, in the
Massif Central; and the Vercors, an Alpine massif between Grenoble
in the Isère and Die in the Drôme.

The battle of Mont-Mouchet, perhaps the most important owing to the
size of the forces engaged, was born of a strategic illusion.

The 2,700 armed maquisards who assembled, on 15 May, among the
Margeride mountains, some 4,500 feet above sea-level, and the 10,000
men who, as in August 1914 and September 1939, obeyed the order for
a levy in mass, issued on 20 May 1944 by the regional commander of
the Auvergne F.F.I., Coulaudon, alias Colonel Gaspard, were convinced
that Mont-Mouchet was a reduit to which an Allied airborne corps,
known as Force C, was to be flown in by parachute and glider.

In the terminology of the French headquarters in London, there
were three forces. Force A consisted of the French detachments which
were to take part in the landings in the north; Force B consisted of the
French troops who were to form de Lattre's army for the landing in the

south; while a third force was to be sent into the interior of occupied France and there liberate a zone which, once captured and heavily fortified, would make it possible for advanced elements of the C.F.L.N., representing French sovereign power, to begin to exercise their functions without waiting for the complete evacuation of the country. This plan had been originated by the internal Resistance, and had been considered between February and April 1944 by the C.O.M.A.C., on the suggestion of General Revers, head of the O.R.A. In April, Guillain de Benouville and Bertin-Chevance, both of whom were to become local generals, went to London to discuss it. After study, the plan was discarded by Supreme Headquarters. The maquisards, however, were never told of this decision and continued to believe that it would be carried out.

Some time during the latter part of April, at Montluçon, Colonel Gaspard met an Englishman, called "Philippe," who had been parachuted in. He believed him to have "an important job in the southern zone." In fact, "Philippe" seems merely to have been one of the many Jedburgh liaison officers who were at that time being sent to the Resistance movements.

During the course of their conversation, Gaspard mentioned his difficulties, the enthusiasm of his troops but their lack of weapons. "Philippe quietly made notes. . . . Could he count on this mass of volunteers, which Gaspard estimated at 15,000 men over the four adjacent departments, when the landings took place?" He could. Upon which "Philippe" drafted a long signal to London. He was full of enthusiasm for the Force C plan and promised to do everything in his power for the F.F.I.

Gaspard presumed that everything had been settled. At an isolated house near Paulhaget, he assembled the leaders of the Resistance organizations. Combat was represented by Ingrand (alias Rouvres), the future Commissaire de la République, as well as by Gaspard himself; there were representatives of Libération, Francs-Tireurs, and the M.O.F. with Raymond Perrier; of the F.T.P. with Roger Vallon; and of the Socialist and Communist Parties with Aufouvre, alias Carlos, and Eldin, alias Charles. This "Grand Council of the Resistance of Auvergne" also included the leaders of the other departments in Region R6: Blaise for the Haute-Loire, Pierre for the Cantal and so on. Ingrand, who took the chair, asked Gaspard to explain the Maquis plan of operations in support of Force C.

Three reduits were planned, one in the Margeride mountains, where extensive forests lent themselves to guerrilla warfare, another on the borders of the Haute-Lozère, with its twisting roads, and a third in the Lioran massif. The operation would require 10,000 to 15,000 men, whereas at the moment only 2,700 had arms. But "Philippe" was expected to supply the deficiencies.

"Do you approve the proposed plan?" Gaspard asked. "Do you undertake, when the signal is given, to send all your men to the reduits allotted you?"

There was unanimous assent. It merely remained to plan the details of the operations and to await the landings which were expected to take place during the last fortnight in May or the first fortnight in June.

During May, the troop concentrations were planned and executed. Gaspard made a reconnaissance of the terrain. For his headquarters and concentration area he selected a forester's lodge, called Mont-Mouchet, in the Margeride hills. It had a sound tactical position. Lying in the heart of an extensive forest, whole companies could be concentrated in the area with no risk of detection from the air. It was also at the intersection of a number of roads and was in communication by telephone to suitable places for advanced posts. This, it was hoped, would prevent the enemy taking them by surprise. It was a big house and had one very large room in which the staff was installed. Officers and other ranks lived a communal life and there reigned an atmosphere of good-fellowship. Everyone wandered in and out of the office regardless of the staff's confidential discussions or, indeed, of the screams of captured Gestapo agents being put to the question in the next room.

To assist Colonel Gaspard, one of the three or four senior Regular officers, who had decided to join the Maquis from the military region of Clermont-Ferrand, arrived in the month of May. Colonel Garcie said: "I want to join you as a soldier not as an officer. Use me as you think best, I simply want to serve."

Garcie, however, became Chief of Staff. His rather finical concern with detail and sometimes excessive regard for regulations were not without their use among these unorthodox and rather undisciplined soldiers. It was also in May that Gaspard made contact with one of the most extraordinary of the Resistance *corps-francs*. Its very name was significant: "*Les Truands*".[1] And the pseudonyms its members adopted were an extraordinary mixture of the historical and the melodramatic. Their leader, who styled himself "Chief of the Corps of Francs-Tireurs of the Volunteer Division of the Auvergne Resistance," called himself "Judex"; his second-in-command "Danton"; and other members "Spada" after the Corsican bandit, "Barberousse," "Tonio," "Milou" and "Irma." They numbered thirty, were born fighters and had already created a legend. It was said of them that they shared everything in common,

[1] "The Vagabonds".

including women, particularly female prisoners; and that to become a "*sacré Truand*" there was an initiation ceremony at which the neophyte had to drink a mixture composed of three-quarters of a litre of red wine, three-quarters of a litre of white wine and three-quarters of a litre of brandy. After which, presumably, he was in a proper state to set about campaigning. In action, the Truands certainly lived up to their reputation. On 23 April, they opened the sabotage campaign in Auvergne. So as to paralyze German war industry, which in the Massif Central, in the valley of the Loire, and even in part of the Paris region, depended for its power on Monistrol, they were mainly responsible for blowing up 147 high-tension pylons within a few hours. Another day "Danton," with ten men and two sub-machine-guns, made a raid on Langeac and bluffed over a hundred Germans in the barracks to surrender.

During rest periods, these "odd chaps" liked to stay in the old châteaux round Saint-Flour, whose aristocratic proprietors they were apt to scandalize. In the fighting at Mont-Mouchet, they distinguished themselves by their courage under fire. Over two-thirds of them were killed. When the Liberation came, their unit, which had been re-formed, was among the first to enter Vichy. The ostentatious entry of "Judex" into the temporary capital of France marked the end of the régime.

While still establishing contact with these shock troops, at the beginning of May, Gaspard received a parachuted mission consisting of three British members. Captain John seemed at first rather distant and reserved, but quickly became friendly; Andrée was a square-shouldered, rock-solid Englishwoman with a loud voice, who nevertheless had a French mother and had lived for a long time in Marseilles; while Denis, a successful London actor, who had escaped from the Gestapo, though not before they had broken his teeth with a mallet and pulled his ankles out of joint, was despite these tortures an exhilarating and agreeable companion. The mere fact of their presence nourished Gaspard's illusions. If his conversation with "Philippe" had led London to send him reinforcements such as these, surely it was because the plan had been agreed and Force C was being made ready.

The Mont-Mouchet position was organized under the command of Garcie. Two concentration areas were set up, one in the Cheires de Pont-Gibaud for the men who absconded each night from Clermont-Ferrand, and another at Vins-Haut, where a new Maquis was formed. The units already organized camped in the forest by the streams on the high plateaux. The only trouble was that at 4,500 feet the weather was cold and wet, there were still snowdrifts in places, and the new soldiers were often short of warm clothes.

Nor was Colonel Garcie content till he had set up a proper staff at Mont-Mouchet. He made Colonel Mondange, alias Thomas, his assistant Chief of Staff, and organized the headquarters into the four classic staff sections. He also set up mechanical, medical, transport, sabotage, engineer, supply, *corps-francs*, liaison, information and signal departments. There were armourers' shops, garages and stores. Indeed, it was as if Colonel Garcie had brought all the departments of the 13th Military Region, if not their personnel, in his knapsack.

On 20 May, now that he had an organization for the proper reception of volunteers, Colonel Gaspard issued the order for a levy in mass.

Order No. 1.

The Army of the Liberation has now been formed in the heart of the Auvergne mountains.

I must remind responsible leaders that, apart from men who have some special job (sabotage, purging, intelligence), it is the duty of every man without exception (whether sedentary or in the Maquis) to join us.

Defaulters will cease to be members of the French Forces of the Interior of the Liberation.

Each man must bring with him:

His best pair of shoes and clogs;

Socks and body linen;

One or two warm blankets;

Arms, if he has received them;

If possible, a tent or tarpaulin to every ten men.

The leaders of groups must make sure of a truck for the transport of their troops.

It is important that the men should join at once before the roads are closed and the German plan (black list) is put into effect.

In the Maquis,
20 May 1944,
The Regional Commander of the F.F.I.
GASPARD

N.B. Prepare a list of the men whose departure may entail a demand for help for their families.

It was no less than an order for general mobilization. No longer was it merely a matter of recruiting volunteers, but of ordering up Reservists. The military machine was being set in motion on the orders of an improvised officer, a reserve list sergeant in the Medical Corps, now playing the part of a senior commander.

Of those called to the colours, there were some, as always, who obeyed with no great enthusiasm. They went because they were ordered to, because they were afraid of sanctions, or because public opinion in their village brought pressure to bear on them. There were too, during these first days, many who lined up at the Mont-Mouchet dispensary, hoping the doctor would discharge them.

The F.T.P. did not comply with the order at this time. They waited till June, till after the battle of Mont-Mouchet and the fighting in the Cantal, before joining the main body of troops. The reason for their recalcitrance is made clear in an intercepted message: "The Gaullists are shortly taking to the mountains; we must stay in the towns to seize power."

But most of the men called up reported with enthusiasm.

The mobilization brought the personnel at Mont-Mouchet alone to over 3,000 men. Nos. 7 to 12 Companies were formed. A hand printing-press was set up and a newspaper, *Le Mur d'Auvergne*, published.

Food had to be procured. A foray on Montluçon, some 250 kilometres away, resulted in ten tons of sardines for the Maquis.

The Laurent group, in the Lozère, captured 6,000 leather jackets "manufactured for the Marshal," which clothed all the maquisards of the Margeride and the Truyère. There were also regular air drops of bazookas, machine-guns and sub-machine-guns.

The first battle took place on 2 June. The Germans, who were clearly unaware of the strength of the Maquis forces, mounted the attack with an S.S. battalion from Mende. It consisted of 800 men and, on arriving at Paulhac, was sent straight into the attack supported by a number of mortars. No. 2 Company received the weight of the attack. When their ammunition ran short, the Truands brought up further supplies. After some hard fighting, the attack was halted early in the afternoon. A counter-attack on their rear forced the Germans to abandon the field, leaving their dead and wounded behind them.

This was the Mont-Mouchet Maquis' first victory and it occurred four days before the landings in Normandy.

Between 2 and 10 June, taking advantage of a respite they knew could be only temporary, the Maquis set about organizing the defences. Roads and bridges were mined, dugouts built or improved. To "purge" the district of its numerous spies and militiamen, a military tribunal was set up. Its verdicts were without appeal.

Volunteers continued to flow in. From the mobilization centre at Vins-Haut, they were sent to the neighbouring reduit of Truyère, where 1,500 men were assembled, or to Saint-Genès, where Commandant

Mabrut had concentrated more than 2,000 volunteers, who soon increased to 6,000. Arms, alas, still continued to be in short supply for some weeks. Nevertheless, taking into account the contingents from the Haute-Loire, amounting to 800 men, the total number of effectives concentrated in the reduits in this part of the Massif Central amounted to over 10,000 men. Colonel Gaspard had assumed the responsibilities of a general.

However, the little German observation plane, known as the "Mouchard," was continually flying over the districts were these concentrations were taking place. But at night the sky belonged to the Allies as they dropped the Maquis arms.

It was clear that the big battle was imminent. The messages, so long awaited, for putting into execution the Green and Violet Plans were broadcast; then the landings were announced. Which would arrive first, Force C or the Wehrmacht?

On the morning of the 10th, the fifteen companies of Mont-Mouchet and the three *corps-francs* were attacked by a German division: over 11,000 men, supported by armoured cars, against less than 3,000, armed with only light weapons.

There were many heroic actions in this unequal battle. Near Ruines and Clavières, the German armoured cars forced the roadblocks, though the leading one turned over. The maquisards repelled the attack in hand-to-hand fighting.

Elsewhere, Lieutenant Fred and twenty of his men were killed "when audaciously attacking the enemy, who was in immensely superior numbers, and refusing to retreat, even though they were then partly and eventually completely overrun."

Their sacrifice enabled No. 10 and No. 14 Companies to contain the enemy till nightfall.

The result of the day's fighting was very creditable to the Maquis. At Monistrol, the enemy was driven back and abandoned two guns and one armoured car, leaving many dead on the field. At Pinols, they retreated; and they evacuated Clavières, Lorcières and the farms in the valley.

Nevertheless, it was clear that the Maquis must begin their withdrawal that night. Owing to the firm stands at Pinols and Monistrol, the road to the south was still open. Orders were issued to evacuate the transport, and the reserves of food and clothing to the Truyère reduit during the night, to break off contact next day and retreat through the woods to avoid further casualties.

During the night, the Maquis Intelligence learned that 200 German trucks were on their way from Clermont-Ferrand, carrying some 4,000 to 5,000 men. In the morning, these fresh troops came into action in the Clavières sector.

The Maquis could do no other than hold out till nightfall. Orders were issued to the companies to fire with deliberation. The evacuation was fixed for 22.00.

All units fought well throughout the day. The machine-gunners of No. 10 Company killed hundreds of Germans as they advanced in close formation. No. 14 Company both suffered and inflicted heavy losses.

Through field-glasses, the besieged could see the German ambulances laden with dead and wounded going back and forth between the front and Saint-Flour. This was no guerrilla fighting, but a pitched battle.

At 22.00 the withdrawal began. Harassed but in good order, the 3,000 maquisards, whom artillery, aircraft and 15,000 [1] well-trained and well-armed men could not overrun, moved to their new positions in the Truyère massif.

The battle cost the Germans 1,400 dead and 1,700 wounded. On the French side, the Truands, Colonel Thomas's battalion, and Nos. 3 and 14 Companies were the hardest hit. They lost 160 dead and 100 wounded.

There was an even greater concentration of men in the Truyère than at Mont-Mouchet. At Saint-Genès, a reception Maquis, men called to the colours were still continuing to arrive. Apart from the troops evacuated from Mont-Mouchet, they soon numbered 6,000 of which barely 800 were armed. Still more were due to come in from Mont-Dore, Latour, Besse, Touves and Bourboule. At the news of fighting the whole country was on the move. Message after message was sent to London asking for arms and air support. Colonel Gaspard set up his headquarters at Saint-Martial, a loyal village, which suffered greater destruction than almost any other in the Cantal. In a neighbouring wood, the parachuted containers of arms, ammunition and explosives were unpacked, sorted and distributed. Contact was established with the Corrèze Maquis, of whom one of the leaders, Captain Duret, paid a visit to Saint-Martial.

With more weapons available it became possible to increase the number of effective combatants in the Truyère to thirty companies totalling approximately 4,000 men. On 18 June 1944, the fourth anniversary of de Gaulle's appeal, an extraordinary ceremony took place in the little square of Saint-Martial. Everyone was well aware of the danger threatening, of the weakness of the Maquis' resources and of

[1] This figure is the Maquis' own estimate of the size of the German force engaged.

7. *Michel Debré,*
"the Commission."

8. *Georges Bidault.*

9. General Pierre Koenig, commanding the Free French Forces in Great Britain and the French Forces of the Interior.

10. Colonel Passy (foreground, second from right), head of the B.C.R.A., conferring with Colonel Marceau of the Brittany F.F.I.

11. Jacques Soustelle, head of the D.G.S.S.

Soustelle, Passy, and Koenig were the three heads directing the National Insurrection.

12. Jean Prévost of the Vercors, a few days before his death.

13. André Malraux, alias Colonel Berger.

how precarious was the freedom that made such an assembly possible. Yet, in this village vowed to destruction, in the presence of a crowd of civilians, many of whom were to suffer a worse fate than that of the fighting men themselves, there took place, under a sky continually traversed by enemy aircraft, an impeccable parade of the troops of the Resistance. Henri Ingrand, Commissaire de la République of a region still under occupation, made his first official public speech.

Then Gaspard spoke: "Soon we shall go down into the towns and the death of our comrades will be avenged by the liberation of our country and the utter defeat of the German forces."

The F.F.I. marched past. "A section of Truands came by with a swinging step. Tough though they were, they could not that day hide their emotion; they had lost many of their original members in the fighting at Mont-Mouchet: Danton, Spada and Fred had sacrificed their lives to hold up the German advance and make the withdrawal possible. During the march past, a German aircraft flew over the village and gave it a burst of machine-gun fire. It was a reminder of the dangers which threatened."

The next day, 19 June, the situation grew even more complicated. Young men began trying to reach Saint-Martial from all the neighbouring villages. The local leaders had misunderstood the orders, or misinterpreted the B.B.C. messages, and had begun to recruit men who had never previously been in touch with the Maquis at all. It was a general mobilization. The same thing happened south of the Puy-de-Dôme, where there was a complete levy in mass. Hundreds of volunteers who could not possibly be armed caused considerable congestion at Saint-Genès.

From this massive influx of recruits, with most of whom he did not know what to do, Gaspard with some difficulty sifted out a few of the more promising and formed three further companies. But they needed to be trained before they could be used in battle.

But time, it was clear, was running out. German troops were moving up. There were Intelligence reports of convoys coming from all directions. The besieged, numbering 4,000 men, divided into thirty companies, had ammunition sufficient for only one day's fighting and the terrain was suitable for enemy tanks.

On 20 June, the battle began. Nearly 20,000 men, supported by tanks, artillery and aircraft, attacked 4,000 maquisards armed only with light weapons. No. 7 Company held the main weight of the enemy attack throughout the day; giving way only at nightfall.

At 22.00, in the Saint-Martial headquarters, which had been machine-gunned by Messerschmitts, the staff drew up orders for withdrawal. A ten-year-old boy, known as Porte-Plume, was acting as secretary and he typed out the orders for retreat by the light of an electric torch. They were sent out by liaison officers in cars, on motor-bicycles or on foot.

Since he was without precise information as to the strength of the German forces or their plan of attack, Colonel Gaspard left a wide initiative to his companies. He envisaged a star-shaped withdrawal and merely indicated to each company its first stage.

The withdrawal took place towards the Lioran massif that night and without serious casualties.

There was one tragic incident. Eighty-five wounded maquisards, of whom eighteen were serious cases, made their way to a wood where they hid as best they could. A French traitor showed the Germans their hiding-place. Nine of the more seriously wounded were dispatched and the Germans paid the traitor 400,000 francs for his services.

The casualties at Mont-Mouchet and in the Truyère, according to the figures claimed by the F.F.I. after the Liberation, amounted to 3,500 German and 350 French. Colonel Gaspard never forgave the Allies for not keeping their promises over the parachuting of arms and, in particular, over Force C, which had in fact never existed. Having learned from experience, the Auvergne F.F.I. gave up fighting pitched battles and devoted itself entirely to guerrilla action.

The F.T.P. and the O.R.A. continued the fight. An agreement putting an end to their differences was signed on 14 July at the Laigles dam. Henceforth their activities could be co-ordinated. The Mont-Mouchet F.F.I., most of whom had escaped from the German attempt to encircle them, were able to continue the struggle to liberate Auvergne.

2. THE VERCORS

The men who fought in the Vercors suffered a very different fate.

Of all the episodes of the Liberation, none is more shocking, none more mysterious. Overwhelmed by the enemy, the maquisards believed they had been sacrificed and betrayed for partisan reasons. Though some of the accusations made are extravagant, it is difficult to prove that the attitude of many of the survivors and of the families of the dead is altogether unjustified. When politics become mixed up with a matter of this kind, passions are unlikely to be calmed or thought clarified.

On 21 July 1944, in the middle of the battle, two radio messages to London and Algiers were sent from Chapelle-en-Vercors. One was from the military commander of the Vercors, Colonel Huet. Transmitted by Captain de Nadaillac, it read more or less as follows: "We shall not forget the bitterness of having been abandoned alone and without support in time of battle." From Regular officers such a message speaks volumes.

The other was even more outspoken. Chavant, the civilian head of the Vercors, did not mince his words: "If you do not take immediate action, we shall be at one with the local population in saying that you people in London and Algiers have entirely failed to understand the situation in which we are placed, and we shall consider you to be cowards and criminals. Repeat cowards and criminals."

The Vercors is one of those places that might have been specially created for partisans to fight in. Its configuration for once justifies the term "natural fortress." There are other districts in France that lie behind steep approaches forming a natural line of resistance to an invader; he may turn them, but he cannot cross them. Such is the massif of the Grande-Chartreuse, not far from the Vercors, which also became a hide-out for the maquisards. But the Vercors seems to have been constructed by nature as the perfect citadel; indeed it might almost have been designed by Vauban. It is a precipitous quadrilateral, some fifty kilometres from north to south, and varying between fifteen and twenty from east to west. The only break in the rampart to the high plateau is towards the valley of the Isère, in the direction of Grenoble, where Saint-Nizier is the one weak point in the natural defences.

In all, eight roads penetrate to the plateau. Two surmount passes of over 3,000 feet, while the others run through cuttings or tunnels hewn in the living rock. They can all be easily denied to an enemy. There are also some twenty mountain tracks, all well known and easy to defend. Finally, there are the water-courses, in summer full of loose stones and in winter of snow water. A few armed mountaineers are sufficient to guard them.

In some places the plateau is broken by deep, perpendicular valleys. To have driven roads through them was a considerable feat of engineering in the old days and the names of the engineers were commemorated by plaques. Today, the names of the maquisards who died in the defence of these valleys are similarly recorded. This chaos of rocks, with their perilously clinging trees, assumes here and there, at certain times of the day, strange outlines. There is a "Virgin of the Vercors"; and elsewhere three needles of rock are known as "The Three Maidens." The "Maidens" stand not far from Saint-Nizier and were used as an observation post during the first battles. There are also a few valleys running longitudinally and parallel to each other. In these the contours are less steep; they are served by fairly good roads and are an attraction to tourists, for which some of the villages cater. They also support a certain amount of dairy farming, potato growing, and the usual Alpine agriculture.

Between the valleys lie extensive forests. Consisting mostly of fir trees, there is also a kind of ash which is peculiar to the region; its deciduous leaves form the mould for the evergreens, and its comparatively hard wood is used for making clogs.

In the north, the villages and farmlands of the Vercors look typically Alpine; while, in the south, the influence of Provence is apparent in the flat roofs and the aspect of the fields. There are relatively few towns, but many villages and isolated farms. The Vercors has an air of self-sufficiency, as if it were a sort of island fortress anchored between the valleys of the Rhône and the Isère. Once the lair of Mandrin, the famous brigand chief, in 1944 the Vercors once again became the refuge of the outlaw, but now he was serving his country.

The Vercors first became a bastion of the Resistance towards the end of 1942 and the beginning of 1943 due to an alliance between two still rather embryonic organizations.

The Dauphinois section of the Franc-Tireur movement with which the original Vercors group, under Doctor Ravalec, had become amalgamated, had begun to recruit defaulters from the S.T.O. and concentrate them in the woods at Ambel (1 January 1943), then at Meaudre, Autrons and Vassieux.

There was also a little group, formed by a surveyor, Pierre Dalloz, which had reconnoitred the massif from the viewpoint of its becoming a reception area for the underground and a concentration zone for Allied airborne forces.

In November 1942, "Franc-Tireur" began directing defaulters to the plateau. They were mostly labourers, artisans and students. A few officers and other ranks from the Army of the Armistice helped organize and train them, but as individuals and not on any organized basis.

Generally speaking, the Resistance organizations of the army, in spite of the pressing demands of certain Regular officers, such as Commandant Pourchier, refused to compromise themselves by forming cadres for the Maquis. In November 1942, after the invasion of the free zone, whole units from Grenoble, complete with the headquarters staff, took to the Maquis. But instead of doing the natural thing and joining the

Maquis in the Vercors, they set off towards Uriage and had very soon to turn back.

In the first instance, therefore, it was civilians who came to their help. Besides Doctor Martin, the socialist mayor of Grenoble, whose official position did not prevent his taking risks and becoming one of the principal supporters of the Vercors, the real founder of the Maquis was Aimé Pupin, alias Mathieu, the proprietor of a little café in the Rue de Polygone in Grenoble. His assistants were known as Ernest and Clément. Ernest, whose real name was Eugène Samuel Ravalec, was a doctor who had had to give up his practice and had become a chemist at Villars-de-Lans. He had raised the first Resistance groups in the Vercors. Having been put in touch with Mathieu by Doctor Martin, he became his second-in-command and replaced him at the head of the Maquis on 28 May 1943, when Mathieu was arrested. Clément, whose real name was Eugène Chavant, was also a café proprietor. At the start, his job was to recruit personnel for the Maquis. He interviewed the candidates and allowed only those of whom he was sure to go up the mountain. He held his secret meetings at the Allemand ironmonger's in the Rue Lediguières in Grenoble. He eventually became the civilian head of the Vercors with the rank of sub-prefect and it was he who sent the famous last signal.

Chavant, though something of a local politician, was not much of a diplomat; he was forthright, rather abrupt in manner and had had a splendid record in the First World War. He was typical of the fierce spirit of the Vercors Resistance. Guard dog to a portion of French soil, or rather a wild boar emerging from the forest with the determination to drive the enemy from the plateau, he was never interested in the political aspects of the extraordinary adventure through which he lived. The fierce simplicity which made of him so heroic a fighter served him ill when he visited Algiers in May 1944 and had to negotiate with high officials and Allied leaders. One of his more fantastic dreams was to set up a radio transmitter near Villars-de-Lans and get de Gaulle to come and broadcast.

The original team also included a tax collector, a bank manager, a journalist, an ironmonger, a railway employee and a taxi driver. They were all peaceable people in a comparatively small way whose patriotism brought them unaccustomed responsibilities. However dissimilar they might be, they all put their shoulders to the same wheel. Indeed, in one village the priest and the local pimp fought side by side.

By and large, the Vercors was politically Left, but not of the extreme

Left; the elected representatives had been radical socialist or socialist for a long time past. There were few Communists.

Under the leadership of these men, the Vercors became just one more Maquis among so many others, better served by the terrain, no doubt, but with no ambitions beyond being a refuge to the disaffected till the Liberation and then harassing the retreating German Army.

However, on the edge of the plateau, in an isolated farm in the Sassenage hills, a more ambitious fate had been in preparation for the Vercors for over a year.

In March 1941, by the dim light that filtered into the farm, a man was busy writing. He was an architect, had once been a mountain climber, and his name was Pierre Dalloz. Having abandoned his profession during the Occupation, he was filling his days by translating Saint Bernard's *Considération*, "authentic spiritual dynamite," particularly in a period of occupation. When the cold numbed his fingers, he went out with an axe into the snow-bound forest and got warm by felling a tree.

In this retreat of his he was often visited by two friends who were both to be killed in the Resistance. One was a professor called René Gosse and the other the writer Jean Prévost. Jean Prévost was at that time writing a book on Stendhal and often came to do research in the Grenoble library.

In March 1941 Pierre Dalloz and his wife received a visit from Jean Prévost and his wife, Claude. During the course of this visit, Dalloz and Prévost had a conversation which was to determine the fate of the Vercors. Pointing to the rocks above them, Dalloz said: "There's a sort of island fastness up there, two cantons of plateau protected on every side by a great wall of China. The approaches to it are few and all cut out of the rock. They could be barred, and with the advantage of surprise whole battalions of paratroops could be dropped there."

The idea appealed to Jean Prévost, who from then on was continually turning it over in his mind, at first merely as an intellectual problem, but later as a real military possibility, and indeed this young writer, one of the most gifted of his generation, was to die in a valley of the Vercors.

The idea began to take shape in Pierre Dalloz's mind too. In December 1942, he talked it over with a young friend, Jean Lefort, who knew the plateau well and had explored its cliffs and caves.

The next night, at the farm, Dalloz wrote a two-page memorandum: "The plan had ripened in my mind. My ideas fell into shape on the paper without difficulty."

A few days later, in January 1943, he took the Lyons train with Jean

Lefort. He had an appointment with an important Resistance leader, Yves Farge, the talented painter and art critic, who was at that time concealing less aesthetic activities behind the façade of his editorship of the *Progrès de Lyon*. The meeting took place in the Brasserie du Tonneau in the Rue de la République, not far from the newspaper's offices. Dalloz had his memorandum on the Vercors in his pocket. Farge promised to submit it to Jean Moulin, alias Max, de Gaulle's representative in France. The following week, on 31 January, Farge came to Grenoble. He said: "Max is enthusiastic about your plan. Here's some money. Get to work at once."

On 12 February 1943, Dalloz and Farge met General Charles Delestraint, the highest military authority in the Resistance. Delestraint, though now sixty-five, was still a first-class soldier. Of a religious turn of mind, and ascetic in his habit of life, he possessed a dynamic vitality which was the envy of his juniors. He had been one of the first senior officers to grasp the importance of the ideas put forward by the pre-war Colonel de Gaulle. Nor was his admiration for, and deference to, his junior ever affected in the least by the relative number of stars they wore on their respective sleeves. Entirely free from both fear and prejudice, to join the Resistance seemed to him an inescapable duty, while the Maquis, though it might fail to conform to the drill book, was nevertheless the proper and necessary form for the struggle against the occupying power to assume.

He was short and round-faced, with a healthy pink and white complexion. He held himself very straight and had an air of authority, intelligence and determination. He met Dalloz off the Lyons train at the platform barrier at Bourg Station. They were able to recognize each other because Dalloz was carrying a copy of *Signal*, and the General was wearing a grey overcoat with a white silk handkerchief in the breast pocket. They held their meeting in an insurance office; the shutters were closed and the atmosphere peculiarly stuffy.

General Delestraint, whose real name was Vidal, had no personal knowledge of the Vercors. Dalloz answered his questions and showed him his plan, which consisted of three typewritten pages, together with a map, a tourist guide and a number of photographs. These the General took with him to London at the next moon.

Dalloz informed the General of two most disappointing interviews he had had with senior regular officers.

"Leave them to their sleep," said Delestraint. "I'll take charge of the Vercors. Which is the largest group there?"

"Franc-Tireur is the only group, *mon Général*."

"In that case, we must support Franc-Tireur. You can use my name to stamp on anyone who tries to interfere. The Vercors must be treated on a national military level. From now on we'll forget the name of Vercors and refer to the operation as 'Montagnards'."

A fortnight later, the General was in London. In his farm at Sassenage, Pierre Dalloz was listening one night, as usual, to the B.B.C. Suddenly there was a "Personal Message" that concerned him: "The Montagnards must continue to climb the peaks."

This was proof that headquarters in London had been persuaded by General Delestraint to agree to his plan. It was a decisive stage in the history of the Vercors.

The Montagnards plan, as conceived by Pierre Dalloz, was at once large in scale, precise, audacious and coherent. It was not their intention to play at being soldiers against the Occupation forces with their great superiority in arms and numbers. The Germans would undoubtedly have the last word. To set up a reduit, a permanent fortress isolated in occupied France, was precisely the sort of temptation that must be resisted. The examples of the plateau of Glières, where the battle, however heroic, ended in disaster, and that of the Auvergne Maquis, which only succeeded in continuing to exist by giving up too ambitious a plan, were to show that Pierre Dalloz's judgement was only too correct. His plan, of which both General Delestraint and London approved, was quite different. The Vercors must be made ready to fight at any moment; but it was not to go on to the offensive till the right moment came; and this was in conjunction with the landings in the south of France, when it would attack the shaken Wehrmacht in the rear. In these circumstances, the natural fortress and the troops garrisoning it could be used with the maximum effect and would have the best chance of success. It would obviously be a tough assignment, but the battle would be short and sharp. It was recognized, of course, that the combatants of the Vercors, in spite of all the care taken to train and arm them, could have neither the stubbornness nor the fire-power even of a shaken Wehrmacht. But the Germans would be involved at the same time with an adversary at least as strong as themselves in the Allied armies. And for these final battles the combatants of the Vercors, operating in the rear areas and on the German lines of retreat, could be reinforced by airborne troops, which Pierre Dalloz had made it quite clear were essential to his plan.

"If the Vercors plan can be put into effect," wrote Pierre Dalloz, "it must be done by surprise and against a distressed and disorganized enemy. . . . It will not be a matter of attacking an enemy in full possession of his resources, but of intervening to aggravate his disorder. It will not be a matter of taking root in the Vercors, but of using it as a springboard from which to attack. It will not be a matter of holding out, but of driving forward in all directions."

In fact, exactly the opposite occurred due to a tragic misunderstanding.

When, in March 1943, London broadcast the phrase accepting the Montagnards plan, a fourfold agreement was implied.

(1) That a sufficient number of men should be mobilized round the nucleus of the existing Vercors Maquis to create an effective force for intervention when the moment came.

(2) That enough arms to equip light units to harass the enemy would be parachuted in.

(3) That offensive action would be ordered only within the framework of the impending general operations and that this intervention would be short and sharp.

(4) That airborne troops would be sent in support.

General Delestraint, on his return from London, confirmed that there were no misunderstandings between the Allied staffs and the B.C.R.A. on the one hand, and between the maquisards and Pierre Dalloz on the other.

In April 1943, he went to the Vercors. He visited Dalloz at the Sassenage farm and assembled a fighting committee, which immediately undertook the work of organization.

The first stage was to co-ordinate the committee, the Maquis on the plateau and the defaulters' camps.

Aimé Pupin, who had recently become leader of the local Franc-Tireur movement, when approached by Dalloz expressed relief at the thought of obtaining financial and administrative support for his camps. He accepted the proposal and became a member of the committee.

The committee at this time consisted of Yves Farge, Pierre Dalloz, Commandant Marcel Pourchier, who was soon to leave the Vercors for the Alpes-Maritimes, only to be deported and die, Captain Alain Le Ray, François Mauriac's son-in-law, Rémy Bayle de Sessé, and Pupin.

Four specific duties were distributed among the members of the committee:

(1) To enlist the assistance of anyone who could contribute usefully to the common effort (Farge, Dalloz, Bayle de Sessé);

(2) To organize regular liaison with the government of Algiers (Farge);

(3) To draw up a detailed plan of operations (Le Ray);

(4) To organize recruiting, training and the administration of the camps (Le Ray and Pupin).

Many local contacts were also made with influential people and organizations such as the Ponts et Chaussées, the Eaux et Forêts, and the hydro-electric works. Haulage contractors helped with the transport of supplies and arms.

By this time, there were nine camps of defaulters on the plateau, containing in all about 350 men. Officers and non-commissioned officers of the demobilized Army of the Armistice began to arrive in the Vercors, and played an increasing part in its organization.

Unfortunately, on 27 May 1943, a raid on a gasoline store failed and fourteen young Francs-Tireurs from the plateau were arrested by the Italian Bolzano battalion. Under interrogation by the Italian secret service, the O.V.R.A., they broke down. As a result, Bayle de Sessé, Aimé Pupin and their principal assistants were arrested. Pourchiers, who was in danger, escaped to the Alpes-Maritimes, where he organized other Maquis. Farge, whose wife was arrested, left Lyons for Paris, where he became president of the secret committee for action against deportation. And Dalloz, in agreement with General Delestraint, went to London taking with him the detailed Montagnards plan.

Of the first leaders of the Vercors, who had done the basic organizing and the negotiating with London, there remained only General Delestraint, Le Ray and Chavant. Then, on 9 June 1943, General Delestraint was arrested by the Gestapo in Paris as he came out of the Pompe métro station, where he was to meet René Hardy. After being a prisoner for twenty-two months, he was killed in Dachau on 22 April 1945, a few days before the arrival of the Americans. His arrest, which deprived the Montagnards plan of its principal guarantor, was an irreparable disaster for the Vercors.

Captain Le Ray and Doctor Ravalec, second-in-command to Pupin, who had also escaped the disaster, now made contact with each other. And through Ravalec, Le Ray also got into contact with Chavant, who was at this time the Vercors representative in Grenoble, and now agreed to go up to the plateau. The Vercors began to reorganize itself for D-day, planning as ever for the moment when the Germans would be in difficulties and could be attacked with the help of the Allied airborne force. Until the very end, this airborne force was to the maquisards of the Vercors what Grouchy's corps had been to Napoleon at Waterloo. It was discussed, awaited and prepared for, till, at the last, it was actually seen to be arriving—only, alas, it turned out not to be the Allies.

From the military point of view, the Vercors was divided into two

The Vercors

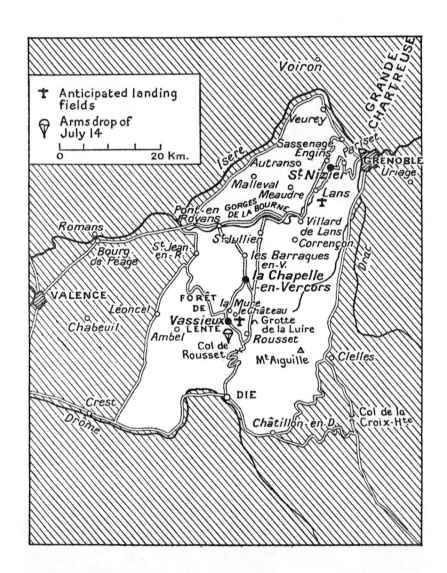

Anticipated landing fields

Arms drop of July 14

0 ____ 20 Km.

Voiron

GRANDE CHARTREUSE

Veurey

Sassenage
Engins
Autrans
Malleval
Meaudre
St Nizier
Lans

Villard
de Lans
Corrençon

Pont-en-
Royans
GORGES DE LA BOURNE

St Jean
en-R.

St Jullien

les Barraques
en-V.
la Chapelle
-en-Vercors

Isère

Romans

Bourg
de Péage

VALENCE

Léoncel

Chabeuil

FORÊT
DE
LENTE

Vassieux

Ambel

Col de
Rousset

la Mure
le Château

Grotte
de la Luire
Rousset

Col de
Rousset

Mt Aiguille

Clelles

DIE

Châtillon-en-D.

Col de la
Croix-Hte

Crest

Drôme

Pariset
GRENOBLE
Uriage

Drac

sectors, occupied by groups who frequently failed to agree. The northern sector was under the command of Commandant Costa de Beauregard, alias Durieux; the southern under Commandant Geyer, alias Thivollet, whose headquarters were near Chavant's. In June 1943, a second fighting committee for the whole of the Vercors was formed with Chavant, Jean Prévost, Doctor Ravalec, Le Ray and Costa de Beauregard. From December 1943 onwards there were a few parachute drops of light weapons, sub-machine-guns, rifles, grenades and explosives for sabotage. Static groups were formed in the villages in the Vercors and the towns in the surrounding plain, in particular at Grenoble. These were reserve units, which the Maquis leaders exercised in weapon-training and mountain warfare during the winter.

"On Sundays," writes an officer of the Vercors, Roland Bechmann-Lescot, "you would often see a bus stopped on a lonely road in the Vercors. You would hear firing. It was the volunteers of the civilian companies come from Grenoble, Romans or Die to do their military training under Maquis instructors."

This "phoney guerrilla warfare" gave the maquisards such a sense of security that even lectures were organized. "Resistant intellectuals came into the Maquis to give talks to keep the maquisards informed of the political situation and the progress of the war, maintain their morale and help to make them feel less isolated." One of the most assiduous lecturers was Beuve-Méry. At the same time, to keep the troops on their toes, raids were organized on gasoline, clothing, weapon and ammunition stores. Some of them were conspicuously daring and successful. One of these raids was on the Doua barracks at Lyons. Maquis trucks drove up during the night and rescued the Senegalese prisoners who were acting as batmen to the German officers. Next morning the Germans had to go on parade with dirty boots; but the Vercors had acquired a unit of colonial troops who fought to the last man and the last round in the battles to come. During another, the maquisards acquired a stock of policemen's uniforms from a store at Grésivaudan. It was wearing these new uniforms with their silver braid that the men of the Goderville (Jean Prévost's) Company sacrificed their lives in the fighting at Saint-Nizier.

In December 1943, Captain Le Ray, the military leader, was summoned to another appointment. He was the last representative of the original military group.

On 5 January 1944, Commandant Pourchier was arrested. After being moved from camp to camp and prison to prison, he was shot in the back of the head during the night of 1 September 1944.

The Germans soon began mounting attacks against the Vercors organization. In January 1944, the Malleval Maquis was surprised and
scattered. A handful of F.T.P. sacrificed their lives to save their comrades. During a skirmish at Barraques-en-Vercors, the Germans burnt
the village, as well as part of the village of Rousset. In March, Saint-
Julien-en-Vercors was attacked, where the regional headquarters of
Colonel Descours, a Regular officer, was surprised by the Germans—
the warning organization had failed to function. Six officers were killed,
as well as several civilians. The Germans had hardly left, when information came through that there was to be an arms drop. It took place
without incident by the light of the burning houses.

In April, the Militia and the Garde Mobile descended on La Chapelle-
en-Vercors and Vassieux for a whole week. They made many arrests,
executed a number of resistants on the spot, and handed others over
to the Gestapo. Many neighbouring farms were burnt.

And so hostilities in the Vercors began little by little. By 6 June, a
third of the Resistance cadres had already fallen in these guerrilla actions. The rest were still making preparations for the reception of the
airborne force. They blocked the roads and, under cover of repairing
them, the Grenoble public works department mined the tunnels of the
Goule Noire in broad daylight; while other groups helped the F.F.I. to
set hidden charges and fuses at suitable points on the roads by night.

It was obviously essential to prevent the Germans erupting into the
reduit while the airborne force was arriving and during the subsequent
days of battle. But there was no question of organizing fortifications for
a long siege. The comparatively gentle slope of the Saint-Nizier access
to the plateau was not fortified at all.

The Vercors F.F.I. still implicitly believed that the Montagnards plan
would be put into execution.

"We gather," one of the F.F.I. wrote on the eve of D-day, "that we
shall be reinforced when the moment comes, in accordance with the
plan, and that we shall receive the means of defending the plateau for
the few days during which we shall have to prepare for the arrival of
the Free French and Allied forces." (Roland Bechmann-Lescot.)

This impression was confirmed on a visit by Eugène Chavant, the
"civilian chief" of the Vercors, to Algiers by submarine during the last
days of May. Among the ministries and staffs of the provisional capital,
"the wild boar of the Vercors" was not wholly at his ease. The civilians
in Algiers, he said on his return, spent their time at parties or in political
intrigue. He felt lost among the office intrigues, and in the negotiations with the various Service staffs. At the Hydra inter-allied head-

quarters, which was concerned with supporting the F.F.I. in France, Colonel Constant, previously of the B.C.R.A., took him under his wing. The colonel tried in vain to make him see the complexity of the problems involved, as they appeared in Algiers. To the topography of the terrain, as Chavant explained it to him, he countered with the infinitely greater complexity of the Lycée Fromentin, the headquarters of the government and its various departments.

Chavant stayed five days in this atmosphere which was no doubt less salubrious than that of his plateau. He came away rather bemused, but still quite certain—and this was the essential point as far as he was concerned—that the Vercors could count on the support of an airborne force on D-day, and that the Montagnards plan was to be carried out. When he got back to his headquarters on 5 June, he reassured the F.F.I. and Huet, their military commander, by confirming that everything was in train.

He was being over-optimistic as a result of his ignorance of what was then going on in London. When Pierre Dalloz, at the end of 1943, left the Vercors for Algiers, taking the Montagnards plan with him, he had seen the officers of the B.C.R.A., Passy, Manuel, Rémy, Fourchaud, Combault, and also Colonel Billotte. Though made very welcome, he had nevertheless got the impression that there was some misunderstanding between them and the Maquis. He felt, particularly during his conversations with Passy, that they were more interested in people's political affiliations than their military capabilities. Passy seemed more concerned about the political orientation of the Vercors than in the tactical role of the reduit. Was it a Communist Maquis? And he had almost a phobia about them. Or was it purely Gaullist? Since the conversations were continually being turned in this direction, they seemed to Dalloz unsatisfactory and he felt he was wasting his time in Algiers.

However, when Passy suggested two months later that he should go to London and take over control of the Maquis at the B.C.R.A., Dalloz accepted at once. He felt that in London, closer to the headquarters from which the war was being carried on, he might be able to be useful. Unfortunately, on arriving, he found himself involved in an internal squabble among the Free French staffs. There was a conflict of authority between the B.C.R.A., which was very anti-Communist, and the Ministry of the Interior which, under Emmanuel d'Astier de la Vigerie, was more sympathetic towards the Party. Both camps wanted to annex him as a Maquis representative.

But he could get no co-operation from either side. He was disappointed by the off-hand way his information was received, and by the

prevailing atmosphere of unreality. What could he do? As a mere lieutenant of the Reserve he lacked standing among the staff officers. He
realized that, on his own, he could neither influence the policy of the
B.C.R.A. nor bring any pressure to bear. He went to see Manuel, and
obtained permission to go back to Algiers. But it was now March 1944,
the ban had been imposed, and he could not leave Great Britain.

He vegetated in London for three months. He had withdrawn from
the B.C.R.A. and worked unofficially with Georges Boris in the Services de l'Intérieur. Meanwhile, being tenacious, he wrote a report on
the Oisans, Chartreuse and Devoluy Maquis. In May 1944, he sent it
to Manuel at the B.C.R.A. and discovered to his great surprise that
though Manuel knew about the Montagnards plan, he was completely
ignorant of the complementary project of using the Oisans Maquis.

During the afternoon of 5 June, Dalloz got a sudden telephone call
to go immediately to Queen Anne Street, the B.C.R.A. operational
headquarters.

He arrived about three o'clock and was received by Colonel Combault, head of operations, and Colonel Miksche, a Czech, who was serving in the French Army and had been through the École de Guerre.

These two officers had just learned from Koenig's staff that the "Personal Messages" for all Metropolitan France had been sent to the
B.B.C. It meant that the landings were imminent and that the Maquis
was to start operations not only in the northern zone but also in the
mountainous districts of the south. They showed Dalloz a big map of
the south-east. "Tell us all you know about the Alps," they said.

Dalloz gave them an account of the situation based on his reports.
The Alps of Haute-Savoie were unsuitable as a base for operations
since they were too far north and backed on to Switzerland and Italy.
In the south, Provence was suitable for harassing operations but not
for mounting an operation of any size. With the Montagnards plan in
mind, Dalloz pointed out that only the Dauphiné, with its two natural
citadels of the Vercors and the Oisans, was a suitable base for cutting
the German lines of retreat at the right moment. "But," he said, "you
must have seen my reports on the Vercors." "Yes," replied the officers,
"but we don't know where they've got to. We've been looking for them
but can't find them." "What about my report on the Oisans?" A report
on the Oisans? They had never even heard of it.

Dalloz made inquiries. He discovered there were two offices on neighbouring floors in the same block doing the same work.

On the upper floor was the operational staff of the B.C.R.A., which
considered itself solely responsible for operations in France. On the

floor below was General Koenig's operational staff section which, having recently been set up and placed in command of all the F.F.I., had similar pretensions.

The reports Dalloz had made on the Vercors had been sent to the upper floor, since Koenig had not yet been appointed, but the B.C.R.A., who had not foreseen that the Resistance would go into action over the whole of France at the same time, had been studying at their leisure operational possibilities in other regions such as the Ardennes, Brittany and the Massif Central, which appeared to have priority. So far they had not considered either the Alps or the Midi. Dalloz's report on the Vercors had been put in a pending file, and there it was eventually discovered.

But his reports on the Oisans, which he had sent in after Koenig's appointment, had gone to the floor below, and the B.C.R.A. had not been informed of them.

Dalloz went downstairs and met Colonel Zigler, alias Vernon. They fortunately had much in common since they were both members of the Club de la Haute Montagne.

Zigler looked out the reports and Dalloz took them upstairs, having incidentally established liaison between the two floors.

The B.C.R.A. now had all his reports and set about having them duplicated. But it was the evening of 5 June and the next day was D-day. How could the Montagnards plan be put into execution at this late date and the Vercors held in reserve till the landings in the south had taken place and an airborne force organized to support it?

Inevitably, in the circumstances, the Vercors did the same as every other Maquis in France. It received orders that night for sabotage and guerrilla action. But since it believed that the Montagnards plan had been agreed by the headquarters, it took the messages to imply the imminent arrival of airborne troops and landings in strength on the Mediterranean coast. On 6 June, under the influence of this twofold illusion, the Vercors began to execute their part of a combined operation which the staffs in London had never even studied.

These were the basic causes of the tragedy.

On receiving the "Personal Messages" on the evening of 5 June, the Vercors mobilized. The reserve companies, which had till then merely been undergoing instruction and training exercises reported to their concentration areas. Colonel Destours, commanding Region R.1, set up his headquarters on the plateau. "From all directions," wrote an eye-witness, "from Grenoble, Romans and Die, from every district and by every means of locomotion, on foot, by car, by the busload, bringing with them numbers of vehicles that were to be invaluable for liaison work, many of which had been stolen from the Germans, the volunteers, on being summoned by the leaders of the Vercors, assembled under the very noses of the Germans. They flowed in with an enthusiasm that was evocative of the conscription of 1793. They were concentrated in previously planned mobilization centres and, after a medical examination, they were issued with arms and equipment and sent to their units." (Roland Bechmann-Lescot.)

Five companies were formed, approximately tripling the initial numbers, which had consisted of some 500 combatants. One company, known as the Brisac, was formed in Grenoble itself. In the Vercors another company, known as the Goderville, was to be commanded by Jean Prévost. The rest came from neighbouring districts and were concentrated at Villars-de-Lans or at Saint-Jean-Royans. During the night of 9–10 June, they went up to their positions on the Vercors, which were sited to defend the approaches.

The mobilization of the Brisac company took place as follows: on the morning of 9 June, the captain, who was living in concealment in Grenoble, was visited by the liaison agent who gave him the order for mobilization. In the afternoon, his 150 men assembled according to plan at the lime kilns, at the bottom of the hill leading from Sassenage to Villars-de-Lans. This position was on the edge of the Vercors plateau, which they had been detailed to defend. For the night they bivouacked at an isolated farm, the Croix-Lichou, and after dark requisitioned trucks brought them arms.

In the morning, the company took over its positions on the slope above Saint-Nizier, the only approach by which the Germans could debouch on to the plateau. There it joined the Goderville Company, with which it was to share the defence of this important sector.

On the afternoon of the 10th, the companies cut off all contact between Saint-Nizier and Grenoble, whose houses they could see from their observation posts, while Grenoble could see the French flag flying from a staff. They stopped the little tramway from going down, and from this the Germans realized that Saint-Nizier was occupied. But there was no need to worry about that. The F.F.I. were not expecting to remain there long, nor to have to withstand an enemy attack on their own. They were awaiting, from hour to hour, or at least from day to day, the arrival of the airborne troops of the Montagnard plan. This misunderstanding endured to the very end, for a period of nearly two months.

Meanwhile, the F.F.I. companies made contact with the proprietors of the Hôtel Touriste, which lay half-way up the slope, and which the Germans were to use as their headquarters during the battle. Through the hotel people the F.F.I. were to be kept informed of enemy movements.

To deny access to the plateau, the two companies took up positions at approximately 3,000 feet on a front three kilometres wide between the Engins gorge and the Vercors cliff. The Goderville Company held the left to a line a few hundred yards north of the cemetery, in which the defenders of the Vercors who died in June 1944 now lie. The Brisac Company was on the right.

Neither of the companies dug themselves in during the two days of respite before the German attack. Expecting the arrival of the airborne troops, they did not want to attract premature attention to themselves by field works. Nor did they think they would have to fight a defensive battle; their role, they imagined, would be to advance out of the reduit and guide the regular troops on to the enemy's rear.

During the morning of 13 June, 1,500 Germans arrived in trucks at Pariset and prepared to attack Saint-Nizier. The 250 maquisards of the Brisac and Goderville Companies became heavily engaged and the battle lasted all day. There was hand-to-hand fighting, and the enemy was beaten off with grenades.

In the middle of the battle a platoon of ex-chasseurs of the 6th Battalion of Chasseurs Alpins, under the command of Sergeant-Major Chabal, came up in support of the two companies singing the *Marseillaise*.

The Germans retreated. The Maquis had lost ten men. The enemy's losses were heavier. At the Fontaine Bridge, between Saint-Nizier and Grenoble, the agents of the Resistance who, like the rest of the inhabitants of Grenoble, had been watching the battle through field-glasses, saw the truckloads of dead and wounded on their way to the hospitals. As for the German headquarters, as it evacuated the Hôtel Touriste, it could not conceal its surprise at the number of maquisards and machine-guns. It was expecting the Maquis to take the offensive in the direction of Grenoble.

The next day, 14 June, arms, which had been urgently asked for, were parachuted in; they consisted of Hotchkiss machine-guns, which were not very practical for fighting in the Maquis, excellent English sub-machine-guns, but still no mortars, which were essential for mountain warfare. The same day, the Germans ranged their artillery on the French positions.

On 15 June, the battle began again at five o'clock in the morning, preceded by an artillery preparation. Three thousand Germans went into the attack against 300 F.F.I. militiamen, pretending to be members of the Resistance, infiltrated the French lines, and shot down the F.F.I. at point-blank range. The enemy attacked on the flanks. The left of Jean Prévost's company was overrun. An order to withdraw arrived at ten o'clock. A non-commissioned officer, called Itier, who was mortally wounded, insisted on being left behind with a sub-machine-gun. His dog stayed with him, licking his wounds. When his comrades had retreated some hundreds of yards, they saw the Germans appear and heard a last burst of fire from the dying man.

The maquisards, covered from attack by the excellent Thivollet Maquis, retreated over the hills or along the roads. The valleys of Lans and Villars became no-man's-land.

The new line of defence along the wooded crests of Croix-Perrin, by Bois Barbu and Corençon, was impossible to defend with the means available. But, once again, their belief in the imminent arrival of an airborne force caused them to throw prudence to the winds. It seemed essential to hold the flat ground on which aircraft and gliders could land. The Vercors sacrificed its safety to the airborne landing in which it still firmly believed.

The respite this time lasted over a month. Volunteers continued to pour in. Their total force now amounted to nearly 4,000, including officers, ex-soldiers and policemen from all the neighbouring districts, workmen from Romans and Grenoble, peasants from Royans and Diois, lumbermen from Trièves, even students from Lyons and Paris, and a certain number of foreigners.

They shared out the arms as best they could, for they were still in woefully short supply, though London and Algiers were continually being asked over the radio for new deliveries. There were still no mortars. Meanwhile, the "Republic of the Vercors" was set up. Under Yves Farge, the secretly appointed Commissaire of the Republic, an embryo administration came into being within these few square miles.

For a whole month, this vulnerable fragment of France maintained its existence. A transport service was organized with buses, mechanics and repair shops. Engineers, who had the resources of several private firms at their disposal, laid minefields and blocked roads. There was an internal telephone service between the front and the villages, and wireless communication direct with London and Algiers.

Commissariat, police and courts martial were organized. At La Chapelle-en-Vercors, the police station became a concentration camp for militiamen and collaborators. When the evacuation took place, most of them refused to leave their improvised jail.

The medical services, which were particularly well organized, had a devoted personnel and sufficient equipment; for the moment, they were quartered in houses and hotels, but had reconnoitred caves in which to shelter the wounded when the fighting began again.

Meanwhile, there were some stirrings of political life in the tradition of the Third Republic. Yves Farge, at La Chapelle-en-Vercors, received a visit from two citizens of eminently respectable appearance.

"Monsieur le Commissaire de la République, we should like to have a private word with you."

Yves Farge took them into the mayor's office. They made quite sure the doors were properly shut.

"Can you give us permission to reopen our Lodge?"

They were elderly Freemasons; and had not the freedoms of the Republic returned?

Meanwhile, during this period of calm between two storms, the Vercors became aware that it was becoming famous, indeed that its fame was increasing more rapidly than its stock of weapons. The Allies were more prodigal of praise than mortars. However, during the last days of June and the beginning of July, the Vercors received parachuted reinforcements. An inter-allied mission, an American commando, and young French instructors from Algiers, parachuted in on 21 June and 7 July, brought moral support. The B.B.C. continually stressed the feats of arms of the Vercors Maquis, whose real situation was so unhappily precarious. Spectacular parachute drops took place by day on a landing-ground which was being made ready at Vassieux; but the Vercors' repeated demands for the bombing of the German airfield at Chabeuil, five minutes away by air and from which the enemy bombers and observation planes came, were ignored.

All the Vercors celebrated the 14 July. There was a banquet at La Chapelle-en-Vercors; in the Lente forest, a parade was held out of sight of the enemy observation planes; there were memorial services for the dead of Saint-Nizier; and a parade at Die. But the most spectacular incident, which the leaders of the Vercors had not expected and would certainly not have approved, took place at the airfield being prepared at Vassieux. At noon, from a clear sky, some eighty American aircraft dropped red, white and blue parachutes with arms' containers. Needed though the arms were, the whole thing was much too obvious, and the Germans reacted violently.

That very afternoon the Germans bombed Vassieux and La Chapelle-en-Vercors with incendiaries.

This was the beginning of the end of the "Republic of the Vercors."

In London, meanwhile, Pierre Dalloz was continuing his fruitless efforts. On 10 June, having recovered his reports together with the copies of them made by the B.C.R.A., he went to see General Béthouart. The General, whom Dalloz had known as a captain in the Chasseurs Alpins at Grenoble, listened sympathetically to his story. Dalloz told him what was happening in the Vercors and what difficulties he had encountered in London. "Leave your reports with me," the general said. "They interest me and I'll have them studied. Come back in three or four days' time. Then we can have a talk." Unfortunately Béthouart, preoccupied with the landings in the north, had no time to study the matter himself, and his staff was equally overburdened. Dalloz returned to Carlton Gardens on the appointed day to discuss his reports. He was received by a subordinate, Colonel Thiébaud, who merely handed them back to him. "Colonel Billotte has told me to inform you that *your* Vercors is already engaged with the enemy," he said.

This was news to Dalloz; and he realized only too well that, if operations had begun, they were bound to have a tragic outcome. "The Vercors," he replied, "is not *my* Vercors. And if you think this is good news, you're wrong; as far as I'm concerned, it's most disturbing." After this, Dalloz was completely out of touch; and all the news he had of *his* Vercors were from the newspapers. On 19 June, the British and French press in London and Algiers published most disquieting reports of the fighting. The Germans had penetrated the defences of Saint-Nizier and occupied Villars-de-Lans. Pierre Dalloz, who knew what this meant in terms of the actual terrain, was greatly distressed. Death in his heart, he hurried round to the B.C.R.A., where he saw Colonel Manuel. "I'm extremely concerned at the news," he said. "The Vercors cannot possibly hold out for even a few weeks. You're throwing away one of the best cards in your hand for operations in the southern zone." Manuel tried to reassure him. "Don't worry so much; we're not children. I can tell you that your reports are as sound as any we've received during the war. All your predictions have come true." This was not the sort of flattery to reassure Dalloz. On 6 or 7 July, when the ban had been lifted, he got permission to go to Algiers.

The situation in Algiers was no more satisfactory.

On 12 June, an alarming and outspoken signal had been received from France. It had been sent by Colonel Henri Zeller, alias Colonel Joseph or Faisceau according to circumstances. The C.O.M.A.C. delegate in the south-east, he was one of the Regular officers who understood the Resistance and did most to help it. Zeller, much concerned by the tragic situation of the Vercors, Ubaye and many other Maquis, insisted that headquarters should shoulder its responsibilities.

On 13 June, Fernand Grenier, Commissaire for Air in the provisional government of Algiers, began to consult his colleagues about air support for the Vercors. The French air force, of which he was the official head, had few aircraft; and most of them were serving under Allied command either in Normandy or Italy. By scraping the bottom of the barrel, appealing to the old hands now acting as instructors, and sending for the few aircraft allotted to the Middle East, it seemed just possible to form a makeshift squadron of twenty-eight aircraft (sixteen Douglas A.24, six Douglas D.B.7, six Glen Martins), for an operation, named Patrie, to support the Resistance. But most of the aircraft were unsuitable since their radius of action was limited merely to the return journey from Algiers and no more.

Nevertheless, Fernand Grenier prepared orders for the formation of the squadron and for the appointment of Lieutenant-Colonel Morlaix, who had been a distinguished fighter pilot, to command it. These orders were submitted to General de Gaulle for signature, but remained unsigned throughout the six weeks that the operations in the Vercors lasted.

This was the basis for Grenier's accusation of betrayal. Before subscribing to that conclusion, however, the reasons why Grenier's proposal could not be put into effect need to be analyzed. The reasons were purely military. At that time the French armed forces, and the air force in particular, were so entirely dependent technically, tactically and for supply on Allied headquarters, a dependence Grenier himself admitted, that it seemed more realistic, as well as much quicker, to bring pressure on the Americans to help the Vercors direct. This was the policy pursued by the B.C.R.A. and in particular by Soustelle. He succeeded in getting a considerable number of parachute drops to the Vercors, both from Algiers and London. From Algiers fourteen drops were made during the night of 23–24 June, and further drops on 28 and 29 June, on 6, 7 and 8 July, and on 11, 16 and 17 July. From England 2,160 containers of arms were parachuted between the 25 and 28 June. No doubt having recourse to the Allies had certain inconveniences. The British and Americans had a tendency to look on the F.F.I. as terrorists whose military value was extremely doubtful. They were not much impressed by reports of districts being spontaneously liberated and of free republics, for they were reminiscent of Tito's communistic activities in Yugoslavia. The arms they supplied to the Maquis, therefore, tended to be limited to guerrilla weapons, and excluded nearly all heavy or semi-heavy weapons, in particular mortars, of which the Vercors had urgent need.

However, the French headquarters in Algiers and London had no option but to apply to the Allied staffs. Fernand Grenier's plan seemed more spectacular than practical. In a letter of 26 June to de Gaulle, the Commissaire for Air appeared to attach great weight to propaganda gestures. Besides the air operation Patrie he suggested that the battle-ship *Richelieu* should take part in the capture of Cherbourg which, he said, would "resound among the French."

And this was the basic cause of disagreement between Grenier and de Gaulle. Grenier seemed concerned not only with military reasons, but also with political ones. When he mentioned propaganda, he uttered precisely the word which was best calculated to arouse distrust. In the minds of de Gaulle and the majority of the other ministers, propaganda in Grenier's mouth meant Communist propaganda.

Grenier, at the Ministry for Air, and Billoux, commissaire for the liberated departments, were the two Communist ministers whom de Gaulle, for the sake of national unity, and also perhaps for diplomatic reasons, had taken into his government. But even before they entered the government, it was clear that they were not precisely as other ministers. From September 1943 to February 1944, there had been continuous conflict between de Gaulle and the Communist Party on the method of selecting Communist ministers. De Gaulle, as Prime Minister, insisted on selecting the ministers himself, while the central committee of the Party wanted to impose their nominees on him. In the end, by a mixture of astuteness and tenacity, de Gaulle won the day; he appointed Grenier and Billoux and they were accepted by the Party. But de Gaulle was fully aware that the two Communist ministers did not consider themselves responsible to him alone. He wrote: "Fernand Grenier and François Billoux, the first rather abrupt, the second clever, and both capable, divide their care and attention between their respective posts, Air and the Commissariat d'État, on the one hand, and their Party, which keeps an eye on them from outside, on the other."

They were loyal to the Party. They kept it informed of their activities. When important decisions had to be taken, they consulted it. Though their patriotism and loyalty to de Gaulle were not in doubt, their Party affiliations naturally aroused suspicions. The Allies were particularly suspicious of them; and the B.C.R.A. watched them closely. De Gaulle, who could neither get rid of them nor openly admit his distrust, was compelled to manœuvre to limit the powers with which he had had officially to invest them.

Fernand Grenier was therefore in a somewhat paradoxical situation and it was understandable that it should irritate him. In spite of his attachment to a party that was subservient to Moscow, he maintained that he was, and indeed he felt that he was, as good a Frenchman as the next man. The Communist Resistance in France was sparing of neither effort nor blood in the struggle against the common enemy. And Grenier, the official head of the air force, should have been able to direct it in the battle against Germany. And yet, whenever he wished to exercise his prerogatives, though he invariably encountered to begin with agreement and encouragement, at the last moment, when his plans were about to be put into execution, something always happened to frustrate him, people seemed to shift their ground and change their minds, beginning with de Gaulle himself.

As Commissaire for Air, he was a member of the Committee of National Defence, which was responsible for directing the struggle in France. This committee was composed of the appropriate civilian and military leaders. It consisted of General de Gaulle, General Béthouart, and the Chiefs of Staff of the army, navy and air force, as well as the Service commissaires, Jacquinot (navy), Diethelm (army) and Fernand Grenier (air). On the face of it, this was an extremely important committee which should have exercised supreme power. In fact, it appeared that because one of its members was a Communist the committee was merely a façade and had abdicated its executive functions to a committee of the B.C.R.A. which had no Communist member. This was the Committee for Action in France, whose secretary-general was Soustelle. It consisted of officers of whom most were members of the B.C.R.A. and it was this committee that was really responsible for military plans in Metropolitan France.

This was typical of General de Gaulle's usual tactics when faced with Communist infiltrations into one of the directing organisms of the Resistance. He would either create or take over a parallel organization, pack it with his own nominees and see that power was transferred to it.

Grenier thus found himself short-circuited and felt that he was suspect. Though he wrote letter upon letter and memorandum after memorandum to the General and his staff, he obtained no satisfaction. And he was constantly quarrelling with Soustelle over matters of detail.

It was at a meeting of the Committee for National Defence, held on 26 June, that Grenier apparently hoped to get his plans for the Patrie squadron agreed. No decision was made. According to Grenier it was because the agenda consisted only of minor matters of no importance, while Soustelle maintained that it was because Grenier was extremely reticent about the formation of the unit.

In these circumstances it is practically impossible to arrive at the truth. But it is clear that there was a great deal of mutual suspicion and recrimination. It is clear, too, that de Gaulle had good reason for his suspicions of his Communist ministers; while conversely, and this is confirmed by non-Communist sources, Grenier was quite right in accusing some of the Service staffs of failing to understand the Maquis and of underestimating its importance. In a letter to de Gaulle, dated 26 June, he wrote: "I think that some of our senior officers are not yet entirely convinced of the effectiveness of the fighting being done by the French Forces of the Interior. Nothing in their military training is conducive to their comprehension of this new aspect of modern wars which brings all the vital forces of a nation into play. A statement about the F.F.I. from you at the beginning of our meetings would help to enlighten our chiefs of staff on this important aspect of the battles now going on."

Throughout the last hours of the Vercors the airborne force was still expected.

On 19 July, the plateau was surrounded by two German divisions—approximately 20,000 men. They methodically set about the assault of the natural citadel whose armed garrison was no more than a sixth of their numbers.

The Germans first made sure of the defiles that led through the cliffs. These breaches in the natural defences were guarded by small isolated groups of maquisards. They were reduced one by one, after heroic resistance in every case. One of the most splendid episodes took place at the Pas de l'Aiguille.

A stream of warm water flowed through the Pas de l'Aiguille, and beside it was a hut with a corrugated iron roof that gave only precarious shelter. There were also two caves, one of which had a wide mouth and not much depth; it was used as a ration store. The other was more habitable and its entrance was better concealed. A section of eighteen men, with two lieutenants and three non-commissioned officers, took up their position there for the defence of the defile.

On 21st, waves of assaulting troops advanced up the defile. They were met with rifle and machine-gun fire and grenades, and withdrew, leaving their dead in front of the cave.

In spite of this first success, the maquisards' situation was desperate. They had the choice of being killed in the cave or of leaving it under enemy fire as soon as darkness fell.

Night came, but unfortunately lit by a bright moon. At about 23.00, to see if the enemy was on the watch, the little garrison threw out stones to simulate the sound of footsteps. The response was immediate. There were flares and bursts of machine-gun fire, while grenades were dropped in front of the entrance from the cliff above. It was hopeless to think of coming out.

By next morning, after a night without food or sleep, both sides had dug themselves in. A maquisard, Gilbert Galland, had set up a machine-gun in front of the entrance to the cave. The Germans had brought up a mortar. They fired two bombs, almost at point-blank range. Galland fell dead beside his broken machine-gun.

There was now no hope of getting away. The besieged lit a fire and threw on to it the photographs of their dear ones whom they never expected to see again. "That was perhaps," said a survivor, "the most painful moment of the appalling siege."

The Germans came into the attack two or three times during the course of the morning. They got near enough to the cave to throw grenades into it. One burst, causing a few minor wounds, the others were thrown back at them by the defenders.

Changing their tactics, the Germans let a rope down from the top of the cliff with a melinite bomb attached to it. The object was to explode it in front of the mouth of the cave.

The first time, the defenders were taken by surprise and the bomb burst, but without doing much damage. Further attempts were met by a man cutting the rope with a knife and throwing the bomb away. The Germans then thought of an even more unpleasant scheme. They lowered a twelve-pound box of melinite. When it came level with the entrance, a man dashed out to cut the rope. But the Germans pulled the box up, its fuse sizzling, and quickly let it down again. The man had barely time to lie flat. There was a terrific explosion, the cave shook and bits of rock flew all over the place. Most of the defenders were deafened by the percussion. However, no one was seriously wounded, though there were many scratches, and they all felt shaken and asphyxiated. When night came, by which time four more F.F.I. had been killed by German bullets or grenades, the besieged decided to make a dash for it whatever the cost. It took them a quarter of an hour to make their preparations. They paid the tribute of a minute's silence to the five bodies of their comrades they must leave behind. Then they rushed out, running desperately down the rocky slope.

The Germans were taken by surprise and sent up flares. But the mist deadened them. Ten minutes later, the eighteen survivors were safe and sound in the defile, wondering why they were still alive.

The other defiles fell to the Germans one by one. But the decisive battle was to take place in the centre of the Vercors. During the morning of 21 July, the workmen, who were hurriedly levelling the landing-ground near Vassieux for the airborne force, saw forty gliders appear towed by aircraft. They came in from the south. Everyone thought at first that they must be coming in from Algiers. But it was soon to be realized that this was merely a deception.

The men on the landing-ground were beside themselves with joy. The anti-aircraft machine-guns never opened fire. There was cheering and waving for the long-expected reinforcements. Then, suddenly, the F.F.I. realized their mistake. The forty gliders came down vertically towards them. The machine-guns opened fire; but it was too late. One glider was hit and crashed with a terrific noise. The troops in another were killed or wounded. But the rest landed safely and Germans jumped out of them. In some, there were ten men, in others twenty-five or thirty. There were 500 men altogether, wearing S.S. uniforms. They dispersed on a prearranged plan and occupied the village of Vassieux, and the two neighbouring villages of Mure and Château.

They were armed with mortars and heavy machine-guns, which the Maquis lacked, and carried a great quantity of ammunition.

The French machine-guns were quickly put out of action. The Germans soon became masters of the terrain. Captain Hardy, a young officer of twenty-three, was killed. Captain "Paquebot" was wounded but, with great presence of mind, succeeded in hiding in a hole full of water for twenty-four hours and eventually escaped. The S.S. searched all the houses in the villages and killed everyone they saw. Officers and men of the Maquis, civilians, the old, women and children were all callously dispatched. They were hanged, impaled, hacked in pieces, quartered and suspended from hooks in the butchers' shops. At Château, a little girl of seven was left with her foot crushed between the beams of her ruined home, lying on the bodies of her parents whom the S.S. had assassinated.

For five days and nights, the child screamed for water. The Germans, who were busy drinking fifty yards away, paid no attention. On the fifth day, the curé of Vassieux found and rescued her. She was taken to the hospital, but her leg was infected and she died soon after.

A letter from a German soldier, intercepted shortly after the operation, described the holocaust:

"There were terrible hours during the engagement. How savagely we massacred these people. We completely wiped out a hospital full of partisans, with all the doctors and nurses. There were forty of them. The wounded were dragged out and killed with machine pistols. It may have been atrocious, but these dogs deserve no better. And, in one village, two companies of Germans and one of Russians were engaged.

The latter probably destroyed everything: men, women and children were slaughtered. . . . We marched from morning till night every day. But not even a mouse was left alive when we had passed. You can't find a single undamaged house. Cows and horses are running free all over the district."

This tragic mistake about the origin of the gliders was the end of the Vercors.

During the afternoon of the 23rd, after two days' fighting, the Germans broke through the defences and penetrated on to the plateau. The 20,000 Germans overcame the desperate resistance of the 3,500 F.F.I.

For the F.F.I. there was nothing left but to signal their anger and disappointment, and to try to evacuate their fortress.

On 23 July, orders were issued to disperse and take to the Maquis. Many took refuge in the forests or on the heights, far from roads and passes. They suffered hunger and thirst, but the Germans dared not pursue them. A month later, they took part in the liberation of Grenoble and Romans, and afterwards joined de Lattre's army. Others split up into small groups and tried to break through the enemy lines to join other Maquis in the neighbourhood. But the Germans kept good watch.

This was how Captain Jean Prévost, Captain Loisel, Lieutenants Veyrat and Julien de Breuil, and Corporal Leizer were captured and executed by a German post at the exit of the Engins gorge as they were trying to join one of the Isère Maquis.

The wounded of the Saint-Martin hospital (among whom were officers of the Regular Army) had been evacuated to the Luire cave, but were massacred by the Germans together with the doctors, Fischer and Ullmann, and the chaplain, Father de Montcheuil. The nurses were deported.

So finished the battle of the Vercors. Of the 3,500 combatants, hundreds lie in the cemeteries on the plateau, side by side with the civilian inhabitants who were massacred. On the Vercors memorial, a sober monument in the Saint-Nizier pass, these simple words are inscribed: "To the seven hundred and fifty combatants and martyrs of the Vercors."

The tragedy of the Vercors and the dispersal of its Maquis gave the Germans no respite, however, neither in the immediate neighbourhood nor in the rest of the southern zone. In the Isère itself, the big Maquis of Oisans, Chambaran, Chartreuse and Trièves welcomed those who had escaped. The Oisans Maquis, on the strength of their reinforcement, spread all over Belledonne and Grésivaudan, where the Stéphane

Company was formed. Constantly on the move from one end of the department to the other, it gave the Germans no rest. These Maquis never stopped fighting till the Liberation. They entered Grenoble and Briançon, and took part in the battles for the Maurienne.

It is impossible to mention all the Maquis which, in every region of France, contributed to the defeat of the Wehrmacht. Many of those which took part in the campaigns of the regular armies or in the liberation of the great cities are mentioned elsewhere. As a whole, they formed an essential element in the victory and their importance was recognized not only by the French but also by the Allies.

Figures bear witness both to the effort made and the sacrifices endured. The *official* number of maquisards armed by the Allies amounted to 140,000, to whom must be added all those—and their number is much more difficult to estimate—who acquired arms from units of the Wehrmacht, the Militia and from official or secret depots organized by the Army of the Armistice.

The *official* number of maquisards killed in battle amounted to 24,000 men.

Chapter IV

DE GAULLE BEFORE PARIS

By 22 August 1944, when General de Gaulle reached Rambouillet, the last stage before his entry into Paris, his position had changed profoundly since the landings in Normandy. The provisional government of the French Republic had been recognized by the Allies as the *de facto* authority administering the liberated regions. A French formation, the 2nd Armoured Division, was moving in the vanguard of the battle towards the capital through the Chevreuse valley, while the First French Army, consisting of five divisions, was fighting in the south under the command of General de Lattre de Tassigny, together with an American corps of three divisions. The headquarters of the F.F.I. in London was no longer merely an annex of Supreme Allied Headquarters; it had achieved independence, and since 17 July had been installed in a house in Bryanston Square. The French sections of the Allied staffs had joined it there and come under the command of General Koenig, whose military authority was no longer limited. General de Gaulle, who had been kept in ignorance of the plans for Overlord, the Normandy landings, had, as head of the French government, been in close touch with the plans for Anvil, the landings in Provence, on 15 August, and had been able to insist on certain alterations. Nor had there been any question of AMGOT or American "false money" in the south.

No doubt, the recognition of French sovereignty was still limited. France had not yet achieved complete Allied status; de Gaulle had not been invited to attend the great Allied conferences. Indeed, on 23 August 1944, while he was waiting at Rambouillet to enter Paris, Churchill, referring to a telegram to the American Secretary of State suggesting a meeting of foreign ministers on future world organization, wrote: "I hope the French will not be admitted to such a discussion until they have broadened their government."

And now, on the eve of the entry into Paris, though the Allied tutelage against which de Gaulle had protested for so long still existed, it was much relaxed. De Gaulle himself had been recognized with enthusiasm by all liberated France, and the setting up of his administration had so far prevented any serious disorder in these provinces. Moreover, whatever reservations concerning him there may still have been among the Allies, no one was now contemplating putting forward an official rival to him. French unity was being restored round the government of which he was president.

This was an essential factor in the events that were to culminate in the liberation of Paris and in the safeguarding of the city. The recognition, sometimes implicit, sometimes overt, of General de Gaulle as head of the government was the determining condition for the prevention of disaster during these difficult days of August 1944. It was not a last-minute improvisation, but the result of the threefold policy, military, administrative and diplomatic, which de Gaulle had been pursuing for four years and, during the last two and a half months, with increasing success.

General de Gaulle had always insisted that Paris should be liberated by a French unit.

On 30 December 1943, during a visit to de Gaulle in Algiers, General Eisenhower expressed himself in the following way: "I had been warned against you in unfavourable terms. Today, I recognize that that judgement was wrong. For the impending battle I shall need, not only the help of your forces, but also the assistance of your civil servants and the moral support of the French population. I therefore need your support. I ask you for it."

This was the first unofficial recognition of General de Gaulle by the Allied Supreme Commander. De Gaulle took the opportunity of discussing the liberation of Paris: "It is essential that French troops take the capital. For the purpose of this operation, it is necessary that a French division be sent over to England in good time, as we French have demanded." And Eisenhower agreed.

Talks then took place between the various staffs. During the negotiations, which were completed only a short while before the landings, Koenig got S.H.A.E.F. to agree that the French division which was to enter Paris should be held in reserve till the advance towards the Seine began. He wanted the citizens of Paris to see fresh, enthusiastic and well-equipped troops as their first impression of the French Army.

This division was also to be one of the best in the renascent French Army. The 2nd Armoured Division was commanded by one of the great soldiers of the period, General Leclerc, whose real name was Jacques-

Philippe de Hauteclocque. He was a professional soldier and had given proof of his rare ability before 1940. A real leader, cool, and decisive in action, endowed with a creative tactical imagination, which he had first shown as a cavalry lieutenant in Morocco, and again during the campaign in France in 1940, when a captain on the staff of the 4th Division, he was also both cultivated and humane.

The 2nd Armoured Division landed on Utah beach in Normandy, on 1 August, to the cheers of the American troops. Leclerc, when attacking the retreating Wehrmacht in force, sent a signal to de Gaulle: "I had the impression . . . of reliving the 1940 situation, but in reverse—total chaos among the enemy, complete surprise of his columns."

On 7 August, the division, under command of XX Corps of the American Third Army, helped to check the German counter-attack on Avranches. On 8 August, it reached Le Mans. On 12 August, it advanced towards Alençon and to take the town made an enveloping movement in the purest of Napoleonic traditions. On 13 August, it was in the suburbs of Argentan.

On 22 August, orders were received to march on Paris. Leclerc's instructions were "to seize the bridges across the Seine in Paris and most urgently those of the lower bend; in case of resistance, the 2nd Armoured Division should halt and go on to the defensive; it will be supported on the right by the 4th American Infantry Division."

The next day, the 23rd, at dawn, the columns of the 2nd Armoured Division took the road to Paris. Leclerc was in constant contact with de Gaulle, who was at Rambouillet. He sent de Gaulle, for whose safety he was responsible, two armoured cars for his entry into Paris. The General must not be said to have entered the capital in foreign vehicles. From the military point of view, de Gaulle had won the day.

The last two months had also been administratively successful.

The plans made in London and Algiers to prevent disorder after the landings had succeeded in reducing the difficulties of this period of transition to the minimum.

There were, of course, both in Normandy and Brittany, certain isolated attempts at sedition and some excesses which were mostly due to the settling of private vendettas.

The liaison officers of the M.M.L.A. had often to work hard to prevent incidents. One of them, Colonel Lion, hurried from town to town, from liberated village to liberated village. At Flers, he encountered subversive elements; he had to get a grasp of local politics in a few hurried moments if he was to prevent bloodshed. He gave a luncheon to the opposing leaders and, backed by the Tricolour, the sacred flag of union, appointed the new mayor.

At Argentan, he had to sack the Vichy sub-prefect to prevent rioting. At Évreux, he installed the Gaullist prefect in office.

The liaison officers had to be perpetually on the alert as they advanced with the Allied armies. They were not, however, solely responsible for maintaining order. There was also Colonel de Chevigné's organization.

Chevigné was one of the first two high officials whom de Gaulle introduced almost secretly into France during his visit to Bayeux on 14 June, the other being François Coulet. Chevigné had the title of Military Delegate to the northern zone. Educated at Saint-Cyr, he had become a Regular soldier but had retired. Called up in 1939, he had twice been wounded during the few months of the phoney war and the battle of France. After the Armistice, he had gone to London and had become Chief of Staff to General Koenig with the rank of colonel.

From 14 June 1944 onwards, he accompanied the forward troops of the Allied advance to make sure that the German departure did not leave revolution behind it.

For the purpose he had a mobile column, which had been organized in Algiers and had passed through London, consisting of police, gendarmerie and supply officers, the essential personnel for getting the administration going again; an escort of Senegalese with French officers; and the members of a court martial.

As soon as a district was liberated by the Allies, Colonel de Chevigné moved in with his column. The first step was to find out whether the administrative officials appointed by Algiers were on hand. If, from amid the crowds and the ruins, someone appeared to claim that he was the prefect, sub-prefect, commissaire of the Republic or the mayor, Chevigné checked his name on the lists prepared in London and appointed him.

To help the new official take over, he would detach police, gendarmerie or supply officers according to circumstances. They would recruit further personnel on the spot. The column could afford to detach only the minimum number of officers at each stage, often indeed no more than a single inspector of police to build up the local force and administration.

In this way the column moved stage by stage from Bayeux to Thionville, by Cherbourg, Rennes, Tours, Angers and Paris, and then through the north. It was a continuous process of improvisation, of organizing with whatever materials were at hand; and it received its orders exclusively from General de Gaulle or his delegates, never from the Allies.

The duties of the military escort, apart from protecting the column and Chevigné himself, were to prevent the F.F.I. and F.T.P. from committing outrages against innocent but unpopular people, among whom were very often the managers of the branches of the Bank of France. By force of circumstance, these unfortunate officials had had to have relations during the Occupation with the German authorities and the Militia, who had indeed often requisitioned their paper currency. This, in many towns at the Liberation, seemed sufficient excuse for undisciplined elements to go to them without any authority whatever and say: "You've got plenty of reserves. How much exactly? Here's a requisition order. We'll take the money." Terrified by sub-machine-guns and revolvers, the wretched man would be compelled to exchange banknotes for scraps of paper signed by such untraceable names as Colonel Charles or Commandant Arthur. In such circumstances, the judicious use of a few Senegalese made an effective dam against inflation.

As for the mobile court martial, it was a remarkable innovation in the judicial life of France. It was the first occasion, at least in modern times, that a court martial had ever been attached to an individual, for these courts are usually attached either to an army or to a district.

It was due very largely to this curb imposed on the wilder elements by Colonel de Chevigné's column that the Liberation took on such different forms in the northern and southern zones.

North of the Loire, the M.M.L.A. or Chevigné's column appeared to keep order as soon as the fighting was over. The fomenters of disorder were deterred by the rapid installation of an administrative organization: a prefect, a commissaire of police, an officer of gendarmerie, and a municipality supported by bayonets. There was no vacuum of power. And to this was due the relatively peaceful character of the Liberation in the northern zone.

South of the Loire, on the other hand, things were rather different. Some considerable time often elapsed between the departure of the German troops and the arrival of the Allies. In the absence of a Gaullist administrative organization many excesses were committed.

By the time de Gaulle reached Rambouillet, where he stayed before entering Paris, the almost total lack of disorder in the liberated northern zone had given proof of his authority and the soundness of his administration to the Allied staffs and governments; while the active participation in the fighting of the 2nd Armoured Division and the French First Army was the justification of his military policy.

During the two and a half months that elapsed between Bayeux and

Rambouillet a third factor had encouraged the Allies to recognize him. His intensive diplomatic activity during June and July 1944 considerably improved his standing.

He made two highly successful journeys abroad. The first was to the Vatican, where the highest spiritual authority in the free world recognized him as President of the provisional government of the Republic of France. The second was to Washington, and led to a similar recognition by President Roosevelt.

The visit to the sovereign pontiff was no improvisation. During May, de Gaulle had made a tour of inspection of the French troops in Italy and Sardinia; and he was already contemplating a gesture of deference to the Pope to coincide with the entry into Rome of the Allied armies. On 29 May 1944, on his return to Algiers, he wrote a letter to Pius XII, assuring him "of the filial respect of our people and its filial attachment to the Apostolic See." He assured him that military operations would be conducted with all the respect due "to the dearest memorials of our Christian faith, and to the religious, intellectual and moral heritage they represent."

On 30 June, General de Gaulle was received in private audience by the Pope. It lasted twenty to twenty-five minutes. His suite, consisting of General Béthouart, General de Rancourt, Palewski, head of his private secretariat, and Diethelm, Commissaire of National Defence, waited outside with the cardinals, who expressed their surprise at the unusual length of the audience.

When the private audience was over, General de Gaulle introduced his suite into the Pope's study. The Pope addressed them in impeccable French and gave them his blessing.

This audience undoubtedly meant a great deal to de Gaulle. It was in keeping with his sense of spiritual values, his lofty outlook and his sublime conception of history. "Pius XII," he said, "judges things from a higher plane than the enterprises and quarrels of men."

He then returned to Rome to fly to Algiers by Naples and Corsica. In Naples, an incident took place of which the General is probably unaware even today. The officer in charge of the luggage discovered to his horror that the General's brief-case had been left behind in Rome. It contained important documents and it was clearly desirable that its loss should be kept from the General. Fortunately, it was recovered and reached Naples at one o'clock in the morning. The General had not missed it or, if he had, he said nothing about it.

The party then went on to Corsica, where the General inspected French fighter squadrons. But his stay was cut short by an unexpected telegram from Roosevelt officially inviting him to Washington. After the Vatican, the White House: things were moving.

The preliminary negotiations had been long and difficult. Roosevelt and de Gaulle had little in common; and they were estranged further by certain complex, if minor, political issues.

The fact was that Roosevelt did not like de Gaulle. He had been biased against him by de Gaulle's representative in America. Adrien Tixier, who represented de Gaulle till the arrival of a diplomatist, was the type of Frenchman who should be kept for internal consumption and never exported abroad. Left wing in politics, he was apt to view world problems in terms of French party quarrels, and to confuse the horizons of his constituency with more universal perspectives. He was brave, sincere and forthright, but also tactless, abrupt and irascible. His contacts with the French in America, who were divided, often from mere opportunism, into rival clans, brought out the worst in him. He irritated the Americans, who did not understand the dissensions among the French, and had, anyway, more important matters requiring their attention.

De Gaulle shared in the discredit of his official representative and was blamed for his abrupt methods when negotiating with the United States. Roosevelt, as an American patrician, tended to look down on de Gaulle, before he had ever met him, as typical of the kind of half-baked political fanatic France is apt to produce and which gives her such a bad name abroad.

And then there was also in the President's attitude perhaps a certain jealousy as between "stars." Roosevelt was vain of his world leadership. As the greatest among the great, meetings with heads of states—apart from those with Churchill and Stalin—made him uneasy; they were apt to rebel against his superiority, to filch some of the rays of his glory.

The result of all this was that American diplomacy spent much time trying to discover alternative expedients to recognizing the one man who was becoming day by day increasingly irreplaceable as the head of the French government.

In 1943, it backed de Monzie, who lacked the necessary standing to be able to respond to the veiled summons formulated on the other side of the Atlantic. In 1944, it backed Albert Lebrun, president of a fallen republic, who had quietly abdicated in July 1940, and had been living ever since in the Château de Vizille, as stripped of influence as if he were still in the Elysée. At the time of the Italian surrender, some officers from the defeated army came to see him and suggested taking him to Rome, where he would be at the disposal of the American troops.

It was no doubt a tempting offer, but Lebrun, most constitutionally, refused it.

There is not much point in discussing the American Secret Services' somewhat bizarre proposal—one they believed to be of extraordinary diplomatic subtlety—to subsidize a secret anti-Gaullist newspaper for the French Resistance. Nor is it worth analyzing at any length the part played in Algiers by that most enigmatic of diplomatists, Robert Murphy. Indeed, he was so enigmatic that he gave every appearance of puzzling himself. This curious man often gave the impression of not understanding the issues involved; perhaps this very fact enhanced his reputation. He was everybody's friend. Right wing with the Right, Left wing with the Left, he reflected all the prejudices and errors of American diplomacy. Indeed, he not only reflected them, he exaggerated them. In him, Roosevelt found a mirror that magnified the image of his own characteristics.

For, indeed, everything emanated from Roosevelt. He was the real chief of American diplomacy: "The President is his own Secretary of State." And since he considered de Gaulle *a priori* an ogre and France "fallow ground," the preliminary negotiations to their meeting were not without difficulty.

Throughout the spring of 1944, Churchill and the British Chiefs of Staff had been bringing pressure to bear on the White House to recognize de Gaulle and his "group" as the provisional government of France. Roosevelt was prepared to allow the leader of the Free French a lowly place beside the great ones of the earth provided de Gaulle solicited it. But the General's stature and his French pride made sitting below the salt intolerable to him.

On 14 and 17 April 1944, Duff Cooper, British Ambassador in Algiers, gave de Gaulle messages from Churchill. In an attempt to ease the relations between the C.F.L.N. and the Americans, Churchill offered to transmit to Washington a request from the General for a meeting with the President. He guaranteed that the reply would be favourable. There was one word in this amiable suggestion which irritated the General. "Request" a meeting? De Gaulle was no supplicant. He cared little for American recognition. What mattered was to be recognized by the French nation, and he had need of no one to achieve that. This first attempt failed.

A month later another attempt was made; this time it was initiated by the Americans themselves. Admiral Fénard, head of the French Naval Mission in the United States, who was well thought of at the White House, arrived on 27 May with an unofficial message from the

President. Roosevelt had asked him to inquire *unofficially* whether de Gaulle would accept *unofficially* an invitation to come to Washington. An *official* reception could then be organized through the usual diplomatic channels and no one would know who had taken the initiative. It was a remarkably cautious message. Roosevelt wanted to see de Gaulle, but without losing face by giving an appearance of having changed his policy towards him. De Gaulle could hardly refuse such an offer but, taking his line from the President, he accepted without accepting, or rather he accepted in principle but procrastinated. He told Admiral Fénard "to make a temporizing reply." He acknowledged the invitation, but since he had to go to England and then to France, he was not in a position to give a firm and precise answer.

De Gaulle then left for London, where the atmosphere was not indeed altogether favourable to the smooth maturing of diplomatic projects. On 10 June, however, at the height of his squabbles with his British allies, he received a visit in Carlton Gardens from General Bedell Smith, Eisenhower's Chief of Staff. That the Supreme Commander should have sent his Chief of Staff at this particular time, when the operations in France had just begun, was a clear indication that the situation was altering for the better. Indeed, Bedell Smith literally entreated de Gaulle to agree to meet the President. It was essential to the American troops in France that an agreement should be reached with the only political leader recognized by the liberated population. Having tried to place him in the position of a supplicant, they were now entreating him. It was not a reversal of roles calculated to displease the General. Having consulted with his government, he accepted, but on certain conditions. The conversations in Washington were to be merely "a reciprocal exchange of views on world problems of interest to both countries." The General's visit to Washington was "to have the significance of an acknowledgement by France of the American war effort and of a proof of the enduring friendship between the two peoples." The more precise problems, about which de Gaulle might have demands to formulate, in particular the recognition of his government, were to be discussed through the normal diplomatic channels. It was thus made quite clear that de Gaulle was being invited to the United States on American initiative.

His stay in Washington lasted three days, from the 6th to the 9th; and he spent 10 July in New York. Then he left for Canada, where he spent an hour and a half in Quebec, an evening in Montreal, and a day in Ottawa.

On the evening of the 13th he returned to Algiers.

There were many vivid incidents during his stay in the United States. On landing, the General found to his surprise a guard of honour of French Air Force cadets. The French Air Attaché had had the happy thought of getting these young Frenchmen up from their training camp. De Gaulle was much touched by this.

The General went straight to the White House and took tea with Roosevelt. The President, accompanied by his wife and daughter, received the General in his invalid chair. He deployed all his charm to obviate any possible embarrassment there might be at this first meeting. De Gaulle was rather cold and reserved. There was no other meeting that day. De Gaulle stayed at Blair House, opposite the White House, where the President always puts up his important guests.

The next day there was a certain thaw. Roosevelt gave a formal, but most cordial luncheon in honour of his guest. But, above all, there was a dinner given by Forrestal, Secretary of Defence. Forrestal made a speech which was a model of concision, but none the less expressive for that: "When we invited General de Gaulle to come here, we expected an ogre, but we have found a man." He then sat down. The victory was to the Frenchman; he had won the day.

And he not only won it at this dinner, but also at the two private interviews he had with Roosevelt. The President found in de Gaulle a man who shared his wide humanitarian views and who, whatever may have been said about him, showed himself to be as democratic as he was himself.

He also won the day with the newspapers at a press conference in New York. The epithet of ogre was more applicable to the American journalists than it was to the General. They harassed him with questions, and tried to trip him up. But it was in vain. Though he knew English perfectly well, he pretended not to, and asked for an interpreter to translate the questions. It gave him time to consider his answers; and he came through the ordeal with flying colours.

The President was most forthcoming and seasoned world politics with touches of personal friendliness. A visit to his swimming pool would succeed an explanation of his policy towards Russia. Though, no doubt more precise about the details of the former than the latter, his attitude towards his guest was not only hospitable but friendly. Before leaving Washington, the General gave Roosevelt a model of a submarine, beautifully made at the Bizerta arsenal. The President thanked him in a charming letter and sent him his photograph inscribed: "To my friend General de Gaulle." The ink on it was scarcely dry, however, before Roosevelt sent Churchill an account of his conversations with de Gaulle and said: "I think he is essentially an egotist."

Nevertheless, things had gone very well at the White House and, on 7 July, the President ordered John J. McCloy, Assistant Secretary for War, and Daniel W. Bell, Assistant Secretary of the Treasury, to draw up an agreement recognizing the French Committee of National Liberation as the *de facto* authority for civil government in France, which even permitted the committee to issue currency.

For once the government offices were expeditious. De Gaulle had scarcely left America when he was informed of the recognition. As soon as he arrived back in Algiers, on 13 July, he decided to attend the next day's ceremony. There was an impressive parade. The General placed a wreath on the war memorial and walked smiling and unescorted through the cheering crowds.

The next month, before his return to France, was marked by a number of incidents that gave proof of how much stronger his position had become.

Before the landings in the north, for instance, de Gaulle had been kept in ignorance of the forthcoming operations, but now he was kept informed of the plans for invading the south and was in a position to give advice.

Yet another sign that the Fates were with de Gaulle was his journey from Algiers to join the leading troops outside Paris.

De Gaulle normally travelled in a little, two-engined Lockheed Lodestar. He intended going to France in this aircraft, which was painted with the French colours and the Cross of Lorraine. But the American authorities, in the person of General Canone, who was then in Corsica, absolutely refused to allow this on the grounds that it was far too dangerous a journey for an aircraft of such limited range. For reasons of security, the route was by Casablanca and Gibraltar, and then along the coast of France by night, avoiding Brittany, which was not yet entirely liberated, and making a long detour via England before turning south to Cherbourg.

The American General determined to lend de Gaulle his personal Flying Fortress. The Lockheed would join de Gaulle in France, if it could make it.

Though reluctant, de Gaulle could do no other than accept. He therefore waited in Algiers for the Flying Fortress to arrive, having made it a condition that the French colours and the Cross of Lorraine were to be painted on its fuselage during the night he was to spend in Casablanca.

The huge American aircraft left Corsica for Algiers, but a whole series of mishaps was to make it plain that it was unwise to ignore the General's wishes. On arriving at Maison Blanche, the Algiers airfield, it made a bad landing, ended up half-way across the road, and was seriously damaged. No matter, said General Canone, another Flying Fortress would be sent to Casablanca. The flight from Algiers to Casablanca presented no danger and de Gaulle could make use of his Lockheed thus far.

On 17 August 1944, therefore, General de Gaulle left Algiers in his own aircraft, as he had always wished to do. He arrived safely at Casablanca, where the second Flying Fortress reached him, this time without mishap.

From Casablanca the two aircraft set out for Gibraltar. The General went in the Fortress with General Juin and Gorse, while Colonel de Rancourt, piloted by de Marmier, travelled in the Lockheed. The Lockheed, however, reached Gibraltar long before the Fortress. Colonel de Rancourt was in time for luncheon. General de Gaulle and his two companions arrived late in the evening, just in time to dine with the governor. As they landed one of the tires burst. The British inspected it, and decided it could not be repaired in time. The General's mechanic, however, said he would mend it himself, and did so during the three or four hours the stay lasted.

But the governor refused to allow de Gaulle to proceed in the Fortress. The tire might have been repaired, but it could be only a temporary repair and was bound to burst again on landing. The General's life was far too valuable. If he insisted on continuing his journey, he must do so in his private aircraft; though no doubt less powerful, it at least had sound tires.

De Gaulle therefore set off alone in the Lockheed with his senior pilot, while the Fortress took Juin, Rancourt and Gorse to Cherbourg. The Fortress had no luck. Lightning destroyed its radio and the American pilot lost his way. They found themselves flying over a coastline, but could not tell whether it was that of England or France, in Allied or German hands. Colonel de Rancourt ordered the pilot to fly very low; he wanted to see to which side of the road the traffic kept. From the traffic, and from the shape of a steeple, which differs on opposite sides of the Channel, they discovered with relief that they were over England. They were flying over Plymouth, which was a long way from the planned route. The American pilot turned south towards Cherbourg, where they landed at last three hours after the General's Lockheed.

In Normandy de Gaulle was joined for this last stage of his journey to the outskirts of Paris by General Koenig and Le Troquer, the designated commissaire for the liberated territories of the northern zone.

On his arrival in Cherbourg, de Gaulle went to the Hôtel de Ville, where a reception was held in his honour. In the afternoon, accompanied by General Koenig, he flew to Eisenhower's headquarters at Saint-Lô. There he deliberately behaved as the detainer of political power in France, and no one was prepared to contest it.

On his return to Cherbourg, he set out for the capital, accompanied by Koenig, Le Troquer, Colonel de Chevigné with his column and escort, and also by a commissariat officer, Commandant de Lignières, who during these last stages on the road to Paris, and eventually in the capital itself, organized accommodation for de Gaulle and his suite.

The convoy progressed by Argentan, Le Mans and Chartres, where de Gaulle went to the cathedral, to Rambouillet, the last halt before Paris. And when the General flew in his little aircraft, as he did on occasion, over this countryside so familiar to Péguy's pilgrims and Sunday excursionists, he was able to see Leclerc's troops marching on the capital.

In the courtyard of the château at Rambouillet, he found Commandant de Lignières awaiting him. This officer had had no easy task; and the Germans were still only four kilometres away. The château, which was in normal times the President's country residence, had been occupied by the Wehrmacht for four years. The building itself had not been much damaged and the furniture was intact. But Commandant de Lignières, on arriving first in the little liberated town, had discovered that there was no electricity.

He searched the cellars and found a mobile power unit abandoned by the Germans. But it needed repairing. Fortunately, Lignières was temporarily billeted with the town's electrician. Somehow or other, current was persuaded to flow into the electric lamps left by the Third Republic.

But he had also to organize the impending entry into Paris. Lignières requisitioned *gazogène* Paris buses, which had been parked in a depot at Dreux, while awaiting events. He mobilized a fireman, who exchanged his uniform for a chauffeur's livery. One way and another, he managed to organize a convoy to take the important personalities to Paris. The General would lead the way, escorted by two of Leclerc's armoured cars. To smarten the convoy for the historic part it was to play, the buses were hurriedly sprayed pale green and the Cross of Lorraine painted on them.

These privileged persons, who were to see the Eiffel Tower again before any of the other exiles in London and Algiers, tested both Lignières' patience and ingenuity. Le Troquer led him aside and said: "My dear Commandant, would you do something for me? I should so like to take something with me to Paris. My family, you understand." And Lignières gave the chauffeur two boxes of food containing sugar and chocolate. Other similar demands were met by getting the keepers to shoot rabbits for the liberators' tables.

There was, of course, no question of minor services of this kind for de Gaulle. Lignières, standing to attention in the courtyard of the château, felt a sense of satisfaction at duty well done. He had prepared the best bedroom in the château for the General, the room which was traditionally the President's. He informed de Gaulle of it. At that moving moment, the shades of MacMahon, Fallières and Félix Faure were all about the Commandant. Would they welcome their successor? Would their successor allow himself to be made welcome by such predecessors?

The General spoke. Lignières trembled. There was a certain edge of dissatisfaction to the General's voice: "Intendant de Lignières, do you mean to say you have made ready for me the bedroom and dining-room of . . ." (the name has not been recorded). "You don't really imagine, do you, that I'm going to sleep in the President of the Republic's bed?"

And the poor commandant had to allot de Gaulle another room less charged with Elysian memories.

Thus it was that on his arrival outside Paris, the General refused to appear either as the restorer of an abolished régime, or as a usurper. He was de Gaulle: that sufficed.

Meanwhile, if one may believe a still unpublished private diary, Marshal Pétain, who was on the point of leaving France under pressure from the Nazis, said to a woman friend: "I thought the French nation incapable of serious effort; these hundreds of thousands of men who have risked their lives for the Liberation have given proof of a heroism in which I no longer dared to believe.

"I knew that de Gaulle was intelligent, but I never would have thought he could succeed in so splendid an undertaking."

Part Four

THE LIBERATION OF PARIS

Chapter I

PARIS AWAITS ITS LIBERATION

In the extraordinary adventure Paris lived through in August 1944, there were almost as many episodes as there were houses or storeys in them. From the little old man the F.F.I. vainly tried to prevent going into the street in the middle of a battle and who replied, paraphrasing with dignity one of Maupassant's characters: "But I'm telling you, it's my time to go fishing," to the boy of thirteen who was killed throwing Molotov cocktails at German tanks, there was not a Parisian whose life was not affected to some extent by this stupendous event.

On the morning of 19 August, René Coty, the senator, came out of his house on the quays. He turned into the Boulevard Saint-Michel. There he saw a crowd gathering in front of the posters of the Committee of Liberation. It was, he thought, reading them without much enthusiasm. But René Coty, at that solemn moment, had other cares than merely to observe what was going on in the streets. Determined to do his best to safeguard Republican institutions, he was anxious to know if the Senate, of which he was a member, was in a fit condition to receive him and the twenty resistant senators who, for several months past, had been secretly discussing the details of a constitution and whether Louis Marin or Queuille should be head of the State. Having with some difficulty passed through two barricades, he called on the Senate's architect in the Rue de Vaugirard. The latter told him that it would be some time before the building could be used. It was an historical monument and an examination would first have to be made. Explosive charges had been placed in it. The conference hall had been transformed into a dormitory. The chamber would be in bad condition. This was René Coty's first disappointment under the Fourth Republic. Before leaving, however, he insisted that at least one room should be made ready as soon as possible for his colleagues. A senator of his group commented on the news somewhat bitterly: "It seems to me that these historic hours lack all interest for those who have to live through them."

They certainly lacked amenity. Paris was hungry and in imminent danger of starvation. The food rations had not only been much reduced but were no longer being regularly distributed; and black market prices had soared.

The situation, already difficult, became precarious during the following month, and catastrophic in August.

We have an official report for July 1944 made by a neutral, Dr. Jean-Marie Muzy, former President of the Swiss Confederation, and Delegate of the International Red Cross in France.

"From the moment he arrives in Paris," wrote this great friend of France, who did much to protect the city, "the traveller becomes aware of an atmosphere of melancholy weighing heavily on the great French capital. . . . Month by month, life becomes more difficult; many essentials are already lacking and those he can find are in general very expensive. Prices have risen fantastically; for instance a tie today costs the same as a shirt two years ago. . . . A slice of meat costs a hundred francs. For the poor, it is already black misery. This is apparent when you realize that junior employees and minor officials earn about two thousand francs a month." Reviewing the staple foods, he continued: "Bread has often run out in the bakers' shops before all the customers have had their rations. . . . It has already happened that on certain days a whole district has lacked bread.

"As for milk, of which there was a daily consumption before the war of approximately one million two hundred thousand litres, the daily average, from 6 June to 17 July, has been no more than two hundred and twenty thousand litres a day. There are at this moment twenty-five thousand undernourished babies in Paris. The fact that the nursing mothers also lack essential nourishment entails early weaning. Concerned by the increasing infant mortality, the Office of Public Hygiene consider it urgent to supply every child with an extra half-litre of milk."

The list of scarcities continues for pages. Since 25 May, "only a quarter of the potential consumers were able to be supplied with potatoes," and "you could search Paris in vain for a dish of fried potatoes." The distribution of wine was completely suspended in July.

Undernourishment was greatly affecting the health of the population. Parisians had no more than half the necessary calories. Deaths from tuberculosis were increasing disquietingly, particularly among the young. Novel and rapid forms of phthisis were beginning to appear. Investigations made in certain dispensaries revealed an increase of from twenty-five to fifty per cent of patients infected with bacilli.

Means of improving the food situation were almost entirely lacking.

Ten thousand trucks were needed to supply the capital, but the Germans had authorized no more than two thousand five hundred; and even these often returned empty from the countryside.

The condition of the railways was deteriorating from day to day. From Bourget-Triage, the centre commanding the capital's traffic, an average of some five hundred trains departed daily in July 1943. Now, the very maximum was twenty and they were in very bad condition. Of the one hundred locomotives belonging to the depot, sixteen had been machine-gunned, eleven bombed, one sabotaged, four blocked in various stations, and two derailed. Twenty-one were being repaired, and six were being used by the Germans. Seven had been sent to other depots. There were in all scarcely thirty available.

The eastern network, which had had two thousand four hundred locomotives available in 1940, had no more than one thousand five hundred by the end of 1943, and six to seven hundred by May 1944. On 12 August, some railway workers were shot for striking. As a result, the eastern network resumed some semblance of working the next day.

Bombing further paralyzed transport round Paris. There were no means of distinguishing between trains serving the Wehrmacht and those feeding the civilian population. For a whole month, the Paris-Orleans network tried to send trains to Paris from Chartres and never succeeded in getting a single one farther than Limours. Trains coming from Paris in the opposite direction could get no further than Étampes. Since the bombing on 30 May of the Canardière viaduct, outside Chantilly, Creil-Compiègne-Brussels line was unusable.

To aggravate the situation still further, the German civilian and military authorities mercilessly increased their demands as it became ever more difficult to satisfy them.

The total number of Germans, both civilian and military, receiving rations in France had been one million three hundred thousand in May 1944, but by June the figure had increased by three hundred and fifty thousand. By the end of the month, the military personnel alone had reached a million and a half.

The official requisitions also contributed to deprive the French of the little food that remained to them. In May 1944, twenty-five thousand head of cattle were sent across the Rhine.

There was also considerable plundering by individuals. German troops seized stocks of flour and tinned food without the knowledge of their headquarters in Paris. As a result, reserves of condensed milk were dispersed and concealed by municipal authorities, who did everything they could to hide such stocks of food as still remained to them.

Indeed, Paris was famished; and in danger of dying from hunger due to the paralysis of its essential services. And not only of dying, but of being unable to bury its dead. For, as the fighting drew nearer, the undertakers refused to go out to the suburban cemeteries which were gradually absorbed into the battle zones. Rarely had Fate pressed so hardly on the city. There were, moreover, social and economic circumstances which might become disastrous at any moment.

Till the summer of 1944, the Paris region had been one of the principal arsenals working for the war effort of the occupying power.

There were many war industries in Paris; and though by the end of July some were gradually slowing down, others were still in full production. Some were coming to a halt through lack of raw materials; some had been damaged by bombing; while others had been sabotaged by their own workers.

The result was that, during July and August 1944, unemployment began to make its appearance amid a population which could not get enough to eat even when working full time. The Gnôme-et-Rhône factories had laid off their nine thousand workers for lack of electricity. Renault had dismissed six thousand of their ten thousand workers, again for lack of electric power and raw materials. Then, one after the other, the Amiot aircraft factories, the Rateau pump works, and the Radio L.M.T. factories closed down. German organizations were already moving back across the Rhine and leaving their French workers unemployed.

The whole of social and economic life became tragically difficult; and work or unemployment became immediately dependent on military operations, and were linked to the progress of the liberating armies. During these days of waiting, the Paris of the children who still played in the squares, the Paris of art exhibitions and meetings of the Institut, which still attracted a certain public, the Paris of alternating work and holidays became a strategic position, at once a German arsenal and a gigantic Maquis for the French who were making ready to liberate themselves. Would Paris be defended or not? After their reversals in Normandy, where would the Germans' next line of resistance be? This was the question on which the future of the city depended; and the responsible authorities in Paris were asking it with anxious concern. The Intelligence services whose headquarters were in Paris—and there were many of them—were all searching feverishly for information. There was not a truck driver or a cyclist, a policeman or a black-marketeer, a resistant or a mere traveller who had not some information to impart on his return to the city. Paris watched its outskirts and the

Ile-de-France with the anxiety of a patient waiting to be told the doctor's diagnosis of his disease and his chances of survival. The familiar countryside, in which children played and young people made love, the woods, so humanly littered on Sundays with the debris of picnics and avowals of eternal passion, seemed suddenly to have become oppressed by brutal forces, and no one knew when or where they would strike.

In the Seine-et-Marne, headquarters of the Wehrmacht seemed to be proliferating. It was reported that there was one at Maison Rouge, four kilometres from Nangis; another, which had withdrawn from Paris, was at Bourron; another, withdrawn from Rouen, had selected Rouvray between Condé and Saint-Légères in the Seine-et-Oise; another was at the Château de Montjeon, near Wissous, where eighty tanks were parked; and yet another was at the Château de Saint-Chéron, in the valley of the Chevreuse. As for Rommel, his headquarters remained at La Roche-Guyon in Seine-et-Oise.

In July, the airfields of Villacoublay, Toussus, Guyancourt and Orly were still in German hands, ready for any eventuality. German units, still uncertain of the part they would have to play, were fortifying their areas. Activities of this kind were reported from Marly-le-Roy; and on the road from Cuny-la-Ville to Versailles anti-tank ditches and machine-gun posts were being organized at every twenty-five yards.

But it was the Seine-et-Marne which was the most highly organized, not so much for resistance, but rather to assure the eventual evacuation to the east of the German forces. If the Wehrmacht were prevented from withdrawing through Paris because of the city being occupied by the Allies, an insurrection, or blown bridges, there was a railway, running parallel to the front through Moret-sur-Loing and Provins, by which the German troops could be moved. And this was the reason for the concentration of German forces and the proliferation of defensive positions. Meanwhile, the F.F.I. increased their forces in the district. The Maquis took up positions in the forest of Fontainebleau, where the local police were soon to join them.

Information such as this, gathered by many thousands of eyes and transmitted to many thousands of ears—inevitably undergoing much deformation in the process—nevertheless finally formed a basis of hypotheses as to the probable fate that awaited Paris. There were two possibilities: either Paris would be part of the last line of resistance the retreating Germans would hold before the Rhine, or their line of resistance would be far away in the north-east, on the Somme or the Aisne, in which case Paris would be no more for the Wehrmacht than a corridor that would have to be kept open for a few days and then abandoned. In the first case, the capital would be in danger of destruction. In the second, it might emerge with no more than a few skirmishes in the streets.

By mid-August, the general situation of the Wehrmacht in France was becoming clearer. The three German armies fighting on the western front had been separated by the tactics of the British and Americans into two distinct masses.

In the north was the Seventh Army, which according to Intelligence consisted of eighteen divisions, half armoured and half motorized. It was retreating on Lisieux and Bernay, and was trying to reach the area of Rouen and the east of Rouen so as to cross the Seine. It was not interested in Paris, and would cross the river some hundred and fifty kilometres downstream.

In the south, the other two German armies, consisting of twenty-two divisions, had retreated on Paris, one to the west to try to reach the right bank of the Seine by Pontoise, and the other to the east of Paris, to cross the river in the neighbourhood of Melun.

To ensure the withdrawal being carried out in good order and that equipment was evacuated, the Germans had placed some eight to ten divisions on a line that ran from Poissy, through the forest of Saint-Germain-en-Laye, to Saint-Cyr, Trappes, the valley of the Chevreuse by Orsay, the neighbourhood of Massy-Palaiseau, and the forest of Fontainebleau to the forest of Sénart. When fighting broke out in the capital, it was estimated that ten German divisions had already crossed the river. South-west of Paris, in the district through which the Allied advance-guards were approaching, there therefore remained only a weak cover of German troops, and these soon retired through Paris, the last possible route to the north. In Paris itself, to assure withdrawal through the city, the Germans still had one division of Panther tanks which, on 12 August, left the city by the Porte d'Orléans without its supply column, from which it was deduced that it was taking up positions nearby, ready to intervene within the city itself should it prove necessary. Within Paris there were two crack S.S. regiments of the Adolf Hitler division. Two Wehrmacht regiments were in the neighbourhood of the Luxembourg. The Palais-Bourbon and the Tuileries were occupied. And, finally, two hundred and fifty trucks, the transport of a German unit, were parked in the Cité Universitaire.

Generally speaking, these troops were still well-disciplined. Yet, from time to time, signs of disintegration became apparent, and there were scenes in the streets which would hitherto have been inconceivable. A

German soldier, one of a section of five men under the command of a non-commissioned officer, in the Métro, on being addressed by an officer, said: "Shut up, you swine!" The officer summoned the non-commissioned officer, who merely shrugged his shoulders in a gesture of impotence. Pale with anger, the officer got out at the next station. A more frequent event was the commandeering of bicycles. German patrols set traps for cyclists. The patrol would split into two. One half of it would advance some hundred or two hundred yards, and let the cyclists pass so that they ran into the second half. Those who turned back fell into the arms of the first half. Some cyclists escaped by pretending their bicycles were out of order and carrying them on their shoulders.

It was from such facts as these that Paris, during these days of waiting, tried to determine what the German intentions were and what incidents were likely to occur between the civilian population and the occupying troops under whom they had suffered for the past four years.

Paris, starving, undergoing a social and economic crisis, transformed into a garrison town, and now in the front line, was also preparing for insurrection.

In the shadows of the captive city, there were conspirators of every party and every persuasion, whose secret plotting caused grave anxiety to the Intelligence services.

Those who wanted to short-circuit de Gaulle and install a patched-up Third Republic were neighboured by men whose only concern was to take advantage of a change of régime to do good business.

Among the first, the S.R. of the National E.M. of the F.F.I. in Paris reported, though naturally somewhat guardedly, the existence of a group calling itself "Comité National des Corps Élus de la République" and which declared itself to be composed of elements which had played an effective part in the Resistance. In fact, it consisted largely of people who had sat on the fence, were not too compromised by their support of the Vichy government and now, being in touch with the Americans, believed their hour had come. Monzie, Frossard, Bonnet and Paul Faure, among others, were promoters of this suspect movement. Chautemps and Monzie, in indirect contact with Admiral Leahy and Robert Murphy, were being very active at this time. It was even asserted later that this new committee was trying to maintain Marshal Pétain in power, while using Members of Parliament who were notoriously anti-Pétainist. "This new movement," concluded the Intelligence bulletin of the S.R. of the F.F.I., "recruits in particular regular officers who have been sitting on the fence. In any case, it appears from a report of Brinon's that the Anglo-Americans have already given certain personal assurances to some Vichy elements."

Indeed, many shameful intentions were attributed to the Allies. They were even suspected of meddling in French affairs. At least this was what the S.R. of the Resistance said: "A new and secret financial association is in process of being set up; it claims to be under the protection of the Americans. It is managed by a former deputy of the Vosges and by two Parisian marquises. This group of people has been successively collaborationist, *attentiste*, and has now naturally become resistant."

Numerous groups set up by the P.P.F. and the Militia also claimed to be "under the protection of the Americans."

Up to what point was this true?

What was more important was the secret planning for insurrection being carried on by the Resistance. Paris, dispossessed for the last four years, was secretly recovering its role of capital city, which was to be officially confirmed by the arrival of General de Gaulle.

The headquarters of the new power were distributed more or less all over the city and suburbs. Indeed, it had a gift for ubiquity that rendered it undiscoverable. For instance, François de la Noë, who controlled the political S.R. of the M.L.N., had three houses, five offices and four secretaries, who were as itinerant as he was himself.

The Jesuit, Father Chaillet, was in charge of the finances and the welfare organization of the Resistance. He lived in a servant's room at 185, Rue de la Pompe. He used a bicycle for his job and carried on it bundles of bank-notes, which were furnished him, somewhat irregularly, by a senior Treasury official called Bloch-Laîné. One evening, when utterly exhausted, the Father parked his bicycle, as he usually did, at the bottom of the stairs. He went up to the sixth floor, fell on his bed and went to sleep. In the morning, on awakening, he suddenly remembered the money. He had left it downstairs. He hurried on a few clothes and ran down to rescue it. The precious parcel was fortunately still on the carrier.

How was the money for the Resistance acquired? Let us turn to Bloch-Laîné.

He was an Inspector of Finance, a high official of the Rue de Rivoli, and combined his official functions with others that were less official. He was a member of the C.O.F.I., that is to say of the Financial Committee of the Resistance, with Félix Gaillard, Michel Debré, Chaban-Delmas, René Courtin and Debray, of the Banque de Paris et des Pays-Bas, in whose house the committee met. How did the committee procure its funds? Parachutings, organized all over the country by Algiers, dropped packets of bank-notes and Treasury bonds. The bank-notes came from the reserves of Gaullist banking houses outside France, and their utilization presented no problem, since most of the money parachuted into the countryside never reached Paris. More often than not the C.O.F.I. never even saw the colour of it.

The Treasury bonds were issued by the government of Algiers and had no official currency in France; turning them into cash was to be a great source of trouble to the C.O.F.I. In the first place, they often bore no presentation date, which did not inspire confidence. Secondly, the people who might have been prepared to underwrite them and change them for normal Bank of France notes, hesitated to make such hazardous investments till the month of June. From the beginning of June their exchange value rose. On 6 June they boomed. And, after the breakout at Avranches, when the Allied armour took the road to Paris, the demand for these bonds became so great in Parisian financial circles that Bloch-Laîné had often to refuse offers of finance that were obviously inspired by motives of personal profit. The C.O.F.I. suddenly rose from penury to affluence.

The clandestine government had also organized a medical service to deal with casualties from possible street-fighting. Professor Debré was head of it for the Paris region, while his colleague, Pasteur-Valléry-Radot, was the national head. When operations began, Debré was to set up his headquarters in a sewage station in the Rue Gay-Lussac, which was scarcely evocative of antiseptics. He had organized a group of secret stretcher-bearers, often recruited from his students, who were to wear white overalls and Red Cross brassards, and pick up the casualties during the street-fighting. Since he had received very few medical supplies by parachute, he made arrangements with the Red Cross and the Public Assistance hospitals, which, when the German inspectors had gone, would be able to receive his wounded. He had not enough stretchers to supply all his first-aid posts, so he arranged for three cyclists to be permanently at his side for liaison purposes; through them he could arrange for stretchers to be sent to wherever fighting was taking place. One of his students was to be killed bringing in a wounded man near the Place Meubert. Not far from there, on the Place Saint-Michel, during firing from an F.F.I. barricade at some German engineers who had taken cover on the other side of the Seine in a restaurant called the Soleil d'Or, Professor Debré directed operations in person from a café near the Rue Saint-André-des-Arts. He telephoned one of his secret posts to ask for an ambulance. At that moment, a German car drove on to the Place; two French policemen in plain clothes, belonging to the Honneur de la Police movement, ran towards it. There were revolver shots. One policeman fell dead on the running-board. A German collapsed over the wheel.

Professor Debré hurried across to give first-aid to the dying men. Some men, who till then had taken no part in the affair, emerged from their cover and tried to stop him attending to the German: "He's a bastard, let him die. . . ." Debré paid no attention and attended equally to both men, though he was unhappily unable to save them.

Apart from the central organizations, the National Council of the Resistance (C.N.R.), the Paris Committee of Liberation (C.P.L.) and the General Delegation, of which we shall have more to say when we come to the insurrection, such were some of the important services which were beginning to function in secret.

Hunted as they were by the Gestapo and the Militia, how did they manage to communicate with each other?

Ensuring liaison was one of the most characteristic difficulties of this extraordinary period. In July 1944, when the Germans created a special police force in Paris, called the Public Gardens Police, it was not because they feared infringements of the ordinary regulations, but because they thought subversive elements frequented them.

One day, one of the heads of the F.F.I. Deuxième Bureau went to meet a leader of the Resistance in the gardens below the Trocadero. It was, of course, to be a secret meeting. But when he arrived he saw a man on a bench in animated conversation with another "suspect," while all around, on chairs and benches, were a dozen resistants who had been summoned for the same hour and were awaiting their turn for an interview. It was a fatal imprudence on the part of the man who had made a habit of arranging his interviews in this way.

Other episodes took place in working-class districts. Tollet, President of the Paris Committee of Liberation (C.P.L.) and a member of the Communist Party, wished during the days which immediately preceded the Liberation to place the archives of his secret organization in safety. He hired a van and sent his and Carrel's secretaries with two loyal policemen, who were members of the National Front. The van was unfortunately followed by the Gestapo. It drove towards Montreuil where the hiding-place had been arranged, but the driver did not know the district and turned into a dead-end. Before the Nazis could drive up, the local inhabitants, warned by the policemen, gathered round the van and emptied it of its contents in a few seconds. All the papers had been concealed in neighbouring houses by the time the Gestapo arrived. They interrogated the policemen; but the two secretaries collected the documents next day.

To ensure liaison was not enough, its personnel had to be protected, as had the various headquarters.

The Communists were past-masters at this. They knew how to partition their activities, arrange water-tight doors as it were in their organizations, so that if one section was caught, the others would not suffer the same fate. They had fixed and regular places for their meetings which took place once or twice a week. If there was any sign of the place being watched, they dispersed at once and assembled at an alternative meeting-place, which had been arranged long before.

The non-Communist F.F.I., at least in the early days, were less skilful. As a result, the Gestapo caused them greater losses during the early months. But they learnt from their disasters and became more prudent; in the end, their secret services and their communications functioned as smoothly as did those of the Communists.

There was an example of this in Paris itself, where Aron-Brunetière was head of the Intelligence department of the Deuxième Bureau of the F.F.I. headquarters.

The department had a gallant young woman as chief liaison officer. She had three agents, whom she met every day at different times and places.

Each agent had two or three accommodation addresses, both for outgoing and incoming mail, which were dealt with separately.

These accommodation addresses were generally shops, usually grocers or drapers. The agent never entered the shop unless he saw some particular object displayed in the window, a pot of mustard or a pair of pyjamas, informing him either that there were communications for him, or that it was safe to hand in his own.

Each accommodation address was in touch only with the liaison agent specially appointed to it and dealt with no one else.

An ultimate precaution, which became common form with the Resistance, was that each meeting-place must have an alternative. No one ever waited more than ten minutes for the person he was due to meet.

These were *Les Mystères de Paris* of a novel kind, and during these days before the liberation they haunted the purlieus of the city.

Indeed, disaster seemed to be lying in wait for Paris. The population was hungry and exasperated; the working class was largely reduced to unemployment and distress; the battle was drawing ever nearer to its suburbs and streets; and clandestine activities were seething among every class in preparation for insurrection.

Rarely had the capital known such dangers. Every necessary ingredient for an explosive mixture seemed to be present. One clash, one unconsidered action, might lead to irreparable disaster. It seemed that only a miracle could save the city from destruction.

Of the days preceding the liberation, there were three on which it seemed that destiny was going to give the capital a chance of safety.

The first was at the end of July 1944, or at the beginning of August.

The German General von Choltitz, who was commanding the 84th Corps in the Normandy battle, was appointed by Hitler to the command of Greater Paris, where he replaced General von Stulpnagel, who had been compromised in the plot against the Führer on 20 July. Choltitz was utterly faithful to the ancient traditions of the German Army. Fifty years of age, he had in his youth been page to the Queen of Saxony. He wore the traditional eye-glass which gave an accent to his round, high-coloured face; he was something of a martinet in the service, and though ruthless in battle hated the looting and cruelty of the S.S. In his opinion they were fanatics who dishonoured the German uniform and were leading Germany to disaster. He was short, stout, in normal circumstances placid, and enjoyed a joke. He had much common sense, and some sense of humour, not always of a wholly delicate kind, though sufficiently *gemütlich*. He had a terrible reputation as the destroyer of towns. According to legend, he was responsible for the destruction of Warsaw with 277,000 dead. One of his staff officers said of him: "During the last four years Hitler has ordered him to destroy every town that he did not want left in enemy hands, and he has never disobeyed."

Von Choltitz dared not give the lie to his appalling reputation, even if he knew it was exaggerated and untrue. His wife and children were in Germany, at Nuremberg, and their lives might depend on his implicit obedience to the Führer. In fact, he had not been at Warsaw when it was destroyed; he had been commanding an airborne regiment in the west, in the Siegfried Line.

He had, however, become a prisoner of his reputation and was obliged to appear to conform to it so as to avoid disaster; and towards the end of July, or the beginning of August, Hitler summoned him to his headquarters to give him instructions as to how he should conduct himself as the Commander of Greater Paris.

Hitler was still suffering from the physical and psychological shock resulting from the military plot of 20 July. Nevertheless, Choltitz had not expected to find him so unhinged. Eyes staring into vague distances, or glowing insanely, Hitler was living on a mixture of stimulants and barbiturates. His talk was visionary, and there was a continual froth at his lips; he seemed almost epileptic. His orders to Choltitz were in keeping with his appearance: "Paris must be utterly destroyed. On the departure of the Wehrmacht, nothing must be left standing, no church, no artistic monument. . . . On his departure, Choltitz must leave a scorched earth behind him. He must also leave typhus and cholera." Hitler gave orders that the water supply be cut off, so that "the ruined city may be a prey to epidemics."

Choltitz felt he was dealing with a lunatic. In a letter, written in May 1947, addressed to a compatriot and intercepted by the French censors, he wrote: "As far as I am concerned, it was a piece of luck that I had scarcely met Hitler before and that now, finding myself in his presence for the first time in my life, I realized I was face to face with a lunatic. This naturally relieved my conscience as a soldier, and I therefore put no single one of his orders for destruction into effect." But if Hitler was a lunatic, he was a still powerful lunatic, and one whose extravagancies were still coherent. Throughout the month of August, he continued to send Choltitz written instructions reminding him of the mad verbal orders he had given him.

The first orders transmitted during the battle of Paris emanated indirectly from Hitler and were signed by General Model, the German Commander of the Western Front.

A message dated 20 August said: "Your troops must hold their ground, so as to permit the elements of the Army of the West to cross the Paris bridges."

A message of 22 August read: "You must hold your ground up to thirty per cent casualties." And a few hours later: "Hold your ground up to forty per cent casualties."

On Wednesday 23 August, Choltitz received a still more imperative order, emanating this time not from General Model's headquarters, but from the Führer himself. It was conceived in horrific terms:

Order.—(1) The Commander of Greater Paris will carry out the most extensive possible demolitions in the area under his command, and, in particular, blow sixty-two bridges;

(2) He will take the most extensive and bloody reprisals if shots are fired at German troops;

(3) He will evacuate Paris when these demolitions are completed and if the German losses amount to thirty per cent.

How did such orders become a dead letter? Fortunately, on his decisive visit to the Führer's headquarters, Choltitz had not been limited merely to meeting the dictator. He had also met officers of the Wehr-macht, who were far from sharing the leader's frenzy. He either saw von Brauchitsch and Speidel personally, or, through trustworthy inter-mediaries, was informed of their opinions which were fortunately very different from Hitler's.

At that time von Brauchitsch was no longer on the active list, having been relieved of his command for disapproving the Führer's strategy in December 1941. But the former Commander-in-Chief, who had once been a pupil of the French Lycée in Berlin, still had much influence over his former subordinates.

In July 1944, he received a visit from President Muzy, who was travel-ling in Germany on behalf of the Red Cross. He told Muzy that the German Army would fight in front of and behind Paris, but not in the capital itself—an assurance that was in complete contradiction to Hit-ler's instructions.

As for General Speidel, Chief of Staff to Army Group B, which in-cluded the Greater Paris area, it is to be presumed that Choltitz was aware of his intentions towards Paris and realized that they were very different from the views expressed by Hitler. At the moment when the final decisions were being made, Choltitz and Speidel were able to hold a guarded telephone conversation, which would have been impossible unless it was based on previous talks.[1]

To sum up, Choltitz's interview with Hitler had precisely the contrary effect to that which the Chancellor intended. On the one hand, the German general, horrified by the leader's extraordinary paroxysms, haunted by the spectacle of a lunatic, had from then on one intention only—not to compromise his honour as a soldier by such a tragedy. On the other hand, he realized that in spite of the bloody failure of the plot of 22 July, the ditch that already existed between the Nazi Party and the Wehrmacht had become an abyss. From his colleagues, the German general officers, he had learnt in particular that the plans for the destruction of Paris, as drawn up by the Führer, were far from corre-sponding to the views of the General Staff. He considered himself re-lieved, not from his military duties, but from the criminal role the Führer wished to impose on him.

One of the more curious episodes of the liberation of Paris made avail-able the orders Choltitz issued to the units under his command. The French General Malraison, in August 1944, was instructed by the F.F.I. to organize the defence of the Bank of France in Paris. The Germans

[1] Cf., page 279.

had transformed the vaults into a wine and rum store, comprising thousands of bottles.

Having saved this obviously valuable loot, Malraison took part in the seizing of the Hôtel Meurice, which was the Greater Paris headquarters. He saw a van full of papers catching fire. It contained Choltitz's archives. He was able to put the fire out, saved the documents, sorted them, translated them and, fourteen years later, was kind enough to put the more important at our disposal.

It is clear that Choltitz was trying both to ensure the safety of his troops and the protection of the civilian population.

In his General Order No. 1, 19 August 1944, the second paragraph reads:

"I order the Second Stage of readiness to be put into immediate effect for the whole of the Greater Paris zone.

"Notice of operations will be posted.

"The commanders of the tactical groups will take merciless action in their zones, and wipe out all important centres of resistance.

"Troops must be warned to avoid useless firing."

In Order No. 2, dated 19 August:

"Quiet and order must be restored by every possible means. Civilian life must be interrupted as little as possible during the day." [Which did not prevent that] "the security of the troops and their strong-points must be assured; all armed resistance will be mercilessly suppressed. . . . Houses from which there is firing will be destroyed."

In Order No. 3, dated 22 August:

"In the City of Paris, combat groups will adopt a prudent and intelligent attitude, at once effective and disciplined, in any action they take against the over-excited young men who are in open revolt. It must be remembered that they are divided into numerous political and ideological tendencies."

This was happily far removed from Hitler's frenzies. The orders were naturally neither particularly amiable or kind, but they were precisely those which, in the circumstances, a military commander was bound to issue. He had in the first place to ensure the safety of his troops, and only in the second the preservation of the city.

On the evidence of certain trustworthy witnesses, though there are no typed archives to support their statements, Choltitz went even further than this. In his desire to spare Paris, he apparently went so far as to get in touch with the Allies and inform Eisenhower of his intentions.

If he did not himself make these overtures directly, they were at least made by one of his subordinates, Major Bender, second-in-command of the German Secret Services in Paris. He was an exceedingly strange character. He claimed to have been involved in General Giraud's escape in 1942 and to have accompanied him to Switzerland in the assumed role of an American agent. "He was certainly," writes Henri Danjoy, basing himself on information which has been confirmed to us by a member of the Intelligence Service in Paris, "at the centre of the diplomatic mysteries which surrounded, and will perhaps continue to surround for a long time to come, some of the secrets of the defence of Paris."

Together with a certain Austrian Baron von Poch-Pastor, who was also at Choltitz's headquarters, Bender wanted to save the capital. Was it without his commander's knowledge, or with his approval, that he informed Eisenhower of Choltitz's humanitarian intentions? In any case, there can be no question that the information influenced Eisenhower's decisions. Till then he had wanted to spare his troops from having to fight their way through Paris, but now he suddenly changed his mind, and turned his armour in its direction.

In its consequences, both immediate and delayed, the Commander of Greater Paris's visit to Hitler proved to be one of the decisive days preliminary to ensuring the safety of the city.

The second day was 17 August, and the site the Hôtel Meurice in Paris. On that day, Taittinger, President of the Municipal Council, accompanied by an interpreter, Madame Fontenille, was shown into General von Choltitz's office in the Hôtel Meurice.

General von Choltitz was sitting in a chair. On his right, Councillor Eckelmann, a sort of German Super-Prefect for Greater Paris, was standing. Despite his scarred face, the result of student duels, his appearance was far from martial; and he was wearing what might well have been a non-commissioned officer's tunic. He seemed shy, talked in a low voice, and blushed like a girl. The German police criticized him for being too sensible to the charms of Parisian life.

On the General's left was his Chief of Staff; behind them stood several officers representing the different staff services, in particular von Gunther of the Medical Services.

It was an impressive gathering. The officers stood immobile about their commander. Their expressionless faces reflected immutable decisions. There was but one favourable sign: Taittinger could see no representative of the Gestapo in the gathering. There was therefore a chance that the interview, painful though it might be, would at least take place between honest men.

Choltitz spoke first. "His words," says Taittinger, "were forthright; he spoke harshly and to the point; his attitude was that of a man who had thought things over and made a decision." He spoke as a military commander:

"My duty is to see that the Wehrmacht holds Paris without opposition; I must therefore inform you that I have decided to apply collective sanctions for every act committed against the representatives of the German Army."

And, pointing to a map of the capital, he said: "If there is any shooting, repressive measures will be taken at once. Look at this for yourselves. My dispositions are quite simple. Imagine that a shot is fired at one of my soldiers from a house among, for instance, the odd numbers of the Avenue de l'Opéra, between the Rue Gomboust and the Rue des Pyramides, I shall have all the houses in that block burnt, and I shall shoot all the inhabitants."

There was an impressive silence. For some minutes the General sat perfectly still at his desk.

Then he screwed his eye-glass into his eye and leaned back in his chair. He replaced his finger on the map of Paris. To what new threat of destruction was this the preliminary?

"I have at my disposal twenty-two thousand men, mostly S.S., one hundred Tiger tanks and ninety bombers.

"If any act is committed more serious than an isolated rifle shot, I shall increase the zone of punishment. In the case of insurrection or riot, I shall call on the air force and destroy the whole district with incendiary bombs. . . . You see, it's a perfectly simple matter."

It was indeed perfectly simple, tragically simple. Paris was threatened with the fate of the Polish capital, which had been entirely destroyed, and two hundred and seventy-seven thousand of its inhabitants massacred.

But the General had not yet finished with the map of Paris. His finger was now following the windings of the Seine.

"You are an officer, M. Taittinger, and you must be aware of the measures I must take for the security of the troops for whom I am responsible. I am now talking to you as a soldier, you understand? The bridges, the power stations, the railway stations . . ."

Then he suddenly said, in a quieter voice, which contrasted with the severity of his words:

"It is my duty to delay the advance of the Allied Forces."

Having delivered himself of this, he became more co-operative:

"If I can help you in the matter of supplies, I shall, as indeed Herr

Eckelmann has often done before. We can help you to maintain your trucks and can even lend you, if they would be of any use, a certain number of Wehrmacht trucks."

There was nothing Taittinger could do but thank him for his somewhat tardy solicitude. He had met the attack without flinching. But now the moment had come for a counter-offensive. Taittinger began by saying:

"If any district of Paris is set on fire, or if there are any mass shootings, the German Army can expect Parisian Vespers, similar to the famous Sicilian Vespers. Every German soldier will be marked down and killed when the moment comes by a revolutionary and patriotic Paris. Do you want to run such a grave risk, when you can so easily avoid it?

"My country," Taittinger went on, "has suffered in body, mind and heart from the war and the Occupation. If you wish to lay the basis of better times to come, leave Paris with the memory that a man such as yourself understood."

Paris was a city of refuge in which the inhabitants of many bombed towns had taken shelter. Was their Calvary to begin all over again? Moreover, Paris was sheltering one hundred and twenty thousand children, forty thousand sick, a great number of the old, and of women and wounded, among whom were twenty-five thousand Germans, who could not be moved and would have to be abandoned by the Wehrmacht on its departure.

The fate of many other towns could support Paris's case.

"As far as I'm concerned," Taittinger went on, "I was most distressed when Westminster Abbey was savagely bombed, and I deplored the fact that Cologne Cathedral was set on fire. Paris is one of the few great cities of Europe which remain intact; you must help me to save it."

Choltitz fell silent for a moment. Then, in a low voice, which was no longer threatening, he told Taittinger that he felt great sympathy for the Parisian population "which seemed so very well behaved."

"You see," he said, "that instead of surrounding the Hôtel Meurice by strong-points armed with guns and machine-guns, I have limited myself merely to defending the approaches with white barriers, which I have ordered to be kept open so that the public may continue to circulate."

The General rose to his feet and went over to the window. The sight of the Place de la Concorde and the Tuileries Gardens reminded him of what the real stakes were in the game they were playing. It was as if he were rediscovering Paris, and as if Paris, unaware of how crucial the moment was, were displaying before him all her charm, her youth, her joy of living.

The German commander, extending his hand towards the city, pointed to a brood of children who, accompanied by their mother, were going to the sand-pit in the Tuileries Gardens.

"I like to see," he said, "all these people moving freely about under my windows."

Moving away from his staff, Choltitz led Taittinger on to the balcony overlooking the Rue de Rivoli.

The Frenchman said: "Generals rarely have the power to build, they more often have that of destroying. . . .

"Imagine that one day—for as far as I'm concerned the die is cast, and the war is coming to an end—you return to the Hôtel Meurice as a tourist and that you come out on to this balcony on which we are now standing; you look to the left, at the Perrault colonnade, with the great Palais du Louvre on the right, the Palais de Gabriel and the Place de la Concorde. And among these splendid buildings, each one charged with history, you are able to say: 'It was I, von Choltitz, who on a certain day had the power to destroy them, but I saved them for humanity.' General, is not that worth all a conqueror's fame?"

Choltitz seemed moved by the thought—which was indeed realized— that one day he might return to lean upon that very balcony. He set a limit to his demands:

"There is one thing," he said, "on which I absolutely insist, there must be no attacks on the five posts defended by the army: my headquarters in the Hôtel Meurice, the Avenue Foch, the Place de l'Opéra, the Palais du Luxembourg, and the barracks in the Place de la République. As for the rest, I'm prepared to close my eyes to individual acts— I say *individual* advisedly—and I put my faith in the good sense of the population of Paris."

Taittinger made an ultimate appeal to the General to take steps to avoid last-minute violence. Choltitz dropped his eye-glass from his eye.

"You're a good advocate for Paris, M. Taittinger; you're doing your duty very well indeed. But I have my duty as a German general. I shall go as far as I can to respond to your appeal concerning the destruction of strategic buildings and the shooting of hostages. . . . We shall do the best we can to live in harmony during the few days we have still to spend together."

The third episode which contributed to the safety of the capital took place against a very different background.

It was on the first floor of a small tavern in Saint-Maur that half a dozen men met on 7 August 1944 to hear what a seventh, suspected of intelligence with the enemy, had to say for himself. It was an important meeting. The Paris Committee of Liberation (C.P.L.), which was in fact the secret Municipal Council of Paris, were gathered to hear Flouret, Councillor at the Cour des Comptes, Commander of the Legion of Honour, who had been appointed by de Gaulle's General Delegation in France to be the future Prefect of the Seine.

The C.P.L. was one of the Resistance organizations in which the Communists had seized power. They counted on it to attain a double end: on the one hand, in default of taking power at once, which was not in accordance with Stalin's immediate policy because of his obligations to the British and the Americans, it gave them an opportunity to fill positions that one day might permit them to attempt in Paris what was later to be known as the "Coup de Prague."

Secondly, it enabled them to make things as difficult as possible for the Wehrmacht, and to poison the relations between the population of Paris and the German Army, even if it resulted in damage to the city. And this was no mere contribution to the defeat of the Germans on the western front, but was intended to prevent their sending troops from the west to fight the U.S.S.R. on the eastern front.

The Communists of the C.P.L. wanted the liberation of Paris to be accomplished by insurrection. Since the Wehrmacht was obliged to retreat through the city, they wished to see its passage disputed by force of arms.

Some of their opponents have said, or let it be understood, that the Communists wished for the destruction of Paris. This is a ridiculous libel. The Paris Communists were as much attached to their city, their monuments and their homes as was anyone else. It is, however, true to say that, as Communists, they were involved in a wider strategy which entailed greater risks for Paris than did the strategy of the other parties of the Resistance.

This was the basic cause of the differences between the C.P.L., represented by Tollet, its President, Carrel, who was in charge of military questions, and the General Delegation, represented principally by Parodi, the direct representative of General de Gaulle in France, and Closon.

During the fighting at the liberation these disagreements affected the truce which the General Delegation supported and the C.P.L. refused to acknowledge.

In this period before the liberation, and particularly on this 7 August 1944, when the C.P.L. met in a suburban tavern, in which the Impressionist painters would have felt at home, the discussions concerned the appointment of the men who, after the Germans had gone, would hold the positions of real authority: the Prefect of the Seine, and the Prefect of Police. Were they to be appointed by the President of the C.P.L., that is to say would they be Communists, or by the General Delegation, that is to say Gaullists? Would they therefore be in favour of intensifying the fighting in Paris itself, with all that must entail in the way of insurrection and destruction, or would they take the opposite view and thereby give the capital a greater chance of safety? There was clearly an important matter of principle at stake.

The President of the C.P.L. was Tollet, a trades union leader, who had lead a courageous and adventurous life as a militant worker. This former upholsterer with his expressive looks and flashing eyes, his working class accent, and the mocking vehement manners of the French working class, had one enemy, Germany, and one rival, the General Delegation, presided over by Parodi.

Flouret, who had come to meet Tollet at Saint-Maur on a bicycle had had a very different career from that of the clandestine President. He was neither a member of the proletariat nor a revolutionary, but a high official whose career, both in peace and war, had always been irreproachably conscientious.

In January 1937, he was appointed a Commander of the Legion of Honour for his work in the Ministry of Finance; and this had facilitated his appointment as designate Prefect of the Seine by the General Delegation. His bicycle and his riband were therefore the bases of his attaining to a position of power.

For this was the matter under discussion on 7 August in the tavern at Saint-Maur. The C.P.L.'s candidate for the Prefecture of the Seine was the Communist Marrane, one of the most intelligent and, to all appearances, most moderate members of the team. He was a magnificent resistant and was the best type of French worker. He might well have come straight from the barricades of 1848. He was good-natured, humane, and even kind. But, in spite of these good qualities, his appointment would have constituted a grave risk to the capital.

The General Delegation, in agreement with General de Gaulle, had nominated Flouret for the post. This created considerable ill-feeling in the C.P.L. It was not that they were personally hostile to Flouret, for he was an affable man, who disliked making enemies, and knew well how to avoid doing so. But in the eyes of the Communists of the C.P.L., he had the unpardonable fault of being nominated to a key post the Party claimed.

The Communist Party was to make use of familiar tactics against him. Through the National Front, they put disgraceful calumnies about him into circulation. He was, they said, a Pétainist, if not a collaborator. It was rumoured that he had held a press conference in his office at the Cour des Comptes to journalists in the pay of the Germans, at which he had announced and discussed measures to be taken against the Communists.

If this was true, it was clear that Flouret could not expect to become Prefect of the Seine and would have to give way to Marrane. The General Delegation declined to believe such infamous stories of so prudent a man, and demanded that an inquiry be held to discover the truth. Léo Hamon, who though no Communist was Left wing and on good personal terms with the Party, was placed in charge of it.

Hamon made inquiries at the Cour des Comptes. He questioned people of every grade. He interviewed a Président de Chambre, a conseiller maître, a conseiller référendaire, an auditeur, and the secretary of the Union of Administrative Employees.

The evidence was unanimous: no one had heard of the press conference. There was no reason why Flouret should not be appointed.

The minutes of the C.P.L. for 31 July contained the following entry:

A report of the inquiry made by U.D., F.N., O.C.M., and C.D.L.R., concerning the character of Février (Flouret) was presented to the C.P.L.

The report made it clear that the accusations against Février should be rejected.

F.N. apologized for having spread these accusations. The C.P.L. took note of this.

Lib, C.D.L.R. and Vallat (Jean Mons) protested at the careless way in which the F.N. had behaved in the matter.

The C.P.L. decided to invite Février to attend its next meeting. . . .

The next meeting was that of 7 August. Flouret, in spite of the prejudice against him, made a very good impression. He was at once vital and diplomatic; he seemed to be the perfect type of prefect. Here are the minutes recording his proposals:

Février announced his desire to work with the C.P.L. He declared that he had never wished to compete against a Communist Party candidate and stated that he would submit happily to the Government's decision, if it went against him.

He intended to work in close and confidential contact with the C.P.L. and the Paris Assemblies. His secretariat would be organized on this basis.

His first care would be to purge the administration as rapidly and energetically as possible. He intended to make it energetic and place it at the disposal of the population of Paris. Questions involving personnel would be negotiated with the representatives of the union concerned.

To conclude, Février gave an account of the plans he had already considered to meet the essential questions that were bound to arise at the time of the liberation.

The incident was closed. The Communists were appeased: in the absence of one of their own people at the Prefecture of the Seine, the post would be held by a man who would clearly give them no trouble.

It was on his now prefectorial bicycle that Flouret returned to the Cour des Comptes.

But there was another obstacle barring the narrow path that Paris must follow to achieve liberty intact.

The worst was no longer certain; but it was still possible, and at the mercy of some chance exasperation or imprudence. There was no lack of indications during these last days before the liberation that it was still very much to be feared.

Before its departure, the Gestapo, or its henchmen, had intensified their atrocities. At the Santé prison, a Militia court-martial had shot ten prisoners. The prisoners detained in Fresnes prison had been evacuated, no one knew where. On 17 August, the bodies of thirty murdered French civilians were found in the Bois de Boulogne.

At the same time, looting took on all the appearance of a razzia, not only by isolated individuals, but organized by the German authorities, who would not be in authority much longer.

The Paris banks received an order to remit all their holdings in gold and paper money to Lloyds Bank by the 16th. The gold would be paid for at the rate of three hundred and eighty francs a *louis*, whereas on the free market the *louis* was worth four thousand.

The atmosphere of anxiety was shot through with strange events: the German censorship—who would have believed it?—forbade the distribution of a number of *Je suis Partout* because of an article by Rebatet entitled "Loyalty to National Socialism." Shaken by this most unexpected impediment to their freedom of expression, the gentlemen of the Paris press ordered the Garage Royal, in the Rue de Berri, to make their cars ready for flight.

Other departures took place in a calmer atmosphere. The German commissioners and controllers, who for the last three years had been directing French industry, wished to part with the French industrialists and officials who had been compelled to work with them on good terms. They pointed out, clearly on orders from above, how "polite, accommodating and indeed useful" they had been and, as they departed, seemed to be saying: "Good-bye, see you soon. . . . We shall do even better next time."

All this presaged the end of the drama. What was to be its dénouement?

One morning, the firemen on watch in the Tower of the Sacré-Cœur saw Allied shells falling on Châtillon and Maisons-Alfort. Would they stop outside the gates? Would they spare the city?

Chapter II

THE LIBERATION OF PARIS

1. THE PRELIMINARIES

PUBLIC transport including the Métro ceased to function; the Parisians asked mockingly that at least four stations be reopened:

Bienvenue, for the Allies.

Cambronne, for the Germans.

Concorde, for the French.

Père-Lachaise, for the collaborators.

On 14 July, there was a mass demonstration in the east of the capital, in the districts of Belleville, La Nation and La République, which were at that time the areas in which the Left held their big meetings. It was organized by two militant Communists of the Union des Syndicats, Toudic of the Builders Union and Grodzinski of the Interbranche S, which included public services, insurance and transport. The Germans, supported by the French police, who, however reluctantly, were still obeying orders, tried in vain to stop it. But the demonstration, protected by the F.T.P., and headed by Colonel Froger, filled the street for three-quarters of an hour.

On this same day of national festival, the Union des Syndicats organized a demonstration of railway workers which marched from the Vitry depot to the statue of Rouget de Lisle at Choisy, a distance of some kilometres. The intention was to obtain the liberation of imprisoned comrades, as well as a raise in pay and a distribution of preserved foods to manual labourers. The French police made no attempt to intervene; but the Germans dispersed the demonstration at the statue of Rouget de Lisle. There were several arrests, but no casualties. This first insurrection paved the way for that of 10 August which was the beginning of the fighting of the liberation.

Meanwhile, the population was carrying out a number of plans which, if less overt, were no less effective. Steel workers manufactured a large quantity of special nails to burst the tires of the retreating German convoys on the road to Meaux, while a chemist called Chisnier was busily preparing Molotov cocktails to deal with the tanks when they had been immobilized.

During the first days of the month of August, Bonffet, the Prefect of the Seine, received delegates of the Paris transport demonstrators, who had assembled on the Place de l'Hôtel de Ville. On the surface this demonstration was merely a claim for higher wages and so on, but in fact it was a cover for operations of a more serious kind.

Meanwhile, in the factories working for the Germans there were some four hundred sabotage groups at work. And at Villeneuve-Saint-Georges, the railway workers set the goods siding that dealt with German stores on fire and caused several million francs worth of damage.

On 12 August, the railway workers went on strike. It was an important event and a prelude to insurrection.

The railway workers from the Batignolles, who were one hundred per cent on strike, went to Pont-Cardinet and stopped all traffic by lying down on the permanent way. At Villeneuve-Saint-Georges, where they were also on strike to a man, they unbolted the rails.

Five employees from the Ivry depot went to the Gare d'Orsay; armed with three pistols between them, they prevented the drivers of the electric locomotives from working.

The movement soon spread over the whole Paris region, and not a train ran.

To break the strike, the Germans proceeded to make arrests; while the French government, represented in Paris by Marcel Déat and Brinon, thought the best policy was to grant several days' holiday dating from 15 August.

At the Halles, there was severe fighting on 19 and 20 August; the F.T.P. of the Bara Battalion having got control of the "stomach of Paris," the Germans tried to retake it by every means in their power. The battalion headquarters, which were in Pavilion 2, issued orders to barricade the Boulevard de Sébastopol and the Rue de Rivoli with overturned trucks, which had been captured from the Germans. Inside the market, they requisitioned all the employees and shorthand typists; on the first floor they hurriedly set up tables, desks, typewriters and duplicating machines to deal with the accounts of the orders for supplies. At the same time, they obtained "with irrefutable arguments, agreement from the big butchers to free the stocks of meat." The same thing was done for flour to the advantage of the bakers of the district.

Thus nationalized, the Halles resumed its normal functions. It fed the population and all the groups of combatants throughout the Paris

The Defence of Paris According to the Orders of General von Choltitz, August 19–22

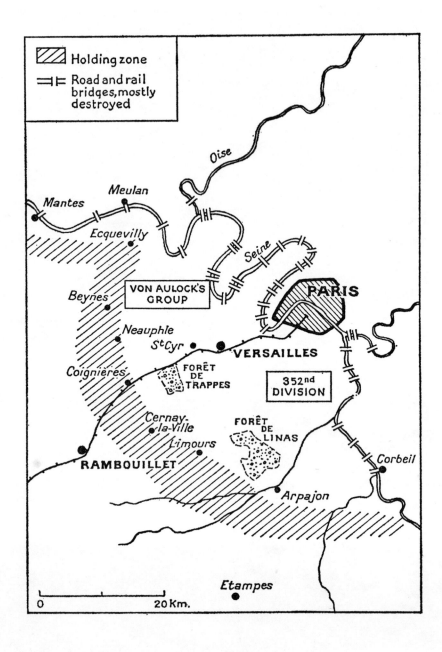

Holding zone

Road and rail bridges, mostly destroyed

Oise

Mantes

Meulan

Ecquevilly

Seine

VON AULOCK'S GROUP

Beynes

Neauphle

St Cyr

PARIS

VERSAILLES

Coignières

FORÊT DE TRAPPES

352nd DIVISION

Cernay-la-Ville

FORÊT DE LINAS

Limours

RAMBOUILLET

Corbeil

Arpajon

0   20 Km.

Etampes

region. Captured trucks, using German gasoline, circulated through Paris and the suburbs supplying institutions, among which were the public hospitals.

The police were also preparing to go on strike. They had had a very difficult role to play throughout the occupation. On 14 June 1940, the date on which the Germans entered Paris, the police had received orders to give military salutes to the officers of the Wehrmacht. During the four years of the occupation, they had often unwillingly had to carry out the enemy's orders: at the 'Vel d'Hiv' they had taken part in rounding up Jews; in the streets they had suppressed student demonstrations against the Germans. . . . As a result, they felt considerable resentment at having been placed at the service of the despots. And out of this resentment three Resistance movements emerged which, during these last days, included the great majority of the police. Their members were distinguished by wearing a red shoulder-lanyard.

These three organizations were Honneur de la Police, which had no particular political colour, though inclining towards a moderate radical socialism, Police et Patrie, also without political alignment, though more or less socialist, and Front National de la Police, which was controlled by the Communists.

Police officers whose behaviour had been in any way dubious were excluded from these organizations. The inspectors of the Special Squads, who often treated Resistance suspects disgracefully, were not to be found among them. "In the corridors," declared one who had suffered their attentions, "one could hear screams from the rooms on each side in which people were being beaten. A woman of seventy was beaten for having harboured a defaulter from forced labour, whose address they wanted to extract from her.

"Women were tortured and handed over to the Germans, indeed suffered such harsh treatment that it can only be qualified as sadistic."

Evidence which was confirmed, alas, by many other witnesses, even by Bussière, the Prefect of Police: "I am heartbroken at the thought that men could have done such things at the Prefecture of Police. I have told you, and I repeat it, that I could never have believed that men could commit such abominable deeds."

Also excluded were those officers who from cowardice had handed their Resistance colleagues over to the Gestapo. Among the German interpreters in the Prefecture, who were almost all Alsatian by origin and very anti-Nazi, there was one, Durand-Berger, who was denounced by B—— of the General Intelligence branch. Durand-Berger, who was a fine swimmer, often went to the Molitor Baths. When they saw him arrive in plain clothes, the staff of the baths at once put him into a cabin which had already been assigned to a German soldier. It is improbable that they did so by inadvertence. Durand-Berger quickly changed into the German's uniform and, postponing his swim, hurried off to the German prisons where, thanks to his Wehrmacht uniform, he was able to free the prisoners.

B—— of the General Intelligence section betrayed him. There was a reward of 5,000 francs for denouncing "a criminal."

The days preceding the liberation were to bear witness to the combative spirit of the police, as well as to the distrust with which the Germans viewed them.

On 13 August, they disarmed 375 police at Saint-Denis, Saint-Ouen and Asnières as a precaution. As a result, the Prefecture of Police, which feared other similar measures, issued orders to all the police to lay down their arms and get out of uniform so as to escape eventual arrest. There were soon no police to be seen.

Hennequin, director-general of the Municipal Police, made contact with the German authorities and obtained an assurance that no new measures would be taken against his subordinates. At eleven o'clock he asked them to resume their normal duties, which they did at 13.30 hours. But these servants of the law had meantime learnt the savour of illegality, after which, so it is said, no one is ever the same again.

Bussière, who was a good man, if rather too conformist for these exceptional circumstances, tried to pacify them.

"At 12.15," relates Ferrol, an Inspector of Police, "I was in the mess at Bertin-Poirée with about 500 inspectors and constables. About half-past twelve Bussière arrived. . . . He climbed on to a table and spoke more or less as follows: 'My friends, I have a piece of good news for you; I have obtained new credits for your mess from the Minister of Finance. I ask you to return to duty. . . . Just think what will happen if the Gestapo or the Militia take over your duties. I know that you've been told the Americans are about to arrive. . . . If they ever do arrive. . . .' Bussière's speech created some wavering among those present."

But the wavering ceased when the order for an immediate general strike was issued by the Paris Police Committee of Liberation. It ran as follows:

Order for a General Strike by the whole of the Paris police.
The Gestapo has issued orders to disarm the Paris police and intern them.

In response to this provocation, the whole personnel of the Prefecture of Police, both active and sedentary, will cease work on Tuesday morning, 15 August, at 7 o'clock.

Those on duty will stop at once.

Police who do not obey this order to strike will be considered traitors and collaborators.

In no circumstances will our comrades allow themselves to be disarmed.

In the ultimate battle we shall all go forward with the people of Paris.

Front National de la Police—Police et Patrie—Honneur de la Police.

On 15 August, on the orders of the Resistance, the police of all ranks left their posts and their uniforms. The Prefecture and the police stations were entirely paralyzed.

In an attempt to arrest the movement, Bussière dismissed Hennequin, whom the police disliked because of his supposed harshness in the service. Godard de Donville replaced him; but in vain. The Resistance was not going to change its orders for a mere detail of this kind.

On 16 August it was estimated that 99.7 per cent of the police force had obeyed the order to strike. Fifteen thousand guardians of the law in plain clothes, but carrying arms, strolled peacefully about Paris. Traffic control had ceased.

If the police were on strike, the diplomats were busy. Such diplomats, that is, who had remained in Paris, for most of them were in Vichy. They thought up a number of fantastic plans.

In May, an Italian journalist, Domenico Russo, who wanted to play at being an *éminence grise* and who claimed to be on terms of intimacy with the Jesuit, of German origin, who was the Pope's confessor, wrote: "The Pope should leave Rome, which would create a profound impression on world opinion." He should go to Lisbon and summon to that city a conference of the belligerent powers, which would be preceded by an armistice.

It was an absurd proposal, but Russo succeeded in interesting a few out-of-work politicians in it. However, it went no further, "many reasons, political, military and religious" having made Russo sceptical about the chances of Papal intervention being successful.

Taittinger preferred to act through neutrals, and selected Dr. Jean-Marie Muzy, former President of the Swiss Confederation, who was at the moment on a mission from the Swiss government and the International Red Cross, for the purpose. Muzy approached Marshal von Rundstedt with the object of having Paris declared an open city. He obtained assurances. In gratitude, the Municipal Council gave him, in July 1944, a medal representing the "Heart of Paris." It was the only recognition this great friend of France ever received.

In this same month of July, Taittinger also approached Lequerica, the Spanish Ambassador to France. But the Ambassador did not believe in the imminence of a German defeat and thought there was plenty of time for negotiations about Paris.

Nevertheless he agreed, as did the other neutral diplomats, to transmit to his government a message from the highest authorities in Paris: Cardinal Suhard, Victor Constant, President of the Council of the Department of the Seine, and Pierre Taittinger, President of the Municipal Council of Paris. This message was addressed to the Pope, to King Gustav of Sweden, to President Salazar and to General Franco. "We would be profoundly grateful to Your Excellency," it ran, "if you would take up this question and invite your government to intervene with the governments of the German Reich, Great Britain and the United States of America so that some measures may be taken to ensure the indispensable minimum of food for the daily subsistence of the French population."

Among all these representations, many of which were absurd, one diplomat played an important part and greatly deserved Paris's gratitude: this was Raoul Nordling, the Swedish Consul-General. Nordling had spent his whole diplomatic career in Paris, had lived there all his life, and was a former pupil of the Janson-de-Sailly Lycée. Though his father was Swedish, his mother was French, from a Burgundian family. This, in the circumstances, was a most suitable background for interceding for Paris with the neutral powers. Besides holding his official position, he was also managing director in Paris of the S.K.F. ball-bearing factories, in which Sweden had an interest. In the summer of 1944, these factories created difficulties with the British and Americans because they were clearly working for the enemy. Indeed, his diplomatic activities were sometimes hindered by the fact that too many ball-bearings were going to Berlin. He was also to have difficulties after the Liberation, though they were purely theoretical ones, with the organizations set up to inquire into economic collaboration.

At the end of May 1944, Nordling returned from Sweden, where the King had talked to him at length about a plan to which he was much attached for mediation by the neutrals. It would seem that the Reich would not have been displeased at this time to see this project realized, for on his arrival in Paris Nordling received a visit from a colonel sent from Hitler's headquarters to find out what was in the King's mind.

Interpreting the visit as a possible overture from the Third Reich,

Nordling and Domenico Russo decided to go to Vichy and ask the Marshal to intervene personally with Chancellor Hitler. Nordling and Russo had a difficult journey. On reaching Vichy, they saw successively two of Pétain's closest collaborators, Louis-Dominique Girard and Commandant Tracou. They both confirmed that it was impossible to ask for an audience with the Marshal without Laval's authorization. Laval then received them, but only to tell them that, though he was interested in their plan for mediation by the neutrals, he could do nothing without the authorization of Abetz. Abetz, informed in his turn, had to refer the matter to Ribbentrop who, obviously, could do nothing without Hitler's consent. The whole procedure seemed so protracted that Nordling and Russo realized that Paris would be—either liberated or destroyed long before negotiations even began.

The Swedish Consul-General, therefore, approached the authorities in Paris, Taittinger and Choltitz, on whom the fate of the city directly depended.

Both sides received him so well that, on 19 August, in the middle of the battle for liberation, during his last hours in office, Taittinger got the German general to agree that next day, 20 August, he would receive at the Hôtel Meurice the Swedish Consul-General, two leaders of the F.F.I. and himself to discuss a truce. The interview took place, but without Taittinger, who had meanwhile been arrested by the very people who were due to accompany him to it.

There were other last-minute negotiations in Paris. During these final days of his political power, Laval displayed an energy and an imagination equal to the best periods of his astonishing career. But, in the context of the moment, when everything on which he had staked was collapsing, he was rather in the situation of a defeated general who, at the very moment of capitulation, prepares a grandiose plan for an offensive. His struggles were in vain and were bound to fail.

Laval's manœuvres were intended to have two phases. In the first place he would purge the government of the ultra-collaborationist ministers, Marcel Déat, Darnand, Bonnard and Brinon, and on the strength of their dismissal himself appear once again as at least relatively a democrat. At the same time, through the agency of Bussière, the Prefect of Police, who was entirely devoted to him, he would endeavour to win over the support of the Paris police. He also intended to take severe measures against the Militia, even arresting certain of their leaders if necessary. After which, he would convoke the National Assembly to Paris, and welcome the Allies on their arrival from the rostrum of the government bench.

It was on this basis that Laval formulated the second phase of his plan. Having broken his ties with Vichy, he would renew his links with the members of the Third Republic, and restore its parliamentary basis.

On 13 August, at five o'clock in the morning, a procession of six cars arrived unheralded in the courtyard of the Hôtel de Ville.

There was a ring at the flat door of the Prefect of the Seine, Bouffet. Five o'clock in the morning, when dawn was breaking, was the usual time for Gestapo arrests. But, on this occasion, precisely the opposite was taking place. The cars in the courtyard had not come to take a prisoner. They had freed one, and an important one. They had brought Édouard Herriot and his wife, whom Pierre Laval had removed from the Hospice de Maréville, near Nancy, where they had been under house-arrest.

Édouard Herriot was delighted to be back in Paris. Both he and his wife sniffed at the bouquets of flowers, decorated with the traditional blue and red, which the Municipal Council presented to them as soon as it knew of their arrival.

He was delighted to be able to send for his usual tailor and order a suit. He savoured, as a man long deprived, the witty and intellectual conversation at which he was himself so adept. But he showed great reserve about the political projects with which Laval wished to associate him.

For three days, during which he refused to take part in political negotiations, he talked of Madame Récamier or the Normandy Forest. He allowed himself to be invited to luncheon and dinner by Laval and Abetz. But during the night of the 16th he was awakened by Roland Nozeck, head of the Political Branch of the Gestapo, who came in full uniform to give him the order to return to Maréville. And this allowed Herriot to make, in theatrical terms, an "exit" of a most convenient kind, which was no doubt precisely what he secretly desired. He declared, in substance: "I have asked nothing from you; my return to Paris took place under the guarantee of Ambassador Abetz. Just when you told me I was free for good, you imprison me again. You cannot play with a man's dignity in this way. It is true that it is not the first time Germany has broken her word, and it will not be the last. . . ."

No Republican statesman could have been more dignified. But it would seem, in reality, that Herriot was delighted to be able to escape from the snare Laval had set for him, and that he had no other wish than to live in peace in his asylum.[1]

[1] Cf., the final telegrams from Grandval, page 169.

The two principal agents of the liberation were on the one hand the French 2nd Armoured Division, whose columns were approaching, and on the other the secret organizations which were beginning to take over.

In order to avoid fighting in Paris, Eisenhower had planned an encircling movement, so as to force the garrison to capitulate without a battle. This plan was conceived for both humanitarian and tactical reasons: "At the moment," he wrote in his *Crusade in Europe*, "we were anxious to save every ounce of fuel and ammunition for combat operations, in order to carry our lines forward the maximum distance." It was not expected that the capital would be taken before the first days of September.

To put this plan into execution, the U.S. Third Army entered Orleans and Chartres on 15 and 16 August. Dreux was taken on the 18th. But, meanwhile, Paris had risen. And, since the Wehrmacht still had 20,000 men, 80 tanks, 60 guns and 60 aircraft in the Paris district, the few thousand police and Paris F.F.I., with no arms but rifles or revolvers, would not be able to hold out for long.

On 21 August, General Leclerc, whose units were before Argentan, was informed of the rising. On his own initiative, he sent a strong reconnaissance force towards Paris. Meanwhile, he asked General Bradley to authorize his whole division to advance with the utmost speed towards the capital.

On 23 August, after an advance of 200 kilometres, he reached Rambouillet. And there he received the orders to march on Paris for which he had been waiting for four years.

Leclerc divided his force into three groups: one under Langlade who advanced to Sévres; a second under Billotte, who moved from Arpajon towards the Panthéon; and a third under Dio, who remained in support.

At 17.00 hours, Leclerc sent a message by reconnaissance plane to the Prefecture of Police: "Stand firm, we're coming." The same day, at 19.30 hours, at Croix-de-Berny, he saw Captain Dronne's detachment, consisting of three tanks, and eleven vehicles, returning down the road to Orleans.

There was a brief dialogue:

"What are you doing?"

"I'm returning on to the axis, according to orders."

"You're not to do anything of the kind. Make for Paris at once, for the centre of Paris."

And so it was that that very evening, guided by Parisians from the suburbs, Dronne arrived with his detachment outside the liberated Hôtel de Ville.

For months, in spite of the unity of action displayed against the occupying power, there had been two main opposing tendencies in Paris: the Gaullist resistance and the Communist resistance. The Communists, who had the preponderance in the C.O.M.A.C., the military organization, and a great influence in the C.N.R., the political organization, were also predominant in the Paris Committee of Liberation, the future municipality of Paris. Gaullist power was represented by the General Delegation, whose chief was Parodi, and whose members had been appointed directly by de Gaulle from outside the area of Communist manœuvres.

Which of the two was going to win the day? The decision did not rest only with the central organization, the C.P.L., but also with the liberation committees of the arrondissements, who would install themselves in the mairies and form the basic organization for the administration of Paris. They consisted of twenty-one members, but were in fact controlled by an inner committee, which was limited to six. Within these inner committees, the Communists began the same manœuvres that had already been successful within the C.P.L.

The liberation of Paris, therefore, had a two-fold aspect, military and political.

Militarily speaking, there was no doubt that sooner or later, by 25 August or perhaps 1 September, the retreating Wehrmacht would abandon Paris. And this posed two questions, not concerning the event itself, but the circumstances in which it would take place. Would Paris be liberated entirely by the regular armies, or would it take part in its own liberation? And, secondly, would Paris be destroyed in the process or not?

From the political point of view, on the other hand, there was one overriding question: would liberated Paris be under Communist influence or not?

This was the great concern both of General de Gaulle, who was approaching the capital, and of Parodi, who was awaiting him within it. It was the question on whose answer the future of the country depended. During the month of August 1944, there was a struggle for power between the two sides.

Rol, the Colonel commanding the F.F.I. for the Paris Region, was a Communist. His second-in-command, Colonel de Marguerittes, alias Lizé, was not. He was a Regular officer, deeply religious, and inimical to materialism. Would Rol or Lizé win the day? The latter was also given a second-in-command, appointed by Rol, a man called Massiet, who was a fellow-traveller; and it was not by chance that he was appointed to Colonel de Marguerittes.

The President of the C.P.L., as we have seen, was the Communist Tollet. But, when the city was liberated, his opposite numbers would be Flouret, the new Prefect of the Seine, and Luizet, the new Prefect of Police, both appointed on General de Gaulle's orders.

There was the same alternation on every level. Nor could either party gain power, as in normal times, as the result of a majority of votes.

In which direction would Paris turn during the course of the fighting; on which side would Paris be after its liberation?

2. THE FIGHTING

The liberation lasted a week, from Friday, 18 August, to Friday, 25 August, inclusive.

There were two previous events that need mentioning. On 16 August, the National Military Delegate, Chaban-Delmas, returned from London with precise orders. The Allies, so he had been told at Koenig's head-quarters, did not expect to reach Paris before 1 September at the earliest. They had decided to break through to the north-west and south-east of the capital and to bring about its fall by an enveloping movement. De Gaulle and Koenig therefore instructed Chaban-Delmas to transmit orders to Parodi that in no circumstances was there to be a premature insurrection, which would both compromise the safety of the capital and embarrass the Allied plans.

Despite these imperative orders, Colonel Lizé, in agreement with Colonel Rol and the Communist leaders in the Paris district, spent the afternoon of the 17th with his Chief of Staff, in the Rue Montalivet, dictating a series of operation orders for the occupation on the 18th of government offices, factories, public services, power stations, banks, the Métro, and water reservoirs in Paris and its suburbs.

Thus, on the eve of the first battles, the responsible leaders of the armed forces of the Resistance in Paris were issuing orders which were at variance with those received by the Delegate General, who repre-sented de Gaulle in France and was in charge of political affairs. This was all the more important since the armed forces in Paris were neither numerous nor well armed. According to Rol, who was in command of the whole Paris district, there existed at the beginning of the fighting arms for no more than 400 men. Moreover, these arms were of various makes and far from modern, consisting mainly of old revolvers and rifles. According to *Grand Strategy*, the official British account of operations in France, the Allied air forces, between February and 15 May 1944, had parachuted into France 76,290 Sten guns, of which only 114 were for the Paris district, and 27,961 pistols, of which 18 were for the capital.

To attack in these circumstances seemed suicidal. Rol accepted the risk for political reasons, and Lizé because he was one of those courageous and offensive-minded soldiers who believed that his duty in face of the enemy could never be to remain inactive.

On 18 August, the Liberation Committee of the Paris Police decided to go into action. During the evening, the leaders of the three Resistance movements ordered 3,000 police to assemble in the neighbourhood of the Hôtel de Ville the next day.

On the 19th, at seven o'clock in the morning, armed but in plain clothes, they seized the Prefecture of Police without a shot, and in the name of General de Gaulle took over the command posts.

The former Prefect, Bussière, was put under guard in his flat. The new Prefect, Luizet, who had just reached Paris from Corsica, took over his job in a somewhat irregular manner.

At ten o'clock that morning he was due to meet certain leaders of the Resistance at the corner of the Rue de Dragon and the Boulevard Saint-Germain. Hugging the walls, he made his way to the meeting-place. It was an unnecessary precaution. Two F.F.I. vehicles, bristling with sub-machine-guns, came to meet him and carried him triumphantly to the Prefecture of Police.

Together with Colonel Rol, commander of the Île de France F.F.I., he left the Prefecture to call on Parodi.

At lunchtime, since no arrangements for food had been made, and the sector seemed fairly calm, the police went home to eat. Having thus kept to their usual timetable, even in a period of insurrection, most of them returned to their police stations in the afternoon.

There was indeed a singular atmosphere about the police headquarters which had been so swiftly liberated. The former officials no longer showed themselves; the new were often excited amateurs, young people having a holiday, who much enjoyed doing jobs for which they had no qualifications.

Pisani, later a most energetic senator, had no job, nor any particular situation in life, except for his membership in the N.A.P. (Novautage des Administrations Publiques), under Yves Bayet. Hearing that the Tricolour was flying over the Prefecture of Police, he came to have a look, went inside to see what was happening, and mingled with the idle crowd of police in plain clothes. Looking for Yves Bayet, he went into an office and discovered him in conversation with two men whom he did not know; in fact, one was the Prefect Luizet and the other Colonel Rol.

All three had been summoned to the Rue de Grenelle by Parodi, and were on the point of leaving the Prefecture. But Luizet, anxious that the organization he had taken over within the last few minutes should function, was looking for someone to answer the telephone, the man whose usual duty it was having failed to appear. Pisani came into the room. Perhaps he would do. Luizet told him to look after the telephone. Then, at ten-thirty, he left. Pisani, in this somewhat subordinate post, represented authority by the mere hazard of events.

He began by refusing to pass calls to the former Prefect, Bussière, who was shut up in his flat. Later in the afternoon, he received a delegation, who looked and talked like Communists, and declared that they had come to take over the Prefecture. Pisani, without reflecting on the political implications of what he was saying, and unaware of its historical precedents, replied decisively: "I am here to look after the telephone. And I'm staying." The visitors were impressed and withdrew. Pisani had saved Republican liberties.

Another young man, who played an historic part on this decisive day, was a journalist. Roger Stéphane was celebrating his twenty-fifth birthday. He had spent the last few years in the service of the Resistance. Arrested and deported in May 1942, he had escaped in November, and had organized the first service of false papers in Paris. Arrested again in March 1943, he had escaped once again on 8 June, and was active with Hervé and Morandat in the ranks of the M.L.N.

On 19 August, he was to have a birthday luncheon with Jean Cocteau, near the Palais-Royal. But just as he got there, he saw a police car drive down the street with young men armed with revolvers clinging to the wings. His taste for the exciting and the unusual was aroused; giving up his luncheon, he turned back and, going by the Rue de Rivoli, joined a crowd which was on its way to see what was happening at the Hôtel de Ville.

He saw the Tricolour hoisted on the building and some two thousand people in the Place, waiting and watching. He went into the Hôtel de Ville: "I want to see the Prefect," he said. "The Prefect?" They looked at him in bewilderment; no one knew whether there was a Prefect, or indeed whether there were two. To the evasive replies of the *huissier* on duty, who was wondering whether he was to retain his chain of office, Stéphane answered angrily: "If I don't see someone at once, there'll be trouble." The secretary-general was brought to see him. "You'll shut the gates of the Prefecture at once, and have the people in front of it dispersed. I'll give you ten minutes, otherwise we shall take stern measures." Who were the "we?" Stéphane himself had no idea. But the official was impressed and promptly obeyed.

Dressed in a light-coloured suit, which André Roussin had lent him when he came out of prison, Stéphane then went to the Prefecture of Police. He was placed in command of the side of the building facing Notre-Dame. He would have to take cover behind heaps of sand. Realizing it would do his borrowed suit no good, he found a workman's blue overalls and this he wore throughout the insurrection. Bullets were flying about all over the place; and during a sortie he was wounded in the arm in the Place Saint-André-des-Arts. He was taken to the Hôtel Dieu, where he was bandaged and given an anti-tetanus injection, after which he went back to the Prefecture of Police, his arm in a martial sling made out of a Hermès scarf, to be greeted as the first hero.

"Have you been wounded?"

"Yes, but it's nothing."

"Are you up to capturing the Hôtel de Ville?"

"Of course I am."

"Go on then."

The next morning, with twenty-five men, Lieutenant Roger Stéphane, or perhaps he was by then a captain, entered the Hôtel de Ville. He remained there until the arrival of General de Gaulle.

In face of this irruption of new chiefs, the permanent officials seemed not over-perturbed. The Prefects were of course well guarded; but their subordinates took it all quietly enough.

Madame Toesca, of the Prefect's Secretariat, went to her office that morning on a bicycle, dressed in a white summer frock: she had been invited to a picnic that day. Alas, she had hardly sat down to her desk, when Colonel Rol arrived. He took over the Prefect's office, and his secretary, a tough and militant female, came with him.

The unfortunate Prefect Bussière, who was expecting the early arrival of the Americans, and had had his full dress uniform prepared for the occasion, was brought in and interrogated by his successor, Luizet. The *huissiers* and the police on duty waited with some anxiety to see how events would turn out, but when they saw that taken all in all things were not going too badly they gradually began to cheer up. There was still the burning question of the picnic: would Madame Toesca be able to go to it?

She soon realized she would have to give it up. Rol's secretary locked her in. No supporter of the Ancien Régime, in a "bourgeoise" summer dress, must be allowed to contaminate the passages and their new occupants. But the locked door did not confound Madame Toesca. She knew the building better than Rol's secretary. Going out by another door, she presented herself smiling affably before her inexperienced jailer and asked the astonished woman whether there were any letters to take.

Being told there were none, Madame Toesca went back to her office; and there she remained immured for three days, with nothing to do but telephone her friends.

This day of 19 August, which brought such changes to the life of the municipal buildings, was also that on which insurrection and truce were successively decided. And this brings us to the heart of the political problem of this extraordinary period.

At about eleven o'clock in the morning, in a house in the Rue de Grenelle, there was a meeting of the C.N.R., attended by the Delegate General, Parodi, the new Prefect of Police, Luizet, and members of the C.P.L. among whom was its president, Tollet. The C.N.R. and the General Delegation had received a demand from the C.P.L., which was predominantly Communist, to issue orders for insurrection. The C.N.R. had discussed it and decided by a majority to reply in the affirmative. Parodi alone represented the General Delegation which, through Chaban-Delmas, had received orders from London to gain time and oppose an insurrection. He found himself in the presence of a majority of resistants, who were not all Communists but who, for various and often admirable reasons, wished to start the fighting at once.

What was he to do? Which view was he to support? The atmosphere of Paris was oppressive. As a Parisian, who had always lived in Paris, and had remained there throughout the Occupation, he could not but be aware of the temperature of the city and realize that the Parisians had come to the end of their tether and had decided to act. For Parodi, a calm, cautious and intelligent man, who emerged from the Liberation with increased stature, this presented a problem whose various possibilities had to be carefully considered.

What were the risks, if he agreed to insurrection in spite of the orders from London? Paris might be destroyed, its population decimated, and its combatants, without uniforms or arms, uselessly massacred. It was no light responsibility, and if he failed the reproaches of his conscience and his superiors could never be lived down.

Conversely, if he strictly obeyed the orders he had received, and refused to give his consent, what would the political consequences be? There would very likely be a breach between the National Council of the Resistance and himself. There might indeed be a breach between his delegation and all the internal Resistance movements, Communist or not, who had decided by a majority to fight.

The result would be that the Paris insurrection would appear as an enterprise both inspired and executed by the Communists and, henceforth, the influence of the Party would be overwhelmingly predominant in the Resistance.

It was not that Parodi, who had seen them fighting, and had been collaborating with them for months in the secret organizations, had, like certain offices in London and Algiers, a phobia about the Communists and a horror of their intrigues. But he considered his principal task was to maintain the unity of the Resistance in face of the enemy. He wanted de Gaulle to find no dissension on his arrival and to be welcomed by representatives of every movement and every party.

The situation was therefore grave and the choice decisive. On that Saturday morning of 19 August, Parodi disobeyed the instructions he had received and gave his consent to the order for insurrection

He did so with no light heart. Nor did he do so without reservations. Circumstances had forced him to make the decision (the strike had already become general), but he hoped to be able to limit its consequences, perhaps even to render them null and void.

The afternoon of the same day first increased his uneasiness, and then brought him some hope of being able to escape the consequences of his decision.

First, during a full meeting of the Delegation in the flat of his secretary, Mademoiselle Raffalovitch, in the Avenue Lowendal, Parodi, as he expected, was violently attacked by Chaban-Delmas about the attitude he had adopted that morning: "Why did you ignore the fact that you had orders forbidding you to launch an insurrection?" Parodi gave his reasons, and pointed out that the decision had been made and that it was no use going back on it.

After this meeting, which had revived his anxieties, Parodi received a visit which was to some extent to relieve his mind. A mysterious character belonging to the British Intelligence Service called on him and told him of his personal fears at the prospect of Paris being destroyed. He asked the Delegate General's permission to signal London asking for the Allied arrival to be hastened on. Parodi immediately gave his authorization, which inaugurated a series of demands to the Allied authorities for rapid intervention. The mysterious messenger then left; nor was he ever seen again.

Meanwhile, a new actor entered the drama. Nordling, the Swedish Consul-General, was to have a decisive influence on the negotiations for a truce.

Two days before he had seen von Choltitz at Bussière's request to plead the cause of the French prisoners: "You cannot be an executioner!" he said to the German General. And Choltitz had finally made Nordling a proposal: "I suggest," he said, "an exchange. I will hand over the prisoners to you, but on condition that the Germans in French prisons are also freed."

The Swedish Consul realized that the number of Germans arrested by the F.F.I. must be very small in comparison to the French detained by the Nazis. He therefore accepted the offer but immediately tried to increase its scope. Choltitz's proposal would affect only the prisons in Paris and the immediate neighbourhood. "Oh," he said, "we have forgotten Compiègne!" "Where is Compiègne?" Choltitz asked. "It's in the outskirts," Nordling replied. "Very well then, I agree," said the German.

Fearing a counter-order, Nordling hurried to Cherche-Midi, Fresnes and Drancy, where he had the prisoners set free. He reached Romainville just at the moment some prisoners were going to be massacred by their drunken jailers, who were Russians of the Vlassov Army. He just succeeded in preventing the tragedy. At Compiègne, alas, he arrived too late: the last train of deportees had just left for Germany.

During the course of the day, Raoul Nordling got 4,213 prisoners freed, among whom were the F.F.I. detained at Neuilly, and the police surrounded in the Grand-Palais.

Having acquired this first claim to the gratitude of Paris, he proceeded to deserve still better of it by trying to protect the capital.

During the day of 19 August, Nordling had seen Ambassador Otto Abetz also to ask him to intervene on behalf of the French prisoners. Abetz had brutally refused: "Yes, I know," he had said, "among the prisoners are pupils of the École Normale Supérieure. But, Monsieur le Consul de Suède, do you know what the École Normale Supérieure is? It is a den of terrorists. There can be no mercy for terrorists."

Abetz was a complex character. He felt a sincere attraction towards France and her culture. Indeed, he loved France rather as a peasant does the livestock he will one day eat. This was the cause of the frequent variations in his behaviour towards France.

A few hours after his vehement refusal to Nordling, Abetz called on Choltitz, who had only met him once before, on the occasion of his taking over command.

The Ambassador had now calmed down and said: "Can I be of any use to you, General?"

"My dear Ambassador, in what way could you be useful to me?"

"I could send to headquarters and to Ribbentrop a signal condemning your brutal behaviour in Paris."

Choltitz was startled, but soon realized that Abetz wanted to cover him with the more fanatical Nazis and thereby give him a chance to take action to save Paris.

"Would you really do that?" Choltitz replied. "Are you really one of us?"

And Abetz said simply: "I want to do it."

Abetz thus prevented Choltitz being recalled to Germany or liquidated. "He gave me," the General recognized, "time to carry out my task; and his gesture was of indisputable assistance to the city of Paris."

Thanks to the diplomat's spontaneous intervention, there was now no reason why the Commander of Greater Paris should not enter into negotiations with Nordling, that is to say with the French themselves through his mediation.

Nordling then called on Choltitz. Before receiving him, the General telephoned Abetz to ask his opinion of the Swedish diplomat. Abetz replied without hesitation that he considered him a man of perfect sincerity and integrity.

Parodi meanwhile was anxious; he had received military reports during the afternoon that were far from encouraging. The Prefecture of Police was threatened by a movement of tanks which, however, had provisional orders not to attack. The French police were short of ammunition. On both sides a truce for the night was declared to cover all the buildings occupied by the Resistance. It was renewable for the following day.

By the evening of 19 August, Parodi was therefore well aware of the tragic circumstances which might result from insurrection; but he also knew that there was a chance of a truce palliating its worst consequences. Harassed by contrary opinions, and hoping for a truce while the military leaders of the Resistance wanted to continue fighting, how could he maintain so unstable an equilibrium during the hours to come?

At 22.30 hours, he had to give further pledges to the supporter of action. A council of war was held at the Prefecture of Police, in the office of the Secretariat. Besides the defenders of the Prefecture, there were present members of the General Delegation, of the C.N.R., and of the C.P.L. It was now that it was decided to take the Hôtel de Ville the following morning, when the episode of Roger Stéphane took place.[1]

It was also during this night that the insurgents received—or thought they received, for contact was unsatisfactory and their imaginations excited—a radio message from the British government wishing them good luck. The insurgents replied: "Send no more messages, but send us weapons to fight with." Upon which, knowing from experience that it was better to help oneself, they seized before dawn some of the semi-heavy weapons they required. In particular, at Vitry-sur-Seine, where a patrol of F.F.I. took mortars from a wagon.

The 20th was filled with serious incidents. Fighting was going on in some districts at the same time as the negotiations for a truce.

In the rooms of the Prefecture of Police, transformed into dormitories, where Madame Toesca had slept in an armchair, it was reveillle at 05.00 hours. Luizet, the new Prefect of Police, Flouret, the new Prefect of the Seine, Albert Bayet and Léo Hamon, accompanied by all their companions in arms, went to the Hôtel de Ville. They numbered about two hundred, half of whom were police and the rest young militants from the Équipes Nationales. With them were a large number of women, secretaries and liaison officers from the Resistance movements, none of whom were armed.

A group of Gardes Mobiles, urgently summoned, joined them in front of Notre-Dame. They went to the Hôtel de Ville and entered it by a door on the quay. Other Gardes Mobiles, recognizing colleagues among the assailants, did nothing whatever to prevent their entering.

By seven o'clock, all was over. Léo Hamon was in occupation of the inside courtyard. He went to the Prefect's office: "In the name of the Paris Committee of Liberation, and on behalf of the provisional government of the French Republic, I take possession of the Hôtel de Ville." Pétain's bust was removed. Bouffet, the Vichy Prefect of the Seine, received the insurgents in spite of the early hour, and counselled them to moderation. It was wasted breath; he was arrested and taken to the Prefecture of Police.

The Hôtel de Ville had now to be put in a state of defence. Commandant Leperc, future Minister of Finance in de Gaulle's government, assisted by Captain Stéphane, who now had under his command a garrison of three hundred men, mainly composed of Équipes Nationales and Gardes Mobiles, was placed in charge.

At the same time, the functioning of the civil administration had to

[1] Cf., page 261.

be assured. By chance the telephone was still working and continued to do so. The Hôtel de Ville made contact with the capital's public services. The new Prefect of the Seine took possession of his office and secretariat. The Hôtel de Ville was thus organized to hold out during the three days and four nights of the insurrection.

At seven o'clock there was a meeting of the General Delegation with Chaban-Delmas at 15, Avenue Lowendal. The Assistant Delegate General for the northern zone, Roland Pré, brought the latest information. He had spent the night in the Prefecture of Police. The Hôtel de Ville was in French hands. As for the Germans, they had asked for a suspension of hostilities and had fixed eleven o'clock for a meeting of negotiators with Nordling at the Swedish Consulate.

Parodi had therefore rather less than four hours in which to make his point of view prevail.

Moreover, at nine o'clock, the C.N.R. was to hold a plenary session. Parodi, Chaban-Delmas and Dassault also attended this decisive meeting. In fact, they did not find the C.N.R. in full session: only six members out of sixteen were present. The majority were not supporters of the Communists; and it would therefore be easier to persuade them that there must be a truce.

Present were Bidault, the President, who would play the part of arbiter, Blocq-Mascart of the O.C.M., Ribère of Libé-Nord, Tessier of the C.F.T.C., and Avinin of Franc-Tireur, none of whom were Communists. Opposed to them was one single Communist or fellow-traveller, Villon of the Front National. Meanwhile Léo Hamon, Roland Pré and Saint-Phalle had had a short interview with the Swedish Consul, in his office, to draw up the text of the announcement to be made by loudspeaker vans in the eventuality of a truce. They handed the document to Parodi, who put it to the vote at the C.N.R. meeting.

The National Military Delegate, Chaban-Delmas, gave an account of the military situation which he represented, in perfectly good faith, as being far more critical than in fact it was. The Germans had an undoubted superiority in arms and men. The Prefecture of Police was isolated and lacked munitions. The Germans had received an order to destroy Paris if the population rose in mass. On the other hand, there was no reason to suppose that the Allied plans had been altered and that help could be expected in under a week.

From the text of the proclamation brought by Léo Hamon and to be made if a truce were agreed to, the following points emerged:

(1) That the F.F.I. would be recognized as regular combatants;

(2) That the occupation of public buildings taken by the F.F.I. would not be contested;

(3) That the Germans should rapidly evacuate the capital by routes selected by the F.F.I.

In the discussion that followed, Pierre Villon was naturally alone in opposing a truce: "The people of Paris have risen and are ready to liberate the capital themselves. To make them lay down their arms would be to curb their spirit and baulk them of their victory."

By five votes to one, the members of the C.N.R. decided to send at once a delegation consisting of three men to the Swedish Consul; these were Chaban-Delmas, Roland Pré and Léo Hamon.

Since the session of the C.N.R. had lasted longer than expected, and the delegates' only means of transport were bicycles, they arrived at 11.10 hours, some ten minutes late, at Nordling's. Though impatient himself, he had succeeded in making the Germans wait and had already communicated the text of the proclamation to them.

As soon as they arrived, the three Frenchmen were shown into a room. The Germans were in another. The Swedish Consul-General acted as liaison between them.

To create a favourable atmosphere, the Germans first proposed to supply the Resistance with a load of meat which was held up at La Villette. Very much on their dignity, the French refused it. Nordling deployed all his diplomatic skill. The Germans would give him the meat; and he would hand over to the French any excess there might be over his personal needs.

By midday, agreement had been reached. The Germans would evacuate Paris by the external boulevards. They would recognize the F.F.I. as regular combatants. They would accept the occupation of the Prefecture of Police, the Hôtel de Ville, the mairies and the police stations. On the other hand, they would continue to hold the points which Choltitz had named as essential to him at his meeting with Taittinger: the Hôtel Meurice, and the quadrilateral formed by the streets of Rivoli, Castiglione, Saint-Honoré and Saint-Florentin.

A truce had now therefore been concluded; but the difficulties were only beginning. During the next few hours it was impossible to inform either Colonel Rol or Colonel Lizé, and the fighting continued.

At 14.00 hours a dramatic event occurred. General von Choltitz, in his office in the Hôtel Meurice, heard over the telephone a hoarse and excited voice, which certainly did not belong to any of his usual staff, say:

"Herr General, we have arrested three men who call themselves ministers of de Gaulle. Shall we shoot them?"

"You have, of course, every right to shoot them; but bring them to me, I should like to see them."

He at once telephoned Nordling to tell him of the arrest of the three "ministers" and inform him that they were being brought to the Hôtel Meurice. He asked him to come across as quickly as he could.

A few minutes later, a tall, tough-looking officer of the Feldgendarmerie entered the General's room, saluted him, and placed a brief-case, stuffed with documents, on his desk.

"Herr General, I have the honour to inform you that I have brought the three men who call themselves ministers of de Gaulle. From the documents found in this brief-case, it appears that the armistice is about to be broken."

Von Choltitz ordered the three men to be brought to him, and dismissed the officer: "Thank you, you have done very well, you can fall out."

The three prisoners were brought in; they were Parodi, Laffont, and Roland Pré. On leaving the meeting of the C.N.R. at which the truce had been decided, they had set off by car and, owing to the driver missing his way, they had fallen into the hands of a German patrol in the Rue de Lille before the loud-speakers had finished announcing the cease-fire. Arrested and searched, they were found to be carrying secret documents (plans of German military installations in Paris, an account of the interview between Herriot and Abetz, information about the Allied advance, and orders for the Resistance to continue the fighting . . .). They were taken to an office in the Avenue Henri-Martin and then to a villa in Saint-Cloud, which the Secret Services and the Gestapo used for carrying out executions. Before shooting them, an officer of the Feldgendarmerie had informed Choltitz over the telephone with the result that the police had had to hand over their victims.

This was the first time that Choltitz had been in the presence of the real leaders of the internal Resistance.

There was complete silence in the room. Beside the General were two officers of his staff, one to act as interpreter, the other to record the conversation for the report.

A few minutes later, Nordling arrived with two interpreters. Between these nine men were to be decided, not only the fate of the three prisoners, but—and this time definitively—the fate of the capital.

On entering the room the Consul-General glanced briefly at the prisoners and Choltitz realized that they were not unknown to him.

To test Nordling's integrity, Choltitz asked him: "Do you know these gentlemen?"

Nordling replied that he did.

Choltitz then told Nordling of the contents of the brief-case. These left the bellicose intentions of the Resistance in no doubt. Among other documents there was a warlike appeal to the population of Paris which was completely at variance with the agreement drawn up the day before between Choltitz and Nordling.

The German General asked why such an appeal had been launched after the agreement had been concluded. What could Parodi say? He could not explain the true reason and tell Choltitz of the divergencies of view within the Resistance. He could not tell him that Colonel Lizé, when informed of the truce, had declared that he considered all negotiations with the enemy to be "an act of treason." Nor could he deny that fighting was continuing, that serious skirmishes had taken place in the Place d'Italie, the Boulevard de l'Hôpital, the Avenue des Gobelins, in the neighbourhood of the Hôtel de Ville, and at the Neuilly mairie.

He tried to evade the question and replied that the incriminating document had been written before and not after the conclusion of the truce, and that the date was due to a typing error.

"You will permit me," Choltitz replied contemptuously, "not to believe that."

The conversation then went on for two hours. Things might have gone very badly for Parodi if the two interpreters, even though they were wearing the uniform of the Wehrmacht, had not been in contact with the Allied Secret Services. Bender, though officially head of the German counter-espionage in Paris, had assisted General Giraud to escape from Germany in 1942. The Austrian Baron von Poch-Pastor, though officially a member of the German transport services in Paris, a few days later changed his uniform and went on a mission to Allied Headquarters.

These two interpreters justified the adage: "Traductore, tradittore." Their translating on this day was a betrayal of the truth in the service of the French. Parodi answered Choltitz in terms which, had the General been better served by the interpreters, he would have found intolerable. When Choltitz offered food from the German reserves for the Paris population, Parodi replied that the Parisians, who had "starved" for four years, could well wait another four days for the German defeat.

Choltitz was well aware that his overtures were being received somewhat coldly. But unaware of the precise terms the Gaullist "minister" had used, he seemed reasonably satisfied. At any rate, he learned the real position of the F.F.I. command: "Parodi told me straight out that as a general I was commanding troops on whose obedience I could count, whereas their men, recruited from many disparate groups, represented a variety of opinions and that it was difficult to maintain uniform discipline among them."

Such frankness, though it was rather late in the day, nevertheless pleased Choltitz. For the first time, he was meeting effective opponents: "For once," he wrote, "I had to do with men of great intelligence."

Choltitz also showed himself to be a man of quality. Incomplete though Parodi's authority might be, there was none other that could be exercised in support of the truce. He therefore set him free, with a few words that showed remarkable intelligence:

"Mr. Consul-General," he said, "I find it painful to take advantage of the situation in which these gentlemen find themselves. I do not propose to examine in detail the documents contained in this brief-case. You stand surety for our agreement; and I pray you to take charge of these gentlemen's documents. See if there are any personal papers among them, and if you find any documents whose terms are in violation of our agreement, keep them yourself."

After which, having declared them free to go, he held out his hand to Parodi, who refused to take it. "Nevertheless," concluded Choltitz, "the Consul-General thanked me in the most sympathetic terms."

No doubt, Choltitz thought his generous gesture would help towards maintaining the truce. In fact, on being set free at 18.30 hours, Parodi found that the situation had grown worse during the six and a half hours he had been detained.

The National Council of the Resistance, which was to have met at 18.00 hours to take a decision, had adjourned in Parodi's absence till the next day. Meanwhile, Colonel Rol had announced at 16.15 hours that, so long as the Germans were in Paris, he stood by the order to fight. In the middle of the night, the C.O.M.A.C. adopted a resolution against the truce.

Finally, at 22.31 hours, Jean Guignebert, Pierre Crenesse and Pierre Schaeffer made the first broadcast on the liberated radio. The *Marseillaise* was played. The little red lamp on the microphone lit up. Pierre Crenesse, alone in the studio, uttered in a strangled voice the few words that made up the whole of the broadcast: "This is the radio of the French nation." The red light went out: it was enough for that night.

The next day, Monday the 21st, hostilities broke out again at various points on local initiative, both French and German, in violation of the

14. Manning the barricades in Paris.

15. *Raoul Nordling, Consul General of Sweden, mediator between the Germans and the Paris F.F.I.*

16. *Colonel Rol, commandant of the Paris F.F.I., with his staff.*

truce. In turn, the Elysée, the Ministries of the Interior, War and Agriculture, the Gare de l'Est, the Halles, the Bourse du Travail, the printing presses, and the telephone exchanges either fell to the insurgents or remained in their hands.

Parodi, who was desirous of affirming the continuity of government action, was specially concerned about the Hôtel Matignon, the normal seat of the Presidency of the Council. He wanted to hold a sort of council of ministers there in the late morning, with the provisional secretary-generals, who had been secretly appointed in the spring of 1944, to make sure that the ministries functioned during the interval between the departure of the Germans and the arrival in Paris of the provisional government.

But it was essential that the secretary-generals should be able to reach the appointed place without undergoing adventures similar to Parodi's of the day before.

The Delegate General sent one of his young assistants, Yves Morandat, aged twenty-six, who was in charge of the political relations of the General Delegation, to the Hôtel Matignon, to take possession of it in the name of the government. Morandat and his secretary set off on bicycles. But neither of them were Parisians. They thought the Hôtel Matignon must be in the Avenue Matignon near the Elysée. They saw a building with "Hôtel" written on it. It must, they thought, be the right place. However, they discovered it to be full of Germans and requisitioned by the Wehrmacht. The porter set them right: the Hôtel Matignon was on the Left Bank, in the Rue de Varenne, nor was it an "hotel" in the ordinary sense of that word.

The two cyclists set off again. They had to crawl across the Champs-Elysées, which was being swept by bursts of German machine-gun fire. They then proceeded to the Left Bank.

They found the Hôtel Matignon, which they recognized by the sentry-box outside it, with its doors closed and windows shuttered. There were still German patrols in the street. Morandat drew from his pocket the F.F.I. tricolour brassard, the only badge of office he had. He put it round his left arm, and then knocked at the little side-door. A window opened: "What do you want?" "To talk to the boss," said Morandat, who had no idea who might, at that moment, be in command. The door opened. The whole courtyard was full of uniforms. It was Pierre Laval's personal bodyguard, wearing black caps and gold grenades on their collars. It was four days since Laval had left for Germany, and they had been idly lounging in the courtyard awaiting a new patron ever since. A senior officer, wearing four stripes, accosted the new arrivals: "What do you want?" "I am the representative of the provisional government of the French Republic," replied Morandat, with a sense of his own importance, but amused by the adventure. "I have come to take possession of the premises in its name."

The officer clicked his heels and stood to attention: "I place myself under your orders, Monsieur le Ministre; I have always been a fervent Republican." Morandat and his secretary crossed the courtyard with dignity between two rows of Laval's bodyguard, who presented arms. On entering the building itself, they were met by civilians welcoming the new régime. The staff-manager came to ask for orders, and was soon followed by the steward and the butler.

Morandat gave instructions that the council chamber be prepared for the meeting that afternoon; and that bedrooms for himself and his staff, who were to spend the night in the palace, be made ready.

The next day, Tuesday the 22nd, Morandat, detailed to reopen the Republican ministries, was involved in a difficult episode at the Ministry of the Interior in the Place Beauvau. When Morandat asked the major-domo to arrange a dinner for twelve of his friends from the Resistance, the man looked rather sullen and replied dryly: "Impossible, Monsieur le Ministre." "Why is it impossible?" The man was silent for a moment, hesitated, then thinking he had better make a clean breast of a matter that had been weighing on him for several days, said: "I must tell you, Monsieur le Ministre, that I have seen, during the course of my career, many ministerial crises. But never one like this." And when Morandat questioned him, he went on: "It is the first time that I've ever seen a Minister go and take the silver with him." The last occupant of the Ministry had apparently made a clean sweep on leaving for Germany.

On the afternoon of the 21st, when the secretary-generals assembled at the Hôtel Matignon, Parodi was involved in another and even angrier meeting about the truce.

At 18.00 hours, the committee of the C.N.R., this time complete with all its Communist members, met in a little flat near the Denfert-Rochereau station. Also present were the National Military Delegate, Chaban-Delmas, and Parodi. There were altogether twenty men present, of which the luckier found seats on the worn Louis XV chairs. It was very hot; and they were all in shirt-sleeves.

The first item on the agenda was the truce. Was it to be denounced at once, as the Communists wished, or prolonged for at least twenty-four hours, as Parodi wanted?

Chaban-Delmas, who was a supporter of the truce, spoke first, as

National Military Delegate. He had just learnt that the Germans held 150 Tiger tanks in Paris. What could the ill-armed F.F.I. do against such weapons? To recommence the fighting would be to invite disaster and sacrifice uselessly the famous buildings of Paris.

The Communist Villon replied furiously that the truce was a disgrace and nothing more nor less than an act of high treason. "Monsieur Chaban-Delmas talks like a coward," he cried angrily. Chaban-Delmas remained calm under the attack. But Parodi got to his feet, put on his coat, picked up his hat, and threatened to walk out if Villon did not apologize at once to Chaban-Delmas.

It was asking too much of him. Villon would go no further than to say: "I did not call Chaban-Delmas a coward. I meant merely to say that he has behaved like a coward."

The over-subtle distinction did not satisfy Parodi, who got to his feet again, picked up his coat which he had put down while waiting for Villon's answer, and asked his Communist colleague who the hell he thought he was talking to.

The meeting was suspended amid considerable excitement. When it was resumed, Villon apologized to Chaban-Delmas, saying that he was tired and overwrought, having worked all night.

And the discussion continued. Bidault finally proposed a compromise which was accepted. The truce would be denounced, but only at 17.00 hours the next day. An appeal to the population of Paris would be posted at that hour, and drafting it took up the last minutes of the meeting and restored unanimity.

Paris, 21 August, 1944.

Parisians,

The insurrection of the people of Paris has already liberated numerous public buildings in the capital. A first great victory has been achieved.

The struggle continues. It must be prosecuted until the enemy is driven from the Paris region.

More than ever now, all must take part in the fight.

Respond to the general order of mobilization. Join the F.F.I.

The population must use all means of preventing the movement of the enemy.

Cut down trees, dig anti-tank ditches, erect barricades.

It will be a victorious people who will welcome the Allies.

The Paris Committee of Liberation.

The respite Parodi had obtained was, in any case, extremely precarious. The truce continued to be observed only somewhat approximately. At 19.30 hours, Colonel Lizé, though he was not a Communist, issued orders to erect barricades in Paris.

The 22 August was the first day since the insurrection on which the military events provided the main interest. These had two aspects: on the one hand, the development of the F.F.I.'s offensive despite the truce, which was due mainly to the action of the Communist leaders; and, on the other, a number of joint appeals to the American generals to hasten their advance on Paris.

Under the influence of Marrane who had seen the effectiveness of the road blocks when on his way from the country; and also under that of Colonel Rol-Tanguy and other officers of the F.F.I., who had learnt the lessons of the Spanish War and were practiced in revolutionary street-fighting, a general thrust by the F.F.I. and the F.T.P. opened a new phase of the Paris insurrection.

The F.F.I. command of the Île-de-France had units in reserve, which were now soon to be committed. There was the F.F.I. Métro group, whose job it was to protect the stations. It was to intervene at the Châtelet and at Saint-Michel to cover the buildings in the Cité held by the insurgents. There were the Cévennes group, the group of Ceux de la Résistance commanded by Vasseur, the Barat group, which had occupied the Halles, and Colonel Fabien's group. There was also the Sidi-Brahim, which Rol-Tanguy was to use as reinforcements to restore the situation in threatened areas.

The F.F.I. and the F.T.P. went on to the offensive and forced the Germans to take up defensive positions in the Caserne de la République, in the Luxembourg, and in the districts of the Opéra and the Porte Dauphine, that is to say more or less in the redoubts which Choltitz had told Taittinger must remain in his possession.

On the evening of the 22nd, Colonel Rol-Tanguy gave orders to increase the number of barricades; he set the Cévennes group to building them.

In this atmosphere of fighting, the truce passed into second place. In the morning, Parodi was visited at the Prefecture of Police by Chaban-Delmas, who admitted that his information about the 150 Tiger tanks was inaccurate. He was soon followed by Colonel Rol-Tanguy, who brought the same news. Rol-Tanguy told Parodi that, as Delegate General, he alone could decide whether to continue the truce or not; Rol-Tanguy would accept his decision.

In response to this recognition of his authority, or rather General de Gaulle's, Parodi immediately took the decision the F.F.I. leaders desired. In the presence of two Communists, Kriegel-Valrimont and Colonel Rol-Tanguy, he signed the order to renew the insurrection without referring it to the C.N.R. Without the 150 Tiger tanks, Paris ran far less risk of being destroyed.

The ultimate military conflict between the Communist and non-Communist elements of the Resistance was now settled. Both camps had achieved what they wanted. They had each, in their own way, contributed to the astonishing fact that Paris was liberated undamaged.

But what part did the truce and what part did the insurrection play in this amazing event?

General de Gaulle had disowned the part played by his Delegate General in interrupting the fighting. Nevertheless, his action brought certain advantages. In the first place: Paris did not become a second Warsaw. And in the second: the Resistance had time to become organized. Indeed, it became a reality to the whole population, and the order to renew the insurrection was obeyed with an enthusiasm and a resolution it might otherwise have lacked. And finally, on the Monday or Tuesday morning (opinions vary as to the day), Parodi was able to hold at Matignon a real council of ministers with the secretary-generals. Owing to the truce, these officials were able to take over their ministries, assuring the continuity of government and avoiding a power-vacuum. Posters bore witness to the effectiveness of the Resistance, and the new press had begun to publish newspapers.

As for the insurrection, it had advantages that even Choltitz recognized in his memoirs, when writing of the Resistance from his own point of view. He naturally did not believe that the F.F.I. had notably influenced the development of the campaign, or constituted an important military factor. "The enemy," he said, "had, I knew, neither heavy artillery, nor even 20 mm. guns; in the information I received there was scarcely mention of heavy machine-guns. From time to time inflammable liquid was thrown from house-tops on to my supporting tanks as they escorted my patrols. It was tiresome, but it did not lose us a single tank. . . . None of my strong-points was ever attacked. . . ." This is a somewhat over-optimistic appreciation and is contradicted by several episodes we shall record later on.

He did not conceal from himself the serious risks created by the insurrection:

"I have always wondered," he wrote, "if, rationally speaking, there can be any advantage in the secret mobilization of civilians, even taking into account the most favourable results they can possibly achieve, when you consider the sea of blood and tears that results from their activities.

When the soldier feels himself attacked from the rear he loses all control of himself and defends himself by every available means. This has always been true in every period of history. . . ."

But at the same time he recognized the gallantry of his clandestine adversaries.

"However that may be, of this I have no doubt, there were courageous combatants in the ranks of the Resistance: students, workmen, officers. They fought with the exaltation of idealism."

Even the German military commander admitted that the great merit of the Paris insurrection was to have given the liberation of the city a certain epic quality, and thus restored to the capital its prestige.

Aware of the true meaning of the exalting event, de Gaulle, on 2 April 1945, at the Hôtel de Ville, uttered this precise and splendid phrase: "It is true to say that Paris at her liberation lacked nothing that was needed to make her worthy of France."

On this Tuesday, 22 August, there were also numerous approaches made to the Allied leaders to expedite their advance on the capital. The first was made by Commandant Gallois, of Colonel Rol's staff, when he met General Bradley. De Gaulle and Koenig, on receiving signals from the General Delegation, made several approaches to Eisenhower: they pressed him to succour Paris which, for three days, had been supporting alone the weight of the fighting against the German garrison.

In the afternoon, in agreement with General von Choltitz and Luizet, the new Prefect of Police, a mission left Paris to inform Bradley and Eisenhower of Choltitz's precise intentions. It left by the Porte de Versailles, flying the Swedish flag. Originally, it was to have been led by the Consul-General, but he was suffering from a heart attack and his place was taken by his brother, Roll-Nordling, who was French by nationality. Among its members were also Saint-Phalle, a banker who was representing Parodi, A—, alias Colonel O—, one of the heads of the Paris Intelligence Service, Jean Laurent, former head of General de Gaulle's Secretariat in 1940, and von Poch-Pastor, representing General von Choltitz, whose loyalty to the Nazis was certainly not beyond doubt. The delegation was accompanied to the German advance-posts by the mysterious Major Bender, of whom the least that can be said was that he was playing a double game.

The cars reached Trappes, where a German officer refused to let them go through: "There are," he said, "orders from generals which should not be obeyed!" His attitude to the travellers was one of such suspicion that they thought their last hour had come. They were about to be searched, which would have been fatal to them, for Poch-Pastor had in his pocket orders for the mission signed by the French staff, when the fortunate arrival of some American aircraft over Versailles created an opportune diversion. The search was postponed, which gave Bender time to telephone Choltitz, who gave categorical orders for the convoy to be allowed to proceed.

The results of these various approaches soon became apparent. During the night of Tuesday to Wednesday, Leclerc received from Patton the order to advance with the 2nd Armoured Division. At dawn the next morning, Wednesday, 23 August, Chaban-Delmas was informed that Leclerc was on his way.

On that same day of the 22nd, Choltitz received by radio another order from Hitler, which was even more lunatic than the previous ones:

"Paris will be transformed into a heap of rubble. The General Commanding in Chief will defend the city to the last man and, if necessary, will be buried beneath it."

Choltitz put the signal in his pocket and telephoned Lieutenant-General Speidel at Army Group Headquarters near Cambrai. Their conversation, whose authenticity has been confirmed by a French resistant, ran as follows:

Choltitz: "I am telephoning you to thank you for the splendid order you have transmitted to me."

Speidel: "What order, Herr General?"

Choltitz: "The order to reduce Paris to a heap of rubble, of course. Would you care to hear the dispositions I have made? Three tons of explosives have been placed in the Cathedral of Notre-Dame, two tons under the dome of the Invalides, one ton in the Chamber of Deputies. I am preparing to blow up the Arc de Triomphe to clear the field of fire."

Wondering what to make of this, Speidel sighed anxiously into the telephone.

Choltitz: "Well, my dear Speidel, I take it you agree?"

Speidel (stammering): "Yes . . . all right, yes . . . Herr General."

Choltitz: "But surely you ordered me to do this?"

Speidel (indignantly): "No, no, we haven't ordered anything of the kind, the order came from the Führer."

Choltitz: "Forgive me, you transmitted the order. And it is you who will bear the responsibility for it in the face of history. . . ."

Speidel made no reply to this.

Choltitz (continuing imperturbably): "I can tell you other dispositions I have made. We shall blow up the Madeleine and the Opéra at one go."

Speidel began to understand what lay behind Choltitz's fantastic proposals. Might it not be that he had no wish to carry out Hitler's order and that he was sounding him to see if he, Speidel, would eventually cover him for failing to do so.

Choltitz, suddenly inspired, increased the dose. In a calm and precise voice, he made the most grotesque suggestion of all, the one most likely to make Speidel grasp the point:

"I shall blow up the Eiffel Tower and its iron girders will deny access to the bridges which would have been previously demolished."

Speidel realized that Choltitz was not being serious and was asking, if not for his agreement, at least for his complicity.

Using a phrase with a double meaning for which he could not be reproached if the Intelligence services had tapped the lines and reported the conversation to Hitler, he said: "Herr General, how lucky we are to have *you* in Paris."

It was enough. As they hung up their respective receivers the two Generals knew that they had reached mutual understanding.

The 23 August was the day of the most violent fighting; there was no further question of a truce.

The Paris Committee of Liberation was sitting continuously in the Hôtel de Ville. It saw Parodi, Chaban-Delmas and, in the afternoon, Bidault. Booty captured from the enemy during the street fighting was littering the courtyards. The military commanders of the Hôtel de Ville, Leperc and Stéphane, issued an ultimate order to their troops:

"This order of the day will be the last.

"The F.F.I., comprising active volunteers, G.M.R.s, Équipes Nationales, and Gardes Républicains, have magnificently defended the Hôtel de Ville. They have victoriously repelled four enemy attacks and have never ceased to harass him.

"The results of their action are as follows: twenty-four Germans killed, twenty-eight prisoners, ten wounded.

"The booty captured includes: one armoured-car, one scout-car, seven trucks, two thousand litres of gasoline and arms and ammunition of all calibres.

"The Commandants Landry and Roger Stéphane are proud of having commanded such men."

Other battles were raging in every district in Paris.

In the afternoon, Chaban-Delmas attended a meeting of the C.O.M.A.C. He informed it that the 2nd Armoured Division was on the way to Paris; and arranged with Colonel Rol to increase the number of attacks, harass the enemy continually, and throw all available forces into the battle.

It was a day of false rumours and information that could not be checked. The Hôtel de Ville, which had wireless and a telephone exchange that still functioned, heard over the B.B.C. that Paris was liberated. To check up, they telephoned various police stations but none of them had heard the news and they all thought it premature. It was learnt that the Germans were retiring into their strong-points.

Their tactics now consisted in merely keeping open the routes between these points. They would send out a few tanks, which would fire a burst or two. But no one in the Resistance yet realized how precarious the Germans' situation had become. Apart from the members of the administrative services, who remained at their desks till they surrendered, Choltitz now had under his direct command no more than four tanks, seventeen armoured-cars, a battalion of engineers, consisting of three hundred men; and, what was more, he could no longer be sure of them or of their discipline.

General von Aulock, who in front of Paris was commanding a delaying force, newly formed of seventeen-year-old recruits, some of whom were not even in uniform, informed Choltitz that he considered he had accomplished his mission and was intending to break off contact with the enemy.

And Choltitz was having difficulties in his own headquarters. During the evening of the 23rd, a colonel of the Street Police asked him to send the garrison away. "If our trained troops," said this singular officer, "have not succeeded in beating the enemy in Normandy, the few German soldiers in Paris, ill-armed and ill-trained as they are, will certainly not succeed in doing so."

Choltitz ordered all the officers to be paraded. "Gentlemen," he said, "I have just seen a mutinous officer for the first time in my life. This officer has tried to force his Commander-in-Chief to issue orders he does not approve. . . .

"The Führer appointed me to Paris, and it is I alone who have responsibility here; my orders will be precisely carried out. I shall force obedience, pistol in hand, on anyone who rebels. Let everyone go to his post and await my orders. Should I be killed, I order Colonel Jay to take over, and my Chief of Staff, von Unger, to give him every assistance."

Thus Choltitz dealt with the defeatists; he was to deal similarly with the fire-eaters inspired by Hitler.

The Chief of the German Air Staff telephoned him.

"Herr General, I have orders to discuss with you the carrying out of an air-attack on Paris."

Choltitz was taken aback, but he could not show it.

"I am in entire agreement. I hope you will send day bombers."

"No, we can't do that."

"Very well," Choltitz replied, "you're proposing, are you, to set the city on fire by night with ninety bombers? How do you conceive the operation?"

"We have orders to discuss it with you. You will indicate the objectives."

"And you guarantee to hit the objectives I indicate by night?"

The Chief of Staff replied that the objectives would have to be whole districts.

"Very well," Choltitz said, "go ahead. But, in that case, I shall certainly have to withdraw my troops from Paris. You can hardly expect me to allow you to burn my soldiers up. I suppose you know about the order I have received to remain in Paris. If I have to leave the city, it will be your responsibility."

There was a pause. Then the airman said: "In that case, the bombing can't take place."

"That is also my view," Choltitz said. And then hung up.

The 24th was the radiant day on which Paris was rewarded for all her sufferings. The city continued to fight round the strong-points in which the Wehrmacht was concentrated. The few remaining tanks seemed now to be conforming to a precise programme: they had their individual routes, and patrolled them at almost exact times. In the 6th arrondissement, the tanks from the Sénat emerged each evening. They went down the Rue de Tournon, and crossed the Rue de Seine, where they exchanged a few shots with a barricade. They disappeared for a few hundred yards into the labyrinth of streets between the boulevard and the Seine.

At the corner of Rue Jacob and the Rue de Buci, they would shake the façade of a Louis XVth house with their firing, then, returning to the Boulevard Saint-Germain, they would enfilade it and spray the houses from which they had been fired on. There were skirmishes all round the Luxembourg. People watched the operations from their windows.

The 24th was marked, apart from many skirmishes, by two strong attacks mounted by the F.F.I. and the F.T.P., the first against the Prince-Eugène barracks at the République, the second against the Buttes-Chaumont tunnel and the trains parked in it.

The Petite Ceinture, that peripheral railway network which was not normally used except for a very short piece of line, could be used by the Germans for transporting troops across the capital. It was reported that among other movements, three trains had been sent from the Gare de Lyon to the Gare du Nord. The F.F.I. on the 19th and 20th arrondissements received as reinforcements units from other arrondissements, among them the 3rd Groupe Franc which, till then, had been operating in the Rue de Neuilly and the Boulevard Diderot. By 15.30 hours, they had won the battle. 137 Germans had been taken prisoner and an important booty captured.

The battle in the Place de la République took longer and was fought by a larger number of men. The F.F.I. of the 10th and 11th arrondissements decided to attack this Wehrmacht strong-point, which they knew was strongly held and armed. They were sent reinforcements. With one accord, Colonel Rol, in his headquarters at Denfort-Rochereau, and Colonel Lizé, in his at the Hôtel des Monnaies, sent such units as they had at their disposal. The Saint-Just Group took up its position in the Rue Fontaine-au-Roi; while a detachment of F.F.I. of the 12th arrondissement, the Armour Group Franc from the suburbs, the P.H.5 Group from Montrouge, and two detachments of F.T.P., Guy Mocquet and Garibaldi, went into the battle. The Germans had a crushing superiority of weapons. Towards 13.30 hours, the Germans counter-attacked with six armoured-cars and two tanks; they advanced as far as Saint-Ambroise, where the police and the Patriotic Militia stopped them. At 21.00 hours the terrain was retaken. But the fighting went on throughout the following day, until the arrival of a tank from Leclerc's division, which opened fire on the barracks.

Hour by hour the perimeter of General von Choltitz's command was being reduced. He scarcely left the Hôtel Meurice at all. Occasionally he would go out into the Rue de Rivoli to inspect the troops immediately guarding his headquarters. He was no longer in contact with his subordinate commanders. During the afternoon, his telephone rang and he heard an unknown voice, which gave no indication where it was speaking from, ask if he were ready to receive a letter from the General Commanding the Allied Troops, which would invite him to surrender. "Nothing can be done till the fighting stops," Choltitz replied. "I shall exchange no letters with enemy generals."

That night, he had his last dinner in the Hôtel Meurice. With him were his Chief of Staff, his Chief of Operations, his A.D.C.s and his two faithful secretaries. His dinner was served, apart from the hotel staff, by his servant who had been with him in all his campaigns for the last seven years.

The General later recorded his feelings at that time: "I thought that our ancestors had never had to face such battles, nor had ever been abandoned as we were. I knew that my wife and children were in Germany, with no means of defence against a régime which menaced their liberty and even their lives."

After dinner, he went with his companions into a little room from which he saw through the open window the last night of his command fall over Paris.

Suddenly bells started ringing from all directions.

"Herr General," exclaimed one of his staff, "what does that mean?"

"What does it mean? It's the Franco-American Army making its entry into Paris."

Choltitz immediately asked on the telephone for the Army Group Headquarters.

"Good evening, Speidel."

"Good evening, Herr General."

Choltitz: "Will you listen, please?"

Choltitz held the receiver to the open window. He then asked: "Did you hear that?"

Speidel: "Yes, a sound of bells."

Choltitz: "That's precisely what it is. The Franco-American Army is entering Paris. . . ."

After a silence Choltitz asked: "Speidel, what are the Army Group's orders for the General Commanding in Chief without troops?"

"Herr General, you know very well that we are no longer in a position to give any orders. . . ."

Choltitz: "Well, my dear Speidel, there is nothing left for me to do but to say good-bye to you. Look after and protect my wife at Baden-Baden, and my children too."

Speidel: "We shall do so, Herr General, we give you our word."

Meanwhile, at the Hôtel de Ville, the *Marseillaise* was ringing out. It was 22.00 hours. The first tank from the 2nd Armoured Division, the *Romilly*, had just drawn up under the windows. Two men got out of it, Captain Dronne and a young soldier.

The Captain, exhausted, ill-shaven, covered with sweat and dirt, was being embraced by Bidault, when suddenly there was a sound of firing, cries and tumult. The chandelier was switched off. When quiet had been restored, the light was turned on again and it was discovered that there were two or three wounded, one of them seriously.

From the Prefecture of the Seine, Dronne, in his *Romilly*, went to the Prefecture of Police. His welcome there was more solemn: the Police

Band played the *Marseillaise*. Over the radio Parodi said: "I have beside me a French captain who has just entered Paris, the first. He has a red face, is dirty and unshaven, and yet one wants to embrace him."

Guignebert, who was in charge of the broadcast, then said he was going to interview the young soldier, who was much moved.

"You will now hear," he said, "one of our own young chaps . . . an ordinary private soldier . . . a sound young Frenchman. . . . Where were you born?"

And history, which occasionally condescends to humour, has recorded for posterity that the first young soldier to be interviewed in Paris over the liberated radio replied shyly: "I was born in Constantinople."

During the night of the 24th to 25th, there was little sleeping done in Paris. Guns were firing continuously, and machine-guns rattling. Balconies and windows were hung with flags and standards that had been secretly made ready.

In spite of the curfew set for 21.00 hours, the streets were full of people in search of news; among them Captain Kergall, head of the F.F.I. Intelligence for the Paris region. His secret office was next door to his official office, in the Rue de Rome, at the Central Committee for the Supply of Fruit and Vegetables, of which he was secretary-general.

At 21.00 hours, after hearing the bells, he prowled round the Hôtel Meurice, to see if there was any German activity. But there was none. Neither cars, nor despatch-riders. He was able to confirm that the Commander of Greater Paris was taking no effective part in these ultimate operations, and that he had no overall plan for opposing the entrance of the Allied troops.

Having ascertained the position, at 23.00 hours Kergall went to the Prefecture of Police and entered the office of the F.F.I. Liaison Officer, who had a direct line to the 2nd Armoured Division. He knew the division was to set out for Paris at 07.00 hours in the morning and that, unless ordered otherwise, the order to march would be issued at 03.00 hours. It was therefore important to inform Leclerc at once as to what was going on in the various districts of the capital.

The two officers telephoned all the police stations in Paris and the suburbs. They asked each of them the same questions: "What's going on in your district? Have you seen any German troop movements?" The reply was always the same: nothing to report.

At three o'clock in the morning, they telephoned to Palaiseau. Just as the division was about to start moving, they transmitted to Leclerc's staff the following reassuring news: "No troop movements in Paris. The Germans shut up in their last strong-points. Go to it; you can march by the three arranged routes." At 07.15 hours the 2nd Armoured Division marched on Paris.

Each of the three brigades of which it was composed had its particular objective: Billotte's was to enter by the Porte de Gentilly, and make for the Prefecture of Police where it would find Captain Dronne, while Langlade's was to enter by the Porte de Saint-Cloud and make for the Étoile. They were both then to join up, taking the axis of the Rue de Rivoli, the Concorde, and the Champs-Élysées. It was they who in passing cleaned up the two German headquarters in the Majestic and the Meurice, where von Choltitz was.

At the Majestic, Commandant Massu, on the orders of Colonel de Langlade, received the surrender. Massu, according to Adrien Dansette's description of him, was "a colossus of six foot three, a sort of huge wood-cutter, who scarcely seemed predestined for the graces of diplomacy." He made his way into a room full of German officers and, by way of negotiation, shouted: *"Heraus! Heraus!"*

The Dio Brigade entered by the Porte d'Orléans. It split into two groups. Rouvillois went by the Gare Montparnasse, made for the Invalides and seized the Latour-Maubourg barracks; he then attacked the Palais-Bourbon and the Quai d'Orsay. Noiret reached the Pont de Grenelle by the outer boulevards, went up the Seine and made sure of all the bridges as far as the Invalides. Then he made for the École Militaire.

It was these two half-brigades that had the hardest fighting. Some of it took place round the block constituted by the Ministry of Foreign Affairs, the Presidency of the Chamber and the Palais-Bourbon. The principal attack was mounted at the corner of the Esplanade des Invalides and the Rue de l'Université. Rouvillois lost one tank; and the French had to set fire to the Ministry which the Germans were defending.

Further fighting took place at the École Militaire where it took five hours to force the garrison of 250 men, fifty of whom were killed, to surrender.

Hour by hour, and almost minute by minute, the aspect of Paris changed. At 12.30 hours, for the first time since June 1940, the Tricolour flew from the summit of the Eiffel Tower. Shortly after 14.00 hours, a huge standard was hoisted to the top of the Arc de Triomphe; the first French officers were saluting the Tomb of the Unknown Soldier, when a shell fired by a German tank passed under the Arch and another damaged Rude's *La Marseillaise*.

The population of Paris surrounded the newcomers; each of Leclerc's soldiers had a group of people round him. When Colonel de Langlade received the surrender of the Hôtel Majestic, the German officers noted that his cheeks were covered with lipstick. Elsewhere, a woman climbed into a tank and took part with its crew in the last fighting in Paris. The Paris police also participated; policemen on bicycles preceded Massu's half-brigade, as if it were an official procession.

Many of the newcomers had friends in Paris. When they reached the city, the soldiers handed down notes from their tanks to the welcoming crowd giving their names and telephone numbers to which their arrival should be announced. A young officer, Second-Lieutenant Bureau, telephoned to his father himself: an hour later, he was killed at the Quai d'Orsay before he had had time to see him.

Indeed, the battle was no make-believe, even if it was accompanied by shouts of joy and bursts of laughter: on 25 August alone, admission to the public hospitals numbered 127 French killed and 714 wounded, 27 Germans killed and 233 wounded. During the whole of the fighting for the liberation of Paris, there were 901 F.F.I. and 582 civilians killed, against 2,788 Germans. And there were 1,455 F.F.I., 2,012 civilians and 4,911 Germans wounded.

And yet the life of the city went on. On this 25 August, when blood was flowing and buildings were burning, when the Tricolour was beginning to fly once again, and the Germans, whether in uniform or plain clothes, were surrendering or dying honourably, most Parisians had luncheon at their usual hour.

Among these luncheons of 25 August 1944, there were two in particular which form a contrast: Choltitz's luncheon, in the Hôtel Meurice, from which in a few hours' time he was to emerge a prisoner, and Leclerc's luncheon, at the Hôtel de Ville, where he received the surrender of the German General with the coffee.

The last night at Choltitz's headquarters had been very quiet. In the morning, accompanied by his Chief of Operations, Jay, the General, who had prudently spent the night at Neuilly, inspected the defences of his headquarters. He placed a guard on the ground floor of the hotel, then went to his office to await events. From his balcony, at about ten or eleven o'clock, he heard artillery fire and tanks, followed by the rattle of machine-gun fire. He saw American tanks, carrying French soldiers, crossing the Rue de Rivoli. At midday the battle ceased, but he learned that the Allies were already at the Opéra.

That same morning, at 11.00 hours, Colonel Billotte, who to impress Choltitz had assumed the rank of general, sent an ultimatum to the Commander of what remained of Greater Paris:

Paris, 25 August, 10.00 hours.

The General commanding the French 1st Armoured Brigade to General von Choltitz.

During yesterday, my brigade crushed all the German strong-points opposed to it. It caused them severe losses and took numerous prisoners.

This morning, I entered Paris and my tanks are occupying the Cité. Large armoured units, French and Allied, have joined me.

From a strictly military point of view, I consider that the resistance of the German troops cannot hope to be effective.

In order to avoid useless bloodshed, it is your duty to put an immediate end to resistance.

Should you insist on continuing a battle which cannot be militarily justified, I am determined to prosecute it to total extermination.

I await your reply within half an hour of your receiving this ultimatum.

BILLOTTE

This document was taken by armoured car to the Swedish Consulate in the Rue d'Anjou. From there, Nordling and the German Major Bender, in plain clothes, set off to the Hôtel Meurice. In the Rue Royale their car was stopped by the Germans. Bender went on alone to the Hôtel Crillon where, after a telephone call, he received a visit from Lieutenant von Arnim, Choltitz's A.D.C.

Von Arnim refused to accept the ultimatum: "The General knows what is in the letter, but he will not accept it." Nevertheless, he added that, honour having been safeguarded, if the General were personally made prisoner, he would give the order for surrender. It was a question of not losing face.

Thereupon, von Choltitz sat down to his last luncheon in the Meurice. We do not know the menu, but we do know that he was gloomy. As usual, the General sat with his back to the terrace which gave on to the Rue de Rivoli. His Chief of Operations, hearing a stray shot, suggested he sit elsewhere. "No," replied Choltitz, "particularly not today."

After luncheon, which was quickly over, Choltitz went up to his room, washed and changed his uniform.

About 14.00 hours, a violent fight began round the hotel. Tanks of American make came into action, escorted by F.F.I. infantry. The German staff cars, parked under the arcades of the Rue de Rivoli, caught fire.

The hotel became full of smoke; and orders were given to close the windows. Allied troops burst into the hall with smoke-bombs. The hotel was now cut in two. The ground floor was liberated, the upper floors still occupied.

The moment had come for negotiations. Choltitz ordered Colonel Jay to send an officer to make contact with the French in the hall. Lieutenant Post was sent. His mission was to get a French officer to come upstairs to Choltitz.

Suddenly the door of the room in which Choltitz was waiting burst open. A haggard-looking civilian appeared, his finger on the trigger of a sub-machine-gun. Behind him was Colonel Jay and the Counsellor of Embassy, Dr. Eckelmann.

The three Germans were nonplussed. They had no doubt they were face to face with a "terrorist."

Levelling his weapon, the man said: *"Sprechen Sie Deutsch?"* (Do you speak German?) To this absurd question, Choltitz replied, not unreasonably: "Probably better than you do." The conversation did not seem to have begun well. Fortunately, at that moment, the door opened again and two French officers came in, Lieutenant Karcher, who had just shot a last German rifleman in the hall, and Commandant de la Horie, Colonel Billotte's Chief of Staff, who had been selected as plenipotentiary. The two officers began by turning the civilian out.

Then Karcher said to the General: "Do you surrender?"

"Yes."

"Lay down your arms."

The officers put down their arms.

Commandant de la Horie then said: "You refused the ultimatum which was sent to you this morning. You have fought. You are defeated. But there is still resistance going on elsewhere. I demand that you give the order to all your commanding officers of the centres of resistance to cease fire."

"This was the procedure in 1940 on the Maginot Line," observed Lieutenant Karcher.

"Yes," replied Choltitz, "but I insist that we be treated as soldiers."

"Follow me."

The three men went down by the service stairs and walked to Choltitz's car. It was in front of the door, but the key had disappeared. The other cars were still burning.

La Horie, Karcher and Choltitz took the Rue de Castiglione and reached the Rue de Rivoli. There Choltitz was joined by his servant, who brought his valise.

Armed civilians hurled themselves on him, snatched the valise and searched it. Suddenly, a woman wearing the brassard of the Red Cross appeared and stood between the two Germans and their attackers. She accompanied Choltitz to a car which was parked at the other end of the building. La Horie invited the General to get into it.

Before doing so, the General saluted the woman, thanked her, shook her hand and said: "Madame, like Joan of Arc"—a sibylline remark. Was it a last hit at the British?

Meanwhile, Leclerc's luncheon was a great deal gayer. Welcomed by Luizet at the Prefecture of Police, he was taken to a table laid with all the luxury with which the city of Paris is accustomed in peacetime to entertain its honoured guests: a white cloth, splendid china, and masses of flowers from the municipal hot-houses. Leclerc sat down, but the fighting was still going on and left him little leisure to appreciate the meal. He remained at the table for only ten minutes, merely tasting a single dish, while receiving reports from despatch-riders about the progress of his troops through Paris. He was concerned at the fact that they were still encountering resistance and was impatiently waiting for Choltitz to be taken prisoner.

During these few minutes, Leclerc exchanged a few words with the civilians round him. During the four years he had been fighting outside France, had he not rather lost contact with the population? Did he understand the true attitude of the people? Had he not, during the course of his exile, fashioned for himself an imaginary France which was not the true one? And Leclerc concluded the brief discussion with these wholly sensible, if apprehensive, words: "Well, we shall have to relearn France."

At the same time, he took note of the weaknesses of some of the people present; and, two days later, on 27 August, when he wrote to de Gaulle to give him an account of his impressions of Paris, he said: "The leaders, even those appointed by your government, are . . . very timorous. This, I think, is one of the cruxes of the problem. It is no affair of mine. I am merely a soldier. But, having witnessed certain scenes, I must tell you what I think. Your task will be none the easier, General."

For the moment, his concern was the arrival of von Choltitz. He eventually arrived at 15.00 hours with Colonel Billotte, who had attended him on his journey to the Prefecture and now showed him into the Prefect of the Seine's billiard-room, where the headquarters had been set up. Von Choltitz and his officers had crossed the courtyard to the Prefecture under the protection of twenty police in uniform.

When Choltitz came into the room, Leclerc said: "I am General Leclerc. You are no doubt General von Choltitz. Why did you refuse to receive my letter?"

Choltitz replied in German: "I was under no obligation to receive a letter before the end of the battle."

Choltitz sat down at a table and the conversation continued through an interpreter, Captain Betz, whom the German General declared "not quite up to his job."

Leclerc produced a typewritten Act of Surrender. The two Generals examined the paragraphs one by one. With them were Colonel Billotte, General Chaban-Delmas, Colonel Rol, two other officers of Leclerc's staff, Commandants Repiton and de Guillebon, and Choltitz's chief signal officer.

Betz read the Act of Surrender first in French and then in German.

The Provisional Government of the French Republic.

Act of Surrender concluded between the Divisional General Leclerc, commanding the French Forces of Paris and General von Choltitz, Military Commander of the German Forces in the Paris Region.

All the articles here below apply to the units of the Wehrmacht throughout the command of General von Choltitz.

(1) Immediate orders will be issued to the commanders of the strong-points to cease fire and fly the white flag: arms will be collected and troops will be mustered without arms in the open, there to await orders. The arms will be intact.

(2) The order of battle, including mobile units and depots of materials throughout the command, will be handed over. The depots will be handed over intact with their books.

(3) A list of the destruction to works and depots.

(4) As many German staff officers as there are strong-points or garrisons will be sent to General Leclerc's headquarters.

(5) The conditions in which the personnel of the Wehrmacht will be evacuated will be arranged by General Leclerc's staff.

(6) Once these articles have been signed and the orders transmitted, members of the Wehrmacht who continue to fight will no longer enjoy the protection of the laws of war.

Paris, 25 August 1944.

There were two arguments before signature: one with Colonel Rol who, as head of the F.F.I. of the Paris Region, demanded to sign the document with Leclerc. Leclerc refused on the grounds that he was designated in the Act of Surrender as commanding the whole of the French Forces of Paris. The other was with von Choltitz over paragraph (6). The German General pointed out that there might be troops passing through Paris who were not under his command and were therefore not subject to the Act of Surrender. Leclerc agreed to add three lines to the original text:

"Nevertheless, the case of any German soldiers in or crossing Paris who are not under the General's command will be fairly examined."

Having appended his signature, Choltitz was taken in an armoured car to the Gare Montparnasse, the headquarters of the 2nd Armoured Division. During the journey Leclerc stood in front of him, his A.D.C. behind.

Arrived at the station, Choltitz had a slight heart-attack due to emotional strain and the nervous tension of the last few days. He asked for a glass of water from one of the little shops in the station hall. He then took a pill from his pocket. A French interpreter hurried up: "Herr General, I hope you're not trying to poison yourself." "Oh, no, young man," replied Choltitz, "we don't do things like that."

When he felt better, the General was taken into one of the offices where he wrote out the order for the cease-fire:

Order: Resistance in the sectors of the strong-points, and within the strong-points themselves will cease at once.

The General Commanding in Chief:
VON CHOLTITZ, General of Infantry.

These instructions were transmitted throughout the city by German officers escorted by French officers.

At Montparnasse, the question of Rol's signature was reopened by Kriegel-Valrimont, of the C.O.M.A.C., who insisted to Leclerc that the F.F.I. leader's signature should appear on the Act of Surrender. Leclerc, unaware of the political dissensions which existed within the Resistance, finally agreed. He altered the heading of the document and even allowed Rol's name to precede his own.

At 16.00 hours, General de Gaulle arrived at the Gare Montparnasse from Rambouillet. He was met by Leclerc and Rol-Tanguy. When he was shown the final draft of the Act of Surrender, he disapproved of the F.F.I. leader's name appearing beside that of the commander of the 2nd Armoured Division as having received the enemy's surrender: "It is not true. Moreover, in this affair, you are the senior officer and therefore solely responsible. Furthermore the demand made to you to agree to this wording proceeds from an unacceptable tendency." And to put Leclerc in the picture de Gaulle showed him a proclamation emanating from the C.N.R. and published that very morning, which made no allusion either to the provisional government or himself.

It was thus that on his very first arrival in Paris, de Gaulle found himself faced with a situation which he had both feared and, for a long time past, had been making preparations to meet. There was, if not antagonism, at least rivalry between the political leaders of the internal Resistance, of whom many were of Communist obedience, and the provisional government, the government of national unity, which was represented in Paris by Parodi and the General Delegation.

On 23 August, from Rambouillet, de Gaulle had written a brief letter to his Prefect of Police, Charles Luizet, which left his intentions in no doubt:

"Monsieur le Préfet and dear Friend,

"I have received your messengers and your letter today.

"Tomorrow will be decisive in the sense we wish.

"When I arrive, I shall go straight to the 'centre.' We shall at once organize the rest with Quartus (Parodi), and with you. . . ."

The "centre" to which de Gaulle intended to go immediately on his arrival in Paris was the Ministry of War, in the Rue Saint-Dominique, the government building in which he had decided to take up his quarters to show that he represented the State, and that the State, without any cessation of continuity, was returning to its proper domain.

Having stopped at the Gare Montparnasse, where he wanted to meet the General commanding his army in his headquarters, de Gaulle then set out for the Rue Saint-Dominique. The journey was not entirely uneventful. As he was going down the Rue Eblé, near Saint-François-Xavier, there was firing from the houses, and he decided to change his route and go by the Rue Vaneau and the Rue de Bourgogne. At 17.00 hours, he re-entered the Ministry he had left with Paul Reynaud on the night of 10 June 1940. After four years, it looked the same, exactly as if nothing had happened. In the courtyard, a platoon of the Republican Guard presented arms as in the old days. The furniture was intact. The same *huissiers* were still there. The switches of the house-telephone still bore the same names. In appearance, nothing had altered; and yet, as he preceded the General into the building, Commandant de Lignières, the supply officer we have already met at Rambouillet, was aware, poor fellow, that all was not well.

Sent on ahead by Colonel de Chevigné, he had received as orders only these few brief words: "De Gaulle will sleep tonight at the Ministry in the Rue Saint-Dominique. Arrange quarters and a meal for fifty people for this evening."

On reaching the Rue Saint-Dominique, Lignières was not well received. A man, dressed in overalls, refused him entrance. As luck would have it, fire broke out in the Ministry. Lignières had friends in the Paris fire-brigade. When the firemen arrived, they took him in with them.

Inside, he found the building entirely full of F.F.I. It was the

C.O.M.A.C. Its members looked on a regular supply officer with suspicion, particularly when he arrived to organize quarters for General de Gaulle.

There was much argument. In the end, Touya, a colonel of gendarmerie, and a future diplomat accredited to the Sultan of Morocco, persuaded the F.F.I. to make room for the General. They evacuated a few offices, and freed the grand staircase. All that now remained for Lignières to do was to find food for fifty people and a cook to cook it.

He met a woman in a passage who told him that she knew a master cook who was out of a job. He had been waiting for someone else to arrive who was now no longer coming. Summoned at once, the man presented himself, somewhat intimidated: "Are you a cook?" asked Lignières. "Yes." "Where were you before?" "At Vichy." "What are you doing in Paris?" "I was sent to the kitchens of the Élysée to await the arrival of the Marshal." He was an ex-cook to the Presidents of the Republic, and after four years' loyal service to the Vichy government he now offered to prepare the first meal in Paris for the provisional government. Delighted with his find, Lignières now set out to find chickens to requisition. These, accompanied on the menu by American rations, foie gras and vegetables, proved to the General that in passing from one régime to another Pétain's cook had not lost his skill.

These incidents in the Rue Saint-Dominique were premonitory signs of the difficulties de Gaulle would himself have to surmount.

When he reached the Ministry with Le Troquer and General Juin, he was joined by Parodi, his Delegate General, who had never met him before. Parodi wished to be properly introduced and was accompanied by one of his assistants, Morandat, who had known General de Gaulle during a stay in London. De Gaulle greeted him in a friendly way: "Hullo, Morandat! I thought you had been arrested." The mistake was due to a cipher error in a signal sent to London. The General, who was always loyal to his companions and interested in their fate, was relieved.

Parodi, who came from the Hôtel de Ville where the C.P.L. and the C.N.R. were awaiting the General's arrival, realized from his first words that he would have some difficulty in persuading de Gaulle to visit the leaders of the Resistance.

The General refused curtly. He would be received neither by the C.N.R. nor the C.P.L. in the municipal building. He represented the State and was the head of the government. He would await a visit from the Resistance authorities in a government palace.

Parodi, much "discouraged" by this welcome, was wholly unable to resolve the conflict. He produced argument after argument: the General had nothing to fear from anyone; all Paris was at his feet. In a word, his prestige was such that nothing could diminish it. He talked of the enthusiastic crowds waiting at the Hôtel de Ville. Were they to be disappointed in this first hour of regained liberty? But it was wasted effort. Parodi, for all his convictions, did not know de Gaulle well enough to find the right arguments to persuade him to change his mind.

It then occurred to Morandat to telephone Luizet, at the Prefecture of Police, and ask him to come over at once. Luizet, whose loyalty in Corsica had been much appreciated by the General and who had been part of his team for a long time, might perhaps carry enough weight to make him alter his decision.

Luizet hurried round. He backed up Parodi's arguments, and de Gaulle allowed himself to be persuaded. If it was necessary, he would go to the Hôtel de Ville, but only for a moment, and after passing by the Prefecture of Police, a government building closely in touch with the "centre."

At the Prefecture of Police, the General inspected the Paris police while the band played the *Marseillaise* and the *Marche Lorraine*. From there he went on foot, through the cheering crowd, to the Hôtel de Ville.

The atmosphere seemed charged. Georges Bidault was stamping with impatience, muttering that never in his life had he been kept waiting so long. Other and more serious incidents had during the course of the day increased the general exasperation.

During the afternoon, two hours before the General's arrival, Colonel Aron-Brunetière, of the S.R. of the Parisian F.F.I., had warned the military commander of the Hôtel de Ville that two militiamen had entered the building with the intention of assassinating the General.

Everyone not a member of the F.F.I. was immediately screened. Each was asked: "Are you armed?" "No." "Swear it." After this first formality, they were locked in various rooms and searched.

Pistols were found on two of them, and the militiamen confessed their intentions. One of them was called Mansuy, and had been one of the assassins of Georges Mandel. The other was called Boutier and had also been on the staff of the Militia. They both stood to their guns: "We'll get you all the same: in a fortnight, the Militia will be back and then you'll be in for it." They were shut into two little offices, and guarded by sentries with sub-machine-guns. They were executed next morning.

De Gaulle arrived. A rumour preceded him to the reception rooms on the first floor: "The General . . . here's the General." The C.N.R. and the C.P.L. were assembled in the Prefect's office. Flouret, the Prefect of the Seine, went down the first flight of stairs to meet the General.

He had never met de Gaulle before; but there could be no doubt: the stature, the uniform, the tunic with no other decoration but the two insignia, that of the Free French (the Cross of Lorraine) and that of the Free French Forces (the red sword and blue wings on a white ground), which Paris did not yet know, but whose meaning could be guessed; and then that sovereign air. Hardly had de Gaulle and Flouret climbed the first steps of the staircase, which was crowded with people and resounding with acclamations, when the General asked a political question: "How far have you got with the purge?" "The committees are being organized as planned, General." "The important thing," de Gaulle went on, "is that it be done quickly. The whole business must be finished within a few weeks." The Prefect understood that the Head of the Government wanted sanctions to be limited to the small number of the principally guilty, and the whole problem dealt with quickly, since it was one which might well poison French political life.

When they reached the Prefect's office on the first floor, the General, whose face was drawn with fatigue, received an extraordinary welcome. With tears in their eyes, the combatants presented arms. There was a thunder of cheering. Now that they saw him, the members of the C.N.R., the C.P.L., and so many of his supporters, all forgetting their dissensions, became united in what they hoped from him. Marrane spoke first for the Paris Committee of Liberation. On behalf of Tollet, he welcomed the General, with great amiability and patriotism, in the name of the new Municipality. Then Bidault spoke on behalf of the C.N.R. "Here is the man," he said, "whom we have been awaiting for four years. . . . It is splendid," he concluded, "that we should be assembled here in the heart of the Cité, on the day of Saint Louis, close to Notre-Dame de Paris, where Saint Geneviève kept watch, and where our ancestors defended the dignity and independence of the Cité over the centuries. We shall continue to do so as, indeed, we have done only yesterday."

Then de Gaulle spoke: "Let us not conceal the emotion we all feel, both men and women, who are now here and at home in a Paris that has been roused to liberate itself and has done so of its own volition. No! This profound, this sacred emotion must not be hidden. This movement is one that surpasses the poor lives of all of us."

After this exordium, everyone expected he would thank the Resistance, whose leaders were assembled about him. Instead, he read them a lecture and appealed to them for that unity of which he was the guardian, the sole incarnation: "The nation will not permit, in the situation in which it finds itself, that this unity be destroyed. . . . The people are well informed, and during their 2,000 years of history, the French people have decided, by instinct and reason, that two conditions must be satisfied for without them nothing great can be achieved. And these are order and ardour. Republican order, under the only valid authority, that of the State; organized ardour, which alone can result in the legal and fraternal building of the edifice of renewal. The enthusiastic acclamations of our towns and villages, now purged at last of the enemy, mean this. And this is what the great voice of liberated Paris is proclaiming."

These words had a nobility which was perhaps greater than the gathering was at this moment expecting. Georges Bidault, for instance, was concerned that the Republic, in conformity with the call to insurrection issued by the C.N.R. on 19 August, should be "proclaimed" in the presence of the people of Paris.

Bidault asked the General to appear on a balcony and proclaim the Republic. De Gaulle was prepared to do the former but not the latter. What was the use of proclaiming the Republic when, for the last four years, it had been maintained in London and then in Algiers, when thousands of men had died in its service, when almost the whole Empire beyond the seas had taken part in its defence? Indeed, there were two objections to proclaiming the Republic: it would mean admitting the legitimacy, if only temporary, of Vichy's interruption of it. And it would also mean recognizing as government organizations those councils of the Resistance, which seemed to be unaware of the exclusive power of de Gaulle's government. De Gaulle was determined to stumble into neither of these snares. His voice, as he replied to Georges Bidault, was peremptory: "No, the Republic has never ceased to exist."

Then he stepped over the sill of a window, to the horror of those standing round who feared he might fall. The Place de l'Hôtel de Ville was filled with a cheering crowd. De Gaulle spread wide his arms in a gesture that was at once an appeal and a dedication. Every eye, cry and gesture rose to him as if to a saviour.

Then, leaving the balcony, de Gaulle quitted the Hôtel de Ville without allowing the members of the C.N.R. to be introduced to him.

Next day was, so to speak, his apotheosis, despite a few rare clouds in the sky.

In the first place, the C.N.R. was not happy. It had neither been informed of, nor invited to, the procession down the Champs-Élysées and the march to Notre-Dame. This did not, however, prevent Bidault from trotting along beside the General; and, while de Gaulle repeated the characteristic gesture of the day before, of spreading wide his arms in greeting to the popular enthusiasm, Georges Bidault was seen to be twisting a pair of gloves in his hands, as if, in his own minor key, he wished to appear to be conjuring with the historic acclaim.

The Americans and, in particular, Gerow, who was in command of the corps to which the French 2nd Armoured Division belonged, were no better pleased. Gerow, in a general order, had forbidden the Leclerc division to take part in the ceremonies in Paris.

"Operating, as you are, under my direct command," he wrote to Leclerc, "you will accept no orders emanating from any other source. I believe you have received orders from General de Gaulle for your troops to take part in a parade this afternoon at 14.00 hours. You will pay no heed to this order and you will continue to carry out the mission to which you are at present assigned to clean up all resistance in Paris and its neighbourhood, within your zone of action.

"The troops under your command will take no part in the parade, either this afternoon, or at any other time, except on orders personally signed by me."

To this de Gaulle replied that he had agreed to lend one of his divisions to the American command and that he had a perfect right to use it to enter his own capital. The incident was quickly smoothed over: Gerow did not insist and the 2nd Armoured Division was alone in keeping order throughout the day of the 26th; after which, it returned to Gerow and set off once more to fight under the American General's command.

The afternoon of 26 August was a unique moment in the history of the capital.

At 15.00 hours, de Gaulle arrived at the Arc de Triomphe, where he found by the flame of the unknown soldier his two "ministers," Parodi and Le Troquer, Resistance leaders, among whom were Bidault and Tollet, generals and admirals, Juin, the conqueror of Rome, Koenig of Bir-Hakeim, Leclerc, leaning on the legendary walking-stick that had accompanied him since Chad, Thierry d'Argenlieu, who commanded the naval forces, Valin, who commanded the air force, the two Prefects of Paris, Flouret and Luizet, and innumerable combatants and leaders of the F.F.I. A unit from the 2nd Armoured Division, the Chad Infantry Regiment, provided a guard of honour at the tomb. The General placed a Cross of Lorraine in rose gladioli on the grave, then, contrary to all protocol, on foot, preceded by four tanks, police, soldiers and F.F.I., who stretched with arms linked from one side of the avenue to the other, at once alone in the crowd and yet a part of those millions of human beings, he proceeded down the Champs-Élysées. Luizet, Prefect of Police, who was far from unaware of the dangers presented by so great a crowd, which was at once impossible to canalize and impossible to infiltrate, had sent out loud-speaker vans. "General de Gaulle," they shouted, "confides his safety to the people of Paris. He asks them to assure order among themselves and to help the police and the F.F.I., tired from five days of fighting, in their task."

There was no danger to him at first, nor indeed for the whole length of the Champs-Élysées.

In the Place de la Concorde, however, at the entrance to the Rue de Rivoli, when the General had entered his car, which was preceded by that of Colonel Peretti, in charge of his security, a few shots aroused a stir of emotion through the crowd. It was a false and brief alarm, which merely made Colonel Peretti hasten the pace a little.

De Gaulle stopped a moment at the Hôtel de Ville, where the band of the Garde Républicaine, in full dress, played *Gloire immortelle de nos aieux*. At 16.15 hours, he got out of his car in front of Notre-Dame. He took a few steps towards the door, and was receiving a tricolour bouquet from two Alsatian girls, when there was a sudden burst of firing. There was panic among the crowd. People lay on the ground; others fled towards the cathedral; and others again raised their weapons and began firing wildly.

De Gaulle, who had been pinned against a column to the left of the principal door, was rescued by Peretti, who fought his way to him through the crowd. Then, his impassivity completely unruffled, he entered the cathedral where he was received with acclamation. He had advanced only a few yards, when more firing was heard. The General continued to walk calmly and unhurriedly up the nave to where a chair had been set for him in the north transept. Parodi, Le Troquer and Colonel Peretti took their places behind him. The firing continued and appeared to be coming from the galleries at the end of the choir. It did not prevent the congregation singing the *Magnificat*; but it was thought best for reasons of security to cut the ceremony short and omit the *Te Deum*.

Who had fired, and why? And at whom? No one present heard the whistle of bullets. Was the firing directed at the roof, not to commit an assassination but to create the illusion that one was intended, and thereby provoke reprisals?

At the same time firing broke out all over Paris, and did cause casualties. It was heard, or thought to be heard, in the Place de l'Hôtel de Ville, at the Gare d'Orsay, in the Champs-Élysées, near the Étoile, and in the Rue de Presbourg, among other places. During the afternoon, the

Hôtel-Dieu admitted 120 wounded, of whom at least as many were due to panic as to bullets. But some of the wounds were undoubted, and due to the "*tireurs des toits*," as they were at once called.

Who were these "roof-firers?" According to some, they were Germans from the Brandenburg Division, but none was ever found. According to others, they were Militia, which may well have been true in a small number of cases. Others, again, put the whole business down to collective hallucination, and the fact that the F.F.I. discharged their weapons from nervous tension. It was said that, at Notre-Dame, the pigeons nesting in the inside galleries had been alarmed by the acclamations, taken flight with a great noise of wings, and that the troops had opened fire on them. While still others maintained that the shots fired into the air were a deliberate provocation by extreme elements of the Resistance to justify reprisals and harsh repressive measures.

In any case, this last is the explanation which de Gaulle, in his *Mémoires*, seems to have accepted twelve years after the event. At the time, his impression was quite otherwise. In an unpublished letter, of 27 August 1944, the day after the ceremony at Notre-Dame, he wrote as follows:

"The 'fusillade' of Notre-Dame was, in my view, a vulgar piece of showing off. Many people (F.F.I. and others) walk about with arms. Excited by the fighting of these last days, they are always ready to fire at the roofs. The first shot starts a wild fusillade. We shall fix this too."

Whether attempted assassination or a piece of showing off, no fusillade of this sort could interrupt the homage paid by the capital to the man who had liberated it.

During the night of 1 September, the *concierge* of the Prefecture at Le Mans saw a convoy of jeeps draw up in front of the gates. Someone tapped at his window. "What do you want?" "To see the Prefect." "This is scarcely the right time. Who are you?" "The members of the French government." "You can't take me in like that. They tried to pull that one over us last week." And the *concierge* shut the door.

However, it was in fact the provisional government of the Republic come from Algiers and on its way to Paris.

As soon as he had entered the liberated capital, General de Gaulle had sent summons after summons to the Ministers who had remained in Algiers under Vice-President Queuille. Letter upon letter and signal upon signal demanded the immediate return of the members of his government to take over the Ministries in Paris, where the secretary-generals were carrying on.

It appeared to him that his admonitions were being received without enthusiasm. Nothing happened. When, on 2 September, de Gaulle at last met Queuille in Paris, he made no attempt to hide his displeasure: "I really think your state of health demands a long stay in Corrèze where you can rest."

It may indeed have been true that some of the Ministers regarded an immediate return to Paris, where there were a certain number of V.1s about, without apprehension. But the true reason for their delay, which was indeed not very prolonged, was not their fault.

The Allies in Algiers, whose first concern was with military transport, were in no hurry to repatriate these fifteen civilians, among whom were André Philip, Commissioner of State concerned with relations with the Consultative Assembly. Queuille and Billoux, in charge of the liberated territories, François de Menthon, Commissioner of Justice, Jacquenot at the Ministry of Marine, Grenier at the Ministry of Air, Mendès-France at the Ministry of Finance, Henri Bonnet at the Ministry of Information, René Mayer at the Ministry of Communications and in charge of the Merchant Marine, Henry Frenay at the Ministry of Prisoners, Adrien Tixier at the Ministry of Labour, Giaccobi at the Ministry of Food, and René Capitant at the Ministry of Public Education.[1]

Louis Joxe, secretary-general of the provisional government, had asked the British for aircraft to transport their Excellencies to France. But the British major with whom he was in contact saw no reason for haste. Joxe made strong representations to him but could obtain no more than a vague promise which was never kept.

Jacquinot fortunately remembered his ships. From those which had just taken part in the landings in the southern zone, he selected an old cruiser, the *Jeanne d'Arc*, which in normal times was a training ship. Her commander, Captain Hourcade, was ordered to prepare to receive the government on board.

This was no easy matter. Some of the Ministers, indeed, made demands that were difficult to meet. Adrien Tixier, who had been badly wounded in the war, and was often in great pain, wanted his wife to accompany him. But the regulations forbade the presence of women on board men-of-war in wartime.

The passengers installed themselves as best they could in the available space. Tixier slept in the officers' dining-room. Jacquinot, as Minister of Marine, had a right to a cabin, but gave it up to Queuille, the senior

---

[1] Parodi and Le Troquer, Commissioners of State for the Liberated Regions, were already in Paris. René Pleven, Commissioner for the Colonies, arrived in Paris by air on the 28th or 29th. Massigli, Commissioner for Foreign Affairs, took over the Quai d'Orsay, on 30 August, on arriving from London.

member of the government. He himself slept in the ward-room next to the dining-room.

After passing the Straits of Gibraltar, they ran into bad weather, and during the night the Ministers, lying on mattresses, began rolling in unexpected directions. Adrien Tixier one night rolled into the ward-room and bumped into Jacquinot. The separation of powers, advocated by Montesquieu, did not suffice to stop their invective.

In the Bay of Biscay, during an appalling storm, the dishes at luncheon were thrown from the table and the lunchers were thrown to the floor. Giaccobi, the Minister of Food, finished the meal in intimate contact with the mashed potatoes.

The *Jeanne d'Arc* was so seriously delayed by the weather that by the time she reached Cherbourg she had been given up. As soon as they landed, the Ministers found a café where they drank one of those "national mixtures" to which their fellow-countrymen who had remained in France had become so accustomed. Somewhat restored, they set out for the Sub-Prefecture, where they woke up the Sub-Prefect, who took them in. In the end, the American authorities took pity on the travellers. They supplied them with rations and a convoy of jeeps to take them to Paris.

The next stage was Le Mans where the government was also not expected. They had to sleep in a barracks which had been only recently vacated by the Germans; and there the Ministers, men of some age and distinction, had to spend the night in a barrack-room like ordinary soldiers. The bunks were double-tiered; the younger took the upper ones, the more elderly the lower. It was an absurd scene and the younger Ministers renewed the old traditions by having a pillow-fight.

The next morning, Queuille and Jacquinot were invited to the Prefecture where the Prefect's wife gave them a cup of coffee. Then they set off for Paris, where the convoy, with the Ministers somewhat crumpled and ill-shaven, though delighted to find themselves in the capital again, waited for some time in the courtyard of the Rue Saint-Dominique for the General to receive them. They were greeted with a few words of welcome, which did not conceal the General's impatience at their delayed arrival. After a brief visit to the Hôtel Claridge, where rooms had been reserved for them, the Ministers met in council under the chairmanship of the Head of the Government.

Then they went to their Ministries where the secretary-generals handed over to them.

Such was the inauguration of the Fourth Republic in the liberated capital.

While the new régime was being installed in Paris, which had once again become the capital of the Republic, another was breaking up at Vichy, the seat of the government of the moribund État Français.

On 17 August, in a café at La Tour d'Auvergne, twenty kilometres from Mont-Doré, Ingrand, the Commissioner of the Republic, and Colonel Gaspard, regional commander of the F.F.I., both still working underground, met an emissary from Marshal Pétain, who had come to negotiate his abduction by the Maquis.

The negotiations had been going on for several days. On 9 August a first messenger had sounded the F.F.I., who had not refused point-blank.

On 13 August, an officer of the Maquis, Commandant Lassauzet, had been invited to luncheon by the Marshal. Sitting on his right, during the luncheon which lasted an hour and a half, he noted how calm and lucid the old man was, and that he seemed perfectly relaxed and happy. After the meal, he had gone with the Marshal into another room, where the Marshal had slept for twenty minutes. On awakening, he had continued the conversation. The head of the État Français had wished to make the acquaintance of the officer who was to abduct him.

Five days later, when Gaspard and Ingrand met the second messenger, all the details of the operation had been worked out. The Marshal would go for his usual daily motor-drive along the Puy-Guillaume road. He would out-distance his escort. A few kilometres from Puy-Guillaume, a light car belonging to the Maquis would come to meet him and the Marshal would change cars, under the protection of some of his personal guard, who had recently gone over to the Resistance.

"Would you ever have believed," said Ingrand to Gaspard, after they had seen the messenger, "that when we began our little secret Resistance in 1941–1942, we should live to see this historic moment: Pétain, a Marshal of France, offering to surrender to the Maquis." "Why not?" replied Gaspard. "Only a few days ago we met the Swiss Minister; nothing can surprise me any more."

Gaspard agreed to undertake the abduction, but on one condition: he would do it himself with one of his men. Indeed, the negotiations with the Marshal would have seemed so scandalous to most of the maquisards, had they known of it, that Gaspard feared for Pétain's safety, and perhaps also for his own. It was therefore agreed that the Marshal would be taken to a secret place; and the operation was arranged for two days later, the afternoon of 20 August. Confirmation would be brought by a motor-cyclist from Vichy.

But he never arrived. Doctor Ménétrel, the Marshal's personal physician, objected to his taking part in such an adventure. On the morning of 20 August, the Marshal was removed by the Germans, and sent under military escort to Sigmaringen, without being given a chance to escape.[1]

In the days following on the liberation, the Hôtel du Parc was the scene of an episode, on which it would seem that little light has been thrown till now. Former members of the Marshal's entourage distributed to a few journalists and officials the proclamation which the Marshal had prepared against his return to Paris.

Here is the complete text:

THE MESSAGE WHICH SHOULD HAVE BEEN READ BY THE MARSHAL FROM PARIS IF THE GERMANS HAD LEFT HIM LIBERTY OF ACTION.

Frenchmen:

It is from Paris that I am addressing you. From Paris where the French flag is floating from all the buildings of the Élysée, the traditional home of the Head of State, of which I have retaken possession.

Today the destiny of France is reborn. Once again the gates of hope are open before her, for the German armies have already evacuated the greater part of France.

But in the middle of our happiness I wish my first words uttered in freedom to proclaim in the face of the world the inalienable rights of our country.

France is a sovereign nation. As the legitimate representative of its sovereignty invested with supreme power by the National Assembly, I assert her right to dispose of herself and to preserve intact the integrity of her metropolitan territories and of her empire.

No pact or treaty is valid except with the approval of the legitimate power. This independence is for us Frenchmen the most sacred of rights.

The first act of our recovered liberty will be to salute the Anglo-American armies whose victories have brought about the retreat of the German armies and to wish them welcome to our land.

On this day we shall forget the destruction of our towns, of our factories, of our means of transport, the number of our dead and wounded, and the attacks made on our fleet, to think only of the brotherhood of arms, born in 1914–1918 and in 1940 on the battlefields of Belgium and Dunkirk.

My second thought concerns those Frenchmen who are exhausting themselves in internecine conflict.

France is today in such a state of impoverishment and internal destruction, that our first duty is to remake its spirit and its body.

Above all else, I wish to restore the unity which has apparently disappeared among Frenchmen. For the divisions which have sometimes led to bloodshed are due much more to divergence of view about means than

[1] Cf., The author's *The Vichy Regime*.

17. General de Lattre de Tassigny.

18. General Dietrich von Choltitz, commander of the German garrison in Paris, signing the papers surrendering that city to the Allies.

19. Maurice Thorez at a Communist rally in Paris.

20. General de Gaulle and Sir Winston Churchill in Paris for Armistice Day, 11 November 1944.

about the end itself, which is for all of us the salvation of our country. Some, aware above all of the necessity of saving the country from that internal degeneracy which led us to the abyss, have wanted to work first of all for the restoration of authority in our institutions and for the transformation of the social structure. And to attain this end, they accepted the circumstances born of the war and have even gone so far as to collaborate with the occupying power. Others have set aside every consideration for that of total war against the invader and have gone so far as to accept an alliance with Communism and with those who were responsible for our defeat in 1940. These contrasting positions have led Frenchmen to armed opposition, sometimes even to rebellion against all authority and progressively to the most painful of civil wars. But the dangers that both sides have been prepared to run, and the number of dead they count in their ranks, are proof of their good faith. And the population, which has cruelly suffered from the sometimes culpable excesses of both sides, who were often blinded by their exclusive passion, must itself make an effort to understand that these are the ineluctable consequences of the Government's inability to lay down each one's duty and to have available sufficient means for maintaining order.

From now on there must be peace between Frenchmen. It is only by legally constituted justice that crimes must be punished. I wish to save France from foundering in the slaughter of a civil war, after having suffered, even to bloodshed, the consequences of the occupation and the battles which are being fought on our soil. I shall do all in my power to see that reprisals are not exacted, either individual or collective. Vengeance belongs only to God, and punishment can be meted out only by the regular tribunals, with all the guarantees that are implied by a sound administration of justice.

Acts of reprisal will be considered as crimes in common law and will be punished as such, whoever their authors may be.

There exists in France only one civil and military authority, that of the State.

In consequence, and with the object of restoring without delay the conditions necessary to the maintenance of order, and with the object also of preparing the organization of the French forces, I order general mobilization and place all the forces or armed factions, other than the police forces, under the authority of the military High Command. They will be integrated in the new army whose first task will be to restore, throughout the whole of the territory of France and her empire, a respect for discipline, and the protection of individuals and their goods.

I shall summon the National Assembly as soon as circumstances permit, so as to inform it of the conditions in which I have had to govern during these four years without the power, more often than not, of making known the real reasons for my decisions and to submit to its ratification the constitution which it is my duty to prepare.

For it is essential that, without waiting any longer, the Government should receive a form more appropriate to the new situation. I shall appoint to assist me ——— who will be charged under my control with the co-ordination of the actions of the Ministers.

The new Government will consist of only four Ministers, among whom the Secretariats of State will be distributed. These Ministers will be tried technicians who have already given brilliant proofs of their worth and of their French independence of mind.

The command of the armed forces and military affairs ——— Economy ——— Interior ——— Foreign Affairs.

To these I shall appoint ——— for social questions, ——— for Production and Communications, and ——— for Food.

Thus France will throw her efforts into the tasks of reconstruction and peace, but she must also accomplish another mission. Exhausted by the wealth she has had to furnish, bruised by the fighting that has been taking place on her soil for nearly five years, it is not by reason of the authority which material strength might give her that she raises her voice today to adjure the belligerents to find some means of stopping this most horrible of wars. What France has suffered in the silence which has been imposed on her, what her prisoners are still suffering, is the image of what will fall successively on all the various nations if the conflict is prolonged and is still further aggravated by the appearance of ever more fearful arms and methods of fighting. How can one not be appalled at the unleashing of hatreds and violence which make what has been called our civilization seem like a new barbarism, this time mechanized? It is time the peoples of the world went home, and ceased the factions which tend to prolong the conflict. It is time they met together to draw up treaties which will put an end to the most terrible crisis the world has ever known.

Frenchmen, the day has come to take up once again the course of our destinies; let each one of us in his place do his duty without personal ambition and with the object only of serving the country.

I count on you. Together we will remake the unity of France.

P. PÉTAIN

By the time the few people who received this document, which is attributed to the Marshal, were able to read it, the Head of the State was a prisoner of the Germans and had abdicated his power.

Part Five

THE LIBERATION OF THE SOUTH

Chapter I

THE PRELIMINARIES
TO D–DAY IN PROVENCE

PREPARATIONS were being made by the American Seventh Army, commanded by General Patch, to land on the seventy kilometres of coast between Cavalaire and Saint-Raphael on 15 August 1944.

This force consisted of the French Army B, numbering 286,000 men, under the command of General de Lattre de Tassigny, and the American VIth Corps, commanded by General Teuscott, which numbered rather less than 100,000 men.

This operation, which was first given the code name of Anvil and, later, from 1 August, to deceive the German Intelligence, Dragoon, was to bring about the liberation of the whole of the South of France in record time. But it had preliminary difficulties. Within the Anglo-American command, as between it and the French, there were three sorts of arguments, which imperilled not only the success but indeed the very existence of the operation.

In the first place, the very principle of the landing was criticized both on political and military grounds.

There were two opposite points of view. Although the Quebec Conference, held in August 1943 to decide on the second front, had also planned a landing in the south, to be timed in conformity with that in Normandy, and the Conference at Teheran in December 1943 had confirmed the plan, operation Anvil was increasingly contested as the date for its accomplishment grew nearer. At the end of May 1944, the Italian front was broken by the French expeditionary force under General Juin; and General Alexander's army rapidly exploited the success. Rome fell without a battle. The German Army fell back in disorder towards Florence, and reformed only on the Gothic Line. Was there not here both a strategic and political opportunity to seize? Was there not a chance, if the forces detailed for Anvil were given to the Army of

Italy, of breaking through the German front and advancing by forced marches to Trieste, Istria and Vienna and occupying Central Europe before the Soviet divisions could reach it?

Churchill, who looked at the whole business from a statesman's point of view and was well aware of the problems that were bound to arise after the war, proposed that Anvil should be abandoned in favour of an advance into Austria. He discussed this plan with the military leaders, General Eisenhower and General Marshall; and also and more particularly, with the political leaders, President Roosevelt and his personal adviser, Hopkins. "Let us resolve," he wrote, "not to wreck one great campaign for the sake of another. Both can be won."

On 28 June 1944 he roundly condemned operation Anvil: "The more I have thought about this, the more bleak and sterile it appears." And he concluded: "Whether we should ruin all hopes of a major victory in Italy and all its fronts and condemn ourselves to a passive rôle in that theatre, after having broken up the fine Allied army which is advancing so rapidly through that peninsula, for the sake of 'Anvil,' with all its limitations, is indeed a grave question for His Majesty's Government and the President, with the Combined Chiefs of Staff, to decide."

Among the British, Churchill clearly had the agreement of Generals Alexander and Montgomery. Among the French, who necessarily had every reason to want to see Anvil put into effect to deliver their country, Churchill found a supporter, General Juin. "A bad strategic orientation," the latter wrote, "risks grave consequences, and, it must be feared, the severe judgement of history."

General Eisenhower, for military reasons, utterly opposed these arguments. As Commander-in-Chief of the invading Allied Armies he declared that a landing in the South of France was essential, not only to hold the German forces in the south, but because he had absolute need of the great port of Marseilles and the important route along the Rhône, so rich in roads and railways, to supply the divisions with which he would have to do battle with the German Army before penetrating into the heart of enemy territory.

Roosevelt made his decision in a note of 29 June 1944. His arguments were of unequal value. Some were of a diplomatic nature and seemed indecisive: "Since the agreement was made at Teheran to mount an 'Anvil,' I cannot accept, without consultation with Stalin, any course of action which abandons this operation." Similarly there would have to be negotiations with the French for a new use of their forces. The others dealt with the military requirements: "I am impressed by Eisenhower's statement that 'Anvil' is of transcendent importance"; then he too appealed to history, which usefully lends itself to contradictory interpretations: "Now that we are fully involved in our major blow, history will never forgive us if we lost precious time or lives in indecision and debate. My dear friend, I beg you to let us go ahead with our plan." He concluded: "Finally, for purely political considerations over here, I should never survive even a slight setback to 'Overlord' if it were known that fairly large forces had been diverted to the Balkans." Anyone but Winston Churchill would have accepted this. But the Prime Minister was tough. On 7 August, only eight days before D-day in Provence, he made one last attempt: Could not the landing planned for the South of France take place in direct support of Overlord in Brittany, or in the Bay of Biscay?

The Americans were not pleased. Eisenhower let it be known that he was keener than ever on the landing in Provence. Roosevelt replied with a curt negative. Churchill had to accept it. On 8 August, he signalled Roosevelt: "I pray God that you may be right." But he continued to dislike the operation.

However, having gone to Italy, Churchill was present at the landing in a British destroyer. He reported to the King: "From my distant view of the Dragoon operations, the landing seemed to be effected with the utmost smoothness. How much time will be taken in the advance first to Marseilles and then up the Rhône valley . . . are the questions that now arise."

Apart from the basic argument as to whether the landing should take place at all, there were further ones about the methods to be employed. These involved the French leaders with their Anglo-Saxon allies. There were two main questions: What part was the French command to play in the landing? What was the French Army to consist of? These two questions, which were hard fought at times, never however became as bitter as the quarrel between the Gaullist authorities and the Allied governments and command at the time of Overlord.

The appointment of General de Lattre as Army Commander, at the same time as that of Generals Béthouart, Mast and Blaizot as Corps Commanders, was decided in Algiers on 16 November 1943, despite the opposition of Le Troquer, the Commissioner for War, who judged it "inopportune."

De Lattre had no intention of being a passive subordinate within the Allied Command. He was the Commander of a French Army, the only combatant French Army, and looked on himself as the responsible head of the renascent French Forces, which was on occasion to entail certain divergencies of view with his American colleagues.

On 27 June 1944, General de Lattre called on General Patch, commanding the American Seventh Army, at 15.00 hours at his headquarters. "The discussion, as well as the one that followed it, took place, it must be admitted, in the most friendly and courteous manner," records a hitherto unpublished report of the interview drawn up by de Lattre's Troisième Bureau. But, after the preliminary courtesies, and Patch's congratulations to de Lattre on the success of his conquest of Elba, there followed embarrassing questions.

"General de Lattre . . . asked whether operation Anvil had already been definitely decided on.

"The American said no, but added that he expected orders to put it into effect to be issued shortly.

"General de Lattre asked what future employment there was for Army B should Anvil not take place. And the American General replied that Army B would accompany the American Seventh Army to whatever theatre of operations it might be employed in . . . no doubt this would be on the Italian front, in the direction of Austria.

"General de Lattre remarked that this eventuality seemed to him to be entirely contrary to the views the Head of the French Government had expressed to him the day before.

"General de Lattre then went to call on General de Gaulle, who received him at 16.30 hours, and was given directives which, an hour later, he explained to General Patch during the course of a second interview."

During this second interview, at which de Lattre asked the question as to whether the French Army would be a satellite or autonomous, there appears to have been a certain heightening of tone and no precise answer was given by the Americans.

Here is the hitherto unpublished letter which, two days later, on 29 June, General Maitland Wilson's [1] Chief of Staff, F. G. Beaumont-Nesbit wrote to General de Lattre, who had asked for an interview:

My dear General,

I have informed the Supreme Allied Commander of General de Gaulle's regret that General Marshall nearly missed his day in Algiers. I have also informed General Wilson that General de Gaulle desired an immediate firm reply—yes or no—about operation Anvil. In these circumstances, I informed him that you had been ordered by General de Gaulle to ask for

[1] General Maitland Wilson had succeeded Eisenhower on 8 January 1944, as Supreme Commander of the Mediterranean Theatre.

an interview with General Wilson with the object of explaining to him General de Gaulle's point of view.

The Supreme Allied Commander has requested me to point out not only that such an interview seemed to him very difficult to arrange at the moment, but also that when he is in a position to give a firm answer, which is not the case at the moment, his intention is to meet General de Gaulle.

Not perhaps a very courteous refusal; but it is evidence, in the first place, that on 29 June operation Anvil had not yet been decided on, or at least that the commanders had not yet been notified—which in the circumstances is not surprising—and, secondly, that de Gaulle was still at this moment, that is to say before his journey to the United States, under the impression that he was being left out of the Allied decisions, and moreover that the British Commander-in-Chief looked on a mere army commander, as in his eyes de Lattre was, as insufficiently important and had decided to discuss matters with the Head of the French Government when the moment came.

It is a revealing document as to the disagreement that existed, until the official recognition of the G.P.R.F., about the role of the French command.

There was also another matter under discussion: the actual constitution of the French Army which was to take part in the operation.

At the end of January 1943, at Anfa, Roosevelt and Giraud had agreed to rearm eleven French divisions, of which three were armoured, with American equipment. At the time of the landing, the French Army in Provence consisted of only seven divisions, of which two were armoured. To these must be added the 2nd Armoured Division which was to enter Paris. Why had the number of divisions been reduced by three?

The French command, when considering effectives, was largely concerned with combatant units. It was anxious, considering the relatively small number of men it had at its disposal in North Africa, to place almost the whole of them on the battlefield, even if it meant reducing the supporting services, or placing the responsibility for them on the Americans. A large part of the French who had escaped from France, veterans of the first Gaullist troops, or professional soldiers, would have thought themselves dishonoured to have fought the campaign in a workshop, a store or an office.

The Americans took an opposite view. Much aware of the technical needs of modern war, they attached primary importance to the base and supply services necessary to the maintaining of the fighting troops. In their view, a repair company or a store of vehicle parts was as important as a fighting unit or a parachute regiment. It refused to rearm the French divisions so long as they had insufficient supply services recruited from their own nationals.

De Lattre found this argument in full swing on his arrival in Algiers in January 1944. On 7 January he drafted a first memorandum on the subject of the organization of the army of which he had been placed in command. He pointed out the deficiencies in fighting men, which amounted to 10,850 for the divisions then being formed; and also the insufficiency of the services the Americans considered indispensable. "It is therefore apparent," he concluded, "that the suppression of two formations in the general programme has become an immediate necessity, if it is desired to create within the time given a French force sufficiently equipped to take part in the forthcoming operations.

"The two formations to be suppressed must be infantry divisions."

The two divisions suppressed were the 10th Colonial Infantry Division and the 8th Algerian Infantry Division. But this sacrifice, which reduced the French Forces to nine divisions, proved insufficient. On 19 January, the American Command sent the French a veritable ultimatum, which implied the dissolution of two further units.

Faced with these demands, the French Command could do no other than agree and reduce to seven, of which two were armoured, the number of divisions engaged in operation Anvil. A third armoured division, the 2nd, continued to figure among the units planned for Overlord. Meanwhile, the cadres of the dissolved French units had to be informed of the reasons for the decision.

General de Lattre drafted a "note on the dissolution and transformation of units" with the object of "dissipating the uneasiness affecting the morale of the cadres of these units."

Here is the conclusion of this hitherto unpublished document:

The cadres' attention must be drawn to the following points, and they must be explained to them so that they in their turn may explain them:

The present war is a war of coalition.

This implies conditions which are apt to change as time goes on.

We, Frenchmen, are not the masters and are often on the receiving end. . . .

We must submit.

It is the price we must pay to be able to participate in the liberation of France.

This was how the difficulties which arose between the Anglo-Saxons and the French over the preparations for Anvil were resolved. When the operation began, all traces of these had been effaced, and the landing in Provence took place in complete accord between the Americans and the French.

The tactical preparations for the landing had begun long before. They concerned not only the regular army but also the F.F.I. whose activities, in this southern region, had often a picturesque side to them. Commander Ullmann, alias Urban, a former tank officer who had been one of the first to believe in the employment of armoured divisions and, as a result, had had both the future General de Gaulle and the future General de Lattre for witnesses at his wedding, was Chief of Staff of the Secret Army of the Alpes-Maritimes. In 1943, shortly before the surrender of the Italian Army, Colonel Groslieu, Vichy Military Attaché to Ankara, who was on leave, had made contact with him. He offered to put him in touch with a staff officer of the Italian Army of the Alps, who liked champagne and hated the Nazis. These were the two reasons he gave for being ready to negotiate with an officer of the Maquis.

A meeting was arranged three days later, at eleven o'clock in the morning, at Grasse, in the American Bar, which was not very well situated since it was opposite a Militia headquarters. No matter. The interview was to be a secret one; and the Italian would be in plain clothes. Ullmann, as a recognition sign, would have a newspaper in each outside pocket of his coat. There could be nothing suspicious about that. Alas, fate took a hand, in the shape of Tino Rossi. Before the war, Ullmann had been a film producer. When he reached the American Bar, he found a film company making a film between the Militia and himself. Gathered round the famous singer were technicians who had worked with him in the past. They recognized him. "Monsieur Ullmann, how are you? Monsieur Ullmann, have a drink?" He had no alternative but to do so under the eyes of the Militia; but he decided it was safer to make off without waiting for the Italian.

A little while later, contact was renewed and an agreement negotiated. To every Italian soldier who joined the Maquis with his arms, the F.F.I. guaranteed a suit of plain clothes, a false identity card and a ration card. Ullmann also negotiated the purchase of two trucks loaded with light weapons for fifty thousand francs each. As a result, the Lécuyer Group which, when Dragoon took place, amounted to three thousand men between Saint-Raphael and Nice, was in a position to assist the French and the Americans in their advance.

Besides these unofficial proceedings to arm the F.F.I., there were official preparations by the Allied authorities in view of the landing.

On 23 May 1944, in Algiers, the staff of A.F.H.Q. (African Forces Headquarters) set up a special organization to organize the Resistance for the landing in the South of France. It was called S.P.O.C. (Special Projects Operation Centre) and consisted of British, American and French officers of the Special Services.

In the following months the S.P.O.C. was to reorganize R2, the F.F.I. region in which Dragoon was to take place. It consisted of the Mediterranean coastal departments of Alpes-Maritimes, Var, Bouches-du-Rhône and those immediately inland, Basses-Alpes, Hautes-Alpes, Gard and Vaucluse. These seven departments had a total of 13,194 men affiliated to the Resistance, of which, by 10 April 1944, 3,333 were armed, and 9,861 were awaiting arms by parachutings, which were considerably stepped up immediately before the landings. 100,000 containers of arms were dropped in the south by the Allied heavy bombers in June and July.

Of these maquisards, of whom a census was taken at the beginning of April, a good third were F.T.P. and of Communist obedience. Of the 3,333 who were armed, 1,360 were F.T.P. Of the 7,533 awaiting arms, 2,270 in R2, as in the neighbouring region of R1 (Rhône-Alpes), had refused to be integrated with the other F.F.I.

Great care had to be taken in organizing the maquisards in a region where such problems existed if they were to play an important part in supporting the landing in Provence. In the days immediately preceding the landing, the command of R2 was entirely reorganized. On 2 August, a new D.M.R., Cloître (Widmer), was parachuted in near Apt, in the Vaucluse. On 11 August, he was joined at his secret headquarters by Lieutenant-Colonel Constant, alias Saint-Sauveur, also parachuted in from Algiers. Meanwhile, the S.P.O.C. had parachuted into R2 and its neighbourhood seven Jedburgh teams: "Chloroform" landed in the Drôme on 29 July, "Novocaine" in the Basses-Alpes on 7 August, soon to be followed by teams with less anaesthetic names: "Graham" reached the Vaucluse on 9 August, "Citroën" the Basses-Alpes on the 10th, and "Sceptre" and "Cinnamon" were parachuted respectively into the Alpes-Maritimes and the Var on the eve of the landing, 14 August.

These Jedburgh teams, reinforced by three operational groups (O.G.S.) with names borrowed from chemistry ("Aluminium" and "Arsenic" in the Basses-Alpes, "Nitrogen" in the Vaucluse), had as their first duty to carry out sabotage and organize the F.F.I. They took part in the capture of Apt on 22 August, and in that of Avignon on 24th.

Their second duty was of a political nature, and consisted in countering Communist influence. The Military Committee of Action, the

C.O.M.A.C., who, under the National Council of the Resistance, the C.N.R., had charge of military affairs, had, as we have seen, passed under Communist control. It claimed to have exclusive control of Maquis operations. "The C.O.M.A.C.," wrote Villon, in August 1944, in a note entitled "National Insurrection and Military Organization," "was and remains the supreme authority in France. . . . The choice of means is up to the C.O.M.A.C., as well as all appointments in the F.F.I., appointments then confirmed by General Koenig." It was to reduce the F.F.I. headquarters in London, under Koenig, to be no more than a relay station for administrative orders. And it was due to this that the C.O.M.A.C. and the Communists were hostile to the special missions and Jedburgh teams sent from London and Algiers to direct and organize the Resistance.

Therefore, by parachuting these operational groups and Jedburgh teams on the eve of the landing in Provence, the Allied Command was pursuing two objectives which, by and large, were attained and reveal to what extent S.H.A.E.F., between Overlord and Anvil, had become aware of the Maquis' peculiar problems, and of the role which it could play during the course of an operation.

In the event, the effectiveness of the Maquis was much greater than the American Command had expected. Centred round the Command Posts, which in the form of Jedburgh teams had fallen from the sky at the last minute, there was a real army to go into action beside the regular troops. The American General Devers, who, in September 1944, was to take command of Sixth Army Group, estimated that the support of the French Forces of the Interior, during his advance to the north, had been worth four to five divisions to him. During the course of the campaign in the south, the F.F.I. alone took 42,000 prisoners.

Beside them, Army B played a primary part.

De Lattre was a remarkable leader. He doubtless had his faults, but they were the defects of his singular merits. Moreover, these defects were trifling when compared to his great qualities. He knew, and had always known, how to take responsibility, which sometimes led him to infringe on that of others. The account, in his *History of the First French Army*, of operation Anvil and the victories which followed on it is perhaps sometimes a little self-centred. Some of his generals could probably show that the "Chief" on occasion takes the credit for decisions and successes which had in fact been conceived and executed without his concurrence.

The fact was that de Lattre, in whom Lyautey admired an "animal of action," with all that that implies of instinct and intuition in the service of the Intelligence, had that extraordinary virtue, that gift reserved to the strong and radiant of being a magnetic personality. It was as if waves of power emanated from him, affecting both men and events. He believed in his destiny, he believed in his luck, his "baraka" as his African soldiers said when they saw him emerge unscathed from an expedition into dissident territory among armed rebels. He knew that wherever he was, wherever he intervened, his mere presence polarized all the forces that were working for France, and turned events in a direction that was to his country's advantage. "Never submit" was his motto. The 14th Division which he commanded during the campaign of France, in May and June 1940, was continually successful amid the general confusion of the French Army. And when it was drawn in spite of itself into the general retreat, and passed through first Limoges and then Clermont-Ferrand, it did so in impeccable order and preceded by a band.

He had therefore a magnetic effect both on events and people, a precious gift for the great *accoucheur* of the future that a war-leader must be. One may say what one likes about war: it is atrocious, savage and barbarous. It kills off the young men and often falsifies problems while pretending to resolve them. But this does not alter the fact that, in blood and tears, perhaps even through blood and tears, it is one of those rare collective incantations by which men may alter their destiny.

And for such incantations, incantators are necessary. Jean de Lattre de Tassigny was certainly one, and though his devices were sometimes apparent, his spells often visible, he may be forgiven them, for their effect was certain and they were in a class of their own.

The General knew how to run risks. He had, too, a sense of the telling phrase and the picturesque gesture. After his troops had taken Toulon and Marseilles, he sent a lapidary signal to de Gaulle: "In the sector of Army B, today D + 13, their remains no single German who is not either dead or a prisoner." On escaping from France, he landed at 16.30 hours, on 20 December 1943, at the airport of Maison-Blanche near Algiers. Informed on his arrival that General de Gaulle would see him next day, he at once demanded to be received that same day, even if it were only for a few minutes. He gained his end. And these were the first words that de Lattre, former Chief of Staff to the Fifth Army in 1939, and de Gaulle, former Tank Commander in that great formation, exchanged:

De Gaulle: "You've grown no older."

De Lattre: "And you have grown in stature."

De Lattre's army was a wholly modern one. Each of his two armoured divisions had 5,000 vehicles, and each of his five infantry divisions 2,500. In the infantry divisions, where in the past the troops had had to march, and the artillery and supply had been horse-drawn, every unit was motorized except for the three regiments of infantry. And for these the division possessed a pool of troop-transporters by which it could move each of its regiments in turn.[1]

Such wholesale motorization entailed certain consequences. It did not much matter that the first French soldiers to land in Provence were, due to their transport, taken for Americans by their fellow-countrymen who greeted them with such tags of bad English as they could remember from their schooldays. During the course of the campaign, however, the movement of such a force presented an appalling fuel problem. In the rapid advance on Épinal and Belfort, during the first days of September, the First Army used over 130,000 gallons of gasoline in twenty-four hours.

This First French Army, which was so lavishly equipped, was distinguished also by the quality of its troops. It could be described without exaggeration as an army composed both of volunteers of the Year II and of veterans of the Empire. "Indeed," wrote General de Lattre, "it is a really magnificent army that has been forged, an army such as France has seldom known, for it combines the knowledge of those who deserve the title of 'veterans'—the veterans of the Free French Forces, of the battlefields of Tunisia and Italy—with the enthusiasm of the volunteers of 1792, that is to say of the F.F.I. who were to come and join it."

Among the veterans were those of the 1st Free French Division, which was commanded by General Brosset, who was killed in a jeep, the victim of his own temerity, and then by General Garbay. They were survivors of the 13th Demi-Brigade of the Foreign Legion, of the Infantry Battalions and the Marines, who had been fighting continuously since June 1940. They remembered their first victory at Bir-Hakeim with the same enthusiasm as the cadets of Saint-Cyr celebrate the anniversary of Austerlitz.

To reinforce these "Free French," who had been in action since 1940, other war-conditioned troops took part in the landing. These were the African divisions. Besides the black soldiers of the 1st D.F.L. and the 9th Colonial Infantry Division, there were the 2nd Moroccan Infantry Division and the 3rd Algerian Infantry Division, who had been fighting in Italy, where they had broken the German line at Cassino. There

[1] Marshal de Lattre: *Histoire de la 1re Armée Française*, page 11, note 1.

were also the 4th Moroccan Mountain Division, the 1st Infantry Division, and the Moroccan "Tabors" Groups, in which the various races of North Africa were amalgamated for the first time. There were Frenchmen by birth, both volunteers and conscripts, who were making a great contribution to the reconquest of Metropolitan France, and natives, animated by the same spirit, who rivalled them in their desire to liberate the country.

This amalgam of races and religions had a picturesque and often moving aspect. At Marseilles, in the fighting round Notre-Dame-de-la-Garde, the Algerian Infantry advanced towards the church, along the Rue Sainte, the ancient Martyrs' Way by which the Christians in the year 410, at a time when Islam had not yet been founded, climbed towards the Monastery of Saint-Cassien, and when they reached the gardens of the bishop's house, several wounded infantrymen were succoured with a devotion they were always to remember by the Catholic prelate, whom they called "the Grand Marabout." At the same place, or nearby, other infantrymen mounted guard at the foot of the sanctuary of "Saint Fatima of the Christians." Whether they were Mohammedan or Christian, whether believers or not, a similar fervour inspired the veterans of the First Army, and it also sustained the newcomers to battle, who, having escaped from Metropolitan France to the number of 20,000, had joined them by way of the Pyrenees and the Spanish prisons.

Face to face with troops animated by such a spirit, how did the German Army react?

Realizing that it was threatened with landings in France, in 1944 the staff of the Wehrmacht had a choice of several solutions.

By concentrating in the west all the divisions that were temporarily unemployed, they could have set up a mass of manœuvre which could at any rate temporarily have arrested the advance. With the twenty-five divisions employed in the defence of the Baltic States and the eighteen divisions in Norway, they might have been able to strike a possibly fatal blow at Overlord and Anvil. It would seem that Marshal Keitel, head of the Oberkommando of the Wehrmacht, considered, contrary to Rommel's advice, that it would suffice when the moment came to draw on reinforcements in France, principally from the German garrisons in the south-west, the south-east, the centre and the coasts. A conception that was clearly wrong in itself, and that the activities of the F.F.I., which held up the movement of the German divisions, rendered still more ineffective.

Reduced to its local resources of troops quartered in France, the German Command had at the most only ten available divisions to oppose the invasion. One formed part of the German First Army, whose head-quarters was at Bordeaux, and whose duty it was to hold the Atlantic coast from the Loire to the Spanish frontier. It took no part in the operations in Provence. The other nine were attached to the German Nineteenth Army, whose headquarters was at Avignon. Commanded by General Wiese, an energetic and competent officer, its principal duty was to ensure with these nine large formations the defence of the whole Mediterranean sector from Italy to Spain. In fact, Wiese had no more than seven divisions to repel the invasion since the 9th Panzer Division, which had been in garrison at Arles, had just left for the Northern Front, while one infantry division was holding the Alps, where it was wholly occupied in fighting the Maquis.

The seven remaining divisions were deployed along the Mediterranean coast; three of them were very thin on the ground west of the Rhône, while the other four were to the east of the river. It was these last which had to sustain the first shock. The 157th and 148th Divisions were be-tween Menton and Saint-Raphael, the 242nd was between Saint-Raphael and Bandol, and the 244th between Bandol and Port-de-Bouc. These first-line divisions had reasonably numerous extra-divisional reserves available, consisting of infantry, artillery and elements of the Kriegs-Marine.

Altogether this force amounted to 250,000 men. They were of unequal quality, but generally speaking sound troops and with excellent com-manders. These were all the troops the Germans had available to repel the 300,000 men of the Franco-American Forces.

The numerical superiority was in favour of the Allies: the French Army alone equalled in numbers the German Nineteenth Army. Apart from the numbers of troops involved, however, the state of the coastal defences and the air forces must be considered, for these are necessarily of the first importance in a landing operation. The former were slightly in favour of the Wehrmacht, but the latter was almost catastrophic for the Germans.

The Germans were strong in artillery, its maximum concentration being round Toulon and Marseilles. In Toulon the fortifications in-cluded 200 guns of medium and heavy calibre, and there were very nearly as many in Marseilles. Apart from these strong-points, there were 45 coastal batteries in position to the east of the Rhône, besides the divisional artillery: between Cavalaire and Agay alone, there were 150 guns of 75 mm. or more. As for heavy artillery, it was estimated that the Wehrmacht had a total on the coast of 500 guns, as opposed to the 650 of the Allied warships. The Wehrmacht was entrenched in a "continuous, dense and solid Mediterranean wall," which consisted of a whole range of blockhouses, bunkers, personnel shelters, headquarters shelters, minefields, obstacles and barbed wire, and had at its disposal a fire-power almost equivalent to that of the Allies. It was clearly in a good position to resist a landing.

Or rather it would have been if the Allies had not had a crushing superiority in the air. The Luftwaffe had to fight in a proportion of one against nine. In all it had 230 aircraft (70 fighters, 130 bombers and 30 reconnaissance planes) against 2,100 Allied aircraft. As for the Kriegs-Marine, it had no more than some 10 submarines and 30 small surface craft as opposed to the 250 warships which made up the Western Task Force, under the command of the American Vice-Admiral Hewitt. Of this total, the French Navy, under the command of Rear-Admiral Lemonnier, amounted to 35 ships: the battleship *Lorraine*, 9 cruisers among which were the *Duguay-Trouin*, the *Émile-Bertin*, the *Georges-Leygues*, the *Gloire*, and the *Montcalm*, 5 destroyers, 5 escort destroyers, 6 despatch boats, 4 frigates, 2 auxiliary cruisers, and 3 fuel ships. The Allies therefore had command of the sea. And their command of the air was uncontested.

On this basis, there seemed to be little doubt of their victory.

How costly would the victory be? In order to arrive at an estimate, it was necessary to know what the German Army was still worth in August 1944. It had been fighting continuously for five years and, since the Allied landings in Italy and France, on three fronts. Anvil would present it with a fourth.

In general, it was still an impressive war machine, but it was beginning to show cracks. Wherever it was engaged in a battle on more or less equal terms, it still fought with a furious obstinacy; but it no longer had the energy of despair or the unit morale which so often redresses an apparently hopeless situation.

In August 1944, the 2nd Moroccan Infantry Division took three prisoners immediately on landing. Taken to the dirty little room the Intelligence officer was using as his office, they clicked their heels and stood to attention. Their discipline was apparently unimpaired. The Intelligence officer had their army paybooks in his hand. In each of them, stuck to the first page, was a notice enjoining them, in case of capture, to give no more than surname and Christian name. Despite these orders, the prisoners, though at first apparently rather ashamed, gave the name of their unit, and then, little by little, told all they knew. "When the interrogation was over," the witness reported, "they clicked their heels and gave an impeccable salute before leaving the room. The external discipline of the Wehrmacht was clearly still strong; it was the vigour of conviction that was beginning to fail." And it was failing not only among the troops but also among the officers. According to the prisoners, about half of them no longer believed in a German victory. No doubt there were still some who maintained their faith, such as a certain Major Otte, whose battalion had been decimated and who had been taken prisoner. When he was brought before an Intelligence officer for interrogation, he said: "I shall tell you nothing more than my name. I absolutely refuse to give you the name of the unit I command." "It is your right to refuse to talk," replied the French officer, who had got all the information he needed from previous interrogations. "Anything you could tell me would be without interest. We know very well who you are: you commanded the 2nd Battalion of the 115th Panzer Grenadier Regiment. . . . For the last two months your regiment has been stationed at P—, then it moved to X—. . . . There you issued the following orders. . . . A little while later you were sent back to the front at ———. . . . Your plans for the battle today were as follows . . ." "*Schweinerei!*" shouted Major Otte. "It is a disgrace! We have been betrayed."

Pale, furiously angry, his eyes flashing with hate, he was taken back to the prison camp though doubtless drawing an obscure relief from his conviction that an officer of the Wehrmacht could not be defeated unless he was betrayed.

At the time of the landing in Provence, the Wehrmacht no doubt still had officers of this temper. But it also had others, who were more sceptical, more aware, and already demoralized. In Italy, there was a General Ringel, whose witticisms were celebrated. The last attributed to him reveals his feelings: "We lost the 1914–1918 war, and we shall win this one in the same way."

In mid-July, Marshal Rommel, Commander-in-Chief of the Armies on the Western Front, sent Hitler a report in which he demanded an immediate armistice because he considered the war lost. It is not known whether the report reached Hitler or whether, like so many communications of the sort, it was intercepted by Marshal Keitel at the Supreme Headquarters of the Wehrmacht. On 20 July, a dramatic event created doubt and confusion among the German High Command. It was the attempted assassination of Hitler organized by generals of the old staff corps of the Wehrmacht, who were becoming increasingly angry at being subordinated to the Nazi Party and the S.S. The attempt failed, and Hitler believed he had been saved by Providence. But the profound shock of the event brought in its train serious consequences and disciplinary measures even in the fighting units.

Nor were the troops at the height of their form at this time. For the most part, they were exhausted by five years of campaigning and their average age had increased. This meant that nearly two-thirds had been long enough in the Wehrmacht to have undergone the appalling fighting on the Russian front.

More than half the effectives had already been wounded. Thirty-four per cent once, 11 per cent twice, 6 per cent three times, 2 per cent four times, and 2 per cent more than four times.

And this army, which was no longer first class, was completed by new elements, which were definitely second rate.

There were boys, far too young, whose training had been hurried on and was incomplete. "Before the retreat," said a prisoner under interrogation, on 12 November 1944, "the training of the young recruits lasted six weeks, after which they were sent to a fighting unit."

A German general, Burky, received the young soldiers with the words: "It is clearly extremely regrettable that you should be sent into battle after so short a period of training."

There were also the old, deficient and infirm. There was one unit, for instance, composed entirely of deaf men, commanded by sick officers. Here is a description of the battalion given by a prisoner:

"The battalion (Marschbataillon Z.B.V.Ing. [Ohren] 636) is composed entirely of men with diseases of the ear, transferred from various units. They were assembled at Herford by the Ersatz und Ausbildung Bton (Ohren) 286. . . . Their morale was very bad. Most of the troops made no attempt to fight, and some prisoners said that the composition of such a battalion was as good as an act of sabotage against the Wehrmacht and their going into the line suicide." An officer of the battalion, who was also taken prisoner, completed the picture of this disinherited unit. "Our men are all deaf. The officers suffer from heart, arthritis or liver diseases. We are defeated. May we at least have peace and the right to live."

The Reich also forcibly enlisted foreigners: Austrians, Poles, Yugoslavs, of whom many had fought against the Germans in 1940 and were now compelled to risk their lives on behalf of the invaders of their country. There were also men from Alsace-Lorraine, who deserted whenever they could to rejoin the French Army.

Other non-Germans formed autonomous units which, originally seduced by the Nazi ideology, imagined they were fighting only against Bolshevism, though they soon realized that the High Command was using them indiscriminately against all Germany's enemies, whether they were loyal to the Kremlin or not. For instance, the Flanders Legion, recruited in August 1941 from Flemish Catholics. In 1942, they were ordered to take the S.S. oath. They protested. They were dispersed among German units. Most of the Flemish officers were killed. By May 1942, there were only two left. The legion was then re-formed under German officers and sent to the Russian front. The end of its adventure bears witness to the Odysseys to which the Wehrmacht's auxiliaries were exposed: "The Tarnopol-Lemberg road being cut, it went south, crossed the Russo-Rumanian frontier, passed through Cerno-vitz, crossed the Carpathians, Hungary and Slovakia and arrived in the district of Joslo (in Poland). After a week, it set off again for the camp at Beneschau-Knowitz (800 kilometres from Prague) at the end of April 1944. There remained scarcely 800 men and they had lost prac-tically all their equipment."

Demoralized by the ordeals suffered at the front, and by the length of the apparently endless war, the Wehrmacht was not reassured by the news it received from inside Germany.

A soldier from Hamburg gave a letter for his mother to one of his comrades who was going to that town on leave. On his return, the man told his friend that he had been unable to find his family, and that the house in which his mother lived had been bombed out. The soldier asked for leave to go and look for his relations. It was refused him. He protested. He was threatened with a court martial. In the end, he determined to desert.

The majority of this sorely tested army no longer believed in victory, though no doubt there were still fanatical Nazis, fresh from the Party mould, who were still ready to sacrifice themselves for Hitler.

Among older soldiers, morale was becoming bad. "Insufficient food, a total lack of warm clothing in spite of reiterated promises, lack of news, terror bombing and, recently, the creation of the Volksturm, which was for them an ultimate admission of the man-power crisis and the final proof of Germany's military impotence." From all these indica-tions, it became increasingly clear, that at the time of Anvil-Dragoon, the forces of morale had changed camps. During the first years of the war, they were perhaps greater in the conquering German camp. The belief in National Socialism and the confidence in the predestination of Hitler animated the combatants. An order from the Führer was in-contestable truth. When he ordered some threatened territory to be held at all costs, when he forbade the surrender of an inch of terrain, no one even thought of questioning his will, and the soldier died where he was. In August 1944, too many imperative orders of this kind had been followed by retreats or routs. Hitler had lost his reputation for infallible invincibility. What inducement had the fighting man now to undertake the appalling efforts that were still being demanded of him?

What had the subjects of a totalitarian state left when their belief in their monolithic party and in their all-powerful leader had disappeared? What was left to the Nazis when they no longer believed in Hitler?

During the fighting for the liberation of Marseilles, there took place a revealing episode, which was symptomatic of the confusion into which some of the German troops were falling. Two officers met for a last attempt at negotiation. One of them was a French captain and a priest in civilian life. The other was a German officer from the Reserve, a professor of philosophy and a disciple of one of those doctrines which had been annexed and disfigured by the Nazi theoreticians. "I am a follower of Nietzsche," he admitted.

And the German went on: "*Ich sterbe hier.* I shall die here, but I have a young wife and four children at home. You who have faith in Her"—and he pointed to the golden statue of the Virgin on the summit of Notre-Dame-de-la-Garde—"pray for my children, for my unfortunate country and for me about to die." "I promise I will," replied the priest, "but why don't you pray to Her yourself?" "*Ich kann nicht,*" was the answer. "I cannot." And covering his face with his hands in a gesture of despair, he went back to his battery, as one damned.[1] A few days later he shot himself through the head.

Without wishing to reduce the whole drama of the Nazi collapse to this anecdote, it was nevertheless a sign, among many others, that morale had abandoned the German camp. The French, of whatever philosophic or religious obedience they might be, had no difficulty from now on in feeling more confident than their conquerors of four years before. This was the most profound and the truest sign of revenge for 1940, and this was what the French Army's assault on Provence became.

[1] Commandant Crosia: *Marseille 1944, Victoire Française*, page 61.

Chapter II

THE LANDING AND THE PURSUIT

THE concentration of forces for the landing began during the night of 10 August 1944. In the case of Overlord,[1] it had sufficed to give the signal for sailing on the eve of D-day, since crossing the Channel took only a few hours. But the invasion forces for Anvil were scattered all over the Mediterranean coasts, the two most important groups being in southern Italy, at Taranto and Naples. But there were also troops in Sicily, near Oran in Algeria, and commandos in Corsica.

The problem was to make the two thousand ships, which constituted the greatest armada that had ever been seen in the Mediterranean, converge at the right moment off the coast of Provence, while setting a course which would keep the enemy guessing till the last moment as to the precise points selected for landing. Some units set sail on 10 August. Others at various times during the following days. During the last day before the landing, 14 August, most of the fleet gave the impression of sailing towards Genoa, as if the intention was to land behind the Gothic Line and attack the German Army in Italy from the rear.

A timely German reconnaissance plane flew over the fleet and returned to France with the information that the Allied landing was to take place in Italy. As soon as the aircraft had disappeared over the horizon, escort and convoy altered course and sailed through the night towards the Saint-Tropez peninsula.

Though the first wave of the assault was composed almost entirely of American troops, and the mass of the French divisions was not to land till the next day, 16 August, it was nevertheless a French commando, led by Lieutenant-Colonel Bouvet, to whom Allied Headquarters gave the honour of landing first in France. During the night of 14 to 15 August, on board the L.S.I. (Landing Ship Infantry) carrying the commando, the radio issued the following order of the day: "Rear-Admiral Davidson, the officers and crews of the Allied Fleet salute Lieutenant-Colonel Bouvet and his troops, who are to have the honour

[1] Cf., page 3.

of setting foot first on the soil of their country to liberate it. May God keep and protect them!"

These were sober and heartfelt words. Nor was the battlefield the French units were approaching one of those distant, indifferent lands which are remembered only for the names of the battles fought in them. It was their native land, a terrain of truth.

And General de Lattre, in a preliminary proclamation, concealed neither the emotion it inspired, nor the problems it would present. The land of France was also the land of Frenchmen, who had suffered, been divided, and tried so hardly for four years. De Lattre, who had been sharing these trials less than ten months earlier, desired to inform those of his men who had not had so recent an experience of them. As a proclamation preliminary to battle, it is one of the most humane and sincere that a general ever wrote:

This is a question of France, of fighting in France, of liberating France. It has this peculiar difficulty, that here it is not merely enough to fight, but also of making ourselves loved. And I must put you on guard against your own emotions. Justly proud of your efforts and the sacrifice of too many of your comrades, you will tend to expect gratitude, and will look upon yourselves as liberators. No doubt. But do not forget that the French who have remained in France have also suffered, with a less apparent suffering perhaps, but often as greatly and perhaps as usefully. Try not to force upon them your claims to fame, which is a matter of chance. Above all, you will meet and find at your side men of the French Forces of the Interior. Take care not to underestimate their contribution. Though come later to the struggle, their rôle is a no less decisive one; they will tell you of their exploits; talk less of yours. You are sons of the same mother and soldiers in the same cause.

These were the feelings which animated the French troops when, on 15 and 16 August, in the morning mists, they breathed from off shore the scents of their own land, its pines and aromatic shrubs, and watched the coast draw nearer.

Wherever possible, the Americans made way for them to land first. From the humblest soldier to the most senior officer, there was a similar deference: "After you, gentlemen of France."

On board the Catoctin, Admiral Hewitt's flagship, the French Admiral Lemonnier, during the night of the 14th to 15th, was interviewed by war correspondents, of whom he remarked: "Each one was already writing in flamboyant terms the story of the battle that was about to be fought."

When, next day, 16 August, the senior commanders landed, these, according to Admiral Hewitt, were the circumstances: "When we reached the beach, General Patch and I stood aside to allow Admiral Lemonnier to step first on to his native soil. I think I never saw a happier man."

There is an amusing echo of this delicate courtesy in a letter to Admiral Lemonnier from Forrestal, the American Secretary of Defence, written after they had attended together the welcome of the population of Saint-Raphael:

My dear Admiral,

. . . I shall not soon or easily forget the memorable scene of which I was a witness this afternoon on the Place at Saint-Raphaël. When the war is over, I very much hope to return to your country and find you Mayor of Saint-Raphaël, so that you can find me a small but permanent sinecure in that delightful town. A bientôt. And with all good wishes.

Most cordially yours,
JAMES FORRESTAL.

But it was perhaps among the crews of the warships and the detachments about to land that the most moving scenes took place.

On 15 August, at 00.45 hours, on board the ships taking up their positions in sight of the coast of Provence, the engineers and stokers, who would have to spend the whole day below with their engines, the gunners and electricians, who would be in the turrets and magazines, came up "to cast a last glance and breathe a last breath of air before disappearing down the ladders to their action stations." [1]

Their luckier comrades, who were to fight in the open air, at the machine-guns, searchlights and light guns, measured their country's approach on their telemeters.

At the landing in the bay of Cavalaire, a witness speaks of the French soldiers "massed in the bows of the ship, fascinated by the beach; they jumped down with a single bound, bent down to pick up a handful of sand, then skipped like madmen to the nearest pine trees, where they regrouped, shaking each other's hands, or embracing like brothers meeting again after a long absence."

For the combatants who were about to liberate it, the land of France was thus at once strategic and welcoming, at once abstract and real.

They manifested a care and concern unusual among soldiers for this country of theirs disguised as a battlefield.

[1] Admiral Lemonnier: Cap sur la Provence, page 18.

"Their constant anxiety," wrote General de Lattre, "was to spare the country which had suffered so much, and been so mutilated, further loss in human lives, as well as further destruction to its towns and villages." When they reached Marseilles, orders were issued to draw the enemy into the outskirts to avoid "fighting in the streets, the destruction it would entail and the grave risks it would cause the civilian population." In the fighting round Notre-Dame-de-la-Garde, the enemy had no scruples about dropping shells in the neighbourhood of the church, while the French artillery indulged in no such sacrilege. At the same time, de Lattre sent a light brigade to seize immediately the Roquefavour aqueduct to the west of Aix to protect the Marseilles water supply.

Care was even taken not to damage the vineyards. "Above all, don't crush the vines," was the order, reminiscent of the France of another day, and the tanks in Burgundy scrupulously observed it. In their anxiety to protect the country, the regular troops were helped by the F.F.I. Thanks to them two thousand yards of quay were saved from destruction in Marseilles. At Sète, the ships that were to block the entrance canals were sunk by the F.F.I. in places where they did not interrupt traffic, and the harbour facilities were on the whole preserved. Indeed, the liberation of Provence was not merely a military victory; it was a civic success, an intimacy reborn between Frenchmen who had been separated.

The French Army began by attacking Toulon, the leading naval port, and Marseilles, the leading commercial port and the second city of France.

On 6 August 1944, General de Lattre concluded his "Personal and Secret Instruction No. 1 for Operation Dragoon." These orders reveal his intentions: "Above all, speed is the factor essential to success, speed in the constant search for opportunities of breaking out of the perimeter of the terrain, speed in the determined exploitation of every favourable occasion for rapid manœuvre." In obeying this directive, the French forces upset the American Command's timetable. This had placed the liberation of Toulon at D+20 (4 September), that of Marseilles at D+40 (24 September), and that of Lyons at D+90 (15 November). Estimates which were anticipated for the first of these towns by seven days, for the second by twenty-six, and for the third by seventy-two.

On 18 August, two days after his landing on the coast of France, General de Lattre had as yet only some 16,000 men, 30 tanks, and 80 guns of medium calibre available. He had to wait another eight or ten days to complete his army. The German garrison of Toulon consisted of 25,000 men, protected by 30 forts and innumerable casemates. Nevertheless, de Lattre was of the opinion that operations should be begun at once.

From a naval officer, Sub-Lieutenant Sanguinetti, who had been parachuted into France two months before, de Lattre learnt at 22.00 hours that same night that according to the Resistance Intelligence networks the Germans were reinforcing their fortified camp with feverish haste. They were equipping the old works on the north to oppose the assault threatening them from the land side. They were blocking the passes and blowing up the buildings of the arsenal to clear a field of fire. They were also awaiting reinforcements from Marseilles. These should clearly be forestalled.

De Lattre also received information about the forces of the Resistance and the situation of the civilian population. The Department of Var had two principal centres of F.F.I., Draguignan in the north, and Toulon in the south. The latter's various groups comprised altogether some 2,000 combatants. Moreover, the population of the naval port, which had suffered the humiliation of the German occupation, and the tragic scuttling of the fleet in November 1942, was eager to fight at the side of the regular troops. At the same time, the situation of the civilian population was becoming increasingly critical; from 24 November 1943 to 6 August 1944, the town had suffered no less than eight heavy bombings. Since 6 August, it had been caught between two fires; incessant alerts and an intensive pounding by the Allied Air Forces in preparation for the landing, while at the same time the Germans were carrying out demolitions.

Many of the terrified inhabitants, since it was summer, were able to spend their nights outside the town among the pine trees on the slopes of the Faron or among the olive groves in the countryside. Others took refuge in cellars.

On 16 August, when the landing was announced, a proclamation by the "Militarbefehlshaber in Frankreich" was published in the newspapers instituting a state of siege. At midday, the electric current was cut off, and there were no more lights or radios.

On the 17th, the newspapers failed to appear. Bombarded and paralized, the town was completely isolated. In anticipation of a critical situation, the authorities had taken certain measures. Fau, in charge of shelters and refugees, whose headquarters was in the former Priseco Store, where the mairie had taken refuge, opened seven canteens for the civilian population. Elsewhere, Bionconi, leader of one of the F.F.I. groups, set up bakeries in the old quarters of the town, and organized, under police control, the sale of flour and vegetables against tickets. Dr. Robert, Director of the Institute of Municipal Hygiene, set up a First Aid Post in the centre of the town at the house of his friend, Dr. Sauvet. During four days and three nights, he attended to 311 seriously wounded and 1,400 slightly wounded people. He dealt with 72 French and 120 German dead. He had to turn the Municipal Theatre into a morgue.

All this pointed to the urgent need to relieve the town. On the 19th, at dawn, after a sleepless night, de Lattre received a visit from General Devers, the American second-in-command to Sir Maitland Wilson, the Supreme Commander in the Mediterranean Theatre. He told him of his plan to take immediate action. At 09.00 hours he visited General Patch to obtain authority to launch the assault. He was given it. At noon, he returned to his headquarters and issued the orders.

On 20 August, a significant and concise signal reached headquarters. It consisted of merely two words: "Le Revest-Linarès." It was the report of a victory and meant that Colonel de Linarès' infantry regiment had reached the village of Le Revest, thus completing the investing of Toulon.

The battle was to last a week. The last Germans surrendered on 28 August. During these eight days, street fighting, which so many towns had suffered during their liberation, reached a rare intensity. Here, as elsewhere, the F.F.I. fought side by side with the regular troops.

On the 21st, in the suburban village of La Vallette, "the country of strawberries and violets," the F.F.I., accompanied by many young men, contained the enemy who had surrounded the place. They awaited the arrival of the infantry, who had been delayed by minefields. Two days later, on 23 August, since the battle for possession of the village still continued, the Municipal Council decided to mobilize part of the population. Armed with whatever weapons were available, civilians joined the soldiers in the defence-posts.

Within Toulon itself, there was a curious mixture of war and normal life. "A really most extraordinary sight," wrote Admiral Lemonnier. "The town was still full of enemy; some streets were deserted while others were crowded with the civilian population who strolled about as if the battle were taking place kilometres away." [1] Passers-by signalled to the officers which objectives to attack, and where the enemy strong-points threatening the French advance were located. Elsewhere, a woman crossed the lines to give information about enemy dispositions.

But the war that was taking place in these familiar surroundings was

[1] Admiral Lemonnier: *Cap sur la Provence*, page 177.

no laughing matter. Toulon, at once a naval port and a fortified city, was subjected to the effects of an intense artillery duel between the Germans holding the forts and the Allied warships.

Hitler had given orders to the German garrisons of the ports to defend them to the death and, in the last resort, to blow them up. In Toulon, Admiral Ruhfuss, commanding the citadel, took these instructions literally. "We shall fight," he announced, "till the last round."

The coastal batteries directed their fire at the Allied ships and made use of a novel method of observation: their shells contained chemicals which coloured the explosions. As a result, when several batteries were concentrating their fire on the same target, each could recognize its own shots. On board the battleship *Lorraine*, which was subjected to a violent bombardment from 340 mm. guns, Commandant Rué suddenly became aware that his uniform had turned violet.

The Allied ships returned the fire of the German batteries. But they had also other targets, which seemed macabre enough to a sailor—the wrecks of the ships scuttled in November 1942. It was suspected, though wrongly, that the Germans had reconditioned the heavy guns so as to be able to turn them on the environs of the harbour. Salvoes of shells fell on the *Strasbourg* and *La Galissonnière*, still further damaging these ships already *hors de combat*.

Below the trajectories of the shells criss-crossing above the infantry advance, the battle for Toulon resolved itself into three phases, which were defined by de Lattre as follows:

"First the phase of investment (20 and 21 August) during which Monsabert's troops drew a net round the north and west of Toulon, while Larminat's approached from the east, together forming a large semicircle round the objective from Hyères to Bandol.

"Then the phase of dismantling (22 and 23 August) consisting of the painful but systematic advance of the 1st D.F.L. and the 9th D.I.C. across the eastern exterior perimeter of the town, which the shock troops and infantry of the 3rd D.I.A. were also harassing.

"Finally, the phase of the definitive reduction of the internal defences, which was mainly the job of the 9th D.I.C. and came to an end on 27 August, at 23.45 hours, with the unconditional surrender of Admiral Ruhfuss and his last forces."

Within these phases there were numerous dramatic episodes.

General Brosset, going ahead of his troops, drove into Toulon alone in a jeep. He then returned to find his leading troops. "Get a move on," he shouted to them. "I've already kissed at least two hundred girls." There was nothing laggard about that division.

A German-speaking colonel succeeded in tapping the interior telephone lines of the Cap Brun Fort. He asked for the commander, told him to shout Heil Hitler three times, and then blow up his guns and surrender with his whole garrison. These, he said, were new orders from the Führer. The commander obeyed.

Guerrilla warfare, stratagems of war and sporting exploits all contributed to clean up the town and clear its approaches. Before the liberation of Toulon had been completed, General de Lattre and Diethelm, Commissioner at the Ministry for War, decided, on the 24th, to take over the old headquarters of the sub-division. They reached it, but only by crossing the railway line on all fours.

On the 25th the French debouched on to the port. The Malbousquet Fort, which dominated it, surrendered.

The next day it was the turn of the Mourillon Arsenal, the Six-Fours Port, and the Brégaillon battery.

During the morning of the 27th the victorious French troops marched past Diethelm and Jacquinot, Commissioner at the Ministry of Marine. But the sound of cheers was still broken by that of gunfire. On the farther side of the roads the peninsula of Saint-Mandrieu was still holding out. Admiral Ruhfuss had still not surrendered.

He surrendered that evening at 23.45 hours; and the next day, at 08.00 hours, a column of 1,800 sailors marched out into captivity. These were the last German combatants.

General de Lattre interviewed Ruhfuss himself. It was to tell him to produce a detailed plan of the minefields within three hours. After the time-limit was up, he would answer with his life for every Frenchman blown up on a German mine.

The German Admiral complied. The liberation of Toulon was complete. It had cost the French 2,700 killed and wounded of which 100 were officers; it had cost the Germans thousands of dead and 17,000 prisoners.

On 13 September the French fleet entered Toulon. Most of the ships had taken part in retaking the great port. Their crews were drawn up on deck, flags floated from every mast, and the ships also flew the long war pendants used on returning from battle. Seldom had that emblem greater justification or been saluted with more emotion. The Tricolour also flew from the *Philadelphia* and the *Sirius*, the flagships of the American admirals.

The fleet entered the deserted roads, which were encumbered with wreckage and the scuttled ships. The forts commanding the harbour were in ruins, and the buildings of the arsenal rubble. The ships berthed along the quays amid the debris. The sailors for shore leave hurried to the entry ports. But they landed only to stare aghast at the immensity of the destruction, over which the Tricolour was now flying.

It was thus, one month after the Liberation, that they saw the first French city to be liberated by Frenchmen.

The second was to be Marseilles.

Its liberation followed an "extravagant week of assaults, bluff and manœuvres," which lasted from 20 to 27 August. One of its most decisive episodes took place in the peaceful surroundings of a hotel for tourists.

General Sudre, who was commanding the advance-guard of the French Army (7th Regiment of Algerian Infantry, 1st combat command of the 1st Armoured Division and two Moroccan Tabors), in conformity with the orders de Lattre had extracted from General Patch, had made contact with the enemy in front of Aubagne on 21 August at 08.00 hours. He had set up his headquarters at Gemenos, at the Relais de la Magdeleine which had been placed at his disposal by the owner, Madame Marignane. He worked on his maps in the hotel's shady courtyard.

During the afternoon of 22 August a stormy council of war,[1] attended by de Lattre, Larminat, Monsabert, Guillaume and Sudre was held in the big sitting-room of the Magdeleine.

It was stormy for two reasons. In the first place the hotel, though being used as a headquarters, had nonetheless retained many of its customers. When the generals arrived to discuss the war, they saw "a pretty terrace with chairs and sunshades, where idle civilians in summer clothes were nonchalantly drinking apéritifs with beautiful blondes."[2] The girls were scantily clothed and the drinks were iced. As for the men, they seemed "indifferent to the soldiers fighting and dying a few kilometres away."

As he put it himself, de Lattre "began by putting a little order into the décor." This no doubt entailed a certain curtness towards the summer visitors. A minor incident, of course, but it was the prelude to another and more serious one.

General de Monsabert and General de Lattre had a heated argument. The former, on information he had received from units of the 3rd Algerian Infantry Division and, in particular, from Colonel Chappuis, commanding the 7th Algerian Infantry Regiment, wanted to enter

[1] Commandant Crosia: *Marseille 1944, Victoire Française*, page 33.
[2] P. Ichac: *La bataille de Marseille* in *La France et son Empire*, Vol. III, page 102.

Marseilles at once, seize the centre of the town with a small force and endeavour to surprise the Germans into surrendering. His leading units had already made contact with the population and he knew he could count on its enthusiastic support. It was known that the F.F.I. had issued orders for insurrection as long ago as Saturday, 19 August.

General de Lattre de Tassigny, though no laggard, was not in favour of this venture. Militarily speaking, it seemed to him absurdly imprudent; and politically, it seemed also to have certain drawbacks. According to Crosia, an Intelligence officer of the 3rd D.I.A., he feared "that the troops would be contaminated by the disorder of a city in a state of insurrection," and he had little liking for the risks involved in exposing his advance-guard to street-fighting and his infantry to being arbiters or hostages in political brawls.

He began therefore by refusing, preferring to invest Marseilles before sending his troops into it. General de Monsabert violently opposed his army commander's plan. In the end, he banged the table and said: "The day after tomorrow I shall drink a pastis on the Canebière."

De Lattre still would not agree. But Monsabert, when transmitting the General's orders to Colonel Chappuis, said with a smile: "These are the orders, but should you have the opportunity . . ." Chappuis saw the point. He let himself be "sucked in by the southern crowd among which the tanks and infantry had some difficulty in clearing a way for themselves, and plunged straight into the city." [1]

On the 23rd, at five o'clock in the morning, two battalions of the 7th Infantry coming from Saint-Julien reached the crossroads of the Madeleine. Despite the hour, windows and doors flew open. Flags appeared on the houses. The population of this suburb of Marseilles crowded round the columns of infantry. Wine and fruit were brought out. Seldom had so copious a breakfast been served amid such wild excitement.

At eight o'clock, at the Madeleine crossroads, Colonel Chappuis and General de Monsabert joined the 1st Battalion. In the middle of the afternoon, Monsabert, escorted by his tanks, installed his headquarters in the Prefecture. The Belzunce and Saint-Charles crossroads and the Bourse were cleared of enemy. But he was still out on a dangerous limb amid the enemy positions. Marseilles was far from liberated. The Canebière was still under German artillery fire and it was clear that Monsabert would drink no apéritif there today.

The French amounted to approximately 800 men amid 15,000 Germans. But they were in Marseilles, a city of wild cock-and-bull stories.

[1] De Lattre: *Histoire de la Première Armée*, page 92.

And now Crosia, who was acting as Intelligence officer to the 7th Infantry, in agreement with Monsabert, tried to bring off an extraordinary, indeed heroic, piece of bluff. Representing a mere handful of men amid the whole German garrison, he was prepared coolly to propose to the Wehrmacht that they surrender. The first problem was to establish contact with enemy headquarters. It occurred to Colonel Chappuis and Crosia simply to ask for it on the telephone—an expedient which turned out to be wholly successful.

The two principal telephone exchanges, Garibaldi and Colbert, were in enemy hands and heavily guarded. Crosia, in the uniform of a captain, marched first into one and then the other. "*Nicht schiessen!* (Don't shoot!)" he cried; and then explained that he merely wanted to put through a telephone call.

The Germans were dumbfounded. On the telephone, Colonel Chappuis arranged with General Schaeffer, commanding the troops and fortifications in Marseilles, a meeting with Monsabert, who was prepared to give him the opportunity to surrender.

At 13.00 hours, during a local cease-fire, "the Vieux Port of Marseilles, which had seen many a good joke in its time, witnessed an astonishing sight: a little French General with white hair standing at the gate of the Saint-Jean Fort . . . , accompanied only by three officers, of whom one was a Marine, amid a crowd of Germans armed to the teeth.

"Standing before him was a tall, thin German General, to whom he politely suggested unconditional surrender. The German General had 15,000 men . . . behind concrete walls. He had 200 guns and all the necessary ammunition. The French General had no more at that time than an artillery group and two battalions of infantry, while his first tanks were only just beginning to enter the town." [1]

The negotiations between the Generals were not easy. Schaeffer did not want to surrender, but to spare the civilian population he was prepared to accept an armistice. Monsabert, suspecting a trap, replied that the only way in which Schaeffer could show his humanitarian intentions was to capitulate. The German General then entered on a long digression about the outrages committed by the F.F.I. Monsabert had no difficulty in refuting him and incidentally reminded him that he had been condemned to death by a Soviet court-martial for atrocities against the civilian population.

The thrust went home. Schaeffer turned pale and fell silent. The interview came to an end. Monsabert returned to his headquarters behind the Prefecture, in the very centre of the German positions.

[1] P. Ichac: *La bataille de Marseille* in *La France et son Empire*, Vol. III, page 102.

The least that could be said about his position was that it was some-what confused, due not only to the Germans, but also to his turbulent neighbours occupying the offices of the Prefecture nearby.

The Resistance in Marseilles was at once active and effervescent. The city had suffered under the Occupation as much as any other in the southern zone. The Germans had destroyed the Vieux Port district. Moreover, the headquarters of Darnand's Militia were at Nice, of Bucard's Francisme at Aix-en-Provence, and of Sabiani's P.P.F. at Marseilles, with their gunmen, their spies in the pay of the Gestapo, their black-marketeers and their informers. On the other hand, Marseilles and the coast generally had an active Resistance though their effective numbers were no doubt less than appeared after the liberation. This clandestine army consisted of 3,000 men of the Lécuyer group, who fought mostly between Nice and Antibes; while in Marseilles itself, in April 1944, there were more than 2,000 members of the O.R.A. (the Resistance Organization of the Army) of whom some small proportion were armed. In the Department of the Bouches-du-Rhône, the F.T.P. and the O.R.A. each had about 1,000 members, of whom a third were armed.

As soon as the regular army approached the city, about 500 F.F.I. began an insurrection. On Saturday the 14th, the Resistance, mostly F.T.P., occupied the Prefecture, without indeed encountering much resistance, and set up there a "committee of insurrection," which was only to hand over its powers to the official "liberation committee" on Tuesday, 22 August.

The Prefecture presented a somewhat unusual spectacle. A variety of individuals, with more or less authority, installed themselves in the offices and reception rooms; ragged-looking men broadcast a smell of wine. Self-styled officers, who had seldom been seen to take part in the exploits of the Maquis, took up their quarters in the regional pre-fect's office, among others a certain Commandant Cocot who, a bar-man in normal times, now set about arresting on various pretexts peo-ple he considered suspect and shutting them up in the attics. There were prisons in the cellars too. The Patriotic Militia filled them with unwilling guests.

Besides these more or less authentic resistants, there were a certain number of people whose presence was surprising owing to their notoriety. A lawyer, who had compromised himself by collaborating with the Germans, installed himself in the former bureau of Jewish affairs and immediately renamed it the "Movement against Racialism," which was perhaps better adapted to these revolutionary circumstances. Everyone simply put on his door any label he thought suitable.

In this new administration there was one qualified and authentic representative of the F.F.I. But on the 28th, after the parade which followed the liberation, he was seen collapsed over his desk, moaning: "Who the hell are all these people?" He had witnessed, parading before Monsabert, 1,500 men wearing brassards, about three times the number there had been a week earlier. There had also been a large number of cars with the letters "F.F.I." chalked on them.

Among these post-liberation F.F.I., there was a certain one-armed commandant, whose manner aroused so much suspicion that he was imprisoned and searched. Concealed under his clothes was found a second arm wrapped in bank-notes to the value of twelve millions.

These details serve to give something of the atmosphere, but they formed only one aspect of the situation. The authorities appointed to take over when the city was liberated quickly undertook the conduct of affairs. On 22 August, the insurrection committee handed over its powers to the liberation committee, presided over by François Leenhardt, deputy S.F.I.O. On 24 August, the Commissioner of the Republic, Raymond Aubrac, a mining engineer, took over the Prefecture and by much public-spirited hard work managed to set a limit to the havoc. One of his first acts was to appoint new prefects. Flavien Veyren, director of Public Assistance, became Prefect of Bouches-du-Rhône, and Pierre Massenet, a civil engineer of the Aeronautique, Deputy-Prefect of Marseilles.

Monsabert's headquarters, in the offices of the Military Region, near the Prefecture, were surrounded by enemy posts. The Germans were within 700 or 800 yards at Notre-Dame-de-la-Garde and near the Post Office. They were within a kilometre, or a kilometre and a half, at Fort Saint-Nicolas, Fort Saint-Charles and the Prado. The very pavement outside was placed in a state of defence. Two half-tracks and machine-guns were in position behind barricades of paving-stones and bags of cement. On the Place Paradis, below the Prefecture, tanks were drawn up. In spite of these precautions, Monsabert came under fire when going from his headquarters to the Prefecture.

Marseilles was not going to lose such a splendid chance of rioting in the streets and showing its spirit round this strategic point, which lay in the very centre of the city. "Dominating the devastation made by humans," relates the diary kept by a Marseilles woman during the liberation, "the hills were bathed in the splendid light of this country. Nothing could alter that. The heaviest guns, the biggest bombs could do no more than scratch the great bare serene mass of them." But within this immutable frame, the atmosphere was far from peaceful; indeed it was often unbreathable.

It was unfortunate that the sirocco blew continuously for three days. There were also districts where there was an intolerable stench of hot oil. The oil works had been bombed by the Americans and spread their stench across the city.

In private homes violence and fear erupted into the permanent avocations of the housewife. Here is an account which by its very simplicity achieves a certain grandeur:

"A thunder of artillery which gives me cold shivers down the spine, the tomatoes are nearly done, the soup ready. We took advantage of a quiet moment to make the soup. But the fire had to be got to draw. We had to clean it out. But cleaning it out meant soot. So we washed the pictures and scrubbed the kitchen. A good day in the feminine tradition which takes little account of the folly of men. And the men said: 'That's just like a woman. She cleans and cooks, so that if everything's destroyed it'll be done in order and cleanliness.'"

All round people's homes the battle thundered in the streets, as though it were merely a new and almost normal part of the city's life.

A man in the suburbs would lean nonchalantly from his window. Was it to take the air or warm himself in the sun? With a seemingly casual gesture he would cut the telephone line which passed across the façade. He would be isolating a German strong-point, which could now no longer take part in the operations of the Wehrmacht.

The exuberant heroism of the districts and suburbs of the city became concentrated during these three days round the Wehrmacht's points of resistance.

In the first place, of course, round Notre-Dame-de-la-Garde. The church was attacked on 25 August at 08.45 hours by two companies of Algerian infantry and a troop of tanks of the 2nd Dragoons. "Beware, there is firing from the church," said a notice at a crossroads by the Vieux Port. There was no artillery preparation; the intention was to spare the church. But smoke shells supported the advance.

It progressed up the steep streets, the Rue Montée-de-l'Oratoire, the Place Sancta-Maria, and up the steps. At 11.30 hours two tanks, the *Jourdain* and the *Jeanne d'Arc*, went into action. The first reached the foot of the steps leading to the church and was blown up on a mine-field, three of its men being wounded. The tank commander, Sergeant

The Landing in Provence

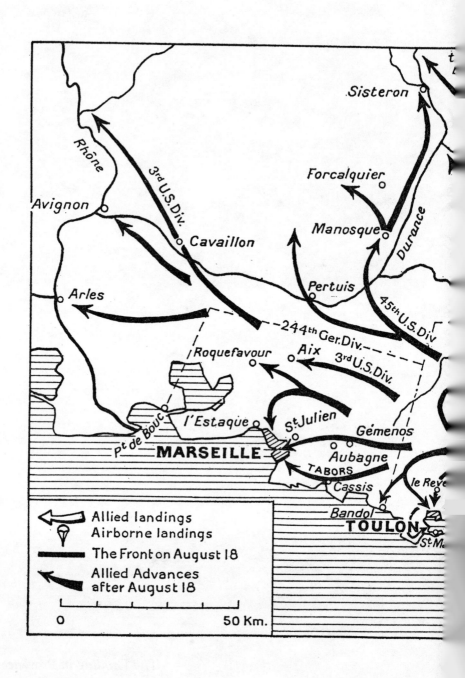

Sisteron

Rhône

3rd U.S.Div.

Avignon

Cavaillon

Forcalquier

Manosque

Durance

Arles

Pertuis

45th U.S.Div.

244th Ger.Div.

Roquefavour

Aix

3rd U.S.Div.

l'Estaque

St.Julien

Gémenos

Pt de Bouc

MARSEILLE

Aubagne

TABORS

Cassis

le Reve

Bandol

TOULON

St.M

Allied landings
Airborne landings

The Front on August 18

Allied Advances
after August 18

0   50 Km.

Lolliot, who was himself wounded, got out of the tank, crawled up to the church and attached a flag to the gate, being thus the first man to fly the French flag from the building. But the flag was too small to be seen from a distance.

Almost at the same moment, the *Jeanne d'Arc* tank caught fire, having been hit point-blank by a German shell. Four of its crew were burnt to death, a fifth was wounded.

Fire broke out in the crypt of Notre-Dame. The Germans evacuated it and took refuge in the sacristy. Suddenly, at 14.00 hours, the building was surrounded by a great cloud of smoke; the Germans had brought flame-throwers into action. Was it by mistake, or was it a last effort to repel the assault?

The French seemed to be held up, but they sent three patrols to attack the building. Few though they were, they succeeded in putting an end to the German resistance.

At 16.30 hours, Aspirant Ripoli, of the 7th R.T.A., reached the church. He went up into the tower of Notre-Dame and hoisted a flag which on this occasion could be seen by the whole city. The news spread that the church was liberated. But all was not yet over. The forts still in German hands could sweep the promontory of Notre-Dame-de-la-Garde with cross-fire.

During the evening of the 25th, General Schaeffer sent a letter to General Monsabert in which he said that "if the French continue to occupy the neighbourhood of the church, he would be obliged to open fire on them and this might result in damage to Marseilles." The French General replied at once: "The French are occupying the positions held a few hours ago by the Germans. The responsibility for the destruction of Notre-Dame-de-la-Garde will rest entirely on General Schaeffer. . . . Such destruction can neither defer nor alter the fate of the German garrison of Marseilles."

Meanwhile, and during the two following days, further German strong-points in the city and its suburbs fell to the combined military and civilian forces. The whole population of the city had stopped work and stood about watching the battles. "A militiaman or a German firing at all the passing military vehicles from the roof of a house drew an interested crowd to the Rue Paradis, till a salvo of air-bursts emptied the district. There was nothing to be seen but a girl in a white dress and cap walking calmly towards the battle, waving a little Red Cross flag above the head of a boy pushing a stretcher."

Command posts were set up in a number of buildings, among which was the Hôtel Terminus, near the Saint-Charles station. There were patrols out in the streets. Military and civilian bearers of flags of truce did their best to demoralize the enemy and persuaded the last pockets to surrender.

The culminating event of the reduction of the German defences took place on 27 August, when Fort Saint-Nicolas surrendered. Its thick walls prevented the effect of shelling from being decisive. The Goumiers had to advance up to the barracks before General Shaeffer, compelled by force of circumstances to disobey Hitler's order to resist to the last round, sent Monsabert the following letter of surrender:

Monsieur le General de Division de Goislard de Monsabert,

The situation of my forces, as a result of the fighting during these last days, is totally different from what it was at the time of our conversation on 23 August. Most strong-points have surrendered after an honourable resistance.

In face of the superiority of the forces in action against us, the continuation of the battle seems to me pointless. It would result in the total annihilation of my remaining forces.

I ask that between 21.00 and 08.00 hours tonight there should be an armistice during which the conditions for an honourable surrender for the morning of 28 August may be worked out. Otherwise, we shall fight to the last man.

SCHAEFFER.
General of Division.

Since the 244th German Division had behaved most gallantly, Monsabert had no reason not to grant it an honourable surrender. He authorized Schaeffer to keep his personal arms.

The next day, at 13.30 hours, the 244th Division marched out to the Sainte-Marthe camp, which had been turned into a prison camp.

Within General Schaeffer's headquarters, the French officers searched the underground passages by candlelight. There were lateral galleries full of beds and shelves covered with bottles.

In one room, still brightly lit, there was a plan of Marseilles on a big table. Beside it were two telephones and a plate of Gruyère cheese. Three men were sitting there with bowed heads. The oldest, "his eyes sunken with fatigue and his face ravaged, got to his feet. His two companions gave a military salute, he gave the Hitler salute." [1]

It was General Schaeffer constituting himself a prisoner.

"Tomorrow," said General Monsabert, "there must be a march past

[1] P. Ichac: *La bataille de Marseille* in *La France et son Empire*, Vol. III, page 106.

on the Vieux Port of the F.F.I. of Marseilles, they have well deserved it. . . ."

Marseilles, the second city of France, had been liberated at the same time as Toulon. De Lattre's audacity, Monsabert's astuteness, and the efforts of the whole population had achieved victory.

But it was a victory dearly paid for: there were 4,000 French killed or wounded. As for the Germans, they lost several thousands killed, and 37,000 prisoners, of whom 700 were officers.

The port of Marseilles was in ruins; the nine docks of La Joliette were a chaos of steel, concrete and cables. All the quays had been blown up by no less than 2,000 large mines. Fifty thousand square metres of warehouses had been destroyed as well as all the railway and electrical installations.

The principal entrance to the harbour was obstructed by the hulls of eleven large ships, among which were the Atlantic liners *Massilia* and *Iméréthie*. There were 170 wrecks in other parts of the port. The transporter bridge had been destroyed. 257 cranes had collapsed.

Nevertheless, in the same way that on 13 September the return of the fleet had marked the liberation of Toulon, only two days later, on 15 September, large transports entered the port of Marseilles through a channel opened in the obstructions.

Nine liberty ships entered the docks or came alongside the quays, while forty-eight others unloaded in the roads.

Seventeen days after the liberation, 10,000 men and 3,000 tons of material were put ashore.

During the eight following months, troops corresponding to fourteen divisions were to disembark in the port and 17,000 tons of food were landed each day.

The event justified Eisenhower's strategic views about the value of Operation Anvil.

After Marseilles, it was to be Grenoble and Lyons.

On 19 August, Colonel Henri Zeller landed at Saint-Tropez in the aircraft belonging to General Cochet, who commanded the F.F.I. of the southern zone. A tall British officer handed him a message: "Tomorrow, we shall begin to put plan Faisceau into effect." Zeller, alias Faisceau, was the author of the new plan General Patch had adopted after their recent meeting. Of the three American divisions composing the American VI Corps, only one, the 3rd Infantry Division, followed the original route and advanced along the plain of the Rhône where the Germans were still masters of the terrain. It encountered, as Zeller had predicted, strong resistance, and had got no further than Aix by 20 August. But the two others, the 36th and 45th Infantry Divisions, supported by Task Force Butler, advanced towards the north by the mountains, where the Maquis were surrounding and pinning down the garrisons of the Wehrmacht as planned. By the 19th, they had liberated most of the Basses-Alpes, and were holding Manosque, Forcalquier, Sisteron, Digne and, in pursuance of plan Faisceau, were hurrying on to Grenoble by the Route Napoléon.

The maquisards were punctual at the rendezvous Zeller had arranged with the Americans. The F.F.I. of the Isère, who had been fighting in the high valleys since 1943, had mobilized and armed since 6 June 1944 a force of approximately 2,000 men. They had isolated the Germans by sabotaging the railways and communications; all traffic was interrupted between Grenoble and Chambéry. Elsewhere daily traffic was limited to one or two convoys escorted by armoured and repair trains. In Grenoble itself the atmosphere was dramatic. This was how Commandant le Ray described it: "The city, which was closed from six o'clock in the evening, shut within its belt of German posts whose job it was to examine everything that went in and out, was alive with patrols who in their panic fired thoughtlessly at passers-by, doctors visiting patients, railway workers, night workers, at windows, lamp-posts and stray dogs. From curfew onwards there was a continual noise of shots, shouting, isolated cries, tramping boots and then, towards two o'clock in the morning, the explosion of 'the bomb,' which everyone had been expecting while wondering what objective had been assigned to our men that night."

On 14 November 1943, the Secret Army destroyed the Wehrmacht artillery park. The Germans replied by taking 300 hostages from the civilian population. The maquisards sent the German authorities an ultimatum demanding the immediate liberation of these innocent people. The Germans refused. At 08.30 hours on 2 December, the Bonne barracks, in which artillery units were lodged, blew up. 220 soldiers were killed and 550 wounded.

On another occasion, for two Germans killed, ten hostages, arrested in the Vercors, were executed in the Cours Bériat. They were six young non-combatants who had been waiting for months in a barracks in Grenoble to know their fate. The S.S. took them from their cells, telling them they were to be set free. The boys got happily into the trucks. When they reached the execution ground, in the very centre of the town, in the early hours of the morning, the guards made them get out and killed them one by one with a shot in the neck. Their bodies lay on the pavement till noon as an example.

At the same place, on the day of the liberation, nine young militia-men suffered a similar fate as a reprisal for the cruelty of the Nazis. Among them was a young man from Uriage, who, being out of work, had taken a job as gardener at the Militia headquarters. It was his only Militia activity. But he was shot with the others in the Cours Bériat, under the pouring rain, in the presence of a howling crowd.

The maquisards of the Isère, whether F.T.P. or A.S., Communists or not, made common front. In June and July, the enemy losses in the Isère (exclusive of the Vercors) amounted to 416 killed, 281 wounded and 35 prisoners, while the F.F.I. had 28 killed and 17 wounded.

In August, five days before the landing in Provence, the Wehrmacht tried to reconquer the district. The 157th Infantry Division launched an attack by Romanche, the Valbonnais, and the Lautaret and Glon-don passes. Until 13 August, small posts of F.F.I. held out to allow the main body of the troops to retreat into the hills. In these delaying actions the Germans lost 200 dead and 180 wounded, while the F.F.I. had 21 killed and 27 wounded. After 18 August the German offensive was checked and the Wehrmacht had to retreat.

Two days later, on 20 August, the first American elements, making forced marches along the Route Napoléon, reached the pass of Luz-la-Croix-Haute. The battle for Grenoble began. It was brief. During the night of the 21st, the Germans blew up the ammunition dumps in the town; and on the 22nd, the day for which the leaders of the Maquis had planned a general assault on the town, they learnt to their disap-pointment that the Germans had withdrawn.

On the 23rd, the combined action of the Americans and the F.F.I. brought about the surrender of the last Germans, who were surrounded in the Gresivaudan, and completely cleared Grenoble, which the Ameri-cans then entered.

The Wehrmacht was now threatened with encirclement. Coming from both the north and the south, the invading armies of Overlord and Anvil were approaching each other. Patton reached Orléans at the same time as Patch reached Grenoble. A huge vice was threatening to close in round the two German armies, the First and the Nineteenth. On 20 August, the German commanders had become aware of their danger. General Wiese, commanding the Nineteenth Army, which was holding the Mediterranean coast, ordered the garrisons of Toulon and Marseilles to resist to the end so as to permit the withdrawal of his other units towards Lyons. General Blaskowitz, commanding the First Army on the Atlantic coast, issued orders to retire in the direction of Dijon.

On 28 August, the pincers were closing in from both sides. Paris, which had been liberated two days before, saw the passage of Allied divisions, of which some were moving to the north-east of France and to Belgium, while others were moving towards Dijon. The fall of Marseilles and Toulon freed de Lattre's army, which then moved along the Rhône with the American divisions. On that same day, General Patch issued his Field Order No. 4, which marked the end of the Mediterranean phase of Operation Anvil, and opened its European phase. The first objective was the junction of the Allied armies of Provence and Normandy. To achieve this, he had to march on Lyons.

Since June 1940, Lyons, which together with Dijon formed the boundaries of the trap in which the Wehrmacht might be taken, had been playing an essential rôle in France. Capital of the Resistance, it became, as a result, the capital of repression, terror and sometimes discord. In July and August 1944, Lyons was the scene of Nazi atrocities followed by reprisals on the part of the maquisards.

The Resistance had been organizing itself in Lyons since the Armistice. From June 1940 to 11 November 1942, the date on which the Germans occupied the free zone, it had taken two forms, one military and the other civilian. The first, organized within the Army of the Armistice of which Lyons was one of the principal centres, was led by a few officers who were preparing revenge within the regular units they commanded. In general, it remained loyal to Pétain, and though necessarily operating secretly, it claimed to be legal. The other form of the Resistance was principally civilian, against the government, hostile to the Marshal, and was soon to rally to de Gaulle.

The military Resistance had great facilities in the Lyons region. It was from there that a major part of the only army to have escaped the disaster had been recruited. The Army of the Alps, which during the last days of the campaign had victoriously opposed the Italians, had known neither defeat nor captivity. Demobilized in the normal way, its officers and men, before going to their homes, had been listed and registered to facilitate remobilization. The men so recorded were designated "elements for the maintenance of order." Regimental societies provided a useful cover. In Haute-Savoie, Savoie and the Hautes-Alpes, their members were ready to form several "Alpine fortress battalions." In the Rhône, as in the Isère, three fighting battalions were formed; one was formed in the Drôme; and two artillery groups were ready to be formed in Grenoble.[1]

Another card-index for mobilization was organized under cover of the "National Service of Statistics" for population. Clothing for the reservists was arranged by a supplementary uniform being issued to every man in the Army of the Armistice.

On 11 November 1942, the Free Zone was occupied. On 27 November, the Army of the Armistice was dissolved. Liquidating organizations handed over all the unit's stores to the Germans. The secret stocks of arms were seized, often through informers. All that could be saved were a few motor trucks which had been farmed out to civilian transport companies, as were the gasoline stocks which for a long time served to move contingents of the Maquis. Military Resistance ceased to have any regular existence. But during these years civilian Resistance was born. It first appeared in Lyons by the issuing of pamphlets, then by secret newspapers, of which the most widespread were *Combat, Libération, Témoignage Chrétien*, and *La Voix du Peuple*. Their distribution was much helped by the closely knit population of the old districts of Lyons, and by the maze of little streets that made up so much of the town. In 1941, the Lyons region made its first contact by air with London and received its first parachuted arms for the benefit of the Libération movement. But till November 1942, the civilian Resistance was still insufficiently concentrated. It operated mostly by direct contacts and personal relations. Its main concern was propaganda and information, though there were a few rare sabotage operations in the Chambéry district against radio-detection vans and railways.

In November 1942 the two forms of Resistance became united. On the civilian side, Combat, Libération and Franc-Tireur were grouped in the Mouvements Unis de Résistance (M.U.R.). Such regular officers or officers of the reserve who considered themselves released from their loyalty to the Vichy government formed the Organization de Résistance de l'Armée (O.R.A.). In October 1943, owing to the influence of Colonel Descours, alias Bayard, the fusion took place between the movements of civilian origin (with the exception of the F.T.P.) and the O.R.A. A joint command was set up. On 27 July 1944, before the Liberation, Descours became military assistant to the regional head of region R1, called Rhône-Alpes, thereby replacing the previous holder of that position who had been assassinated by the Germans. The regional head was

[1] This information and much of what follows appear in an unpublished report by M. Galimand.

Alban Vistel, one of the leaders of the F.F.I., who did more than any-one to prevent the politicizing of the Resistance and to limit the wast-age and losses among its indispensable members. Thanks to him R1 had one of the best organizations of the internal Resistance. It had assured contact with London and with the military leaders of the various departments. Its network comprised two fixed radio posts in Saône-et-Loire, two in the Ain, two in Haute-Savoie, two in the Isère, one in Savoie and one in the Loire, without counting the mobile posts of the Allied teams parachuted into the region. It had an Intelligence service which kept the German order of battle minutely up to date and was often able to warn the F.F.I. of threatening dangers in time. Thus the Tarare Maquis was warned that Police Commissioner Cussonac was preparing to attack it. It had state employees who gave it information, such as a Post Office official in the Drôme, called Bastia, who passed on all the communications of the Kommandantur, or a railway official who informed it of the movements of trains. In November 1940, it set up a factory to mass produce false papers—Laboratory TO/VX—which had 620 different seals and made 50,000 false ration cards and 30,000 identity cards for the benefit of the F.F.I.

The battle began on 22 August. On the American side it was fought by a brigade of motorized cavalry, Task Force Butler, and the 36th Division. On their side, the F.F.I. of the Drôme blocked the roads through their department to the German troops. The Wehrmacht put all it had into the field. The 11th Panzer Division used all its Tiger and Mark 5 tanks. They set off along the road from Montélimar to Crest, reached Clein which they set on fire, and came within five kilometres of the headquarters of the 36th Division; north of Montélimar, two battalions of F.T.P. contained the Germans for thirty-six hours, while waiting for the American armour to come up.

The Germans, who had managed to force a crossing of the Rhône at La Courcoude, were stopped on the Drôme where the bridge had been blown. Most of their infantry succeeded in crossing the river. But they had to abandon their equipment. Between 20 and 29 August, 1,500 vehicles were destroyed on the road from Montélimar to Loriol, and nearly 200 were taken intact. 3,000 prisoners fell into Allied hands; 1,000 dead were left on the field. Such was the result of the combined efforts of the F.F.I., who had first barred the way, of the American armour, which had come to the rescue, and of the American airmen, of whom one, on returning from bombing the incredible target, declared happily: "This has been the best day of the war for us."

By the 28th, the German Nineteenth Army had to all intents and purposes ceased to be a fighting force. The valley of the Rhône south of Lyons had been cleared, and the battle for Lyons began.

On 27 August, Colonel Descours, alias Bayard, commanding the F.F.I., had met General Truscott, commanding the American VIth Corps at Aspres, and one of his assistants, Colonel Huet, the defender of the Vercors, had conferred with the French Generals Touzet du Vigier and Brosset, commanding the 1st D.F.L.

On 28 August, Descours concentrated all the F.F.I. of the region round Lyons. He divided them into three groups: the first, to the west of the Rhône, co-ordinated the battalions of the Ardèche and the Loire; the second, north of Lyons, consisted of elements from the Rhône and the Ain; and the third, whose headquarters was at Bourgoin, consisted principally of the F.F.I. from the Isère. These troops were to concentrate to the west of Lyons, at the same time as General du Vigier's 1st Armoured Division. The Maquis and the regular troops were to deliver together the assault on the right bank of the Rhône while the Americans were to attack the left bank. Meanwhile, during the days preceding the liberation, the F.F.I. inside Lyons were fighting and sabotaging to hinder the concentration and evacuation of the Wehrmacht.

On 2 September, General Monsabert entered Saint-Étienne from where he was to direct the offensive. D-day was fixed for 3 September and H-hour for 06.00 hours. But early in the afternoon of the 2nd the enemy troops round Lyons withdrew to the town with the French, who reached the bank of the Rhône at 16.00 hours, hard on their heels. Unfortunately, the river was difficult to cross since the Germans had blown the bridges at 09.00 hours.

Of the town's twenty-eight bridges across the Rhône and the Saône only two remained intact, the Homme-de-la-Roche Bridge and the Saint-Vincent footbridge, both over the Saône. Moreover, both these bridges could carry only light weights, the first up to a maximum of two and a half tons, and the second a great deal less.

Among the bridges the Germans had blown, however, there were some which could be sufficiently repaired fairly rapidly to take a limited amount of traffic.

Early in the morning of Sunday, 3 September, repairs were made to the Wilson Bridge over the Rhône, which had only been damaged in spite of four attempts to demolish it. A few jeeps were able to cross from one bank to the other.

The next day, the American engineers put a thirty-yard Bailey bridge over the blown arch of the Guillotière Bridge which allowed one-way traffic for vehicles up to 30 tons.

On 12 September, road traffic was temporarily re-established over the viaduct of the Perrache railway, of which the Germans, not realizing that it had been doubled shortly before the war, had blown up only the older part.

On 16 September a footbridge four yards wide was established on the Wilson Bridge. On 23rd, a second Bailey bridge was erected on the La Guillotière Bridge allowing two-way traffic to vehicles up to 30 tons.

Thus, little by little, traffic was organized, but only slowly and precariously. On 11 September, Commandant Calloud, departmental Chief of Staff to the F.F.I., when coming to place his men at the disposal of André Mook-Aray, the engineer of Ponts et Chaussées, excused himself for being late by saying that he had had to wait an hour and a half for his turn at the Wilson Bridge.

But this is to anticipate the return to normal life. On 2nd September, protected by the obstacle of the river, the Germans evacuated the city. On the morning of the next day, the F.F.I. of the western sector, supported by Vigier's division, entered Lyons, while the F.F.I. of the left bank, crossing the footbridge which had remained intact, reached the peninsula between the Saône and the Rhône and began cleaning-up operations. At the same time General Brosset's 1st D.F.L. reached the suburbs.

Between 500 and 600 Germans were killed during these last battles. Of those who managed to escape, most were captured in ambushes set on the roads to Bourg and Mâcon.

Thus Lyons played its role of capital of the Resistance to the end.

But at the same time the Nazis had made it the capital of repression. On 29 June, 724 men were deported to Germany. On 1 July, 33 women. On 22nd July, 35 men and 20 women. At the beginning of August, ten trains, with locked wagons, carried away their tragic loads. On 11 August, 80 men and 17 women, most of whom were waiting to appear before the special section of the Court of Appeal, were removed from the Saint-Paul and the Saint-Joseph Prisons; they were sent to an unknown destination. Many people disappeared, never to be heard of again.

At the same time, throughout the whole region, prisoners were being "eliminated." In June, 122 prisoners were massacred at Neuville-sur-Saône, Saint-Didier-de-Formans, Saint-Laurent-de-Mure, Roche, Dagneux and Villeneuve. On 8 July, there were thirty executions at Porte-les-Valence. On 12 July, 28 people were shot at the edge of a wood in the Toussieu commune. On 19 July, 52 were executed at Châtillon d'Azergues.

In Lyons these horrors took place in the open street. In the centre of the town, on the Place Bellecour, during the night of 26 July, at about midnight, an explosion took place inside Le Moulin à Vent café, which was requisitioned by German officers and police, though civilians were also allowed to use it. Considerable damage was done, but no one was hurt. The next day, at noon, German soldiers in khaki, without helmets, but with sub-machine-guns and rifles, got out of a truck in front of the restaurant. They stopped all traffic in the street and cleared the northern pavement of foot passengers.

Coming by the La Guillotière Bridge and the Rue de la Barre, from the direction of the Montluc Prison, a grey car drove quickly up and stopped. The right door was opened; five bare-headed young men in plain clothes got out. They were immediately shot down, four on the pavement, and one in the street who fell with his head in the gutter.

These hostages were resistants who had been arrested in June and July, 1944, and could not therefore have taken part in the incident.

There was another appalling execution in the Rue Tronchet.

On evacuating a military school, the Germans authorized the French to use the supplies left behind: "They would rather they had them, than the Americans." The news spread. Two hundred and fifty to three hundred people gathered in front of the building. Loaves of bread, chocolate, biscuits, sheets and blankets were thrown down to them from the windows. Suddenly, as the result of a police report, a German truck drove up. Soldiers got out of it and opened fire with rifles and sub-machine-guns, killing twenty-six people and wounding twenty-one.

On 26 August, at Villeurbanne, an industrial suburb of Lyons, in the Place de la Bascule, where some young men had erected a barricade, a German patrol surrounded a block of houses and set it on fire. The inhabitants tried to escape, but the Germans fired on them to drive them back into the flames. After the Germans had gone, eight dead and three wounded were found. It would appear that no shots had been fired at them from the houses.

The same day, an armoured-car and a truck full of troops drove along the Quai du Rhône, between the Pasteur and Mualtière Bridges. There was the sound of an explosion, which it was later realized was due to a bursting tire. As a reprisal the Germans opened fire on a neighbouring house, smashing the door down with anti-tank guns. The house was soon in flames. The inhabitants took refuge in the cellars. The besiegers allowed them to come out, promising them their lives. In fact they killed five, as a punishment for a burst tire.

Terrible as these stories are, they are surpassed in horror by two killings that preceded the Germans' departure.

The Bron airfield had been bombed by American planes, and it had to be repaired. One hundred and nine prisoners from the Montluc Prison, two-thirds of whom were Jews, were taken from their cells and sent to the airfield. That evening, when the work had been done, seventy-three of them were shot by the Germans, and the rest by the Militia. Their bodies were heaped in a common grave which was found after the Liberation.

But the worst crime of all was committed at Saint-Genis-Laval, not far from the outskirts of Lyons.

On 19 August, in the late afternoon, about one hundred prisoners from the Montluc Prison were called out "without baggage" (they knew what that meant). Among them were a few women and two priests, the Abbé Larue, Professor of Science at the Lazarists' College and a battalion commander on the Reserve of Infantry, who during the Occupation had most courageously carried out his double duty of priest and soldier, and Canon Boursier, vicar of Sainte-Thérèse de l'Enfant Jésus at Villeurbanne.

They were tied together in couples, and pushed into trucks.

An hour later, at 08.30 hours, the inhabitants of Saint-Genis-Laval saw five or six cars and two trucks arrive.

The vehicles turned right into the village street and, after a brief halt to ask the way, set off along the road to Fort Côte-Lorette, a disused fort flanked by an empty guardhouse to the west of Saint-Genis-Laval.

A neighbour, who had climbed a tree, saw the trucks go in through the door. A little while later, salvoes of shots rang out, and were repeated at intervals during the next three-quarters of an hour.

Three prisoners tried to escape through the ground floor window of the guard-house. Germans in uniform and French in plain clothes fired at them. Only one succeeded in escaping, though wounded in the knee. The other two were recaptured, shot down, and thrown into the house which had been set on fire.

By ten o'clock that night it was entirely in flames. Forty-five minutes later, the two trucks full of Germans drove back through the village followed by the cars containing the French collaborators who had murdered their compatriots.

The vehicles had scarcely left, when a series of explosions began and continued from 10.45 to 14.00 hours. The guard-house was blown up by delayed action bombs which had been placed in the ruins to scatter and destroy the charred bodies.

Abominations such as these provoked reprisals. Yves Farge, the still clandestine Commissioner of the Republic responsible for R1, sent the following letter to the Regional Prefect, the President of the Red Cross, and the Swedish Consul, after the killing at Saint-Genis-Laval.

Lyons, 21 August, 1944.

Monsieur,

Our letter of 20 August informed you of the reasons obliging us to consider as hostages the 752 German prisoners taken by the Forces Françaises de l'Intérieur in Haute-Savoie, on 17 August last.

During the evening of 20 August, the German police took from the Montluc Prison at Lyons eighty French whom they shot at Saint-Genis-Laval. As a result, we have issued orders to the headquarters of the F.F.I. in Haute-Savoie to execute eighty German prisoners held in that department.

This order will have been carried out by the time this letter reaches you. We ask you to communicate this decision to the German military authorities, and to let them know that the F.F.I. of the Loire have captured a contingent of German police commanded by a certain Buhl, accompanied by his interpreter Leuman. From now on we shall consider these prisoners as hostages and we ask you to notify Colonel Knapp, head of the German police at Lyons, that Buhl and Leuman are at the top of the list of hostages who will be shot immediately if further French patriots are executed.

We apologize for the painful mission we are asking you to undertake, and assure you, Monsieur, of our distinguished sentiments.

The Delegate of the French Government
MAILLET.

The Regional Commissioner of the Republic
YVES FARGE.

The Colonel appointed by Headquarters
to the Southern Zone of Operations
BERNIQUET.

Such was the atmosphere in Lyons at the time of the Liberation. Moreover, various irregular tribunals were set up during the weeks which preceded and followed it. The original ones were intended to punish acts of resistance, but from 3 September they were replaced by others which tried people accused of being supporters of Vichy or of having collaborated. Three phases can be distinguished in this succession of judicial anomalies.

The first corresponded to the courts-martial set up by the Militia in January 1944. Their jurisdiction (if one may call it that) appeared to be entirely illegal. The judges were confined to no procedure. The accused had no benefit of counsel. The court-martial sat secretly in the prison in which its victims were held. The members of the court were militia-men in uniform, and they turned up the collars of their tunics so that their badges might not be identified. The accused did not even appear before his anonymous judges; and the verdict had already been agreed and the order for execution issued even before the court sat. When this parody of justice had been completed, the accused was brought into the room in which the court-martial sat for the first time. It was merely to be told that he had been condemned to death and would be executed forthwith.

The second phase began on the departure of the Germans. The Militia courts-martial were replaced, sometimes in the same localities, by ir-regular tribunals set up by the Resistance. These "People's Tribunals" sat in the Place of a suburb, or in the courtyard of a barracks recently recaptured from the Germans, and pronounced hasty and often ir-reparable sentences. It was thus that popular anger gave rise to a People's Tribunal at Saint-Fons, in the suburb of Lyons. No magistrate or pro-fessional lawyer sat on it, and its composition is still a mystery. Similarly, members of the F.T.P. constituted themselves into a tribunal and dis-posed of the lives of those who only the day before could have disposed of theirs, and with no greater formality. They sat in the barracks of Part-Dieu. Collaborators were taken to it, briefly interrogated, and taken to the Jonage canal where they were executed; no record of the court's deliberations was made, nor were even the names of the prisoners recorded. The number of their victims is estimated at twenty or thirty, but no one really knows. Three remand prisons were also used as courts, as were the Forts of Montluc, Saint-Paul and Saint-Joseph, where the summary sentences echoed the appalling executions the Militia and the Nazis had carried out there. What was to happen in Lyons if all the murders perpetrated in the town and the district by the Germans and their collaborators were to entail similar reprisals, if the 14,311 arrests, the 4,342 murders, the 290 women and girls raped, the common graves, which were being discovered all over the place now that the Germans had gone, were to incite the liberators to reply to evil with evil and to crime with vengeance? Would anyone in Lyons be able to break the vicious circle of reprisal and counter-reprisal?

Yves Farge, the Commissioner of the Republic, became the chief official of the region after 3 September. He was a man overflowing with vitality and ideas, whom Lucie Aubrac depicts walking "up and down, his pipe in his mouth, his black hair in disorder" in the offices in which, according to the period, he hid in secret, or worked as an official. He was a revolutionary of typically French temperament and tradition, even if later, when disappointed in the Fourth Republic, he drew nearer to Communism. In 1944, at the time of the collapse of the Vichy government, of the national rising of the population, and of the crimes committed by the Gestapo and the Militia, there was something about him of the Commissioners to the Armies of 1792.

He was unwilling to see "his" liberation, the liberation for which so many of his comrades had sacrificed their lives, spoilt either by the lukewarm or the over-excited. He wanted it to keep a balance between idealism and common sense, between what could be achieved and what must be achieved. In this respect, the composition of the staff he had gathered together as Commissioner of the Republic during the last days of the Occupation, in his little secret office in the Rue Bugeaud, was significant.

It was a sort of cocktail in which there were ingredients making for order side by side with others that were less so. Three lawyers' clerks, who, *a priori*, were not agitators, worked together with two Communists. There were also a trade unionist, a retired tramway employee, a professor of law who knew procedure, and a general who knew discipline. The head of his secretariat was one of the three lawyers' clerks, while his principal private secretary was one of the two Communists. Similarly, among the high officials who worked with him, the new Prefect of Lyons, Longchambon, curbed possible excesses. These ingredients were apparent in the balanced and lucid orders of Farge issued concerning measures of repression.

It was not that he was either indulgent or soft. The Republic, which was to come out of the turmoil, must, he said, be "pure and hard." But it must also be just. "There is no excuse for blind vengeance," he said, "but all these crimes explain it." It was therefore necessary to speak out clearly and forthrightly to prevent reprisals and curb disorder. He himself, on the day of the liberation, had been arrested in the streets of Lyons by individuals without authority who mistook him for a collaborator. A fortnight later, during a tour of inspection in Haute-Savoie, he had been arrested six times as a suspect. It was altogether too much. Such "stupidities" must cease.

To limit the excesses, Farge reorganized the tribunals, and this was a third phase in the evolution of these courts. To restore order, though it was still necessarily a revolutionary order, he took four decisions. First, he suppressed the illegal tribunals which were too often composed of irresponsible elements of D+1 F.F.I., or to use an abbreviation Farge employed, the R.D.S. (Resistants of September).

Secondly, during the first week after the liberation he set up an official court-martial which alone could try collaborators. It began to function on 9 September.

Thirdly, he had all the criminal records drawn up by the Committees of Liberation in the eight departments of R1 brought to the office of the Commissioner of the Republic in Lyons. They were investigated by two or three commissions whose duty it was to separate the prisoners arrested during the first days for valid reasons from those who had committed no serious offence. The latter were set free.

Fourthly, he introduced a system of "administrative arrests," each to be subject to his personal approval. His object was to place the guilty and the suspect in a place of safety, sometimes to prevent their escaping, but sometimes also to protect them from the anger of the populace. Some of those he imprisoned later came to thank Farge or his staff for saving their lives.

Finally, he assumed the power to reprieve prisoners condemned to death by the court-martial.

All this did not yet mean that justice was assured; but the setting up of such a judicial system at least made it a possibility, within the limits that the turmoil of the liberation allowed. It was a step towards a return to normal justice, a step which necessarily involved many imperfections and delays, but which had to be taken in difficult conditions. Within a few days, 1,800 prosecutions for collaboration were filed. It was certainly a great many, perhaps too many, but it was better than condemnation on verbal denunciations.

The right of being defended having been restored, every accused had the assistance of counsel. However, counsel often found the conditions far from favourable for the exercise of his functions. The documents were often sent him only a day or two before the hearing. Moreover, the atmosphere of the sessions was not always serene, nor the procedure legal.

One advocate was summoned to Montluc by the president of the court-martial. On handing him the documents in the case, he said: "The prisoner belonged to the action groups of the P.P.F. You can say what you like, but he'll be condemned to death."

On another occasion, a barrister summoned to appear before the tribunal was addressed as follows: "You will be given the brief at eight o'clock. The case will be heard at nine. The execution will take place at 16.00 hours." The barrister exclaimed: "Do you mean to say you have prejudged the case?" No one bothered to answer him.

There was a revolutionary atmosphere apparent in the repressive measures taken against collaborators; it was apparent too in the social measures which Farge, as an anti-capitalist, soon took against the big industrialists.

In most cases the Commissioner of the Republic had no sympathy with the capitalists. Two days after the liberation, on 5 September 1944, a decree sequestrated the Berliet Motor Co. and appointed, the former directors having been imprisoned, a young engineer called Mosnier to run the business.

This was an experiment in workers' democracy which Yves Farge, out of loyalty to what he considered to be the spirit of the Resistance, undertook spontaneously and brought to success. According to him the results were excellent.

With Farge, one of the principal regions had at its head a man whose conception of the Resistance was at once formidable and exacting. The Resistance must be militant, pitiless but pure, proud of its great deeds, jealous of the blood it had spilt and the suffering it had known; it must be determined to lead the country back into paths that were proper to it. But its destiny was a picture painted in contrasting colours, they were aspirations, ambitions too high and too noble for realization and there was blood too, and disappointed hopes, and justice denied. The men who came to power in such circumstances were neither choir-boys nor electoral agents. But their severities were backed by reason, and their errors by impersonal ambition.

When, on the morrow of the liberation of Lyons, the aircraft with the Cross of Lorraine bearing General de Gaulle landed on the Bron airfield, Farge was there to meet him. He told him the programme for the day: "The leaders of the Maquis will welcome you. You will see our teams of young people: the liaison agents of the Resistance. Tonight, you will dine with all the original resistants."

The General interrupted him to ask a question.

"What about the authorities?"

To which Farge replied in the most natural way in the world:

"In prison, General."

During the morning of 12 September, Gaston Merle and his wife set out on bicycles along the road to Châtillon-sur-Seine. As proprietor of the tobacconist's shop in the little village of Nod, in the Côte-d'Or, he was going, as he did every ten days, to fetch from the principal town in the canton the rations of cigarettes and tobacco for its two hundred and fifty inhabitants.

By 12 September the fighting was coming to an end. The encirclement of certain elements of the Wehrmacht was almost complete, though the majority had succeeded in escaping.

In the south, on 4 September, the 1st D.F.L., which had taken part in the liberation of Lyons, entered both Mâcon and Tournus without firing a shot. On the 5th, after a long day of manœuvring, it occupied Chalon-sur-Saône and Chagny. On the 7th, at Paray-le-Monial, reconnaissance elements, commanded by Colonel Demetz, established contact with the 25,000 F.F.I. from the south-west, the Schneider column, which had been pursuing the Germans all the way from the Pyrenees. On the 9th, Autun was defended yard by yard by General Blaskowitz. In the hard fighting that ensued, Bernard de Lattre de Tassigny, the General's son, who had enlisted at the age of sixteen by special permission of General de Gaulle, fell on the outskirts of the city, gravely wounded by a bullet. On the 11th, the Wehrmacht evacuated Dijon, which was occupied by patrols of the 3rd Chasseurs d'Afrique.

Nod lay on Route Nationale 71, which led from Châtillon-sur-Seine to Dijon. Monsieur and Madame Merle, so as to fetch supplies for their customers, were following the last strategic road which, theoretically, was still in German hands.

On reaching Châtillon, they were surprised to see in the first houses of the town, men in khaki uniforms watching the approaches. They went forward and found Frenchmen of Leclerc's division, who had come from the north after liberating Paris, and were now trying to make contact with the 1st D.F.L.

They could not know at Nod that the evening before a first contact had been made by air between the 2nd Armoured Division and the First French Army. A Piper-Cub, carrying an officer of Leclerc's division, had landed at Sombernon, within the lines of de Lattre's army. It had brought information about the advance of the southern detachment of the 2nd Armoured Division, which was on the extreme right of Patton's army, at Château-Villain and Châtillon-sur-Seine.

The Merles hurried forward. "How glad we are to see you," they cried. An officer came up. "Have you come along the Dijon road?" "Yes." "We have orders to advance as far as Chamesson. Are there still Germans there?" "We've come from Nod, the village beyond Chamesson. We've not seen a soul. You can advance as far as Nod." It was thus that on information given by a tobacconist the 2nd Armoured Division advanced four kilometres farther than had been expected; and that Nod usurped from Chamesson the privilege of becoming part of history.

When, at noon, the Merles returned to Nod, Captain Gaudet of the

12th Cuirassiers, commanding a detachment of some fifty men, with one tank, and several trucks and armoured cars, was already there.

Route Nationale 71 passed below the village. The tank took up its position at the southern entrance to the village, where the main road crossed the road to Céramique, in the direction of the Seine, which was low and narrow in these summer months. The armoured cars concealed themselves under the trees of an orchard which lined one of the outer roads of the village, a small steep lane called d'André. Two men with a bazooka took up their positions in a ditch a few hundred yards towards Aisey, the first village in the direction of Dijon, while another section watched the junction of the Bon-Espoir and Quicogne roads.

On the main road, immediately opposite the place where the commemorative stone was later to be erected, in front of the windows of Pierre Garnier, the architect who was to erect it, a wireless truck tried to get into communication with the 1st D.F.L. "N for Nicholas, O for Oscar, D for Desire," chanted the signaller, not wanting to mention in clear the fact that he was at Nod.

The population of the village had crowded down to the road. Food and bottles of old wine had been taken from their hiding-places. From the main road the soldiers could see the flags, which had been prepared against such an eventuality, flying from the houses. A Parisian F.T.P., helped by the Merles' son, climbed up the bell-tower of the church and hoisted the Tricolour. Everyone was eagerly awaiting the arrival of Leclerc's division.

It had not arrived by four o'clock. The inhabitants, leaving the children where they were, went up to the tobacconist's shop to hear on the radio a speech by General de Gaulle, which had been announced for that afternoon. But at 16.30 hours, the children came running back. The officer had sent them to warn the mayor, Bernard Huguenin, that the junction had taken place. All the village went down the hill, just in time to see Captain Guérard, of the 1st D.F.L., shake Captain Gaudet's hand at the foot of an ancient elm. "Mr. Mayor, have a temporary placard placed at once at the foot of this tree, so as to show the exact spot where the junction took place; it is an event that will have its place in history."

The mayor, accompanied by Pierre Garnier, went up the hill to Gaston Merle, who was also a carpenter. He selected a sheet of three-ply, and wrote the text of the notice: "Here, on 12 September 1944, took place the junction between de Lattre's army and Leclerc's division."

While the main junction was taking place at Nod, other contacts were being established between the two divisions. Twenty kilometres to the south, on the same Route Nationale 71, at Courceau, a patrol of the 2nd Armoured Division met a detachment of three cars of the 1st D.F.L. opposite the Café de la Seine. In one of them was General Brosset, and Lieutenant Eve Curie, who was a member of his staff.

The General followed the main road as far as Saint-Marc, eight kilometres from Nod. There he visited an elderly aunt who received him in her garden. Half an hour before there had been the sound of firing. She gave him a glass of wine, and then the General returned to his headquarters, leaving Lieutenant Curie to go on to Nod. While passing through Aisey, she met a half-track belonging to the Chad Regiment of the 2nd Armoured Division standing in front of the presbytery. "The modest vicarage," wrote de Lattre in his *Mémoires*, "was the scene of this historic encounter."

Between Lyons and Dijon, therefore, the trap was closing round the Germans. Its military results were to be the surrender of a column of 20,000 men, and the capture of one of the worst war criminals.

When orders for a general withdrawal had been issued on 20 August to the First Army then occupying the Atlantic coast, eighty thousand German soldiers set out for the east. They left behind them only the garrisons of the pockets of Royan, La Rochelle, Lorient and Saint-Nazaire. Their objective was to cross the Loire at Nevers and reach Dijon before the First French Army, which was moving up from Marseilles.

Most of them, after being involved in heavy fighting, particularly against Bertrand's group, which consisted of nearly five thousand men,[1] had succeeded in crossing.

But there remained a rear-guard of some 20,000 men, whose head had only reached Châteauneuf. This was the Elster column.

General Elster had under command three brigades of about 6,000 men each—sailors, airmen, coastal defence troops—well equipped with transport, armoured-cars and guns. These units had been on the march for a fortnight. For security reasons, they moved at night, marching stages of 30 to 40 kilometres on foot. Some men rode stolen bicycles. They halted each morning at dawn.

Towards the end of this exodus, in the neighbourhood of Châteauroux, the column crossed a village which had been bombed by American

[1] Colonel Bertrand, who before the disbanding of the Army of the Armistice had commanded the 1st Regiment of Infantry, had brought 1,800 of his men to the Maquis and had there been joined by several groups of F.T.P., the F.F.I. Surcourf Company and the 33rd Demi-Brigade, consisting of two battalions officered by Regular soldiers.

aircraft the night before. German soldiers passing through it had been killed and their bodies were found among the ruins.

Commandant Kühnemann, commanding the sailors, learnt there was an American officer in a nearby château. He went there. "You are a prisoner-of-war," he said. The American replied imperturbably in English: "Which of us is the prisoner of the other?" Kühnemann, unable to resolve the problem, merely destroyed the American's transmitting set and continued his march.

The next day, another American officer approached the column with a big white flag. "We are continuously aware of the position of your troops," he said. "If you want to spare your men the fate of those whose bodies you found in the village, you have only to surrender." Kühnemann had the American officer taken to Châteauneuf-sur-Cher, where his general was. The negotiations lasted for three days.

On 10 September, General Elster left his headquarters at Châteauneuf and went to Issoudun to negotiate his surrender with the Americans. Indeed, by some last professional soldier's scruple, he refused to surrender to irregular troops. An agreement in principle was signed. Informed of this at 18.00 hours, Colonel Bertrand insisted that the German General should surrender directly to those with whom he had been fighting, or there would be no cease-fire. The next day, at the mairie of Arçay, General Elster read him the agreement. His units then marched to Blois, where they were disarmed on 17 September.

This final march, according to the account given us by Commandant Kühnemann and the *Journal de Marche* of the Sologne Maquis, whose territory Elster's column crossed, had one most surprising aspect. The prisoners' march was entirely unsupervised by Allied troops, and they had been permitted by the Americans to keep their vehicles and equipment till they reached the appointed place for being disarmed. For three days they marched in regular formation, with arms, vehicles and colours, to the great astonishment of the Sologne F.F.I.

When a prisoner in America, General Elster was court-martialled by his comrades in captivity for having surrendered without a fight.

Another singular episode took place on 16 September, in Haute-Saône, when General Sudre, of the 1st Armoured Division, saw four French soldiers coming along pushing a baby-carriage. In the vehicle was the German Colonel von Alweyden, Chief of Staff to General von Brodowski, who was responsible for the massacre of Oradour. The four men, who had been taken prisoner by the retreating Wehrmacht, had been ordered to follow at the tail of the column and to look after the Colonel who had sore feet and could no longer march.

They had put him in the baby-carriage. "The Frenchmen pushed and pulled the baby-carriage, lifting the Colonel over the barbed wire. He was not heavy, but despite his complaints, our men purposely took their time over it, gradually lagging even farther behind the enemy column. The baby-carriage was soon alone. The Frenchmen then went to the main road and made their way towards a village whose steeple they could see." It was thus, according to Captain Berthet, that General Sudre learnt that von Brodowski was concealed in the district.

On 19 September, a patrol of the 2nd Algerian Spahis Reconnaissance Regiment was informed that two Germans were asleep in a barn near Corre, fifteen kilometres from Jussey. They hurried off and captured General von Brodowski in his sleep.

The General arrogantly insisted on being taken to Colonel Lecoq's headquarters, and was astonished not to find General Sudre there to receive him. In spite of his protests, the famous war diary containing an account of the Oradour massacre was taken off him. He was then sent to First Army Headquarters.

A few days later, when imprisoned in the citadel at Besançon, he tried to escape and was shot by a Senegalese sentry. And so he suffered in reality the fate he had so often attributed to the victims he had executed contrary to the laws of war by writing opposite their names in his war diary: "Shot while trying to escape."

Chapter III

FROM THE PYRENEES
TO THE LOIRE

In the quadrilateral bounded by the Pyrenees and the Loire, the Atlantic and the Rhône, the Liberation was carried out entirely by units of the Maquis.

On 17 August, Supreme Headquarters, S.H.A.E.F., gave them orders to go into action and seize the big cities and the more important centres of communication, such as Limoges, Poitiers and Châteauroux.

As a result, five military regions of the Resistance were to be liberated by the F.F.I. and the F.T.P. without help from regular troops. Four belonged to the former free zone: R3 (Montpellier), R4 (Toulouse), R5 (Limoges), and R6 (Clermont-Ferrand). The fifth, Region B (Bordeaux), formed part of the former occupied zone.

Of these five regions there were three, R3, R4 and R5, in which the Communists or crypto-Communists had achieved positions of authority. The military leaders, Gilbert de Chambrun at Montpellier, Ravanel at Toulouse, and Guingoin at Limoges, were all attached to the Party. Bordeaux, however, though less Communistic, was nevertheless also an F.T.P. objective. The region of Clermont-Ferrand, where a large Maquis was commanded by and had been recruited from non-Communists, escaped any immediate attempt by the supporters of insurrection to take over power.

The four regions on which the Communists had designs, consisting as they did of twenty-six departments, became subject to two kinds of activity. In the first place, there were military operations against the retreating Wehrmacht to hasten its departure or cut off its withdrawal; and, secondly, there was political rivalry between the Communist and non-Communist elements of the Resistance to acquire control of the liberated territories.

Aware of these dangers to the south-west, General Revers had planned a complete regrouping of the F.F.I. (Plan Caïman), which included the setting-up of a provisional government authority at Toulouse or in the Massif Central. The troops he believed to be at his disposal (A.S., O.R.A., and the Corps Franc Pommiès) were expected to amount to 15,000 or 20,000 men. These non-Communist forces should have been sufficient to clear the whole area and maintain order till the new authorities had taken over. In March 1944, the F.F.I. Generals de Benouville and Bertin-Chevance took the plan to Algiers. The French staff examined it. General Giraud sent la Vasselais as a delegate to France to study the terrain and the German fortifications in the south. On completing his mission, la Vasselais returned through Spain. His report was satisfactory. Algiers adopted Plan Caïman.

In May, Revers set up his headquarters at Languépie in the Lot-et-Garonne. But at the beginning of July he was informed that Algiers had cancelled the operation and he received orders to leave the south-west and go to Paris.

Some vestiges still remained of this still-born plan. In the month of August, the Corps Franc Pommiès moved north in accordance with Revers's plan; while Bertin-Chevance, unaware that Plan Caïman had been abandoned, went to Toulouse with the intention of exerting political influence there.

In fact, when on 20 August General Wiese decided on a general withdrawal of German troops in France, with the exception of those defending Marseilles and Toulon and the units holding the pockets on the Atlantic, the F.F.I. had no overall plan to co-ordinating the activities of the Resistance.

The German retreat began at the Pyrenees. On 17 August, Tarbes gave the signal for a general rising. In the morning, the Militia surrendered to the forces of the Resistance. The next day, after a tentative and unfruitful attempt at negotiation with the German General Mayr, two groups of the F.F.I., of which one, Captain Pierre's, was composed of factory workers, went into action. They arrested the German railway workers at the station. They attacked the depots, and burnt the stores of gasoline. The Germans tried to resist but the Patriotic Militia seized the arsenal and disarmed the garrison.

Unable to hold out against the insurgents, the Germans concentrated their forces, amounting to some 300 men, round the Larry district. There they formed a convoy of thirty vehicles to evacuate personnel and equipment. At 18.45 hours, the column set out for Toulouse. All along the road it was harassed by F.F.I. of the Secret Army. During one of these skirmishes the German General was wounded and taken prisoner as was his Chief of Staff.

The liberation spread like oil. On 18 August, the news of the Tarbes insurrection reached Lourdes, where the head of the F.F.I., commanding the Secret Army of the region, decided, in agreement with the Janot Company of F.T.P., to send an ultimatum to the German garrison. The German Colonel Kuliszcher agreed in principle to surrender on condition of being authorized to do so by his superior in Tarbes. If that town had already surrendered, or if the General commanding it gave him permission, he would lay down his arms.

Two cars, one flying the French flag, immediately set out for Tarbes. The first contained the F.F.I. officers, the second the German officers, bearing a letter asking for orders from their superior commander. They found the town still in turmoil. Firing was going on round the Larry district. General Mayr, on receiving the delegates from his subordinate at Lourdes, could not make up his mind what advice to give. The two cars returned to Lourdes empty-handed.

But the next day, at 13.00 hours, the Germans surrendered unconditionally, with the one reservation that a high official, the Sub-Prefect of Argelès, should countersign the document. A car was sent off to fetch M. de Saint-Pierre, the Sub-Prefect, who appended his signature. Without striking a blow, 167 men of the Secret Army and 25 of the F.T.P., together with a Maquis composed of Spaniards, obtained the surrender of 340 Germans and a colonel of the Wehrmacht.

After these first surrenders had been brought about by the F.F.I., General Wiese issued orders for the garrisons to leave the Pyrenean frontier. The liberation, for the most part, took place without fighting. At Pau, on the morning of Sunday, 20 August, the Germans were preparing to leave. At 14.00 hours, accompanied by many members of the Militia of both sexes, they left the town in eighty trucks by the Bordeaux road.

The F.F.I. entered the town and by evening the authorities appointed by the government of Algiers had taken possession of their offices.

As had happened after Tarbes, the news of the liberation of Pau spread quickly and brought about other liberations in its train.

At Oloron-Sainte-Marie, the train from Pau entered the station on Sunday at its usual hour. The travellers brought with them secretly the first number of the first free newspaper, the 44, which had just been placed on sale in Pau. Early in the afternoon, it was learnt that the garrison at Tarbes, which was retreating towards Oloron, had been attacked on the Montory Hill, and that a battle was in progress. At 16.30 hours, from the Place Clemenceau, in the centre of the town, a thick column of smoke arose. The Wehrmacht was burning the equipment, stores and baggage it did not want to take with it in its retreat.

And suddenly, watched by the delighted population, a German column formed up, crossed the town and took the road to Spain. The Tricolour was hoisted on the balcony of the ex-Kommandantur. The F.F.I. spread through the streets; and the brassard with the Cross of Lorraine was to be seen everywhere. The new Sub-Prefect, Boussard, entered the police headquarters that evening.

On 22 August, it was the turn of Orthez. The Germans, reinforced by the garrison from Mauléon, which had been hastily evacuated, packed their baggage as quickly as they could, burnt everything for which they had no use, and requisitioned bicycles, horses, carts and cars. The next day, at 08.00 hours, the last German had left. At 10.00 hours an official car arrived bearing the Allied flags. And during the afternoon the Vichy municipality was turned out.

By the 24th freedom was flowing northwards from the Pyrenees, and had reached Dax. For three days the town had been in a state of feverish excitement. On 21 August, a heavily armed German column arrived from the south and stopped in one of its squares. It was a short halt, for the Maquis was on its heels. The trucks stopped just long enough to take on board some militiamen and their families before continuing on their way north.

At dawn next day the Germans still remaining in the town began to evacuate the hotels, barracks and offices. They hastily loaded their archives on to requisitioned trucks. They threw hundreds of rounds of ammunition of every calibre into the Adour. Officers requisitioned plain clothes.

In the middle of the afternoon the Germans blew up part of the Post Office and the Saint-Paul telephone exchange before leaving.

On their heels, Léon des Landes, whose real name was Léonce Dussarat, a native of Dax, and head of the Maquis of the Landes, made his triumphal entry with his lieutenants Augé and Lamothe. All the groups of neighbouring F.F.I., even those of Mont-de-Marsan and Tarbes, escorted him to the mairie, into which he was carried in triumph by a crowd of admirers.

It was a scene characteristic of the south-west: the wild cheering, and excited gestures marking the triumph of a son of the region, of whom circumstances had made a hero. It was also a scene most characteristic of the period, of those wonderful days when liberty seemed to have been miraculously reconquered.

Léon des Landes, an iron merchant in a small way, had led a hard life for the last three years. His citations from de Gaulle and King George VI bear witness to it:

Monsieur Dussarat fought with a British organization in the neighbour-hood of Bordeaux, in 1943 and 1944, and became Departmental Head of the Landes. Having refused to reveal the position of an arms' depot, he fled from his house, when an attempt was made to arrest him, and organized throughout the department all the sabotage operations, including the com-plete destruction of a train of munitions at Laluque and of a gasoline depot at Dax.

On 20 August, he personally directed the 700 men of the Maquis who took part in the liberation of the Landes. . . .

Such was Léon des Landes, sturdy of body, decisive in word and ges-ture, imperturbably confident in his star, but not always prudent or diplomatic.

The Wehrmacht's withdrawal not only caused temporary adminis-trators of justice such as Léon des Landes to appear, but brought to light the crimes committed by the Gestapo and its French auxiliaries. These cannot be passed over if the outrages committed at the Liberation are to be understood.

In the Avenue Trespoey in Pau there was a fine villa in the Basque style, two storeys high, with a terrace and a balcony in the middle of a garden. It was the Villa Saint-Albert, the Gestapo Headquarters, and its basement had been turned into cells for prisoners condemned to death. After the Liberation, this sinister place was opened. One of the first visitors gave the following description: "There were inscriptions on the plaster walls. A name, an address, and then dates, a long series of days. In this dungeon, without light or air, a brief and moving prayer had been written up: 'Truber, of Lacq; I leave a wife and two children, look after them.' Farther on, as a last defiance, some firm hand had drawn a Cross of Lorraine in chalk surmounted by the words 'Death to the Boches.' There were signatures all over the narrow wall: an ex-serviceman, a naval lieutenant, a poor boy of seventeen . . . 'My last day. Good-bye.' Some had the magnificent courage to joke; others had turned to religion: 'All things come from God, blessings as well as trials; we cannot understand His designs but as Christians we accept them.'"

There were other discoveries, even more tragic than these graffiti, that incited to vengeance after the German withdrawal. The newspaper *IVe République*, of 30 August 1944, described the common graves, into which the victims of the Gestapo and the Militia had been thrown at random.

Murdered by the Boches, buried alive by the Militia, fifty patriots lay in graves on the rifle range. . . . Four large graves have been discov-ered. . . .

Having covered the bodies with a thin layer of earth, the criminals concealed the grave with branches.

A dozen German prisoners are starting to uncover the first grave which will undoubtedly prove to be one of the most important. From the first strokes of the pick limbs appeared and then, by using the spade with infinite precaution, the first bodies were disinterred.

These bodies were a hideous spectacle. Their limbs were entwined as if they were embracing each other in their appalling death.

As these common graves were being discovered, the circumstances in which the victims had been executed were also coming to light. Nor were they calculated to appease the fury of the French.

When they had been taken out of the trucks, the victims were led one by one to the foot of the butts and there, either standing or kneeling, they were executed with revolvers or bursts of machine-gun fire. The police doctor has discovered marks on the body which show without doubt that these unfortunate people had been tortured before being executed. In particular, several of them had twisted and broken arms. Some still wore the bandages with which their murderers had blindfolded them, and their hands were tied behind their backs. When they had executed their victims, the Germans generally departed, leaving the Militia to bury them. The latter were always informed of the executions and arrived on the scene in cars. The graves had, of course, been previously dug by the patriots who were to be executed. The heap of bodies at the foot of the butts was casually moved to the edge of the graves and kicked into them.

Their macabre duty over, the militiamen returned singing to their cars, proud of their exploit, leaving behind them in the night and the horror of the grave their pathetic victims still convulsed in atrocious agony.

These were the sorts of spectacle that the F.F.I. and the F.T.P. discovered at Pau, and in many other places in the south-west after the Liberation. Horror is also contagious. In the over-heated atmosphere of this summer of crisis, news spread quickly and anger aroused anger, reacting inflammably on the liberation of many towns, the effects varying from department to department.

Between the Pyrenees and the Loire, the Resistance, there left to itself, did not operate in the same manner in all districts. In this region, which amounted to two-fifths of the whole of France, there were columns that manœuvred in much the same way as regular units, and in accordance with a joint strategy. But there were also Maquis who behaved almost entirely as local units, fought in their own department and thought they had done enough when they had liberated their own district and occupied its chief town.

Among the columns which moved in the general direction of the north towards strategic objectives, we have already mentioned the four to five thousand men under Léon des Landes who, reinforced by other Maquis, both Spanish and French, converged on Bordeaux, the capital of the south-west, where decisive political events were to take place. Others moved farther east along the axes of the Wehrmacht's withdrawal, which they were trying to intercept. Their objective was the zone between Lyons and Dijon through which the Germans were endeavouring to retreat.

The most important of these columns was the Corps Franc Pommiès, which played a decisive part in the liberation of the south-west. Colonel Pommiès was a professional soldier. He was forty and had had a distinguished career. He had been responsible for the suppression of sixty-eight officers or agents of the Gestapo and controlled a network, which possessed 3,000 card-indexes of enemy agents or suspects, in the very heart of the German organizations. But this Resistance group's ambition was to fight.

In April 1944, it consisted of four sub-groups in direct contact by wireless with Algiers and London, and amounted to 12,000 men of whom 7,000 were armed. Their uniform was shorts, a blue shirt and a tricolour brassard. After the landing in Provence, the Corps Franc went into action at Pau and Tarbes. In an action lasting from the 19th to the 21st, on the Lannemezan plateau, it took General Mayr and his Chief of Staff prisoner.

After the liberation of Toulouse, the French Command gave the Corps Franc Pommiès the job of preventing the Wehrmacht evacuating the south-west. It was thought at first that it would retreat into Spain, with the Gestapo and the collaborators. Pommiès immediately put 3,000 men into the Pyrenees to occupy the valleys, passes and summit posts. At the same time, to clean up the southern Atlantic coast, he sent 5,000 men to occupy the crossings of the Adour or to concentrate in the Mimizan district.

But it was suddenly learned that the enemy had discarded the idea of taking refuge in Spain and was moving north-east, into the Autun region, in the hope of evading encirclement. The C.F.P. immediately regrouped. It left part of its forces on the Pyrenees to keep watch on the frontier, while another, more numerous detachment, consisting of 4,800 men who made up most of the Schneider column, moved up towards Autun.

The Schneider column was commanded by two officers of the colonial army, Captain Bertin-Chevance, who was promoted to General in the Resistance, and Colonel Schneider. It consisted of an amalgam of the

Toulouse Resistance and the Corps Franc Pommiès. Amounting to 9,000 men, it was almost equivalent to a division. Ill-shod and insufficiently armed, their transport captured from the enemy and often too worn to be of much service, these troops were to attempt a difficult manœuvre against German units which were still strong and organized. Their job was to get between the two axes of the Wehrmacht retreat, one of which ran south-west and north-east through the valleys of the Massif Central, and the other west and east through Touraine and Berri. If the operation was successful, the Schneider column would reach the great turn-table of the Nivernais before the retreating Germans, bar the road to Dijon and the Langres plateau to the enemy, and impede his regrouping to attack the flank of the First Army which was moving on a north-south axis.

It was therefore a true strategic manœuvre these units of the F.F.I. were carrying out.

On 9 September, the Fusiliers-Marins, the advance elements of the regular army, and the Pommiès column entered Autun where there was hard fighting for three days. On the 10th, 5,000 Germans, who were trying to retake the town, were surrounded and surrendered, abandoning to Pommiès the arms and vehicles he needed to complete his equipment. On the 11th, the remainder of the enemy troops, broken, harassed and having blown the bridges across the Charité behind them, burnt such material as remained to them, dispersed, and individually sought routes to the north. The Schneider column, exhausted and its equipment much in need of maintenance, devoted 12 and 13 September to cleaning up the Nivernais-Morvan-Burgundy pocket, while de Lattre's army, having nothing to fear now from its left, continued its advance.

Other columns also took part as organized forces in the campaign to liberate France. By and large, these columns and brigades were properly run by Regular officers, and entirely devoted themselves to fulfilling their strategic role. Since they had moved out of their own departments, they were not tempted to play the part of justiciars or assume political responsibilities. It was not, generally speaking, by them that the disturbances and excesses of the Liberation were committed.

Nevertheless, in most departments of the south-west there were units of the Maquis whose activities were largely limited to their own departments or neighbouring cantons and whose main ambition was to liberate their own territory. Till this was achieved, they fought furiously. Once the chief town had been taken, and occupied, however, they tended to split up. Some of their units accompanied the columns in their strategic manœuvres outside the department. Many others were more anxious to organize or exploit their conquests than they were to join in the operations.

The Dordogne was one of the departments in which the liberation became most dramatic. The Green plan, the Violet plan and the Tortoise plan had been given a thorough preparation there. All the planned railway and telegraphic cuts were immediately put into effect on receipt of the B.B.C. messages. Moreover, the Dordogne was on the route the German units took when moving up to reinforce the north, and among them was the Das Reich division, which was attacked near Souillac and lost several hours.

The result was that, in June 1944, the enemy took reprisals throughout the department; all the evidence emphasizes the number of villages burnt, hostages shot, and other atrocities committed by the Georgians who were incorporated in the Wehrmacht, or by the Militia who were using North African auxiliaries.

On their side, the F.F.I. and F.T.P. led the Germans, their satellites and collaborators a hard life. Apart from frequent ambushes on the roads, there were other incidents which are evidence of the atmosphere of insecurity in which the Germans lived. For instance, a train, which was known to be carrying prisoners, stopped in the station of La Cave on the Bordeaux line. Some F.F.I. got into it, searched the compartments and killed six of the seven Germans. Conversely, ten F.F.I. were surprised by a group of thirty Germans, guided by a local woman. Only one escaped; the other nine were disarmed and shot.

There were some audacious raids at Bergerac. On 2 August, the maquisards entered the powder works to seize some alcohol, wounding or killing the sentries. Four days later, there was another raid, this time on the prison, where they liberated fifteen political prisoners. Again, on 20 August, in the Périgueux district, an attack was made on an arms and ammunition depot from which 300 rifles, sub-machine-guns, 47 mm. and 25 mm. shells, and grenades were removed. The Germans were perpetually on the alert and their life was becoming extremely difficult. It was difficult also for the civilian population which, caught between two or three fires, exposed to reprisals and counter-reprisals, never knew in the morning who might attack them during the day. There was a privately owned château, near Ruffignac, which throughout the period of the liberation was successfully visited by a "white" Maquis, that is to say a non-Communist one, by a "red" Maquis of the F.T.P., and by Germans of the Wehrmacht. The conversation was always bilingual, in French with the first, in German with the last, but also in German with certain elements of the "red" Maquis, which had been recruited from foreigners who could not speak French. Relations between the various groups of the Maquis were often far from cordial. A doctor, who had treated a member of one Maquis, was executed by another. As for the village of Ruffignac, the inhabitants were ordered to evacuate it and the Germans razed it to the ground. The evacuation took place amid such panic that, when the Germans arrived to set fire to the village, they found babies forgotten in the abandoned houses.

There was such an atmosphere throughout the countryside in which the Francs-Tireurs hid and fought that they were bound to be affected by it. The difficulty of controlling often undisciplined troops, the improvised apparatus of military justice which, even when it tried to operate in a regular manner was none the less immediate and subject to political influences, the lack of money which obliged them to make "levies" —all these lent something of an atmosphere of civil war to the liberated districts.

In the towns the situation was perhaps even worse. The Germans, unable to control all the territory of the department, had shut themselves up in Périgueux, the principal town, and in Bergerac, one of the sub-prefectures.

In Périgueux there was a reign of terror which lasted three months. On 7 June, as soon as the landing in Normandy some thousand kilometres away was announced, Popineau, the Prefect of Dordogne, left hurriedly, believing he was already in danger from paratroops. He had also been warned that the maquisards were planning to cut his throat that very night while he was in bed. Callard, the Sub-Prefect of Bergerac, heard over the radio that he had been appointed to replace him. His first difficulty was to take up his new post through the insurrection which had already started. He did so by borrowing an ambulance. His next difficulty was to tell the Maquis that the bed had changed not only its sheets but its occupant. This he succeeded in doing through friends in the Resistance.

For three months, Callard was to find very difficult conditions in which to maintain order and save the town. The German commander of Périgueux was a Balt by origin, a fanatic who shouted and threatened; the atmosphere of siege in which he and his troops were to live during the last days of the Occupation deprived him of the little composure of which he was capable. At a last interview with the Prefect, he dashed into his office and shouted: "I know that the Maquis have infiltrated into Périgueux. If a single shot is fired, I shall burn the town, and kill the women and children." Placing his revolver on the table, he went on: "And I shall begin by killing you, Monsieur le Préfét." Callard opened a drawer, took out a revolver and placed it beside the other. "It's a question," he said, "of which of us fires first."

It is impossible to give any figure for the summary executions carried out by the Germans, the Militia and F.T.P. The Cours Montaigne was one of the places where the bodies of the assassinated were assembled. In turn, the victims of the Nazis and of the "terrorists" washed the same cobbles with their blood.

This lasted from 6 June to 28 August, when the Germans left; and it cannot be asserted that similar conditions did not continue for some time after their departure.

The state of opinion after the Liberation can be gauged from letters from inhabitants of the town which were opened by the Post Office censor. Here are a few extracts:

It has not been pleasant to see all the arrests since Sunday, both men and women, 2,500 women it is said, and each time one is taken, people clench their fists as they go past and cry: "To the gallows! To the gallows!" It is not a pretty sight. . . .

. . . As soon as the town was liberated the traitors were punished. 530 men were arrested and 630 women; 83 were condemned to death and executed, and this continues. Our chief engineer was sacked and thrown into prison as well as other bosses. It was almost a revolution. You saw only thousands of young men with rifles, sub-machine-guns, grenades, etc. . . .

The tendencies which have become apparent are more and more disturbing and make one tremble for the future. A ferment of hatred and envy is developing in frightening proportions and gives rise to disgraceful actions inspired by a spirit of hatred which will stop at nothing; people are killed indiscriminately and the whole thing is appallingly sad. . . .

. . . From the point of view of internal politics, it is chaos. The popular front has come to life again. The Communists believe their hour has come! As for the Catholics, they believe nothing at all, they're merely the sheep being led to the slaughter. . . .

. . . There are two groups of Maquis who think of nothing but defeating each other. One of them, wild, undisciplined and pillaging, has a mortal hatred for the other. How can any reasonable solution be reached without order and without a leader?

After the departure of the Germans, was not another trial of strength beginning with the Resistance?

Chapter IV

THE TRIAL OF STRENGTH

Was there really a trial of strength between the Communists and the Gaullists at the time of the Liberation? Some say that there can be no doubt of it; others say it miscarried.

"The French," wrote Devinat, a Radical-Socialist Minister in Queille's government, in the *Manchester Guardian* at the end of 1948, "have just passed through a profound revolution which has only recently and partially been brought under control. . . . If the action taken by the Provisional Government foiled the Communist Party's basic calculations, it is no less true that the Party succeeded in considerably widening its influence at the period. Numerous departments in the south were in fact for long months under its control. Under cover of the purge, it shook the official hierarchy of the country. Indeed, till April 1947, it had influential representatives within the Government itself and was able to put into practice the methods applied with more success elsewhere, in Czechoslovakia and other countries."

Where a bourgeois politician trembles retrospectively, Communist militants on the other hand were indignant at a failure for which they blamed the French Communist leaders. Duclos, it was declared at the constitutive assembly of the Kominform of Szklarsko-Poreba (22 to 27 September 1947) was suffering from "parliamentary cretinism."

He himself recognized "the small effectiveness of the French Party" since the Liberation.

Thorez, according to a Yugoslav Communist, Marko-Ristitch, who in 1947 was still in the good graces of the Kremlin, was nothing more during these years in which the war was coming to an end than a superpatriot, a chauvinist, for whom, scandalously enough, the French Communist Party "was not under the thumb of Russia."

According, therefore, as to whether one accepts the views of a bourgeois or a Communist, the French Communist Party appears either to have attempted or avoided a trial of strength after the Liberation.

374

In August 1944 there was great risk of revolution.

On the Saturday after the liberation of Paris, General Eisenhower entered the capital accompanied by Bradley. He there met de Gaulle who told him of his "anxieties." Some of these were no surprise to the Supreme Allied Commander. De Gaulle asked for food for the liberated capital, and for uniforms and military equipment for the F.F.I. But, Eisenhower goes on in his *Crusade in Europe:* "A serious problem in view of the disorganized state of the city was the speedy establishment of his own authority and the preservation of order." In his *Mémoires,* the Head of the Provisional Government writes: "I told the Supreme Commander that for reasons both of the morale of the population and eventually of the preservation of order, I would keep the 2nd Armoured Division under my direct command for a few days," that is to say the Leclerc division which had just entered Paris.

But from there on the stories of the two leaders differ. Eisenhower's account seems more precise and complete than de Gaulle's. According to Eisenhower, it was not only the French division de Gaulle asked for but also "the temporary loan of two American divisions to use, as he said, as a show of force, and to establish his position firmly."

Eisenhower had no troops to lend. The best he could do was to promise "that two of our divisions, marching to the front, would do so through the main avenues of the city." He suggested that de Gaulle should review these divisions as they marched through and that General Bradley should stand beside him "to symbolize Allied unity."

On 29 August, the French radio from London announced that a march past of American troops had just taken place on the Champs-Élysées in the presence of General de Gaulle. It was, says Eisenhower, "possibly the only instance in history of troops marching in parade through the capital of a great country to participate in pitched battle on the same day."

It was also perhaps the first example of such a request being made by de Gaulle to his allies. Did the danger of insurrection appear to him so great that it justified such an unusual attitude?

Three months later, during the course of a conversation with General Passy, de Gaulle gave the following reason: "The Communists had seized all the sources of production. I could not subdue them, for to do so I should have had to bring several of our five divisions back from the front. And it was essential that they should be in the battle if France was to figure with honour among the victors." This appears to be the reason for two surprising decisions de Gaulle took at this time: the first was this request to Eisenhower for two divisions, the second, four months later, was a matter of far greater importance, his own journey to Moscow in December 1944: "In order to obtain from the Communist Party the year of respite I needed to get the situation in hand, I had to go to Moscow and sign agreements there." These two apparently quite dissimilar overtures were both to be explained by the threat of insurrection which then hung over the centre of political life in the liberated capital.

The trial of strength seemed also to be imminent in the provinces. There were four regions in the south-west which had been liberated without the assistance of the Allied armies and in which the preservation of order depended on the F.F.I. or F.T.P. Maquis.[1] In these regions, there were four great towns in which the Communists had seized the principal posts. At the Liberation, there was a risk that these towns might secede from the authority of the central power. Bordeaux, Toulouse, Limoges and Montpellier were practically cut off from Paris, where moreover the government was scarcely reinstalled. To communicate from one of these towns with the capital, it was often necessary to employ the secret circuits established by the Resistance, that is to say go through London or Algiers. The local authorities appeared to be independent; and while the Commissioner of the Republic tried to maintain order, the military leader of the F.T.P. often tried to upset it. Between these two lay an uncertain public opinion, a Maquis suddenly swollen by undesirable elements, an insufficient or demoralized police force, the dismissed Vichy authorities, who were often being hunted down, the still inexperienced Gaullist authorities, irregular courts, summary executions, and the paying off of old scores that seemed often to derive from the class struggle. The moment seemed propitious for a trial of strength and favourable to revolution. How was it that in Bordeaux as in Toulouse, in Limoges as in Montpellier, such circumstances should have resulted in a slow but nevertheless definite restoration of order? Each town, in the then dislocated state of the country, presents a particular case, even if the result was to be the same in all of them.

In the days that followed on the Liberation, every hotel in Bordeaux was requisitioned by a different set of clients, who remained grimly isolated from those of the other establishments. The heads of the F.T.P. lived in the Hôtel de Normandie and drank at the Café du Commerce: these were Colonel Martel, the son of a former Communist deputy, and a certain Captain or Commandant "Docteur" of whom no one knew either his exact rank, for he always wore plain clothes, or his precise nationality, for he talked French with an Oriental accent.

[1] Cf., page 363.

The Hôtel de Bordeaux has in its registers (if they still exist) other former clandestine fighters, whose politics were opposed to those of the Hôtel de Normandie: these were "Aristide" and "Triangle."

"Aristide," whose real name was Landès, was an agent of the British Secret Service. He was twenty-six years old, an architect in civilian life, and a major in the war. Only recently become naturalized British, he nevertheless supported the interests of the Crown with a marked British stubbornness. It was almost as if, for him, the Hundred Years War was still going on and he wished to preserve Bordeaux as a British enclave in France. In front of the Hôtel de Bordeaux, the Senegalese, whom he had recruited from prison camps, presented arms in the English manner and marched up and down with all the stamping of sentries outside Buckingham Palace. According to some, his ambitions were more down to earth; it was thought he was trying to recover the millions of pounds worth of merchandise the Germans had stored in the port for the British. Whatever his incentive, he tried to become the real power in the town. His first secret interview, in about May 1944, with the non-Communist leaders of the Resistance was, according to one of them, Gabriel Delaunay, "dramatic."

"When we both arrived, General Morraglia and I, in the Bordeaux Park," he recounted later, "we felt we were in a trap. Indeed, people were clearly watching us from several points and we both thought at the time that the Gestapo were on to us. There was nothing else we could do but go on to our meeting-place. It took place in the southern part of the big park. Christian first came up to us alone; he then went off and brought Aristide back with him. As Aristide came up to us, we realized there were armed men concealed behind the trees and bushes. Aristide's first words, which were not calculated to make a good impression on us, were these: 'Don't move. I've taken my precautions. One movement and you're dead men!' We replied by pointing out that, if we had taken the same precautions and had brought our armed friends with us, a pretty battle would already be taking place. Our discussion took a very bitter turn. Aristide said that he alone was responsible for the south-west and everyone must obey him. Morraglia and I naturally held a different view.

"At one point, the conversation almost led to blows. I remember particularly this phrase of Aristide's: 'You forget that I am an officer of the British Army, and have been decorated with His Majesty's highest honours, and that all the French, whoever they may be, must obey me.' To which Morraglia replied: 'You forget that I am a general, a Commander of the Legion of Honour, and that I have ten French citations which must be worth more than yours.' "

The meeting lasted about an hour and a half, and ended in practically no other result than a declaration of war.

The pre-liberation period in Bordeaux gave rise to a dramatic episode in which a French Resistance leader and a German policeman played the principal parts.

Dhose was a professional policeman who in peacetime had exercised his talents in Stuttgart. Sent to Bordeaux, this extremely subtle man departed from the ordinary methods the Gestapo used towards the resistants. He arrested them, of course, but in the first place treated them with an almost sinister lack of brutality. He conversed about politics with them, asserted his love for France, and his admiration for the Resistance, whose role he thought should not be limited merely to fighting the Germans. Having reached this point in the conversation, he would strike the chord, often a particularly sensitive one, of anti-Communism. Rather than engage in a hopeless struggle against the Wehrmacht, why did the Resistance not prepare, hand in glove with the Gestapo, to fight the common enemy in the east when the war was over? In January 1944, the French radio in London sent orders to execute at once and at all costs an F.F.I. leader called Grandclément. There was scarcely a day when it did not repeat: "Beware of Grandclément! Grandclément is a traitor." It seemed probable that Grandclément was one of this Machiavellian Dhose's victims.

It was indeed the case. Grandclément, leader of the Bordeaux Resistance, was a man of some thirty-five years of age, handsome, charming and intelligent, who had great influence over the F.F.I. officers and the members of his movement, the O.C.M. (Civil and Military Organization). He recruited many of its members among students. From the beginning of 1943, he was in receipt of a great deal of money for his organization, and on the strength of it he achieved a considerable importance in Region B.

He had a staff, of whom most were later deported, five organized groups in the Gironde, the Lot-et-Garonne and the Landes, a parachute team which covered the whole region, a weapon-training school, which carried on secretly at 102, Cours d'Alsace-Lorraine in Bordeaux, Maquis in the Corrèze and the Landes, secret channels for reaching them, radio contact with the War Office in London, and a courier system across the Spanish frontier. He also had considerable arms: more than 2,000 submachine-guns, pistols, grenades and tons of explosives.

In July 1943, Grandclément was in Paris. His wife, who took part in his activities had remained in Bordeaux. Léon des Landes, on the basis of radio messages and messengers from London, told Madame Grandclément that she and her husband were "blown," and suggested she should go into hiding. She refused to believe him, laughed in his face, and remained in her house to await her husband's return. The Gestapo arrived first, took her away, and organized a trap for some of Grand-clément's lieutenants.

However, on 19 September, Grandclément was arrested in a café in Paris, where he had arranged a meeting with a double-agent. He was put in Fresnes for three days and then transferred to Bordeaux on 23 September.

This was how Dhose, speaking of himself in the third person, re-counted his interview with the prisoner:

"He interrogated 'Bernard' all day and all night, showed him the list of persons his organization had arrested, and of those it was going to arrest, among whom were his two lieutenants, Malleyrand and Chazeau, whose families were already imprisoned. He told Grandclément that his organization knew the approximate localities of the parachuting grounds owing to observations made by the Luftwaffe and certain ad-missions, adding that he would be able to find the depots of arms by using the appropriate Wehrmacht machines (detectors).

"He then proposed to stop the arrests in process and free the people already arrested on condition that the arms held by the Resistance were handed over."

Grandclément at first refused this curious suggestion of a "gentle-man's agreement." Dhose gave him a night to think it over. Next day, Grandclément changed his mind. "Personally," he said to Dhose, "I accept your proposal but I must get the opinion of my subaltern officers," and he asked to be set at liberty for a few hours. It was not a responsi-bility Dhose was prepared to assume on his own. He consulted the other heads of the K.D.S., Luther, John and Nerich. Luther went to Paris to submit the case to Knocken, second-in-command to Oberg, chief of the S.S. for the whole of France, who gave his assent.

On his return, Grandclément asked to be allowed out again next day, which was once more agreed to. He returned from this second outing with the agreement of his lieutenants, Malleyrand and Chazeau. A first arms depot, at Sabres, in the Landes, would be handed over at once.

During a halt at Captieux, when on the way to make this first delivery of arms, Grandclément, together with Malleyrand and Chazeau, drafted in proper form the "gentleman's agreement" with Dhose, who was accompanied by Kunesch.

It was agreed that the Maquis would commit only spectacular but ineffective acts of sabotage, and that the maquisards would deliver to the Germans forty or fifty tons of arms parachuted by the British and concealed in 132 secret depots. In return, the Gestapo would release 180 of the 300 resistants it had arrested in Bordeaux, among whom, of course, would be Grandclément himself.

This agreement was clearly signed with enthusiasm, for as soon as the ink was dry the two main instigators conceived a fantastic extension of it. Since Grandclément and Dhose had succeeded in reaching an agreement on the local level, why should they not try to extend their plan to the national level by getting Hitler and de Gaulle to sign a similar agreement? The two enemy camps would be united in a common front against Bolshevism.

The absurd proposal was pursued further. Through Knochen, Dhose submitted his idea to Hitler who, it is said, received it with a marked lack of enthusiasm. But even before they had received the Führer's reply, he had decided in agreement with Grandclément to send two French emissaries of the Resistance to Algiers to "contact" de Gaulle. Inaugurating a method of escape which was to be used again later, they shut the emissaries in a specially arranged boot of a car. Dhose himself drove them to San Sebastian, from where they went on to Algiers. Alas, de Gaulle, no more than Hitler, appreciated their initiative. As soon as the emissaries arrived they were accused of treason and shut up in a concentration camp in southern Algeria.

Months went by. On 22 July, a resistant named Jean Chablin of the Aristide-Triangle group found Grandclément in the Restaurant Volant Doré, in the Rue de Hautoir, in Bordeaux, where he was having lunch with his lieutenant, Duluguet. Jean Chablin told the former head of the O.C.M. that the D.M.R. Triangle suggested he should go to London to justify himself. Grandclément accepted. It was arranged that he and his wife should appear to have been kidnapped from Duluguet's house. In fact, furniture was upset, cartridge cases and traces of revolver bullets were scattered through the rooms as if the F.F.I. had made a raid. After the Grandcléments and her husband had gone, Madame Duluguet waited an hour before informing the German police.

The three prisoners, who still believed it was all pretence, were taken on 27 July to an airfield. The reception committee were armed with daggers, grenades and sub-machine-guns, in case Grandclément had warned the Germans. As the Germans did not arrive, the three travellers were arrested and taken to a cave where they were submitted to a first interrogation. Grandclément revealed all the secrets of his collaboration with Dhose and admitted that he was responsible for the arrest of 3,000 patriots and the execution of 300 of them.

At noon on 28 July, at Belin, he was handed over to Aristide, who interrogated him at length. That very evening, he was shot on an old farm at Muret in the Landes. His wife and Duluguet were executed two kilometres away. There is evidence that Aristide killed them himself.

This bloody episode was the end of Dhose's machinations. But they resulted in the Bordeaux Resistance being decimated and disorganized at the time of the Liberation. Among the forces on which the safety or destruction of the town was to depend in April 1944, it played only a secondary part.

What were these forces? Who were the protagonists in the last-minute negotiations between the French and the Germans? On the side of the Germans there were the administration and the army. On the side of the French there were the civilian authorities of the Resistance and of Vichy and a few elements of the Maquis spread over the vicinity of the town.

The German administration in Bordeaux, which the French had known well for four years, was directed by Major-General Knoerzer who fulfilled the functions of town-major. His relations with the French had on the whole been correct. On the other hand, the troops of the Wehrmacht in Bordeaux lived apart and without service contacts with the French authorities. Neither General Nake, commanding the land forces, nor Captain Kühnemann, commanding the maritime base, were well known to the Prefecture or the mairie. Two or three meetings at official ceremonies had not enabled the Vichy notables to establish relations which could be of use when the Liberation came. The Resistance, of course, they did not know at all.

On the French side were the prefectorial and municipal organizations. At the head of the first was Sabatier, the regional prefect, Castanet, head of his secretariat, and Maurice Papon, secretary-general of the Prefecture of the Gironde. At the head of the second was Adrien Marquet, mayor of Bordeaux, René Caussade, head of his secretariat, and Bricaud, assistant secretary-general. Though Marquet had been able to persuade the Germans to set limits to their repressive measures against the population and had been able to keep the French flag flying permanently from the mairie, he could not officially assume the position of a negotiator in August 1944.

The Resistance, after the Grandclément affair, had never regained its previous importance, at least in the Gironde. Its principal centres had been liquidated, and its parachuting arrangements functioned only very uncertainly. There were, however, in the neighbourhood of Bordeaux, a few local Maquis. In the Blayais hills there were a group commanded by Aristide, and another, commanded by Commandant Rougès, on the right bank of the Garonne, at Senon and Floirac. The new authorities, among whom was Cusin, the Commissioner of the Republic, were still isolated and in the month of August had still made only fortuitous contacts with the authorities in control.

Such was the state of the forces in Bordeaux when the Liberation drew near. Two camps, of which neither desired the worst to happen, the destruction of the bridges and the harbour, were face to face. But they lacked the essential contacts to open the negotiations from which safety might result. How were these negotiations to be begun?

The wine of Bordeaux took a hand in the matter. By chance, the Kriegsmarine postings in France had placed Captain Kühnemann at the head of the maritime base. Fortunately he appreciated claret. Kühnemann, fifty-eight years old, and therefore of a generation previous to Hitler's coming to power, was an officer of the reserve who disliked the Nazis. In 1941, his daughter had been tried in Germany for having made disobliging remarks about the Chancellor. The judges had said her crime was due to an unsatisfactory family atmosphere. Kühnemann himself had always been in professional relations with France and, in particular, with the south-western capital. He was a director of an important wine business in Berlin, which had been founded in 1848 by his wife's grandfather. He knew all the notabilities of the wine trade well, including Eschenauer, whom he called, as did many others, Uncle Louis, and with whom he had been on friendly terms for twenty-five years.

Opposite this German soldier, who liked Bordeaux and its wines, the French principal negotiator was to be a university professor. Jean-Philippe Larrose was Professor of German at the University, and in charge of courses at the École de Santé Navale. He thus had possible access to the Kriegsmarine. Moreover, he was the mayor's interpreter for relations with the occupying power.

These then were the principal negotiators who were to discuss the safety of the harbour and bridges of Bordeaux.

Three attempts at negotiation were made by the French: one, backed by Marquet, had no result. The other two, undertaken on the initiative of Eschenauer and Rougès, commanding one of the Gironde Maquis, were more successful.

On 22 August, at 20.00 hours, the mayor of Bordeaux received information that the Germans intended to defend La Rochelle and Bordeaux and destroy their harbour installations. This alarming news, which Caussade had brought from the Propaganda Staffel, was in keeping with orders previously given by the German Naval Headquarters at Nantes, under whom Kühnemann was. On evacuation, each harbour commander was made responsible for the complete destruction of all port installations, thereby making the harbour completely unusable for a long time to come. This order had been issued as a result of air reconnaissance over Cherbourg. The Luftwaffe had reported that that port had been insufficiently demolished and that the Allies had repaired it with great speed and were using it once more.

On this information Adrien Marquet summoned Larrose and asked him and Caussade, the head of his secretariat, to do everything in his power to save the bridges and harbour of Bordeaux. "The mayor said," related Caussade, "that he could no longer intervene with the Germans about this and asked us to make overtures on a personal basis."

Caussade and Larrose went to the Hôtel Splendide to meet Lieutenant Dornemann, an officer of the Propaganda Staffel, who was their usual contact. They asked him for information about the German intentions and for his support. Dornemann gave them to understand that there was a good chance of the bridges not being blown. On being pressed by the two Frenchmen, Dornemann, betraying what he considered to be a military secret, then told them that as a result of a conference held that day in Bordeaux, it was possible the harbour might also be saved. Alluding to the conversations Caussade had previously held with him on this subject, he added "that it would be known one day what Bordeaux owed to his personal action." There was therefore a gleam of hope; and they tried to persuade Dornemann to keep in contact with the French until the desired result had been definitely attained. The conversation continued on these lines. But at 20.50 hours, a terrific explosion was heard from the direction of the quays. At 21.15 hours, there was gunfire, accompanied by automatic fire. The negotiators went into the basement and the discussion was interrupted.

Dornemann telephoned to find out what had happened. The explosion was that of a blockhouse in the Rue Raze, an ammunition depot which the Germans had intended to use to blow up the bridge and port installations. Its destruction had been effected through the complicity of a corporal of the Wehrmacht named Stahlschmitt. The gunfire was due to the F.F.I. who, to test the German resistance, had fired from the Gare d'Orléans and from the steeple of the Sainte-Marie church at a ship in the roads opposite the Quinconces, and on a detachment crossing the river. The Navy had returned the fire, and some of the shells had landed on a column preparing to embark. Thinking it was being attacked, it had also opened fire. Believing they were being ambushed by the Resistance, the Germans fired at each other in the dark.

At 02.30 hours, after further telephone calls, Dornemann informed Caussade and Larrose that owing to these incidents, the German intentions had been altered. He considered he could now make no further efforts.

Thus the first negotiations were interrupted and had no success. The second and third were more fortunate and obtained results.

Kühnemann, who had no desire to damage the town in which he had so many friends, was moreover continually being lobbied by Louis Eschnauer and his nephew Lung, who had been encouraged to work on the Captain by Cayel, the mayor of Bouscat, whose son Claude was serving under Rougès in the Maquis. He could therefore make representations to Kühnemann on behalf of both commercial Bordeaux and the F.F.I.

Subjected to this double pressure, and perfectly aware of the latest threat contained in it, Kühnemann, who was himself commanding the land-based units of the Navy, went to General Nake, commanding the fighting forces in Bordeaux. He told Nake that there appeared to be no justification for blocking the river by scuttling ships or destroying the harbour and bridges. The outcome of the war was already decided and the senseless destruction of Bordeaux, the fourth city of France, would cost Germany dear both morally and materially.

"Your harbour has nothing to do with me; and it is no part of my duty to take a decision with regard to it," Nake began by saying. In the end, the General, who was an Austrian and no more of a Nazi than Kühnemann, admitted he agreed with him.

Kühnemann then went to see the Engineer-Admiral of the Bordeaux sector. He told him of his vist to Nake and asserted that the General had given him orders not to destroy the harbour and bridges, and to sink no ships in the port.

The Admiral, a highly disciplined officer, wished to put into effect the demolitions ordered by his superior in Nantes. He went to see Nake.

On his return, he informed Kühnemann that Nake was opposed to demolishing the port and bridges, but agreed with the order to obstruct the river so as to make the harbour unusable.

The worst had therefore been avoided. But a second approach to Nake by Kühnemann to stop the scuttling of the ships was unsuccessful.

He had therefore to issue orders to sink the three lost of ships in the river.

To be certain of saving the harbour and bridges, it was now essential to prevent the F.F.I., in their ignorance of the fact that an agreement had been reached, creating an incident which might decide the Germans to take reprisals to protect their retreat. Kühnemann, with the approval of Eschenauer and Lung, now turned his attention to this danger. He persuaded Generals Nake and Knoerzer to summon the civil authorities and get them to inform the population and the F.F.I. of the understanding that had been reached.

On 24 August, at 11.30 hours, at the Greater-Bordeaux headquarters, in the Place Pey-Berland, Generals Nake and Knoerzer, Captain Kühnemann, and Colonel Seiz, commanding Greater-Bordeaux, accompanied by his assistants, Commandant Monscheuer and Captain Schultz, received six Frenchmen: Sabatier, the regional prefect; Castaret, head of the secretariat; Adrien Marquet, mayor of Bordeaux; and Bricaud, his secretary-general, accompanied by two interpreters, Blintz and Lung.

General Nake suggested the French authorities should make an appeal to the population to remain calm; and they agreed on the following text, which was to appear both in the press and on posters. Nake was the only signatory, Sabatier and Marquet refusing to append their names.

Appeal to the Population.
As Supreme Commander of the German troops in the Bordeaux Region, I declare that no destruction will take place in Bordeaux and its neighbourhood, and that the harbour and bridges of Bordeaux, which are mined, will not be demolished provided the population abstains from all acts of sabotage until after the departure of the German troops from Bordeaux and its neighbourhood.

NAKE.
Lieutenant-General,
U. Div-Kdr.

The text was at once sent to the Delmas Press, which delivered the posters at 15.30 hours to Colonel Seiz's headquarters. They were posted on Saturday, 26 August, by Granet, an employee in the mayor's office, and the younger Cayrel, after Nake had been by air to Poitiers and had returned with the German High Command's approval.

The announcement did much to calm the population. Only some accident could now prevent the safeguarding of the harbour and bridges.

But an accident might well take place at the departure of the German troops. To ensure against it there was a third negotiation to conclude a military agreement between the F.F.I. and the Wehrmacht. It fixed the date and conditions of evacuation.

To prevent useless firing which might compromise the whole business, this agreement was transmitted to Colonel Druilhe, who was on the way to Bordeaux at the head of the F.F.I. of the Dordogne. During the afternoon of the next day, 27 August, Adrien Marquet, the mayor, issued a communiqué to the press:

"The Municipal authorities ask the population to fly the French and Allied flags and to celebrate the liberty which has at last been recovered with calm and dignity.

"The Hôtel de Ville will be closed on Monday, 28 August, and the big bell will ring for a quarter of an hour at 08.00 hours and 20.00 hours."

At 20.30 hours a note signed by Triangle and Aristide was brought to Caussade for the mayor; it forbade, on pain of punishment, the publication of the communiqué. Only the regional military delegate and the delegate of the British War Office were qualified to give instructions concerning the entry of the Allies into Bordeaux, the flying of flags in the streets and the ringing of bells.

By this note, the civilian negotiators, to whom Bordeaux owed its safety, were excluded from the ceremonies arranged for the liberation. On 28 August, at 04.30 hours, the last German troops left Bordeaux by the Carbon-Blanc road. The harbour and the bridges were intact.

Two hours later, Colonel Druilhe, escorted by the non-Communist F.F.I. of the Dordogne, and Colonel Adeline entered the town and went to the Military Region Headquarters in the Rue Vital-Carles. From there, they went to the Hôtel de Ville, where at 07.30 hours the Tricolour was hoisted.

Bordeaux was liberated and had nothing more to fear from the Germans.

But in this town in which the Resistance had suffered such extraordinary avatars, in which treason had almost destroyed it, and internal dissensions had divided it, a trial of strength was now to begin. And here we return to the main theme of this chapter.

It was won on the military level thanks to two professional soldiers who were serving with the Secret Army, Colonel Druilhe and Colonel Adeline.

The first had been in command of a force of about 1,800 men in southern Dordogne. When Bergerac had been liberated, he considered the local campaign over. But there were other matters to concern him. He was in possession of a most disquieting secret document addressed to the F.T.P. in Dordogne: "The orders are to wait till Limoges and

Toulouse are taken to proclaim the Republic of the Soviets of the South of France." Did it emanate from the C.O.M.A.C. or from some local headquarters which imagined in its zeal that its desires were possibilities? However that might be, Druilhe foresaw that a decisive game was to be played out in Bordeaux, towards which he knew that quantities of F.T.P. were moving.

It became a race as to who would reach the Gironde first. Three days after leaving Bergerac, Druilhe entered the town with his 1,800 men, just as the Germans were evacuating it. He was appointed to the command of the 18th Military Region on 13 September.

It was he, as we have seen, who hoisted the first flags and took possession of the official buildings. He had won the first round, but there was a long way to go before the game was his.

Bordeaux was indeed in a critical situation. On the one hand, retreating German troops had fortified themselves on the Grave point, from which they could prevent ships using the river and could threaten the city. On the other hand, now that the city was liberated, it had become a centre of attraction for quantities of maquisards.

Some of them were not indeed Communists, but they had joined Aristide and Triangle, and could not make up their minds to accept Druilhe's authority. Among these were the 5,000 men whom Léon des Landes had sent north. Others were more eager to fight the retreating Germans, who were taking refuge in the pockets, than to become involved in political quarrels. Among these, in particular, were the F.F.I. of Arcachon and the Bassin.

But the majority were presenting Druilhe with a serious problem.

There were 6,000 Spanish "guerrilleros," who had come from the Dordogne and Toulouse, where they had fought most gallantly against the Germans. They were refugees from the Spanish Civil War and still imbued with the revolutionary spirit they had brought from beyond the Pyrenees. They were still divided into Anarchists and Communists, and were not prepared either to agree among themselves or to recognize Druilhe's authority.

There were also F.T.P. from the Dordogne and other departments in the south-west, whom Druile estimated to amount to 12,000 men. Some of their leaders, such as Colonel Martel, were prepared to accept his orders and had no desire for a showdown. Others, on the other hand, such as Soleil, Doublemètre and Docteur, were among those leaders of the F.T.P. who had found in the Maquis an opportunity to satisfy their instincts for being outlaws. Docteur, a public works engineer, partly Czech, partly Armenian, and naturalized Russian, placed his remarkable intelligence and ambition at the service of the Communists. Against these, Druilhe, who had far fewer men but had had the luck to install himself first in the official buildings, was to play a subtle and authoritative game which reduced the impending trial of strength to comparatively modest proportions.

When dealing with the Spaniards, he remembered most opportunely a curious flight he had made in an aircraft some seven years earlier. Before the civil war, Druihle had been attached to the French Embassy in Madrid as Directer of the School for Officers of the French Artillery Reserve in Spain. He had organized lectures and indoor tactical exercises in Madrid and Barcelona, which had given him a reputation as a military commander beyond the Pyrenees.

When Franco's rebellion broke out, he had returned to France, and was surprised one day to be called on by a representative of the Republicans, who asked him to go urgently to Madrid. A French aircraft was awaiting him at Barcelona. He went. The pilot introduced himself and said: "Mon Commandant, may I have permission to take another passenger along with us?"

The pilot was Corniglion-Molinier, the extra passenger was André Malraux.

On reaching Madrid, Druilhe had immediately been received by Garcia Prieto, who suggested he should take over a command in the Republican Army. Druilhe refused. Training reservists was a very different matter from being a Spanish general. As a French officer, he could not accept without permission from his government. What he could do, however, was to examine the situation unofficially with the Spanish military leaders, whose headquarters were in Madrid, and give them the benefit of his advice.

Owing to these activities, limited as they were, Druilhe still retained great prestige among the guerrilleros. When, after many adventures, 6,000 of them reached Bordeaux, Druilhe made contact with their leaders, reminded them that he had once nearly commanded them, and spoke of Garcia Prieto. The result was that the guerrilleros remained loyal to Colonel Druilhe whom they regarded as a friendly leader.

To put an end to the F.T.P. threat, Druilhe had successively to use military and diplomatic methods. Docteur was one of their most redoubtable leaders.

One day, Druilhe sent for him. "I've known you for a long time," he said. "You're a splendid, brave, intelligent chap and have done me great service. In recognition of it, I propose to offer you an important post in the 18th Military Region. I want to appoint you to the command of the engineers of the region and I hope you'll accept."

In that salon in the Louis XVI house in the Rue Vital-Carles, which was the headquarters of the military region, and before which Senegalese mounted impeccable guard, Docteur, the irregular, the expatriate, who had no home other than his F.T.P. troop, was suddenly presented with an offer of promotion to a regular rank. Denying his past and his political obedience, he said: "I am with you body and soul, mon Colonel, you can count on me."

For a fortnight, Docteur exercised his new functions as commander of the engineers. The F.T.P. were furious at his defection and disowned him. But, at the end of that fortnight, Druilhe sent for him and addressed him in quite a different tone: "You bastard, why the hell didn't you tell me you weren't French?" (In fact, Druilhe had known this perfectly well.) "What do you think the Minister's going to say about it? Do you realize what it means? You'll give me your resignation at once." Docteur submitted. He had lost the confidence both of the Communists and, if he had ever had it, of the military hierarchy. He was never heard of again.

On other occasions Machiavellianism was not enough to neutralize the F.T.P. In the Château of Thouard, once the residence of the Black Prince, and no doubt still haunted by his ghost, near Talence, in the suburbs of Bordeaux, some F.T.P. elements of the Soleil Group had taken up their quarters. They were behaving far from well. Five or six crimes had already cast terror into the district when Druilhe decided to make an end. He mobilized a battalion of infantry, which had been mostly recruited from liberated prisoners, and then, saying nothing to anyone, not even to Cusin, the Commissioner of the Republic, he confided the command to Colonel Ablard, a Regular officer, and ordered him to undertake the siege of the château.

A captain of gendarmerie summoned the defenders in the regular manner; but the besieged replied with rifle and sub-machine-gun fire.

Druilhe then issued orders to attack. One of the besieged fell under the assailants' fire. The others hoisted a white flag, though one or two of them succeeded in escaping with their pillaged booty. Inside the château, a man was found in a boiler with his feet and hands bound with wire.

The next day, Druilhe was visited by leaders of the F.T.P., armed with sub-machine-guns, who protested against the arrest of their men. Druilhe confronted them with a dilemma:

"Either you support these men who form part of your troops and become the accomplices of murderers, looters and thieves. Or you disown them, and justice will take its course."

This lamentable episode is evidence of the difficulties the non-Communist resistants, such as Druilhe, Cusin, Morraglia and Delaunay, had to surmount to prevent the trial of strength becoming open warfare.

Indeed, it was several months before the situation became stable.

An unchallengeable document, since it is a synthesis of information derived from telephone interceptions between 16 and 23 November 1944, shows that the Communist menace still subsisted nearly three months after the Liberation:

The only political parties showing any signs of real activity are still the Communist Party and the organizations which, on the local level, may be considered its satellites.

(1) National Front: increasing activity, characterized by very numerous telephone communications with its sister organizations: relations increasingly frequent and close with the *Gironde Populaire* (the local daily Communist paper), the Union of French Women, the Communist Youth and the Patriotic Militia (become the Republican Civic Guard). These, by the very fact of their close contact with the National Front, are quite obviously operating on the political level, their 'civic' role being only it would seem a secondary consideration. The National Front is still in contact with the headquarters of the F.T.P. Engineers at the Mondenard barracks, where members of the National Front are invited, if they so wish, to take their meals and draw rations.

The many telephone calls asked for from Régent (the headquarters of the National Front in Bordeaux) by Colonel Martel would suggest that this officer is playing a very active part in support of these parties. It must indeed be said that the National Front sends certain of its members 'to carry out missions in vehicles outside Bordeaux' and which, owing to the very secrecy with which they are surrounded, would seem to bear reference to preoccupations other than the pure and simple pursuit of the avowed purposes of the assembled parties which constitute the National Front.

(2) The Union of French Woman: the U.F.F. is also showing increasingly intense activity. It is in constant contact with the above-mentioned organizations (National Front, Communist Youth, *Gironde Populaire*) without forgetting also its relations with the headquarters of the F.T.P. Engineers which furnishes it with the quantities of gasoline it requires for its constant movements.

(3) Republican Civic Guard (formerly the Patriotic Militia): together with the other organizations, the Republic Civic Guard shows great activity. The gasoline it needs is furnished by the Mondenard barracks (headquarters

of the Engineers). However, it does not appear to get all the gasoline it needs to judge from certain communications which show disappointment at 'failures' for lack of spare parts and gasoline. The Republican Civic Guard seems to count more on money than enthusiasm for recruiting its militants and retaining their support.

The constant usurpations of power in which the Republican Civic Guards indulge (search, requisition, seizure, arrest) are making them increasingly unpopular and some telephone subscribers, owing to the arbitrary way in which the Republican Civic Guards behave, tend in their telephone conversations to compare them to the intolerable memory of the recent occupants.

(4) The Communist Party: the Communist Party is holding increasing numbers of meetings in Bordeaux and the district, and is also in liaison with the National Front, the Union of French Women, the Republican Civic Guard and the headquarters of the Engineers.

. . . Political Youth: the Communist youth is the only existing organization. It is holding increasing numbers of meetings (Pau, Saint-Foy, Coutras, Listrac). It also indulges in searches.

This gives the measure of the danger of the Communist attempt in Bordeaux.

In Toulouse, Limoges and Montpellier, the C.O.M.A.C. had appointed Communist or Communist-sympathizing military leaders. In these towns, unlike Bordeaux, they were the first to seize power.

One morning in 1941, a shy polytechnician entered a secret office of the Resistance in Lyons. Twenty-two years of age, slender, fair, with an honest look and an amiable smile, Second-Lieutenant Asher was eventually to become "Colonel" Ravanel. At about the same time a thin, dark and dynamic thirty-year-old professor of German at Toulouse, called Pierre Bertaux, who had a lively if somewhat ironical expression, called together the leaders of the Resistance network he had founded. Among them were Jean Cassou, a talented writer, Spanish expert and art critic, Nitti, the nephew of the Italian President, Marcel Vanhove and Jean-Maurice Hermann. "I've just learned through Morandat, parachuted in from London," Bertaux told them, "that the landing will not take place in the spring of 1942, but at the earliest in 1943. . . . There are at least another eighteen months to wait. . . . We shall not be able to hold out. . . . You know the risks well. . . . We are all married and fathers of families. . . . Faced with such uncertainty, I give you all your freedom. . . . I myself shall go on, but I want you to feel free to stop." Since no member of the team withdrew, the network continued to function.

It was between Asher and Bertaux that three years later, in August 1944, the trial of strength was played out in Toulouse.

Colonel Ravanel, a Communist who had fought bravely in the Resistance as Commander of a Corps Francs, had been appointed in June 1944 regional head of the F.F.I. by the C.O.M.A.C. His headquarters were in Toulouse. It was on him that the Communist elements of the Resistance counted to hold this key position in the south-west.

Meanwhile, Jean Cassou was appointed by the Algiers government to be Commissioner of the Republic, and Pierre Bertaux, who was working with him, took over La République newspaper, in the much-coveted buildings of the Dépêche de Toulouse. Jean Cassou was himself Left-wing; there were sympathizers with the Party in his entourage; but he had prevented the C.D.L. as he had the future administrative cadres from becoming political.

On 19 August, the German spontaneously began to evacuate the town. Towards the end of the afternoon, there remained only patrols and detachments of the rearguard. During the previous night, the sleep of the inhabitants of Toulouse had been disturbed by explosions. And in the morning a smell of burning paper still lay over the town. During the day, the Germans set fire to the Magasins Gênéraux, to the Hôtel des Postes, to the Collège Saint-Aubin for girls, to the Cafarelli Barracks and to hotels they had requisitioned. The fire-brigade tried to intervene; but the Germans cut the hoses with axes or bursts of sub-machine-gun fire and threw gasoline on the flames. The Saint-Michel Prison in which the resistants, among whom were André Malraux, were detained, was taken by assault by the population. The cell doors were forced open or mysteriously unlocked. Surprised at regaining their freedom, four hundred prisoners went down into the yard; but the last Germans saw them and threw grenades among them, killing one and wounding two more.

During the night of the 19th to 20th, when returning by car from a meeting of the C.D.L., Cassou encountered an enemy patrol. On being challenged, the driver refused to stop. The Germans opened fire and killed him. They then attacked Cassou with their rifle-butts and left him for dead in the road.

The next morning, Sunday, Pierre Bertaux heard the news from his friend Marcel Abraham, who was to have been a member of Cassou's secretariat. He got a lift to the hospital by the first F.F.I. car he saw in the street. He was fired at as he crossed the bridges which the Germans were still holding. He found Cassou, who was registered under a false name, in a coma.

Bertaux, whom Laffon had appointed during the course of a quarter of an hour's interview in Paris as Cassou's assistant, then went to the Prefecture. It was important to take over the Prefect's office first and beat the Communists to it.

Bertaux found there Sadon, the Regional Prefect, sitting at his desk. "I am the Commissioner of the Republic," he said. "Monsieur le Commissaire, I was expecting you to call," replied Sadon. For half an hour, Bertaux discussed the state of the town, the damage done by the Germans, and the reserves of electricity, gas, water, flour and baker's wood. After which he politely said to his predecessor: "You are under arrest. Do not leave your apartments." Sadon rose to his feet to show his successor out, precisely as if he were some ordinary visitor. At the door, he said: "After you, Monsieur le Commissaire." "No, Monsieur le Préfet, after you," replied Bertaux, "I am at home here now." "Indeed, so you are," Sadon admitted, and went out first.

Bertaux and his two companions, Brevan and Charpentier, looked at each other in some perplexity. The essential, of course, was to have forestalled the seizure of power by the Communists. But in what did this power consist and how was it to be exercised? The Commissioner of the Republic had no more than 800 police to keep order in his eight departments, and many of them, uncertain who to look to, were demoralized. He knew that the F.T.P. Maquis of the Lot, commanded by Colonel Georges, had just entered the town. Intended originally for Limoges, they had been deflected to Toulouse by Ravanel, who thought he had insufficient men. During the first night he spent in the Prefecture, Bertaux had only two companions armed with sub-machine-guns to protect him. They slept in adjoining rooms with the doors open.

Certainly, he was sitting in the Prefect's office, but what weight did that carry? And how long would he be allowed to remain there?

Half an hour later, the members of the Committee of Liberation arrived. There were six of them and their demeanour was threatening. "What are you doing here?" they shouted at Pierre Bertaux, whom they had not expected to find. "I am the Commissioner of the Republic." "No, Cassou is." "Cassou is not available, and I am replacing him on the orders of General de Gaulle." The impressive name had its usual effect. The visitors retired grumbling from the office, but they remained in the Prefecture ready to renew their offensive.

Almost on their heels the military leader arrived. Nonchalant, wearing an open-neck shirt, Ravanel also seemed surprised to find that Bertaux had beaten him to it by half an hour. Faced with the accomplished fact, he in turn withdrew after some minutes of argument.

Had he won the day? Would the thirty minutes' start Bertaux had gained over the Communists be sufficiently decisive?

About 18.00 hours, a crowd gathered on the square in front of the Prefecture. An F.T.P. entered Bertaux's office and saluted him: "Colonel Ravanel wishes to inform you that a German column is advancing on the Prefecture and that you will have to defend it with such means as you have at your disposal."

What was he to do? And was the story true? Or was it a stratagem to get Pierre Bertaux to leave the Prefecture? He disposed such companions as were with him as sentries in the courtyard and the adjoining rooms. Having had nothing to eat since morning, he himself crossed the courtyard for a cup of tea and then returned to his office. The situation meanwhile seemed to have grown no worse: there were no Germans in sight.

Bertaux sent for Ravanel and, to establish his authority, persuaded him to talk with him over the radio. Ravanel could hardly refuse. In spite of a militiaman sniper who was covering the neighbourhood of the Prefecture from the cathedral tower, they went out safely and reached the Toulouse-Pyrénées radio station. They each in turn announced the liberation of the town and the departure of the Germans. They wanted to do the same from the second radio station, Radio-Toulouse, but this was occupied by the F.T.P. It was like Barcelona in July 1936: "We do not know the Commissioner of the Republic. We do not know Colonel Ravanel. We are the F.T.P.," they said, their hands on their pistols. Ravanel and Bertaux gave up the broadcast and went away disappointed. "Aren't they your people?" the Commissioner of the Republic asked. "Yes, in theory," replied Ravanel without much conviction.

The chaos lasted a fortnight. Shots were fired in the street as the last Germans left, then the Militia began shooting from the rooftops. The Post Office and the telephone exchange were burnt. Sixty-eight armed F.T.P. were installed in the Prefecture. Bertaux, apart from his few companions and his *huissier*, had no forces under his command. Nor had he, as he said, "any means of knowing what was going on beyond his range of vision." But due to the fact that he was occupying the Prefect's office in the name of General de Gaulle, he succeeded little by little in gaining authority over the disorganized forces in the town.

There were no less than thirty-seven Deuxièmes Bureaux in Toulouse, who had taken the law into their own hands and were busy with the purge. There were also many leaders of bands or Maquis who had crowded into the town.

There was also a British officer, who had been parachuted into the district about a year and a half earlier and had organized the Maquis of Panjas in the Gers. He visited Pierre Bertaux and addressed him as follows: "I am Colonel Hilaire, Churchill's and de Gaulle's representative here; I have several thousand armed men at my back; and in my pocket I have an order signed by Churchill and de Gaulle. Order must be maintained in Toulouse, and if there is any trouble here, I shall merely bang my fist on the table and say: 'I'm taking over command'." In spite of these aggressive words, the man did not look particularly fierce. Bertaux laughed and replied: "In the first place, there is no trouble. Secondly, I'm in command here. And, anyway, I can see you're a splendid chap."

There were also F.F.I. of the A.S., the Armagnac battalion and the Corps Franc Pommiès, who also hoped to take advantage of the situation to seize power. But above all, there were the F.T.P. of the Lot under the command of Colonel Georges, who had been the first to arrive in the liberated town, and whose leader had been appointed town-major by Ravanel.

In face of this, what could Bertaux, deprived as he was of contact both with the central power and the departmental prefectures of the region, do? On Friday, 25 August, he received an unexpected telephone call from Albi. The Prefect of the Tarn asked to speak to him. "What's your name?" Bertaux asked. "Soloniac, a former colonial governor." That afternoon, delighted to know the name of one prefect at least, Bertaux asked the exchange to get him the Prefecture at Albi. "There's no answer," he was told. By chance, an F.F.I. colonel came on the line and was able to give information: "A German column has returned to Albi; the Post Office is burnt down. As for the Prefect, no one knows what has become of him."

That same day, Bertaux learned that there had been incidents in another of his departments, the Ariège. A summary purge had taken place, and in Pamiers alone thirty people had been shot. He sent Bartoli, one of his assistants, to find out what was going on. He returned horrified by what had taken place, but reassured as to the future. He had been much surprised to find a Prefect in the Prefecture and to discover he was no fool.

Nevertheless, Bertaux felt he was walking on a tight-rope. Little by little, he had got to know the people who were living in the Prefecture with him. Ravanel was a hard case, but he was also something of a façade behind which the real inspirers of the Communist game in Toulouse, older, more experienced and more fanatical men, as is often the case with intellectuals who have strayed into politics, were concealed. There was a philosopher, who had succumbed to the temptations of action; he was highly intelligent and extraordinarily dynamic, one of those men who could adapt the Marxist dialect to every situation. He introduced himself as Vernont and told Pierre Bertaux of the arrival of a certain Colonel Montfort, whom he described as being a "great theoretician" of war. Bertaux expected a forthright and imperious warrior. But he was mistaken. Montfort turned out to be a rather dusty little intellectual, the son of a member of the Institut, though he was none the less dangerous for that.

One among the Communists who surrounded him was a sensible man. This was Colonel Georges, whose real name was Noirot. Bertaux took a chance on him. He led him into a window embrasure and said: "What do they want? To turn me out? It would be better to say so straight out." "There's no question of that," Noirot replied. "All the better, because if they want to turn me out, there'll be trouble. I alone represent order here; the Germans are still only a few kilometres away and the Militia are in the town. Tell your comrades that we had better come to an understanding."

Upon this, negotiations began. Bertaux began by giving up a point or two. He agreed to dissolve the Garde Mobile and the Garde Mobile Républicain, on which he knew he could not really count in any case. Then, counting on Georges's loyalty, he asked for 200 F.T.P. from the Lot, to be placed under Georges's command, but under his own personal authority, to maintain order in Toulouse.

Georges had a sense of discipline; for him a prefect was a prefect, and a commissioner of the Republic a super-prefect who represented the government. And the government was presided over by a man whose right no one was prepared openly to contest at that time; not even the Communist Party. It contained two Communist Ministers whom Georges believed to be in whole-hearted agreement with the decisions taken in Algiers. Georges was prepared to obey Bertaux. The latter could breathe again; he had won through.

At the beginning of September, an aircraft from Algiers established a first contact with the government. It brought André Philip and Pierre Bloch, who officially sanctioned the appointment of Bertaux to the position of Commissioner of the Republic.

In mid-September, de Gaulle arrived in Toulouse. It was not one of his better days. Bertaux met him at the airfield, gave him an account of the situation and in particular told him about the Hilaire episode. The General's immediate reaction was: "Didn't you arrest him?" "No, Hilaire had 700 armed men with him." "At least, you haven't asked him to luncheon with me?" "Of course I have, he fought for nearly two years in the Maquis, under the aegis of your name." "Well, you'll tell him I won't eat with him." It was not an easy mission to fulfill and was the prelude to an angry scene between de Gaulle and Hilaire in the Prefect's office.

High words could be heard in the antechamber. Suddenly Hilaire stamped angrily out. The General said to Bertaux: "You'll give him twenty-four hours to quit French soil. If he stays, you'll have him arrested." A threat which was not in fact put into execution.

Other leaders of the F.F.I. were treated with no greater courtesy. To Ravanel, who presented himself dressed as a colonel, de Gaulle said merely: "Ah, Second-Lieutenant Asher." To Georges, who came dressed in overalls like a good proletarian, he said: "And who are you?" "Georges, from the Lot." "Georges? To begin with, stand to attention when you're speaking to a superior officer."

After a few more amenities of the sort, there was considerable ferment in the antechamber. Ravanel was anxious. "He'll be kidnapped," he said to his friends.

Fortunately, the tone changed. De Gaulle received all the leaders of the Resistance in the Prefect's office. They were drawn up in a square. He walked slowly along their lines, asked each one about the actions in which he had taken part, and then made them a brief speech, after which half his audience were in tears. He concluded in these terms: "I am addressing you, and your comrades through you. You will go back to them. You will tell them that I like them well. Good-bye, gentlemen."

After a big luncheon in the Prefecture, Bertaux asked the General his intentions for the future. He got an answer of singular gravity: "As for me, I shall withdraw. . . . I have a mission; and it is coming to an end. I must disappear. France may again one day have need of a pure image. That image must be left with her. Had Joan of Arc been married, she would no longer have been Joan of Arc. I must disappear."

These were strangely prophetic words. In spite of his joy at the Liberation, and his satisfaction at having maintained order in the town confided to him. Pierre Bertaux felt gravely concerned about the future.

At Montpellier the struggle was less overt than at Toulouse. It was perhaps because the military leader appointed by the C.O.M.A.C., Gilbert de Chambrun, alias Colonel Carrel, was not a member of the Party, but merely a Communist sympathizer or perhaps what is known as a "progressiste." And a "progressiste" is to a Communist rather as a parish priest is to a monk: he believes the same things, but his style of life is different. He does not live in a closed and disciplined society, but accepts outside contacts and frequents profane circles. As a result he is sometimes influenced and his behaviour is less intransigent and direct. The real Communists use him, but do not altogether accept him.

Gilbert de Chambrun officially represented the Combat movement in the United Movements of the Resistance (M.U.R.). Algiers thought he was Right-wing; in fact, he was one of those aristocrats who wanted to be on the right side when it came to future Bastilles. In the secret war, he played the Communist game with all the graces of the *ancien régime*. He had a certain nonchalance, inherited from the Regency, towards life, and particularly towards military regulations. His attitude was reminiscent of the days when promotion depended on interest. On one occasion, he appointed 600 second-lieutenants all at once. According to him, he was not laying a duty upon them, but giving them a status, as in times past the king conferred nobility. As a former diplomat whom the Quai d'Orsay were vainly trying to get back from commanding F.T.P., he had a certain prestige with his men. He had prestige, too, in the manœuvres and negotiations he conducted at Montpellier after the Liberation, when Ramadier and Jules Moch, former politicians of the Third Republic, tried to eliminate him; and, again, in his relations with Colonel Zeller who, sent by Paris in September 1944 to neutralize him, arrived in Montpellier without knowing what awaited him.

Four months before the Liberation, after the Germans had executed two Commissioners of the Republic designate, Gilbert de Cambrun had been appointed to that position by Emmanuel d'Astier de la Vigerie, the Commissioner for the Interior, who also sympathized with the ideas of the extreme Left. But within the regional directorate of the M.U.R., over which he had to preside, Chambrun was in a minority. The two other members, Missa and Henri Noguères, were Socialists. Moreover, Henri Noguères, in agreement with Jacques Picard, the regional military delegate appointed by Algiers, commanded the "regional bands of Corps Francs." These numbered some fifty men, were the shock troops of the Maquis, and operated in groups of four, being responsible for all the more difficult operations such as sabotage, reprisals and commando raids. Chambrun could do nothing against them. He tried in vain to dissolve them; but Noguères and Missa succeeded in persuading d'Astier to annul Chambrun's appointment as Commissioner of the Republic. D'Astier in the end appointed Jacques Bounin who, though no descendant of Lafayette as was Colonel Carrel, was nevertheless of more moderate opinions.

The Lozère, which was Chambrun's department, was in ordinary times a reactionary district. During the Resistance, its isolation had made it a refuge for all sorts of turbulent elements. The Prefect appointed by Vichy, and the Captain of the Gendarmerie were shot at the Liberation. The new Prefect, a Communist schoolteacher, wore a red scarf which impressed the commander of the F.F.I. who, in spite of his four stripes, spent all his leisure studying the life of bees. There was no sufficient authority to prevent the settling of private accounts, assassinations, and the pillaging which went on for a long time and proved difficult to suppress. A turncoat regiment of the Vlassov Army, a battalion of Italian deserters, a battalion of the F.T.P. and a battalion of Indo-Chinese made up its somewhat mixed garrison.

Among the departments of the region, the Gard, as we have seen, was one of those which had most difficulty in regaining its equilibrium. Reprisals and counter-reprisals went on for a long time.

At Perpignan, in the Pyrénées-Orientales, the population was not too badly off, and the supply situation more or less satisfactory. Among the numerous soldiers and colonists who had retired there, a former non-commissioned officer of the colonial army, who liked his wine, was appointed to command the sub-division. He was given five stripes and, thus accoutred, died peacefully a year later over his apéritif.

But the real trial of strength took place in the Hérault. Politically, the department consisted both of conservatives and very progressive elements; ranging from "bright red" to what was called "bright white," it furnished, at the time of the Liberation, strong contingents to the F.T.P., as well as a relatively large number of recruits to the Militia. The Prefect, Reboulleau, was a member of the Militia, and wore its uniform even when engaged in his official functions. On 30 August, he was condemned to death by a court-martial at Montpellier and was executed the next day.

The Communists and Communist sympathizers were almost in a majority within the Maquis. From the figures furnished by Chambrun, there were 9,000 men of whom 5,000 were armed, and 3,840 openly declared themselves to be F.T.P. They were supported by Spanish Maquis and by sympathizers belonging to other organizations: 3,000 of these were armed.

During the night of 19 to 20 August, the inhabitants of Montpellier were kept awake by a series of explosions. The Germans were preparing to leave and blowing up their principal installations, in particular the telephone exchange at the Post Office. Throughout 21 and 22 August the Wehrmacht was evacuating the town. "What a procession they made!" relates a witness. "Departmental buses, cars, trucks of all sizes and colours, brought from all over the place, and even dust-carts. One could see a Paris bus go by and even—and this is not a joke—a hearse. Then horse-carts and station trolleys. At intervals in this fantastic cavalcade cyclists appeared in Indian file, and even soldiers on foot, sweating, harassed and limping—unfortunates whose war would end in some not-too-distant ditch."

The population, who had been deprived for a long time past of the spectacle of the Tour de France, watched this curious procession with interest. While this inglorious withdrawal of the occupying troops was taking place, Montpellier was subject to all the dangers of insurrection, though it is difficult to arrive at any precise chronology. All one can say is that the crisis was reached between 23 and 27 August.

While the Militia and the collaborationists were being hunted down and killed in the streets, there were many indications that a trial of strength was imminent. The F.T.P. from the Maquis were leaving their usual operational sectors and were pouring into the towns, in particular Montpellier, Béziers and Sète. It seemed that this must be due to a general order transmitted directly to leaders of the different groups through unofficial channels. Bounin, the Commissioner of the Republic, knew nothing of it. It is not so certain that the same can be said of Gilbert de Chambrun.

Why were these troops flowing towards the towns? Was it not all the more surprising the whole countryside was covered at this moment by German units which the Maquis would normally have endeavoured to intercept? Was the intention to trap the elements of the Wehrmacht then evacuating the towns? From witnesses' reports, it would not appear that the F.T.P. concentrated at Montpellier made any attempt whatever to embarrass the German retreat. For instance, it is reported that units of the Maquis were billeted in a school beside the main road and made no attempt to attack the German columns marching past it. No doubt, when the Germans were rashly indiscreet, or when isolated detachments of the Wehrmacht too overtly threatened the safety of a town or, alternatively, seemed disposed to put their hands up, the maquisards would attack them or gratefully receive their surrender.

On the 23rd, the population assembled in front of the Prefecture.

The new municipality was to be elected by acclamation—a somewhat revolutionary process in itself. The ceremony, however, was somewhat curtailed. Just as he was beginning to make his speech, Bounin, the Commissioner of the Republic, received a pencilled note with the seal of the Regional Committee of Liberation. It ran as follows:

"A telephone communication has been intercepted at the station announcing that a convoy of German tanks is being directed by rail and road to Montpellier."

True or false, the news was scarcely calculated to stimulate his oratory and Bounin cut his speech short. The new municipality was hastily elected by acclamation. It was to be presided over by the actual secretary-general of the mairie, Émile Martin. But, apart, from this elderly, bearded official, who was more concerned with administration than politics, the municipality, called the "General Delegation," had a Communist majority. Of its five members, one was a representative from the National Front, one from the C.G.T. and one from the Party. The Marxists therefore not only controlled the Maquis troops who had entered the town, but the provisional organization which administered it.

For a few days, the situation appears to have remained comparatively fluid. The Communists requisitioned the two Montpellier newspaper presses. Taking advantage of the fact that Noguères had been made prisoner by the Gestapo, they installed Georges Sadoul, one of their own men, as Commissioner of Information in his place. And when Noguères escaped and returned, he found his office in the headquarters of the National Front. The Communists also dominated the court-martial set up to try collaborators. This court pronounced fifty death sentences.

On 27 August, the F.F.I. troops, under the command of Colonel Carrel, otherwise Gilbert de Chambrun, made their official entry into Montpellier. Was this, under the cover of resounding *Marseillaises*, tricolour flags, and the acclamations of the population for its liberators, the prelude to that trial of strength, which seemed always deferred and yet was always threatening? That very evening, Emmanuel d'Astier, the Commissioner for the Interior, arrived unexpectedly in a jeep covered with dust.

What had this Minister with Communist sympathies come to do? Had he come officially to install the representatives of the provisional government, or to replace them by others elected by the "will of the people?" On 28 August, at 14.30 hours, during a ceremony on the Place de la Préfecture, d'Astier defined the duties of the new authorities. They were to begin a purge which must "strike harder the higher it strikes," organize a "French economy in which the interests of the individual must be broken to yield place to the general interest," and, finally, "set up . . . a social structure in which economic power, the power of money, no longer makes the law but is really under the control of the State and at the service of the people."

None of this was of a very good augury for the bourgeois inhabitants but it did not appear necessarily to mean that a trial of strength was imminent.

Aside from these public declarations, one clearly cannot tell what private instructions d'Astier may have given Chambrun. It would appear, however, that he was concerned, on the one hand, not to provoke a disturbance, and, on the other, to allow the revolutionary climate to subsist.

There are two facts which support this hypothesis. When, on 2 September, General de Lattre de Tassigny spent the day in Montpellier, which he had left at the head of his division on 11 November 1942 on the entry of the Germans into the Free Zone to try and organize resistance to them, he received a triumphal welcome in the streets and the squares; but, these festivities over, he had to spend the whole night till four o'clock in the morning explaining to the assembled leaders of the F.T.P. that he was a friend of Bogomolov, the Soviet Ambassador to the provisional government, and that the Ambassador had requested him to tell the inhabitants of Montpellier to stay quiet.

Another event which bears witness to the persistence of the revolutionary climate was that, on 25 September, at Alès, the Commissioner of the Republic's car stopped outside the mairie where the official decrees requisitioning the mines of the district for the nation were to be signed.

Making use of the special powers conferred on the Commissioners of the Republic on appointment, Jacques Bounin had proceeded to the first act of nationalization effected after the Liberation, that of the mines of the Alès basin. Here is part of the speech he made on that occasion:

Two decrees concerning the mining industry are to be signed shortly. The first requisitions the seven mines of the Alès basin and places them at the service of the nation. The second appoints the members of the Consultative Committees of administration and names the directors of the mines.

For a long time past, all political programmes holding your attention have mentioned nationalizing the great enterprises. They promised you to remove from those who owned the means of production, the trusts, those industries which should belong to no one but the nation itself. The Government has announced measures of nationalization. So, by taking this decision today, I believe I am responding both to the wishes of the nation and to the intentions of the Government.

The nation had the wish to own the means of production. How could it acquire this ownership? The law of 11 July 1938 concerning the organization of the nation in time of war admits of requisition. This permits the taking over of both people and property to place them at the nation's disposal.

In pursuance of this law, I have decided to requisition the seven mines of the Alès basin and restore them to the nation. . . .

On 25 September 1944, the mines will be handed over to the workers. It is a date in the history of the Alès mines. It is a date in the history of the mines of France. . . .

In 1629, the peace of Alès, signed by Richelieu in this very town, brought reconciliation to a population divided by the wars of religion. Richelieu had no hesitation in combating the feudalism of those times.

Today the revolution will destroy economic feudalism and bring you social peace in a better and juster world. The revolution is on the march, it will liberate man from his servitude, as you have liberated the territory from the enemy.

Social justice will be given to a district which has gained the plaudits of the world.

Forward!

What, in these circumstances, was the part claimed for Richelieu? Had he covered with his "red robe" the first despoiling of the capitalists, or had he limited it by his ecclesiastical unction and diplomatic genius? However that may be, the revolution, though deferred in its political form, was beginning to take place on the economic plane.

In this month of September, Diethelm, Commissioner for National Defence, ordered Colonel Zeller to take over command of the 16th Military Region which was still held by Chambrun. But Colonel Masson, head of the "minister's" secretariat, warned Zeller when handing him his appointment that it was "all we can give you . . . do your best. Since you've taken part in the Resistance, they may not arrest you." It was an allusion to what had happened at Poitiers, where the regional commander appointed by Paris had been met at the station by the F.T.P. and sent straight back again.

What chance had Zeller against the fellow-travelling military leader? Chambrun had every intention of keeping his appointment, at least until the C.O.M.A.C. had agreed to his replacement, which that organization, controlled as it was by the Communists, appeared to have no intention of doing. At the beginning of October a meeting of the

C.O.M.A.C. was held at Clermont-Ferrand, during which the regional commanders it had appointed received orders to remain at their posts. At the same time there was a meeting of the Regional Committee of Liberation. In spite of a proposal made by Ramadier that they should rally immediately to de Gaulle and place Zeller in command, the C.D.L., by a majority of thirty to twenty votes, decided to continue supporting Chambrun.

The Colonel had no doubt about the tactics to be pursued. He refused to rush things, offend anyone directly, or even assume the rank of F.F.I. General which had been conferred on him from London two months before. He set out to win sympathy and gain influence.

He intended to wait till by the mere circumstances of the case the neophytes to power, appointed by the C.O.M.A.C. to positions for which they had no real competence, were obliged to have recourse to the senior officers of the army and administration. Until then, he was prepared to counteract such dangerous initiatives as might compromise the future by prudently unofficial methods.

As soon as he arrived, therefore, Zeller called on the actual holder of the post to which he himself had been appointed by Paris. Gilbert de Chambrun received him most courteously. "We know what you did in the Resistance. I am most happy to welcome you. Unfortunately, since I have been appointed Regional Military Commander by my superiors, I cannot leave my post until they have appointed someone to replace me. . . . I shall be delighted to have your advice, but I am the commander of the region. . . . If you agree, I will have an office arranged for you adjoining mine. And we shall work in concert."

Zeller therefore behaved as Chambrun's eventual heir. But, for the moment, Chambrun had no intention of abdicating. His policy did not coincide with that of the Gaullist authorities. He wanted to cherish the influence of the Communists. As a single, but revealing, example here is the text of a proclamation addressed to the maquisards of the region, on 2 September 1944, about the forming and despatching of F.F.I. battalions to de Lattre's army. Beneath its Déroulède-like style, it will be noted that the Patriotic Militia, the Communist shock troops, were expressly invited not to leave for the armies.

Dear Comrades,

The High Command calls upon you to furnish it with seven battalions to be despatched to pursue the enemy with the regular army. This is the order you were awaiting and you will receive it with enthusiasm. Once again, you will be in a position to avenge so many of your massacred and mutilated comrades. Our popular army will have a further opportunity of contributing to the liberation of the Fatherland. You will all want to go. But a great number of you, and in particular our valuable Patriotic Militia of the National Front and the National Liberation Movement, must remain in the region to assure the maintenance of public security and to protect our Revolution in its beginnings. There is here an equal duty, both for those who will pursue the enemy to his lair and for those who will mount an active and vigilant guard in our liberated cities. At the dawn of a new era, we repeat fervently: "*Aux Armes, citoyens, formez vos bataillons. . . .*"

Chambrun was therefore playing a double game, according to whether he was addressing Maquis of his own persuasion or not. On the one hand, he was inviting the non-Communist F.F.I. to join de Lattre's army, and on the other was proposing Offenbach's Carabiniers as models to the Patriotic Militia.

Little by little, as Zeller worked with him, he was able to take things in hand. At first, he limited himself to accompanying Chambrun on his tours of inspection which were often peculiar enough. Chambrun liked to play the demagogue. Talking to a corporal, he would call him "comrade corporal." He was prepared to tolerate women in F.F.I. vehicles. When a gendarme refused to obey his sergeant, whom he thought had not been a thorough-going resistant, it was the sergeant who was suspended. However, throughout these somewhat unmilitary tours, Zeller was at Chambrun's side; and Chambrun consulted him increasingly often, making use of his competence. Chauliac, the Chief of Staff, made arrangements to keep Zeller informed of Chambrun's decisions. Some could be put into execution, others had to be adjourned, illegal arrests and the improper appointment of officers in particular. Until 1 December, Chambrun continued to exercise command, while Zeller patiently remained his subordinate to all appearances. By that date, however, the revolution, longed for or feared according to which camp you were in, had not yet taken place. The judicial, administrative, economic and military cadres of the country had been restored. The Patriotic Militia was on the point of being dissolved. Chambrun, who had ceased to receive instructions to attempt a trial of strength, one day came to Zeller and said very properly: "It's time I handed the command over to you. . . . Couldn't you give me a regiment going to join the armies?" The 81st R.I. was formed with some difficulty at Carcassone. Gilbert de Chambrun asked for a Regular soldier as his second-in-command. At the front, Lieutenant-Colonel Bousquet played a similar part to Zeller's at Montpellier. Under this double command, the infantry regiment distinguished itself in Haute-Alsace and Germany.

The Montpellier region had escaped a trial of strength. But it had been a close-run thing.

At Limoges, the Liberation was dominated by the singular personality of an F.T.P. leader, Colonel Guingouin, who seemed to be able to arouse as much hatred as devotion. He was indeed an obstinate and wilful man, with two curiously opposed strains in his heredity. His father, a regular non-commissioned officer, had been killed a year after his birth, in 1914, and had perhaps left him a sense of authority and a taste for command. His mother, a schoolteacher with revolutionary opinions, was excitable and rather unbalanced. She had brought him up and had doubtless persuaded him to join the Communist Youth at the age of eighteen, when he was finishing his studies to become a schoolmaster at Limoges. Both these hereditary strains seemed to have converged in the title Guingouin adopted when he became head of the Resistance in the Limousin in 1943. He called himself "Prefect of the Maquis," and was successful in getting the decrees he posted up under the noses of the Germans, the Militia and the Vichy authorities obeyed.

Guingouin had therefore been a Communist since 1931, and remained one till December 1952, when the Party expelled him. Indeed, he was a Communist in his own way, and it was not always a way pleasing to the Communist Party authorities. Until 1940, he remained a modest local militant, and even in 1936, at the time of the Popular Front, took no initiative. However, after the signing of the Russo-German Pact, and particularly after the invasion of France by the Wehrmacht, he was unable to accept the pacifist attitude which was then the Party's policy. He kicked over the traces and took to the Maquis in the winter of 1940. He was never quite able to forgive the Communist leaders for their policy at that time. After the Liberation he published a pamphlet on the Limousin Maquis, and printed a facsimile of a number of the clandestine *Humanité* to remind people that before Germany attacked Russia the Party had been pro-German and to prove that he himself had been right not to obey the orders of the Communist authorities. Conversely, the latter never forgave the independence displayed at that time by the man who, not without some exaggeration, was called the "Limousin Tito." At the beginning of 1944, the F.T.P. leaders of the region assembled to discuss his case. "Guingouin," they said, "is beginning to annoy us. Either he comes to heel and obeys orders or he must disappear out of circulation." Indeed, Guingouin's behaviour at that time seemed shocking to the Communists, while his authority over the Maquis and the civilian population of the regions he had liberated was great and his name was on everyone's lips. He was the local boy who had achieved rank as a national hero. The Communists decided it was wiser not to break with him; but Guingouin was still to afford them much disappointment.

The Limoges region was far from easy to control. The repression enforced by the Militia was fierce and the Resistance bitter. In these unfortunate circumstances old peasant quarrels came to a head and degenerated into massacres. It was not always known who had killed; it was not often known why. Assassination might be political or not. It was not even known how many executions took place; no one would talk, and the common graves into which the victims were heaped seemed mysteriously forgotten.

The crimes committed by the Militia sowed the seeds of hatred and gave rise to further excesses. The maquisards, more or less undisciplined, indulged in summary executions and bathed the neighbourhood of Limoges in blood. If, at its liberation, the town itself might consider that it had been relatively spared, counting as it did only some twenty executions in the streets and seventy-five death sentences pronounced between 24 August and 6 October by the Resistance court-martial in reprisals for those ordered by Vichy, the countryside round about was the scene of hundreds of murders. There were some spectacular ones; and the memory of them still lies heavily on the public conscience. For example, there was a young bride belonging to an aristocratic family who was arrested on coming out of the church with her bridegroom, the priest and a witness, and was shot at dawn next day in her wedding-dress. She was accused of owning a château and of having nursed wounded militiamen. Other families, both bourgeois and noble, lost many of their members; for instance, six in one case, seven in another.

This banditry was not only directed against the bourgeois and the nobles in the form of a class war. It existed also within the Resistance itself. On occasion the F.T.P. and members of the A.S. would kill each other, sometimes as a result of peasant rivalries.

According to a speech given on the radio, on 12 September 1945, by Chaintron, the Communist Prefect of the Haute-Vienne, there were 210 deaths in the department. But if this figure is admitted to be accurate, it corresponds only to the overt executions carried out by the Maquis of which there are usually records. To approach the real total, the three hundred bodies of executed men discovered in an anonymous grave after the Liberation must at least be added, as well as an estimate of the number of executions of which no trace has been found, either on paper or in the earth. From estimates made by officials, who remained at their posts for fifteen years without ever being engaged on one side or the other, it would appear that the summary executions in Haute-Vienne were not far short of a thousand.

In circumstances where human life appeared of such small account and there was no justice, what attitude could and did Colonel Guingouin's Maquis take? Borne along on the general frenzy, it would be ingenuous to suggest that none of its members had French blood on his hands. At that time, the most peaceful citizens were sometimes drawn into behaving like murderers. We know of a respectable upper-class Parisian who became the leader of a Maquis in the Dordogne. One day, the inhabitants of a village asked him to kill one of their number whom they suspected of being a traitor. If he did not execute the man within the hour, the village threatened sanctions against the Maquis which it sheltered and fed. The unfortunate man was therefore shot. A year later, the very people who had demanded his death laid flowers on his grave to rehabilitate his memory. It is unlikely that Guingouin's Maquis could always avoid such executions, or that he himself could prevent elements of the population not under his control attributing hideous crimes or the personal paying off of scores to the spirit of the Resistance. Had it been the case, he would certainly have been an exception.

But what must be realized, is that this almost fatal behaviour, the result of circumstances and the atrocities committed by the Militia and the Germans, was not without its counterpart. Guingouin was not merely the leader of a band; he had a sense of authority and was aware of his responsibilities. The decisions he took, both to administer the district before the Liberation, and to preserve Limoges at the time of the Liberation, showed that he was anxious to limit the damage. Before the Liberation the "Prefect of the Maquis" took his administrative duties very seriously. He fixed the prices of agricultural produce both to prevent a black market and to assure the farmers a just remuneration: potatoes at 4 francs a kilo, pork at 2,500 francs for 50 kilos, eggs at 28 francs a dozen, and butter at 8 francs a kilo. Any farmer selling above the fixed price was fined the difference between the black-market price and the fixed price. "The announcement of the fine, for which a receipt is given, will be fixed to the door of his house."

Furthermore, the requisitioning of cattle for Germany was stopped. The "Pétain requisition" was itself unable to buy potatoes at the ridiculous price of 1.25 francs a kilo, which did not recompense the efforts of the agricultural workers. So that no one should be ignorant of Guingouin's legislation, his decrees were posted in the villages he controlled.

The author of these decrees had clearly acquired a taste for power. Moreover, on 20 August 1944, when it was a question of liberating the chief town of the department, he interpreted very freely the instructions sent him by the C.O.M.A.C.

In accordance with the Communist policy, the C.O.M.A.C. wanted Limoges to be liberated by force of arms, that is to say by a majority of F.T.P., which for an over-populated town counting 30,000 refugees over and above its 90,000 normal inhabitants, all in a state of feverish excitement from the persecution they had suffered, was taking a great risk. Contrary to his orders, Guingouin decided to negotiate with the Germans so as to enter the town without a shot being fired. In this hazardous plan, he got the support of three very different men, whom fate had brought together. One was the Vichy Regional Prefect, Freund-Valade, the second was the German General Gleiniger, commanding the troops in Limoges, and the third was a Swiss citizen, Jean d'Albis, whose family, long resident in Limoges, owned a porcelain factory there. In August 1944, d'Albis was acting temporarily as the Swiss consular agent.

During the fortnight preceding the Liberation, Freund-Valade made several approaches to the German authorities to spare the town. He was promised by Maier, Chief of the Gestapo, that persons detained in the German prison would not be killed on the Gestapo's departure.

On 17 August, during a visit to General Gleiniger, he refused absolutely to allow the French police under his orders to join the Germans in the defence of the town against the Maquis.

That same day, the Trade Unions in Limoges having issued orders for a general strike, he dissuaded the German from intervening and took the opportunity to tell him a few unpleasant truths: "You do not realize the seriousness of your situation, which will get worse from hour to hour."

On the 19th, continuing his work of demoralization, he saw Gleiniger again to inform him that on instructions from General Perret, Directeur de la Garde at Vichy, the French police and military forces were to evacuate Limoges because of the rapid advance of the American tanks which were then in the neighbourhood of Châteauroux and Poitiers. The General was appalled. Freund-Valade chose this moment to inform him that 15,000 F.F.I. were massed in the neighbourhood ready to attack and that defence was hopeless. It would, he said, be better to capitulate, and he offered his services. Much upset, Gleiniger neverthe-less replied that honour demanded he should fight.

Meanwhile, Freund-Valade had made contact with Colonel Guin-gouin through Trisson, his controller of Economic Affairs. The depart-mental chief of the F.F.I. had not been inactive; during the last eight days his troops had invested Limoges. Two attempts at sorties, one by the Germans and the other by the Militia, had been repulsed. Groups of Maquis were making raids into the town. Guingouin asked by radio for Allied air support and gave them the objectives to bomb. Everything was in readiness for the assault. But Guingouin wanted to avoid blood-shed. He was prepared to negotiate. First, he negotiated with Freund-Valade to arrange for the evacuation of the Gardes and the Gardes Mobiles, which took place without incident during the night of 20 to 21 August. He then negotiated with Gleiniger.

Since Gleiniger refused to have any direct contact with the Maquis, Guingouin asked Jean d'Albis to act as intermediary. In agreement with Freund-Valade, the Swiss consular agent met the German General on Sunday, 20 August, at 12.45 hours. He transmitted to him the condi-tions proposed by the Maquis: "Unconditional surrender of the garrison, in which case the troops' lives would be spared and a guard of honour given the General."

Gleiniger refused. During the course of the discussion, however, Jean d'Albis saw one possibility: if Gleiniger refused to negotiate with the F.F.I., he might be persuaded to meet a mission consisting of inter-Allied officers parachuted in to the Maquis.

The meeting was arranged for the next day, 21 August, at 16.00 hours, at Jean d'Albis' house. In the morning, Gleiniger renewed contact with Freund-Valade, as if he were trying to persuade himself that there were good reasons to surrender. "He asked me," reported Freund-Valade, in a note, dated 13 October 1944, to Boursicot, the Commissioner of the Republic, "if the figure given him on 19 August of the number of F.F.I. surrounding the town was correct. I said it was. He then told me of the difficulties he had felt since our last interview. When I insisted once again on the uselessness of his defending the town, he avoided making a direct reply by saying that he still had time to think it over. But just as he was going away, I nevertheless managed to get him to promise that if he decided to fight, he would not do so inside the town but at the gates of Limoges."

At 16.00 hours, the British Major G. M. Staunton and the American Captain Charles E. Brown, accompanied by two F.F.I. captains, met General Gleiniger, escorted by two officers. The German agreed to surrender on condition that "the Allied officers forming part of the mission would give their word of honour as soldiers that treatment proper to prisoners of war would be guaranteed to all German forces who laid down their arms on the order of Major-General Gleiniger."

It was specifically stated, moreover, that the Militia was not included in the surrender.

That evening, the F.F.I. made their entry. Gleiniger, however, was unable to take advantage of the treatment proper to a prisoner of war since the S.S., infuriated by the surrender, kidnapped him with his staff and obliged him to commit suicide in a wood not far from Limoges. So died a German General because he was not insensible to the fate of the population of a French town. Already, at the time of the Oradour massacre, Hitler had ordered his removal as a punishment for his humane attitude. Had he not authorized Freund-Valade and the bishop to attend a ceremony in memory of the victims? Indeed, on that occasion, he had refused to ally himself with the authors of the crime and had assured the French authorities of his sympathy.

Having entered the town peacefully, Guingouin set about maintaining order. For ten days, until the arrival on 5 September of Boursicot, the Commissioner of the Republic, the municipal authorities appointed by Vichy remained in office. Faure, the mayor, was merely advised for his own safety not to appear too often at the Hôtel de Ville; Mlle. Merlet, a municipal councillor, performed marriage ceremonies in his name.

There were two problems to resolve. In the first place, who was to be president of the Departmental Committee of Liberation? The question was debated during the day of the 22nd in the Café du Commerce. There was a false alarm during the discussion: "the Boches are coming back." There were bursts of machine-gun fire all over the place. It was agreed to give the presidency to Pasteur Chaudier, who was politically neutral.

Secondly, who was to be captain of the Fire Brigade? The former captain had made the mistake of getting his men to sing *Maréchal, nous voilà*. It was a song that had now become subversive; and he was dismissed. A non-commissioned officer, Sergeant Constant, replaced him. He was appointed during the course of the first parade. Three days later the captain ordered an assembly. In front of the assembled company, one of his colleagues, Sergeant Andrieu, who was an enthusiastic resistant, presented him with a document appointing himself captain. Constant returned to the ranks. He emerged from them again two days later, being reappointed at another assembly. The situation became more complicated. Guingouin was asked to arbitrate. Acting the part of Solomon, he decided the two sergeants should command the company jointly.

On the 5th, Boursicot took up his duties as Commissioner of the Republic on appointment from Algiers. Chaintron, a Communist, was appointed Prefect. A new mayor, Doctor Chadourne, a non-Communist resistant, was also appointed.

Limoges had emerged without too much damage from this difficult period. A trial of strength had been avoided.

When, on 13 May 1945, Guingouin, properly elected mayor of the town, arrived to take up his new post, he came impressively in uniform. He placed his revolver, which now no longer struck terror into anyone, on the municipal desk.

Someone irreverently and unjustly nicknamed him "Ubu Mayor."

Events had, therefore, taken very much the same turn in Limoges as they had in Toulouse, Montpellier and, up to a point, in Bordeaux. The forces of insurrection, for which the C.O.M.A.C. had organized the cadres, hesitated to act and the trial of strength was still-born. Ravanel, Gilbert de Chambrun and Guingouin, for different reasons, all failed to attempt the trial of strength for which they had been appointed military leaders of the F.F.I. We have seen the circumstances in which these failures took place. But it was also a general failure. Nowhere, except in a few towns of comparatively minor importance,[1] did the Communists seize power. And for this failure there were more general reasons.

The directing organisms of the Party were far from being in agreement as to how their policy should be implemented. The political direction, the military direction and the regional leaders, all took up different positions. And no doubt this explains the uncertainties of their revolutionary action from August 1944 onwards.

In the political headquarters of the Party, which consisted of Duclos, Frachon, Lecœur and Tillon, there were two different views. Lecœur's and Tillon's was that of the combatants who had remained in France, created the F.T.P., and conducted the armed struggle. They had their troops well in hand and, owing to the disorganization of the whole apparatus of government following on the Liberation, thought there was a favourable opportunity of seizing power.

Duclos's and Franchon's view was that of political non-combatants, who were used to conforming to directives from Moscow. That the Party should acquire certain positions of authority, infiltrate the F.F.I.

[1] In Arles a Communist municipality was appointed by acclamation.

and the administration, and increase the number of its effectives were
not matters calculated to displease them provided these preparations
did not anticipate Stalin's instructions.

The C.O.M.A.C., the military command, knew no such divergencies.
Its attitude was the same everywhere and in every case it was out to
seize power. We have seen it in action in Paris, where through Villon
it was out to impose its own tactics and denounce the truce. We have
seen it in the three regions in the south-west on which it had designs
and where it placed its own people in command of the F.F.I. Moreover, at the Liberation, it disposed its F.T.P. units in accordance with
a central plan which, though not perhaps immediately one of insurrection, was certainly a preliminary to it. Some evidence of these obviously secret orders has transpired. As we have seen, Colonel Druilhe,
the non-Communist commander of the Dordogne F.F.I., knew of the
C.O.M.A.C. order "to proclaim the Republic of the Soviets of the South
of France." Similarly, Colonel Noirot, commanding the F.T.P. of the
Lot, received orders to march on Limoges where the military effectives
of the Party seemed too weak to seize the town.

There was, therefore, at the summit of the military hierarchy of the
F.T.P., both a desire for insurrection and a general plan for distributing
its effectives for the purpose.

To these orders from the C.O.M.A.C. the departmental or local leaders responded in different ways. And it was here that the monolithic
system of the Party was breached. The F.T.P., of whom the majority
were Communist, nevertheless comprised non-Communist maquisards
who had joined them for local reasons or because they did not realize
what their real designs were. There were therefore F.T.P.s of two kinds:
those for whom the Communist cause was more important than the
national interest, or was rather its true emanation, and who therefore
refused to co-ordinate their efforts with those of the F.F.I. and had
tactics, methods of recruitment and sometimes even equipment which
were peculiar to them; and others for whom the fact of having joined
the F.T.P. did not mean that they had lost their sense of solidarity
with the Resistance as a whole. These remained loyal to de Gaulle
and to his government. Besides, did not his government contain Communist ministers? And was not the General therefore the uncontested
leader whom even the French Communists did not dare openly to attack? For these the Liberation of France was the supreme object, whereas
for the F.T.P., who were strictly Communist in obedience, it was but the
first stage. When it was a question of delivering the country, they would
follow the orders of their resistant leaders, whether these were Com-

munist or not. After the liberation of the Dordogne, Colonel Druilhe ordered all the Maquis of the department, F.T.P. and A.S. alike, to march on Bordeaux. They all obeyed equally; the only difference being that the first followed the right bank of the Dordogne and the second the left. And, when they reached Bordeaux, they found themselves united in protecting the town against the menace of the Germans who were fortified on the Pointe de Grave. Without the support of the F.T.P., it would have been difficult to establish a continuous front.

There was not therefore complete unity in the attitude of the F.T.P. at the time of the Liberation. In general, they had similar aspirations and made similar plans, but had no general instructions. It would no doubt have been sufficient for the secretary-general of the Party or the Kremlin to issue orders for insurrection for a trial of strength to take place and a Communist revolution to break out in the liberated territories. But the secretary-general of the Party, Maurice Thorez, was in Moscow. And Moscow had no intention of compromising its relations with the Americans and British for a secondary and premature operation in France.

In 1944, Stalin needed his allies. When de Gaulle visited him in the Kremlin in December, there was an anecdote told which, though no doubt apocryphal, was nevertheless revealing. Talking of Maurice Thorez's return to France, Stalin said to the General with a laugh: "Please wait a little before you shoot him." A wish de Gaulle found it all the easier to gratify since, on his return to France, the rebel of 1939 advocated union and loyalty to de Gaulle.

The insurrection was always on the point of being launched and yet never occurred. There were a staff and troops organized for a D-day that never came, but for which the preparations and preliminaries were often impressive. . . . Was it owing to Communist uncertainties that the trial of strength never came off? Up to a point, this was undoubtedly so. But it was also due to the confidence with which the Gaullists assumed control. While the Communist camp lacked orders and sometimes seemed to be taken unawares by events, the Gaullists of London, Algiers and the Maquis had made detailed preparations and knew in advance what steps would be necessary to prevent subversion. The Commissioners of the Republic and the new Prefects, with the execption of two or three, were sufficiently aware of their responsibilities to have no need of precise instructions on the attitude they should adopt. The military leaders knew well whom they could trust and whom they could not. After the departure of the Wehrmacht and the Gestapo, even when they were cut off from the central power, they took the necessary steps to protect the towns and gradually restore order to the countryside.

On one side was the immense, rigid and monolithic apparatus of the Communist Party, which could have done much had it wished, but received no orders to do so. The result was confusion, haphazarded effort and failure.

On the other side was a new, less experienced, but more supple organization composed mostly of free men, whom orderly and detailed preparatory work had organized without enslaving or embarrassing their initiative. Above all, they were linked by their confidence in an uncontested leader.

In the last analysis, the victor in this abortive trial of strength with the Communists was General de Gaulle. There were certain apparent contradictions in his policy which even today seem to cast a doubt on the true sense of his actions.

He is often blamed for having played the Communist game by including Communists in the government, allowing Thorez back to France, and going to Moscow to sign a Franco-Soviet Pact. But these apparent satisfactions afforded Stalin and the Communists were but so many means of neutralizing action on their part.

With regard to the Communist Ministers, we have seen, when dealing with the Vercors, how the General succeeded in short-circuiting them.

As for his journey to Moscow and the return of Thorez, they entailed consequences which were not appreciated by members of the Party. Their principal civil war-machine consisted at that time of the Patriotic Militia and they were intensifying recruiting to it. All the militants in France were much attached to it. On 27 October 1944, Duclos still declared himself in favour of this organization. A month later, on 27 November, Thorez returned to Paris. On 30 November, speaking at the Vélodrome d'Hiver, he issued these instructions: "Fight the war"; "Create a powerful French Army"; "Reconstruct industry as quickly as possible"; "Unite." These were patriotic words but still too general for their consequences to be foreseen. But, on 21 January 1945, after General de Gaulle's journey to Moscow, the Central Committee of the Communist Party met at Ivry. Thorez made his report and, to the general surprise, supported the disbandment of the Patriotic Militia and Guard: "These armed groups were necessary before and during the insurrection against the Hitlerian occupation and its Vichy accomplices. But the situation is now different. Public security must be assured by the regular forces of the police set up for this purpose. The civic guards and, generally speaking, *all* the armed irregular groups must be maintained no longer."

Here then were the Communist shock troops being dissolved by the secretary-general of the Party himself. It seemed as if Thorez, in making his declaration, was paying to de Gaulle a *quid pro quo* for his return to France and for the Franco-Soviet Pact. Moreover, he was probably not displeased to take the Party he had abandoned for five years back into his own hands by disarming his comrades who had remained and fought in France. A very personal point of view, with which his wife, Jeannette Vermersch, who had returned with him from Moscow, was no doubt in agreement.

In any case, de Gaulle had won. He and his men had prevented the Communist insurrection, not only by their overt action of replacing the administrative and political cadres of the country, but by their necessarily concealed diplomatic activity.

This was statesmanship on the grand scale, and it was able to be conducted at a critical moment and with few means due to the prestige of one man.

Chapter V

THE SUMMARY EXECUTIONS

WE now come to some of the most painful episodes of the period. These summary executions, by which many French died, were not carried out by the Gestapo or the Militia, but by men who seemed to their victims to be among their liberators. Excesses such as these were doubtless inevitable in the dramatic circumstances that accompanied the departure of the Germans. They were often reprisals for the treatment suffered by the Resistance during the Occupation. But this could not alter the fact that they aroused passionate resentments which in some cases still exist and distort the truth. Consciences were troubled and still continue to be so. Any account of them must therefore be objective.

On 20 June 1945, Adrien Tixier, Minister of the Interior in de Gaulle's government, wrote to his colleague, the Minister of Justice: "I must inform you . . . of the serious difficulties the police services are encountering at the present time in carrying out their task in the face of a popular and spontaneous movement which it is often almost impossible to combat."

Thus, ten months after the Liberation of practically the whole country, popular passions were still so violent that the police were not always able to prevent reprisals.

In support of this general picture, here are the official reports, with references, of some of these excesses. In a note to the Minister of Justice, dated 19 October 1945, the Procurator General of the Cour d'Appel of Nîmes reported on the case of a certain Marquis des I—, whom the Committee of Liberation of Carpentras considered to be "an infamous collaborator" and whose château it was threatening to burn down. "It would seem," wrote the magistrate, "that the accused is a victim of local hatreds, due essentially to the fact that he is an important landed proprietor with Royalist tendencies."

At Poitiers, the Court had to deal with a case of summary execution.

Here is the report: "On 28 August 1944, the married couple T— and their daughter were arrested by a group of the F.T.P. 'Paul' and shot in the Mauprier wood, near Lusignan. The order had been issued by A— Paul (alias Paul P—) who is today an orderly officer at the Ministry of Air. He asserts that these three people were tried by a military tribunal, which had been regularly constituted, and were convicted of connivance with the Gestapo. The secretary of the mairie and the assistant to the Mayor of Chaunay declared that in fact there was no tribunal. According to popular rumour the maquisards told the T's to bring with them their money and their jewels, which have not been recovered.

"The people of the district do not seem to believe that the T's denounced Frenchmen, but it appears that they entertained Germans and that the daughter was frequently in their company."

Others were matters of pure and simple banditry. For instance, the crimes committed near Loches, by a gangster called Le Coz, whose *curriculum vitae* is here taken from an official report:

A recidivist, with thirty-six convictions and more than ninety years forbidden residence, he appeared in the region of Loches under the name of Dr. Jean, stayed at Beaulieu, and at Saint-Hippolyte, and was unable to join the Maquis of Épernon (32nd R.I.) since he was known from a general information report and a special enquiry made by Commandant Villeminot. He set himself up as a Maquis leader, and recruited 250 men of all nationalities, Ukrainians, Poles, Spaniards, former Waffen S.S., as well as young men from the Loches district. An inveterate alcoholic, he terrorized the whole district, and with a following of twenty women who were his mistresses, hoped to appear as the scourge of collaborators. In fact, he was a bandit who pillaged, stole and murdered. He occupied Loches from 16 to 20 August, killed Inspector Recco in the main square, and abandoned Loches under pressure from the German Army which reoccupied the town until 2 September.

At the beginning of October 1944, Le Coz and his principal lieutenants left for the Jura to join de Lattre's army, but he was driven back and returned to Loches. The Prefect had been informed, and requisitioned military, police and gendarmerie to set a trap for him. Le Coz was arrested on Sunday evening, 21 October, and imprisoned in Angers where he was tried and condemned to death on 16 October 1945. He was eventually shot in May 1946.

The number of summary executions (those known to the military tribunal of Angers) carried out by Le Coz amounted to eighteen.

There were also many collective crimes. Those responsible were often unknown and the authorities were usually unable to take action.

A common grave was discovered in the Dordogne: "On 6 November 1944, the Public Prosecutor of Riberac was informed by the Mayor of Saint-Aulaye of the exhumation of twenty bodies discovered in a common grave at the place called 'Petit-Bregaut.' The exhumation had taken place on 24 August 1944, on the initiative of the departmental delegate of the Red Cross, M. Van C—.

"They were people of the district, of both sexes, of whom fifteen have been identified, eight being of French nationality, one North African, and six German soldiers; two other bodies appear also to be those of Frenchmen. They have all been placed in coffins and buried in the parish cemetery.

"My deputy immediately ordered an enquiry by the gendarmerie which confirmed the statements of the Mayor. These were persons who had been executed after the liberation of the Canton by two battalions of F.T.P.F., who were stationed in Saint-Aulaye and the neighbourhood on two separate occasions, early in the month of August, though the precise dates cannot be fixed."

In this case, it took the judicial authorities four months to become aware of a collective massacre, which is very indicative of the state of anarchy to which certain districts were reduced at the time of the Liberation.

Even the police was not always innocent of such misdeeds.

On 16 March 1945, the President of the Paris Committee of Liberation wrote to the Minister of Justice to complain that "patriotic" police had been imprisoned after the Liberation. Here is part of the reply from the Minister of Justice in which he details certain brutalities committed by these servants of the law:

(3) The affair of B— and G—.

I have the honour to inform you that the policemen B— and G— have been accused of murder in the following circumstances:

On 1 September 1944, in the Boulevard Jean-Jaurès, at Clichy, near the Place Lecomte, the crowd was attacking a group of three persons, among whom was a man named R— M—, because of shots fired from a window in a house in the Boulevard Jean-Jaurès.

Panic-stricken, the man named R— ran away, but was caught and arrested a little farther on by two members of the F.F.I. While being taken to the police station and making no attempt to resist arrest, R— M— was wounded with two bullets in the head by policeman G— and killed by a third bullet fired by policeman B—.

As a result of this incident, the said persons were arrested and suspended from their duties on 3 September 1944.

This irrefutable official document, of which many more could be quoted, has a twofold interest.

In the first place, they allow some diagnosis of the summary executions to be made. Some were provoked by class rivalries or political quarrels that had no direct relationship to the Resistance. Others were merely vicious or passionate crimes which also had nothing to do with the struggle against the occupying power and its accomplices. Others again were the result of private vendettas and, as we have seen, were all too common in certain districts before the Liberation.

In the second place, these documents reveal the attitude of the authorities born of the Resistance towards summary executions. Though disapproving these excesses, and doing their best in the circumstances to prevent or at least limit them, it cannot be said that their efforts were always effective, at least in the beginning; above all, they were in many cases unable to take the necessary steps openly and had to proceed unofficially, indeed almost secretly, towards re-establishing order.

In the state of anarchy in which France then was, the forces of order, decimated, demoralized and frequently suspect because of the part they had had to play during the Occupation, were often powerless to intervene. The government might launch appeals for order but its instructions remained vain. It sometimes happened that Ministers and high officials had to intervene in person to prevent excesses. At different times the Minister of Justice and Commissioners of the Republic, such as Yves Farge in Lyons for instance, had to protect with their own persons prisoners who were in danger of being hauled from their cells and executed.

In general, as soon as it was possible, the Gaullist authorities restored order and gradually reintroduced normal judicial practices. From the military tribunals and courts-martial which had come spontaneously to birth on the departure of the Militia and the Germans, to the regularly constituted courts of justice, the path towards the re-establishment of legality was often slow and painful.

But, in spite of their desire for order, which in the event could not always be achieved, in spite of the obvious tendency to have done with individuals taking the law into their own hands, the new authorities did not much care for these things being mentioned in public.

This was often due to the fact that they were powerless to get their decisions put into effect. In certain districts, whenever they wished to arrest a former resistant known to be guilty of a crime, the Committee of Liberation would intervene and the population riot. In some cases, it was perhaps also due to prudence. In order to protect a suspect from the vindictiveness of the population the local authorities would often begin by imprisoning him; and one can well see why they had no wish to proclaim their real intentions in these cases. It was also no doubt due to a continuing sense of solidarity with everything that, more or less legitimately, went by the name of resistant, and a feeling of aversion to everything that recalled Vichy and the Occupation.

And then, too, the families of the victims had often been terrorized and preferred to conceal their misfortunes rather than go to the authorities.

The result was that the situation remained confused for a long time and that to the public the government's attitude appeared somewhat uncertain, indeed often contradictory. To see the matter in its true light, it would have been necessary to make a minute and objective study of the facts; and this was certainly not possible in 1944.

There then occurred what always does occur when the authorities fail to take the public into their confidence. Public opinion sought for explanations beyond the official declarations. Individual commentators appeared and revealed, often exaggeratedly, the facts the authorities wished to conceal. In this painful matter of the summary executions, which required to be treated with balance and discretion, articles were written with a lack of objectivity which bedevilled the whole question for a long time to come.

It began with the Allied journalists whose only interest in French quarrels was to derive sensational reports from them. In *The American Mercury* of April 1946, Donald Robinson wrote the following: "Since I was then attached to the headquarters of Civil Affairs of the Seventh Army in Marseilles, I witnessed personally the Communist terror which was established after the German retreat from the South of France. Military security officers estimated the number of victims, executed mostly by the Communists, to amount to fifty thousand. During the summer and autumn of 1944, the revolution, ardently fomented by the Communists, nearly overwhelmed the South of France. Their partial failure had its source in the brake applied by the presence of the American Army. The bitterness resulting from their excesses, and the divisions resulting from their manœuvres, are the source of the present disunion. A people does not blindly forget its Calvary. . . . From Toulouse to Nice, the terror was in evidence. Everywhere in the streets were civilians with a hard look, and armed with a variety of weapons, from knives to rifles, grenades and American weapons. They drove along the boulevards in doorless cars which made shooting on the move easier. Every district, every street was searched, not only for militiamen, but for anyone who had happened to attract their political enmity. Even Americans were among their victims, soldiers were killed or wounded, and I myself was fired at more than a dozen times."

Much in this account would appear unlikely, to begin with its author's remarkable luck in being missed so often. The figure of fifty thousand victims, which some would think excessive and others insufficient, would seem to have no foundation. It is clearly one of those figures adopted lightly in a climate of excitement by which armies in a campaign or frightened civilian populations crystallize their emotions. It was repeated four years later by an English writer, Frank MacMillan, in *The Tablet* of 7 January 1950. He quoted the same figure but gave a different description of the territory to which it applied: "It was calculated by the commander of the historic division of the American Army that approximately fifty thousand persons were put to death in the Mediterranean zone during the years 1944 to 1945."

What does the "Mediterranean zone" mean? Is it simply meant to imply the southern district in which the American troops operated immediately after the landing in the south, that is to say Provence and the valley of the Rhône? In that case, the figure is certainly exaggerated. Or does it mean the whole of the south? If this is meant, what could the Americans know about it except by hearsay, since they never fought in the south-western and central districts where most of the summary executions took place? The whole matter seems very uncertain, and these Allied witnesses merely leave us in confusion.

Certain Frenchmen, on the other hand, informed by a legitimate desire to establish the truth, have cited with proofs some of the most scandalous crimes that came to their knowledge.

One of these was Canon Desgranges in his book *Les Crimes masqués du résistantialisme*. This good and honourable man was obeying only his conscience. Such again were the articles by Jean-Louis Vigier published in 1945 in *Époque*, under the title *"Banditisme et lacheté,"* in which he cites summary executions it would be difficult to contest. These two authors were members of the Resistance and do not plead *pro domo*. Another was Colonel Rémy.

In the opposite camp, among those who were victims of the Liberation, there was one, Pleyber-Grandjean, who made an effort to give an objective account of a number of atrocities in *Écrits de Paris*. The facts he gives are for the most part exact, but he exaggerates the conclusions he draws from them. According to him, the 7,000,000 people who abstained from voting at the elections for the Fourth Republic, though they were on the Electoral Register, corresponded to the number of direct or indirect victims of the Liberation.

However, by and large, these exaggerations do not prevent private evidence from supplementing to a considerable extent the discreet utterances of authority. Public opinion often owed to them the fact that it had any information at all. And the families of the victims owe them a debt of gratitude.

From the historical point of view, however, they are insufficient. Without sufficient means of research, and lacking in objectivity, they can form no basis for the appreciation of the problem as a whole. Indeed, how can the number of summary executions committed at the Liberation be arrived at?

We have been fortunate to obtain some unpublished and indisputable information which allows us to answer this question. On 20 February 1959, we received a reply from the Headquarters of the Gendarmerie and Military Justice to an enquiry addressed to them on 17 November 1958. For the first time, an official source has produced information on which some probable solution to the problems of the summary executions can be based. It consists of "a report drawn up from objective information gathered by units of the gendarmerie." This "report . . . does not cover the whole of metropolitan territory." It excludes the cities of Paris, Orléans, Limoges and Toulouse. Moreover, the information from the cities of Metz, Dijon, Lyons and Marseilles are shown as being only "fragmentary."

Apart from these lacunae, which affect some of the regions most concerned, the number of summary executions committed at the time of the Liberation and reported by units of the gendarmerie amount to 14,468. Taking into account the missing regions, and those incompletely covered, a figure of over 20,000 can be reasonably estimated for the whole of France. If one adds to this the summary executions committed before the Liberation, statistics which the Ministry of the Interior places at a higher figure than those perpetrated at the Liberation, the minimum must be between thirty and forty thousand.

Approximately one Frenchman in a thousand was the victim to the excesses committed at the Liberation—a figure sufficiently high to create a psychosis that will remain forever in the memories of the survivors. It would be vain to try to appease their rancour: all one can suggest—and this would have to be confirmed by a more extensive study of the post-Liberation period—is that without the action, however insufficient, taken by the new authorities, the disorder would have been still greater and the victims more numerous.

We can here thank only briefly the Headquarters of the Gendarmerie and Military Justice, which by its civic spirit and intellectual honesty has established new and important evidence for the study of this painful problem.

Part Six

THE LAST LIBERATIONS

Chapter I

THE ATLANTIC AND THE RHINE

AFTER Paris and the greater part of France had been liberated, there were still two campaigns to be fought on French soil, one in the east towards Belgium and the Rhine, and the other in the west round the Atlantic pockets in which the Germans had fortified themselves.

The advance to the east took place in four stages.

The first stage was the continuation of the battle of France, which ended on 16 September 1944. The Allied advance took three directions.

In the direction of Belgium and Holland, Amiens was taken on 1 September, Arras on the 2nd, Tournai and Charleroi on the 3rd, Lille, Brussels and Antwerp on the 4th, Nieuport and Ostend on the 8th. Elements of four German divisions were enclosed in the redoubts of Calais, Dunkirk and Boulogne.

Towards Luxemburg, the advance took the general line of Lille-Trêves. Louvain, Tirlemont and Namur fell on 5 September, Liège on the 8th. Luxemburg was liberated between the 10th and 15th.

Towards Lorraine, Charleville and Sedan were taken on 1 September, Verdun on the 4th and the western bank of the Moselle was reached on 7 September. Pont-à-Mousson and Épinal fell on 15 September.

Meanwhile, Le Havre was taken on 12 September, with its German garrison of 12,000 men, fortified behind an anti-tank ditch, with concrete pillboxes, and supported by 110 88 mm. guns.

The second stage was the battle of the frontiers, which lasted from 17 September to 15 December. The German High Command refused to withdraw its right wing behind the shelter of the Rhine and the Siegfried Line, which would have allowed the Wehrmacht to economize its forces. But Hitler, for reasons of prestige, refused to contemplate the evacuation of Alsace and Lorraine, which he had always claimed as German territory.

Until November, three Allied armies before Metz, the Vosges and Belfort, tried in vain to pierce the German front and liberate the Moselle, the Bas-Rhin and the Haut-Rhin. The taking of Épinal and Remiremont by the Americans were successes which led to nothing. In November, the Allied Commander-in-Chief launched a general offensive from the North Sea to Switzerland. On the 8th, the American Third Army encircled Metz with two converging attacks. It entered the town on the 22nd, but the forts held out till 13 December. On that date, the whole of the Moselle was liberated.

On 13 November, the American Seventh Army went into the attack. After a difficult start in front of Sarrebourg and Gérardmer, the offensive made ground in the region of Cirey. The French 2nd Armoured Division, which was attached to it, passed through the breach, succeeded in penetrating into Alsace by secondary passes, opened the Saverne Pass, and advanced on Strasbourg, which it took on 23 November. On 14 November, the French First Army had attacked the Belfort Gap. Bypassing the town, it debouched into Haute-Alsace, reached the Rhine on the 19th and liberated Mulhouse on the 20th. The Germans evacuated Belfort, but launched a counter-attack which enabled them to hold their ground between the Seventh Army and the First Army in what was called the Colmar pocket. The American and French offensive had only partially obtained its objective, the Rhine.

The third stage, which then began, took the Allies by surprise. From 16 December 1944 to 20 January 1945, the Germans regained the offensive. It took two directions; one across Belgium towards Antwerp, which was finally halted a few kilometres from the Meuse. The Americans, whose front had been pierced, counter-attacked on 26 December and obliged the Wehrmacht to retreat, with the loss of some 100,000 men. At the same time, however, the Germans advanced in Alsace each side of Strasbourg. So as to shorten their front, the Americans decided to abandon the town. The French were placed in charge of its defence and limited themselves to evacuating the salient of Wissembourg.

On 20 January 1945, the fourth stage, which was the final one, began. The Allies resumed their advance and continued to make progress till they invaded Germany and forced the Third Reich to capitulate on 8 May 1945.

This last battle began on the front of the French First Army which attacked the Colmar pocket. On 2 February, Colmar was liberated and on the 7th the whole of Haute-Alsace was retaken.

French territory had now been reconquered in its entirety, except for the pockets on the Atlantic coast round which the second campaign was in preparation. From the military point of view this front was of secondary importance, but for Germany, as for France, it presented political problems of great importance. According to German signals the garri-

21. & 22. *Pierre Laval (above), Premier of Vichy, France,
and Marshal Pétain, as they appeared at Pétain's trial for
treason.*

23. & 24. German
fortifications along "the
Atlantikwall."

sons of the Atlantic pockets amounted to no more than 69,000 men, of whom 8,000 were in the Royan pocket—5,000 in Royan itself and 3,000 in Verdon—16,000 in La Rochelle, 18,000 in Saint-Nazaire and 27,000 in Lorient. But these comparatively small numbers of troops held positions to which the Führer's pride was peculiarly sensitive. Indeed, they were holding the last vestiges of the Atlantic Wall, which had been one of his great inspirations and had remained his permanent care.

In the summer of 1942 Hitler had held numerous conferences at the Reich Chancellery in Berlin, with Field-Marshal Keitel, General Jacob, Reichsminister Speer and Rear-Admiral Kranke. These concerned the "Atlantikwall." Here, from an unpublished German document, is the gist of the speech Hitler made at the opening of the first session, at 21.40 hours on 13 August 1942. The Führer wished at all cost to avoid the creation of a second front.

"There is only one fighting front, the second can be only a defensive front held by insufficient forces. The army's offensive against Czechoslovakia and Poland was made in these conditions: for the benefit of the eastern front, the western front must manage with relatively weak forces. Russia has not yet been defeated and England may have surprises in store for us at critical moments. To avoid this, the Führer . . . has therefore decided to make the Atlantic and Channel coasts an impregnable fortress . . . which cannot be taken from the front, by encirclement, or even by assaults lasting several weeks. . . ."

To make the Atlantikwall impregnable, Hitler intended that the garrisons should amount to 300,000 or 350,000 men, supported by reserves of approximately 150,000 men. He was therefore allowing half a million men for the 15,000 strong-points of which it was intended the Atlantikwall should consist.

This, then, was the origin of the Atlantikwall.

When in June and August 1944, the Overlord and Anvil operations had confirmed the Führer's fears, the German units in the Atlantic pockets did not consider themselves as defeated troops taking refuge within their fortresses, but as the vestige of a grandiose plan, which might yet be reborn.

If the Ardennes offensive, in December 1944, had succeeded in reaching French territory, the pockets might have formed a new base for departure, a second front directed against the Allies.

A frequent aircraft service linked the pockets to Germany. There was also contact by sea due to 200 ships of small tonnage, a few submarines, and some fifty patrol boats and motor-boats. And when, in February 1945, Lieutenant Weissenborn, with a flotilla of mine-sweepers, succeeded in running the Allied blockade outside Royal and reached Hamburg, he was received as a deserter and court-martialled. The German troops fought energetically till the end. It was perhaps because they were defending in these last battles not only the ultimate hope for their country, but also what remained of the Führer's prestige.

On the French side, at this moment in the campaign, the problem arose of incorporating the F.F.I. into the regular French Army. This took different forms in the east and west, in the First Army, under the command of General de Lattre de Tassigny, which was campaigning towards Alsace, and in the "Detachment of the Army of the Atlantic," under the command of General de Larminat, which was to attack the pockets.

De Lattre at once understood the national importance of the fusion of the F.F.I. with the regular divisions. Immediately after the liberation of Lyons, in an interview given to Madeleine Braun for *Le Patriote*, he made his attitude to the Maquis clear: "We shall never merely absorb the F.F.I. . . . It is essential to preserve their name, their mystique and the pride of their groups. . . . Given the actual circumstances of our fighting army, its structure must not be changed. Individually or in formations, the F.F.I. groups, while preserving their identity, have come voluntarily to join our army. . . . As soon as conditions permit, a synthesis will have to be made between what they represent and what we represent, with the greatest generosity of understanding on both sides. . . . To all the merits and fighting qualities they have acquired during their life in the Maquis, we ask them to make an effort to add order and discipline, so that the country may recognize in them a part of the reconstituted army of tomorrow. . . . I emphasize the fact that it can be no integration in the future, but a synthesis in which they will keep their identity and their autonomy."

No fusion, therefore, but an amalgamation, which corresponded better to the state of mind of the Maquis. The newcomers did not always behave like a regular army. They had shown during the clandestine struggle "revolutionary military virtues," which were not altogether in accordance with regulations. "It would be contrary to the truth," noted de Lattre, not without humour, "to imagine the F.F.I. were all attracted to the army by an irresistible inclination." And, certainly to begin with, the army did not always take a very good view of them.

When, on 23 August 1944, the order was issued that the F.F.I., who wished to continue fighting, should sign up for the duration of the war, in certain Maquis there was an indignant flight from this return to military red tape. On the average, the units lost at that time 35 per cent of their effectives. In some, it was mainly the F.T.P. who departed, but the A.S. was also affected. The celebrated Corps Franc Pommiès was reduced by 50 per cent.

The fact was that the Resistance consisted of soldier-citizens who refused to abdicate any of their civil rights, particularly that of protesting when they felt so inclined.

Their discipline was not like that of regular units. Colonel Cheval described it as follows:

"Public reprimand inflicted by the commander of the unit, the suppression of saluting off duty, the use of the second person singular between commanders and subordinates, and the Tribunal of Honour are some of the measures which may be considered innovations.

"One may find in eight units out of eighteen elements of a new way of life. For example: when in rest one unit holds a short period of physical training on rising. In three units, the officers share the life of the men and eat from the field-kitchen. In four units, men and officers meet in the evening."

The amalgamation did not appear to be taking place under very favourable auspices. Nevertheless, it was successful. Both the regular army and the maquisards had the same fighting spirit and the same desire to get on with each other.

It was in these circumstances that the F.F.I. converged on the First Army from nearly all the liberated provinces. The names of their units bore witness to their origins. The order of battle of de Lattre's army, when in the Vosges and Alsace, in December 1944, included the Languedoc Light Brigade, the Lorraine Tactical Group, the Garonne Light Brigade, the Franche-Comté Regiment, the Bourgogne Regiment, the 1st Morvan Regiment, the 1st Yonne Regiment, the Alsace Mobile Group, the Cluny Commando, the 1st Aveyron Battalion and the Alsace-Lorraine Brigade, though this last had been recruited in the Dordogne under the command of André Malraux.

The Paris contribution was as varied as its population, and as diverse as its districts. Battalions of resistants were formed at the Château de Madrid, at Mont Valérien and at the École Militaire. Another was composed of pupils from the Janson-de-Sailly Lycée in which "the names of the old French aristocracy appeared beside those of the Parisian bourgeoisie." Others again came from working-class suburbs: "The F.T.P. Colonel Fabien, a former member of the International Brigades, who had fought beside Rol-Tanguy at the liberation of Paris, reached Vesoul on 10 December with 3,000 men from Billancourt." Colonel Rol-Tanguy himself joined the First Army in March 1945, while Colonel de Chambrun arrived from Montpellier at the head of the 81st R.I. These reconstituted units, in which F.F.I. and F.T.P., without political distinction, fought the same battle, brought to the First Army an addition of 137,000 men to the 256,000 who had landed on the Mediterranean coast. In battle they often took over from units which could no longer remain in their positions, in particular from Africans, who could not fight in the mid-winter climate of the Vosges mountains and had to be relieved.

This replacing of African troops by others more accustomed to bad weather, this "whitening" of the effectives of the 1st French Free Division and the 9th Colonial Infantry Division was confided to the F.F.I. It concerned a total of 6,000 men from the Cameroons, French Equatorial Africa and Djibouti in the D.F.L., and 9,200 Senegalese in the 9th D.I.C. Their relief by young recruits from the Morvan and Provence, from the Isère and the Charollais, from Langres, Lyons, Chalon-sur-Saône, Besançon, the Ardennes and Brittany was sometimes carried out in camps behind the lines. But, wrote General de Lattre, "the substitution is so general and rapid that more often than not it is carried out in the line. One may then see this extraordinary spectacle: in fox-holes, only a few hundred yards from the enemy, these boys take over from the Senegalese and receive on the spot coats, helmets, weapons . . . and advice."

The amalgamation within the regiments and divisions already existing was completed by February 1945. Then, in deference to the part played by the F.F.I., a division was formed entirely of maquisards. The taking of Colmar and Mulhouse allowed the revival of the pre-war 14th D.I., which became the first F.F.I. division and took its place in the line of battle.

In the Detachment of the Army of the Atlantic, which was fighting in front of the pockets, the use made of the F.F.I. was somewhat different. Originally, the D.A.A. included no regular troops and was entirely composed of elements from the interior, F.F.I. and F.T.P.F. from the Maquis and more particularly from the Maquis of the region. At the beginning of September, Colonel Adeline, who had taken over command after the liberation of Bordeaux, was joined by detachments of F.F.I. from all over the country.

Nine units, amounting to over 12,000 men, moved on Royan, La Rochelle and Rochefort without much co-ordination. They marched in more or less ordered ranks through the liberated villages. In spite of their lack of uniforms, they formed guards of honour at the war memorials, now beflowered for the first time in four years, and decorated with the Cross of Lorraine. Each of these Maquis units had its own particular story to tell of the Liberation.

The one from Arcachon had taken part in a ceremony attended by the resistants of the town on 24 August. There had been present Commandant de Luze, town-major of Arcachon, Colonel Charly, Commandant Duchez, Doctors Monod and Doche, and MM. de Gracia and Dupin. "Three charming little girls, one young republican in a Phrygian bonnet, and two little Alsatians went up to the Commandant and presented him with a bouquet of red, white and blue flowers to the cheers of the crowd. . . ." Then the French, British, American and Russian flags were hoisted over the Hôtel de Ville. Everyone saluted while the band played the *Marseillaise, God Save the King,* the *Stars and Stripes* and the *Marseillaise* once again for their Russian ally, since the music for the new Soviet national anthem had proved unprocurable. . . .

At the start, these "terrorists," as the Germans called them, fought in precarious and demoralizing physical conditions. Their equipment was wholly rudimentary. They carried cartridges in their pockets and attached grenades to their trouser belts. They generally had a haversack in which they carried washing things, a bottle of wine, a spoon or a fork. Most of them had left without a plate, a mess tin, a blanket or a change of underclothes.

Their "uniform" to begin with consisted merely of a white brassard displaying the blue V and the Cross of Lorraine. But the Germans refused to recognize the badge and shot those who wore it. The F.F.I., therefore, soon discarded it and were to be recognized only by the fact that they were carrying arms.

At first these consisted of a very varied collection of light weapons. But the F.F.I. group commanders scrounged arms and uniforms wherever they could. In their "gazogènes" they toured the liberated regions, Bordeaux, Toulouse, Tarbes, Marseilles, Limoges, Châteauroux, Bourges, Orléans, Lyons, Le Mans, Bayeux, Paris and even as far as Lille and Brussels. They raided the stocks of the Vichy Youth Camps and the American depots, each Maquis rivalling the other, sometimes to the detriment of stocks destined for the First Army, which on occasion saw its reserves of uniforms disappearing.

As for artillery, they managed. Luckily the Wehrmacht, on leaving Bordeaux, had abandoned on the quays 150 20 mm. guns, which it thought useless because they lacked gun-carriages. These were manufactured; and in September these guns went into action, shelling the German defenders of Royan with shells that had been destined for the

Allies. Luckily, too, Colonel Adeline had a most valuable assistant in Lieutenant-Colonel Moressée, an artillery officer of the Belgian Army, who succeeded in transforming a regiment of F.F.I., inexperienced infantrymen, into a regiment of artillery.

From the morale point of view, it became increasingly necessary that the F.F.I. should be campaigning in normal conditions. The immediate problem was to obtain their recognition as regular combatants by the Wehrmacht.

On 12 September, a non-commissioned officer and an F.F.I. private were taken prisoner on the Royan front. Colonel Adeline informed the German Colonel Pollmann that "the troops under his command had taken prisoner a number of German officers, non-commissioned officers and men and that these were being treated in conformity with the rules of the Geneva Convention. . . .

"But that he had decided, should any French prisoners be executed, to exact immediate reprisals on these German prisoners to the number of ten Germans for one Frenchman—though he was prepared to consider the question of an exchange of prisoners."

On 13 September, Pollmann replied that the French prisoners interned in Royan were being well treated and proposed a meeting between officers of the two staffs. The meeting took place on 15 September at 10.00 hours in the Médis School, four kilometres south of Saujon.

The French delegation consisted of Lieutenant-Colonel Fray, Chief of Staff to Colonel Adeline, Lieutenant-Colonel Durand of the F.T.P. and an interpreter. The French officers arrived in uniform in an open car bearing a tricolour flag and a white flag. The German delegation, which was expecting F.F.I. leaders in Maquis clothes, was visibly impressed. A detachment of German infantry formed a guard of honour. The Germans, having negotiated an exchange of prisoners, ended by recognizing the F.F.I. as "regular combatants" on condition they wore a red, white and blue brassard sewn on the left sleeve.

Thus, in this first period, the Maquis began to organize itself empirically while besieging the German pockets as best it could.

On 18 September, General de Gaulle, while visiting the F.F.I. leaders at Saintes, gave orders that their groups should be transformed into regular units. A ministerial instruction of 20 September defined a coastal zone in which "the military command has power to take all measures directly."

On 14 October, de Gaulle created the "Command of the French Forces of the West" and appointed to it General de Larminat. He was instructed to deal directly with the Allied Supreme Commander for all questions concerning the preparation and execution of operations.

At this time, the units of the Maquis in contact with the Germans were divided into five sectors, under the command of the leaders who had formed them in clandestine days.

The Morbihan sector was commanded by General Borgnis-Desbordes, the Loire-Inférieure by Colonel Charnel, and the Royan and Pointe de Grave sectors by Colonel Adeline.

Larminat set up his headquarters on 13 November at Cognac, near the three southern sectors. A secondary headquarters, made necessary by the considerable extent of the front (400 kilometres), was opened on the same date at Angers for the two northern sectors.

The total number of F.F.I. amounted to 73,000 men, and they were to fight a hard campaign during the first winter months.

"Submitted without possible relief to the wastage of daily contacts and skirmishes, these formations had to be incessantly active in the mud and cold of a particularly hard winter to fulfil their mission. . . ."

In the Aunis sector, the enemy was particularly aggressive. He kept the initiative and on several occasions succeeded in penetrating into localities near the front, plundering livestock, and sometimes carrying off the healthy male population.

In front of Royal, the Germans improved their positions during the first months of the siege, by taking the Medis-Semussac ridge. From it they could look down to the sea and watch every movement of the French. After this, the front became stabilized.

The Pointe de Grave sector, which on the whole was the quietest, nevertheless had its active moments. In March, S.S. units succeeded in penetrating two kilometres through the lines in the Montalivet district.

In the northern sectors, the German garrisons made a few attacks both at Lorient and Saint-Nazaire. But the F.F.I., supported by the American 66th Infantry Division, contained them.

The war round the pockets became static. It was Larminat's mission to regain the initiative and drive out the occupants.

In December, the First Army was ordered to send reinforcements to the Atlantic front, which it did rather reluctantly. First, rear echelons were borrowed which allowed Larminat to get organized. Depots and supply services of all kinds were set up: ammunition, gasoline, repair shops, food depots and so on.

Meanwhile, de Larminat was reinforced by units of the regular army, which should have been sent to the Atlantic front in December, but had been delayed on the eastern front by the German counter-attacks at the end of the year and the beginning of January. The 1st Regiment of Moroccan Spahis, the 4th Regiment of Zouaves, the 1st Regiment of Marine Artillery, the 5th Antilles Battalion, the Oubangui-Chari Infantry Battalion, the Equatorial African and Somali Regiment, the 6th North African Infantry Battalion, the 1st Infantry Battalion, and an artillery group of the Far Eastern Colonial Division, all veterans of whom many had begun fighting again as early as 1940, now came to reinforce the F.F.I. Moreover, on the eve of operations, which owing to the promising situation in Germany had been fixed for the beginning of April, the Charente sector was completed by the French 2nd Armoured Division, a brigade of American artillery and a considerable part of the American 10th Infantry Division.

The air force consisted of five French groups under the command of General Corniglion-Molinier, and American and British formations under the command of General Doyle. A naval force, the "French Naval Task Force," under the command of Admiral Rié, consisted of a battleship, the *Lorraine*, a cruiser, the *Duquesne*, three destroyers, *Fortune*, *Basque* and *Alcyon*, four frigates, *Aventure*, *Découverte*, *Surprise* and *Neva*, the *Admiral Mouchez* flotilla of minesweepers, and the 31st flotilla of British minesweepers.

Such was the force under the command of General de Larminat for Operation "Indépendence," the first in which units of the Maquis were in a majority. For this reason, its political significance was even greater than its military importance.

Chapter II

THE LIBERATION OF ALSACE

OF all the French provinces Alsace was the last to remain wholly occupied. Its liberation was particularly moving. Indeed, rather than a
liberation, it was a reconquest, a dis-annexation.

On 14 July 1940, the French who were resident in Alsace, but not
Alsatian by origin, had been expelled and dispossessed. On 7 August,
Hitler appointed Robert Wagner, Gauleiter of Alsace, and Joseph
Bürckel, Gauleiter of Lorraine. Alsace was then attached to the Gau
of Baden. The Gauleiter immediately began to take repressive measures;
Alsatians were deported to Germany, others were incorporated in Nazi
formations, and a religious statute was imposed on the Bas-Rhin and
the Haut-Rhin. On 8 May 1941, the young Alsatians were mobilized
into German labour camps. The Gauleiter demanded the dismissal of
the Deputies of the province. Decrees imposed German legislation in
matters of nationality, marriage and inheritance. . . . Forced labour
was instituted on 30 May 1942 at the same time as military service.

Many Alsatians, at the peril of their lives, defaulted and took to the
Maquis. Resistance organizations multiplied and made contact with
the Resistance on the other side of the provisional frontier.

In July 1944, an envoy from London, Colonel "Maximum," was
parachuted into the Ain. On 28 July, he received a telegram from the
B.C.R.A. congratulating him on having crossed into Alsace: "Bravo,
Colonel, for your splendid performance. You were the first representa-
tive of General de Gaulle in Alsace." On 29 and 30 August, notices in
French and German were posted in Alsace. They emanated from
Colonel Grandval, head of Region C, to which were attached the
Haut-Rhin, the Bas-Rhin and the Moselle.

Notice:

The German army is beaten on all fronts. The inevitable capitulation is
near. One must be mad to believe in a reversal of the military situation due
to hypothetical new weapons.

In view of the atrocities committed by certain members of the Wehrmacht and the Gestapo on soldiers of the French Forces of the Interior and numerous civilians without distinction of age or sex, in the name of the French High Command and in agreement with the Allied High Command I address the following solemn warning to all Germans.

For one Frenchman, one Frenchwoman, one French child killed, martyred or massacred, ten Germans, ten German women, ten German children will be executed. For one farm, house, French village pillaged or burnt, ten farms, ten houses, ten German villages will be pillaged or burnt. The Germans count on the humanitarianism of the French to escape the savage treatment they themselves have meted out during the fifty months of the occupation.

Let them be sure that the justice demanded by our martyrs will pursue its inexorable course. It depends on them whether that justice remains strict justice or becomes transformed into implacable vengeance.

> For General Koenig, Commander-in-Chief of the French Forces of the Interior.
>
> Colonel Grandval, Military Commander of the Region.

Such was the anger which marked the end of the German occupation of Alsace. Of a population of 1,915,000 inhabitants, Alsace, together with the annexed part of Lorraine, had had 520,000 people deported and 140,000 forcibly incorporated into the German Army.

In a province which had suffered so much, the fight to liberate it became extraordinarily bitter on both sides. For the Germans, it was a decisive battle, for they had to protect the Ruhr which was the immediate Allied objective. Furthermore, it was a matter of preserving the territory of the Reich, for the Nazis considered Alsace and Lorraine an integral part of it. It was a battle in which the stakes were economic and political, a battle for frontiers stretching from Switzerland to the North Sea; and they devoted to it seven armies, of which one was armoured, consisting of seventy-three divisions of which sixty-eight were in the line and only five in reserve. In spite of the wastage of men and the lack of fresh troops, the morale of the German troops remained high; with their backs to the doors of their own country, they fought with energy, sometimes even with savagery.

Himmler, who carried out the Führer's reprisals, having completed the hecatombs following on 20 July 1944, was appointed in December to the command of the group of armies on the upper Rhine. But the Wehrmacht had not awaited his appointment to take harsh measures against the civilian population. The following announcement was made in the streets of Gérardmer on 6 September at eleven o'clock at night:

"The French male population between fourteen and sixty years of age of Gérardmer, Xonrupt and Longemer will assemble at 08.00 hours tomorrow in front of the Hôtel de Longemer, bringing tools (spades, shovels, picks, saws, axes). Any person refusing to work or failing to attend for work will be shot.

"The women and girls of families in which the men default will be required to replace them."

Similar pressure was brought to bear on the German troops to force them to fight and die to the last man.

On 21 September, Hitler threatened four divisional commanders in the Vosges with death if their units gave ground.

To encourage the troops to fight, the officers told them that German soldiers taken prisoner by the Gaullist troops would be shot on the spot. The Nazi Command turned its soldiers into "war criminals" by persuading them that "if taken prisoner they would be shot; and if wounded they would be finished off" and by ordering them, in reprisal, to shoot enemy prisoners and finish off the wounded.

In this merciless war there were many among the French who were exalted by the idea of reconquering this most sacred soil, both because it was the symbol of revenge, and because of the sufferings its population had endured.

On 19 November, when the tanks of the 1st Armoured Division entered Alsace, de Lattre sent General du Vigier the following signal:

"Bravo, with all my heart. The tanks of the 1st D.B. and the R.I.C.M. have been the first to enter Alsace. What a moving moment, what pride, what joy!"

The Allied forces in action from the coast to the Swiss frontier comprised three million men divided into three army groups: the Twenty-First Army Group, under the command of Field-Marshal Montgomery, consisted of the British Second Army and the Canadian First Army; the Twelfth Army Group, under General Bradley, consisted of the American First, Ninth and Third Armies; the Sixth Army Group, under General Devers, consisted of the American Seventh Army and the French First Army.

From this it can be seen that the French formations composed scarcely more than a tenth of the forces engaged. But de Lattre's army had achieved its autonomy: in September 1944 it had ceased being integrated with the American Seventh Army. It formed an army group with it on an equal footing.

Moreover, the campaign in Alsace was confided largely to the French.

It was not, of course, that the Allies were being inactive: during the months of September and October 1944, they captured territory of greater extent than Alsace: Vesoul, Lure, Remiremont, Épinal, Lorraine as far as Metz, Luxemburg, Belgium, and Holland up to the Meuse. But practically the whole of Alsace was liberated by the French, among other places the Belfort Gap, the Saverne Gap, Mulhouse, Strasbourg, and then Colmar. And it was French troops who reached the Rhine first.

Enthused by what was at stake in the battle, never had French armies fought a more intense and more diversified war. All the resources of modern battle were brought into play: the courage of infantrymen clinging to the terrain and dying there rather than retreat; the dash of armoured units darting like arrows across a countryside still occupied by the enemy, triumphing by their speed; the commander's strength of character, rejecting easy solutions, risking all for victory; and also his Machiavellism, setting traps for the enemy to fall into.

One of the most extraordinary episodes of this part of the war was the dash for Strasbourg.

Leclerc's 2nd Armoured Division received orders during the night of the 22nd of November to help the American VI Corps to take Strasbourg. But the Americans had not yet crossed the crest of the Vosges, while the French, having already seized Saverne, were descending into the plain. In that town they had received an enthusiastic welcome which increased their impatience.

"The town," wrote a witness, "was beflagged as if in a Hansi engraving. There was an intoxication of joy! The people welcomed us with tears in their eyes. The F.F.I. commander told us with pride of the prisoners his men had taken. The police had put on French uniforms which they had hidden for four years. We lunched quickly and I decided to go on at once to Strasbourg. Beflagged villages. The little children acclaimed us everywhere waving flags. . . ."

Leclerc therefore advanced on Strasbourg. It was the objective he had been hoping for for three years. But the fortress, with its garrison, forts, and the Pont de Kehl redoubt, was perhaps rather too strong for one armoured division. It was known, too, that the population of Strasbourg was intermingled with 15,000 German soldiers and officials, who were quite capable of helping to oppose the French advance. Nevertheless, Leclerc used the same tactics at Strasbourg as he had employed for Paris. Sacrificing everything to speed, he debouched from Saverne with his whole force, splitting it up into as many columns as there were roads. "Prisoners," wrote General Faury, "will merely be disarmed and sent westwards; the forts will be bypassed if they are not taken at the first thrust; columns held up by resistance will switch to the most favourable line of advance; the first units to enter Strasbourg will continue without stopping as far as the Pont de Kehl, the supreme objective."

On the 23rd at 07.15 hours, the avalanche left Saverne. At 10.30 hours, divisional tactical headquarters received a signal that the Rouvillois column had entered Strasbourg and was continuing towards Kehl.

"The arrival of the French tanks in Strasbourg created extraordinary astonishment; the garrison was not in a complete state of alert; officers, drivers and fatigue parties were out in the streets going about the business of ordinary life."

Rouvillois crossed the town like a whirlwind, shooting down everyone in German uniform. Officers were killed walking arm in arm with their wives. He got within six hundred yards of the Pont de Kehl, where his advance was halted by energetic resistance.

In the meantime, Massu's column was checked at Fort Foch and switched to Rouvillois's line of advance. Putz neutralized Fort Kléber and entered Strasbourg from the south. Cantarel was checked by Fort Pétain and switched to Putz's line of advance. Debray reduced Fort Joffre, wiped out an enemy column at Lingolsheim, crossed the Ill and occupied the Neuhof airfield, where he captured anti-aircraft and anti-tank guns.

Guillebon entered the town with an American support battalion. He ran up against a fortified barracks. Though he had neither guns nor tanks, he forced the Germans to surrender.

The whole Leclerc division succeeded in entering the capital of Alsace, but it was rather swamped amid a concentration of 200,000 men. There was no other solution but to carry on.

On the 25th, the battle was being fought in Strasbourg itself. The American guns were turned on to the forts that were still holding out. During the afternoon, General von Vaterrode surrendered.

On the 26th, General Leclerc ordered a parade on the Place Kléber: he announced that Strasbourg had definitely returned to France. But his words were supported by a march-past consisting of no more than one squadron of tanks and two companies of infantry, while German aircraft flew over the little ceremony. General Leclerc saluted the colours; the crowd sang the *Marseillaise*; and flags appeared at the windows.

In the middle of October, after the failure of an attempt to push through the Vosges, de Lattre decided to turn the obstacle by the right flank and attack in the Doubs sector along the Swiss frontier. But while drawing up orders for his unit commanders, he also wrote another series designed to deceive the enemy into believing that the new offensive would again be directed at the Vosges. This deception plan was mounted not only on paper but also on the terrain: "Simulated movements of troops and the setting up of national headquarters were ostensibly made in the region of Remiremont. At Plombières, a detachment of the 5th Armoured Division set up signboards and signposts and made considerable use of wireless. None of this activity could escape the notice of enemy spies," concluded General de Lattre, "and if, by chance, they did fail to see it, agents of our own S.R. would be there to open their eyes."

The General, who "was trying to extend the limits of Machiavellism," carried deception by fictitious orders even further. On 20 October, he signed the Secret and Personal Order No. 3 *bis* in which he announced his intention "to continue at once and with the maximum forces available the manœuvre across the Vosges." What did *bis* signify? Merely that the order was not intended for the commanders of the French formations, but for General Wiese, the German Army commander, to whom it was not, moreover, an easy task to get it.

A double agent, who tried to pass through the lines with the "secret" order he was supposed to have stolen, was arrested by the Moroccan infantry and only just escaped with his life.

De Lattre then employed channels through Switzerland, which was swarming with the secret services of all nations. He succeeded in passing a "Direction of Orientation No. 4" in which he stated that an action in the southern sector "would require extremely powerful forces without there being much hope of success in depth," that the offensive must therefore be continued in the Vosges, but that to mislead the enemy units must be moved to the southern zone, where no attack would in fact be made.

To make sure these stratagems were effective, it was not only necessary to get the enemy to believe them, but also, which was more difficult and more painful, to mislead the French troops. On 12 November, after long hesitation, de Lattre issued an order of the day to the First Army announcing that leave would start again in the second fortnight of November. It was the very period for which the offensive was planned. He was extremely reluctant to deceive his own men, but he knew that by doing so the whole of the First Army would become his unwitting accomplices.

Equally distressing was the fact that he was forced to refuse the pathetic appeals reaching him from the other side of the front. Engineers of the Peugeot company passed through the lines at the peril of their lives to tell him that the Germans were beginning to remove

The Liberation of Alsace

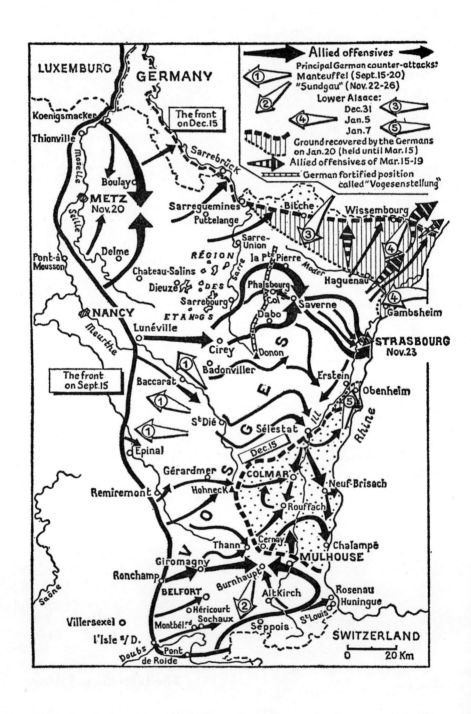

the machines from the Sochaux works and to entreat him to attack. Young men escaped through Switzerland from the still occupied territories and described the terror reigning in them, the shooting of patriots, the deportations, the cruelties of the Gestapo and the Militia, the requisitioning of goods and labour. They entreated the General to start his offensive soon. He could not tell them how imminent it was and, death in his heart, was obliged to let them go back in despair.

This was the price of success. On 14 November, General Oschmann, commanding the 338th Volksgrenadier Division (V.G.D.), which was holding the sector opposite the French Army, carried out the usual inspection of his positions. He thought there was no immediate threat to them. But, suddenly, at 11.20 hours, a bombardment of unparalleled violence forced him to take refuge in a hole with his A.D.C. He had with him personal notes which asserted his certainty that the French Army had no thought of an offensive. . . . After an hour the shelling died down. He emerged from his shelter to find himself surrounded by Moroccans. They shot him down with a burst of sub-machine-gun fire. His A.D.C. put his hands up. He was searched and on him was found a staff map, which confirmed his commander's illusions.

The Secret and Personal Order No. 3 *bis* had reached its intended recipient.

On 16 December 1944, Marshal von Rundstedt had launched a formidable offensive with twenty-eight divisions, of which nine were armoured, on a sector of the Belgian Ardennes, where the Americans were thin on the ground. Surprise was complete, and the Wehrmacht succeeded in creating a salient shaped like an equilateral triangle with sixty kilometre sides. The point of one angle almost reached the Meuse. Their line pierced in the centre, the Americans held the flanks in the regions of Montjoie and Echternach. Within the salient, they succeeded in holding the communications centre of Bastogne by the sacrifice of an airborne division.

On the 26th, with strong air support, they launched their counter-attack. Crushed by the bombing and hard pressed by the armour, the Germans had to withdraw to their starting-point, having lost 100,000 men.

It had been a desperate battle. One of the results of it was that the French 2nd Armoured Division had gone into strategic reserve in Lorraine, to block, in the Puttelange-Sarre-Union region, attacks directed against the American right wing.

But while the Germans were being halted and then driven back in the Ardennes, they attacked in Alsace, north and south of Strasbourg.

They retook the salient of Wissembourg between the Lauter and the Rhine. Bitche, Wissembourg, Lauterbourg, Woerth, Soultz and Seltz were subjected a second time to the rigours of the Occupation.

This new enemy offensive upset the plans of the American Command which was concentrating all its available troops in the Ardennes, where there was a danger of another German thrust. Eisenhower decided to abandon Strasbourg in order to shorten his front.

Strategically, it was a reasonable decision. But politically and humanly it seemed intolerable to the French. Could one go back on the promise Leclerc had made to Strasbourg? Could the population of Strasbourg, which had compromised itself by the enthusiasm with which it had welcomed the French troops, be abandoned to the tender mercies of the Gestapo?

On 1 January 1945, de Gaulle intervened with all his authority.

In a letter to General Eisenhower, he said:

"Without contesting that abandoning Strasbourg may eventually be justified from the strategic point of view for the Allied armies, the French Government clearly cannot allow the city to fall once again into enemy hands without doing all it possibly can to defend it.

". . . I am prepared to send to that area all the French forces in process of formation I can possibly raise in the interior, and in the first instance the 10th Division under General Billotte, whose forward elements are in Rheims. These forces will be placed at the disposal of General de Lattre.

"I am sure you will give them the necessary support.

"Whatever happens, the French will defend Strasbourg."

This categorical refusal was followed by a letter to de Lattre.

In the late afternoon of this same New Year's Day, General du Vigier went to the American Sixth Army Group Headquarters at Vittel. General Devers informed him that the decision to withdraw had been taken by the American Command. Du Vigier flew to Paris and informed General de Gaulle on the morning of 2 January. De Gaulle's reaction was immediate. He ordered General Juin to confirm to de Lattre the order to take over the defence of Strasbourg and to inform Eisenhower to this effect. At Versailles, on 3 January, at 15.00 hours, de Gaulle met Winston Churchill, who had come specially from London, and General Eisenhower. He showed himself completely determined. The French point of view carried the day. At 22.00 hours, de Lattre received a telegram from Juin: "As a result of a conference held at S.H.A.E.F. this afternoon, the Allied Command has decided on new dispositions which will ensure covering Strasbourg. General Devers must have received orders in this sense. . . ." Thanks to the stubbornness of General de Gaulle, and the mutual understanding existing between him and the commander of the First Army, Strasbourg was defended and saved. It was a rare example of what the patriotism and energy of a leader can do to alter strategy and assure victory.

Punctuated by episodes such as these, the campaign in Alsace consisted of five phases, from the arrival of the Allies in front of Belfort in September till the complete liberation of the province. Five long months during which the Wehrmacht shot its last bolt on the western front, and the French army played an essential part in the Allied advance.

The first phase, corresponding to the months of September and October, was marked by a stiffening of the defence and the marking time of the French.

In the Vosges, the "Battle of the Pines" fought by II Corps, under General de Monsabert, reinforced by the 1st Armoured Division and part of the 5th Armoured Division, was one of the hardest of the war. The French progressed step by step towards Gérardmer. It was a "diabolical sector" in which the Germans, who seemed to have learnt lessons from the Japanese, left behind them as they retired specially trained troops, who climbed trees and shot the first French waves in the back.

It was a battle of reciprocal encirclement in which the French had to fight for every yard of ground. One day, 30 October, they occupied a coalfield. Two days later, they infiltrated into the forest and took the Morbien Pass, one of the secondary passes of the Vosges. From there, they descended to the Moselette and pressed on towards the Moselle, gaining two kilometres. On the 8th, a sunny day, the tanks made a reconnaissance, without the support of infantry, and entered two villages. On the 9th, a day of mist and deluging rain, Monsabert's troops were stopped on the heights. They were trying to debouch into the plain. . . .

During eighteen days more this determined advance took place by fits and starts, interrupted by German counter-attacks. On 27 October, the first snow fell. During the night of 27th to 28th it froze; and the North Africans made shelters of logs. The F.F.I., who had not even one blanket, lay out on the frozen ground. It was the end of the offensive, which had driven in the German front, but had not been able to pierce it.

One of the causes of this check was the failure of supplies, both ammunition and food.

During the days of 28 and 29 September, II Corps had itself used 650 tons of ammunition, whereas the whole army received only 500 a day. In comparison with the supplies available to the American units, the French divisions were often very unfairly treated. In a note of 30 September to General Devers, de Lattre emphasized that, between the 20 and 28 September, the three divisions of the American Seventh Army had received an average of 2,102 tons a day by rail, while the five divisions of the French First Army had to be content with 968. In a letter of 19 October, to General de Gaulle, de Lattre reported the results of this first phase:

"The operations undertaken in the Vosges since the end of September have seriously encroached upon the enemy defences without however finding the gap which would have permitted crossing the crests and descending into Alsace. These last three weeks have however achieved 2,000 prisoners and over twice as many killed."

If the objectives could not be reached, others must be substituted. Leaving Monsabert to continue his pressure in the Vosges so as to hold the enemy's attention, de Lattre prepared a new offensive in the south. It was to be the second phase of the campaign which, between 14 and 29 November, was to result in a victory on the Doubs and in Haute-Alsace.

At noon on 14 November, after a short but violent artillery preparation, the 2nd D.I.M. and the 1st D.B., which formed part of I Corps, under the command of Béthouart, attacked between the Doubs and Villersexel. Owing to General de Lattre's cover plan, the offensive took the enemy by surprise; it was not until the tanks went into action, on 16 November, that the Germans realized it was not a diversion. For three days, the Wehrmacht hung on. On the 17th, Héricourt was taken. During the night, after an audacious manœuvre by the 5th Moroccan Infantry Regiment, Montbéliard was outflanked, encircled and overrun, while inside the town the F.F.I. of the Pingouins group seized the bridges over the Lisaine and prevented the Germans from blowing them.

This time, it was a break-through. The First Army had had 273 killed and 1,297 wounded. But it had captured the industrial district of Héricourt-Montbéliard and the Peugeot works at Hérimoncourt, Selancourt and Valentigney.

Béthouart set about exploiting his success. From 18 November, the exploitation took three different directions. In the first place, the reduction of the fortified camp of Belfort by the 2nd D.I.M. The town was not completely cleared till the 25th, after street fighting.

The second axis of advance was towards the Rhine and Mulhouse by the 1st Armoured Division (General du Vigier). On the 19th, at

14.00 hours, after a hard battle which inflicted 50 killed and 100 wounded on the Germans, the Moroccan Colonial Infantry Regiment, under the command of Colonel Le Puloch, began the liberation of Alsace by taking the village of Seppois. Then the tanks pushed on and, at 18.30 hours, French troops were the first to reach the Rhine. At Rosenau, a French battery of the 2nd group of the 68th Regiment of Artillery, commanded by Captain Laire, had the pleasure of firing the first shells across the river into Germany.

On 20 November, at 13.30 hours, the columns began advancing. At 16.00 hours, they were in front of Mulhouse, where the rear headquarters of Wiese's army was situated. The Wehrmacht was in indescribable chaos and the protection battalion was wiped out. In the dark, Colonel Caldairou, revolver in hand, and accompanied only by his adjutant, entered the "Feldpost," where twenty men were quietly sorting letters, and sixty more were "serenely sleeping." The two officers had only to fire a few shots to take eighty-four prisoners. On the left, the 5th Armoured Division ran into strong resistance round Cernay on the road that was to lead them to Colmar.

The battle of Haute-Alsace ended in a brilliant victory. From 20 September to 30 November, the German Nineteenth Army had lost 21,000 dead, 22,500 prisoners, 180 guns and 100 tanks.

Meanwhile, the third phase of the campaign was taking place in Basse-Alsace, conducted by the American XV Corps of which Leclerc's 2nd Armoured Division formed part.

The main attack took place through the Saverne Gap. The German defence line was on the crest of the Vosges hills dominating the valley. Saverne lay below in the plain.

General Leclerc now put into execution a manœuvre which had long been in his mind. He had determined to cross the hills to the north and south of Saverne, go down into the plain of Alsace and take Saverne from the rear; and then, when the town was taken, move on Phalsbourg.

This manœuvre, carried out in the north by the Dio group, and in the south by the Langlade group, took place between 19 to 22 November 1944. It was a complete surprise to the enemy, owing to the secondary routes used in crossing the Vosges, the speed of the advance, and the direction of the attack which took his positions in the rear.

On 22 November at dawn, the Rouvillois group debouched into the plain. It made junction with Massu to the east of Saverne. Meanwhile, Minjounet entered the town from the south, crossed it without incident and took the road to Phalsbourg, which was the road to France. He thus took the second German position from the rear and wiped it out.

At Saverne itself, the situation was quickly liquidated. General Bruhn, commanding the German 553rd Division, was taken prisoner with 800 of his men.

The next day, Strasbourg was taken by Leclerc, who debouched from Saverne with practically the whole of his forces. The 1st Armoured Division had taken Mulhouse on 21 November; the 2nd Armoured Division had taken Strasbourg on the 23rd. These two victories spanned the date of the liberation of Alsace in 1918. They had considerable effect on public opinion.

The fourth phase consisted of fighting in Vosges and in the plain of Alsace, now half liberated, where the Colmar pocket still separated the positions taken in the south and the north. It took place during December and the beginning of January, coinciding with the last German offensives at Bastogne and on Strasbourg.

After the taking of Strasbourg and the victory of Haute-Alsace, the general feeling in France and among the Allies was that the total liberation of Alsace must soon be achieved. The Allied Command left in Strasbourg and the Vosges only two divisions, one French, the 2nd Armoured Division, and the other American, the 36th Infantry Division.

Yet it took two months of unremitting effort to achieve the liberation of the province.[1]

For Hitler, Strasbourg was an integral part of Germany. Nothing must be left undone to recapture it. He relieved General Wiese from his command, holding him responsible for the failures, and replaced him by a man he could trust. Himmler's mission was to arrest the Allied invasion and then reconquer the abandoned territory. The new commander of the German Nineteenth Army was to be his subordinate.

Reinforcements both of infantry and armour were placed at his disposal. They included, in particular, the great armoured formation, the "Feldherrenhalle," and the 2nd Mountain Infantry Division, which arrived from Norway.

"Alsace," declared Hitler, "will be a present to the German people for New Year's Day 1945."

At the beginning of December, the French and Americans were continuing to advance. Béthouart attacked in the direction of Colmar, but made only a limited advance. West of Mulhouse, the Saint-Amarin valley was cleaned up as far as Thann. The Doller was crossed above Mulhouse and the line established on the outskirts of the Nonnebruck forest. East of Mulhouse, the French penetrated into the Harth Massif, but a violent counter-attack took back most of the terrain gained. After

[1] Cf., *La France et son Empire*, Vol. III. Several Studies by General Faury.

the taking of the Schlucht and Bonhomme Passes by the French, and the Sainte-Marie-aux-Mines Pass, Sélestat and Ribeauville by the Americans, the front was stabilized by Christmas. The Germans having attacked in the Ardennes, the Allied Command would authorize no further offensives outside the region where the decision was being played out. At the same time as they were making their principal effort in Belgium, the Germans attacked in Lorraine and in Basse-Alsace to hold down the Allied reserves.

The German offensive was launched towards Haguenau and crossed the Rhine at Gambscheim, from where it threatened Strasbourg.

It was then the dramatic episode of the Allied Command ordering the abandonment of Strasbourg took place. De Lattre and de Gaulle prevented the decision being put into effect. But, on 7 January, the Wehrmacht launched a new attack which obtained results. A French battalion was surrounded and annihilated at Obenheim, after an heroic defence. In general, the French maintained their positions, apart from the right bank of the Ill which they were obliged to evacuate.

By and large, in spite of some tactical successes, the German offensive was contained. The enemy remained enclosed in the region comprised between the Rhine, the Ill and the Kraft canal. Strasbourg was saved.

The Germans made one last effort to the north of the town, and succeeded in enlarging the bridgehead of Gambsheim and taking Kilstett.

But it was too late. They no longer had the initiative. The fifth phase began with a decisive push by the French Army.

Orders were issued for it on 16 January, the day on which Montgomery and Patton effected a junction at Bastogne, thereby putting a decisive end to the German operation in Belgium.

On 20 January, the troops went into the attack. Coming from the north and the south they converged on Brisach on the Rhine, on the level of Colmar, and encircled the town. Béthouart, with I Corps, attacked first in the south, to draw off the enemy reserves. Three days later, Monsabert, with II Corps, took the offensive in the north, where the decisive results were obtained.

The battle consisted of two phases: a battle of attrition which shook the enemy troops, during 2 February in the north, and 3 and 4 February in the south; then a rapid exploitation which ended in the reduction of the Colmar pocket. The town itself fell on 2 February.

On arriving at the gates of the town, the American infantry that Devers had sent as reinforcements to de Lattre's army had the courtesy to move aside and allow the French 5th Armoured Division to enter first.

The Alsace campaign thus ended with a splendid example of Allied solidarity. On the eve of crossing the Rhine and marching into Germany, the victorious commanders expressed their satisfaction.

"I have great pleasure," Devers wrote to de Lattre on 13 February, "in congratulating you highly on the magnificent qualities of leadership you have shown as General commanding the French First Army in the reduction of the Colmar pocket. In spite of the snow and extremely cold weather, followed by an inopportune thaw, which set the watercourses in spate and covered the plain of Alsace with floods, you have directed your troops in a superb manner, and in such a way as to destroy at least 80 per cent of the German Nineteenth Army with very few losses to your own troops.

"Your name will go down in history as the great liberator of Colmar and as the man who restored liberty and peace to the Alsatians."

De Gaulle and Eisenhower added their own congratulations. But the most spontaneous and moving manifestation was what de Lattre called "the plebiscite of the flags." "All the villages awakened to welcome their liberators . . . every house opened its doors to receive the men who had restored them to their country."

Chapter III

ROYAN AND LA ROCHELLE

THE two towns within the coastal pockets faced the last phase of the war in identical conditions, but their fates were very different; when the Germans surrendered in May 1945, Royan had been entirely demolished and La Rochelle was intact.

Royan and the Pointe de Grave facing it block the entrance to the Gironde and can prevent all traffic reaching Bordeaux. The pocket of La Rochelle, which lay between the mouth of the Sèvre Niortaise and that of the Charente, included the harbour of La Pallice and the Aiguillon inlet, where the Kriegsmarine had set up one of its principal bases on the Atlantic. On 18 September 1944, at Saintes, General de Gaulle met Colonel Adeline, who was temporarily commanding the sector before the appointment of General de Larminat, and gave him instructions for operations against the pockets. Referring to the unofficial negotiations by which Commander Hubert Meyer had obtained the evacuation of Rochefort by the Germans without a battle, he said:

I approve, in principle, all you have done up till now, and I congratulate you on the results obtained, notably at Rochefort. Nevertheless, I can in no circumstances approve of a definite local armistice with the enemy.

The German pockets must and will be reduced by force. A French Armoured Division will be sent here in the very near future, though I cannot say precisely when.

For the moment, I authorize intimidating action to persuade the enemy to abstain from executions and demolitions in the pockets.

I emphasize that negotiations must never assume the character of negotiations for an armistice. It is by adopting a firm attitude, if necessary a threatening one, and with the feeling that we are the victors, that the enemy must be brought to surrender.

These instructions in no way prejudiced the manner in which Royan and La Rochelle might be liberated. There were two possibilities: the coastal towns might be liberated as a result of limited negotiations, con-

ducted firmly and "if necessary by threats," or they might be taken by
force as a result of military operations. These two different attitudes
were represented by two French officers.

The negotiations were conducted by Captain Hubert Meyer, appointed by the government of Algiers to command the navy at the naval
prefecture of Rochefort. General de Gaulle laid it down that this officer
was the only one qualified to negotiate with the enemy in the name of
the French Command.

From 22 October, the military operations were confined to General
de Larminat, Commander-in-Chief of the Detachment of the Army of
the Atlantic. From General de Gaulle's instructions it would not appear
that there was any clash between Meyer's and Larminat's roles. The
negotiations were to contribute to the demoralization of the enemy
and to limit the employment of armed forces to the strictly necessary.
Preliminary negotiations followed by a death blow inflicted on the German garrisons by the French Forces should have brought about the liberation of the two pockets with limited destruction.

If things turned out otherwise, it was because Captain Meyer and
General de Larminat had different conceptions of the parts they had to
play. There was also a tragic error on the part of the American Air Force
which, for Royan at least, brought failure to the negotiations.

Captain Hubert Meyer was a native of the district. When he reached
the outskirts of Royan, his first visit was to the Château de Mons, which
belonged to his family. Not far away, at Orignac, near Jonzac, he owned
an estate that had belonged to his ancestors since the eighteenth century. With his roots in the district going back for centuries, the battlefield had for him not only a strategic, but a familiar and human aspect.

General de Larminat, who was a native of the Gard, had fought in
the Near East, the Desert, French Equatorial Africa, Tunisia and Italy,
indeed in all the victorious campaigns conducted by the renascent
French Forces since June 1940. He had commanded with success in the
Desert and before Sienna, in the Levant and in Tunis. He had been with
the French First Army at the taking of Toulon. When, in October
1944, he was appointed with the rank of army commander of the D.A.A.,
there was for him no strategic difference, no lack of continuity, between
the victories in which he had taken part in distant lands and the one
he now intended to win on French soil. It was all part of the same
process, and he remained the victorious General in action.

On 13 September, Captain Meyer met the German Admiral Schirlitz,
who was in command at La Rochelle, for the first time. He succeeded
in obtaining from him certain mitigations of the severity of the occupa-

tion of La Rochelle and drew up a "gentleman's agreement" by which the French undertook not to bomb from the air or endeavour to take the harbour. On their side, the Germans undertook to refrain from all demolitions and to make no attempt to pierce the French lines.

On 20 September, having obtained General de Gaulle's approval, Meyer renewed the negotiations.

"Admiral," he said, "the French Command has authorized me to make the following proposition to you:

"The French Command will fix a security line, slightly behind their actual positions. The crossing of that line by your troops will be considered a deliberately offensive act, which will have the effect of annulling every agreement and will bring down on you an immediate air offensive.

"On its side, the German Command will fix a line somewhat behind its actual advance posts, and our troops will undertake not to cross it.

"Between those two lines there will exist a sort of zone of operations in which actions, which are no doubt necessary to the morale of our respective troops, can take place freely.

"It is understood that during the course of such actions, the humanitarian conventions . . . will be scrupulously observed."

This last sentence concerned the exchange of prisoners and the recognition by Schirlitz of the F.F.I. as regular combatants.

After long and arduous negotiations between the two staffs, the lines were settled and an agreement, without time limit, was signed on 18 October. Each party reserved the right to denounce it after a warning of "four times twenty-four hours, counting from midnight on the day of denouncing it."

As a result, the situation round La Rochelle somewhat resembled the phoney war of 1939. But this time it was to the advantage of the French. The risks to the civilian population from local skirmishes were small, and the inhabitants of no-man's-land very soon got used to the situation. The peasants in the neutral zone quickly realized that it was in their interest to sell their livestock to La Rochelle, where the Germans had robbed the Bank of France and paid in French money, rather than to the F.F.I. who merely gave them requisition receipts. One girl had two lovers, a German and a Frenchman, whom she received alternately as their patrols were in the neighbourhood. On the eve of the surrender of the town, the Frenchman arrived. "It's my turn," he said. His rival protested that the surrender was to take effect only the following morning and upheld his right to that particular night. The Frenchman shot him with his revolver—contrary to the stipulations.

On 2 January, on the strength of this first success, Captain Meyer got Admiral Schirlitz to recommend him to Admiral Michahelles, commanding the Royan pocket, from whom he hoped to obtain a reprieve for several resistants who had been condemned to death by a German court-martial.

When the interview was over, Commandant Seim, Chief of Staff to Michahelles, took Meyer aside and suggested that Royan might well benefit from a similar agreement to that in force at La Rochelle. When Meyer pointed out that the situation at Royan was different because Royan prevented Bordeaux and the south-west being supplied by the Gironde, Seim replied that he was prepared to consider free access to the estuary for ships carrying neither troops or military equipment. . . .

Meyer hurried to Larminat's headquarters at Saintes, but the General was unfortunately away for a few days. General d'Anselme, who was deputizing for him, held out little hope of the German offer being accepted. "It would be very difficult to deny a battle which was so ardently desired and a victory which was so certain to the Army of the South-West which had been straining at the leash with its arms at the ready for months."

Nevertheless Meyer did not lose all hope of obtaining Larminat's agreement on his return. Unfortunately, events decided otherwise.

At dawn, on 5 January, the first disaster to Royan took place.

On 10 December, the American General commanding the Tactical Air Force of the Sixth Army, whose headquarters were at Vittel, had paid a visit to General de Larminat and General Cornignion-Molinier, who commanded his air force, at Cognac. It was of course a secret interview, but it appears that during it the "American general, who was of an enthusiastic temper, had argued forcibly that the Atlantic pockets should be, to use his own expression, 'softened up' by massive bombing attacks." [1]

There could be no question of this at La Rochelle where the Meyer-Schirlitz agreement was in force. As for Royan and the Pointe de Grave, the operation presented such grave risks that the French declined the offer.

Disappointed, the American General spent the evening in an F.F.I. Press Camp, where over the drinks there was wild and irresponsible talk about the population which had remained in Royan. "All those people," they said, "are collaborators."

Thus enlightened, the American returned to the French headquarters

[1] Admiral H. Meyer: *Au secours de la Rochelle, Rochefort et Royan* (22 August 1944–9 May 1945), page 59.

next day and suggested "a marvellous idea which had come to him during the night." Since there were no anti-aircraft defences in Royan, would it not make an admirable training target for certain bombing schools situated in Great Britain?

The French again refused. But, since their visitor insisted, they finally conceded that he might train his bombers by 'softening up' two objectives some kilometres from Royan on the sea, one being the Pointe de Grave on the other side of the river, and the other the Pointe de la Coubre at the extreme north-west of the estuary. Even inexperienced airmen could hardly mistake those two points and Royan would be in no danger.

On 5 January, at fifteen minutes past midnight, Captain Meyer, at Rochefort, was awakened by a fantastic firework display in the direction of Royan. In Royan itself, Admiral Michahelles took refuge in his "bunker," where he received messages about the raid. The bombs were falling principally on the residential districts, indeed far more so than on military objectives. The Germans had very few losses, 90 men in all. There were between 1,500 and 1,800 French civilians killed.

At 05.00 hours, while the massacre was still going on, his unit commanders asked him for orders. "It's no good asking me for orders," replied the German Admiral, who thought the bombing was a prelude to a French attack, "all our lines are cut. The French will be here in a few minutes. If, however, they have not arrived by 08.00 hours, we shall keep to our usual working timetable." At 08.05 hours there were no French, the bombing had stopped, and the Germans came out of their shelters into a town in ruins.

At Larminat's headquarters in Cognac, another interpretation had been put on the noise heard from the Royan direction. It was thought to be a German attack. Lights were dowsed, while aircraft continued to mutter over the headquarters.

Two aircraft collided and crashed nearby. Soldiers rushed out to them expecting to find Germans. To their surprise they found Scotsmen, some of whom were dead and the rest wounded. The survivors explained that they belonged to the R.A.F., that two hundred or three hundred aircraft were taking part in the operation, and that some dozen, being in difficulties, had been ordered to land at Cognac. They seemed very surprised not to be expected. Landing lights were immediately switched on and ten bombers, manned by Scotsmen, proceeded to land.

All this threw some light on the mystery, but there were still many unanswered questions.

In the first place, why had Cognac not been informed of the raid?

There was an American liaison detachment, commanded by a non-commissioned officer, at Larminat's headquarters. At 18.55 hours, the day before, precisely five minutes before he was going off duty, this non-commissioned officer received a signal in code from S.H.A.E.F. It was dinner-time. No important signal had ever come to Cognac. He went to his dinner, thinking there would be plenty of time to decode the message next day. In fact, it was the signal announcing the bombing for that night. But why did the aircraft bomb Royan, when it had been agreed that they should bomb only the Pointe de Grave and the Pointe de la Coubre? This tragic mistake in the objectives to be bombed was partly due to weather conditions and partly to the American commander using out-of-date methods.

The aircraft which bombed Royan had originally received orders to bomb a target in Germany. When it was found that the target could not be reached because of the meteorological conditions, the commander of the Tactical Air Force had issued orders on the radio to return and unload the bombs on the Pointe de la Coubre. How was the objective to be pinpointed? The commander of the squadron was told, when in flight, to have recourse to a method already abandoned three years before which consisted in dropping four flares at the four corners of the objective.

The flares were dropped correctly round the Point de la Coubre. But there was a gale blowing from the north. Indeed, it was so strong that Captain Meyer, at Rochefort, could see the flashes of the explosions but could not hear the noise. Owing to the storm, the flares drifted south towards Royan. And by the time the main body of the aircraft began dropping its bombs, the flares were over the town.

Four-fifths of Royan were destroyed by 1,600 tons of bombs and nearly two thousand of its inhabitants were killed. The American General responsible was sacked and sent back to the United States.

The negotiations directed to sparing the town were replaced by negotiations to succour the victims. Admiral Michahelles allowed the entry of the French services to feed the survivors and evacuate the wounded. In agreement with Admiral Michahelles and Admiral Schirlitz, a company of naval firemen from La Rochelle were sent to Royan to help clear the ruins.

On 28 March, General de Larminat, on the point of launching his attack against Royan and the Pointe de Grave, told Captain Meyer that the agreement made for La Rochelle no longer seemed to him appropriate.

"Are you proposing to attack La Rochelle, General?"

"Don't worry . . . there's no question of it. But you must admit that it would be displeasing to achieve victory with an agreement of which the enemy might make use to acquire all sorts of advantages. It's a question of dignity. And since you tell me that Schirlitz will blow the harbour up only in the last extremity . . . what would you think of my denouncing the agreement forthwith?"

"I think," replied Meyer, "that such a gesture would expose La Rochelle to serious and useless risks."

The two officers were not speaking the same language. One was thinking of the prestige of the renascent French Army which required a victory by force of arms and the unconditional surrender of the enemy. The other was trying to avoid the last battles by negotiation.

On 10 April, Larminat told Meyer to transmit to Schirlitz a letter denouncing the agreement of 18 April. The German Admiral considered one paragraph of it insulting:

The harbours and towns of La Rochelle and La Pallice no longer present any military interest, so that if these places were deliberately damaged, now that the war has reached a decisive point, the French Government would consider that a deliberate act of sabotage had been committed, contrary to international law, indeed a crime that would be subject to the application of the jurisdiction of common law to its authors, whether direct or indirect.

On 12 April, Schirlitz's Flag-Lieutenant, Lieutenant Groupe, handed Meyer the Admiral's answer. Its terms seemed to threaten the destruction of La Pallice.

Très Honoré Monsieur le Général,

I acknowledge receipt of your communication of 10 April 1945, No. 1111, by the terms of which the agreement concluded between the French and German commands, relating to the nondestruction of the port installations of La Pallice, lapses on 16 April 1945, at midnight (G.M.T.). Please accept, Monsieur le Général, the expression of my highest consideration.

                                                      SCHIRLITZ.

As soon as he had read the letter, Meyer on his own initiative asked to see the Admiral. He wanted to persuade him to spare La Pallice. He feared the interview might not be very agreeable, but he could have no idea how pathetic it would turn out to be.

"I saw come towards me," he related, "a man much bent, whose features were drawn and emaciated. He seemed to be overwhelmed and to be making visible efforts to control himself. When he came up to me, I saw that his mouth was trembling. Was it from emotion or anger?

. . . I had the impression that the conversation was going to be difficult.

" 'How can you expect,' the Admiral said, 'that I can have any further
confidence in a man who addresses me so dishonouring an insult and
who breaks his engagements the moment he feels he is the stronger? I
can now only accept the challenge, and prepare to fight and apply the
plans made for the moment when my fortress falls.'

"With these words, the Admiral seemed to imply that the interview
was at an end, or at least he moved away to talk with his companions.
Lieutenant Groupe then came to me and said in a broken voice: 'Monsieur le Commandant, I want a private word with you.' I went aside
with the German officer.

" 'There's an explanation for the Admiral's attitude,' he said. 'The
man has death in his heart and is likely to do something irreparable.
. . . I really don't know how he has had the strength and courage to
come here. He heard this morning that he had lost his wife, his two
daughters and his six grandchildren in the Allied bombing of Kiel.'

"I went to the Admiral and said with real emotion: 'Monsieur
l'Amiral, I have just learnt of the appalling misfortune which has be-
fallen you. Even though we are enemies, allow me to say with what
horror I have heard the news, and to express the sympathy I feel for
you personally. I ask you to permit me to shake you by the hand.'

"Admiral Schirlitz then held out a trembling hand and I saw tears in
his eyes. He coughed, then said in a firm but strangled voice: 'Monsieur
le Commandant, none of the words of sympathy I have received from
those about me has touched me as much as those you have just uttered.' "

The conversation then continued. After difficult preliminaries, during which Schirlitz complained of having been called by General de
Larminat "a criminal in common law," Meyer suggested a personal guarantee in place of the written agreement and gave his word of honour
that the agreement, which had been officially denounced, would be kept
in practice.

On 13 April, Meyer saw General de Larminat in his headquarters
trailer near Royan. He was shown a personal letter which Larminat
had written to the German Admiral. It was drafted in terms of great
courtesy and dignity:

Monsieur l'Amiral,

For secret operational reasons, I have not told you till now of the considerations which led me to denounce the agreement of 18 October 1944.

25. *Royan, following the bombing of 5 January 1945.*

Libération Libération Libérat

LES VOILA
ILS ARRIVENT

"La France écrasée, pillée, trahie, se redresse"

But, now that there is no longer any need for secrecy, I feel I should give them to so honourable an opponent.

I am attacking Royan. I wished to leave your hands free so that you might act in the circumstances in any way that you felt proper towards Admiral Michahelles in the comradeship of battle. I do not wish it to be said one day that, in a battle between soldiers, an agreement of a diplomatic nature had withdrawn part of his forces from one of his adversaries. I want the game to be completely open and frank in the light of day, as I have never personally ceased fighting your country since 1940. If the date of the 16th at midnight seems to you too late, you may consider yourself free to act now.

You will certainly admit that I have personally no interest in denouncing an agreement under whose shelter I could have withdrawn troops from our front to reinforce Royan. It is therefore an honest and honourable fight which is being offered you. If you take it on, you will encounter the best troops in our army.

As for the eventual destruction of La Pallice by the Germans, Larminat maintained his point of view, but this time in terms that could not offend the Admiral.

By this letter Larminat hoped to dispel for good and all the threat to La Rochelle caused by his denunciation of the agreement. In fact, the interview between Meyer and Schirlitz had already done much to reduce it.

That same day, he launched his attack on Royan.

An assertion of prestige and a demonstration of military valour were clearly the determining reasons for the operation at Royan. Unfortunately these reasons allowed little consideration for the civilian population.

The attack was wholly successful. In four days the F.F.I., supported by regular troops and the American Air Force, took the whole of the Royan pocket. On the other side of the Gironde, the Pointe de Grave was taken in six days, and the whole estuary liberated. The Island of Oléron, the last German position threatening the entrance to La Rochelle, was taken between 29 April and 1 May. As for La Rochelle itself, General de Larminat remarked, on 8 May, that "the troops . . . after an eight months' siege, will have the satisfaction of reoccupying a town which is intact with its bridges, and is capable of taking part very quickly in the effort to supply the country."

Why was it not the same for Royan?

The taking of that town, which had cost the Germans 1,000 dead, 800 wounded and 8,000 prisoners, of which 260 were officers, inflicted fewer, but nevertheless serious, losses on the French: 364 dead, 1,560 wounded, and 13 missing.

Moreover, the fifth of the town that had not been destroyed by Allied bombing was almost totally razed to the ground.

La Rochelle, which was liberated undamaged due to the ability of Captain Meyer, was the scene of some extraordinary episodes. Two or three days before the surrender, Schirlitz sent for his Flag-Lieutenant, Lieutenant Grupe. "I have just received a secret signal from the O.K.W.," he said. "A large four-engined aircraft from Germany is going to try to land on the Laleu airfield. It will be carrying a very important person, a new secret weapon and a large sum in false dollars, so that the garrison may be supplied by Spanish sailors. . . . You will meet the aircraft. But you must give me your word not to mention this to anyone." The Flag-Lieutenant went that night to the airfield and had it marked out with hurricane lamps. In the middle of the night, he heard the sound of an aircraft. It circled the airfield and then the noise suddenly ceased. On enquiry it was discovered that the aircraft had fallen into the Aiguillon inlet near the town. Both men and cargo were lost. Grupe immediately went to report to Schirlitz. "This is very serious," the Admiral said, "the aircraft must be fished up at once with all its contents." Grupe at once ordered a rescue squad to get busy and they worked all night. By morning, they had succeeded in finding the wreck and removing from it a courier's bag for the garrison, a sack of false dollars, a bazooka of an unusual design and two bodies, those of the pilot and navigator. The "very important person" had disappeared. No one will ever know who it was.

Schirlitz insisted that the men who had dealt with the wreck should also give their word to keep silent about it.

Who was this mysterious dignitary of the Third Reich? He must undoubtedly have been a very important person, since a long-distance submarine, the *Fuchs*, was waiting to pick him up at La Rochelle and take him to America. An hour after the accident the submarine sailed, but was intercepted off Saint-Nazaire by a British flotilla.

According to some, the personage concerned was Martin Bormann, one of the few important Nazis of whom all trace has been lost. Head of the Party's chancellery, Hitler's confidant, and responsible for the most pitiless acts of the Third Reich when *in extremis,* he may have been trying to escape punishment or had perhaps been charged by the Führer with some ultimate secret mission. But this is only conjecture.

During the last days of the siege, there was another, though less macabre, episode. The German authorities had organized an unusually comfortable internment camp for the French prisoners. It was not due merely to humanitarian feelings. Realizing that the camp was likely to change its inmates in the near future and that they themselves had a good chance of replacing the French after the surrender they were determined to see that the camp was as luxurious as circumstances allowed.

A few days after the surrender of La Rochelle, Meyer visited the camp and inspected the new prisoners. He found them looking fit, fat, rosy-cheeked and well, in spite of the shortages the population was suffering. Rather surprised, he asked: "What did you have to eat yesterday?" "Carrots." "And for lunch today?" "Carrots." "What will you have for dinner tonight?" "Carrots." Upon which the captain exclaimed: "Either carrots have suddenly acquired an unusual nutritive value, or you're taking me for a fool." To make sure, he went to the kitchen and had the ovens opened. He saw carrots, nothing but carrots. On interrogation, the German camp commanders said rather evasively: "You can always manage to get supplementary supplies in a port." Questioned more closely, they finally admitted that they had spent the day which had elapsed between the capitulation and the entry of the French troops accumulating reserves of tinned food behind the barbed wire to supplement the ordinary rations. The Schirlitz-Meyer agreement had not only saved the town from destruction but had preserved the Germans from famine.

The only Germans to escape the amenities of the prisoners of war camp were the crews of three submarines undergoing repairs in the submarine base. After the surrender of La Rochelle, the officers and petty officers had been interned, but the engineers and men remained on board their ships. A few months later, Captain Meyer assembled the crews and told them their ships were to have French commanders appointed. How would the Germans take the news? Faithful to the "Führer-prinzip," they took it extremely well. A petty officer, speaking on behalf of the men in the first submarine, said merely: "We await our new commander and we shall obey him, but we regret that we have no clean uniforms to do him the proper honours." Another, in another submarine, asked if they should wear decorations for the ceremony. "No doubt you should," Meyer replied, "you have won them honourably; they will do honour to your new commander." This singular situation, which in converse circumstances would have been called "collaboration," continued till the repairs were completed. The first sea trials were carried out by a German crew commanded by a French officer.

The final liberation of La Rochelle took place on 8 May at six o'clock in the morning. During the morning of the next day, two other pockets, Saint-Nazaire and Lorient, were liquidated. From these ports, contrary to the terms of surrender, German submarines put to sea and were soon signalled to be off the Spanish coast.

The same day, 9 May, the German Admiral Frisius, commanding the Dunkirk pocket, signed an Act of Surrender. He was an intractable and irrascible man, whose proclamations to his troops were often somewhat terse. Here is an order he issued on 20 February 1945, presumably with the intention of raising the morale of his men:

> To the officers of the Fortress of Dunkirk,
> To the soldiers of the Fortress of Dunkirk.
> Another swine has deserted. By doing so, he has brought indescribable misfortune upon his family. In a case such as this, you can be sure it will be liquidated.

The Admiral did not alter his tone at the surrender ceremony. He was sarcastic and contemptuous, particularly towards the French. In fact, the F.F.I. at Dunkirk had been treated as poor relations till the end. Though they had provided a considerable part of the infantry besieging the town, all the honours were for the British and the independent Czech armoured brigade, which had fought with it.

"The Czechs and the British," wrote Jean Éparvier, in Le Figaro of 10 May 1945, "are alone dealing with the questions of reintegration. They are keeping a jealous watch over Dunkirk where, until now, the Navy is the only French force that has been allowed to reinstall itself.

"They even excluded the French war correspondents from the ceremony, while the Czech, British and American journalists were admitted."

When, on 10 May 1945, at 09.45 hours, the Allied troops entered the last French town to be liberated, only the British and Czech flags were hoisted on the belfry. The 600 or 700 civilians who had remained amid the ruins of the Dunkirk pocket, at the peril of their lives, waited vainly for the Tricolour to appear.

The ceremony took place in the presence of the Czech General Lijka, commanding the Allied forces of Dunkirk, the commanders of the units of his brigade, and a British military attaché. The only French uniform present was that of a liaison officer.

It is not merely to revive an old resentment, which in any case quickly dispersed, that this must be related. But, *a posteriori*, it explains General de Larminat's attitude of mind at the Royan pocket. The circumstances at Dunkirk, the last French town to be liberated, make it understandable that in the spring of 1945 it was not entirely superfluous to show even the Allies that France had taken a considerable part in her own liberation.

Conclusion

THE BALANCE SHEET
OF THE LIBERATION

To understand the consequences of the Liberation as a whole, the demographic facts must be considered. When, between June 1944 and May 1945, France gradually became free of the Occupation, she was suffering from a deficit of adult men, which amounted to approximately one-tenth of the whole population, to one-fifth of the masculine population, or approximately to one-third of the adult masculine population.

Since the beginning of this Thirty Years War, which de Gaulle placed in August 1914, France had suffered successively three haemorrhages of which two were irremediable and the last, happily, only temporary.

Between 1914 and 1918, France had 1,500,000 men killed, and these were among the youngest and bravest of her male population. Had these men survived the First World War, they would have been at the height of their powers during the Second. They would have formed the cadres of the nation; and their loss was all the more grave because it affected generations in which the number of births, even in normal times, had scarcely equalled the deaths.

In June, 1940, there was a second loss of manpower equalling the first. This one was reparable but, at the time of the Liberation, it was still increasing the deficit. It consisted of 1,500,000 prisoners, also from the youth of the nation, and they mostly remained separated from their country until May 1945.

Between August 1914 and June 1941, therefore, three million men, half of them young, and the other half who would have been of mature age had they survived, were withdrawn from the French community.[1]

To these must be added the killed in the campaign of France, during the Occupation and the Liberation. From September 1939 to May 1945, the total amounted to 618,000 men, divided as follows:

[1] These are obviously only approximate figures, but they serve to indicate the size of the problem.

Soldiers: the campaign of 1939 to 1940	92,000[1]
The Free French campaign 1940 to 1945	58,000
The battles of the French Forces of the	
Interior	24,000
Frenchmen forcibly incorporated into the	
Wehrmacht	38,000
Prisoners: died in captivity	39,000
died as a result of captivity	4,000
Political, racial and labour deportees to Germany	200,000
Civilian victims of military operations	133,000[2]
Shot and massacred in France	30,000

[1] This figure includes a certain number from the French Empire.
[2] Half were the victims of bombing.

Between June 1944 and May 1945, therefore, France was in a more critical demographic state than any other occupied country. Indeed, none of them had suffered such a large percentage of losses for 1914–1918 and 1939–1945. These were scarcely normal conditions in which to face the certainly salutary, but also redoubtable crisis of the Liberation. Indeed, France, when the Germans left, was in danger, in spite of the heroism of the Resistance, of suffering from the unhappy consequences of this condition of anaemia. These were of two kinds: in the first place, military and political, due directly to physiological weakness. France was in danger of being considered, both on the battlefield and at the conference table, a partner who no longer carried much weight. Moreover, in her internal political life, a temptation to revolution might be expected to result for her weakness.

Secondly, there were the psychological consequences. Since the rise of Fascism and Hitlerism, France, deprived of the most active part of her youth, felt herself to be outclassed by the totalitarian régimes. She had lost the initiative and had seen it pass to her enemies. Above all, she had witnessed in her own land and in her own politics the adoption of measures which were contrary to her traditions. And from this fact, she might well have a bad conscience at the moment of the Liberation and in the months that followed it; and she might well hesitate, too, as to the procedure to observe and the attitude to adopt in face of painful problems she would have to tackle.

Since 1934, France, as indeed the other democracies, had struggled without success to find some new system that at once suited her and could oppose the brutal systems of the totalitarian states. In 1934, an attempted revolution by the Right failed; in 1936 an attempted revolution by the Left was no more successful.

Despite the fervour which sustained the Popular Front government, it could not introduce the necessary structural reforms. In the years which followed, confusion and weakness marked French political life, in contrast to the brutal certainties and displays of strength of the dictatorships.

More serious still, during the years which immediately preceded the war and the defeat of 1940, was the contagion of totalitarian practices within France's democratic institutions. After 1936, government by decree became almost habitual.

In view of the anaemia from which France was suffering in 1944–1945, how could she entirely guard herself against such weaknesses?

The balance sheet of the Liberation must therefore be drawn up from three points of view, the military, the political, and the psychological, or, if one prefers it, the civic.

Militarily, it was an undoubted success of which de Gaulle was the principal author. It was a remarkable success to have raised in an occupied and a weakened country an army which played so important a part in the last battles. Half a million men, either in the divisions re-formed in North Africa, or in the French Forces of the Interior amalgamated with regular units, took part in the Liberation of France and in these last battles. And thanks to this reconstituted army, France figured among the victors and among the signatories of the German surrender. Who would have dared hope it in November 1942 at the time of the total occupation of the country, the dissolution of the army and the scuttling of the fleet? Politically also, thanks to de Gaulle, France won the game, or more precisely, the two difficult games she had to play in her state of weakness. She won abroad as she did at home.

Abroad, de Gaulle showed himself rigidly intransigent, refusing every concession that might militate against French independence or threaten French sovereignty. He succeeded in persuading the Allies to recognize a French government, his own, and made certain that his government should be the only one to administer France at the Liberation. Who would have dared hope for this in May 1944, on the eve of the landings? And he obtained this result not only by his personal prestige and his remarkable determination, but by the detailed preparation of the political, administrative and judicial cadres that were destined to build a new façade of authority and order on the ruins of the Vichy government.

Meanwhile, he was also making preparations to win the political struggle at home. Who would have dared hope, in July 1944, that France could have entirely avoided subversion from the extreme Left, a Marxist revolution, when the Communists held the principal commands in the interior Resistance, and had placed their militants or allies at the head of several regions, including Paris. That this danger was avoided, that so imminent a risk was not realized, required much determination, much attention to detail, much courage and also, when necessary, much cunning. The General's great merit was that he was able to arouse these essential qualities in his subordinates. By means of apparent concessions, which were in fact manœuvres, by means of scathing refusals and forthright assertions, which meant exactly what they said, he succeeded, by allying heroism with Machiavellism, in disarming in his own camp his adversaries who were also the adversaries of liberty.

This was a masterly labour, whose importance does not seem as yet to have been sufficiently emphasized.

That said, great war leader and great politician as he was, did de Gaulle also succeed, which would have been the crown of his labours, in restoring national unity, not only in the army and the administration, but in the hearts of all the French who, without being adherents of his, had nevertheless not betrayed their country? Did his civic success achieve the same perfection as his successes as Head of State and as military leader?

Between June 1944 and May 1945, there were many factors against him. France, debilitated and scarcely emerging from defeat, felt that contempt for the weak which is so often manifested, through a need for a necessary compensation, in sectarianism and harshness. Many of those who had feared for national independence and often for their own lives ever since June 1940, were ready to condemn those of their compatriots who had not felt these anxieties so keenly. Moreover, the inevitable climate of war, and above all of civil war, necessarily led to the practice of that sort of Manicheism by which people are classed as wholly good or wholly bad, absolute friends or declared enemies—an attitude which justifies every summary judgement and every murderous inclination. And from this, in an atmosphere of reprisals and counter-reprisals, resulted the excommunication by those in power of those who no longer were so.

Such were the fatal consequences of the trials France had undergone since 1940. An attempt could be made to limit their effects, which the new authorities succeeded in doing after the Liberation in many places. They could have been officially condemned, which does not seem to have been done with sufficient vigour; indeed, it was perhaps impossible to do so openly, owing to the bid elements of the extreme Left were making to canalize popular resentments for their own advantage. Here again, it may have been necessary to appear to give the more turbulent elements some limited satisfaction in order the better to neutralize them.

It is not easy to establish the correct proportions between what was done to restore the nation's unity, what might have been done, what ought to have been done and what was not done—proportions which only a detailed and objective history of the purge could establish, and which might incidentally quiet many rancours. However that may be, the civic results of the Liberation were not as incontestably successful as the political and military results. To this, two incidents bear witness, one dating from the Liberation itself, the other from ten years after it. At 21.00 hours, on 26 April 1945, a train stopped at the Swiss frontier on its way to Paris. From a reserved compartment an old couple gazed out of the windows at the shadows of night lying over their native land. Marshal Pétain and his wife were voluntarily returning to France after eight months' captivity in Germany. A few moments after leaving the frontier, the train halted by a main road. There were shouts from hundreds of people of "Down with Pétain! Pétain to the gallows!" The demonstrators soon discovered the former Head of the State's compartment. They rushed on to the permanent way, beat on the windows with their fists, and yelled for his death.[1]

Leaving the Marshal impassive in his seat, his wife went into the corridor and found the guards who were supposed to protect them. "Is this where we are going to be assassinated?" she asked. The police decided to intervene and drove the demonstrators away. The train finally set off again.

It was a disgraceful scene, though it was perhaps inevitable at the time. One could wish that it had not been repeated.

Ten years later, in a town in the centre of France, an inquirer was gathering information from people who had lived through the Liberation. The first day, he met the former leaders of the Maquis, who told him of the sufferings of the F.F.I., of their exploits and their victories. It was a bright picture he was given, and it doubtless corresponded largely to the reality.

The next day, he met a dozen people who had been victims of the maquisards. Their story was a very different one. "The Liberation," said one of them, "was an act of brigandage." And, in support of his statement, he gave instances which were certainly not all without verisimilitude. According to them, the victories of the Maquis existed only in the official propaganda. They mentioned appalling reprisals, and the

[1] From an unpublished account given by Pétain's wife to Y. Garnier-Rizet.

summary execution of Vichy officials, who had saved men from the Gestapo. From one extreme we had passed to another. The people present were undoubted patriots, men who, in normal times, would have held important positions in their province till the day of their deaths. Two of them were senior barristers, a third had been a governor in the colonies. There were also two eminent doctors, one of whom had been Minister of Public Health under Vichy, the President of the Flying Club of the province, a former member of the Committee of the National Union of Combatants, an industrialist, and a land-owner. . . . There was not one of them who could have desired a German victory for a single second. But they were blamed for having continued to serve France by undertaking official duties for the nation under the Vichy government. One of them had been a National Assistance delegate and assistant to the mayor of a big town; in this capacity, he had saved Jews and Alsatians who had taken refuge in the district. One of the doctors had helped a Resistance leader, who had been taken prisoner by the Germans, to escape. Others had organized local cadres of the French Legion of Combatants, which, until November 1942, had still nourished hopes of revenge.

From the patriotic point of view, they were without stain. But all of them, having chosen to work in the camp that was excommunicated in 1944, were harassed, sacked, imprisoned and sometimes tortured at the Liberation.

Such was the horrifying abyss still existing in 1955 between two factions of the population of a big French town. Absurdly, this divergence was, in the last analysis, due to the fact that both sides, first under Pétain and then under de Gaulle, had been successively victims of excommunication.

During the course of this volume, we have seen many examples of the summary judgements which are so contrary to the traditions of French humanism. But it was clearly inevitable that at the time of the Liberation, during a period of reprisals and counter-reprisals, errors such as these would be perpetrated and perpetuated.

It would obviously have been desirable that the new authorities could have dissociated themselves more rapidly and more overtly than they did from these practices inherited from the totalitarian régimes and from which they were in process of freeing the world. But perhaps at the time it could be no more than a pious hope, a purely theoretical wish. Perhaps the only process by which the totalitarian toxins could be eliminated was the slow and progressive one that actually took place.

It may be that now, with the renewed vitality permeating France and with the lapse, which one may hope will be permanent, of certain internal quarrels, all these wounds will be healed.

But this is no proper view for an historian. The most he can do is to end by posing three questions relative to the period he has studied.

Did the extent of the Communist danger in 1944 really prohibit the Gaullist authorities from showing greater indulgence to the supporters of the Vichy government, or would such indulgence have facilitated the hold the extremists were trying to gain over the population?

Was de Gaulle, the war-leader responsible for a country that had been crushed by an early defeat, in a position to practice the subtle virtues of forbearance, qualities so essential to the politics of peacetime?

Finally, and above all, would not the arbitrary acts committed have been even more numerous and bloody if the Gaullist authorities had not been in power to curb excesses?

Since May 1940, France has found herself in the vanguard of civilized nations, facing either totalitarian dictatorships or, in terms more intellectual than material, underdeveloped countries questioning the West's "leadership" in the world. In turn, France's encounter with Nazi Germany and Fascist Italy, the Soviet attempts to sway her public opinion, the wars in Indochina and Algeria, show that for a quarter of a century she has been exposed in the front line to all the dangers known to the free world.

Hence the vicissitudes in her recent history. Hence the often painful misunderstandings between France and her allies who, less directly exposed, have the spare time to give her the advice which, were they in her place, they would doubtless be unable to follow.

But, as there are several great countries in the world whose permanence and independence resist all assaults, and as France is one of these, there always comes a moment when, after the worst trials, equilibrium is reestablished and soundness returns.

This book evokes one of those recoveries of France. Following a terrible ordeal from which she nearly perished, France's resurrection obviously could not be peaceable or easy. It necessarily involved internal quarrels and discord with other countries, even with those to whom she is tied forever and to whom she owes the return of her liberty.

Hence the quarrels among the French and the dissipation of power among rival factions. Hence the attempts from outside to apply pressure on French government and French politics, as noted in this book. Hence the stiffness and ingratitude of the man who came to represent France and who, before a nearly full meeting of Allied nations, refused to give up, at trifling cost, a portion of independence.

France, in this book, like all those seriously wounded regaining their health, appears at times irritable, quarrelsome, and often even unjust. Her allies, like all people who watch by the bedside, appear at times indiscreet and paternalistic.

This book tries to diagnose such extreme susceptibilities and superficial frictions in the hope that it may help the countries collectively responsible for freedom in the world to understand themselves better and to cooperate more easily in the future.

To have survived the ordeals between May 1940 and August 1944, the Atlantic solidarity of France must be profoundly inscribed in its very being. Such is the lesson, constant and necessary, to be drawn today from the history of its liberation.

GLOSSARY

A.F.I.	French Information Agency.
A.M.G.O.T.	Allied Military Government in Occupied Territories.
A.S.	Secret Army.
B.C.R.A.	Central Bureau for Intelligence and Action.
B.I.P.	Press and Information Bureau.
B.O.A.	Air Operations Bureau.
C.D.L.	Departmental Liberation Committees.
C.F.L.N.	French Committee of National Liberation.
C.F.P.	Corps Franc Pommies
C.G.E.	General Planning Committee.
C.G.T.	General Confederation of Workers.
C.N.R.	National Committee of Resistance.
C.O.M.A.C.	Central Committee for Military Action.
C.P.L.	Paris Liberation Committee
D.G.S.S.	Directorate-General of Special Services.
D.M.N.	National Military Delegate.
D.M.R.	Regional Military Delegate.
D.M.Z.	Zonal Military Delegate.
F.F.I.	French Forces of the Interior.
F.N.	National Front Movement.
F.T.P.F.	French Partisan Francs-Tireurs.
G.M.R.	Mobile Police Columns
G.P.R.F.	Provisional Government of the French Republic.
L.V.F.	League of French Volunteers against Bolshevism.
M.L.N.	National Liberation Movement.
M.M.L.A.	Military Mission for Administrative Liaison.
M.U.R.	United Resistance Movements.
N.A.P.	Secret Networks in the Public Services.
O.A.S.	Secret Army Organization
O.C.M.	Civil and Military Organization.
O.G.	Operational Groups.
O.R.A.	Army Resistance Organization.
P.L.M.	Paris, Lyons and Marseilles Railway.
P.T.T.	Posts, Telegraphs and Telephones.
R.C.P.	Chasseurs Parachute Regiment.
R.N.R.	National Popular Assembly.
S.A.S.	Special Air Service.
S.H.A.E.F.	Supreme Headquarters Allied Expeditionary Force.
S.N.C.F.	French State Railways.
S.P.O.C.	Special Projects Operations Centre
S.R.	Secret Services.
S.T.O.	Forced Labour in Germany.

T H E French edition of *L'Histoire de la Libération de la France* (Paris, Librairie Fayard, 1959) contains a complete list of all the sources used in the compilation of this work—oral testimonies, private and official documents, books and periodicals. This covers no less than sixteen pages, four of them in double columns. American readers who wish to use Robert Aron's work for the purpose of historical research are advised to consult the French edition.

For other readers, it was thought best to limit the bibliography to the more important works and to those which are most easily accessible; it is this selection, necessarily somewhat brief, which is to be found below.

General ADELINE: *La libération du Sud-Ouest, Bordeaux, Royan, La Rochelle* (Imp. Baconnier, Algiers 1948).

GEORGES BLOND: *D'Arromanches à Berlin* (Fayard 1954).

—— *Le débarquement, 6 juin 1944* (Fayard 1951).

LÉON BLUM: *Mémoires, 1940–1945* (Albin Michel 1955).

Colonel C. R. BOUVET: *Ouvriers de la première heure* (Berger-Levrault 1954).

General O. N. BRADLEY: *A Soldier's Story* (Holt 1941).

ROGER CÉRÉ and CHARLES ROUSSEAU: *Chronologie du conflit mondial, 1935–1945* (Sefi 1945).

Sir WINSTON CHURCHILL: *The Second World War*, Vols. III–VI. Vol. III: The Grand Alliance; Vol. IV: The Hinge of Fate; Vol. V: Closing the Ring; Vol. VI: Triumph and Tragedy (Houghton 1950–53).

ADRIEN DANSETTE: *Le général Leclerc* (Flammarion 1952).

—— *Histoire de la libération de Paris* (revised edition, Fayard 1958).

GUILLAIN DE BÉNOUVILLE: *Le Sacrifice du matin* (Robert Laffont 1949).

CHARLES DE GAULLE: *Discours et messages 1940–1946* (Berger-Levraut 1946).

—— *Discours aux Français*, Vols. I and II (Paul Dupont 1945).

—— *War Memoirs*. Vol. I: Call to Honor, 1940–1942; Vol. II: Unity, 1942–1944; Vol. III: Salvation, 1944–1945 (Simon and Schuster 1958–60).

Marshal DE LATTRE DE TASSIGNY: *History of the French First Army* (Allen and Unwin 1952).

DWIGHT EISENHOWER: *Crusade in Europe* (Doubleday 1948).

YVES FARGE: *Rebelles, Soldats et citoyens* (Grasset 1946).

ANDRÉ GUÉRIN and MICHEL SAINTMONT: *Normandie, champ de bataille de la libération* (Ed. du Bonhomme libre, Caen).

PAUL GUILLAUME: *La Sologne au temps de l'héroïsme et de la trahison* (Imp. nouvelle, Orleans 1950).

RENÉ HOSTACHE: *Le conseil national de la Résistance* (Presses Universitaires de France 1958).

PHILIPPE KIEFFER: *Béret vert* (Ed. France Empire).

Admiral W. D. LEAHY: *I Was There* (Whittlesey 1950).

Admiral LEMONNIER: *Cap sur la Provence* (Ed. France Empire 1954).

—— *Paisible Normandie* (La Colombe 1954).

RAYMOND MASSIET: *La préparation de l'insurrection et la bataille de Paris* (Payot 1945).

Admiral H. MEYER: *Au secours de la Rochelle, 22 août 1944–9 mai 1945* (Ed. du Cahier de l'Ouest 1955).

HENRI MICHEL: *Histoire de la Résistance, 1940–1945* (Presses Universitaires de France 1950).

HENRI MICHEL and BORIS MIRKINE GUENZEVITCH: *Les idées sociales et politiques de la Résistance* (Presses Universitaires de France).

Field-Marshal VISCOUNT MONTGOMERY: *Memoirs* (World 1958).

Vice-Admiral MUSELIER: *De Gaulle contre le gaullisme* (Ed. du Chêne 1946).

Colonel PASSY: *Souvenirs I:* 2e bureau Londres, juin 1940–décembre 1941 (Raoul Solar 1947).

—— *Souvenirs II:* 10 Duke Street, Londres, janvier 1942–octobre 1942 (Raoul Solar 1949).

—— *Souvenirs III:* Missions secrètes en France, novembre 1942, juin 1943 (Plon 1951).

ERIC PIQUET-WICKS: *Quatre dans l'ombre* (Gallimard 1957).

ROSSI: *Physiologie du Parti Communiste français* (Self 1948).

—— *Les communistes français pendant la drôle de guerre* (Les îles d'or 1951).

—— *La guerre des papillons: quatre ans de politique communiste, 1940–1944* (Les îles d'or 1954).

JACQUES SOUSTELLE: *Envers et contre tout.* Vol. I: De Londres à Alger, 1940–1942; Vol. II: D'Alger à Paris, 1942–1944 (Robert Laffont 1947–50).

Colonel C. P. STACEY: *The Canadian Army, 1939–1945* (Edmond Cloutier, Ottawa 1949).

STANFORD UNIVERSITY HOOVER INSTITUTE ON WAR, REVOLUTION AND PEACE: *Life in France during the German Occupation,* 3 vols. (Stanford University Press & Oxford 1959).

WALTER STUCKI: *La fin du régime de Vichy* (O. Zeluck 1947).

PIERRE TAITTINGER: *Et Paris ne fut pas détruit* (NEL 1956).

THOMASSET: *La vie héroïque de Jean de Lattre de Tassigny, maréchal de France* (Baudinière 1952).

PAUL VEYNET: *Les Catholiques dans la Résistance* (Ed. des St.-Pères 1945).

CHESTER WILMOT: *The Struggle for Europe* (Harper 1952).

(VARIOUS TESTIMONIES): *La France et son Empire pendant la Guerre,* 3 vols. (ELF).

INDEX

Abeille, M., 78
Abetz, Otto, 149, 255, 256, 265–266, 270
Ablard, Colonel, 389
Aconit (corvette), 15
Adeline, Colonel, 386, 434, 451
A.F.H.Q. *see* African Forces Headquarters
African Forces Headquarters (A.F.H.Q.), 316
Afrika Korps, 155–156
Alexander, General, 309, 310
"Algebra" *see* Ely, Colonel
Algiers Committee, 35
Allard, Colonel, 166
Allied Army, 232, 239, 346
    air superiority of, 322
    Atlantic advances, 427–428
    divided into three army groups, 439
    Rhine advances, 427–428
    solidarity in Alsace campaign, 450
Allied High Command, 91
    broadcasts to the Resistance, 89, 92–93
Allied Intelligence services, 151
Allied Navy, Toulon bombardment by, 333
Alma, Colonel, 117
Aloès Mission (headquarters group), 126, 127
Alsace
    German occupation of, 438
    liberation of, 437–450
    phases of campaign, 445
Alsace (fighter group), 16
Alsace Lorraine Brigade, 431
Alsace Mobile Group, 431
Alweyden, Colonel von, 361
American Air Force, 452
American Army, 18–19
    Alsace campaign, 439
    Brittany liberation and, 99, 110, 116, 128–129, 133–135
    83rd Infantry Division, 131
    First, 100
    Lyons attack and, 348–349
    Normandy liberation and, 14, 99, 100–109
    Paris liberation and, 257
    Seventh, 309
    VII Corps, 129
    Third, 100, 116, 128, 257
American Mercury, The (publication), 421
AMGOT, 36, 43, 136, 209
André, Louis, 11–12, 57
Anfra, 313
Ansot *see* Avinin, M.
"Anvil" *see* Operation "Anvil"
"Arc" *see* Chaban–Delmas, M.
Ardennes, 195
"Aristide" *see* Landés, Léon des
Armée Secrète (A.S.), 69, 113, 163, 414
Armin, Lieutenant von, 288

Army of the Armistice, 88, 164, 171, 184, 190, 346
Aron–Brunetière, Colonel, 235, 295
Asher, Second–Lieutenant, 391, 392
A.S. *see* Armée Secrète (A.S.)
Assemblée Consultative, 16, 18, 36, 77
Atlantic front, First Army reinforcements to, 435
Atlantic Wall, 11, 429
Aubert, M., 130
Aubrac, Lucie, 135, 354
Aubrac, Raymond, 83, 399
Audibert, General, 117, 118
Audren, M., 118
Augros, Father, 106
Aulock, Colonel von, 129, 281
Austrians, German Army and, 324–325
Autonomist Party, 136
Aventure (frigate), 15
Avinin, M., 81, 268
Aveyron Battalion, 431

"Banditisme et lâcheté" (Vigier), 422
Bank of France, 213
Banse, M., 48
Barrat, M., 119, 125
Bastia, M., 348
Bastid, M., 81
"Battle of the Pines," 445
Bayer, Yves, 260–261
Bayet, Albert, 267
Bayeux, 3–60
Bayeux Liberation Committee, 11
Bayle de Sessé, Rémy, 189, 190
B.B.C. *see* British Broadcasting Company (B.B.C.)
B.C.R.A., 88, 172, 173, 189, 193, 200
    files of, 158–159
    sabotage and, 144, 147, 151
Bechmann–Lescot, Roland, 191, 192, 196
Bell, Daniel W, 219
Bellan, Vice–Principal, 111
Bender, Major, 240, 271, 278, 279, 288
Benier, M., 78
Bénouville, General de, 364
Berger, Colonel *see* Malraux, André
Bernard, Commandant Pierre–Paul, 172
Bernard, Georges, 101
Bernard, Jean–Guy, 147–148
Bernonville, M., 65
Berrigant, M., 118
Berry (bomber group), 16
Bertaux, Pierre, 83n., 391, 392, 393, 394, 395, 397
Berthaud, Colonel, 111
Berthet, Captain, 362
Bertin–Chevance, General, 364, 369

477